KT-570-030

For
Adam and Julie
who will now have some evidence as to what Daddy has been doing on the weekends
and evenings

Robert H. Rosenfeld

For
Alex and Amy
who are part of the future in the exciting and bewildering world of complex
organizations

David C. Wilson

Contents

Contributors

Robert H. Rosenfeld is a Director of Garner Hall & Company Ltd. He is also a Visiting Fellow in the Centre for Corporate Strategy and Change at the University of Warwick.

David C. Wilson is Professor of Strategic Management at Warwick Business School, University of Warwick.

Christopher W. Allinson is a Lecturer in Organizational Behaviour at the School of Business and Economic Studies, University of Leeds and a Chartered Occupational Psychologist.

Oriol Amat is at Pompeu Fabra University, Barcelona, Spain.

Mats Alvesson is Associate Professor of Business Administration at Stockholm University, Sweden.

P. D. Anthony is a Senior Research Fellow at Kings College, London.

José Maria de Anzizu is Director of the Centre for Organizational Studies at IESE, Barcelona.

Christopher Barnatt is a Lecturer in Organizational Behaviour and Computer Management, School of Management and Finance, University of Nottingham.

J. G. Boerlijst is Professor at the University of Twente, Netherlands.

Richard J. Butler is Professor of Organizational Analysis at the University of Bradford Management Centre, Bradford.

Roland Calori is Professor of Business Policy and Head of the Business Policy Department at Group ESC, Lyon, France.

Tupper Cawsey is Professor of Business at the School of Business and Economics, Wilfred Laurier University, Ontario.

Allan H. Church is Principal at W. Warner Burke Associates, Inc. USA.

Cary L. Cooper is Professor of Organizational Psychology at the Manchester School of Management, University of Manchester Institute of Science and Technology. He is currently President of the British Academy of Management and a Fellow of the British Psychological Society, and is editor of the Journal of Organizational Behaviour.

J. Martin Corbett is Senior Lecturer in Industrial Relations and Organizational Behaviour at the School of Industrial and Business Studies, Warwick Business School.

David Coghlan is a Lecturer in Organizational Development, at the School of Business Studies, Trinity College, Dublin.

Karen Davies is a Director of Garner Hall & Company Ltd.

Gene Deszca is Associate Professor in Management Organizational Behaviour at the School of Business and Economics, Wilfred Laurier University, Ontario.

Iurii I. Ekaterinoslavskii is Professor at the Central Training Institute for Civil Engineering and a founding member of the Russian Academy of Entrepreneurship in Moscow, Russia.

Silvia Gherardi is Professor of Organizational Sociology at the Dipartimento di Politica Sociale, Universita degli Studi di Trento, Italy.

Hugh Gunz is Associate Professor of Organizational Behaviour, Joseph L. Rotman School of Management, University of Toronto.

B. I. J. M. van der Heijden is Assistant Professor at the University of Twente, Netherlands.

David J. Hickson is Professor of International Management and Organization at the University of Bradford Management Centre. He is also the Eldon Foote Visiting Professor of International Business at the University of Alberta, Canada.

Geert Hofstede is Professor of Organizational Anthropology and International Management at the Department of Economics and Business Administration, the University of Limburg at Maastricht in The Netherlands. Professor Hofstede is also Director of the Institute for Research on Intercultural Cooperation at Limburg University.

Dian-Marie Hosking is Lecturer of Applied Social Psychology of Organizations at Aston Business School, Aston University.

Matt Hudson is Senior Manager, Policy Development at Lloyds TSB Group plc.

Phillipe Le Comte is Director of Compensation and Career Development at Otis Elevator International, Paris.

Robert A. Lee was a Senior Lecturer in Organizational Behaviour in the Department of Management Studies at Loughborough University.

Alan McKinlay is Professor of Management at St. Andrews University, Scotland.

Aminu Mamman is a Lecturer in Management at the Graduate School of Business, Northern Territory University, Australia.

Maurice Mazerolle is at the School of Business and Economics, Wilfred Laurier, University, Ontario.

Davide Nicolini is a researcher in Organizational Sociology, Universita degli Studi di Trento, Italy.

Francesca Odella is a researcher in Organizational Sociology, Universita degli Studi di Trento, Italy.

Andrew M. Pettigrew is Professor of Strategy and Organization at Warwick Business School, University of Warwick.

Sheila M. Puffer is Professor of Human Resources and International Business at the College of Business Administration, Northeastern University, Boston, MA.

Abraham R. Sagie is at the School of Business Administration, Bar-Ilan University, Israel.

Stanislav V. Shekshnia is Zone Manager for RusOtis in Moscow, Russia.

Ken Starkey is a Professor of Strategic Management at the School of Management and Finance, University of Nottingham.

Valerie J. Sutherland is a Chartered Occupational Psychologist.

Terry Thornley is Principal Lecturer in Management Studies at the Huddersfield University Business School.

Richard Thorpe is Professor in Management at Manchester Metropolitan University.

Acknowledgements

When we originally put together the first edition of *Managing Organizations*, it was primarily as a response to our own desire to use a challenging and comprehensive text in the courses and programmes in which we were involved. It may sound somewhat naïve, but we were never quite sure if anyone would see its value (aside from us!).

The response to the first edition was exceedingly gratifying and we are indebted to all the readers of the first edition, as well as instructors who very kindly provided us with feedback—most of which was surprisingly constructive! It was the scale of the interest in the text that finally made us decide to update the book with a second edition. So thank you for your patience and interest.

One of the critical success factors for our first edition was the high quality of contributors which we were able to gather together. For the second edition, we wanted to find new readings and perspectives which would offer new insights. Once again we were most fortunate to find many new contributors offering readings and cases. It was difficult for us to make our selections from the array we received. We certainly thank all those who contributed their work.

The first edition was published in 1990. Since then David Wilson moved to Aston Business School in 1993 and then in 1997 back to Warwick Business School. David would like to express his appreciation for the support provided by both institutions for the development of this book.

During the same period, Robert Rosenfeld was involved in starting up a strategy and management development consultancy called Garner Hall & Company Ltd. He has benefitted greatly from the opportunities provided by his clients to review parts of the manuscript and become involved in the many debates this entailed. At the same time, Robert has also been able to remain involved through his academic relationships with both Warwick and Aston Business Schools. He would also like to express his appreciation to London Business School for providing access to their excellent library resources.

For those readers with a keen eye for detail, you may have noticed that the authors have been reversed for this edition. This basically reflects the equality of our long friendship and partnership.

Much of the administration for this edition has been undertaken by the support team at Garner Hall & Company Ltd. In particular, we would like to extend our heartfelt appreciation to Jo Phillips who spent many late evenings patiently putting the work into order and forcing the pace when necessary. We would also like to acknowledge the administrative contribution of Shoni Shulman at an earlier state of the project.

A critical period of development of the second edition was when we cloistered ourselves away for two weeks in Dublin in the summer of 1997 to finish off the manuscript. We wish to express our thanks to Professor Brian Leavey of Dublin City University Business School for being our gracious host. In addition, we would also like to thank Donal Motherway, the Administrative Manager and his team in the Business School for ensuring that our visit was productive.

Our final formal expression of thanks must go to Alistair Lindsay and his editorial team at McGraw-Hill Publishing Company. His support and encouragement throughout the project was crucial to our success. We realize the scale of his task in extracting a manuscript of sufficient calibre and can only hope that we added to his professional stamina and patience.

Finally, we must pay homage to our wives, Jo (for Dave) and Liz (for Rob). Aside from our somewhat dubious rationale for the need to go to Dublin for two weeks, Jo and Liz were constant supporters of our efforts. We know that we could never have completed this task without their support and the co-operation of our children, Alex and Amy (Dave's) and Adam and Julie (Rob's).

We have had a great time putting this book together. We hope that you enjoy it.

Robert H. Rosenfeld
David C. Wilson

Part I
Introduction

About this book

Introduction

This book is aimed at addressing the contemporary issues which fall under the broad title of organizational theory and behaviour. It is also designed with a view to incorporating in one volume text, readings and cases. The text is written to outline the topic areas. It shows to what extent our current theoretical and empirical knowledge can comment upon contemporary themes in organizations. In order to do this, the book's contents are spread across a wide range of topics.

Of course, there are topics which focus on the individual within the organization and the issues of working with others in groups or teams. We also look outside these areas toward more contextually based themes in the subject. In particular, this is the result of teaching and talking with managers, students of business and researching in the discipline. The book is thus led by research and guided by current issues. Therefore, themes of organizational change, control, decision-making and operating internationally are included as a natural part of organizational behaviour.

Organization of the book

The book has seven parts. Each part of the book corresponds to a set of different themes and approaches. Traditionally enough, we begin with you, the individual, in the organization. We look at some of the attributes of individuals and see to what extent these can be reflected in their behaviour in organizations. We also look at how organizations themselves behave toward their markets, their peers and their immediate environment. Linking these perspectives together are the underlying themes of continuity and change in organizations and what these imply both for working within them as well as for their management.

At the end of each part are both readings and cases. The intention is to achieve a further degree of thematic integration. Each reading is written by a leading researcher and academic in the specific topics in each section. The case studies present the reader with organizational scenarios and situations which illustrate the topics in practice as well as posing a set of problems for resolution. They ask . . . 'Given your knowledge in this area, what would you recommend as a course of action and why?' Again, leading authors have contributed cases for discussion. They are real issues from real organizations.

Why another text in organizational behaviour?

The broad ideas which went into compiling this book reflect the experience of the authors (as teachers and researchers) and also the experience, frustrations and suggestions of many of our peers. The teaching of theory and analysis in organizations has changed almost unrecognizably over the past 10 years. The growth of business degree programmes at undergraduate and postgraduate level has placed the question of managing organizations and their human resources at centre stage. Coupled with this expansion comes a recognition of the importance of management education from practitioners. Organizations large and small, manufacturing and service, commercial and voluntary are now seeking education for their managers at all levels.

The role of Business Schools and Management Departments in higher education generally has been to supply this need, often at very short notice. The number of textbooks on organizational behaviour is extremely large, but predominantly North American in origin. There are some British and European texts available, but these are notable exceptions. Even these texts either cover the terrain partially (by design), or force the reader to go elsewhere for relevant case examples or for a wider theoretical lens.

Examples which originate in North America and portray the experience of companies and managers in the United States and Canada have become rather less relevant to European organizations over the same 10-year period. Examples of how it was done in General Motors America is not always helpful in looking at Asea Brown Boveri or Nokia. At the very general level, of course, comparisons are possible. At any more detailed level, comparisons become strained, often to the point of irrelevance. The operating context, the fiscal economy, the regulatory environment, the values, attitudes and beliefs of individuals all differ between the two contexts. Managing organizational change in Europe, for example, necessitates attention to a whole set of characteristics which simply would not apply in North America. The history of the organization, its corporate culture, societal characteristics, levels of unionization are all different.

As stated earlier, the intention with this book is to capture theory and practice within one volume. The cases and readings are intended to show how European organizations face challenges in their operating environment, while the text is aimed at highlighting theories and research results as they apply in the Anglo-European context.

The book's seven parts are all self-contained. This means that the reader can also choose to sample particular sections if these are seen to be of particular relevance. We have also tried to make the text a coherent whole from beginning to end, so that the themes of the book can emerge through different perspectives and levels of analysis. Thus, a complete reading of the book should provide the framework and the foundations for the detailed study of organizational behaviour.

About the second edition

One of the most pleasant aspects of seeing the first edition published was to receive feedback from readers and instructors who have used the book. Based on the comments we received (both positive and negative), as well as our own experience in using the textbook, we started to compile a list of changes, enhancements and additions. When our publisher asked us to consider undertaking the second edition, we felt that it would be a relatively simple matter of making a few alterations here and there. However, as we looked more closely at what our 'ideal' textbook might look like, we realized that a more substantive rewrite was what we wanted.

Since the publication of the first edition in 1990, the field of organizational behaviour has continued to develop. New questions, new research and interesting findings have moved the field on substantially. It was only after a thorough rereading of the contents of the first edition that we realized how much had changed. So the game plan changed for us. Instead of some minor alterations, we determined to undertake a complete review of the book with substantial rewrites of most of the chapters. Many of the readings and case studies used in the first edition have been changed as well. This was not because they were found wanting in any way, but because we wanted our cases and readings to reflect the very latest concerns in our field. The result is now a blend of the 'classic' and the new.

Perhaps the most striking changes in the second edition, compared to the first edition lie in the final two parts: International Management and Managing in the Future. Re-reading the first edition, we were somewhat surprised to note how 'time specific' the material was. The context of organizations and even our own views on future changes had certainly evolved substantially! The slow and somewhat unsteady move within the European Union (EU) towards greater integration is emerging now as a much greater management issue than it was a decade ago. Similarly, the impact information technologies will have on the ways and means we undertake our jobs is becoming much clearer than it was previously.

All in all, we hope that the second edition still retains the attributes which have made the first edition well-liked among its readers. In addition, we hope that the changes we have made to bring the material up to date and improve the general flow of the book will be appreciated by an even wider audience!

A framework for reading this book

This book spans a range of topics and levels of analysis. It is important, therefore, to know how to read it. The route map is summarized in Figure 1.1, which is intended to give a framework for analysis.

Figure 1.1 Studying organizations—a framework for analysis

Level of analysis	Example topics
Societal	• Nature of European context • Sector characteristics • Demographic and social changes
Organizational	• Structure and process • Organizational growth/development • Change/decline • Mergers/demergers/outsourcing
Group	• Human behaviour • Team work
Individual	• People's needs/attitudes/values • Behaviour/learning

No-one is likely to come into your office and say 'Look, have you got 10 minutes, I think we've got an organizational behaviour problem!' It's going to be far less specific and much more ambiguous. Perhaps it is a problem with one department which seems to be declining in performance, or is difficult for others to work alongside. A host of possible solutions and alternative interpretations are possible. As a first step, this book offers the chance to decide the level (or levels) of analysis from which to start. Is it a specific problem with specific individuals in the department? Is it the whole department which is tricky to deal with and there is no differentiation between individuals? Is the problem likely to be the location of the department in the organizational structure, or is it likely to be a much wider problem outside the scope and the control of any single organization?

Asking these questions provides us with four broad levels of analysis:

- societal
- organizational
- group
- individual

Taking the first letters of each gives the acronym SOGI and this is a useful way to think about analysing problems in organizations. This book is organized around the SOGI principle. Characteristics and attributes of individuals are dealt with in Part 2, for example, the operation of groups in Part 3 and so on through the parts, dealing first with organizations themselves and then the environment in which they are embedded. In addition, themes of change, control, effectiveness and competitiveness permeate all sections.

At all these analytical levels, there have been substantial changes since the writing of the first edition. There is no reason to suppose that the rate and pace of such changes will abate. For example, at the level of the individual, changes have taken place in terms of the role of women in the workforce and in the gender balance more generally at the societal level of analysis. In the UK, over 50% of the working population is female (including part-time employment). The 'man' in the word manager cannot (and actually never did) stand for the man—the male. The precise etymology of the word 'manager' is unclear. In Italian, the word would indicate someone who, long ago, looked after horses. In French, the old-fashioned word, *manant*, meant a churl or a boor and always applied to the peasant class. Not especially distinguished; nor always masculine! Perhaps the current French terminology of a 'chef' to denote a manager (*chef du service*) would be better applied in Anglo writings? However, we have had to deal with the 'man' terminology in this book. Terms such as 'economic man' which have been used for many years in the social sciences, are used in this book in their original form. Where we, as authors, use the term of a single gender (he or she) we intend both genders to be included in our description or analysis. We have avoided using the rather ugly s/he terminology.

The number of women in the workforce has increased from 1985 to 1995 by 1.5 million. Working women have a greater degree of purchasing power than their stay-at-home counterparts and their impact in organizations and on the growth of the overall economy will be substantial. The world-wide population is estimated to grow around 30% (1.8 billion) by 2021, but in the UK in the same period the growth is predicted to be 4% (2.5 million). In continental Western Europe, the rate of annual population growth has been falling and, in the UK, there are predictions for a population fall from 2021 to 2031. An often hidden factor in broad population trends is the increasing length and depth of women's careers. Women who occupy senior and middle management roles often have postponed having a family until they are established in their career. They have children later in life and usually at a less fertile time of life. It is likely that the effect of this will be to reduce the number of young people aged between 16 and 34 by 15% (1995–2021) and the number aged 55–64 will increase by 40% (the 1960s' baby boom).

At the level of the group, traditional ways of working in teams are no longer the only ways of working. Physical meetings, face-to-face, are not the only alternative. Rapid advances in communications technology (one of the biggest recruitment markets for students in Europe) have meant that 'virtual teams' can form and interact using electronic mail, video-conferencing and other remote site communications technologies. The effects of all of these factors will be to transform the workplace. Early writers on organization theory did not have to consider that a person working in the UK could, by using technology, communicate in real time with co-workers around the world 24 hours a day (and every day) and do this from home! Offices, too, may become 'virtual'. Theories of how formal organizations used to work may not apply so readily to modern organizations. For example, what will terms such as organizational culture mean? In addition, teleworking will mean that dress codes and the wearing of business attire may become irrelevant. The traditional workplace has already seen a more casual trend. Although the idea of 'dress-down-Friday' is not widespread across European organizations, it was significant enough for Marks and Spencer to comment formally on the practice in their 1996 annual report. Even the formal organizations of today are changing in ways unthought of only a few decades ago.

The future, therefore, is one of the themes of this book as it applies to all levels of analysis (individuals, groups and organizations). There are some changes of huge proportions which will face organizations and their staff in the future. Already, we can see the political and economic tensions associated with the European Union. Beyond these are questions such as the role of technology in taking organizations forward to new levels of efficiency and effectiveness. Or do technological advances such as Computer Integrated Manufacture (CIM) and electronic commerce on the Internet (e-commerce) primarily result in the de-skilling of a labour force which will be increasingly relegated to becoming baby-sitters for computer controlled machines? Will individuals adapt to and cope with teleworking from home? Will existing theories of motivation and job satisfaction be able to tell us anything about the stresses and strains of electronic working from remote sites? There are a host of other questions which impact directly upon organizations and their design and management as we 'crystal ball gaze' into the future. Much of the latter sections of this book have been designed to examining these issues in the context of organization theory and behaviour.

The intellectual terrain of organizational behaviour and this book

Readers familiar with the first edition of this book will know that the greater part of it is best described as organization theory rather than organizational behaviour. For new readers (welcome!) they will find the intellectual focus unchanged. Because social science is inherently multi-level and multi-disciplinary in its focus, the term organizational behaviour seemed to us unduly restrictive to the more psychological perspectives of individual behaviour. Psychologists are really concerned with individuals first and the fact that these individuals work in organizations second. We are less concerned in this book with personality or the characteristics and traits of individuals generally, and are more concerned with the study of social behaviour in organizations (e.g. teams and groups) and in the 'behaviour' of organizations themselves as decision-making systems and as creators of economic wealth (and sometime destroyers of it).

This is not to relegate the perceptions, feelings and beliefs of individuals as unimportant. For the reader interested predominantly in such factors, then they could consult one of the many textbooks in organizational psychology (e.g. McKenna, 1994). In this book, we place the context of organization at centre stage. The analysis of individuals, teams and processes is geared to this view. However, the contributions of at least psychology, sociology, anthropology and economics have to be consulted and drawn upon when taking this perspective. Broadly:

Psychologists	study the personality properties and traits of individuals irrespective of whether they are in formal organizations or not. Feelings, beliefs, attitudes and values are key factors in understanding human behaviour.
Sociologists	study social structures and the impact of social structures (such as work organizations) on individuals. Sociologists also study the inter-relationships between social structures and the questions of hierarchy, power and influence they raise.
Anthropologists	study the systems of societies, especially their customs, histories, prevailing ideas and values. Work organizations for an anthropologist provide a comparable research site to that of the village, the metropolis or the rural tribe.
Economists	study the inter-relationships of supply and demand across a range of factors of production. They study both at the level of individual choice and at the aggregate level of business and social systems (e.g. the level of interest rates, inflation and patterns in trade policies). To examine these factors, economists often have to model their theories in the form of equations. The science of doing this is called econometrics. Inevitably, modelling has to make some assumptions (for example, individuals will always exercise choice in a certain 'rational' way).

This book takes the notion of organization itself to be pivotal. Organization is viewed as an integrating activity in which human behaviour takes place, but where the overall understanding of organization theory is more than simply the sum of its parts (or the sum of individual behaviours). Thus the intellectual focus of the book draws more heavily on the sociological and anthropological than the psychological frames of reference. We also believe that organization theory should seek to explain organizational performance (economic as well as social). In this regard, we also favour the economists' perspective of seeking applied or relevant knowledge.

In each of the above perspectives there are often mutually exclusive theoretical debates and disagreements. There is no room to include the details of these debates in this book. However, students of organization should always bear in mind that virtually all theories of social behaviour rest on often heavily contested theories. There is no one single correct answer to a problem or approach to a problem. This may be a source of frustration for many readers who seek 'the answer' but we hope it will also serve as a source of enjoyment and perhaps a little information for those who seek to understand the problem.

Reference McKenna, E. (1994) *Business Psychology and Organisational Behaviour: A Students' Handbook*, Lawrence Erlbaum Associates Ltd, Sussex.

CHAPTER 2 Behaviour and organizations

Introduction

All organizations are filled with people. They may occupy different positions. Some are managers, others workers; some are owners of their own businesses, others act as trustees of someone else's organization. Whichever is the case, one of the key aspects to understanding what is going on in any organization is to understand the people within it. Why did they choose to apply to that particular organization? How were they selected? What makes them work effectively and enjoy their life in the organization? And what makes them dissatisfied and look for alternative jobs? The answers to these questions and a host of others are the central concerns of organizational behaviour.

What do we mean by behaviour?

Organizations are social collectivities. Behaviour refers to the nature of human interaction and conduct within them. This can be on a one-to-one basis or in groups. The discipline also refers to the behaviour of organizations. We talk of Nestlé's marketing strategy over the next five years, or the new strategies of organizations in the financial services sector. We know that organizations do not really act as if they were a person, yet we often perceive their actions as such. We talk of firms being aggressive or as fair employers and so on. Really, we mean that their managers and staff are moving the organization in these directions. As we shall see, people act on their perceptions, not on objective realities, so the concept of organizations 'behaving' is important. To talk of organizations in this way is called 'reification' (from the Latin word *res*—a thing).

Human behaviour is at the root of organizational behaviour. The discipline draws heavily from the behavioural and social sciences such as psychology, sociology, philosophy, politics and economics. It also shares each of these subject's problems, doubts, questions and logics. However, organizational behaviour is more than just the sum total of these sciences. Because it is the study of human behaviour within specific settings (organizations which have a collective purpose) the aspects of common membership, the collective benefits and maintaining at least some forms of control and performance help to integrate knowledge so that organization behaviour becomes a study in its own right.

What sort of organizations do we mean?

At its broadest, the term organization can refer to any collective social arrangement. It is collective because individuals working alone could not possibly achieve the goals set or the task to be achieved. Thus, Glaxo Wellcome are just as much an organization as the darts team at the local pub. So are groups of musicians, railway enthusiasts' societies and Women's Institutes.

It is the purposeful nature of social groups which makes them describable accurately as organizations. Organizations have to build in to their arrangements the means to achieve given aims (Pugh, 1974) and often have to ensure as far as possible survival of the organization beyond the tenure of its present constituent individuals. Normally, medium and large organizations survive longer than most individuals, although there are exceptions.

This means that specific needs have to be met in these organizations. They must be able to perform effectively and this brings with it the need for some means of controlling what goes on in the organization. There are many criteria of effectiveness. Profit levels, return on investment and working capital are some of the more common measures for business organizations. Control mechanisms also cover a wide range of areas from selection of employees to corporate strategy and direction. These issues have been at the heart of organizational behaviour. In the next section, we outline very briefly the early foundations of the subject.

What is organizational behaviour?

It is the study of the social arrangement of people in organizations. It is concerned with the application of key disciplines such as psychology and sociology specifically to organizations. The subject looks at how social processes are interwoven to form the fabric of organized society and how all these are reflected in the actions of organizations large and small.

The twin themes of control and performance allow us to examine how the subject has developed. What follows is necessarily a very brief and broad outline. For the reader interested in the detail of early theoretical and empirical development in organizational behaviour, Nisbet (1973), Pugh (1974) and Zey-Ferrell and Aiken (1981) would be a fruitful source of ideas.

Scientific management: classical theories

Scientific management is possibly the first approach which set the course for the development of the subject. There are a number of key managers and academics who contributed to the development of scientific management and together we refer to them as the 'classical school' of organizational behaviour. Scientific management (which originated at the turn of the 20th century) is founded on the principles of measurement and precision. There was a concerted effort to identify key aspects of work and organization which could be used to achieve efficiency through immutable principles. Management became a 'science'.

The organization was viewed as a machine which could be made more efficient if universal principles could be applied. Historically, this search paralleled similar developments in the natural sciences. Perhaps the two foremost authors associated with the classical approach were Frederick Winslow Taylor (1911) and Henri Fayol (1949). Their aim was to develop a 'one best way' of organizing.

In a famous address to the House of Representatives Committee in the United States, Taylor outlined the example of the science of shovelling. Having studied the process with respect to iron ore and having identified a 'normal' labourer (Schmidt, by name) Taylor argued that shovelling could be broken down into separate movements each of which had an optimal level of mechanical efficiency. When applied, a consistently greater level of output was achieved.

Taylor also persuaded Frank Bunker Gilbreth (1908) to do the same to analysing the movements involved in bricklaying. By substituting shorter, faster movements for longer, slower ones the output of individual bricklayers was substantially increased. Gilbreth became notorious for being able to speed up almost any routine task. In an era of incentive and bonus schemes based upon productivity rates, his Therblig and Simo charts (which detailed every physical movement in a task) were hailed with enthusiasm.

It should be remembered that there were relatively few models of organization at this time which could act as comparators. The military, the railway companies and the church were the most accessible for comparison. Assumed to be efficient models of organizing, these organizations became role models for many business organizations. Functional differentiation, bureaucracy and specialization were the template for many a company. So was centralization. Fayol (1949) took Taylor's theories of individual working and efficiency and applied them to whole organizations. He wanted to standardize organizational efficiency. It was based on a 'natural order' of centralization in which everything tends toward the brain in living organisms (and all directives come from it). The vocabulary of employment often reflects this model of organization. When advertising for labour, many firms would advertise for 'hands'. Hands were wanted—but not the brains (these were the prerogative of management). And these advertisements were still around in the UK in the 1970s!

Fayol listed his principles of organization as:

- plan ahead
- keep records
- write down policies
- specialize labour and tasks
- ensure commensurate responsibility with authority
- keep managers' spans of control to approximately six people

Many of these principles remain pervasive in today's organizations in the guise of time and motion studies and general ergonomics. Classical theories were subjected to intense criticism on two fronts. First, they were argued to be open to abuse. They could be applied indiscriminately by unscrupulous managers (Gantt, 1919). Second, work organizations proliferated and became large and complex.

The adoption of scientific principles did not appear to work universally, and as general economic depression spread throughout the 1930s, many organizations became patently inefficient and poor performers. Taylor (and Taylorism) became the subject of a Congressional investigation and he was asked to account for himself and his theories. Before this, however, companies like Ford and many other manufacturing firms had adopted wholeheartedly the principles of scientific management and the impact of the whole classical movement can still be felt in modern organizations. Some of the key reasons which led to the demise of scientific management are listed in Table 2.1.

The human relations school

This, as its name implies, was a theory of organizational behaviour which rested more upon human behaviour and less upon the mechanical efficiency of a productive unit. It was well-timed. There was general labour unrest both in America and Britain and the shadow of economic depression was still large and long. Barnard (1938) marks the genesis of human relations

Table 2.1
Key factors in the demise of scientific management

Factor	Reason
Labour becomes a critical force in the organization	As technology increased in complexity, labour became more specialized, taking longer to train in skills. The distinction made earlier by Taylor between manual and mental work became blurred. Labour cost more to recruit and train. Labour became more selective, the power of labour increased and unions and strikes began to appear as powerful antidotes to managerialism
Increasing complexity of markets and products	The need for flexible and adaptive organizational structures became greater. The rigidity of the firm designed on Taylorist principles precluded subsequent change
Political, social and cultural changes	Societal values were beginning to change. No longer were brutal supervision and unquestioned authority considered legitimate features of managerial behaviour
Organizations became large and complex	Firms could no longer be controlled under the direction of one person such as the founding father, for example. A search for good leaders and professional managers became pre-eminent. The focus of achieving good performance and maintaining control turned more toward human factors rather than toward principles of organizational design

theories, although Elton Mayo (1949) and Roethlisberger and Dickson (1939) are equally famous for their experiments in the field and can also be considered founders of the movement. The hallmark of human relations theories is the primacy given to organizations as human co-operative systems rather than as mechanical contraptions. Barnard stressed:

1 *Natural groups* Humans tend to organize themselves into natural social groups which do not always coincide with 'functionally specialized' workgroups. The social thus take precedence over the functional.
2 *Upward communication* Rather than flow 'naturally' from the top of the organization, information should be two-way, from workers to the chief executive. Relevant information comes from the workforce concerning both corporate and individual needs.
3 *Cohesive leadership* Is necessary for the development in executives of the long-term aims of the organization. Good leadership is necessary to communicate these goals to others in the organization. When achieved, this should ensure effective and coherent decision-making.

The year 1939 saw the first large-scale investigations into productivity and social relations. These were the famous Hawthorne Studies which were conducted under the guidance of Elton Mayo. Initially set up to study the effects of illumination intensity on productivity, the studies revealed the importance of informal groups, work norms, the value of human leadership and the important role of psychology in counselling employees (Roethlisberger and Dickson 1939).

The human relations approach generated almost as many questions as it purported to solve. The most famous query has subsequently become known as the 'Hawthorne' effect which is used commonly to describe the influence of experimentation itself as a factor in altering performance levels. The very fact that groups knew they were being studied led to an increase in output. Its assumptions were also subject to question. Did everyone desire freedom at work and the opportunity for self-development to the same extent? Is it possible to prescribe conditions under which groups will be happy? Does social happiness really lead to greater productivity, or are there hidden intervening variables? People also had a life outside the formal workplace. It was not their whole life. To many, a job could be viewed as strictly instrumental in securing money to spend on leisure time.

Debates still rage over these and other questions raised by the human relations approach. It is not surprising, therefore, that subsequent schools of thought began to look outside the single unit of organization for explanations of both human behaviour and organizational performance. Open systems theory, which views a single organization as enmeshed in a much wider environment which has an influence over its functioning and the people within it, is described in more detail in Chapter 17. Socio technical theories also form part of this move away from particularism, human or organizational, and they are covered briefly in the next section. See the list of further readings at the end of this chapter for detailed coverage of these theories.

Socio-technical theories

The focus of these approaches to organization is the relationship between technology and the workgroup. These theories began to gather momentum following the rather wholesale and rapid adoption of the assembly line as an efficient and effective production method.

Socio-technical is a simple concept. It argues that there are two predominant elements to any organization which need management. These are the social and the technical. Bringing in new people or altering the pattern of work does not necessarily mean changing technology, nor does the introduction of new technology mean that social relations in the organization are fixed in one pattern.

Much has been written about the experiences of workers who are subjected to the rigours and restrictions of the assembly line (which was seen by management to be the answer to fast and high-volume production). Some of the best accounts can be read in Walker and Guest (1952) and Terkel (1974).

The results of working on an assembly line are well-known today, but they were not so well known in the 1950s and early 1960s. Workers would become numbed to the job. They would feel drained and lacking in any motivation to work at all. Work was purely instrumental. It paid the bills or it was a job when the alternative was no job at all.

From a manager's viewpoint, the assembly line was a good idea. It made rational economic sense. Economies of scale were soon realized and mass production usually meant mass profits, so that pay levels could be at a higher rate in these plants than elsewhere.

From a worker's viewpoint, the assembly line meant no more seasonal variation in work (no worries about being laid off because of bad weather, etc) and it also gave the security of working for a big company which was less likely to go broke. It also meant more stress and more illness which were related to the pressures exerted by the assembly line.

The assembly line is just one way of organizing activities which are interrelated. The sub-tasks of the whole product are broken down into separate steps and related together so that when they are performed in sequence, the final step of the process produces the final product.

Mass production work is characterized by:

1 a mechanically controlled workplace.
2 repetition
3 requiring minimum skill
4 giving no choice of tools or methods to the worker
5 requiring only surface mental attention

However, volume production of cars does not predetermine the adoption of the assembly line. The use of assembly lines was an overt management decision. At the time, managers gave little attention to considerations of whether the assembly lines were good or bad for employees. In fact, they assumed that the import of new technology made the production process fixed. It was humans who should change.

Fortunately, humans are extremely adaptable. For a time, it looked as if this was a good management decision. Employees adapted to the line and the car factories began to be profitable. Yet developments in the organization and management of coal mining in the UK were beginning to shed doubt on the efficacy of simple assembly line production methods. These studies showed for the first time that managers had a choice in the way they organized the interrelated aspects of work. This kind of thinking was much broader than the human relations school for it looked beyond the individual workplace toward a system of technology in which there was a choice.

In studies of mechanization in coal mining in Britain (Trist and Bamforth, 1951) there were now ways of getting coal from the coal face using new technology. This could loosen more coal per hour than any individual or group of miners working by hand. Coal seams were opened up into what became known as longwalls. A machine could travel along a huge expanse of coal face and hack out all the coal from up to a 100 metre straight run.

Management looked for a way to organize work around this new technology. Previously, miners did all the tasks of coal mining themselves. They:

1 cut the coal
2 loaded the coal on to wagons or conveyor
3 advanced the roof supports and roadways underground

With the new technology, it seemed obvious to borrow from the assembly line mass production techniques for producing coal. This meant that the three stages above were now broken down into three separate jobs. Three shifts meant that it seemed natural to allocate one shift for each task. This soon created unforeseen problems for management:

1 Each shift began to develop different needs and wanted different rewards.
2 The cutters began to be the elite of the shifts with all the rest inferior to them.
3 The pay of each group was calculated on a different basis and each group negotiated separately with management.
4 Management's task was to co-ordinate the production cycle but this proved impossible. Sequencing activities might make sense in theory, but in practice it did not work in the coal mine.

5   The three-shift system led to all sorts of sabotage occurring between the shifts. In order to make the cutter's work doubly hard, for example, the shot-firers would often put only half strength charges in the face. Or they might leave the odd undetonated charge for the cutters to find on their shift. It also led to social grievances being taken into the workplace. The shift system divided people in a way which facilitated getting your own back on someone.

In some mines, the work had to be organized differently since the physical conditions underground did not allow the longwall system to operate fully. Management resisted any changes to the sequential organization of work and tried to impose the longwall three-shift system. This failed. The miners grouped together and formed what we now know today as the Autonomous Working Group (AWG). Characteristics of the group were:

1   *One* group of workers performed all the tasks of the job.
2   Group composition was on a *self-selected* basis.
3   Production became continuous. Each group took over where the last one had finished. It did not matter where each group was on the production cycle.
4   Each individual did not have to possess all the skills required. It just mattered that the group as a whole had the full range of required skills within it.
5   Each group was paid on a common basis.

The function of management on these sites changed dramatically. The autonomous working groups began to operate in a self-regulating way. They effectively managed themselves. Instead of fragmenting the work task and organizing work specialization, the managerial task was now to integrate the activities of the various groups. It also gave managers the time to plan for the future and to look ahead. They were now free from managing the day-to-day activities of the plant and could concentrate on longer-term planning and strategies.

The socio-technical concept has since been developed and replicated all over the world in a whole range of firms. Scandinavian managers did not invent the autonomous working group, but they did invest in it in a big way in many of their manufacturing plants. Saab-Scania, Volvo, Electrolux, and Atlas-Copco have all been recognized for their efforts. Since then, a whole host of firms now uses autonomous working groups.

What is an 'excellent' organization?

Chances are that you have perused the business section of an airport or train station bookshop. If so, you probably couldn't help but notice perhaps the most over-used adjective in the history of organizational behaviour: excellent. Most managers strive to improve their firm's performance and their own behaviour by subtly benchmarking themselves against so-called 'excellent' firms. What defines excellence is largely up to the authors of these terms. The only consistent features of organizations identified as excellent is that such recognition invariably leads to the 'curse of excellence', at which point profits decline, management changes, takeover or bankruptcy loom, etc.

The initiators of the 'excellence' industry were Tom Peters and Bob Waterman, Jr. (Peters and Waterman, 1982). They scoured the US looking for organizations who were perceived to be 'excellent' on a range of measures. They emerged from their research with a 'golden' list of 14 companies: Bechtel, Boeing, Caterpillar, Dana, Delta Airlines, Digital Equipment, Emerson Electric, Fluor, Hewlett-Packard, IBM, Johnson & Johnson, McDonald's, Proctor & Gamble and 3M. Peters and Waterman continued by highlighting nine organizational properties which these companies seemed to share:

- *Staying close to the customer* Innovations arise from listening to the needs of customers. Key management skills here are communicating effectively and spanning the organizational boundary between it and its immediate operating environment.
- *Managing ambiguity and paradox* Change and innovation in the face of external developments must be fostered as a natural knee-jerk response by all individuals in the organization. Key skills are retaining core businesses and at the same time building in strategic flexibility and agility.
- *Stick to the knitting* This reduces the level of complexity and ambiguity faced by managers. Sticking to what you know pays off also by allowing managers more time to think and to experiment.
- *Hands-on, value-driven* Managers must be able to create a sense of purpose and instill commitment in their employees. Key skills require that the manager can also do the job of the employee, not as a substitute, but as a co-worker. Participation and communication are vital aspects.
- *A bias toward action* Not talking problems so intensively that nothing ever is done. Doing something and taking action are essential. This requires a philosophy of accepting mistakes as inevitable, but as a significant learning process, not something to be penalized.
- *Simple form and lean staff* Not to overdo formalization and rules. These should be just sufficient to cover activities and maintain control, but no more than this.
- *Autonomy and entrepreneurship* Excellent companies had an ability to look big but act small though empowering its managers to think and act as if they owned their own 'business'.
- *Simultaneous loose–tight properties* Not quite the paradox it sounds. Basically, this means using tight controls in some areas and not in others. Tight control can be over market analysis and evaluation for example, while fairly loose control needs to be exercised over innovation and idea generation.
- *Productivity through people* This requires cross-functional thinking, collaboration not competition in decision-making, backed up by a highly efficient and over-utilized communication network.

Overall, the resonating theme of excellent companies are its people and its ability to give them just the right amount of responsible autonomy, involvement and commitment. This builds upon previous theories (such as human relations) but differs to the extent that the ultimate criteria for excellence was competitive firms with track records of financial and market success.

However, are the lessons of excellence in the United States translatable to other economic or national contexts? Probably not! Countries such as Japan seemed to treat their employees differently from most Western organizations. For example, Japanese employees were given more trust, more autonomy, were treated as partners in the whole enterprise, enjoyed a lifetime's employment if they wanted and were subject to informal control mechanisms and consensual decision-making (Pascale and Athos 1982).

Many of these aspects have been included in the agenda for re-energizing ailing and flagging organizations in the West. Ouchi and Jaeger (1978) argued that wholesale translation from Japan was improbable given the immense cultural and economic differences between Western countries and Japan, but they argued that a compromise could be reached which included many of the original features. This hybrid was termed by them as the 'Type Z' organization. Features are:

- Long-term (rather than lifetime) employment
- Consensual decision-making
- Individual responsibility
- Informal control
- Holistic concern for employees

Source: adapted from Ouchi and Jaeger (1978: 311).

One of the enduring components of excellent organizations is the emphasis is upon instilling in each member of the organization a sense of strategic vision or holistic view of the direction of the whole organization (Johnston, 1986; Handy, 1987; Kanter, 1984). Commitment is thus achieved through individuals 'internalizing' the culture of their company, rather than through attempts to effect motivation from the 'outside' with the obvious disadvantages of artificiality these bring with them. Chapter 13 discusses the concepts of organizational culture in more detail.

Not surprisingly, the popular business books and their focus on 'excellence' has given rise to its ardent enthusiasts and its strong critics. Enthusiasts argue that adopting such principles as those outlined above are the only way to revive and revitalize organizations facing continual threats and increasing levels of competition. Others argue that all it has done is to provide a set of normative recipes, untried in practice, with little theoretical foundation and with limited utility. Reading 1 by Robert Lee and Reading 2 by P. D. Anthony at the end of Part I neatly summarizes these debates.

Summary

We have explored the foundations of organizational behaviour in this chapter. The last 30 years have seen a massive increase both in theory generation and in research knowledge of many kinds of organizations. Only now is the field beginning to establish its identity as a unique and separate discipline.

The discipline presents a formidable challenge intellectually, for it requires a thorough understanding at many levels of analysis. We need to understand the motives and behaviour of individuals as well as the more global actions [and behaviours] of organizations themselves. Rhetoric and reality need careful distinction as the debates swing backward and forward across a whole array of academic disciplines [economics, psychology, sociology, philosophy to name only some] and cases of organizational practice. From its beginnings in scientific management to today's concerns with sustained competition and change, the subject can look forward to a challenging and stimulating future. The problems and opportunities facing modern organizations bear comparison with those Taylor, Mayo and Trist were grappling with 80, 40 and 20 years ago. They have given us a foundation of knowledge which we can develop and refine in future. The aim of this book is to highlight these developments and to alert the reader to the multitude of contemporary theories and debates.

References

Barnard, C. I. (1938) *The Functions of the Executive*, Harvard University Press, Massachusetts.

Fayol, H. (1949) *General and Industrial Management*, translated by C. Storrs, Pitman, London.

Gantt, H. (1919) *Organizing For Work*, Harcourt, Brace & Hove, New York.

Gilbreth, F. B. (1908) *Field Systems*, Myron C. Clark, New York.

Handy, C. B. (1987) *The Making of Managers*, NEDO, London.

Johnston J. S. (ed.), (1986) *Educating Managers*, Jossey-Bass, San Francisco.

Kanter, R. M. (1984) *The Change Masters: Corporate Entrepreneurs at Work*, Allen & Unwin, London.

Mayo, E. (1949) *Hawthorne and the Western Electric Company: The Social Problems of an Industrial Civilization*, Routledge, London.

Nisbet, R. A. (1973) *The Sociological Tradition*, Heinemann, London.

Ouchi, W. G. and A. M. Jaeger (1978) 'Type Z organizations: stability in the midst of mobility', *Academy of Management Review*, **3**, 305–14.

Pascale, R. T. and A. G. Athos (1982) *The Art of Japanese Management*, Penguin, Harmondsworth.

Peters, T. and R. Waterman Jr. (1982) *In Search of Excellence: Lessons from America's Best Run Companies*, Harper & Row, New York.

Pugh, D. S. (ed.), (1974) *Organization Theory*, Penguin, Harmondsworth.

Roethlisberger, F. J. and W. J. Dickson (1939) *Management and the Worker*, Harvard University Press, Massachusetts.

Taylor, F. W. (1911) *Principles of Scientific Management*, Harper & Row, New York.

Terkel, S. (1974) *Working*, Random House, New York.

Trist E. and K. W. Bamforth (1951) 'Some social and psychological consequences of the longwall method of coal getting', Human Relations, **4** (1), 3–38.

Walker, C. and R. Guest (1952) *The Man on the Assembly Line*, Harvard University Press, Massachusetts.

Zey-Ferrell, M. and M. Aiken (1981) *Complex Organizations: Critical Perspectives*, Scott, Foresman & Co., Glenview, Illinois.

Organizations, management and you

Introduction

The title of this book, *Managing Organizations*, hopefully offers you some indication of our intent to illustrate the breadth of tools, techniques and theories which are used to manage organizations. To some extent, we all manage and are, in turn, managed. Sometimes, being managed provides support and encouragement for the tasks we undertake. At other times, it may seem as if the management process was designed to achieve precisely the opposite effect. The purpose of this chapter is to provide some feel as to how organizational processes are used to manage people. We will consider the typical activities undertaken in many organizations to manage their employees. Sometimes called personnel, sometimes employee relations, we will use the presently popular term: human resource management (HRM).

Human resource management

Human resource management is the process by which organizations seek to generate an acceptable return from their employees' efforts. The term 'human resource management' (HRM) has evolved from 'personnel management' and 'industrial relations'. One of the forces driving this jargon shift is management's recognition that employees are the fundamental asset of any organization and should be actively managed to ensure that maximum value is derived.

The primary driver of HRM practices is to maximize the value provided by the efforts of people working in the organization. By using the term 'value', the adherents of HRM display a key component of their approach to the field. From an organizational perspective, employees are viewed as 'social capital' (Beer, *et al.*, 1985, Caruso, 1992). It highlights the need for the adoption of rational and measurable management techniques to assess the contribution of people in much the same fashion as the finance function would use for fixed assets and working capital. By defining employees in such terms, HRM can offer a perspective on issues such as the 'front-end' investment and the expected return over time. For example, a decision regarding whether to pay more (upfront) for an experienced new employee who could, theoretically, be expected to contribute more quickly to the organization's objectives, or, go for someone with less experience (lower initial salary) but may require on-going investment over time to be brought up to speed.

Continuing the analogy with finance, it is recognized that an organization's fixed assets get worn out over time and therefore require maintenance and care to ensure long-lasting productivity. In HRM terms, this could equally apply to employee needs for on-going training and development as well as creating a positive work environment which should increase personal motivation.

The intention of HRM, as opposed to a more traditional view, is to accentuate the need to force employee management out of the organizational 'backwater' and into the forefront of strategic issues facing the organization. It emphasizes the need to link business strategy with the planning and implementation of HR practices. (Hendry, *et al.*, 1988).

As you might already have anticipated, there have also been concerns expressed regarding the desire to have organizations view its staff in a similar fashion to its machines. One concern that has been expressed (Keenoy, 1990) is that HRM is undertaken as a 'one-way' process insofar as measures and improvements are imposed on employees in much the same way as capital expenditure decisions are conducted.

What do organisations want?

Organizations are intangible legal entities which are surrounded by people, capital and equipment to create itself. Although we may imply that an 'organization' is a tangible, resource allocating decision-maker, it is the individuals within it who make it happen. Given the broad range of individuals who make decisions in organizations, it should not be too surprising to note that there exists a wide divergence of views regarding what is required from employees. At best, we can draw some rough outline of trends in the workplace and extrapolate towards an answer to this question. It would appear that the trend in workforce management is moving towards flexibility. In the final section of this book, we will consider some of the trends in how organizations and employees are reshaping the workplace. However, at this stage it might be sufficient to consider the pull towards ever more flexibility from the organization's perspective as well as the employee's. Blyton (1992) identified four forms of flexibility which he argues are occurring simultaneously in the work environment.

Task flexibility

Increasingly, organizations are looking for employees who are ready and willing to undertake a wide range of tasks in the organization. In some ways, this goes against the established theories of specialization of labour covered in Chapter 2. Flexibility in task refers to overcoming traditional demarcations in workplace practices to create a multi-skilled workforce. From an HRM perspective this permits greater freedom to move a labour resource to where it is most needed. From an individual's standpoint, this can also provide some greater job security insofar as the alternative might be redundancy if the organisation does not value their particular expertise. Another form of task flexibility is vertical capability. For example, many organizations have dramatically reduced clerical and secretarial levels in favour of providing the remaining staff with access to computers, voice mail systems, etc. The result has been that middle-level managers have been forced to undertake their own administration (which they did not have to do in the past).

Numerical flexibility

Given the volatile state of many competitive markets, management teams in many organizations have been looking for ways to vary their staff costs and numbers according to need. This has led to the evolution of HR strategies away from providing job security to employees towards a greater use of temporary and short-term contract workers. In many instances, this shift in attitude has generated serious consequences in terms of motivation, job satisfaction, and leadership. It may even be argued that many of the theories which underpin organizational behaviour can be called into question due to the fundamental changes in defining such established terms as 'a job' or 'an employee'.

Temporal flexibility

Traditionally, employees have been asked to report to work at the same time and place and leave at the same time. From a control point of view, this was desirable as it simplified the human resource planning process. However, advances in technology and HR systems has provided the opportunity to offer employees a greater degree of choice regarding when to work (flexitime) and where to work (teleworking). In theory, this can permit a greater number of people to enter the workforce who were unable to fit in with the established work structures. On the other hand, organizations can reduce costs due to not requiring a workplace for all employees due to teleworking and by employing part-time staff (which are often cheaper than full-time staff, due to the company providing a restricted set of benefits).

Financial flexibility

Previous generations of workers strived to negotiate fixed wage rates with their employers so as to provide security for themselves and their families. However, changing economic conditions have meant that many employees are willing to trade-off a secure wage packet for a more flexible arrangement which permits a greater up-side as well as more freedom to the individual. The increasing use of part-time and teleworkers has encouraged organizations to develop such new reward arrangements. Today it is not uncommon for employees to be offered some mixture of performance-related pay, profit-sharing, share option schemes etc., as a method of creating greater flexibility and reduce the overall cost of labour.

Human resource planning

Whether we work in large or small organizations, the need for developing HR plans is vital. This is not to imply a requirement for specific structures and operating systems. Rather, it recognizes the benefits of co-ordination and communication between business requirements and employee capabilities and capacities. Large organizations undertake such HR planning tasks with greater rigour and defined methodologies than smaller entities, although mistakes and omissions still get made (Torrington and Hall 1987).

Despite the need to develop effective HR plans, experience shows that many organizations—even large ones—do not recognize the benefits. (Torrington and Hall, 1987). In our research and consultancy visits with senior executives in organizations of varying sizes, we have found that asking for an overview of their HR plan can be a real conversation killer. Often we find that senior line managers seek to assure us that such plans do exist, albeit within the HR department. In such cases, we would find that if the plans did indeed exist, they would updated very irregularly and serve to inform only those within the HR function. The most effective HR plans are of course, those which are fully integrated into the organization's business plan. In this way, HR becomes a key component of the structure to deliver successful business strategies.

The topic of HR planning is large and complex and we could not hope to do the subject justice in the space we have available here (see Hendry, *et al.*, 1988 for detailed applications of planning). However, it is important to highlight some key developments. As a field of study, HR planning is evolving rapidly. It has moved from a highly quantitative manpower planning system towards a more integral part of the organization's overall strategic planning process. This is due, in no small part, to the increasing problems organizations face due to skill or competence shortages. As their markets become more competitive and the speed of competitive response becomes vital to survival, organizations are discovering that they require their human resources to be ready and able to contribute much more quickly as well. The cost of not having the appropriate skills or knowledge outweighs the financial costs of developing and maintaining an appropriate labour force.

The remainder of this chapter will deal with some of the managerial dilemmas of comprehensive HR planning. The intention is to highlight where organizational behaviour, as a field of study, links with the application of HRM techniques in organizations. In doing so, we will consider some of the mutually dependent activities associated with:

1 resourcing;
2 development;
3 compensation; and
4 employee relations (Smilansky, 1997)

Resourcing The recruitment, deployment and departure of employees is at the heart of developing an HR resource strategy. The initial step in resource planning is defining what resources will be required in the future. An important contribution in this area has been the work undertaken on the subject of managerial competencies (Boyatzis, 1982).

Boyatzis' original research in competencies was based on identifying 'effective' and 'ineffective' performers and identifying those behaviours which discriminated between them. The methodological dilemma revolves around problems with classifying and identifying 'effectiveness'. The issue is that such definitions are invariably linked with performance in the past as well as under specific sets of circumstances. To extrapolate such measures, particularly if they are subjective, can be somewhat dubious.

A managerial competency framework rests on the ability to identify the functions and demands of a job, define the characteristics necessary for an individual to be successful in this role, and develop a form of determining whether or not the potential job holder has the necessary competencies.

As mentioned earlier, despite the logic of a managerial competency framework, deep-seated doubts exist as to its overall validity (Sparrow, 1996). At the heart of this concern is the uncertainty surrounding the methodologies used to undertake competency-based analyses. Many of the tools and techniques used in competency analysis (and in many other parts of HRM) are used in ways which are outside the scope of their original purpose. As one occupational psychologist commented, 'I didn't realise you were going to make such important decisions on the basis of this (shaky) evidence' (Sparrow, 1996).

A vital part of the resourcing function within an organization is selection. Selection is a systematic attempt to make a very complex decision—filling the right jobs with the right people. As Watson (1989) notes: 'Selection techniques cannot overcome failures in recruitment, they merely make them evident'. Yet most managers will deal with the process of selection as a means of implementing the organization's human resources plan (in whatever form this exists). While relatively few managers get directly involved in recruitment, preferring to leave the task to human resource specialist or consultants, most managers are involved in selection decisions (Institute of Personnel and Development, 1995).

There are a number of standard selection techniques which managers can use to help them reach a decision on the suitability of a candidate for a job. These include:

1 Psychological testing
2 Physical testing
3 Interviews
4 Assessment centres
5 Familiarization courses

In order to use any of the above, the first step is to examine the characteristics of the post to be filled. This process is called job analysis.

Job analysis   This comprises a formal assessment of the skills, knowledge and experience needed to carry out a specific job effectively. For a job which already exists in the organization (that is, not a brand new position) this will comprise observation of employees who are filling comparable roles. Detailed records can then be compiled about the nature of the job and the understanding of any technology involved.

This is usually achieved through observation and interviews, occasionally using specific techniques such as work method study and measurement. The result of all this is a *job description*, which is the basis for the subsequent selection decision. Managers can now specify the characteristics and skill levels required by applicants for the job. For management posts, this usually specifies the number of employees supervised, the scope of authority and position in the hierarchy. For non-managerial posts this specifies the sequence of operations, the average time taken to carry out a task and the methods adopted to perform the task. Job descriptions will also spell out variables such as age, level of education, formal qualifications, level of previous training, experience, physical characteristics, dexterity, literacy and numeracy. Figure 3.1 shows a typical chart used to construct a job description.

Figure 3.1
A typical job description chart (supervisory role)

JOB
Title ....   Production responsibility
Location ....
Number of subordinates ....   Budget responsibility ....
POSITION/AUTHORITY
Responsible to ....   Needs the permission of a senior to
Responsible for ....
RESPONSIBILITIES
75% of time   ....
10% of time   ....
15% of time   ....

Working environment
 	
   Sitting, standing, driving, combination
   Noise, heat, cold, dirt, risk, hours, holidays, etc.

Psychological testing

These tests aim to be able to construct a profile of any candidate on such factors as personality, attitudes, values, intelligence and perception. The idea is to assume that the results obtained on the day of the tests will accurately predict how the candidate will subsequently perform in the organization. According to Cronbach (1970) a psychological test is one which enables a systematic procedure to be followed in assessing and observing a person's behaviour by using numerical scales or a category system.

There are a battery of such tests. Most used are those accredited by the British Psychological Society. Commonly used tests in Britain include the Myers-Briggs Type Indicator (used to identify differences in the way people look at events), the FIRO-B (which examines an individual's needs and likely behaviour in areas of interpersonal relationships, the CPI (which provides scores on 20 different scales such as dominance, sociability, tolerance and flexibility), Cattell's (1974) 16PF (personality factor) test, and Rotter's (1966) Internal–External Locus of Control questionnaire. The latter two present statements and questions in a forced choice format. The individual has to choose one or the other statement in all cases. In the event of ambiguity, the candidate is instructed to choose the statement with which he or she most agrees. The 16PF test comprises 187 questions; the Locus of Control test comprises 29 statements. Both rely on the trait theory of personality which examine the predilections of individuals to act or think in particular ways. These can be inherited or acquired (Chapter 4 outlines these theories in more detail and provides a criticism of them). Figures 3.2 and 3.3 show typical profiles for the 16PF and Locus of Control tests.

Figure 3.2
Personality profiles of female clerks and general managers (mixed sex) using Cattell's 16PF test

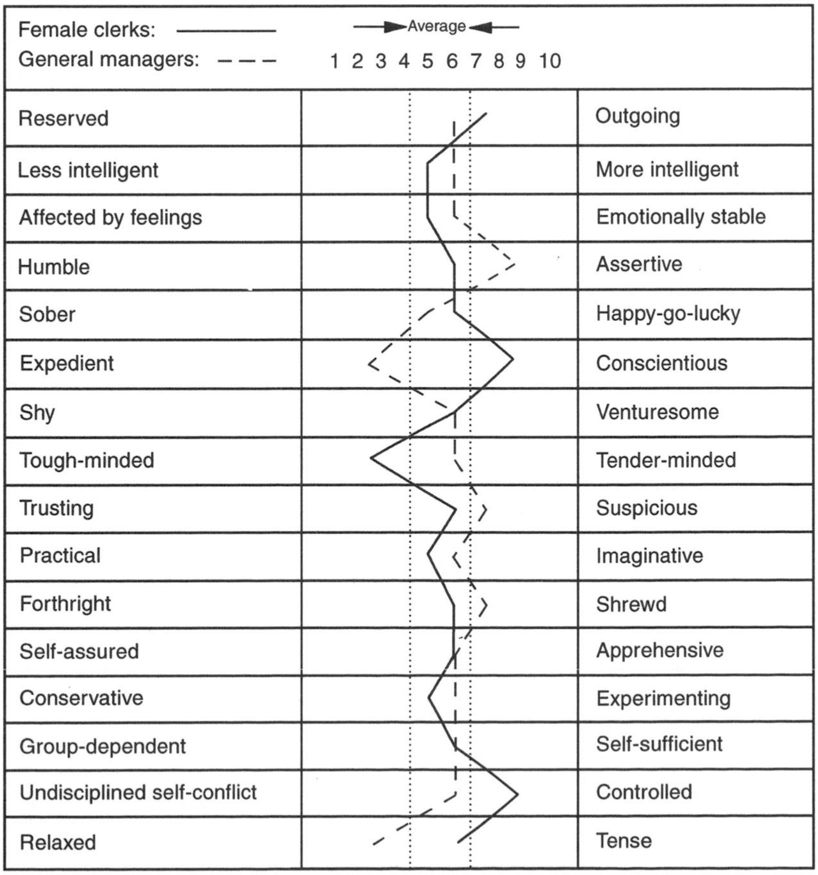

Figure 3.3
Locus of Control
profile using Rotter's
test (2nd year UK
Business Studies
undergraduates)

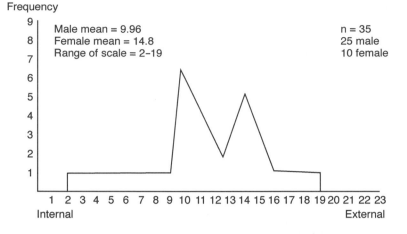

A study conducted (by the authors) of 40 female clerks and general managers (from a financial services organization) revealed the results shown in Figure 3.2. The female clerks tended to be conscientious, tough-minded, controlled and outgoing (persevering, moralistic, with a strong self-image, coupled with a no-nonsense attitude; they are generally self-reliant but are easy-going and warm to others). The general managers tended to be more assertive, expedient and relaxed than the clerks (more aggressive, stubborn, feel few obligations but are relatively easy about it all). Of course, this is just one sample. One could not imply that all clerks and general managers would display similar profiles.

Figure 3.3 shows some results for a small group of undergraduate business students from the University of Warwick. Internals consider that they are in charge of their own destiny: whatever happens to them is a direct consequence of their own actions. Externals feel the reverse. Ill luck, chance and external circumstances will confound whatever they do. So outcomes are not attributable solely to individual actions. Most students clustered around the mean of 11.5, males being generally more internal than the females. Again, this result reflects just the characteristics of that sample and does not necessarily indicate a profile for all British undergraduates.

Reliability and validity

In all cases, tests should be both *reliable* and *valid*.

Reliability of a test is the consistency with which it produces the same score throughout a series of measurements.

Validity is the degree to which a test measures what it is intended to measure. There are a number of facets to determining validity:

1 *Face validity* Does the method feel valid to the tester as well as the candidate? Although face validity is somewhat superficial, it is important in convincing those involved that the results are meaningful. Some selection instruments such as personality questionnaires have a low face validity so that respondents cannot tell which items refer to which personality traits.

2 *Predictive validity* This is the degree of correlation between the outcome of the selection process and the actual ability of the candidate to do the job in question.

> **3** *Content validity* This concerns the degree to which a particular
> selection instrument is actually measuring what the assessors want
> measured. For example, if the assessors felt that good interpersonal
> skills were a key success factor in a job, it would be important to
> insure that whatever selection instrument was used provided a
> measure of this factor. A poor example of content validity in this case
> might be a 'good smile' category on an interview checklist.

Although both the above tests have robust reliability and validity scores,
doubts have still been raised concerning their consistency (see Ghiselli,
1966; Peck and Whitlow, 1975). Changes in the context in which the test is
used can undermine validity despite attempts to standardize conditions and
instructions. Many companies settle for face validity.

The proliferation of psychometric tests in the selection process is
growing rapidly. McHenry (1997) reported that the market for such
instruments was growing at 30% per year. One concern raised by
McHenry is the frequency of cases of misuse of the testing instruments.
This is due to the naïvety of the users, the exaggerated claims of the test
publishers, and the misuse of the tests due to either ignorance or malice.
Another area of concern is the potential for in-built discrimination due to
racial, sexual or national stereotypes. Therefore, it is important for
potential users of such powerful instruments to ensure that the
questionnaire has been fully tested in the 'local' market and does not
contain hidden discriminatory factors. Given the increasing vigilance of
anti-discrimination legislation, naïve or malicious users of such
instruments could leave themselves open to legal prosecution.

Physical and competency tests

Many organizations ask that potential employees submit to a general health
test to see if there are any major problems with cardio-vascular processes,
eyesight and so forth. Tests which examine specific skills are relatively rare.
Airline pilots, police officers, steeplejacks and some jobs in the armed forces
are ones which specify and require certain physical characteristics
(minimum height, fast reactions, above average stamina and physical fitness).

Other physical competencies include static strength, the maximum force
that can be exerted against external objects (e.g., lifting weights), and
stamina, the capacity to sustain maximum effort requiring cardio-vascular
exertion (for example, a hundred metre dash). Once again, the relevance of
these competencies varies from job to job. It is up to the manager to
establish where and how a given competency becomes important.

Watson (1989) points to the problems of reliability in physical tests. He
cites cases of pilots who, having passed the Civil Aeronautics Administration
fitness examination, displayed a 43% disqualifying rate on re-examination!
Neither do physical tests appear to predict future performance (at least not
those tests which are medically oriented). Again, Watson reports the case of
RAF pilots who showed no correlation between their accident rates over a
10-year period and whether or not they met the physical standards required.

Each of us is acquainted with various *competency* tests used to measure
mental aptitudes and abilities. Some of these provide an overall 'IQ' score,
while others provide measures of more specific competencies required of
people entering various educational programmes or career fields. Many
universities which offer MBA degrees now require applicants to take the
Graduate Management Admission Test (GMAT). It supposedly can serve as
an indicator of the aptitude of the applicant for business studies. All such

tests seek to measure mental aptitude or ability and thereby facilitate the screening and selection of applicants.

All selection techniques should provide the recruiter with a greater insight into the probability that the selected candidate will perform to the expected level. The use of psychometric tests and other forms of assessment techniques are designed to lower the risk of incorrect selection. One study examined the overall usefulness of a variety of selection techniques and compared them to selection by chance (that is, 'eeney, meeny, miny, mo . . .'). The results of their assessment are shown in Table 3.1 below.

Interviewing

This (combined with the use of written and verbal references) is the most frequently used selection test of British companies. As a technique it is cheap and easy to conduct, but full of potential problems. In this section we shall outline some of the problems associated with the interview. More structured approaches, such as assessing intelligence and aptitudes during the interview are discussed in Chapter 4.

The interview is the time when the interviewer (usually a manager) meets the prospective candidate face-to-face. The manager can choose the setting to provide a variety of desired contexts. These can range from the threatening (sparsely furnished room with uncomfortable chairs and over-bright or bare lighting) through 'businesslike' to very informal and relaxed, where the candidate can, in theory be him or herself. The crucial point is that the interview is a process where the manager makes a personal judgement about whether the prospective candidate is suitable and will 'fit-in'. This personal judgement relies heavily upon perceptual interpretation. This is how the interviewer perceives the interviewee.

A great deal of research has gone into assessing the interview process. Given the often subjective nature of interviews, it is fraught with problems such as preconceptions, environmental factors, and inefficiency. (Beardwell and Holden, 1994). However, it is difficult to imagine too many managerial appointments being made without some form of interview being conducted. Indeed, the difficulty does not lie in the interview process itself, but in the bundle of emotions, perceptions and subjective judgements that is the interviewer(s).

Barriers to effective selection

The key to an effective and fair selection method is that it should provide information about potential candidates that is relevant, useful and allows comparison between alternative candidates. If cost was no object, a selection

Table 3.1
Selection techniques versus chance selection

Method	Percentage better than chance %
Assessment centres	17–18
Work sample/simulation	14–29
Supervisory/line manager evaluation	18
Mental ability	6–20
Biodata	6–14
References	3–7
Interviews	2–5
Personality 'tests' and other self-report questionnaires	2.5
Graphology	0

Source: Nelson and Wedderburn (1988)

method could be constructed which would permit all characteristics to be evaluated, cross-matched and validated. However, in reality, this cannot often be considered. Therefore, selection processes tend to seek a balance among a variety of factors including:

1 cost;
2 validity and reliability;
3 ease of use; and
4 fairness.

Possibly the most fundamental problem hindering the selection of the right candidate is the human failing of being unable to perceive others accurately. Factors which influence perception include:

- **Stereotyping**   A consistent difficulty in any selection process is the tendency to incorporate some form of stereotyping. The definition of stereotyping is the tendency to form opinions on the basis of very few facts. The problem with stereotypes is that they are oversimplifications of reality and therefore, untrue. Although there may be some grain of truth which lies behind them, they often are the result of some small perceived differences which are blown out of all proportion as a way of distinguishing between ourselves and others.
- **Gender and age**   There have been countless studies which have examined the issue of age and gender bias in organizations (Rosen and Jerdee, 1974). Generally speaking, younger people view older employees as resistant to change, more rigid, less creative, fewer physical abilities, etc. However, when we consider this list again, we might notice that it can apply equally well to young people. The same issues apply to gender-based bias. The problem with gender bias is that it can often be incorporated in an individual's self-perception. For example, a study found that males and females equally ascribe masculine characteristics, attitudes and temperaments as key attributes to a managerial role. (Schein, 1975) This has two damaging effects. First, males may not select females for managerial roles as they do not have the characteristics they perceive as relevant. Second, females may choose not to pursue managerial appointments because they feel that they do not possess the perceived masculine characteristics.
- **Halo effect**   This occurs where the perceiver already has an overall impression of an individual. This may be favourable or unfavourable (that is, good or bad). More specific traits, or isolated events are then placed into this overall context of generalized perception. Thus, someone who is perceived as diligent and hardworking is unlikely to be perceived as lazy and cavalier if he or she 'plays truant' from work for a few days. Another person taking the same action (but someone who was perceived generally unfavourably) very likely would be categorized as lazy. It would be 'typical' behaviour. Evaluation is thus influenced by an overall impression (the halo).
- **Projection**   From a psychological perspective, projection is a human defence mechanism through which we assign our own feelings to others rather than acknowledge this in ourselves. For example, if you are describing a frightening situation you had been in with a partner or friend, you might describe it afterward by saying that your partner was frightened and that you saw them through it.
- **Logical error**   Perception may also be confounded by the tendency to 'fill

in the missing data' about a person. We learn to associate traits together (Asch, 1946). When we perceive some traits in a person, we naturally assume that he or she must also have other traits we associate with them. This is known as *logical error*. It is based on the notion that we tend always to associate certain traits together.

The selection interview: advantages and disadvantages

The majority of jobs in British organizations are filled following at least one face-to-face interview. Advantages include:

1 It is relatively quick. It combines presenting the job to the candidate and the information-gathering process about the candidate's skills in social interaction, verbal fluency and technical knowledge.
2 Interviews are 'expected' by candidates and are easy to arrange in most organizations.
3 It is not easy to specify an equally good alternative way of selecting candidates since most employers want to 'see' their prospective employees and to talk to them.
(Robbins, 1989; Arvey and Campion, 1982).

Disadvantages include:

1 All interviews are subject to perceptual biases. These may be inaccurate.
2 Interviewers often find it difficult to differentiate between relevant and irrelevant information in the interview process.
3 Multiple interviewers are likely to pick up on different aspects during the interview and so reach different conclusions about the candidate.
4 Early impressions (often gained in the first few minutes) are likely to colour subsequent judgements.
(Wicks, 1984)

As a general rule of thumb, selection interviews should be well thought out in advance with a clear structure. If there are a number of candidates being interviewed it is best to adopt as similar a structure and format as possible for each interview.

Assessment centres

As managers become increasingly aware of the costs of getting selection decisions wrong, assessment centres have become increasingly popular. Fundamentally, they consist of gathering together a number of candidates and submitting them to an amalgamation of selection techniques (interviews, simulations, role plays, psychometric questionnaires, etc.) with a number of trained assessors to eliminate personal bias. The idea is that by considering the candidates 'side-by-side', and using a variety of techniques and different assessors, overall selection validity is increased. The fundamental drawback of assessment centres is their cost and overall complexity. Assessors are usually drawn from the senior management population of the organization and need to be trained to focus their attention on particular aspects of the assessment tools. In addition, the assessment centres need to be highly structured and well managed given the number of people involved in the process.

The most common use of assessment centres is for the selection of management personnel, among individuals already employed by the organization. Typically, two to four days will be spent going through psychological tests and exercises such as 'in-basket' exercises and 'leaderless group discussions'.

An in-basket exercise is designed to simulate a large pile of correspondence which a manager is likely to be faced with after a few days' absence. The exercise assesses the candidate's ability to set priorities, to delegate and to use judgement in handling the information. Leaderless groups assess the candidate's ability to be part of (and to lead) a group in making a decision. Candidates are usually judged on how effectively they communicate orally, how persuasive they are, how sensitive they are to others' feelings and on their ability to lead a group.

Evidence suggests that assessment centres are extremely good predictors of future performance in managerial positions (see Gaugher *et al.*, 1987). Although they still do retain the criticism that the factors being assessed are only 'simulations' rather than the job itself. They are more expensive than interviews, but perhaps their demonstrably better performance over interviews makes them cost-effective in the long run. Selecting the wrong managers can be very costly indeed.

Development

Although selection is designed to recruit the most competent individual, he or she is unlikely to remain competent for the whole of their career. As changes take place in technology, knowledge, and innovations, so too will the demands placed upon specific jobs. This is where training and development comes in. First, we need to differentiate between training and development which are often wrongly used as synonyms.

Training is a systematic process whereby an individual learns skills, abilities and knowledge to further both organizational and personal goals. In general terms, training is focused on helping individuals fulfil the requirements of their *present* role.

Development is more future oriented. It is usually intended for those individuals who are perceived in the organization as having the desire and potential to undertake other roles. Although the organization often has a responsibility in creating appropriate development activities and programmes, it relies more upon the individual's initiative to ask questions and to bring out important points for consideration. More precisely, it should be called self-development since the impetus for development is very much grounded in self and not others.

On-site training

The belief here is that employees can best learn the specifics of a job through training in the actual work environment. This can be very effective in learning specific techniques such as in apprenticeships. Skilled crafts such as plumbing, welding, building construction are learned from seasoned and skilled individuals in the organization. Often, the apprentice will have previously learned the basics of the trade at a college of further education. Training increases skill levels and tailors techniques to particular requirements (for example, oil pipe welding, gas rig construction).

Off-site training

This includes any form of training which takes place away from the individual's workplace. One reason for off-site training can be to develop inter-personal or problem-solving skills (rather than technical expertise); another can be that training on site could be both expensive (by slowing production) and potentially dangerous (Robbins, 1989).

In some cases, organizations have training areas equipped with replica machines and tools away from the main production process. This is known as 'vestibule' training. It can also take the form of 'simulation' whereby individuals such as airline pilots can gain knowledge of particular situations without actually flying a real aircraft. Where individuals also have to learn a great deal of new information, then classroom training can also be used as an additional back-up. This includes films, lectures, computer-based training software and so on.

These latter techniques are relatively rare in Britain. Both Taylor (1980) and Keep (1989) point to the enormous preference for apprenticeships in most British companies. In the face of new initiatives to reform apprenticeships from the recessions of the early 1980s, the number of new apprentices in manufacturing has decreased markedly (240 000 in 1964 compared with 7000 apprentices and 2000 new technicians in 1986). As Keep (1989: 181) says:

> Even allowing for the substantial reduction in employment in manufacturing and the changing demands of technology . . . the decline . . . is little short of astonishing.

Despite government rhetoric about other training initiatives, not much progress has been made. It seems that other forms of training have not taken the place of apprenticeships in Britain (such as vocational education and training) and despite some arguments in the data, Britain compares very badly with European countries such as Germany in adult training overall.

Management development

Alongside training, management development is a relatively new venture. For a concise history of management development from the 1940s, see Sadler (1989). Not all of management development is strictly in line with the earlier definition of development. Much of it could be said to be training. There is on-site training (using more senior mentors) and off-site training using business schools, or management and conference centres. Alternatively, in-house management training programmes are conducted by professional trainers brought in specifically for the task.

Training managers, however, does require a great deal of commitment if it is to be effective. Two key reports (Constable and McCormick, 1987; Handy, 1987), emphasize this point. Although many organizations in Britain do offer training and the opportunity for development to their managers, the majority do not. Most managers lacked even basic formal educational training and, on average, received extra training of approximately one day per year. Opportunities for development are very limited indeed. According to Handy (1987) Britain lagged significantly behind competitor European countries and he suggested a 'development charter' for management development which includes a minimum of five days off-site training per year for every manager. We await further initiatives in this area with great interest.

Whether or not management skills can be categorized and assessed in this way is open to question, particularly in the light of Mintzberg's (1973) account of what managers actually do. They interact frequently, deal with many issues per day, spend relatively short amounts of time on each issue and prefer verbal to written communication. It would seem that managerial activity might be too complex, changeable and ambiguous for the measurement of specific and rigid categories of achievement.

Lateral career movement

One commonly attempted development technique is job rotation. This involves moving managers from one department to another to familiarize them with the workings and the demands of each function. Development can occur on at least two fronts. First, managers gain an appreciation of the whole organization rather than just develop a perspective solely from their own function. Second, the 'generalist' experience thus gained can be of immense benefit in developing managers for senior positions in the organization.

Job rotation has had more success in non-managerial positions than with managers in Britain (Buchanan, 1989). It can help relieve the boredom of monotonous jobs and can keep attention levels relatively higher on individual tasks. With British managers, job rotation has not met with the same broad levels of success. Recent studies indicate that managers often view working 'in another function' or alongside others in cross-functional teams with great suspicion. They tend to become protective about information and about their 'own' function (see Tunnicliff, 1988; Davies, 1988). This supports the political perspective of organizations which is outlined in Chapter 11. Chapter 7 gives greater detail on the topic of job redesign and rotation.

Reward management

Reward management is inextricably linked with concepts of motivation (see Chapter 5). As a critical component of HRM, we would only wish to highlight some of the key dilemmas HR managers face when designing or altering reward structures in organizations.

In the broadest sense, reward management covers: developing remuneration strategies, linking these strategies to individual jobs and people, managing the often extensive and complex range of benefits and expenses involved with a workforce and, perhaps most importantly, ensuring that everyone gets paid the correct amount in a timely fashion—all at minimal cost to the organization.

Criticism of reward management systems abound (Kohn, 1997). Rewards are at their worst when they are made artificially scarce—with one winner and many losers. The result of this approach leads to competition followed swiftly by anxiety and is a highly effective way of demotivating all those who believe they stand no chance of gaining the reward.

Rosabeth Moss Kanter (1989) commented that '. . . traditional pay systems . . . are under attack for being neither cost-effective nor motivating people to do more'. A contributing set of causal factors have led many organizations to a 'no-win' situation regarding reward management. First, the reward systems which have been put in place are usually inflexible. Second, there has been a tradition of setting pay and benefits by reference to national or regional agreements which does not allow flexibility either. Third, many organizations view rewards as consisting almost solely of pecuniary benefits—which also limits flexibility and creates expectations in the minds of employees.

One topic which is taxing the mind of HR managers and their consultants is the link between pay and performance. A growing number of organizations are moving towards performance-related pay packages (Sparrow, *et al.*, 1994) The essence of this approach is to combine a relatively low fixed salary component (60–80%) with a variable 'top-up' depending upon any number of organizational, departmental or individual variables. These might include: individual bonuses (based on individual performance), team bonuses (attaining some team performance level, with all team members sharing the bonus pot in some predetermined fashion), organizational bonuses (based on the organization hitting predetermined objectives, with the rewards being distributed in some fashion—usually related to a percentage of basic pay).

A rule of thumb regarding the design of reward systems is: 'If you can't measure it, you can't pay for it'. Therefore, organizations are forced to develop appraisal systems which link performance and pay in a clear and easily measured way. Given the overall importance of establishing a fair and equitable link, it may come as somewhat of a surprise to learn that 80% of UK organizations are dissatisfied with their appraisal schemes (Sparrow, 1996). A fundamental flaw to any appraisal scheme is that the appraisal process is designed to motivate you for the future, despite rewarding you for the past. The implication is simple, you will probably perform in the future as you did in the past. Perhaps you might work harder, but it would be unlikely that you would look for ways to work differently. As such, it does not really offer the individual much encouragement to change or try new ideas.

The most recent approach to reward management is through the use of competencies. The general idea is that we should pay employees for developing and using their own competencies. As long as organizations can identify and measure competencies, then they can reward staff on the basis of their presence and relative strength. Although the idea is attractive, there are some methodological flaws which limit its take-up. First, it can be complex to administer given the need to identify the key competencies, establish a 'price' for each exhibited competency, and measure the presence of the competency in individuals.

Second, there is a need to evolve the critical competencies over time as the needs of the organization changes. As markets and the competitive environment forces organizations to adapt ever more quickly, employees are finding that highly valued competencies of the past are now less desirable. In such situations, conflict, demotivation and a loss of employee morale can create an undesirable situation where new recruits (with the newly fashionable competencies) are resented by the existing staff. The results are predictable and usually negative.

Employee relations

The on-going maintenance of the workforce and their role in the production process falls within the broad umbrella term of employee relations. It includes: organizational and job design, change management, internal communication, trade union relations, health and safety, equal opportunities, grievance and dispute arbitration, counselling and employee welfare, and general HR consultancy to line managers. It should be pointed out that this activity is often distributed in organizations among many different functions. Although larger organizations will often have individuals or departments responsible for each of the above mentioned areas, this is unlikely to be true in small firms.

Career management

A career is the (usually) linear sequence of steps taken by an individual through a number of organizational positions. Career correlates strongly with age (Hall, 1976) so the potential for substantial developments is likely to become less as the manager gets older:

Early career During this stage, individuals are just completing their transition from education to occupation. Their personal lives are also subject to change—moving home, getting married, having children, etc. Career plans for this stage include mobility and the stretching of one's abilities. Potential for development is high.

Mid-life transition   Around late 30s and early 40s career becomes an overwhelming concern. Often there is a conflict between demands of family and career for both men and women. Frustration and cynicism toward the 'system' (the organization) that is, are often the result. Potential for development decreases.

Late career   Around the 50s and onward, the individual will more or less have become resolved to the demands and the operation of the 'system'. Ideals and objectives will have mellowed and cynicism may have increased to a point where development is virtually impossible.

The moral of the career stage analysis seems to be 'start developing managers as early as possible'. There is research evidence to support this view, also indicating that managers who receive particularly challenging jobs in their early career go on to be more successful, stay with the organization longer and carry on the process of self-development (Berlew and Hall, 1966; Van Maanen and Schein, 1977).

Summary

The importance of the individual as a resource for the organization has been the keynote of this chapter. We have concentrated upon how organizations can attract and select the kind of individuals they would like (or need). Examining this deceptively simple process reveals that a large number of psychological processes are likely to confound selection. Largely this is because humans tend to distort the information coming to them from the outside world and from other people. Perception in all its guises comes into play.

Once in an organization, the focus of attention becomes the progression of individuals both in terms of training and development. There are some predictable results from research in this area. For example, managers become increasingly harder to train and develop as they get older. There are some unpredictable results too. Britain does not fare very well in comparison to European competitors in the extent to which it invests in the training and development of its managers. Only a handful of organizations take this seriously and have formal, systematic programmes for their managers. This is despite government and private initiatives to increase the level and scope of training since 1980 to the present day.

So far, we have not discussed the pool of labour from which even the imperfect selection processes and training methods we have described have to draw recruits. This is particularly poignant given demographic predictions for the 1990s. These indicate a drop of 20% in young people available by 1995, particularly in the range 16–19 years old. The overall size of the available labour force is increasing, however, around 80% of this net increase comprising women returning to work after having had a family. The 'balance' of the labour market will alter and will bring with it the need for recruitment and selection processes to be sensitive to these changes alongside changes in training and employment practices. These demands of the future are discussed in more detail in Part VII of this book.

References

Arvey, R. D. and J. E. Campion (1982) 'The employment interview: a summary and review of recent research', *Personnel Psychology*, Summer, **35**, 281–322.

Asch, S. E. (1946) 'Forming impressions of personality', *Journal of Abnormal and Social Psychology*, **41**, 258–290.

Beardwell, I. and L. Holden (1994) *Human Resource Management: A Contemporary Perspective*, Pitman, London.

Beer, M., B. Spector, P. R. Lawrence, D. Quinn Mills and R. E. Walton (1985) *Human Resource Management: A General Manager's Perspective*, The Free Press, London.

Berlew, D. E. and D. T. Hall (1966) 'The socialization of managers: effects of expectation and performance', *Administrative Science Quarterly*, September (10), 207–223.

Blyton, P. (1992) 'The search for workforce flexibility' in B. Towers (ed.), *The Handbook of Human Resource Management*, Blackwell, Oxford.

Boyatzis, R. E. (1982) *The Competent Manager: A Model for Effective Performance*. Wiley, New York.

Buchanan, D. A. (1989) 'Principles and Practices in Work Design', in K. Sisson (ed.), *Personnel Management in Britain*, Blackwell, Oxford.

Caruso, R. (1992) 'Human resources as capital' in K. Bradley (ed.), *Human Resource Management: People and Performance*, Dartmouth Publishing, Aldershot.

Cattell, R. B. (1974) 'How good is the modern questionnaire? General principles for evaluation'. *Journal of Personality Assessment*, **38**, 115–129.

Constable, R. and R. J. McCormick (1987) '*The Making of British Managers*', A Report for the BIM and CBI into Management Training, Education and Development, BIM, London.

Cronbach L. J. (1970) *Essentials of Psychological Testing*, 3rd edn., Harper & Row, New York.

Davies, J. (1988) 'Organizational development and the management of change', MBA Dissertation, University of Warwick.

Gaugher, B. B., D. B. Rosenthal, G. C. Thornton and C. Bentson (1987) 'Meta-analysis of assessment center validity', *Journal of Applied Psychology*, **2**, 493–511.

Ghiselli, E. E. (1966) *The Validity of Occupational Aptitude Tests*, Wiley, New York.

Hall, D. T. (1976) *Careers in Organizations*, Goodyear, Santa Monica.

Handy, C. B. (1987) *The Making of Managers*, NEDO, London.

Hendry, C., A. M. Pettigrew and P. Sparrow (1988) 'Changing patterns of human resource management', *Personnel Management*, November, 37–41.

Institute of Personnel and Development (1995) *Personnel and the Line: Developing the New Relationship*. IPD, London.

Kanter, R. M. (1989) *When Giants Learn to Dance*, Simon & Schuster: London.

Keenoy, T. (1990) 'Human resource management: A case of the wolf in sheep's clothing', *Personnel Review*, **19** (2), 3–9.

Keep, E. (1989) 'Corporate training strategies: The vital component', in J. Storey (ed.), *New Perspectives on Human Resource Management*, Routledge, London.

Kohn, A. (1997) *Punished by Rewards*, Houghton Mifflin, New York.

McHenry, R. (1997) 'Tried and tested' *People Management*, 23 Jan., 32–37.

Mintzberg, H. (1973) *The Nature of Managerial Work*, Harper & Row, New York.

Peck, D. and D. Whitlow (1975) *Approaches to Personality Theory*, Methuen, London.

Robbins, S. P. (1989) *Organizational Behavior: Concepts, Controversies and Applications*, Prentice-Hall, Englewood Cliffs, N.J.

Rosen, B., T. H. Jerdee (1974) 'The influence of sex-role stereotypes on evaluations of male and female supervisory behaviour. *Journal of Applied Psychology*, **59**, 9–14.

Rotter, J. B. (1966) 'Generalized expectancies for internal versus external control of reinforcement', *Psychological Monographs*, **1** (609), 80.

Sadler, P. (1989) 'Management development', in K. Sisson (ed.), *Personnel Management in Britain*, Blackwell, Oxford.

Schein, V. E. (1975). 'Relationships between sex role stereotypes and requisite management characteristics among female managers', *Journal of Applied Psychology*, **60**, 340–344.

Smilansky, J. (1997) *The New HR*, International Thompson Press, London.

Sparrow, P. (1996) 'Too good to be true', *People Management*, **2** (24), 22–27.

Sparrow, P., R. S. Schuler and S. E. Jackson (1994) 'Convergence or divergence: Human resource practices and policies for competitive advantage worldwide' *International Journal of Human Resource Management* **5** (2), 267–299.

Taylor, R. (1980) 'The training scandal', *Management Today*, July, 46–51.

Torrington, D. and L. Hall (1987) *Personnel Management: A New Approach*, Prentice-Hall, London.

Tunnicliff, A. (1988) 'A study into cross-functional awareness at British Sugar plc', MBA Dissertation, University of Warwick.

Van Maanen, J. and E. H. Schein (1977) 'Career development', in J. R. Hackman and J. L. Suttle (eds.), *Improving Life at Work*, Goodyear, Santa Monica.

Watson, T. (1989) 'Recruitment and selection', in K. Sisson (ed.), *Personnel Management in Britain*, Blackwell, Oxford.

Wicks, R. P. (1984) 'Interviewing: practical aspects', in C. L. Cooper and P. J. Makin (eds.), *Psychology for Managers*, BPS & MacMillan, Basingstoke, Hants.

There is nothing so useful as an 'appropriate theory'

Robert A. Lee

An 'appropriate theory' is one which is used by an educator, even though it is known to have inadequacies in terms of the scientific supporting evidence underlying it and even though it is known to offer a simplified view of reality, because it is perceived as a useful way of encouraging insights which will help when coping with practical situations. This reading addresses issues relating to the use of 'appropriate theory' in management education. The reader is invited to consider the theories which are being taught on their current management programme and their 'appropriateness'.

Theories and theorists in management education

Anyone who teaches management, and anyone of even moderate intellect and experience who is subjected to such teaching, soon becomes aware that the theories used are often of limited scientific validity in terms of the explanations or predictions which they offer. At best they are partial; applied in the wrong way, without understanding of the necessary complementary ideas, caveats and provisos, they may even be misleading. Nevertheless they are essential for the proper education of managers. It is the widespread use of such theories which is responsible for many of the attacks from our peers directed at those of us who teach and study management. Our discipline is not seen as academically respectable by our colleagues who are concerned with more traditional areas.

It is almost possible to classify management lecturers into three groups, those who try to satisfy traditional academic criteria, those who are happy to develop and use any ideas provided they help to achieve their teaching objectives and, of course, a sizeable group who try, with varying degrees of success, to find an acceptable middle ground. In this paper it will be argued that any such schism within the broad church of management education is resolvable if appropriate theory is accorded its rightful place, worthy of equal respect, alongside efforts of a more strictly scientific nature. Lewin's dictum that 'there is nothing so practical as a good theory' is capable of more than one interpretation.

At a fundamental level it can be argued that all social-science theories have limitations. None is a total explanation of 'reality'. All are based on particular assumptions about such matters as nature of knowledge, the nature of people and the nature of reality itself. Nevertheless there are many researchers who are trying to develop what we may call 'scientific theory' which comes as close as possible to explaining reality within its own inherent assumptions. It can be argued that it is necessary when one is developing theory primarily for use by particular actors, rather than for traditional scholarly purposes, to accept that there will always be a gap between what any theory can offer and what the practitioner needs to know. This may render a different type of theory as appropriate for many educational purposes.

The gap between what theory can do to explain the practitioner's reality and what she or he needs to know may be called the 'experiential learning gap', it is represented in Figure R1.1.

Figure R1.1
The experiential
learning gap

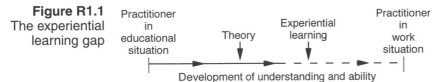

The 'experiential learning gap' is only partly explained by the simplifying assumptions inevitably underlying all theories. There are several other factors involved:

1   Theories are often designed within particular perspectives which do not conform to those of the practitioner. Any perspective, be it Marxist, Buddhist, Green, pluralist or whatever, may be of limited use to the practitioner if its fundamental tenets are rejected.
2   Theories are often not addressed at issues with which the practitioner is concerned. All theories will throw light on some aspects of reality but inevitably leave others in shadow.
3   The practitioner is concerned with unique situations which involve many variables that no general theory can accommodate; most significant among these will often be the practitioner and other actors who are engaged in a complex and dynamic social interaction.

To illustrate these points let us take the well-known subject of motivation. The would-be practitioner, away from the workplace, may be taught some simple ideas such as the hierarchy of needs developed by Maslow (1954) and the two factor theory of Herzberg (1966). None of us is naïve enough to believe that on returning to work the practitioner would now have anything more than a very slightly improved understanding of the motivation of subordinates and perhaps an even more limited improvement in ability to effect change. The 'experiential gap' which the individual has to jump is very large. Referring to the factor above we can see that the theories taught may be less effective if the manager does not accept the motivation of subordinates as the major issue but rather influencing peers and senior colleagues. In any event the specific behaviours required of the practitioner will have to be tailored to a unique situation with a unique history and context and involving particular actors.

Experiential training of various types can be used to overcome some, perhaps all, of these problems. This is part of the strong case for experiential training. But what must not be forgotten is that the argument so far also has implications for the nature of theory itself, particularly where this is developed primarily to be used in conjunction with experiential work.

A supporter of the exclusive pursuit of 'scientific theory', on viewing Figure R1.1 may argue that what is required to bridge at least some of the gap is 'better' theory which can come closer to explaining the practitioner's 'reality'. There is merit in this point. To return to our earlier example, most management educators nowadays go way beyond Maslow and Herzberg and introduce ideas from, for example, the various cognitive process theories. Provided such theories can be introduced *in appropriate form* they offer valuable insights which will assist the experiential learning process. But they will never be sufficient in themselves to bridge the experiential learning gap and if they are not taught in appropriate form they may actually prevent the gap ever being crossed.

For example, if we apply 'scientific theory' related to snooker which is concerned primarily with applied mechanics, would it be useful to a practitioner to learn the detail of these theories? Probably not. Some simple 'appropriate' ideas about the use of cues and game tactics are sufficient.

It is argued that where theories are too complex or are designed for *ex post facto* explanation rather than for use by practitioners they may lead to confusion and the phenomenon which may be called *the paralysis of analysis*. There is always a danger, if the complexity of life is overemphasized, and if the need to understand fully is placed ahead of the need to act effectively, that managers can be turned into interested spectators rather than proactive participants.

Making scientific theories appropriate

Many of the theories currently used by management educators are appropriate versions of more complex theories which their originators intended to be scientific. The hierarchy of needs is an excellent example: Maslow himself would probably be disconcerted to see how his work is grossly simplified in order to provide some language and basic ideas in the middle of a conventional management programme. The same may be true of the human-relation theory of Roethlisberger and Dickson (1964), the leadership theory of Fielder (1967), the structural theory of Lawrence and Lorsch (1967), and the expectancy theory of Lawler (1973), to name but the tip of the iceberg.

In most cases the appropriate versions take the core ideas of their parent theory and present them in some simple way without too much jargon. There is clearly danger here. Important caveats may be dropped and attempts to increase impact and teachability may lose or distort the meaning of the underlying theory. Sometimes this is to be deplored; more often, when the educator is a skilled professional, the underlying ideas have been converted to something which is in effect a new, more appropriate, theory.

New appropriate theories

Much management theory is never intended to be scientific. Its *raison d'être* from the outset is that it is a reasonable reflection of reality as perceived by the practitioner and it can be used to assist in the development of personal conceptual frameworks which will be of value in the pursuit of practical goals. Support for appropriate theory can and often does include the existence of related scientific theory and the range of research sources which would be required for scientific validity but such support, while desirable, is not essential. The best kind of support for appropriate theory is its widespread acceptance by practitioners because of its high utility to them, but until that is achieved it is possible to argue for ideas on the basis of experience or other anecdotal evidence. What the theorist must beware of, in situations where there is no other support available, is any inclination to overlook counter-evidence or alternative approaches.

Clearly, theory which is supported in this way will always be disputable and subject to frequent development. It is fairly easy to be critical of what exists and to expound something new to replace it. Furthermore, each educator can have a personal variation around a few widely used core ideas. None of this is problematic if we remember that the aim of appropriate theory is not to be 'right' but to be useful. The context of management is changing so rapidly that new ideas are always required to help provide insights relevant to new issues. Each educator has a unique style and different conceptual variations will have different learning effects depending on how the learning situation is designed and also the particular participants involved.

A recent example of appropriate theory which unashamedly purports to be nothing else is that presented by Peters and Waterman (1982). Their 7-S Framework (to understand and manage an organization effectively you have to understand and manage effectively: Staff, Style, Skills, Systems, Strategy, Structure and Shared values) is embodied in a simple figure in which each of the basic concepts is, with a bit of stretching, cutting and fitting made to begin with the letter 'S'. Their ideas are reduced to a handful of catchy guidelines in the form of appealing generalizations and the theory they represent is supported by a hotchpotch analysis of crudely researched and anecdotal data, sprinkled with a large amount of name-dropping and a small amount of discussion of relevant scientific research. And it is good stuff! Easily understood, exciting, and likely to stimulate the reader to some kind of rethink from which new insights about their own reality will emerge.

Peters and Waterman make no apology for their style, 'Anthony Athos at the Harvard Business School gave us the courage to do it that way, urging that without the memory hooks provided by alliteration, our stuff was just too hard to explain, too easily forgettable' (p. 9).

A recent critic of appropriate theory

At this point it seems necessary to acknowledge the arguments against the use of appropriate theory which have recently been put forward by Anthony (1986). Most of these arguments are summarized in Reading 2 of this book. He discusses issues related to teaching which he sees as having 'intellectual and academic respectability' as opposed to that which is aimed at enhancing 'vocational and practical skill'. He states that the latter involves 'some degree of slippage from the demands and standards of academic rigour' but does not accept that what is put in the place of these conventional academic virtues on programmes for experienced managers should be held in equal regard. This leads him to be highly critical of current MBA programmes in a manner which, if the thesis of this reading is accepted, is quite unjustified—'The conclusion is hard to avoid that postgraduate courses in management are designed for beginners rather than masters' (1986: 119). He later states:

> The rigorousness of academic work is valued because its results are more likely to be reliable. The alternative choice of what is called 'practical' is at best made by men who are too busy to insist upon reliability or, at worst, by those who are too stupid to understand the methods by which it is attained (p. 135).

Anthony discusses *In Search of Excellence* (Peters and Waterman, 1982) directly. 'The authors market ideas rather than examine them,' he states, 'Memory hooks are necessary to the marketing of ideas to a managerial readership with serious intellectual deficiencies.' He concludes, 'The search for excellence continues a well-established tradition of management writing: it will not make its readers think' (p. 163).

Anthony's objectives are entirely laudable. He sets out to emphasize the need for managers to be encouraged to question their own values and to rethink the legitimacy of their position of influence over much of the nation's resources. He attacks the managerialist ideology which many management theories unquestioningly accept. This process, however, need not rely on perpetuating an undesirable academic snobbery; indeed it will probably be enhanced if Anthony produces an 'appropriate' form of his own ideas!

Conclusion

Those who use appropriate theories must be aware of the dangers beyond those discussed above. In the first place, there is the seduction of simplicity. It is one thing knowingly to make assumptions and to neglect certain complexities where their introduction would not serve the desired educational purpose but it is quite another to cling to an obviously unsatisfactory theory just because of its attractive simplicity. This is related to the danger of adopting theories because they are teachable rather than because they are effective. It is too easy to cobble together a programme based on a 'successful' combination of appealing ideas without considering the true nature of the 'experience gap' for the particular participants and tailoring theories to specific teaching objectives.

The existence of these dangers is not in any way an argument against the use of appropriate theories. This short reading is an attempt to how their vital importance to management education. There is just one more serious concern to express. It concerns the relationships between members of the management academic community and the lack of widespread acceptance of the need for both types of theory. This has several undesirable effects which can be highlighted by imagining management as a discipline without each in turn.

If the management academic community were to neglect the pursuit of full explanations of complexity then true academic progress would be impossible. Colleagues have been heard to bemoan the tedious treatment of narrow questions in certain journals and subsequently to dismiss totally the value of such endeavour. Rigorous research will always be essential; it will, among other things, serve to test and develop fundamental ideas from which appropriate theories can be developed.

Without appropriate theory there would be very little communication of the insights of scientific theory to practising managers. It will never be possible for busy practitioners to draw their own insights from the meticulous complexity of most research papers and it would not be possible to design management programmes around them.

The importance of appropriate theory should not, however, be seen entirely in terms of management development. Scientific theory itself can be improved by drawing on the many rich ideas within appropriate theory. Those who are at the sharp end of management education and management consultancy are likely to identify new issues of importance early and, by the nature of their work, they will often be exposing current ideas to the true test of application. It is easy to see the value of scientific theory for appropriate theory but the fact that this relationship can work in reverse must also be emphasized. It is desirable for exponents of both scientific and appropriate persuasions to keep abreast of developments in each other's wisdom.

References

Anthony, P. D. (1986) *The Foundation of Management*, Tavistock, London.
Fielder, F. F. (1967) *A Theory of Leadership Effectiveness*, McGraw-Hill, New York.

Herzberg, F. (1966) *Work and the Nature of Man*, World Publishing, Cleveland.

Lawler, E. E. (1973) *Motivation in Work Organisations*, Brooke/Cole, Monterey.

Lawrence, P. R. and J. W. Lorsch (1967) *Organisation and Environment*, Harvard Graduate School of Business Administration, Cambridge, Mass.

Maslow, A. (1954) *Motivation and Personality*, Harper, New York.

Peters, T. J. and R. H. Waterman (1982) *In Search of Excellence: Lessons from America's Best Run Companies*, Harper & Row, New York.

Roethlisberger, F. J. and W. J. Dickson (1964) *Management and the Worker*, Wiley, New York.

In defence of the appropriate

P. D. Anthony[1]

Any argument against appropriate theory is disadvantaged by its title, an illustration of the technique of influential naming in which opponents must espouse 'inappropriate' theory and begin by defending the apparently indefensible. A further difficulty is that 'appropriate' is used in two ways. Appropriate theory is theory which, despite scientific inadequacy, is useful for the development of insights in practitioners who are not themselves scientists (Lee, 1987), and it is theory which, although accurate, is complex so that it has to be introduced to practitioners in appropriate form. The first meaning might be termed the theory of useful error, the second of necessary simplification. Lee's argument confuses the two; inappropriate theory (damned by its appellation) becomes appropriate (and blessed) when its presentation changes so that those to whom it is presented come to understand it—but it may still be wrong and there is an alarming suggestion that it needs to be wrong to be understood. We are now discussing both the theory, the students of it and their teachers. Stupid students, or inappropriate students, may not understand it if it is presented by good teachers who do understand it. Some may think they understand it when it is presented wrongly but with simplicity. Lee says this may not matter, may even be an advantage. We must hope that these students do not become practitioners although their error will be of more consequence in some areas of practice than others. Practitioners, for the most part, need to get it right, at least we must hope so if they are going to practise medicine upon us.

What do management practitioners need to get right? Well, if they are taking examinations in management they need to get the answers right. Generally speaking their teachers see to it that they have a fair chance of getting them right by asking them appropriate questions about appropriate material that they have been taught. The material does not change very much. Every year examination papers in personnel management regurgitate the proper conduct of selection procedures while acknowledging that they are not very appropriate to prediction of success. Every year students of Organizational Behaviour (OB) repeat the 'simple ideas' (Lee, 1987:249) of Maslow (1954) and Herzberg (1966). Every year students in organizational behaviour, organizational development, industrial relations (or all three) repeat that open participative systems are best and that industrial democracy works while decrying the lack of enthusiasm for such ideas of practitioners in management who are still stuck in bad old theory X. What happens to the students who give the appropriate answers about appropriate theory when they become practitioners of management?

What, indeed, do managers need-to-know? Who says what they need-to-know? Lee tells us that theories used in post-experience management education—even though they may be of limited validity, may be applied in the wrong way, and in fact may be downright misleading—are nevertheless:

... essential for the proper education of managers [but] it is the widespread use of such theories which is responsible for many of the attacks directed at those of us who teach management in the academic world. Our discipline is not seen as academically respectable by our colleagues who work in more traditional areas (Lee, Reading I: 38).

My own case is not that these activities are not academically respectable; it is that they are not respectable at all, and that the disrespect for them that has accrued contributes to the low status of management, the weakness of its authority and the disinclination of good and intelligent young men and women to take it up—not because of a 'contempt for the useful' but because on the whole, they would rather practise medicine.

The ultimate test of management theory is 'that it is a reasonable reflection of reality as perceived by the practitioner' and that it can assist in the development of personal conceptual frameworks which will be of value in the support of practical goals' (Lee, Reading I: 40). We need not raise awkward and boring old questions of a traditional kind like: whose practical goals are the ultimate determinants of the usefulness of conceptual frameworks: the goals of the individual manager in getting on, of the shareholders, the directors, or satisfying, or surviving, of getting by or getting through? He, our practitioner hero, will know about practical goals (unless he is a foreman, God help him) and he will tell us what he needs to know. Well, not quite, according to Lee, because we, his teachers, know more than he does. Not about practical goals we don't, of course, but we know more about organization and social relationships and a great deal more about control techniques and an awful lot about motivational theory and conceptual frameworks. We have to go easy with all this because we must not confuse our practitioners by over-emphasizing the complexity of life lest they become interested spectators (Lee, Reading I: 40). What we need is a useful dialogue between us clever chaps and the sturdy practitioners who know about their practical goals but could do with help in hitting them. The useful dialogue demands that we bridge the experiential learning gap.

This particular educational phenomenon is, according to Lee, explained by differences in the perspectives of the theorist and the practitioner, by lack of relevance of theory to particular issues which concern the practitioner and by his (*sic*) involvement in unique situations which 'no general theory can accommodate' particularly when he is engaged in a 'complex and dynamic social interaction'. These are revealing explanations. The argument about lack of relevance has confronted every management teacher and is often expressed in the form, 'It's all right in theory but it doesn't work in practice.' For the most part that old saw is nonsense; if it does not work in practice there is something wrong with the theory and its failure in practice is a classic case for theoretical verification and revision. Quite often, however, if the theory of metal fatigue is well founded it is the practice of box-girder bridge design that is at fault. There is an intimate and necessary relationship between good theory and good practice, except when you come to instances of theoretical perspectives which are rejected and of complex and dynamic social interactions. Here, I suggest, we are not dealing with theory at all.

In the first instance, where the practitioner rejects Marxist theory because he rejects the tenets of Marxism, the practitioner may be right (just as he would be to reject Thatcherism or managerialism). What confronts the practitioner in much (but not all) of Marxism is gross over-simplification, ideological loading and purposive prediction. The practising manager would be right to be gravely suspicious of a great deal of motivational or participative theory as a manipulative device at the length of a production line. In the second instance (the first and the second are often confused in practice) of complex social interactions, there is precious little theory of any level of generalization or predicative value. There is nothing to teach.

It depends, of course, on what kind of managers you are teaching and upon what they are being taught. If a manager needs to understand, in order to practice, the techniques of statistical analysis, you must ensure that he masters chi square theory. He or she may be required to understand the theory of cash-flow discounting, of multivariant analysis, of critical path analysis, of linear programming. If the theory is sufficiently simplified—made appropriate to his or her own experience to the extent that it is deliberately misinterpreted—our practising manager may end up bankrupt or in prison. If he is a colliery manager who was taught an 'appropriate' version of the theory of roof support or of gas suppression, he may well kill himself and his subordinates. The less he is dependent upon specific techniques and procedures, the more of a general manager he is, the more likely he is to need to exercise judgement, social and political skills. And it is in this, the most responsible and influential area of management, that there is precious little theory to help him to cope with confusion and complexity. What is available to him is a ready battery of consultants' advice, of educational programmes compounded of recipes and simplifications, distillations of general explanation of human behaviour, catalogues of the best ways to 'handle' people, select them, promote them, motivate and control them. None of it may relate to the constantly shifting situation and the arcane complexities that confront him but the advice is to hand, it is simple, it provides comfort and, above all, it is appropriate to his understanding. The 'theory' from which it was distantly derived was not, could not have been, appropriate, but the images in which it is presented must be acceptable and be deemed to be appropriate. The practitioner must and can be convinced that there is an appropriate mode of behaviour (Theory Y, 9.9: problem-solving, participative, supportive) that he can acquire which is not conceptually difficult; he just has to try.

What the management educator is trying to do in these areas is to change the behaviour of the practitioner-manager and that needs time—less, perhaps, if the practitioner is an idiot, more if he is a manager of intelligence and experience. But the time is not needed because complex theory has to be adapted, made appropriate, to the manager; it is needed to wear him down, to dull his critical senses, to condition him. It is not that the management 'educator' is wrestling with the explication of grand and complex theory to a practitioner who needs to understand it but rather that the educator is trying to convince him, to manipulate and mould him, much as Marx and Mrs Thatcher have tried and are trying to make us see the world as they do. They must all simplify, address us in terms and in language appropriate to our experience, ensure that they do not shock us into hostility. They are, all of them, engaged in the rhetoric of persuasion.

In a previous publication (Anthony, 1986), I suggested that this aspect of management education was mistaken in its conception and abortive in its consequence. What managers need is to apply critical and analytical intelligence to their environment; the ordinary expectation of education is to encourage and nurture these facilities; the function of management education is to suppress them.

Finally, Lee flatters me not only by the attention he gives to my views but by suggesting that I have advanced a theory that deserves an appropriate expression. That is kind of him but I must disclaim such ambitions. There *is* little or no theory and I have made no contribution to it. I have only submitted a polemic and an argument; my claim is that that is sufficient.

Note   1   Reprinted by permission Lee (1987: 255–9).

References   Anthony, P. D. (1986) *The Foundation of Management*, Tavistock, London.
Herzberg, F. (1966) *Work and the Nature of Man*, World Publishing, Cleveland.
Lee, R. (1987) 'The use of "appropriate theory" in management education', *Management Education and Development*, **18**, (4), 247–54.
Maslow, A. (1954) *Motivation and Personality*, Harper, New York.

A hitch-hiker's guide to job security: the portfolio career as a response to job market chaos

Tupper Cawsey, Gene Deszca and Maurice Mazerolle

What comes to mind when we think of careers? Normally, we think of patterns: integration around a theme; orderly, sequential development; hierarchical progression in status. Implicit in these images is a ladder or pyramid metaphor which symbolizes career and career progress. This pattern no longer holds for many and the metaphor is false. Lay-offs, rightsizing, decruitment, downsizing, re-sizing, etc., caused by the recession, global competition, information technology, shedding of overhead, demands for higher profit performance etc., have meant that the 'normal assumptions' around careers are invalid.

Viewing oneself as having a portfolio of skills offered to a portfolio of organizational client (a portfolio career[1]), provides a new way of thinking about and framing the relationships between work, organizations, payment and value for an individual. This concept, explored below, provides a new set of assumptions to help people cope with the uncertainty and chaos of the job market.

In today's world, there are many people who find themselves in the unsecured or contingent labour market. If they are not currently in a career, they are searching for phantom start points or credentials that 'guarantee' a career. Witness, for example, the devaluation of a law degree to the level of a certificate that too many others have. Teaching, and other sectors that have not been as affected are in the process of developing entry barriers which require extraordinary academic achievement, as if that were some guarantee of the empathy and skills needed to be an excellent teacher today. Many graduates find relief in part-time or voluntary positions planning, plotting, predicting that these will lead to better things. But often they don't. As has been recently reported in *Fortune magazine*:

> The era that traded loyalty for job security is virtually dead. The new contract is: 'There will never be job security. You will be employed by us as long as you add value to the organization, and *you* are continuously responsible for finding ways to add value. In return, you have the right to demand interesting and important work, the freedom and resources to perform it well, the pay that reflects your contribution, and the experience and training needed to be employable here or elsewhere.' (*Fortune*, 1994).

This new deal kills the traditional notion of career: one company or one profession—one person. This view may be the 'wave of the future' but is it likely to be one that a majority of individuals will willingly buy into. Will this 'wave' in fact be a wave good-bye? To answer this, let us look at some of the underlying premises upon which this new contract is built.

The first assumption is that organizations are trustworthy. You as an individual must first deliver value added and only then does the organization entertain training you for your next job. This has the individual bearing all of the risk. Even if a person performs but things just don't work out for reasons not related to performance, the most one could hope for would be a good reference.

This presumed contract also says 'You have the right to demand interesting and important work . . . and training to be employable here or elsewhere.' While one might have the *right* to demand the foregoing, it is difficult to imagine how one might enforce such a right. Also, how does one ensure that the training the organization proposes for you will be what is required to make you super-mobile? Even those who are not overly cynical will view this proposed bargain with a grain of scepticism.

As well, this new contract assumes employment to be within organizations. In this age of contracting out, network organizations, virtual companies and ethereal alliances *á la* internet, it is increasingly likely that this assumption is incorrect. According to the National Association of Temporary Services, interim professionals now comprise 24% of temporary workers. Henry Conn and Joseph Boyett, authors of *Workplace 2000: The Revolution Reshaping American Business*, estimate that the average American beginning his or her career in the 1990s will probably work in 10 or more jobs for five or more employers before retiring (Henkoff, 1993). A more succinct restating of this new contract might be: 'Depend on us now so that we can prepare you to never have to depend on us again'!

How are individuals handling this upending of expectations? How are they coping with the trauma of new rules in a new game? For many, the methods of coping are inappropriate and ineffective. Some are psychologically damaged and cannot cope effectively, while others become alienated and bitter, losing their effectiveness as a consequence. Still others adopt a 'duck' philosophy—feather my nest, keep my head down and perhaps I won't get shot. Many without work simply assume 'There are no jobs' and stop looking.[2] Many, however, are adopting a pattern of behaviour which has been labelled the portfolio career.

The portfolio career

Webster's dictionary defines a portfolio as:[3]

A list of stocks, bonds and commercial paper owned by a bank or investor.

This definition suggests that a portfolio is a variety of things with value, held for the purpose of increasing that value. In a portfolio career, an individual has a portfolio of skills which he or she sells to a portfolio of clients. Like the financial portfolio, the purpose of the portfolio is to manage risk. The financial portfolio handles risk by having various stocks with differing risks for differing parts of the economic cycle. The career portfolio minimizes risks by having skill sets which can produce a variety of value-added activities. If one skill is not in demand, another might be. As well, risk is minimized because the individual deals with several clients—if the relationship with one client ends, the cost is not extreme. The dependence on one employer is eliminated. Paradoxically, this results in job security being acquired not on the basis of loyalty and commitment, but by detachment and diversification.

The concept of the portfolio career is significant because it provides a new way of viewing our relationship to work. Many of us have the perspective of 'job' equals 'career'. However, if there are no 'jobs' it is easy for us to be frozen into inaction. Re-thinking the structuring of work into projects provides much more flexibility to the individual and to the organization, with the possibility of mutual gain. For example, the individual can earn his or her way into ever increasing skilled contracts, while at the same time organizations can have work done, perhaps even a long-term relationship, without the long-term commitment.

Skills risk

In a portfolio career, individuals recognize that their value to organizations comes about because of the skills they hold which can produce results. The risk of obsolescent skills is reduced by acquiring proficiency in a variety of skills and continually developing new ones.

A skill or skill set can be viewed as having a product life-cycle akin to that of a consumer good. This is complicated somewhat because the development of the skill is related to both the expressed and perceived needs of clients. However, the following categories of skills might be considered:

- A *developing skill* is a skill or skill set that the individual has decided is worth pursuing and developing. Thus, an individual who is familiar with internet and has international contacts may believe that they could conduct market research via the internet. Their skill is not at the stage where the individual feels confident and would not be ready to 'sell' the skill on anything but a results basis (that is, payment would be for results not for time or effort).
- A *mature skill* is one that is fully developed and can be sold to organizations. For example, a university graduate could well have excellent skills in report writing. This craft would be of value to organizations in communicating to their internal or external publics.
- A *post-maturity skill* is one that is either no longer in demand by clients or is subsumed by other more complex skills by the individual. Thus, skill in using particular computer packages may be valueless because of new software developments. Or the individual's skill levels may grow and this particular skill is not worth pursuing.

To reduce skills risk, individuals must begin to see themselves as holders and developers of skills. Skills have a life-cycle of usefulness. The process of development, maturity and decay is essential for the renewal of the individual's skill set and the minimization of risk.

Many managers or university graduates see themselves as 'holders of degrees' or 'specialists in'. These perceptions are limiting and block the insights possible from a skills orientation. Thus, most arts or humanities students have skills in researching, analysing, synthesizing, writing, etc—all valuable skills in the knowledge society which Nuala Beck (1992) claims we are moving into. Graduates need to become aware of their skill sets and their value.

Client risk

The second risk that 'career portfolio-ists' need to manage is their client risk. As one shifts orientation away from 'one company and one career' to 'many jobs and contracts with many skills', the risk is minimized by having a variety of clients in your portfolio. With one company and one career, the individual is betting that the organization will continue to view his or her skills as valuable and that the organizational environment will continue to be positive for that organization. In today's world, it is not sufficient to merely add value to the organization, this is now a requirement for individual survival. However, even this offers no protection if the organization has problems.

To minimize these risks, an individual must develop a set of clients that, in effect, mirror an individual's skill sets. These clients can be categorized as:

- *Money clients* Money clients provide the money needed to pay the bills. The skills used for these clients are generally not particularly unique or valuable. Individuals have these clients out of necessity not choice. Little learning takes place doing work for money clients.
- *Learning clients* Learning clients provide opportunities to learn new skills and concepts. Doing these activities the individual learns the skill set which will provide him or her with the 'next generation' of skills to market. Generally, concrete or extrinsic rewards are not the focus of these skills. If payment is made, it will be for results since the individual is learning on the job and developing their skills as they work.
- *Niche clients* Niche clients result from the matching of developed skills with a significant need. Here the individual can market or sell his or her skill at an appropriate price. Niche clients also allow you to develop your reputation and network for future work.

An alternate way of viewing this is to classify clients according to the amount of learning on the job or the amount of pay received. Figure R3.1 classifies high and low learning situations versus high and low pay situations. Individuals should strive to work in cross-diagonal areas; that is, areas of low pay and high learning or areas of high pay and low learning. Areas of low pay and low learning should be avoided whenever possible since the rewards will be low or non-existent. Areas of high pay and high learning appear attractive. However, they are also areas of high risk. It is possible that the client will expect more than the individual can deliver since he or she is just in the learning phase. Individuals should strive for both types of work: high pay and high learning but recognize the balance of each which is desirable.

Figure R3.1
A matrix of client attractiveness

	Low pay or $ rewards	High pay or $ rewards
High learning	**Attractive:** Developing Intellectual Capital, perhaps some $ gain	**Risky:** May not deliver the goods
Low learning	Avoid unless necessary	**Attractive:** Using intellectual capital for gain

In a similar vein, Handy (1989) describes five types of work: wage work, fee work, home work, gift work and learning work. Wage work is work where payment is for time or effort. Fee work is work where payment is for results. Home work is that done in the home: child-raising, lawn care, etc. Gift work is voluntary or charitable work. Learning work is studying, learning a new skill. At times voluntary work will lead to wage or fee work. Learning work creates the next generation of skills which provide wage or fee work.

In a portfolio career, increasing amounts of work will be done in the learning and fee categories. While many individuals will strive to have wage work, this is not the direction being taken by many of today's firms. Instead, as both employers and career portfolio-ists recognize the value of contract work, a combination of market forces and contract negotiations will assign a value to the task to be performed. Skilled, high-demand portfolio-ists will bargain for premium rates—including payment for uncertainty. Learning or low-skilled portfolio-ists will suffer from market surpluses and pay the penalty of low wages and dull jobs.

Implications of portfolio careers

While organizations have been quick to accept the benefits and inevitability of contracting out, temporary jobs, and part-time employees, perhaps they need to consider if this is going to be beneficial in the long run. In a global context can US and Canadian firms compete against Japanese and European rivals that often retain the lifelong loyalty and commitment of their employees. How does one build a collaborative effort if every one is working for themselves? (*Business Week*, 1991).

Drucker recently pointed out the dramatic power shift that occurs in the knowledge society (Drucker, 1994: 71). For the first time, 'The employees—that is, the knowledge workers—own the tools of production.' The tools of production become the knowledge held by the individual and the skills to implement that knowledge. While the cry for generalists is often heard, Drucker states that contributions of knowledge workers can only be accessed through their specialty, the skills held in their portfolio. And these skills are best utilized in teams working together tapping into the expertise of each.

The paired forces of globalization and information technology imply an increased likelihood that teams of people will be working together across great distances requiring yet another type of relationship skills. Workers who are able to flourish in this new environment may be so prized by employers that companies will go out of their way to build a new corporate loyalty (Sherman, 1993). Reducing the risks associated with unemployment through longer, more frequent, or more interesting contracts should enable companies to attract creative and productive employees. Furthermore, if training and development is used to teach knowledge that is less firm specific and more generalizable employees will recognize the value of these skills. This ironically may produce more committed workers and higher performance.

Should companies choose this approach, then there needs to be some re-thinking of the rules concerning both the explicit and implicit psychological employment contracts. For example, here is Apple Computer's written employment contract with every full-time employee.

> Here's the deal Apple will give you; here's what we want from you. We're going to give you a really neat trip while you're here. We're going to teach you stuff you couldn't learn anywhere else. In return we expect you to work like hell, buy the vision as long as you're here. We're not interested in employing you for a lifetime, but that's not the way we are thinking about this. It's a good opportunity for both of us that is probably finite (Ettorre, 1994).

If this 'new age' Apple deal is a harbinger of things to come as far as employment contracts go, one has to ask if this is enough? Besides interesting work and the opportunity to learn, how might firms respond to ensure that these highly valued types of individuals are there when needed? The answer might, in part, be found in some of the approaches that so-called new age firms are bringing to the employment relationship. In a recent *Harvard Business Review* article, Nichols (1994) observed that creating meaning may be the true managerial task of the future. Common values, and a shared sense of purpose can turn a company into a community where daily work acquires a deeper meaning and sense of satisfaction. But is this really going to be possible given the emergence of borderless, faceless, nameless groupings of individuals pursuing portfolio careers?

In order to overcome this paradox, organizations must recognize the need to form and reform teams capable of accomplishing great things. If this is the case, then so-called 'people' skills or process skills become vital. Recruitment systems must be transformed in order to handle the increased volume of contract and temporary work while identifying the critical core employees who will be 'permanent'. Induction and orientation mechanisms must be revamped so that they quickly and smoothly make newcomers aware of essential information on a need-to-know basis and not much else. Outplacement or ending mechanisms must be reconfigured to provide for intermittent continuity.

At the individual level, the career portfolio-ist must reframe his or her definition of a job or career along a skills/client basis: 'What am I good at? What are organizations willing to pay for?' The facing up to these questions will be the start for the portfolio-ist. Each of us must undergo a form of self-assessment in order to know the state of our skills. Once we have taken stock, these skills have to be benchmarked in relationship to the marketplace. Self-understanding, determination, and a tolerance for ambiguity will become the basics of portfolio careers. Finally, each person who undertakes a portfolio career must learn to structure uncertainty in order that ambiguity be lessened.

In *The New Individualists: The Generation After the Organization Man,* social researchers Paul Leinberger and Bruce Tucker (1992) contend that the communities of the future are going to emerge from far-flung networks of professionals battling time-zone differences. For these authors, true community doesn't grow out of a shared higher purpose but evolves through the pragmatic need to solve common problems. Can these new 'self-careerists' be as committed to the solution of problems and the seizing of opportunities as the old-time 'organizational careerists'? This may, in fact, be the ultimate test facing portfolio careerists.

Notes

1 The term portfolio career was first used by Handy in his book, *The Age of Unreason* (Handy, 1989). Our usage is similar but stresses the match between skills and clients.

2 See, for example, *The Kitchener-Waterloo Record* article, 'Jobs Unfilled at Student Employment Centre', August 3, 1994.

3 Webster's dictionary has a second definition of a portfolio: 'A flat, portable case usually of leather for carrying loose sheets of paper, manuscripts or drawings'. This might serve as a metaphor! Many of us have been flattened by the recession and downsizing that has occurred in organizations. We have become aware of how portable we are—far too often an involuntary exit form of portability. We become cases or incidents not employees or people. We wish we mere made of leather to withstand the wear and tear. And we carry inside us valuable things, the skills, knowledge and abilities that enable us to accomplish things.

4 For a discussion of the relationship between dependence, independence and interdependence, see Covey, 1989.

References

Beck, N. (1992) *Shifting Gears: Thriving in the New Economy,* Harper-Collins Publishers Ltd., Toronto.

Business Week (1991) 'I'm Worried About My Job', *Business Week,* October 7.

Conn, H. and J. Boyett (1992) *Workplace 2000: The Revolution Reshaping American Business,* New York: Plume Books.

Covey, R. (1989) *The Seven Habits of Highly Effective People,* Simon & Schuster, New York.

Drucker, P. F. (1994) 'The Age of Social Transformation', *The Atlantic Monthly*, November. 53–80.

Ettorre, B. (1994) 'The Contingency Workforce Moves Mainstream', *Management Review*, **83** (2), February.

Fierman, J. (1994) 'The Contingency Work Force', *Fortune*, January 24.

Handy, C. B. (1989) *The Age of Unreason*, Harvard Business School Press, Boston, Mass, 183–85.

Henkoff, R. (1993) 'Winning the New Career Game', *Fortune*, July 12.

Kitchener-Waterloo Record (1994) 'Jobs Unfilled at Student Employment Centre', *Kitchener-Waterloo Record*, August 3.

Leinberger, P. and B. Tucker (1992) *The New Individualists: The Generation After the Organization Man*, Harper-Collins, New York.

Nichols, M. (1994) *'Does New Age Business Have a Message for Managers?'* Harvard Business Review, March–April.

O'Reilly, B. (1994) 'The New Deal', *Fortune*, June 13.

Sherman, S. (1993) 'A Brave New Darwinian Workplace', *Fortune*, January, 25.

Part II
The Individual

CHAPTER 4 Attributes of individuals

Introduction

This chapter will examine two key themes which predominate in organizational behaviour. First, are people different? Do they have separate, unique characteristics which make them the kind of person they are? Second, is the really important thing how we perceive others? Since we act upon our perceptions, then the study of perception rather than personality should be our focus.

This perception/personality debate is one of many which permeate psychology. There is insufficient space in this chapter to reveal the complexities of these debates, but the interested reader should follow up the literature cited in the references at the end of this chapter (see particularly Dubrin, 1990). Many aspects of perception, as they relate to the HR management process (recruitment, selection, etc.) were dealt with in Chapter 3. Here, we look at values, attitudes, needs, expectations and personality.

Values, attitudes, needs and expectations

Dealing with aspects of the individual in organizational behaviour leads naturally into an examination of values, attitudes, needs and expectations. Put simply, these fundamental building blocks of human behaviour explain why individuals are motivated to strive for certain things and why they try to satisfy themselves in certain ways.

Values

Values is the term which is used to identify the importance individuals place on something. These 'somethings' could be wide-ranging: religion, ecology, education, sports, relationships, etc. The degree of importance we attach to anything is part of our 'learned behaviour', that is, we incorporate these values into our own beliefs by observing how other people behave and either incorporating or rejecting them. According to Rokeach (1972) values are concerned with conduct and desired end states:

> To say that a person 'has a value' is to say that he has an enduring belief that a specific mode of conduct or end-state of existence is personally and socially preferable . . . once a value is internalized, it becomes, consciously or unconsciously, a standard or criterion for guiding action . . . for morally judging self and others.
>
> Rokeach (1972: 160)

The value system of classical organization theory represents an individualistic, rational approach to life which sets the highest values on achievement, aggression, and affluence. Historically derived from Calvinism, this work ethic presumes that an individual is predestined either to heaven or hell and that the ticket is made out according to how well he or she manages the stewardship of worldly goods that come his or her way. Values provide the yardstick by which that stewardship might be judged.

This pervasive value system seeped into every aspect of life, defining attitudes towards everything, particularly anything that smacked of enjoyment (for example, pay-day has traditionally been on Fridays, which was favoured as a drinking night for the working classes because it provided the least chance of upsetting the work week).

Attitudes

Attitude may be defined as the predisposition or tendency of a person to evaluate some symbol, person, place, or thing in a favourable or unfavourable manner. The person's opinion constitutes the verbal expression of an attitude. In essence, an attitude is a state of mind which people carry around in their heads, through which they focus on particular objects in the environment, such as foreigners, communists, pornography, the unions, men or women, students or academics.

Attitudes are made up of three elements:

1 cognitive
2 affective
3 conative

The dimensions of an attitude are presumed to follow a sequence such as (1) cognition ('I see rising unemployment as a threat to our society'), (2) emotion ('I feel strongly that everyone has a right to a job'), and (3) behaviour ('I will actively campaign against rising unemployment'). This sequence of cognition, emotion, and behaviour, may be followed in some circumstances, but not in all, as the three elements interlock and interact (see Lovejoy, 1950; Hilliard, 1950). For example, in Chapter 5 we will consider processes which change people's work behaviour patterns, which can also change their attitudes. This often occurs when an individual is promoted to a managerial position and then has to supervise former peers with a new perspective.

Needs

The most uncomplicated behaviour is found in infants. When they are hungry, thirsty, or uncomfortable, they cry; when they are happy, they smile or giggle; and when they are sleepy, they sleep. Through observing and studying infants, psychologists have learned a great deal about the forces governing behaviour. Not many adults cry when hungry or thirsty. Whether or not they cry when in pain depends upon what they learned as children. But at least people still smile and laugh when they are happy, and some people even go to sleep when they are sleepy. Although people tend to complicate the ways of meeting these basic human needs, the needs must still be met—survival depends on it.

In order to survive, one must have enough air, water, food, protection from physical dangers, and so forth. The infant obviously is dependent upon others to have survival needs met—the best it can do is give some signals of hunger, thirst, or discomfort. Survival needs can be met in fairly universal ways. Even as they grow and mature, people develop fairly similar methods of meeting these needs. Tastes and preferences develop, but the basic ingredients for survival are more or less universal.

Humans are also social beings and therefore require interaction with others. For infants, this need is initially met by the immediate family. The important ingredient is a kind of support base which provides a sense of belonging and the beginnings of feelings of personal worth. While the individual might survive the absence of such a support base, it is not likely to be a very healthy existence and can set the stage for a lifetime of desperately seeking a state of social belonging or of apathetic withdrawal from human contact.

Like survival needs, the social needs do not disappear from the scene once they are provided for. They continue to exert important influences on individuals' behaviour throughout their entire lives. When threatened they tend to prompt people into some kind of definite action. When you have felt alone, isolated, or deprived of the kinds of warmth and support that human contact alone can offer, you are likely to seek out your friends or your family or even casual acquaintances. When it gets really bad, you may go to a public place just to be in the presence of others.

Unlike the survival needs, the social needs do not seem to demand immediate gratification, at least among most adults. When necessary, a person can await the return of a valued friend, although a letter or even just thinking about the other can provide some degree of comfort. Also, social needs are satisfied in a greater number of ways than are the more basic survival needs. Look at the variety of social systems people live in, the differences in family relationships, and the varying patterns of friendship and social groupings. In short, the social needs of people seem to have some relation to survival but not quite the critical character associated with air, water, food, safety, etc. And while they exert powerful influences on all our behaviour, they are subject to wide variations in style. We explore the motivational aspects of these needs in Chapter 5.

Expectations   Usually, before you make a choice, you appraise the situation and decide which alternatives are likely to result in self-enhancement. Few people like to waste their efforts and even fewer wish to engage in behaviour that goes against their values, attitudes, and needs. To deal with the matter of choosing the best course of action in a situation your appraisal takes the form of a kind of prediction—'The chances are that if I do this, I will achieve what I want.' You make a statement (implicit or explicit) of your expectancy regarding the probable outcome. It is like being your own personal scientist, making hypotheses, testing them out, revising them when they prove wrong, and holding on to the ones that prove accurate. Outcomes that are rewarding tend to create and reinforce the expectancies that are positive. Conversely, outcomes that are unrewarding or punishing lead to expectancies that are neutral or negative.

In general, the behaviour most likely to occur is that which the person expects to most enhance self-concept (Nadler and Lawler, 1977). When the expectancy and the self-concept fit together no dilemma is experienced. But what happens when an anticipated outcome involves some risk to self, yet no alternatives exist to meet goals?

For example, suppose you see yourself as bright and as capable of putting your ideas into words very clearly. Your goal is to be outspoken in departmental meetings at work so that you can have some reaction to your ideas from your supervisors. You now find yourself in a department in which the supervisor refuses to entertain questions until the reports are given; but you also find that there is no time left for discussion at the end of the meetings. You can choose to keep your mouth shut, expecting a negative reaction should you speak up, or you can say something anyway in order to move towards your goal. In order for anyone to predict what you are likely to do would require them to know:

1   the strength of your goal to speak out;
2   your expectancy regarding the negative consequences of speaking out; and
3   your expectancy regarding the positive and negative consequences for your self-concept in not speaking out.

Trait approaches to personality

Personality can be summarized as the pattern of traits and dispositions which distinguish one individual from another and determines how he or she adjusts to their environment. Such traits and dispositions are enduring and some psychologists have argued that they are almost impossible to change except for some fine-tuning at the edges (Wiggins, 1973; Rokeach, 1972). Others have argued that personality is predominantly a function of heredity which then is subject to change depending upon the environment in which the individual works and lives (Gilmer, 1984; Holden, 1980). Holden's work demonstrated that genetics appeared to play a central part in determining personality. A study of identical twins, separated at birth, all placed in different environments displayed strong similarities and traits. Their pattern appeared to be the same or very similar. They married spouses often with the same first name; they liked to wear similar kinds of clothes; they both smoked and they favoured similar or the same names for their children.

The structure of personality

Systematic ways in which psychologists have looked at personality include a wide range of psychoanalytical approaches, typologies and trait theories.

Psychoanalytical theories highlight the tension between nature and nurture (that is, the dynamic interplay of ourselves with our immediate environment). Freud (1933) is perhaps the most well-known theorist who adopted this approach. Freud concentrated on the conflicts which arose between what he termed 'libido' (the basic nature of us all to seek pleasure in all its forms) and the norms, values and mores of wider society. Technically, this is the conflict between the 'ego' (self) and the 'superego' (societal values). Freud also proposed the concept of the 'id' which is generally held to describe the variety of impulses and desires which we seek to gratify often subconsciously.

Erich Fromm (1941) argued that personality structures were the product of man's interaction with society. Despair, pessimism, aggression for Fromm all stemmed ultimately from man's inability to cope with the expectations and demands of wider society.

Typologies and trait theories both attempt to classify different personalities based on a set of factors or characteristics on which we can all be compared. Freud described the 'obsessional' type of personality (critical and sceptical), the 'erotic' (sociable and self-dramatizing) and the 'narcissistic' (concerned with self and self-satisfied). Based on the work of Carl Jung, a German psychologist, Eysenck proposed two dimensions of personality:

Introversion–Extroversion
Neuroticism–Stability

Based on the idea that personality is essentially genetic in origin, Eysenck describes a number of personal dispositions which correspond to his two dimensions. See Table 4.1 for examples.

It is important to emphasize that none of these is an exclusive category. Most individuals fall between the extremes outlined in Table 4.1. The

Table 4.1
Eysenck's two
dimensions of
personality

Personal disposition	Description
Extroversion	Expressiveness/impulsiveness/risk-taking behaviour/sociability/practicality/expressiveness/ irresponsibility
Introversion	Carefulness/reflectiveness/unsociability/inhibition/ control/inactivity/responsibility
Neuroticism	Low self-esteem/little autonomy/unhappiness/ anxiety/obsessiveness/hypochondria/guilt
Stability	High self-esteem/autonomy/happiness/tranquility/ health and well-being/calmness/quiescence

Source: Eysenck and Wilson, 1975.

structure of personality is hierarchical according to Eysenck. Individuals who exhibit particular traits (such as anxiety or obsessiveness) are also likely to possess other predictable traits (such as hypochondria and guilt). You can find the questionnaire test designed by Eysenck in Eysenck and Wilson (1975).

There is no 'good' or 'poor' pattern of personality as measured by Eysenck's traits, although some personalities are likely to be more socially acceptable in particular settings. A neurotic extrovert, for example, would possibly be considered out of place in an environment which favoured solitude and reflective behaviours (such as a library or research establishment).

Apart from questionnaires, personality can be tapped by a number of other methods. One of the more widely known, though somewhat dubious method is the Rorschach 'ink blot' assessment. Based on the assumption that each individual will interpret ambiguous stimuli in a different and unique way, the Rorschach test examines the interpretation of ink blots and similar blotches of indefinable shape (see Rabin, 1958). A Swiss psychiatrist, Rorschach recorded both why individuals interpreted the ink blot as they did as well as precisely what it was they saw. The test is ridden with difficulties in scoring and it is neither reliable nor standardized.

The Thematic Apperception Test (TAT) relies upon the idea that we all project situations into the future in our own separate ways (Holmes, 1974) The most common form of this test is for the candidate to make up a story having been shown a picture which portrays a person (or people) in an ambiguous setting. Twenty such pictures are shown and the 20 stories are examined for themes and consistently held personality traits. The test is widely used and is seen as more reliable than the ink blot tests, although it too is subject to rigging by candidates taking the test. Some of the major factors which comprise personality are shown in Figure 4.1.

Environmental approaches to personality

The structural/trait approaches to personality neglect to consider the impact of the environment or situation on individuals. The role played by the environment includes socialization, imitation and ideology. The culture in which we grow up (for example, family, social groupings and friends) influences personality. What is considered to be ideologically acceptable behaviour in one culture does not always easily translate to another culture. Mead's (1935) work in primitive societies illustrates that differences in child socialization led to differences in subsequent behaviour (the males took on what we would consider female roles in Western cultures). This would not

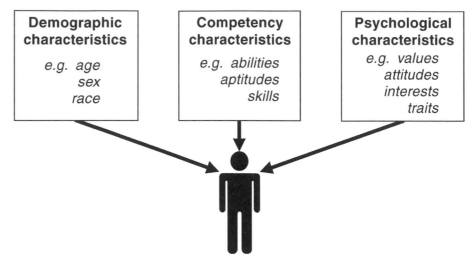

Figure 4.1
The major
components of
individual personality

easily translate to 'traditional' Western cultures which instil in the male
aggressive, competitive and independent behaviour.

Mischel (1973) argued that the situation played an important part in
shaping personality. While there may be underlying stability in personality
(through traits, for example) it was open to change in different situations.
Each situation demands a different personality response. Mischel argued
that the same situation can provoke different responses from different
individuals and that different situations can bring out similar responses from
the same individual. Although compelling, we do not know enough about
these theories to say if they have any kind of substance. Problems include:

1   a lack of substantial empirical work;
2   difficulty in classifying the enormous number of situational variables;
3   problems in isolating and controlling for an individual's previous experience
    with similar situations, or prior knowledge of a forthcoming situation.

Following point 3 above, the effect of stereotyping begins to emerge.

Stereotyping and prejudices

In news bulletins and magazine articles, the terms prejudice and
discrimination are generally used as synonyms. More analytically, prejudice
can be defined in the following way. It is an attitude (usually negative)
toward the members of some specific group (racial, ethnic, sexual, etc.)
which causes the person holding it to evaluate others solely on the basis of
their membership in that group. When an individual is prejudiced against
the members of some group, we mean that he or she tends to evaluate such
persons in a negative manner simply because they belong to that group—not
because of their individual characteristics or behaviour.

The cognitive component of prejudice refers to beliefs and expectations
held about the members of a particular group. Often, these beliefs form
clusters of preconceived notions known as stereotypes. Stereotypes are of
major importance, for once formed, they exert several powerful effects.
First, they lead individuals to assume consistencies which do not really exist.
For example, they can give rise to the belief that all members of a given
racial, ethnic or other group possess similar traits or invariably. Second, they
exert a powerful impact upon the processing of new social information.
They shape the interpretation of such information so that it is perceived as
offering support for the stereotyped beliefs, even if this is not actually so.

Unfortunately, stereotypes are both common and persistent. They change very slowly, even over the course of several decades. They exist with respect to racial groups, sex, occupational groups, geographical upbringing, age, education, social class, and even physical beauty (Cash, Gillen and Burns, 1977). (Burrell, 1984: 97) argues that the field of organizational behaviour itself stereotypes organizations as sexless places. He argues that novels and biographies possibly reflect a more rounded reality of organizational life.

In discovering the origins of prejudice, several different answers have been offered. Among the ones receiving most attention have been the suggestions that prejudice stems mainly from:

1 inter-group contact;
2 the presence of certain personality traits;
3 from learning experiences occurring early in life.

With respect to inter-group conflict, it has been proposed that prejudice often arises when different groups strive for the same jobs, housing, and other resources. Since their contacts under these conditions are largely hostile and competitive, it is not surprising that these interactions give rise to strong, negative attitudes. Research evidence has been obtained from a number of different studies which suggests that when groups must compete, negative feelings akin to prejudice often emerge (see Sherif *et al.*, 1961; Kerrington, 1981). Conversely, when contacts between various groups are largely friendly and co-operative in nature, such reactions are reduced.

It has been proposed that certain personality traits predispose individuals toward prejudices. It has been suggested that prejudice is often related to a cluster of personality traits termed the 'authoritarian personality' (Adorno *et al.*, 1950). Briefly, authoritarian individuals are people showing a pattern of submissive obedience to authority, punitive rejection of groups other than their own, and rigid thinking. Either you are a member of the group and are for them, or you are a member of some other rejected group, and must be against them. Authoritarian individuals are far from rare, and you will probably encounter many during your career.

A final view is that stereotypes are learned. Basically, it suggests that children acquire negative attitudes toward various social groups either simply by observing such reactions on the part of their parents or through direct reward and training for expressing such views. While parents, teachers, and peers are probably most important in this respect, the mass media, too, may play a role. Until recently, members of racial and ethnic minorities appeared only rarely on television and in films. Further, when they did, they were often shown as holding low-status jobs, as living in slums, and as speaking with a heavy and incomprehensible accent. Given repeated exposure to such material, it is far from surprising that many children soon acquire negative attitudes toward such persons, even if they had never met any in real-life situations.

Cognitive theories of personality

Psychological characteristics of individuals

Another category of individual attributes is psychological characteristics. While there is a wide range of these characteristics, they share a common tendency to predispose an individual to behave in predictable ways. These predispositions have a substantial influence on behaviour. Extroverted salespersons, for example, are likely to see things differently than introverts and to be seen differently by others. These differences will influence their behaviour and the sales they are able to generate. There is not enough space in this book to deal with the many psychological and cognitive studies of individuals. Two broad dimensions which have important implications in work organizations are internal–external orientation and problem-solving style.

Locus of control: internal–external orientation

The internal-external orientation measures the extent to which a person feels able to affect his or her life (Rotter, 1966). Chapter 3 dealt with locus of control with respect to using its results for selection. Here, we are more concerned with its cognitive aspects. People have general expectancies about whether events are controlled primarily by themselves, which indicates an internal orientation, or by outside forces, characteristic of an external orientation. 'Internals' believe they control their own fate or destiny. 'Externals' believes much of what happens to them is uncontrolled and determined by outside forces. Two examples of questionnaire items which have been shown to distinguish internals from externals are:

1 **a** Many of the unhappy things in people's lives are partly due to bad luck.
   b People's misfortunes result from the mistakes they make.
2 **a** As far as world affairs are concerned, most of us are the victims of forces we can neither understand nor control.
   b By taking an active part in political and social affairs, people can control world events.
      Source: Rotter, 1966.

Answers 1a and 2a reflect an external orientation while individuals responding with 1b and 2b show an internal orientation. Rotter's scale of locus of control is produced by asking 29 such forced choice pairs of statements. Given six 'filler' pairs, the scale ranges from 0 (purely internal) to 23 (purely external). Most populations score around the mean although closer study of particular groups can reveal marked differences in locus of control. Table 4.2 shows some of the ways in which internals and externals have been found to differ.

Problem-solving style

This examines the way in which a person goes about gathering and evaluating information in solving problems and making decisions (Hellriegel and Slocum, 1976). In the problem-solving process, information gathering and evaluating are separate activities. Information gathering is the process by which a person organizes stimuli or data for use. Styles of information gathering vary from sensation to intuitive. Sensation-type individuals prefer routine and order, and emphasize well-defined details in gathering information. Intuitive-type persons prefer the big picture, like solving new problems, and dislike routine.

Evaluation involves making judgements about how to deal with information once it has been collected. Styles of information evaluation vary, from an emphasis on feeling to an emphasis on thinking. Feeling-type individuals are oriented toward conformity and try to accommodate themselves to other people. They try to avoid problems that might result in disagreements. Thinking-type people use reason and intellect to deal with problems. They down-play emotional aspects in the problem situation.

It is likely that people with particular problem-solving styles may be better suited to certain jobs than others. For instance, intuitive-feeling or intuitive-thinking individuals are likely to be better counsellors than sensation-feeling or sensation-thinking individuals. Given a fit between the

Table 4.2
Some ways in which
internals differ from
externals

Characteristic	Description
Information processing	Internals make more attempts to acquire information, are better at information retention, are less satisfied with amount of information they possess, are better at utilizing information and devising processing rules
Job satisfaction	Internals are more satisfied, less alienated, and less rootless
Self-control and risk behaviour	Internals exhibit greater self-control, are more cautious, and engage in less risky behaviour
Expectancies and results	Internals see a stronger relationship between themselves and results, what they do and what happens to them, expect working hard to lead to good performance, feel more control over how to spend time, perform better
Preference for skill versus chance achievements	Internals prefer skill-achievement outcomes, externals prefer chance achievements (e.g. winning a lottery)
Use of rewards	Internals more likely to use personally persuasive rewards and power bases; less likely to use coercion
Response to others	Internals are more independent, more reliant on own judgement, less susceptible to influence of others, they resist subtle influence attempts and are more discriminating in information acceptance. Information is more likely to be accepted on own merits rather than based upon prestige of its source. (e.g. your instructor!)
Leader behaviour	Internals prefer participative leadership; externals prefer directive

Adapted from: Schemerhorn, Hunt and Osborn (1982:90). Reprinted by permission

problem-solving style and the information processing requirements of a job, it is plausible that a person should be more productive and satisfied than when there is a lack of fit.

Job satisfaction

Work plays a dominant role in our lives. It occupies more of our time than any other single activity. For most of us, it is central to our self-concept: we define ourselves, in part, by our careers or professions. We say we are an accountant or an operations manager when asked 'What do you do'? Rarely do we answer 'I play the piano or I'm quite a good painter' if these are our hobbies. The definition of work takes precedence in our self-description.

Most people can readily report feelings, beliefs, and behaviour tendencies relating to their jobs. In short, they hold strong and well-established attitudes towards their work and specific aspects of it. Such attitudes are generally known as job satisfaction.

Job satisfaction is of central concern to organizational behaviour researchers. One major reason for this interest in job satisfaction is obvious: positive and negative attitudes toward work may exert powerful effects upon many forms of organizational behaviour. However, while job satisfaction is closely related to some forms of work-related behaviour, it does not seem to play a direct role in others.

As is true of other attitudes, job satisfaction can be measured by several different techniques. By far the most common approach is by administering to individuals a set of rating scales on which the respondents simply report their reactions to their jobs. A large number of different scales have been developed. Items similar to those used on one (the Minnesota Satisfaction Questionnaire) are presented in Table 4.3.

Table 4.3
One type of attitude scale

In my present job, this is how I feel about:	Not at all satisfied	Slightly satisfied	Satisfied	Very satisfied	Extremely satisfied
. . . the variety of tasks I perform	1	2	3	4	5
. . . my responsibility for planning my work	1	2	3	4	5
. . . opportunities for advancement	1	2	3	4	5
. . . my rate of pay	1	2	3	4	5

The Job Descriptive Index (JDI) is a similar scale. Individuals completing this scale are presented with lists of adjectives and asked to indicate whether each does or does not describe a particular aspect of their work. (Respondents indicate their reactions by placing a 'Y' for yes, 'N' for no, or '?' for undecided next to each adjective.) One interesting feature of the JDI is that it assesses reactions to five distinct aspects of the job: the work itself, pay, promotional opportunities, supervision, and people (co-workers). Items similar to those included on the JDI are shown in Table 4.4.

Table 4.4
Items similar to those on the JDI

Place a Y (for yes), an N (for no), or a ? (for undecided) next to each word to indicate whether it does or does not describe your job:	
Work	**Pay**
_____ Interesting	_____ Fair
_____ Unpleasant	_____ Appropriate to my level
_____ Useful	_____ More than I deserve
_____ Simple	_____ Adequate for my current life-style
_____ Tiring	_____ Related to my performance

Another technique for assessing job satisfaction is the critical incident procedure. Here, individuals are asked to describe incidents relating to their work that they found particularly satisfying or dissatisfying. Their replies are then carefully analysed to uncover underlying themes and reactions. Finally, job satisfaction can also be assessed through interviews. Unfortunately, such procedures are often long and costly, therefore they have not been used for this purpose very often. Regardless of the specific approach adopted, the goal in assessing job satisfaction remains the same: uncovering the feelings, beliefs and behaviour tendencies of employees towards various aspects of their work. Further details of attempts to increase job satisfaction by redesigning or enriching jobs are outlined in Chapter 7.

One of the key features of any job is its ability to be stressful to the individual. All jobs have the potential to be stressful rather than give satisfaction. We explore stress in the next section.

Stress

Have you ever found yourself in a situation that seemed to be more than you could handle? If you have ever driven in frenzied commuter traffic, delivered a speech to a large, unfriendly audience, or looked frantically for your flight a few minutes before take-off in a bustling airport, your answer is certain to be yes. These situations share a common feature: they threaten literally to overwhelm our ability to handle or cope with them. When conditions of this type exist, we experience stress. As McGrath (1976) argues:

> . . . there is a potential for stress when an environmental situation is perceived as presenting a demand which threatens to exceed the person's capabilities and resources for meeting it.

While our reactions to stress vary greatly (everything from damp palms and shaking knees to intense feelings of despair), most fall under three major categories. First, we respond to stress physiologically. This includes a rise in heart rate and blood pressure, increased respiration, and a diversion of blood to skeletal muscles—the ones used in 'fight' or 'flight' situations.

In addition, we react psychologically. We experience such feelings as fear, anxiety, and tension. We actively seek to evaluate or appraise the stress-inducing situation, to determine just how dangerous it really is. Finally, we also respond to stress overtly, with a variety of coping behaviours. These range from attempts to gather more information about the stressful situation through direct steps to deal with it, and may also include intra-psychic strategies—ones designed simply to make us feel better (for example, taking a drink, convincing ourselves that there really is not much danger).

Stress can emerge from every aspect of our daily lives. In this brief discussion of the topic, we will focus on two groups of factors that produce or influence stress: ones relating to aspects of organizations and ones involving the personal characteristics of individuals. It is important to emphasize that trying to detail objective situations and variables to describe a situation as stressful is fraught with difficulty.

Stress is largely a perceived phenomenon (Lazarus, 1966). Only the individual experiencing the stress can identify the specific set of factors which are causing stress. They may not, however, be aware of all of them and we begin this section by looking at common situational causes of stress found in the organization. Reading 4 by Valerie Sutherland and Cary Cooper at the end of Part II fleshes out some of the ideas particularly with respect to the characteristics of individuals perceiving stress.

Organizational causes of stress

Occupational demands Some jobs are more stressful than others. Systematic evidence on this issue is provided by a recent study of the level of stress in more than 130 occupations (National Institute for Occupational Safety and Health, 1978). The results of this survey indicate that several occupations for example, physician, office manager, foreman, and waitress/waiter, are all relatively high in stress. In contrast, other jobs, such as craft worker, maid, farm labourer, and university lecturers, are much lower in this regard.

Role conflict Stress from conflicting and often irreconcilable demands. When individuals join an organization, they are generally expected to behave in certain ways. Such expectations constitute a role—a general set of guidelines indicating how persons holding certain positions should behave. In many cases, the presence of roles is beneficial: they save you the trouble of deciding what constitutes appropriate behaviour in many situations. Often though, roles can be the source of considerable discomfort and stress. This is especially likely in situations where different groups of people with whom an individual interacts hold contradictory expectations about how he or she should behave. Under these conditions, role conflict exists, and the person in question may find him or herself being pulled in different and incompatible directions.

Role ambiguity This is stress from uncertainty. Even if an individual manages to avoid the strain associated with role conflict, he or she may still encounter this even more common source of on-the-job stress. It occurs under conditions where individuals are uncertain about several matters pertaining to their jobs: the scope of their responsibilities, the limits of their authority and that of others, company rules, job security, and the methods used to evaluate their work.

Overload and underload Doing too much and doing too little. When the phrase 'job stress' is mentioned, many people imagine a harried executive who is attempting to dictate a letter, talk on three telephones, conduct an interview, and write a report simultaneously! This is referred to as 'overload', and while it rarely reaches this extreme, more than half of all white-collar workers report experiencing it to some degree in their jobs (French and Caplan, 1972).

Conversely, being asked to do too little in one's work can also be quite stressful. Such 'under-utilization' generally results in monotony and intense boredom. Stress occurs since, most persons wish to feel useful and needed, and by doing nothing in their job, their self-esteem is threatened. Individuals also appear to have a strong need for stimulation, and their preferred state is definitely not that of staring blankly into space (Katz and Kahn, 1978).

Responsibility for others This is often perceived by individuals as a heavy burden, although it is often encouraged in organizations as a part of career development. In general, being responsible for other people (dealing with them, motivating and making decisions about them) creates potentially higher levels of stress than positions in which such responsibility is absent (McLean, 1980). Such persons are more likely to report feelings of tension and anxiety. And they are also more likely to develop the 'classic' symptoms of stress, such as ulcers and hypertension.

The basis for this difference is easily discerned. Supervisors and managers must often deal with the human costs of their decisions. They must witness the anguish of persons who are sacked or passed over for promotion, as well as witness the reactions of those given negative feedback on their work. In families, the same stress due to responsibility can be seen in both mothers and fathers (over children's schooling, nurturing them for some preconceived future, etc).

Lack of participation This situation can cause stress from a perceived absence of input. Lack of employee participation in decisions which affect them and their job can serve as a source of tension and stress for two reasons. First, many employees feel 'left out'. Second, individuals may also experience feelings of helplessness or loss of control. These reactions often intensify the impact of other stressful events. Stressors are additive. An individual experiencing all six of the above situational conditions would be more prone to suffer the symptoms of stress than an individual experiencing one of the above situations. However, we must not neglect the interpretive nature of the stress–individual relationship. Certain individuals may not feel stressed at all, but will be in perhaps two or three of the above situations (see Reading 4).

The individual and stress

Lazarus (1966) argues that a better way to study stress and its effects is to study both situational events and their respective perception by different individuals. Much work has been conducted in this area. In this section we concentrate on three major fields of study:

1 Impact of life change, such as the death of a loved one, divorce, etc. (Holmes and Rahe, 1967).
2 Maintaining a hard-driving, high-pressure life-style. This is sometimes referred to as 'Type A' behaviour (Pittner and Houston, 1980).
3 Perceived control and reactions to stress. Events which are under your control (in terms of scheduling, etc.) cause less stress than those externally set (Rotter, 1966).

Life events and the individual

'Whenever a major change in state takes place the need arises for the individual to re-structure his ways of looking at the world and his plans for living in it' (Murray Parkes, 1971). The idea that we all have to adapt and change to various events has been a keystone of much research linking the onset of stress-induced illness to life changes.

The most well-known research into life changes is that of Holmes and Rahe (1967) who devised the 'Social Readjustment Rating Scale'. Respondents are asked to rate a series of life events according to their relative degrees of perceived necessary readjustment. It is argued that the greater the level of adjustment required, the greater the level of stress, accompanied by a high possibility of subsequent illness (physical and/or mental). The scale is shown in Table 4.5. The rank order was derived from a total of 394 American subjects, equally split male-female, predominantly Caucasian and between 20–60 years old. As our society has changed in many ways since the original study was conducted in the mid-1960s, it is also likely that our 'felt stress' due to these factors may also have altered. For example, our society's attitude towards divorce or taking on a mortgage has changed significantly and hence, may not produce as much 'stress' as it did to a previous generation.

For the respondents, marriage was given the arbitrary value of 500, and they were asked to complete the remaining 42 life events allocating scores to the extent that they believed the event needed more or less readjustment than marriage. Mean values such as those in Table 4.5 can then be calculated across any sample.

Holmes and Masuda (1973) categorized the life-change units (LCUs) as:

1 Mild life crisis (mild stress)   150–199 LCU
2 Moderate life crisis (moderate stress) 200–299 LCU
3 Major life crisis (high levels of stress) 300 + LCU.

It would appear that there is consistency across different nations using the Social Readjustment Rating Scale. Rank order correlation coefficients are shown in Table 4.6.

In this research area, cross-national research supports similarities rather than differences. The correlation coefficients in Table 4.6 are consistently high. This is quite remarkable. Western Europeans, for example, have a culture embedded in the democratic ethic, bolstered by internalized Western moral values for the most part. Asian 'Eastern Culture' is embedded in a hierarchical system which emphasize family-oriented, externally sanctioned rules of ethical conduct. Yet perception of stressful life events is very similar.

Table 4.5
The social
readjustment rating
scale (Results for
394 Americans)

Rank	Life event	Mean value
1	Death of spouse	100
2	Divorce	73
3	Marital separation	65
4	Jail term	63
5	Death of close family member	63
6	Personal injury or illness	53
7	Marriage	50
8	Sacked from work	47
9	Marital reconciliation	45
10	Retirement	45
11	Change in health of family member	44
12	Pregnancy	40
13	Sexual difficulties	39
14	Gain of new family member	39
15	Business readjustment	39
16	Change in financial state	38
17	Death of close friend	37
18	Change to a different line of work	36
19	Change in number of arguments with spouse	35
20	Mortgage over £100 000[1]	31
21	Foreclosure of mortgage or loan	30
22	Change in responsibilities at work	29
23	Son or daughter leaving home	29
24	Trouble with in-laws	29
25	Outstanding personal achievement	28
26	Wife beginning or ceasing work	26
27	Begin or end school (formal education)	26
28	Change in living conditions	25
29	Revision of personal habits (dress, etc)	24
30	Trouble with the boss	23
31	Change in work hours or conditions	20
32	Change in residence	20
33	Change in schools	20
34	Change in recreation	19
35	Change in church activities	19
36	Change in social activities	18
37	Mortgage or loan less than £90 000[1]	17
38	Change in sleeping habits	16
39	Change in number of family get-togethers	15
40	Change in eating habits	15
41	Holidays	13
42	Christmas	12
43	Minor violations of the law	11

[1] Figures updated to reflect 1998 prices!
Adapted from: Holmes and Rahe (1967) by permission of Pergamon Press Ltd.

Of course, this does not mean that every individual who scores over 300 LCUs will definitely suffer stress to the point where illness will inevitably result. There are many intervening factors such as personality, locus of control and Type A behaviours. We have covered personality in this Chapter and Chapter 3. Locus of control is summarized in Table 4.2. We discuss Type A behaviours briefly in the next section.

Table 4.6
Cross-Cultural
comparisons of rank
ordering using the
Social readjustment
rating scale.[1]

Cultural group	Japanese	West European	Spanish	Black American	Mexican
Caucasian American	0.752	0.884	0.847	0.798	0.735
Japanese		0.884	0.836	0.816	0.724
West European			0.849	0.772	0.754
Spanish				0.848	0.767
Black American					0.892

[1] Spearman's Rank Order Correlation Coefficient.
Adapted from: Masuda and Holmes (1967), Komaroff (1967) and Celdran (1970)

Type A behaviours

These can be classified as individuals who are:

1 extremely competitive: always striving for achievement;
2 always doing things in a hurry [walking, working, eating];
3 aggressive and restless: are impatient at the pace of most things around them;
4 are keen to take on responsibility: leisure time is difficult to cope with;
5 often set themselves objectives to achieve both in domestic and working life.

Some cultures (such as North America and, to a lesser extent, Britain) value such behaviour highly in managers and thus reinforce Type A traits. A study of 236 managers revealed a connection between Type A behaviours and symptoms of stress, such as high blood pressure and high cholesterol levels (Howard, Cunningham and Rechnitzer, 1976). Other studies, however, have found little support for this association (see Brief, Schuler and Van Sell, 1981). It is certain nevertheless that Type A individuals experience more stress both at work and at home.

Type B behaviours are the opposite of Type A. They will experience much lower levels of stress. Type B characteristics are:

1 little sense of urgency or impatience;
2 enjoy leisure and do not feel guilty about it;
3 can play sports and games without always being competitive;
4 feel little need to advertise their achievements.

Personal strategies for coping with stress

Self-improvement and self-help have been popular themes during the past two decades. Many techniques for coping with the harmful impact of stress (and for creating 'wellness') have been suggested. Some of these focus on physical strategies and others on psychological or behavioural approaches. Examples are:

1 *Physical strategies*
   ● exercise
   ● good diet
2 *Psychological strategies*
   ● develop networks of social support within the organization
   ● plan ahead, be prepared with alternative proposals
   ● take a holiday
   ● try meditation and relaxation training

Organizational strategies for reducing stress

While personal strategies for coping with stress differ greatly, all rely on giving individuals techniques they can use for dealing with stress when it occurs. Support provided by the employer for managing individual stress should seek to minimize those factors which are potentially stress-inducing in the work setting. Many of these involve changes in structure. Others focus primarily on changes in the nature of specific jobs. These include:

1 *Changes in organizational structure or function*
   ● decentralization
   ● adjustments to the reward system
   ● improved techniques of training and placement of employees
   ● arranging for employee participation in the decision-making process
   ● improved lines of communication in the organization
2 *Changes in the nature of specific jobs*
   ● job enlargement (see Chapter 7)
   ● job enrichment (see Chapter 7)

Judging from the list above, you can safely conclude that working within an organization is stress inducing! It is a high compliment to those who are able to devote decades of their lives to working within such sub-optimal conditions! As a society we have created organizations which do function and achieve their aims. Nevertheless, it is clear that greater development of the organizational form needs to occur if we are to maximize the results they offer. Part VII of this book looks toward such future developments in organizational structure and job roles to see if improvements are on the horizon.

Summary

This chapter has introduced a number of key issues in the study of organizational behaviour. In particular, the question of whether behaviour is situationally determined, or is largely determined by perception is important. For example, all jobs have the potential to create a stressful situation, so we would expect all individuals to experience stress. Yet, people's perceptions differ. They appraise the same situation in different ways. From this perspective, some people may experience very little stress, while others experience a great deal.

There are no hard and fast answers to these questions. There is empirical support for both social action explanations (everything can only be explained in terms of how any one individual perceives his or her world) and for environmental determinism (where the characteristics of the situation are argued to take primacy in explaining behaviour). Although introduced here at the individual level of analysis, this debate will be seen to run centrally through many of the following chapters.

References

Adorno, T. W., E. Frenkel-Brunswik, D. J. Levinson, and R. N. Sanford (1950) *The Authoritarian Personality*, Harper, New York.
Brief, A. P., R. S. Schuler and M. Van Sell (1981) *Managing Job Stress*, Little, Brown & Co., Boston, Mass.
Burrell, G. (1984) 'Sex and organizational analysis', *Organization Studies*, **5**, (2) 97–118.
Cash, T. F., B. Gillen, and D. S. Burns (1977) 'Sexism and "Beautyism" in Personnel Consultant Decision Making', *Journal of Applied Psychology*, **2**, 301–10.
Celdran, H. H. (1970) 'The Cross-Cultural Consistency of Two Social Consensus Scales: The Seriousness of Illness Rating Scale and the Social Readjustment Rating Scale in Spain', *University of Washington Medical Thesis*.

Crandale, R. and P. L. Perrewé (1995) *Occupational Stress: A Handbook*, Taylor and Francis, Washington D.C.

Dubrin, A. J. (1990) *Effective Business Psychology*, 3rd edn., Prentice-Hall, Englewood Cliffs, N.J.

Eysenck, H. J. and G. Wilson (1975) *Know Your Own Personality*, Harmondsworth, Penguin.

French, J. R. P. and R. D. Caplan (1972) 'Organizational Stress and Individual Strain' in A. J. Morrow, (ed.), *The Failure of Success*, AMACOM, New York.

Freud, S. (1933) *New Introductory Lectures on Psychoanalysis*, Norton, New York.

Fromm, E. (1941) *Escape from Freedom*, Rinehart, New York.

Gilmer, B. von H. (1984) *Applied Psychology: Adjustments in Living and Work*, 2nd edn., McGraw-Hill, Tata, New Delhi.

Hellriegel, D. and J. W. Slocum (1976) *Organizational Behaviour*, 2nd edn., West Publishing, Minneapolis.

Hilliard, A. L. (1950) *The Forms of Value*, New York, Columbia University Press.

Holden, C. (1980) 'Identical Twins Reared Apart', *Science*, March, 1323–1324.

Holmes, R. H. and M. Masuda (1973) 'Life Change and Illness Susceptibility', *Separation and Depression*, **12**, 43–65.

Holmes, T. H. and R. H. Rahe (1967) 'Social Readjustment Rating Scale', *Journal of Psychosomatic Research*, **11**, 213–218.

Holmes, D. S. (1974) The conscious control of thematic projection, *Journal of Consulting and Clinical Psychology*, **42**, 323–9.

Howard, J. H., D. A. Cunningham and P. A. Rechnitzer (1976) 'Health patterns associated with Type A behaviour: a managerial population', *Journal of Human Stress*, **4**, 24–31.

Katz, D. and R. Kahn (1978) *The Social Psychology of Organizations*, 2nd edn., Wiley, New York.

Kerrington, S. M. (1981) 'Inter-group Relations and Nursing', *European Journal of Social Psychology*, **11**, 43–59.

Komaroff, A. L. (1967) 'A comparative study of Negro, Mexican and White Americans', *Journal of Psychosomatic Research*, **12**, 25–36.

Lazarus, R. S. (1966) *Psychological Stress and the Coping Process*, McGraw-Hill, New York.

Lovejoy, A. O. (1950) 'Terminal and adjectival values', *Journal of Philosophy*, **47**, 593–608.

McGrath, J. E. (1976) 'Stress and behavior in organizations', in M. D. Dunnette (ed.), *Handbook of Industrial and Organizational Psychology*, Rand McNally, Chicago.

McLean, A. A. (1980) *Work Stress*, Addison-Wesley, Reading, Mass.

Masuda, M. and R. H. Holmes (1967) 'The Social Readjustment Rating Scale: A Cross-Cultural Study of Japanese and Americans', *Journal of Psychosomatic Research*, **12**, 10–24.

Mead, M. (1935) *Sex and Temperament in Three Primitive Societies*, William Morrow, New York.

Mischel, W. (1973) 'Toward a Cognitive Social Learning Re-Conceptualization of Personality', *Psychological Review*, **80**, 252–83.

Murray Parkes, C. (1971) 'Psycho-Social Transitions: A Field for Study', *Social Science and Medicine*, **5**, 21–45.

Nadler, D. and E. Lawler (1977) 'Motivation: a diagnostic approach', J. R. Hackman, and L. W. Porter (eds.), *Perspectives on Behaviour in Organizations*, McGraw-Hill, New York.

Pittner, M. S. and B. K. Houston (1980) 'Response to stress, cognitive coping strategies, and the Type A behavior pattern', *Journal of Personality and Social Psychology*, **39**, 147–57.

Rabin, A. I. (ed.), (1958) *Projective Techniques in Personality Assessment*, Springer, New York.

Rokeach, M. (1972) *Beliefs, Attitudes and Values: A Theory of Organization and Change*, Jossey-Bass, San Francisco.

Rotter, J. B. (1966) 'Generalized expectancies for internal versus external control of reinforcement, *Psychological Monographs*, **80**, 609.

Schemerhorn, J. R., J. G. Hunt, J. G. and R. N. Osborn (1982) *Managing Organizational Behaviour*, Wiley, New York.

Sherif, M., O. J. Harvey, B. J. White, W. R. Hood, and C. W. Sherif (1961) *Intergroup Conflict and Co-operation: The Robbers' Cave Experiment*, University of Oklahoma Press, Norman.

Wiggins, J. S. (1973) *Personality and Prediction: Principles of Personality Assessment*, Addison-Wesley, Reading, Mass.

CHAPTER 5 Theories of motivation

Introduction

Motivation is one of the earliest concerns of organizational behaviour. Links between a motivated workforce and increased performance (often assumed, and with surprisingly little empirical support) led managers to strive toward 'motivating' their workforces in an attempt to reduce alienation.

> *Alienation* is where the individual feels that work is a necessity imposed upon him or her. Working under such conditions means abandoning one's control over doing the job or of developing it.
>
> *Motivation* is where the individual feels that work is sometimes good and sometimes bad, but that it is fulfilling, satisfying and capable of development in all ways.

The dominance of linear thinking (motivation of staff leads to increased performance of the firm) has been challenged by Durst (1987) who argues that most managers mistakenly think that motivation leads to success, but it is more likely that organizational success produces motivation. The question of whether managerial agency or organizational performance are key influencers of motivation remains unresolved, but it does ask critical questions of much 'traditional' motivation theory.

A precise definition of motivation is elusive since the concept comprises both the characteristics of individuals, characteristics of the situation, and the perception of that situation by the individual. Yet we can usually spot the motivated individual with relative ease. He or she usually works harder, is interested in the task, is alert, bright and full of enthusiasm and ideas. Motivation then is characterized by a certain level of willingness on the part of an individual to increase effort, to the extent that this exertion also satisfies some need. In using this definition, we must distinguish between *motives* and *needs*.

> *Motives* are the internal drives and energies of an individual. They direct behaviour. This behaviour results in outcomes. Any single outcome (such as the purchase of a sports car) may be the result of multiple motives (I like the speed; I like the image I think it portrays; I only need two seats in my car; I like being my own mechanic etc.).
>
> *Needs* are also internal to the individual. They can be physiological (I need sleep, warmth, food) or social (I like working with others and talking to them) or self-esteem needs (I need to gain the respect of others for what I do).

Figure 5.1
Assumptions which form the basis for content theory

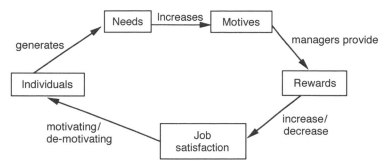

It is the interaction between the situation and needs and motives which forms the basis of most theories of motivation. In this book we shall be concerned with this interaction in the workplace, although clearly motivation is not limited solely to life in work organizations.

Theories of work motivation are largely grounded in the field of psychology. Psychologists, in turn, rely substantially upon the philosophical tradition of hedonism in their theory-building efforts—people seek to maximize pleasure and minimize pain in their day-to-day lives. Two categories of motivation theories evolve from this starting point: *content* theories and *process* theories.

Content theories

Content theories provide a link between individual needs and work rewards. They offer a perspective based upon the relative value people place on various rewards. Content theorists make a number of important assumptions about the relationship between an individual's motivation and job satisfaction (Maslow, 1943, 1970; McClelland, 1961). The first assumption is that needs are both physiological and psychological in origin. Second, that managers have the facility to alter rewards to suit individual preferences—thereby satisfying individual needs. Figure 5.1 illustrates the key factors which concern the content theorists.

Maslow's Hierarcy of Needs

This theory assumes that man is basically a wanting animal seeking to satisfy needs both in social and working life. Man is motivated toward satisfying these needs and does so in a predisposed and logical order. This hierarchy, usually displayed as a pyramid with higher order needs at the apex, is listed in Figure 5.2.

According to Abraham Maslow, needs which are satisfied are no longer motivators. This means that managers who constantly provide the same rewards cannot expect increasing levels of motivation from their staff.

Individuals are only driven (according to Maslow) by needs which remain unattained. Maslow's *Hierarchy of Needs* assumes that an individual can only progress through the five levels by satisfying each one in turn. For example, until one's safety and security needs are satisfied, status-based rewards would have little effect.

The highest level in Maslow's hierarchy is self-actualization. Given the somewhat 'existential' nature of this highest-order need, Maslow argued that it could never be completely satisfied. That is, individuals would continue to be motivated by challenging jobs and creative task demands. This is what would happen in an ideal situation according to Maslow. In most organizations and other aspects of social life, this ideal is rarely attained. In

Figure 5.2
Maslow's Hierarchy
of Needs

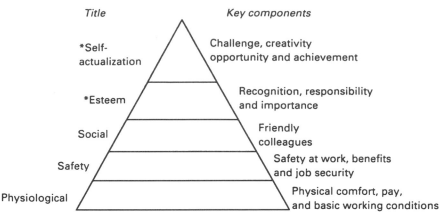

* denotes a 'higher order' need
Source: Adapted from Maslow (1943)

practice, individuals trade off needs rather than pursue them in a strictly ordered hierarchy. For example, it is possible to self-actualize, but at the expense of safety, the love of others and higher levels of pay.

McClelland (1961) also falls into the category of content theorists. His acquired needs theory focused on needs similar to the higher-order needs identified by Maslow. Specifically, McClelland argued that individuals have needs for:

1 achievement (nAch)
2 affiliation (nAff)
3 power (nPow)

Figure 5.3
Identification of
McClelland's needs

1. Do you like situations where you personally must find solutions to problems?
2. Do you tend to set moderate goals and take moderate, thought-out risks?
3. Do you want specific feedback about how well you are doing?
4. Do you spend time considering how to advance your career, how to do your job better, or how to accomplish something important?

If you responded to yes to questions 1–4, then you probably *have a high need for achievement*.

5. Do you look for jobs or seek situations that provide an opportunity for social relationships?
6. Do you often think about the personal relationships you have?
7. Do you consider the feelings of others very important?
8. Do you try to restore disrupted relationships when they occur?

If you responded yes to questions 5–8, then you probably have a *high need for affiliation*.

9. Do you try to influence and control others?
10. Do you seek leadership positions in groups?
11. Do you enjoy persuading others?
12. Are you perceived by others as outspoken, forceful, and demanding?

If you responded yes to questions 9–12, then you probably have a *high need for power*.

Source: Based on Steers and Porter, (1979, 57–64).

Table 5.1
Idealized job attributes and individual needs

Individual need	Job attributes	Typical jobs
High nAch	Greater responsibility Challenging goals	Commission-based e.g. stockbroker, insurance salesperson
High nAff	Friendship, teamwork	Social workers, sporting teams, volunteer worker
High nPow	Clear structure, authority and influence over others	Military ranks, politicians, plant managers

Although each person has all of these needs to some extent, only one of them tends to motivate an individual at any given time. To give you a rough idea of how these needs are determined, Figure 5.3 helps you to identify your own predominant need at any given time.

In contrast to Maslow's view that individuals are born with a well-ordered hierarchy of needs, McClelland argued that individual needs vary over time and as a result of their life history. From a practical point of view, McClelland felt that by manipulating the work environment, managers could satisfy different distributions of employee needs for achievement, affiliation and power.

As can be seen from 5.1, McClelland's approach allows a potential linkage between different individual needs and idealized job attributes.

This theory was derived in the 1950s by Frederick Herzberg and his associates at the University of Pittsburgh (Herzberg, Mausner and Snyderman, 1959) where they examined the models and assumptions proposed by Abraham Maslow. In a research study involving 200 engineers and accountants, the subjects were asked to describe times when they felt especially satisfied or dissatisfied with their jobs. Careful analysis of the incidents described yielded an intriguing pattern of findings. Incidents involving the work itself, achievement, promotion, recognition, and responsibility were often mentioned as sources of satisfaction, but rarely as a source of dissatisfaction. In contrast, incidents involving inter-personal relations, working conditions, supervisors, salary, and company policies were frequently mentioned as causes of job dissatisfaction, but rarely as a cause of satisfaction. The result of Herzberg's work was termed the Motivation–Hygiene Theory (M–H). The basic attributes of this theory are:

1. There are two types of motivators, one type which results in satisfaction with the job (called motivators), and the other one which merely prevents dissatisfaction (called hygiene factors). These two types of factors are quite separate and distinct from each other.
2. The factors that lead to job satisfaction (motivators) are:
   - achievement
   - recognition
   - work itself
   - responsibility
   - advancement
3. The factors which prevent dissatisfaction (hygiene) are:
   - company policy and administration
   - supervision
   - inter-personal relations
   - money
   - status
   - security

Criticisms of content theories

Both Herzberg's and Maslow's findings were soon investigated in a large number of studies conducted by other academics. Unfortunately, these replicative studies failed to offer strong support for the content theories. While some studies did yield findings similar to those reported by Herzberg, many others reported sharply contrasting results (see, for example, Schneider and Locke, 1971). In this study it was found that hygienes and motivators exerted powerful effects upon both satisfaction and dissatisfaction—contrary to Herzberg's basic assertion that these positive and negative reactions stem from different distinct clusters of variables. Several studies which sought to substantiate Maslow's theory also failed to find support for the needs hierarchy (see Lawler and Suttle, 1972; Rauschenberger, Schmitt and Hunter, 1980).

In view of this evidence, acceptance of Maslow's hierarchy of needs and Herzberg's theory as fully adequate theoretical frameworks does not seem justified. This is not to say that they are of no value. The M–H theory served to call attention to the importance of psychological growth as a basic condition for lasting job satisfaction. Attention to this fact, led in turn to much work concerned with the question of how jobs might be designed to foster such growth. This led to models such as the Job Characteristics Model (Hackman *et al.*, 1975). This is discussed in Chapter 7. In terms of motivation, the model provides a framework for enriching jobs to cater for the needs of individual workers, especially to give autonomy, feedback of performance and results and a sense of accomplishment (it is perceived as significant by the worker).

Maslow's theory has been criticised as being static, descriptive and ideologically biased. Like Herzberg, it cannot predict behaviour through analysing needs. Needs could be argued to reflect a cosy set of middle-class values rather than a rigorous theory (see Chapter 4). Both theories are full of methodological problems and they would not meet the criteria demanded by modern social science research.

Research was not conducted under controlled conditions. Respondents' data were evaluated by numerous researchers so that immense amounts of subjectivity permeated the results. Respondents themselves compounded this subjectivity. When asked to think of a time when they felt very good or very bad about their jobs, respondents tended to attribute the good things to themselves, and the bad things to the situation. We will re-visit this attribution of blame to external factors in Chapter 10, where groups also display the same phenomenon. Finally, not all individuals respond in the same way to having more challenging work or a greater sense of accomplishment (see House and Wigdor, 1967 for a review of critiques of the M–H theory).

Process theories

Process theories attempt a more dynamic approach by striving to understand the thought processes of individuals which act to influence their behaviour. They are thus more linked to the process of developing motives rather than to a static analysis of needs. Two process theories which offer significant implications for motivation in work organizations are *equity theory* and *expectancy theory*.

Equity theory

The basis of equity theory lies in the process of individual comparison. If individuals feel they are being rewarded unfairly for what they do, the result

Figure 5.4
The equity theory of
motivation: the
comparison process

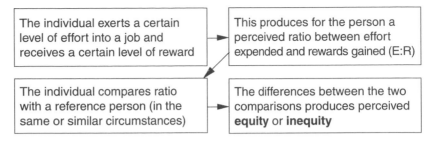

is more likely to be alienation or de-motivation. This process is very similar
to the more general sociological theory of social comparison (Adams, 1963).
Figure 5.4 outlines the major stages in the comparison process.

The most obvious form of inequity exists when a person doing a
particular job compares what he or she earns with another person doing the
same job in another, but similar organization. If they receive different levels
of pay or benefit, for example, the person who receives less will feel negative
inequity (see Figure 5.4). Equally, an individual who receives significantly
more pay and benefits than others doing the same job will also experience
inequity. This time, positive inequity exists. Both states represent an
imbalance which is perceived by the individual. The result is that they try to
achieve a balance (or equity).

The relevance of equity theory to studies of motivation is that it explains a
rationale for human behaviour which is not tied into need hierarchies or to
specific kinds of individual drives. On the positive side, equity theory helps
explain a potentially limitless list of factors which can lead toward motivating
behaviour. On the negative side, its basis as a theory of motivation places
great emphasis upon managers whose task becomes that of changing the
levels of reward in order to satisfy others' perceptions of equity. This is not
an easy task, both physically and mentally. It means that managers must infer
inequity from the behaviour (or complaints) of others and must choose the
most appropriate form of changes to achieve stability. The behaviours of
individuals who perceive inequities cover a wide range. Some of the more
common responses include:

● negotiating for higher levels of reward
● altering the bases on which comparisons are made
● looking for alternative employment

Managerial action designed to overcome negative inequity among staff
might include:

● better communication regarding how rewards are calculated
● commitment to rectify any real inequities brought to light
● constant monitoring of the comparisons which matter most to individuals

Fundamentally, managers must be sensitive to how others perceive their
working environment. For example, I might recognize that I am in an
inequitable position with regard to my peers in other organizations. They
may be promoted faster, earn more money, or work fewer hours (in the worst
case, all three!). Nevertheless, I might not perceive this as inequity since I
derive satisfaction from other factors, such as where I live, or loyalty to the
organization and friends. The argument that every employee in a work unit
will view their annual pay raise as fair is simplistic. It is not how a manager
feels about the allocation of rewards that counts, it is how the individuals

receiving their rewards feel or perceive them that will determine the motivational outcomes of the equity dynamic.

Expectancy theory

Expectancy theory, also known as the Path–Goal (P–G) concept, received its initial thrust from the work of Victor Vroom, an organizational psychologist at Yale University. Vroom (1964) argues that performance is a multiplicative function of motivation (M) and ability (A):

$$[\text{Performance} = f(M, A)]$$

Motivation to perform a task can be assumed to vary with:

1 the utilities of outcomes associated with the performance of that particular task (*valence*);
2 the *instrumentality* (belief that performance and outcome are linked) of performance for the achievement or avoidance of particular outcomes;
3 the *expectancy*, which determines the amount of effort expended by the individual in pursuit of a number of desired outcomes (such as gaining money to spend on a new car or house).

Basically, this is a hypothesis about decision-making. The presumption is that people can make intelligent and rational estimates about the consequences of particular choices and how such consequences will affect their own interests. Thus, the P–G model presupposes that people can estimate expectancies (in terms of probabilities that range from 0 to 1) in regard to both whether they can carry through particular tasks and the likelihood that their efforts will be noticed and rewarded accordingly. This 'logic' is illustrated in Figure 5.5.

Vroom's theory is important because it avoids the general error of the previous approaches which put the cart before the horse by arguing that enhancing human satisfaction always leads to improved task performance. The P–G/expectancy model gets the horse and cart in the right order by arguing that getting the task right determines human satisfaction. In application of P–G theory, the emphasis must be on carefully investigating what employees' expectancies, utilities, and instrumentalities are; and then, setting out to change the structure of the situation to provide what management and workers want. This may be very difficult to achieve in practice. It is also notable that expectancy theory is, like much work on motivation, highly skewed toward male workers and data from males generally. Lambert (1991) describes the common assumption that although men and women find the same job features equally attractive, women have lower expectations of the workplace and are therefore more satisfied than men under similar job conditions. In her research, Lambert found no

Figure 5.5
The path–goal sequence

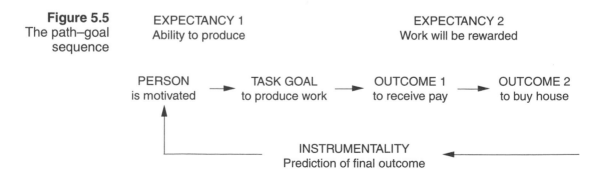

support for this assumption. Expectations were less important than values. Testing a sample of male and female employees, she found that whether one values what one receives is a key variable in motivation. She tested to see if social conditions made any difference (for example, if one's partner also worked) but concluded that this had little significant effect on motivation. More important were the conditions of employment which had a direct relationship to individuals' motivation at work.

Expectancy theory is also peculiarly context-free (as is the case with the majority of motivation theories). The assumption is that there is some homogenous, standardized individual with a relatively small range of expectancies, most of which can be predicted by management. Not so. According to Dawson and Dawson (1990) for example, the influx of women with children, the rising number of men in dual career families, the inclusion of various minority groups into work have irreversibly changed the demographics of the workplace and the expectations they hold about work. Equity theory, in particular, will be subject to the scale and scope of such demographic changes which fundamentally alter the bases of social comparison and what is expected and not expected from the workplace. In summary:

Content theories
- are based on the concept of hedonism
- assume individuals seek to satisfy all needs
- assume homogeneity of needs and individuals

Process theories
- focus particularly on choice behaviours
- rely on assuming a strong causality between means and ends
- are often impractical to implement in practice
- often are over-simplified since they neglect intervening factors such as egocentric behaviour and differences in individuals' perceptions.
- treat the decision-making processes of individuals as if they were homogenous and context-free.

Reinforcement theory: a situational approach to motivation

The reinforcement theory of motivation is based upon the notion that the likelihood of a particular behaviour being repeated is a function of its expected consequences (Thorndike, 1911). If you do something which results in a pleasant reward, then you are more likely to do it again. Similarly, if you undertake something which has unpleasant consequences (negative reinforcement), you may be less likely to repeat it.

A simple illustration could be if a new employee joins your work group. To welcome this new member, you may go out of your way to be friendly and jovial with him or her. However, if the new colleague does not respond with similar friendly behaviour, it is unlikely that you would continue putting effort into being friendly for very much longer. By not receiving any positive reinforcement, you would not be motivated to continue your behaviour.

Essentially, there are four kinds of reinforcement. *Positive reinforcement* is to provide a pleasurable reward following a desired behaviour. *Negative reinforcement* is a way of increasing a particularly desired behaviour by offering individuals an opportunity to avoid an unpleasant consequence. For example, to avoid criticism from your manager, you might adopt those behaviours which you know he or she wishes to see. *Extinction* is the withdrawal of reinforcement which was previously provided to encourage behaviours. An example would be if a manager would make it a point to criticize employees who arrived late for work. If, for whatever reason, the boss was no longer able to provide this negative reinforcement, the gradual extinction of the desired behaviour (that is, arriving on time) might be the result. The final type of reinforcement is *punishment*. Rather than reward good behaviour, punishment is the imposition of some unpleasant consequences as a result of undesirable behaviour.

Predicting performance and satisfaction

There is no simple relation between job satisfaction and performance. A widely held belief of human relations theory (see Chapter 2) is that improving job satisfaction directly improves performance. Thus, improving employee morale is argued to cut down labour turnover, absenteeism and increases production.

The current view is that satisfaction is not related to performance or, if it is, the correlation is very small. Some statistically oriented psychologists, for example, believe that a low, but consistent relationship exists (for example, Lawler and Porter, 1978). The question is why job satisfaction is such an important variable. Probably the most important reason is that there is some evidence to suggest that high job satisfaction reduces absenteeism and turnover. In path–goal theory terms, it can be argued that the satisfied individual is motivated to work where their important needs are met. Lawler and Porter (1978) state:

> It may well be that a high general level of job satisfaction of needs like self-actualization may be a sign of organizational effectiveness. Such a level of satisfaction would indicate, for instance, that most employees have interesting and involving jobs and that they are probably performing them well. One of the obvious advantages of providing employees with intrinsically interesting jobs is that good performance is rewarding in and of itself. Furthermore, being rewarded for good performance is likely to encourage further good performance.

Managing pay as an extrinsic reward

The development and maintenance of a fair and appropriate system for providing pay for work performance can be a major, and often frustrating challenge for managers and organizations. If it is not well-managed, pay dissatisfaction can lead to some potentially troublesome consequences (see Figure 5.6).

Figure 5.6
The consequences of pay dissatisfaction

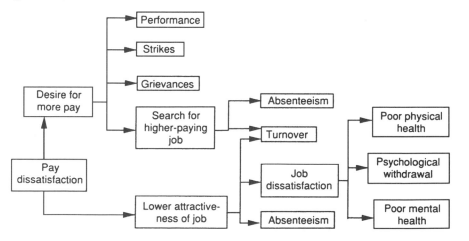

	What is Pay?	According to . . .
Table 5.2 The multiple meanings of pay as viewed from a job satisfaction perspective	Pay is a flexible reward which can satisfy a number of needs. First, it can overcome immediate 'lower-level' needs. Second, it provides the medium through which 'higher-level' needs are addressed	Abraham Maslow
	Pay is, primarily, a hygiene factor. When it is seen as too low, an individual would feel dissatisfied. Under certain circumstances, pay can also be a motivator since it can be seen as a form of recognition for merit, etc	Frederick Herzberg
	For high nAch individuals, pay increases are a form of feedback. For high nAffil people, elements of pay which are derived from meeting group targets can be a source of motivation. For individuals with high nPow, pay might be viewed as a function of their position in the organizational firmament	David McClelland
	Pay is one of the more important 'yardsticks' people use in organizations to assess their position *vis à vis* others. Based on their assessment, work effort may be altered accordingly	J. S. Adams
	When an individual believes that improved performance will lead to more pay (instrumentality), higher levels of motivation will result. Similarly, if an individual understands how much extra effort must be expended to attract more pay (expectancy), then the individual can make a decision whether or not to work harder	Victor Vroom
	Providing pay can be a positive reinforcement of desired behaviour. Alternatively, pay on a piece-rate or commission basis can be seen as having elements of negative reinforcement	E. L. Thorndike

Dissatisfaction with pay received can seriously affect the longer-term ability of an organization to survive. If the better employees start to leave or work less, coupled perhaps with difficulties in recruiting new, qualified staff, then the organization's ability to regenerate itself is thrown into question. Thus the motivation of employees via pay can have a direct effect on organizational performance and survival.

Earlier in this chapter, we outlined six of the major theories of motivation. Each has its own unique interpretation of why people perform the way they do. In each theory, pay is seen as an important element of the reward system. Nevertheless, it is interesting to note the different interpretations offered by each theory as to why pay is important. Table 5.2 summarizes the concept of pay according to the various schools of thought.

Pay and motivation

The basic assumption behind appraisal schemes, performance-related pay, merit schemes, profit-sharing and employee share ownership (among other variants) is that people are motivated by money. According to Wright (1986) financial sharing schemes can lead to greater levels of motivation by:

- creating a 'better' organizational climate;
- stimulating employee interest in profits and financial performance of the firm, therefore;
- encouraging more effective work.

Given even the early work on motivation theory, such as Herzberg or Maslow, such schemes would seem rather naïve and partial in their assumptions. To date, the evidence concerning to what extent employees are motivated by money is very mixed indeed. One problem lies in the limited extent to which such schemes are used in practice. Another problem is that the links between motivation and pay (if any) are hard to determine. For example, Poole (1988) conducted a national survey of 1125 firms in the UK looking at to what extent they had implemented profit-sharing and employee share ownership schemes. He indicates that, overall, around 22% of UK firms have some type of scheme. The majority of UK-owned publicly held organizations have schemes while 80% of private firms have none at all. Firms in the financial sector have significantly more schemes than other sectors.

In a study of 41 UK firms, quoted on the stock market and which all used employee profit-sharing schemes, Richardson and Nejad (1986) found that there was no significant direct link between these schemes and employee motivation. They did find, however, that there was a significant relationship between share price movements and the use of financial participation schemes. Firms with schemes had a faster increase in their share price. The authors did not study whether such increases were then associated with subsequently higher commitment and motivation levels by their staff. Poole and Jenkins (1991) suggest, however, that there was little or no direct link. They found that intervening variables, such as rate of growth, competitive position of the firm and the varied expectations of the workforce all confounded any simple relationships between shareholding and profit-sharing schemes with motivation. Poole (1988) also noted that managerial style and employee financial participation were positively related. Firms with predominantly consultative managerial styles also had greater levels of employee financial participation. In other words, managerial style may be a greater factor for employee motivation than financial sharing schemes.

Cable (1988) found that in German engineering firms, the use of financial participation and consultative management styles were rarely found together in the same firm. Firms using financial sharing schemes were rarely characterized by consultative management styles. Although the data are partial, Cable (1988: 136) does indicate that productivity gains (presumably from a more motivated workforce) seem to be greater in firms which use consultative management styles rather than profit-sharing schemes. Florkowski (1987) however shows that measuring the extent of profit-sharing is a problem in the North American firms he studied and can affect levels of motivation. Factors such as how extensive is participation; what amounts and kinds of participation are allowed; what unit of assessment is used to measure profitablity (the business unit or the whole organization, for example); the quality of participation in decision-making all affect how importantly employees view profit-sharing and how motivated they feel by potentially increased pay.

In a gloomy analysis of performance-related pay in UK organizations, Drennan (1988) argues that most company merit schemes motivate only the minority. Managers, he argues, often do not perform the appraisal process properly and often give more rewards than are deserved to avoid conflict and arguments. By definition, exceptional performance is the preserve of the few and these are the employees who will receive money and perhaps promotion. The greater majority will remain at their current level and may become demotivated at the sight of their colleagues' advancement. They will also become disenchanted at rewards given indiscriminantly or in ways they perceive to be unfair.

Summary

Theories of motivation are appealing at the intuitive level but when subject to analysis, none appear to offer substantial empirical evidence as to their efficacy. Content theories are possibly more useful at identifying basic values and needs in human beings than as theories of motivation in the workplace. Even here, there is an untenable assumption of homogeneity in all content theories. All people do not have identical needs in an identical pattern. Sayles' (1963) study of a variety of work groups points out that Herzberg's theories might well apply to many managers and to achievement-oriented work groups, but it is inapplicable to apathetic or conservative work groups which want to remain as they are.

Extending motivation theories into choice behaviours, rather than studying individual needs, merely complicates the issue even further. Expectancy theory and its derivatives make sweeping assumptions about causality and about individuals' capacities to specify future desired states clearly, in rank order and without ambiguity. Furthermore, even if this were possible, the degree of change or restructuring required in both organizations and individuals which would have to take place to accommodate motivation through process theories, is unrealistic to achieve in practice. Organizational and perhaps national contexts, too, will also confound the simple linearity of expectancy–outcome models.

It is likely that any single or unified theory of motivation is impossible to articulate. Individuals themselves are complex enough in their needs, values, beliefs, perceptions and attitudes. Add to these the additional factors of an individual's interaction with an organization and the analysis of what motivates him or her becomes very complex indeed.

Nevertheless, theories of motivation lie at the heart of much organizational practice. Equity theory can be seen in action in the guise of pay bargaining, for example. It is often assumed by both trades' unions and management that achieving parity in pay across various sectors will achieve equity and will lead to increased productivity and performance. Herzberg underpins virtually every job enrichment or satisfaction approach, while Maslow has permeated all levels from health and safety at work to the self-actualizing need of creative leaders, currently fashionable in management literature.

References

Adams, J. S. (1963) 'Toward an understanding of inequity', *Journal of Abnormal and Social Psychology*, **67**, 422–36.

Cable, J. R. (1988) 'Is profit sharing participation? Evidence on alternative firm types from West Germany', *International Journal of Industrial Relations*, **6** (1), 121–37.

Dawson, K. M. and S. N. Dawson (1990) 'How to motivate your employees', *Human Relations Magazine*, **35** (4), 78–80.

Drennan, D. (1988) 'Motivating the majority', *Management Today*, March, 88–92.

Durst, M. (1987) 'The "three Rs" of motivation: responsibility, recognition and reward', *Systems/3X World*, **15** (7), 120–21.

Florkowski, G. W. (1987) 'The organizational impact of profit sharing', *Academy of Management Review*, **12** (4), 622–36.

Hackman, J. R., G. Oldham, R. Janson and K. Purdy (1975) 'A new strategy for job enrichment', *California Management Review*, **15** (3), 96–7.

Herzberg, F., B. Mausner and B. Snyderman (1959) *The Motivation to Work*, Wiley, New York.

House, R. J. and L. A. Wigdor (1967) 'Herzberg's dual factor theory of job satisfaction and motivation: a review of the evidence and a criticism', *Personnel Psychology*, **20** (4), 369–89.

Lambert, S. J. (1991) 'The combined effects of job and family characteristics on the job satisfaction, job involvement and intrinsic motivation of men and women workers', *Journal of Organizational Behavior*, **12** (4), 341–63.

Lawler, E. E. (1971) Pay and organizational Effectiveness: A Psychological View, McGraw-Hill Book Company, New York.

Lawler, E. E. and J. L. Suttle (1972) 'A causal correlational test of the need hierarchy concept', *Organizational Behavior And Human Performance*, April, 265–87.

Lawler, E. E. and L. W. Porter (1978) 'The effect of performance on job satisfaction', in D. W. Organ (ed.), *The Applied Psychology of Work Behaviour: A Book of Readings*, Business Publications, Dallas, Texas.

Maslow, A. H. (1943) 'A theory of human motivation', *Psychological Review*, **50** (4), 370–96.

Maslow, A. H. (1970) *Motivation And Personality*, 2nd edn., Harper & Row, New York.

McClelland, D. C. (1961) *The Achieving Society*, Free Press, New York.

Poole, M. (1988) 'Factors affecting the development of employee financial participation in contemporary Britain: evidence from a national survey', *British Journal of Industrial Relations*, **26** (1), 21–36.

Poole, M. and M. Jenkins (1991) 'The impact of profit-sharing and employee shareholding schemes', *Journal of General Management*, **16** (3), 52–72.

Rauschenberger, J., N. Schmitt and J. Hunter (1980) 'A test of the need hierarchy concept by a Markov model of change in need strength', *Administrative Science Quarterly*, **25** (4), 654–70.

Richardson, R. and A. Nejad (1986) 'Employee share ownership schemes in the UK and evaluation', *British Journal of Industrial Relations*, **24** (2), 233–50.

Sayles, L. R. (1963) *Behaviour Of Industrial Workgroups*, Wiley, New York.

Sneider, J. and E. A. Locke (1971) 'A critique of Herzberg's incident classification system' *Organizational Behaviour and Human Performance*, **6**, 441–57.

Steers, R. M. and L. W. Porter (1979) *Motivation And Work Behavior*, McGraw-Hill, New York.

Thorndike, E. L. (1911) *Animal Intelligence*, Macmillan, New York.

Vroom, V. H. (1964) *Work And Motivation*, Wiley, New York.

Wright, V. (1986) 'Does profit sharing improve employee performance?', *Personnel Management*, **18** (11), 46–50.

Concepts of learning and behaviour

Introduction

Much of the application of motivation and learning theories falls under the general heading of behaviour modification (BM). This is the attempt *to try and control individual behaviour by systematically reinforcing those behaviours deemed to be desirable.* It thus draws heavily upon concepts of learning, reinforcement and conditioning. Many texts in psychology deal in depth with these concepts (see, for example, Hilgard, Atkinson and Atkinson, 1975). In this chapter we shall only touch upon these debates. Our major concern is to illustrate the role of BM in work organizations. First, we must examine the basic building blocks of BM: learning, reinforcement and conditioning.

Learning, reinforcement and conditioning

The concept of learning is so common that many people take it for granted and never really stop to think about how it is accomplished. Learning is a crucial component of BM. Without learning, there would be no reason to expend energy on changing behaviour patterns. In very general terms, it is by learning that behaviour is modified. As one would expect there are countless definitions for learning. One working definition is that: *learning is a relatively permanent change in behaviour that results from reinforced practice or experience.* The implication is that if the reinforcement process can be controlled, then learning can also be controlled. Learning can be subdivided into two distinct processes: learning through insight and latent learning.

Learning through insight

Learning through insight involves a three-stage process. First, one must understand a particular situation and identify what the problem is which needs to be solved. The second stage requires some thinking about the problem and its context. During this time, no learning may be apparent as one searches for a potential solution. The third stage is the brilliant flash when a solution becomes evident. A feature of learning through insight is that solutions derived in this manner are frequently used in a variety of other situations as well. Once a solution has been found, it is continually applied to try to resolve other problems. This can also have important negative effects upon creativity in decision-making (see Chapter 10).

Latent learning

Latent learning is slightly more complex. It derives from the ability to use knowledge from past experience to guide behaviour in a totally new situation. Latent learning is the accumulation of knowledge which does not have any immediate reward but which, in a particular context, can be recalled to guide behaviour.

Reinforcement

Reinforcement is the process through which certain consequences strengthen behaviour. Consequences which encourage particular behaviour are called reinforcers. Behaviour is positively reinforced when positive consequences are applied or accepted. Behaviour is *negatively reinforced* when negative consequences are applied or accepted. In a similar manner, behaviour can be extinguished when positive consequences are withheld.

Positive reinforcement is a strategy of accentuating the positive in order to eliminate the negative. By complimenting an individual on a success and/or providing some other form of recognition, the successful behaviour may be strengthened and more likely to re-occur. Positive reinforcement can be material (pay, promotion, privileges), verbal (compliments) and non-verbal (a smile, paying attention).

Negative reinforcement means inducing desired behaviour by withdrawing a particular undesirable condition upon improved performance. For example, if an employee works harder to prevent his or her boss from nagging, then negative reinforcement has occurred (Luthans and Kreitner, 1974). One way to consider negative reinforcement is as a type of 'blackmail' (Luthans, 1981). The principle is that people will behave in a particular way to avoid punishment.

Extinction means that an identifiable behaviour can be stopped if a particular reinforcement is withheld. For example, if a crying child is ignored and the behaviour eventually stops, then extinction has occurred. If people refuse to laugh at off-colour or racist jokes, then the behaviour of telling such jokes will eventually be extinguished. In work organizations, it is difficult to incorporate extinction in any deliberate policy. The problem is that by withholding reinforcement, the undesired behaviour may increase in the hope of regaining attention. A result could simply be further escalation of the situation.

Punishment should not be confused with negative reinforcement. Negative reinforcement increases the frequency of a desired behaviour, while punishment is intended to decrease the frequency of undesired behaviour. Punishment involves the imposition of a negative consequence upon a particular response. Since negative outcomes tend to be avoided, this should reduce the likelihood that the undesired behaviour will re-occur. Alternatively, punishment can also mean the withdrawal of a pleasant consequence. The theory is that if an individual values a particular consequence, the withholding of it is a punishment and has the effect of decreasing the likelihood of the undesired behaviour happening again. To be effective, punishment tactics should observe the following five points: (Hellreigel, Slocum and Woodman, 1983).

1 Tell the person what he or she has specifically done wrong.
2 Tell the person what is right. This is an attempt positively to reinforce correct behaviour.
3 The punishment should follow as soon after the undesired behaviour as possible.
4 Punish in private, praise in public.
5 Be fair, make the punishment fit the 'crime'.

Conditioning

Though the two terms are frequently interchanged, conditioning is not the same thing as learning. Conditioning is the *process* by which learning occurs.

Learning is the *result* of conditioning. Conditioning describes the various reactions to an individual's behaviour, and the modifying effect these reactions have upon the individual's behaviour in the future. If the person's behaviour changes, then we can say that the individual has been conditioned. There are two basic types of conditioning process, *classical* and *operant* conditioning.

Classical conditioning

The most famous demonstration of classical conditioning was conducted by the Russian physiologist Ivan Pavlov in the 1880s, see Schultz and Shultz (1992). Pavlov had noticed that dogs began to salivate at the sight of food. To test this reaction, Pavlov constructed an experiment in which a bell was rung shortly before the dog was given food. After this procedure had been followed for a number of times, Pavlov found that he was able to trigger the dog's salivation just by ringing the bell. The conclusion was that Pavlov was able to induce a reflex action by providing a particular stimulus. In terms of classical conditioning, this can be expressed as:

Prior to conditioning

An unconditional stimulus (i.e food)
cause
an unconditioned response (i.e. salivation)
At this stage, ringing a bell would be a neutral stimulus
(i.e. it would have no effect at all)

After conditioning

A conditional stimulus (i.e ringing the bell)
cause
a conditioned response of salivation
(irrespective of food being present)

Classical conditioning appears to explain a number of behaviours. For example, phobias can be argued to be the conditioned response to an early childhood trauma. In advertising, many television commercials use imagery which has less to do with the product and more to do with implanting a favourable image into the consumer's mind. For example, the strikingly beautiful scenery used in many car advertisements triggers a subconscious connection between the car (the product) and scenic beauty (image) even if the majority of driving will be along congested urban roads! Equally, motor car advertisements utilize lifestyle and sexual imagery deemed to be attractive to potential consumers. You can be a good driver, get the partner of your choice (or in some cases, get rid of the partner for someone new) by buying this make of car. The image and the product become intertwined.

Generalization can also occur. A similar, though unrelated stimulus brings out a conditioned response. With Pavlov's hungry hounds, it was found that salivation occurred (to a lesser extent) at the sound of a metronome as well as a bell. Commercially, this occurs regularly. For example, individuals have a response to particular product brand names. A good (or bad) experience with a product made by one manufacturer would very likely provide the consumer with a conditioned response to the manufacturer's entire product range. For firms operating globally on the strength of international brand names (such as St. Michael or Marlboro cigarettes) consumer response to the brand is crucial.

Operant conditioning

Classical conditioning is the study of how particular stimuli affect responses, $S \rightarrow R$. Operant conditioning looks at the process of responses affecting stimuli, $R \rightarrow S$. This has become known as the 'Skinnerian' approach after the work of the psychologist B. F. Skinner (Skinner, 1961).

Operant conditioning imitates the process of evolution. This is achieved by patiently waiting for a particular response (R) and then rewarding the person with a stimulus (S) to reinforce the continued behaviour. The underlying theory is that behaviour is strengthened or weakened by its consequences. The classic experiment used by Skinner to demonstrate this effect was to place a hungry rat in a box which contained a lever. When the lever was pressed, a pellet of food would drop into the box. When first placed in the box, the rat would explore and eventually, by chance, it would press the lever. Skinner found that the rat would then press the lever more and more frequently to obtain the food.

In work organizations, Skinner's work has potentially highly manipulative implications. The argument is that by controlling the consequences of particular actions, it is possible to change peoples' behaviours. By strengthening, maintaining or reducing the consequences of particular activities, the likelihood of a behaviour can be altered. Hamner and Hamner (1976) and Luthans and Kreitner (1974, 1975) have related Skinner's ideas to a number of work organizations in North America and results are significant. Both approaches are very similar. They involve a step-by-step analysis of performance-related behaviours and the application of a managerial strategy to motivate and to reinforce changes in individuals' behaviour.

In Hamner and Hamner's (1976) work, there is an attempt to outline a series of guidelines by which positive reinforcement can be achieved in work organizations:

1 Management sets organizational goals for each worker. These are reasonable, attainable, focus on behaviour and are measurable.
2 Each individual keeps a record of job performance so that the relationship between the organizational goal and actual performance is clear.
3 The manager identifies behaviour which appears to be associated with positive performance and rewards this (by praise, for example). Negative behaviour/performance links are not criticized. The absence of praise is sufficient for negative reinforcement and is argued to prevent the individual feeling overly controlled. The key to this approach is the extrinsic approach to applying concepts of motivation. Praise leads to a desire for more praise and thence to the achievement of performance-related goals.

Luthans and Kreitner (1974, 1975) have also adopted a similar stance. Like Hamner and Hamner, they take a highly managerialist view to how employees might be controlled and manipulated. Thinking and doing are separated in both models. Managers do the thinking (and the controlling) while employees get on with 'doing'. The element of Luthans and Kreitner's model are:

1 Identify the particular behaviours which are necessary for good job performance. These are those behaviours which may take up relatively little effort or time for an individual, but which are very effective for performance. These are called critical behaviours.

Table 6.1 Typical rewards to support behaviour modification in work organizations

Work Design	Social	Institutional
Private office	Free lunches	Preferential services (e.g. cheap loans)
Redecoration	Pub/wine bar get-togethers	Profit-sharing
Provision of windows/music	Friendly greetings	Free membership of private schemes (e.g. health insurance)
Action on suggestions	Informal recognition	Share ownership schemes
Job rotation	Public praise	Use of firm's recreation facilities (e.g. sports grounds)

2 Measure both the strength and the frequency of such behaviours by keeping a record.

3 Where changes are necessary, managers should design an intervention strategy to achieve the desired behaviours. This will involve the explicit giving of rewards to individuals or groups and may also involve changes to work design, organizational structure, etc. This model applies rewards as motivators. It thus pays little attention to the more perceptually based theories of expectancy in motivation (see Chapter 5). Typical rewards are shown in Table 6.1.

4 The new state should be subject to constant monitoring to sustain the behaviour modification.

The above methods of modification rely heavily upon the processes of *shaping* and *modelling*.

Shaping

Shaping involves taking a large, complex task and breaking it down into small components. Each of the components can then be taught separately until the entire sequence has been learned. Shaping is the way we learn to walk, ride bicycles, play tennis, etc.

In organizations, shaping involves the application of positive reinforcements as the individual becomes increasingly adept at each step of the learning process. The role of a manager in a shaping process is that of a teacher, a coach or helper. Rather than saying what was wrong, the 'shaping' manager will clarify how to do a task correctly. When the individual has completed the task, some appropriate reinforcement is provided (praise or other reward) and then the next sequential step is attempted.

Modelling

Though related to the concept of shaping, modelling adopts a different method of communicating the desired behaviour to the individual. The basis of modelling is to illustrate the 'ideal' form of behaviour and then ask the individual to model him or herself along the same lines. Positive reinforcement is provided as individuals become more adept at imitating the desired behaviour.

There are a wide number of ways to use modelling in organizations. Training exercises which involve role playing as well other forms of feedback oriented exercises (such as experiential learning) all incorporate some form of modelling.

Applications and limitations of behaviour modification

To many people, the term behaviour modification implies manipulation, coercive control and other 'Orwellian' management methods (see Robertson and Cooper, 1983). Others have argued that theories based upon simple stimulus–response relationships (getting dogs to salivate at the sound of a bell, chickens to ring bells and mice to run mazes) are overly simplistic and inapplicable in organizations.

Behaviourists and cognitive psychologists fundamentally disagree about putting BM into practice in organizations.

Behavioural psychologists   argue that all behaviour is learned through a process of experiencing rewards and punishments. Individuals can learn to do something without necessarily being motivated to act voluntarily.

Cognitive psychologists   argue that individuals think before they act. Therefore the key to modifying behaviour lies in motivation. Learning can be achieved by motivating individuals to act in particular ways. (see Locke, 1977)

It is likely that neither of the above views are right, but that the truth is contained in both statements. We know from Chapters 3 and 4 that we can better understand behaviour from examining both the individual and the context or situation. Behaviour modification is central to this interaction between person and context.

Despite academic scepticism, behaviour modification seems to have been extremely successful, especially in North American organizations such as B.F. Goodrich, General Electric, Collins Food, Standard Oil Ohio and Emery Air Freight. In Britain, behaviour modification has seen some success in safety and hygiene applications. Getting people to wear protective clothing and masks both for their own safety and for the safety of others has never been easy, especially where there are no direct penalties for not conforming. By changing management styles and giving rewards for wearing protective clothing etc., its acceptance has become far more widespread. In the food industry, this was also reinforced by increased legislation on cleanliness in the workplace, so differentiating cause and effect in this case becomes difficult.

It is arguable that even in universities and perhaps especially, business schools (in the UK and continental Europe) behaviour modification practices are at work to standardize the organization. Ritzer (1992), for example, has argued that the majority of organizations in societies are becoming 'McDonaldized'—that is the predominance of the retail metaphor and the standardized way of delivering the product or the service. Universities 'sell' their service to the customer (the paying student). In order to give efficient and effective service, academic staff must behave in particular ways and espouse particular values. These do not always fit the 'traditional' behaviour patterns and actions of academic staff. The public demonstration of internalizing and acting upon the new principles of service delivery are rewarded with discretionary pay awards, merit schemes and, sometimes, earnings additional to the basic salary, (Prichard and Willmott, 1997).

Summary   Behaviour modification in work organizations is the process in which
performance-related behaviours are identified and managed; desirable
behaviours are strengthened and undesirable behaviours are weakened. This
process is contingent upon reinforcement and conditioning.

The controversy surrounding the use of BM techniques in organizational
settings has become intense in recent years (see Locke, 1977; Gray, 1979;
Locke, 1979; Ritzer, 1992). Views on BM tend to be at either of two extremes:
for it or against it. The cognitive theorists propose that individuals engage in
complex thought processes before behaviour occurs. Behaviourists have
tended to exclude the issue of thinking from their model. Another criticism
is that BM focuses attention on explaining behaviour rather than predicting
it. Champions of BM respond that the observation of how people respond to
environmental stimulus provides the most important clues to how they will
respond in the future.

There are four primary concerns upon which critics of BM have focused
their energies. They are:

1   *Control*   These are the ethical issues raised when managers are provided
    with tools designed to control subordinates. Managers themselves can
    often feel uncomfortable with the thought of having control over
    someone else's behaviour. There is a large element of authoritarianism
    built into BM. It presumes that the controllers of behaviour (the shapers,
    the modellers, the reinforcers and the punishers) all have unquestioned
    control and authority.
2   *Reinforcements*   Successful BM is limited by the degree to which the
    manager can control the reinforcements. If a manager cannot influence
    events which the employee finds rewarding, then the manager will not
    have much influence over employee behaviour. In many organizations,
    managers are restricted in the amount of freedom they might have to
    alter such devices as pay scales, benefits, promotions, disciplinary
    procedures and firing.
3   *Group behaviour*   BM tends to focus on the level of the individual.
    However, group demands may conflict. For example, suppose an
    employee's job is altered to provide for greater responsibility and it is
    expected that this will result in the individual working harder and
    achieving greater job satisfaction. This outcome might conflict with a
    work group norm which might exist that restricts the actual amount of
    work which someone does. From the employee's perspective, a decision
    has to be made regarding the relative attractiveness of the two conflicting
    reinforcements—job satisfaction or group acceptance.
4   *Identification*   BM has consistently focused upon lower hierarchical levels.
    Little research has been conducted at more senior managerial levels.
    Also, managers often are unable to identify what employees find
    reinforcing (Kerr, 1975). While there are many things which might be
    favoured by the employee (more pay, benefits, etc.), it is possible that
    these do not function to reinforce the desired behaviour. Unfortunately, a
    manager cannot just ask the employee what the best reinforcer might
    be—there is no guarantee that the answer will be complete or even
    correct. There are many reasons why this is so. Individuals may feel
    foolish to admit the things which they most desire or they may distrust the
    manager's motives. In the final analysis, the best way to isolate effective
    reinforcers is to deduce what the employee has responded to in the past.
    To do so consistently requires managers to be acutely aware of the

problems of cause and effect—which is, essentially, the problem in the first place!

References

Gray, J. L. (1979) 'The myths of the myths about behaviour mod in organizations: a reply to Locke's criticisms of behaviour modification', *Academy Of Management Review*, **4** (1), 121–29.

Hamner, W. C. and E. P. Hamner (1976) 'Behaviour modification on the bottom line', *Organizational Dynamics*, **4**, 3–21.

Hellriegel, D., J. Slocum and R. Woodman (1983) *Organizational Behaviour*, 3rd edn., West Publishing, St. Paul, Minn.

Hilgard, E. R., R. C. S. Atkinson and R. L. Atkinson (1975) *Introduction To Psychology*, 6th edn., Harcourt Brace, New York.

Kerr, S. (1975) 'On the folly of rewarding A, while hoping for B', *Academy Of Management Journal*, **18** (4), 769–83.

Locke, E. A. (1977) 'The myths of behaviour modelling in organizations', *Academy Of Management Review*, **2** (4), 543–53.

Locke, E. A. (1979) 'Myths in the myths of the myths of behaviour mod in organizations', *Academy Of Management Review*, **4** (1), 131–36.

Luthans, F. and R. Kreitner (1975) *Organizational Behaviour Modification*, Scott, Foresman, Glenview, Illinois.

Luthans, F. and R. Kreitner (1974) 'The management of behavioural contingencies', *Personnel*, July–August, 7–16.

Luthans, F. (1981) *Organizational Behaviour*, 3rd edn., McGraw-Hill, New York.

Prichard C. and H. Willmott (1997) 'Just how managed in the McUniversity?', *Organization Studies*, **18** (2), 287–316.

Ritzer, G. (1992) *The McDonaldization of Society*, Pine Forge, Newbury Park, CA.

Robertson, I. T. and C. L. Cooper (1983) *Human Behaviour In Organisations*, Macdonald & Evans, Plymouth.

Schultz, D. P. and S. E. Schultz (1992) *A History of Modern Psychology*, 5th edn., Chicago: Harcourt Brace Jovanovich.

Skinner, B. F. (1961) *Analysis Of Behaviour*, McGraw-Hill, New York.

The quality of working life: jobs and job design

Introduction

In contrast to *ex*trinsic rewards, which are the central focus of most motivation theories, job designs such as enrichment, enlargement, teamwork and empowerment refer to those rewards which are *in*trinsic. The assumption is that the rewards for individuals are a function of the job itself. The assumption of the job design approach, therefore, is that ways in which jobs are organized will have a direct effect on whether they motivate or de-motivate individuals. Although the notion of adequate reward will be subject to some degree of perceptual bias, organization theory is full of attempts to increase intrinsic rewards and to increase job satisfaction.

There are two broad distinctions on the literature. Early theories were concerned with the design of individual tasks (such as routine or shop-floor jobs). They focused on increasing efficiency and the level of reward (where possible) from individual tasks. Later theories were more concerned with examining how jobs fitted into the wider context of individuals' lifestyles (typically flexible working hours or choosing work sites to suit family and other commitments). Both approaches assume that motivation arises primarily from doing the job itself rather than from any external incentive controlled by management directly. Aldag and Brief (1977) illustrate how individuals may receive quite low salary levels, but receive immense satisfaction from their jobs. Volunteer workers, artists, musicians, teachers and some public service workers would fit into this category. Intrinsic rewards come from the nature of the job itself. Craftsmen and artists generally are examples. Helping others without expecting commensurate reward oneself (altruism) may represent a very high degree of intrinsic reward. However, the approaches to job design outlined in this chapter are not without their own ideological bias. The planning of jobs, decisions over how much autonomy and personal freedom to give staff and whether or not to value intrinsic rewards are fundamentally imbued with managerial ideologies. A manager who views labour antagonistically and as needing to be controlled will manage very differently to the humanistic, more egalitarian, manager (Braverman, 1974).

Job Design: a theory of intrinsic rewards

As Umstot, Bell and Mitchell (1976) note, job design is the deliberate, purposeful planning of the job. This means not only perhaps rearranging how tasks are done (their sequence, for example) but also examines how more social or informal aspects of the job might affect perceived rewards and satisfaction. The question of who designs and plans particular jobs has long been a central debate in organization theory. Leaving this solely to management implies that workers should have little say over how their jobs are organized. However, empirical evidence points to the ability of many workers to organize and design their own jobs with varying degrees of participation from management (see Chapter 2 and socio-technical approaches). Results indicate that where individuals have the autonomy to design their own jobs (within the limits of feasibility) then both job satisfaction and levels of job performance increase. Yet, early days of job design took a very different view, arguing that jobs should be standardized and mechanized as far as possible. This was called job simplification.

Job simplification: Taylorism

Job simplification emphasizes the reduction of a job to its component parts, and then a reassembly of these parts into an optimally efficient work process. Deeply rooted in the tradition of scientific management (Taylor, 1911 and Chapter 2), job simplification emphasizes the following features

1 Mechanical pacing, or the use of an automated assembly line to monitor the speed of production (Walker and Guest, 1952).
2 Repetitive work processes, or designing the work so that individuals replicate the same tasks.
3 Concentration on only a fraction of the product; for example, in automobile manufacturing, one individual might mount the wheel on the stub axle assembly, while another might place the hub cap on the wheel.
4 Predetermination of tools and techniques; that is, describing and prescribing the work process as precisely as possible.
5 Limited social interaction among the labour force.
6 Low skill requirements, or breaking the job down into specific and relatively simple tasks that require minimal training.

Typically, the implementation of work simplification uses industrial engineering methods. To begin, industrial engineers study the exact series of motions in a job, using detailed observation records and drawing extensive diagrams of the work process. Next, they monitor the time required for each part of the job. Third, they identify and then attempt to eliminate all false, slow, and useless movements. Finally, they redesign the job by collecting into a series the quickest and best movements. To accomplish the last step, work simplification typically involves a high use of machines, maximum spacing of rest periods, high specialization of work activities, and matching of workers to jobs best suited to their abilities, experience, and aptitudes.

Jobs which stand most to gain from simplification tend to be those influenced by rapidly changing technology. It is likely that some fully automated manufacturing processes will simplify jobs in the extreme. Workers will become machine-minders, baby-sitters of the factory floor. On the other hand, some workers (but by no means all) prefer less complex jobs. Only diagnosis of a specific situation can determine the functional or dysfunctional nature of job simplification.

Typical dysfunctions are: worker boredom, limited opportunities for individual growth, and mechanization for its own sake. The costs of task segmentation that must be overcome include:

1 moving and repositioning items between operations;
2 assembling separate tasks into a more efficient total process;
3 balancing the line to reduce down-time; and
4 providing additional external supervision and work pacing (Emery, 1975)

Table 7.1 summarizes some of the advantages and disadvantages commonly associated with job simplification.

Table 7.1
Expected
advantages and
disadvantages of
machine-paced
assembly lines

Potential advantages	Potential disadvantages
Increased economy because:	Economy gains not realized because:
• Jobs require little training • Jobs staffed by low-skilled people • Workers interchangeble among jobs • Production quality and quantity easily controlled	• Absenteeism high • Turnover high • High wages required to attract workers • Production quality suffers because workers become bored and frustrated

Source: Adapted from Lawler (1973)

Job enlargement

Taylorism and job simplification were to have a strong influence over the organization of jobs which lasted virtually throughout two world wars. It was in the immediate post-Second World War period that the implications of boredom and repetition became increasingly apparent, especially in machine-paced technologies (see Table 7.1). In place of job simplification, enlarging jobs involved the re-combination of what were previously separate tasks. This proved popular with managers of the era, especially since it effected quite substantial changes in the jobs carried out by workers, but largely left the rest of the organization unchanged (for example, in its overall structure, degree of functional specialization etc.).

Where jobs proved difficult to enlarge, such as where specific technologies prevented the re-combination of tasks (as in the case of assembly lines) the solution of job rotation was an alternative. This involved workers performing a variety of tasks rather than just one and switching between tasks at pre-set intervals. Once again, this changed the workers' jobs radically, but left the rest of the organization virtually unchanged. Today the practice of job rotation is practised at management levels in the guise of cross-functional work, although the extent to which this has really broken down functional barriers is debatable. For workers, job rotation was not always a benefit. They often saw it as just adding one meaningless job to another (Herzberg, 1968).

Job enrichment

The widespread demoralization of staff led to a further search for alternative ways to make work more interesting and intrinsically more satisfying. Recourse to the then current motivation theories seemed to provide an answer. Expectancy theories of motivation (see Chapter 5) became the basis for the *job characteristics model*, widely reported by Hackman *et al.*, (1975). Herzberg's (1968) work on motivation was to provide a second source of enriching jobs by allowing workers more autonomy and responsibility in their daily tasks (see Table 7.2). The main features of the job characteristics model focus on five core characteristics relevant to motivation and satisfying workers who perform the task. The features includes aspects of the job itself (the task) as well as the process by which the job is carried out (for example, different degrees of responsibility and autonomy). A job which scores high on all the core features is argued to have been enriched. The five features are:

The task 1 *Identity* The extent to which the task is one meaningful piece of work. The worker can see tangible beginning and end points to the job.

Table 7.2
The principles of job
enrichment

Principle	Motivators involved
1. Remove some controls while retaining accountability	Responsibility and achievement
2. Increase the accountability for individuals for their own work	Responsibility and achievement
3. Give a person a complete natural unit of work (module, division, area)	Responsibility, achievement and recognition
4. Grant additional authority to an employee in his or her activity, provide job freedom	Responsibility, achievement and recognition
5. Make periodic reports directly available to the worker rather than the supervisor	Recognition
6. Introduce new and more difficult tasks not previously handled	Growth and learning
7. Assign individuals specific tasks, enable them to become experts	Responsibility, growth, and advancement

Source: Herzberg (1968).

2 *Significance*   The extent to which the task directly affects the jobs of others within or outside the organization.

3 *Variety*   The extent to which the task employs the different skills and abilities of each worker. In common parlance, the job becomes more challenging.

The worker   **1** *Autonomy*   The extent to which the individual can exercise discretion over how the job is performed (for example, in time-scheduling or deciding which tools to use).

2 *Feedback*   The extent to which the individual receives direct information concerning how effectively the task has been performed.

According to the job characteristics model, high scores on the core characteristics lead to conditions which promote high levels of task motivation, performance and job satisfaction. Designing in the five features to jobs, therefore, increases the likelihood that performance and job satisfaction will benefit (Hackman *et al.*, 1975). Figure 7.1. depicts extreme cases of job enrichment and their effects upon individuals.

The basis of these assumptions is that the more individuals experience that work is meaningful, the greater is their motivation to work and the more satisfaction they will receive from working. This is achieved by creating a job in which they have responsibility and can see a tangible outcome from their efforts. Empirical support, however, is relatively scarce. Brief and Aldag (1975) summarize job enrichment studies which have been carried out in a variety of settings. One involved looking at the jobs of female telephone operators. Another involved studies of financial service organizations and dental practices. The results are far from clear. Some individuals became anxious about job security and unforeseen difficulties arose where other peoples' jobs not in the experiments were affected. Overall, more managers than workers agreed that job enrichment had been successful.

This approach to job enrichment has been examined in a variety of work

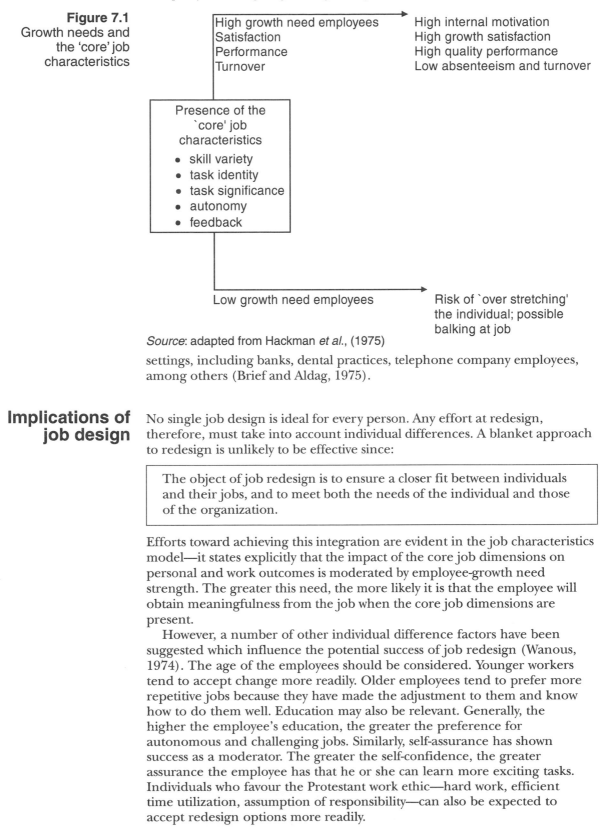

Figure 7.1
Growth needs and the 'core' job characteristics

High growth need employees
Satisfaction
Performance
Turnover

High internal motivation
High growth satisfaction
High quality performance
Low absenteeism and turnover

Presence of the 'core' job characteristics
- skill variety
- task identity
- task significance
- autonomy
- feedback

Low growth need employees

Risk of 'over stretching' the individual; possible balking at job

Source: adapted from Hackman *et al.*, (1975)

settings, including banks, dental practices, telephone company employees, among others (Brief and Aldag, 1975).

Implications of job design

No single job design is ideal for every person. Any effort at redesign, therefore, must take into account individual differences. A blanket approach to redesign is unlikely to be effective since:

> The object of job redesign is to ensure a closer fit between individuals and their jobs, and to meet both the needs of the individual and those of the organization.

Efforts toward achieving this integration are evident in the job characteristics model—it states explicitly that the impact of the core job dimensions on personal and work outcomes is moderated by employee-growth need strength. The greater this need, the more likely it is that the employee will obtain meaningfulness from the job when the core job dimensions are present.

However, a number of other individual difference factors have been suggested which influence the potential success of job redesign (Wanous, 1974). The age of the employees should be considered. Younger workers tend to accept change more readily. Older employees tend to prefer more repetitive jobs because they have made the adjustment to them and know how to do them well. Education may also be relevant. Generally, the higher the employee's education, the greater the preference for autonomous and challenging jobs. Similarly, self-assurance has shown success as a moderator. The greater the self-confidence, the greater assurance the employee has that he or she can learn more exciting tasks. Individuals who favour the Protestant work ethic—hard work, efficient time utilization, assumption of responsibility—can also be expected to accept redesign options more readily.

Although often overlooked by zealous advocates of job redesign, some individuals are actually happier with repetitive and monotonous jobs. When given the opportunity to assume a job with demanding and rewarding tasks, some individuals will opt to remain in their highly repetitive and low-skill jobs. These individuals do not have the strong needs for growth and autonomy or have chosen to satisfy their needs away from the workplace. Many workers look to their jobs as providing the means to allow them to do more gratifying activities outside the work context (Terkel, 1972). To ignore this diversity in the workforce is foolhardy. Efforts to redesign everyone's job in an organization to improve its motivation potential will undoubtedly lead to making some people less happy and less productive.

Goal-setting

Much management time is spent on determining what are appropriate organizational goals and how to get individuals to work toward their targets. Locke (1968) devoted considerable early efforts to understand the various components of goal-setting. Locke argued that well-selected and communicated goals can, in themselves, be a motivating factor for employees. This principle underlies much of the approach taken by Management by Objectives (MBO). According to Locke and Latham (1990), effort expended by individuals in undertaking a desired set of behaviours is a function of four properties of the goals themselves:

1 *Difficulty* This is the extent to which an individual sees goals as challenging but achievable.
2 *Specificity* The greater the precision in defining the goals, the more likely it is that individuals will understand how (and when) they should achieve them.
3 *Acceptance* The degree to which an individual accepts the goals as ones they would like to achieve.
4 *Commitment* The individual is committed to achieving these goals and undertakes, on their own initiative, actions to fulfil these aims.

The principles of goal-setting are closely aligned to theories of motivation. For example, expectancy theory suggests that goals are more likely to be accepted if they are seen as attainable (high expectancy) and that the desired outcome for the individual will clearly be the result (high instrumentality) (see Latham and Ukl, 1975).

Working in groups: self-regulation and autonomy

This aspect of job redesign owes a lot to the work of researchers in the socio-technical school of organization theory (see Chapter 2). Socio-technical redesign complements the other approaches described so far. It responds specifically to the difficulty of introducing new technology into a work system effectively. Researchers at the Tavistock Institute were among the first to note the negative impact of new technology on worker productivity and satisfaction. In both the coal mining (Trist and Bamforth, 1951) and textile weaving industries (Rice, 1958), the introduction of a new technology conflicted with a strong work culture and social system. Car manufacturers experienced similar resistance to the increasing automation of the assembly line, resulting in greater absenteeism, increased sabotage, and lowered productivity (Gyllenhammar, 1977).

To combat such problems, Scandinavian car manufacturers (Saab and Volvo), introduced the concept of autonomous work groups for meeting workers' social needs while introducing technological innovation into work. These work groups controlled their own task assignments and the division of labour within the group.

Volvo and Saab also introduced self-regulating groups, in which employees who perform interdependent tasks work in a common unit (Cummings, 1978). Such work design requires that the workers have the ability to regulate and control their tasks to influence their transaction with the environment, and to differentiate themselves from other groups sufficiently to form a whole. Self-regulating groups perform many roles traditionally assigned to management, such as making job assignments and determining work processes.

The introduction of autonomous or self-regulating work groups had a significant impact. In 1975, for example, a specially built Volvo plant operated at 100% efficiency, as compared to 80% in other plants which were not so redesigned (Huse, 1980). In the mining industry, productivity rose from 78% to 95% (Trist and Bamforth, 1951) and in the weaving industry, from 80% to 95% with a substantial drop in labour turnover in both cases.

Employee empowerment and teamworking

More recently, the ideas of job design and self-regulating work groups have crystallized around two related concepts—empowerment and teamworking. Both are attempts to redesign work to get the best out of committed, expert and innovative employees. The two concepts generally go together. Empowerment is the process of devolving decision-making responsibility and autonomy across and down the hierarchy (even in flat, lean firms there is still a hierarchy). This done, it is rare that individuals in the organization are targeted to make decisions. Most likely it is teams, often specially set up for the purpose.

In theory, empowerment should work. It means releasing the knowledge that is already there in the organization and placing decision responsibility at the point of greatest expertise and knowledge. Chief executives are likely to know less about their firm's customers, for example, than the sales and marketing teams. So why not give these teams the autonomy to make decisions? In effect, redesign their jobs. In many cases, teamworking and empowerment are coupled with quality initiatives in the organization (see Chapter 14). Randolph (1995) argues that empowerment is easier said than done. In a study of 10 organizations that redesigned jobs around empowerment and teams, he argued that there were three criteria which must be satisfied:

1 Open and honest sharing of information with all employees about organizational performance.
2 Creating more (and new) structures rather than less as the teams transfer to self-management.
3 Replacing the traditional hierarchy with teams.

Like many organizational issues, it is easier to have an empowerment policy than to actually implement it. Pascale *et al.*, (1998) imply that empowerment is one of the many fads of management, unlikely to have lasting impact. They indicate that over the last 26 years there have been at least 25 fads in management (mostly around job design and organizational culture and change) and most have ebbed after one or two years. They argue that individual competencies, especially agility to think and be creative, are more important than structural arrangements such as teamworking or empowerment. Certainly, there is much jargon around the ideas. For example, Butman (1993), in assessing the impact of teamworking on senior managers describes the necessary transition as being from 'old world commander to new world flying fox' (whatever that means) and he is by no means alone in creating jargon (see Wilson, 1992).

Yet, there is evidence to the contrary. Some organizations have organized around teamwork and created not only a better working environment, but also produce more effective performance, however measured. These include Boots plc, Nestlé, Radio Shack, Abbey Life Insurance, 3M and Ford Motor Company. In the public sector, many National Health Service Hospital Trusts also report benefits from empowerment and teamworking. What do these organizations do to differentiate them from the empowerment failures? The major factors seem to be:

1 The individuals to be empowered must be capable of self-motivation. Already cynical and demoralized individuals will not receive the news that they are about to be empowered with unbounded joy.
2 The newly formed groups must ensure they do not fall into the traps of conformity (see Chapter 10) or allow 'social loafing' to occur. This is where individuals exert less effort when their efforts are combined in groups than when efforts are individual (see Shepperd, 1993 and Erez and Somech, 1996).
3 Managers should not be tempted to fall into the 'empowerment trap' where an employee, having been empowered, is deemed to have done a job unsatisfactorily by his or her boss and the boss takes the job back.
4 Empowerment should not mean more work, more responsibility with less time to do it and no information on how to complete the task for the newly 'empowered'.
5 Punishment cultures should be avoided and mistakes tolerated.

Alternative work schedules

Another way that work settings may be modified is to rearrange work schedules. There are a variety of ways to do this. Four of the most common are:

1 the compressed working week
2 flexible working hours (time and place)
3 job sharing
4 career breaks

Each of these approaches shares a common concern for making the work day and its time requirements more compatible with individual needs and non-work activities. The compressed working week squeezes the 'standard' week's hours into four days instead of five (for example). Given the number of individuals who commute long distances to the office, this has also become a default option where the individual will stay away from home for four days and nights (living close to the job in a flat, for example) and returning home on the fifth day. Table 7.3 lists some of the advantages of a compressed working week.

Flexible working hours can include 'flexitime' and 'flexiplace'. Flexitime means that workers are free to work any hours they wish, so long as certain core hours are covered. Flexiplace means that workers can be connected electronically to their workplace via a PC and modem, and have little or no need to physically go into the office. They are known colloquially as teleworkers. We return to this topic in Part VII.

	Organizations	Individuals
Benefits	Reduced employee turnover Improved productivity Attractiveness to recruits	Job satisfaction Greater opportunity for leisure
Disadvantages	'Who works Friday' syndrome Fulfilling customer requirements Trade union suspicion	Tiredness Safety at risk Family difficulties

Table 7.3
Benefits and
disadvantages of a
compressed working
week schedule

Source: adapted from Cohen and Gadon (1978).

Job sharing occurs when two (or more) people split a full-time job between them. Such jobs obviously appeal to those who wish to work part-time. Jobs can be shared over a single day or over longer time periods, such as half week/half week, or week on/week off.

Career breaks allows employees to take a break from a job for a specific time (usually two to five years). They then return to work at the same level or grade. Employment is guaranteed on return, but is supported by a training programme which brings knowledge and experience up to date. This scheme needs a good level of communication between the organization and the individual throughout the career break, especially to keep in touch with organizational changes. Advantages include:

- Savings on recruitment and selection by obviating the need to advertise for staff who, without the scheme, would have left the organization permanently.
- Reduction in skill shortages.
- Retention of skilled and experienced staff.
- Maintains a smoother flow of potential successors to senior positions.
- Provides the opportunity of getting good quality applicants in the first place. Firms which offer career break schemes will be more competitively placed to attract good staff.
- Can help reduce stress and absenteeism.
- Provides a role model for other females in the organization for the successful combination of career and family.

Many firms have well-established flexible working schemes in place (for example, Boots plc., Rank-Xerox and Carlsberg) and others use career breaks extensively (for example, BP Oil, Lloyds Bank and British Gas).

Work schedules and demographic trends

It is likely that most organizations will be forced to think about alternative job schedules. From 1988 to 1995, the number of young people in the British labour market fell by around one million, a drop of 20% (NEDO/Training Commission, 1988) and future speculation is for a further drop as we approach the year 2000. The overall size of the labour force will increase significantly, especially boosted by women, many of whom will be seeking re-entry into the labour market having had their families. Job schedules will now have to accommodate the needs of a mother with young children as well as some single fathers with children. European employment legislation is likely to increase the pressure for firms to accommodate job flexibility and firms which neglect to do this will face a severe competitive disadvantage as the labour force takes its skills elsewhere.

Summary

The design of jobs in any organization is not a simple and straightforward task. It involves examining both the organization itself (its structure and its system of operation) and the individuals within it (their motivation to work, the values they hold and their other psychological attributes). There is little research in the area which categorically can suggest 'recipes' for job design, although some authors have presented their results in perhaps too enthusiastic a way. Some aspects of redesign (such as the creation of autonomous working groups or the introduction of flexitime) are also simply not possible in some organizations.

On the positive side, research evidence to date provides a set of choices for the design and the redesign of jobs. Given the increasing rate of technological change in virtually every facet of organizational life coupled with large shifts in the demography of the available workforce, it would seem vitally important not to lose sight of the concept of choice in job design, so that jobs are not unthinkingly subsumed under the banners of rigid work hours, automation and computerized technologies.

References

Aldag, R. J. and A. P. Brief (1977) 'The intrinsic-extrinsic dichotomy: toward conceptual clarity', *Academy of Management Review*, **2**, 497–8.

Braverman, H. (1974) *Labour And Monopoly Capital: The Degradation of Work in the Twentieth Century*, Monthly Review Press, New York.

Brief, A. P. and R. J. Aldag (1975) 'Employee reactions to job characteristics: a constructive replication', *Journal of Applied Psychology*, **60**, 182–6.

Butman, J. (1993) 'Are you an old world commander or a new world flying fox?', *Human Relations Focus*, **70** (2), 6–7.

Cohen, A. R. and H. Gadon (1978) *Alternative Work Schedules: Integrating Individual and Organizational Needs*, Addison-Wesley, Reading, Mass.

Cummings, T. G. (1978) 'Self-regulating work groups: a socio-technical synthesis', *Academy of Management Review*, **3** (2), 625–34.

Emery, F. E. (1975) 'The assembly line—its logic and our future', *National Labour Institute Bulletin (U.S.)*, **1**, 1–19.

Erez, M. and A. Somech (1996) 'Is group productivity loss the rule or the exception? Effects of culture and group-based motivation', *Academy of Management Journal*, **39** (6), 1513–37.

Gyllenhammar, P. G. (1977) *People At Work*, Addison-Wesley, Reading, Mass.

Hackman, J. R., G. Oldham, R. Janson, and K. Purdy (1975) 'A new strategy for job enrichment', *California Management Review*, **15** (3), 96–7.

Herzberg, F. (1968) 'One more time: how do you motivate employees?', *Harvard Business Review*, **46**, Jan–Feb, 53–62.

Huse, E. F. (1980) *Organizational Development*, 2nd edn., West, St. Paul, Minnesota.

Latham, P. G. and G. A. Ukl (1975) 'A review of research on the application of goal-setting in organizations', *Academy of Management Journal*, **18** (2), 824–45.

Lawler, E. E. (1973) *Motivation in Work Organizations*, Wadsworth Monterey, Calif.

Locke E. A. and P. G. Latham (1990) *A Theory of Goal Setting and Task Performance*, Prentice-Hall, Englewood Cliffs, N.J.

Locke, E. A. (1968) 'Toward a theory of task motivation and incentives', *Organizational Behavior and Human Performance*, **3**, 157–184.

NEDO/Training Commission (1988) *Young People and the Labour Market: A Challenge for the 1990s*. NEDO/Training Commission, London.

Pascale, R., M. Millemann and L. Gioja (1998) 'Dinosaurs to butterflies: the quest for organizational agility', *Californian Management Review* (in press).

Randolph, W. A. (1995) 'Navigating the journey to empowerment', *Organizational Dynamics*, **23** (4), 19–32.

Rice, A. K. (1958) *Productivity and Social Organization: The Ahmedabad Experiment*, Tavistock, London.

Shepperd, J. A. (1993) 'Productivity loss in performance groups: a motivation analysis', *Psychological Bulletin*, **113** (1), 67–81.

Taylor, F. W. (1911) *The Principles of Scientific Management*, Harper, New York.

Terkel, S. (1972) *Working*, Wildwood House, London.

Trist, E. and K. W. Bamforth (1951) 'Some social and psychological consequences of the long wall method of coal getting', *Human Relations*, **4** (1), 3–38.

Umstot, D., C. H. Bell and T. R. Mitchell (1976) 'Effects of job enrichment and task goals on satisfaction and productivity: implications for job design', *Journal of Applied Psychology*, **61** (2), 367–79.

Walker, C. R. and R. H. Guest (1952) *The Man On The Assembly Line*, Harvard University Press, Harvard.

Wanous, J. P. (1974) 'Individual differences and reactions to job characteristics', *Journal of Applied Psychology*, Oct, 616–22.

Wilson, D. C. (1992) *A Strategy of Change: Concepts and Controversies in the Management of Change*, Routledge, London.

Attributes of the individual as moderators of stress

Valerie J. Sutherland and Cary L. Cooper

Understanding stress at work

Our understanding of the nature of stress at work increases as data from research into many different occupations form consistent patterns. There have been at least six sources of potential stressors identified with an extensive range of occupations. Although the relative importance of each category varies according to a particular job, stressor categories may be defined as: *intrinsic to the job* (e.g. physical conditions); associated with ones *role in the organization* (e.g. role conflict); *career development* (e.g. over or under-promotion); caused by *relationships at work* (e.g. a difficult boss); or associated with the *organizational structure and climate* (e.g. simply being in the organization; office politics, etc.). These factors cannot be understood unless the stressors identified with the *interface between and work and home* are also taken into account (e.g. life crises; death in the family, divorce, etc.).

Sources of stress of a particular occupation, together with certain personality characteristics, are predictive of stress manifestation. Symptoms of occupational ill health include absenteeism, high labour turnover, poor industrial relations, job dissatisfaction, escapist drinking, and increased cigarette smoking. Job 'burn-out', physical and psychological ill health, accident involvement, and poor performance are consequences of exposure to mismanaged stress.

This interpretation oversimplifies the problem. Although our understanding of potential sources of stress at work is comprehensive, it is less understood why some individuals thrive and cope in an acknowledged, high stress situation, while others have less resilience to stressful events.

Response to stress—an interactive process

An interactive view of stress is that situations are not inherently stressful. The consequences of occupational stressors are the product of particular situations derived from the individual's personality, behaviour pattern and life circumstances. The judgement of threat is dependent on many attributes of the individual. For example, demographics (age, sex, education), attitudes, past experience, values, needs and personality characteristics, influence and affect the perception of a source of stress at work. A situation will only be perceived as stressful when an imbalance exists between perceived demands and perceived abilities. Continuous monitoring of the situation and feedback alters our perceptions and response to a potential stressor. Thus, the effect of a potential source of stress varies between individuals (Cassel, 1976).

Personality, behaviour patterns, needs and values as mediators of the response to stress

The area of study to receive the most attention appears to be that of 'personality characteristics'. This will be discussed first, together with 'behaviour pattern' factors, and the issues of 'needs and values'. Second, the individual qualities of ability and experience will be reviewed as a conditioning variable in the response to stressors in the environment. Third, the issue of ethnicity will be briefly discussed, given the more heterogeneous working population of the 1980s and beyond. Last, the factors of 'age' and 'physical condition' will be considered.

Many personality variables are implicated in the mediation of stress. Table R4.1 indicates some of the attributes that are implicated in the way stress is perceived by the individual.

Table R4.1
Personality characteristics and behaviour patterns as mediators of response to stress

Neuroticism	Anxiety
Emotional instability	Rigid versus flexible
High conformity	Self-esteem
Submissiveness	Locus of control
Seriousness	The 'hardy' personality
Self-sufficiency	Type A coronary-prone behaviour
Introversion/extroversion	Sensation seeking

Using personality tests

Most research in this area has focused on personality differences between high- and low-stressed individuals. This examines the relationship between various psychometric measures, for example, the Minnesota Multiphasic Personality Inventory (MMPI) or Cattell's 16 Personality Factors Scale (16PF), with stress-related diseases such as coronary heart disease (CHD). Findings from several studies (Jenkins, 1971) indicate that patients with fatal CHD tend to show greater neuroticism in MMPI scores than those who incur and survive coronary disease. Studies using the 16PF report findings of emotional instability; high conformity and submissiveness; de-urgency/seriousness and high self-sufficiency. However, most of the studies were retrospective and, thus, the characteristics reported may be a reaction to CHD and not a precursor of it.

Introvert/extrovert

Other dimensions of personality which are likely to interact with stress include introversion/extroversion (Brebner and Cooper, 1979). The extrovert is viewed as 'geared to respond' and will attempt to respond when given an opportunity whereas the introvert may inhibit a response and seek more information. An important point to consider here is the 'self-selection' of individuals into a particular occupation. For example, offshore oil workers could be sensation-seeking extroverts who are attracted to this unique, relatively new situation of the self-contained, hostile environment of a drilling rig in the North Sea or the China Sea. Workers who are compatible will survive best, or longer than others, who will move away or function poorly (McMichael, 1978).

Rigidity and flexibility

The investigation by Kahn *et al.*, (1964) into role conflict and role ambiguity also includes personality measures from a full range of occupations (first-time supervisors and upwards). Response to role conflict was found to be mediated or 'conditioned' by the personality of the individual. For example, anxiety-prone people experienced the conflict as more intense; introverts suffered more tensions and reported more deterioration in interpersonal relations; 'flexibles' (as opposed to 'rigids') were more open to influence from other people and were more likely to become overloaded, but 'rigids' were more susceptible to rush jobs from above (Brief *et al.*, 1981; Chan, 1977; Ivancevich and Matteson, 1980).

Self-esteem

Self-esteem also appears to be an important individual trait in the workplace. Mueller (1965) suggests that individuals with self-reported low esteem were also more likely to perceive greater work overload. Kasl and Cobb (1970) believe that self-esteem acts as a buffer against adverse stress reaction, and CHD risk increases as self-esteem declines.

Locus of control

Another characteristic of the individual which may be an important moderator of stressors in the environment is 'locus of control' (Rotter, 1966). This refers to the extent to which individuals perceive that they have control over a given situation. People who are characterized as 'internals' believe that their decisions and actions will influence what happens to them. The belief that they play a role in determining the events that impinge upon them is viewed as a factor in the expectation of coping with a stressful situation; thus they suffer less threat and fewer adverse reactions than the externally orientated individuals who tend to believe in luck or fate, and that they do not have any control over their environment. However, 'internals' will experience more anxiety in a situation in which they perceive that they have no control.

The issue of *perceived* level of control in the work situation has been extensively studied in relationship to noise as a stressor in the environment. The work of Glass and Singer (1972) highlights the importance of the individual's perception of noise in a given situation. The extent to which the worker believes that he or she is in control of the noise, and the ability to predict or govern its onset, appears to be crucial in mediating disruption of both mood and performance (Graeven, 1975; Jones, 1983). The importance of categorization of individuals as 'internals' or 'externals' may therefore be relevant in that it is acknowledged that subjective experience of noise may be more crucial than the objective measurement of environmental noise.

However, Lefcourt (1976) warns that locus of control is not a trait nor a typology and people are not totally 'internals' or 'externals'.

The 'hardy' personality

Kobasa *et al.*, (1982) have included some elements of 'control' as part of the 'hardy' personality. This is a *conditioner* of the effects of stressful life events. Prospective data from a growing body of research indicates that the 'hardy type' is less likely to suffer illness as a consequence of exposure to stressful situations.

Hardiness incorporates the quality of 'commitment' versus alienation, 'control' versus powerlessness, and 'challenge' versus threat. This cluster of personality dispositions is, thus, viewed as a resistance source. *Commitment* is the tendency to involve oneself in whatever one is doing, whether it appears negative or positive, rather than disengaging. *Control* involves believing and acting as if one can influence the course of events, rather than being a passive victim of events. *Challenge* involves the expectations that it is normal for life to change, and that changes will stimulate personal growth.

Person–environment fit

This 'subjective-experience' factor is the focal point for assessing a job stress measure known as 'person–environment fit' (P–E fit) (Caplan, 1983). P–E fit is assessed by asking subjects to indicate 'desired' and 'actual' levels of work-related factors, such as role ambiguity, workload and responsibility, and looking at the differences between the scores. Misfit is defined as either exceeding a person's capability/capacity or if capability/capacity exceeds what the role requires. Resultant stress manifests in problems such as depression, job dissatisfaction and anxiety (Caplan, 1983).

Type A coronary-prone behaviour

The most frequent cause of death in Western society today is from coronary heart disease and related circulatory disorders. As such, the Type A versus Type B differentiation and its association with an increased risk of heart disease has received a great deal of attention. The 'Western Collaborative Group Study' (WCGS) (Rosenmann *et al.*, 1975) began in 1959 and has examined 35 000 men over the years to produce data of an epidemiological, pathological and biochemical nature, relating aggressive emotion with a high risk of getting CHD (Carruthers, 1980). The study confirms the importance of other factors such as family history of CHD, cigarette smoking, level of education, elevated systolic and diastolic blood pressures, and higher serum levels of cholesterol, beta lipoproteins and neutral fat.

The study classified individuals as 'A' or 'B' types on the basis of structured interviews; none had any prior record of heart disease. Results of follow-up investigations at regular intervals have confirmed the Type A behaviour pattern as a precursor of CHD, independent of the standard risk factor (Rosenmann *et al.*, 1975). Those judged to be Type A at the onset of the study had twice the rate of clinical coronary diseases, were five times as likely to have a second myocardial infarction and had twice the rate of fatal heart attacks experienced by the Type B subjects at follow-up (8.5 year point).

Modification of Type A behaviour patterns

Research continually shows that Type A behaviour may be reliably rated as a deeply ingrained, enduring trait. Beehr and Newman (1978) also discuss the issue of Type A/B as a personality characteristic or a behaviour; however, McMichael (1978) maintains that it is not a trait, but a style of behaviour and a habitual response to circumstance. The assumption is that behaviour can be changed. The extent to which an individual can change, to prevent heart disease, is not fully understood. It should be remembered that neat categorizations are dangerous in that they over-simplify. Often, only individuals exhibiting extremes of behaviour are at risk, whereas most individuals are somewhere in the middle along a continuum of the Type A/Type B behaviour pattern. Categorizations may therefore not be very useful.

The issue of 'self-selection' into jobs that entail a greater exposure to stimulation or stressors needs to be considered. Those with particular personality and behaviour characteristics may seek out a certain type of work environment (Caplan *et al.*, 1975). Type A individuals are more prone to perceive stress in an exaggerated fashion, and experience more stress at work and more CHD, with the latter due partially to the former (House, 1974).

Personality— Innate or learned? Needs and Values— Innate or learned?

Implicit in this discussion is that personality results in a predisposition to respond in a certain way. Therefore personality is an important moderator in responding to a stressor in the environment. The presence or absence of behaviour pattern can increase or decrease the likelihood that a particular event or condition will be perceived as stressful (Quick and Quick, 1984). This also applies to the needs and values of an individual which help to determine the perception of opportunity, constraint and demands of the environment, and the relative importance of the outcomes (Schuler, 1980).

Needs and values identified as mediators in the response to organizational stressors include:

- achievement (McClelland, 1965);
- self-control, certainty and predictability (Zaleznik *et al.*, 1977);
- feedback (Corson, 1971);
- fairness and justice (Adams, 1965);
- inter-personal recognition and acceptance;
- ethical conduct (Kahn *et al.*, 1964);
- responsibility, meaningfulness and purpose (Hackman and Oldham, 1975);
- personal space and ownership (Sundstrom, 1977);
- stimulation (Levi, 1967);
- intrinsic satisfaction (Harrison, 1975).

Knowing an individual's needs and values, whether innate or learned, is necessary in understanding whether the individual will experience stress from his or her perception of the working environment.

Abilities and experience

Research on 'ability' and 'experience' as moderators of the response to organizational stress is scarce, but are seen as important in that they influence perception of opportunity, demand and constraint and, consequently, the choice of strategy to deal with a stressor (Schuler, 1980).

Ability

The factor of 'ability' is incorporated in the research on role/work overload (Kahn *et al.*, 1964). Quantitative overload (French and Caplan, 1973) may be interpreted in terms of the ability of the employee, as well as the time available to do the job. A worker with more ability can accomplish more work in less time than an employee with less ability for the job. Sales (1970) has shown that quantitative overload is negatively related to self-esteem, and positively to tension and heart rate. Qualitative work overload as a source of stress (French and Caplan, 1973) is also related to the moderator variable, 'ability', in that some employees could not complete the work successfully, regardless of the time allowed, because they do not have the skill required to do the job and would thus experience qualitative work overload as stressful.

Experience

McGrath (1970) suggests that 'experience' should also be considered as a moderator of the response to stressors in the work environment. This is in terms of 'familiarity' with the situation. Past exposure, practice and training to deal with a situation can effect the level of and thus modify the reaction to that stressor. This may perhaps explain why the method of role-play is more successful in attitude/behaviour change in training situations (e.g. educational and safety campaigns) than lectures, posters or discussions alone.

Ethnicity

Membership of a particular racial or minority group can have an effect on an individual's response to a stressor in the environment, in addition to being a source of stress itself. Expectations and aspirations of the individual will affect the perception of opportunity, constraint and demand, and may be more acute for members of a minority group where different cultural and social factors may magnify the source of stress; for example, status incongruence in interpersonal relationships at work.

Age and physical condition

Age

Age is an important consideration as a moderator variable of stress. Each stage of life has its own particular vulnerability and coping mechanism (McLean, 1979). For example, career development, over and under-promotion and thwarted ambition, can only be fully understood in relation to the stage of life of the individual concerned. As Levinson (1978) states, 'there are seasons of a man's life which when documented will point to likely periods of stress and why they occur'. A study of middle-aged construction workers (Theorell, 1976) found the measure of 'discord' among employees to be much higher in the 41–56 age group than the 55–65 age group. This suggests that age may perform a moderator role in the experience of job stress, and is linked perhaps, to factors such as expectation and aspiration.

Physical condition

An individual's biological condition may determine how a stressor response is manifested. Physical condition is viewed as part of the process and a logical predictor of illness. Hennigan and Wortham (1975) have demonstrated that individuals in good physical condition, and who are not cigarette smokers, are able to maintain a low heart rate during the normal stress of the work day, whereas stress is more likely to increase the heart rate of others less physically fit.

Conclusion

Individual qualities or characteristics can help to explain the level of stress that an individual might experience. Yet much of the research to date is correlational and leaves questions of causation unanswered (Beehr and Newman, 1978).

Discussion that seeks to review individual attributes as mediators in the response to stress is misleading in that discrete categorization is not possible, and may not be appropriate. Overlap exists and many variables cannot be viewed in isolation. The problem of clarity of discussion is minimal in comparison to the complexity which confronts the stress researcher. Most studies are limited to the investigation of relatively few individual attributes of the individual that may mediate in the response to stress; it simply would not be possible to consider all potential moderating variables in one study.

Acceptance of this may explain the current strategy adopted in stress management programmes. It is not possible to change the environment to suit all personnel, nor is it possible to eliminate all sources of stress. At some stage, individuals in organizations will be required to work under pressure or strain. Response to pressure and coping strategies vary significantly. It is more productive to identify individual strengths and weaknesses and where necessary teach the vulnerable members of the organization to cope more efficiently.

References

Adams, J. S. (1965) 'Inequity in social exchange', in L. Berkowitz (ed.), *Advances in Experimental Social Psychology*, **2**, Academic Press, New York.

Beehr, T. A. and J. E. Newman (1978) 'Job stress, employee health and organisational effectiveness: a facet analysis model and literature review', *Personnel Psychology*, **31**, 665–99.

Brebner, J. and C. Cooper (1979) 'Stimulus or response induced excitation: a comparison of behaviour of introverts and extroverts', *Journal of Research into Personality*, **12**, 306–11.

Brief, A. P., R. S. Schuler and M. Van Self (1981) *Managing Job Stress*, Little, Brown & Co., Boston.

Caplan, R. D. (1983) 'Person–environment fit: past, present and future', in C. L. Cooper (ed.), *Stress Research, Issues for the Eighties*, Wiley, Chichester and New York.

Caplan, R. D., S. Cobb, J. R. P. French, R. Van Harrison and S. R. Pinneau (1975) 'Job demands and worker health: main effects and occupational differences', NIOSH Research Report.

Carruthers, M. (1980) 'Hazardous occupations and the heart', in C. L. Cooper and R. Payne (eds), *Current Concerns in Occupational Stress*, Wiley, London.

Cassel, J. C. (1976) 'The contribution of the social environment to host resistance', *American Journal of Epidemiology*, **104**, 107–24.

Chan, K. B. (1977) 'Individual differences in reactions to stress and their personality and situational determinants', *Social Science and Medicine*, **11**, 89–103.

Corson, S. A. (1971) 'The lack of feedback in today's societies—a psychosocial stressor', in L. Levi (ed.), *Society, Stress and Disease*, 1, Oxford University Press, London.

French, J. R. P. and R. D. Caplan (1973) 'Organizational stress and individual strain', in Marrow (ed.), *The Failure of Success*, Amacon, New York, 30–66.

Glass, D. C. and J. E. Singer (1972) *Urban Stress: Experiments on Noise and Social Stressors*, Academic Press, New York.

Graeven, D. B. (1975) 'Necessity control and predictability of noise annoyance', *Journal of Social Psychology*, **95**, 85–90.

Hackman, J. R. and G. R. Oldham (1975) 'Development of the job diagnostic survey', *Journal of Applied Psychology*, **60**, 159–70.

Harrison, R. V. (1975) 'Job stress and worker health: person–environment misfit', paper presented to the American Public Health Association Convention, Chicago.

Hennigan, J. K. and A. W. Wortham (1975) 'Analysis of workday stress on industrial managers using heart rate as a criterion', *Ergonomics*, **18**, 675–81.

House, J. S. (1974) 'Occupational stress and coronary heart disease: a review and theoretical integration', *Journal of Health and Social Behaviour*, **5**, 12–27.

Ivancevich, J. M. and M. T. Matteson (1980) *Stress at Work*, Scott, Foresman, Glenview, Ill.

Jenkins, C. D. (1971) 'Psychological and social precursors of coronary disease', *New England Journal of Medicine*, **284** (5), 244–55.

Jones, D. M. (1983) 'Noise', in R. Hockey (ed.), *Stress and Fatigue in Human Performance*, Wiley, London.

Kahn, R. L., D. M. Wolfe, R. P. Quinn, J. D. Snoek and R. A. Rosenthal (1964) *Organizational Stress: Studies in Role Conflict & Ambiguity*, Wiley, London, 41.

Kasl, S. V. and S. Cobb (1970) 'Blood pressure changes in men undergoing job loss: a preliminary report', *Psychomatic Medicine*, **32**, 19–38.

Kobasa, S. C., S. R. Maddi and S. Kahn (1982) 'Hardiness and health: a prospective study', *Journal of Personality and Social Psychology*, **42**, 168–77.

Lefcourt, H. M. (1976) *Locus of Control*, Wiley, London.

Levi, L. (1967) *Stress: Sources, Management and Prevention; Medical and Psychological Aspects of the Stress of Everyday Life*, Liveright, New York.

Levinson, D. J. (1978) *The Seasons of a Man's Life*, Knopf, New York.

McClelland, D. C. N. (1965) 'Achievement and entrepreneurship: a longitudinal study', *Journal of Personality and Social Psychology*, **1**, 389–92.

McGrath, J. E. (1970) 'A conceptual formulation for research on stress', in J. E. McGrath (ed.), *Social and Psychological Factors on Stress*, Holt, Rinehart & Winston, New York, 10–21.

McLean, A. A. (1979) *Work Stress*, Addison-Wesley, Reading, Mass.

McMichael, A. J. (1978) 'Personality, behavioural and situational modifiers of work stressors', in C. L. Cooper and R. Payne (eds), *Stress at Work*, Wiley, London.

Mueller, E. F. (1965) 'Psychological and physiological correlates of work overload among university professors', unpublished doctoral dissertation. University of Michigan, Ann Arbor.

Quick, J. C. and J. D. Quick (1984) *Organizational Stress & Preventive Management*, McGraw Hill, New York.

Rosenmann, R. H., R. H. Brand, D. Jenkins, M. Friedman, R. Strauss and M. Wurm (1975) 'Coronary heart disease in the Western Collaborative Group Study. Final follow up experience of 8.5 years', *Occupational Health*, **32** (11), 524–27.

Rotter, J. B. (1966) 'Generalized expectancies for internal versus external control of reinforcement', *Psychological Monographs*, **80** (1), whole no. 609.

Sales, S. M. (1970) 'Some effects of role overload and role underload', *Organizational Behaviour and Human Performance*, **5**, 592–608.

Schuler, R. S. (1980) 'Definition and conceptualization of stress in organizations', *Organizational Behaviour and Human Performance*, **25**, 184–215.

Sundstrom, E. (1977) 'Interpersonal Behaviour and the physical environment', in L. Wrightsman (ed.), *Social Psychology*, Brooks Cole.

Theorell, T. (1976) 'Selected illness and somatic factors in relation to two psychosocial stress indices—a prospective study on middle aged construction building workers', *Journal of Psychosomatic Research*, **20**, 7–20.

Zaleznik, A., M. F. R. Kets de Vries and J. Howard (1977) Stress reactions in organizations: syndromes, causes and consequences, *Behavioural Science*, **22**, 151–61.

Personality and bureaucracy

Christopher W. Allinson

Psychologists have never really agreed on what determines human personality. Some believe it is largely inherited, others that it is a product of environmental influence. Most accept that while mental characteristics are passed on genetically, important developments occur later as individuals learn to respond to cultural and social factors. This learning, or 'socialization', results from role changes throughout life. Although many take place relatively early on, significant shifts in personality may be observed well into adulthood.

Particularly important after adolescence is the influence of the work organization. Organizational socialization has been defined as 'the process by which an individual acquires the social knowledge and skills necessary to assume an organizational role' (Van Maanen and Schein, 1979). It occurs at all stages in the work career, but the first year is crucial (Berlew and Hall, 1966). Former expectations may need to be revised as the newcomer adapts to prevailing conditions. Through its culture, task assignments and supervisory practices, the organization shapes individual attitudes and behaviour (Jones, 1983). After this 'breaking in', changes associated with career progress and technological advancement lead to further socialization, each prompting the development of personality characteristics (Kolb and Plovnick, 1977).

Evidence of organizational socialization is strong. One of the best known is Kohn and Schooler's (1983) survey of over 3000 American men. Their study revealed a marked relationship between 'occupational self-direction' and several psychological dimensions such as social orientation, self-concept and work values. Subsequent examination suggested 'that job affects man more than man affects job'.

Bureaucratic personality

A major concern in the study of the effects of different kinds of organization on personality has been the impact of bureaucracy. The idea that this type of work environment is responsible for a characteristic pattern of attitudes and behaviour has a long tradition. The most convincing theoretical interpretation remains that of Robert Merton, an American sociologist writing almost half a century ago. Merton (1940), though acknowledging the positive attainments of bureaucracy, regarded the emergence of what has become known as the 'bureaucratic personality' as a serious threat to efficiency. It develops essentially as a result of over-socialization. The attitudes and values necessary for the employee to make an effective contribution are adopted with such intensity that the needs of the organization become subordinated to the mechanics of the bureaucracy itself:

> . . . that state of affairs in which one's abilities function as inadequacies or blind spots. Actions based upon training and skills which have been successfully applied in the past may result in inappropriate responses under changed conditions (Merton, 1940).

This is much the same as Dewey's concept of 'occupational psychosis':

> As the result of the day-to-day routines, people develop special preferences, antipathies,
> discriminations and emphases . . . These psychoses develop through demands put upon
> the individual by the particular organization of his occupational role (Merton, 1940).

Attention is diverted from the objectives of the organization to the details of its control system; rules become ends in themselves rather than means to an end. Strict compliance with regulations becomes a ritual, regardless of its appropriateness for particular circumstances. Rigid adherence to formal procedures, and a fastidious insistence on 'going by the book', may cause the bureaucrat to lose sight of the real task in hand. Behaviour becomes so rule-bound that it is often impossible to meet the needs of clients. Acar and Aupperle (1984) cite a case in point:

> Newspapers throughout the United States reported that, on 7 March 1984, Lilian Boff
> died of a heart attack while a Dallas fire department dispatcher wasted precious minutes
> delaying the prompt dispatch of an ambulance to the Boff residence as requested by
> Larry Boff, Lilian's stepson. This dispatcher had been a nurse for 17 years. The delay
> was caused by her insistence to speak to Mrs. Boff before sending an ambulance. She
> paid no attention to Larry Boff's pleas that his stepmother could not possibly be
> expected to carry on a coherent or even audible conversation with the ambulance
> dispatcher while she was gasping for air! Such pleas went unheeded in spite of the
> dispatcher's medical knowledge, and the woman died while her stepson was
> undergoing this Orwellian or Kafkaesque experience.

Little wonder that bureaucracy is saddled with pejorative connotations of red tape and small-minded officialdom. But what is at the root of this syndrome? Merton claimed that it derives from various structural sources:

Career structure   The working life of the bureaucrat is defined in terms of a career plan. Reluctance to lose associated benefits, such as regular salary increases, pension schemes and fixed promotion opportunities, can lead to overconformity, conservatism and timidity.

Esprit de corps   There is a feeling of common destiny among members of the bureaucracy; interests are shared, and since promotion is based on seniority, competition is almost nonexistent. This results in a defensive informal system surfacing whenever the entrenched interests of the group are threatened, possibly at the expense of assisting higher officials or the clients of the organization.

Sanctification   Employees' emotional involvement may lead to bureaucratic norms which were originally intended to encourage administrative efficiency becoming rigidified and sacred. They emerge as values in their own right, divorced from the technical purposes for which they were designed.

Impersonality   Bureaucracy emphasizes the depersonalization of relationships and categorization of cases with which it deals. This norm of impersonality, and the consequent refusal to provide clients with personalized, individual consideration, gives rise to charges of arrogance and high-handedness.

Authority   Sometimes officials allow the authority associated with their position to influence behaviour towards clients, leading to the impression of a domineering attitude. Recourse by the client to other staff is often unsuccessful owing to the prevailing *esprit de corps*. Although customers in the private sector can always turn to another organization, there is no such alternative for the client of a monopolistic public sector institution.

March and Simon (1958) have provided a diagrammatic summary of Merton's model (see Figure R5.1).

Figure R5.1
The Merton model

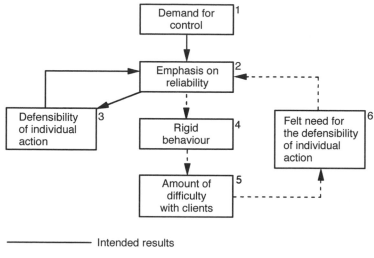

Intended results

– – – – – – Unintended results

Copyright © 1958 by John Wiley and Sousine
Source: adapted from March and Simon (1958).

The process begins with a *demand for control* (1) from those at the top. This is met by an *emphasis on reliability* (2) of behaviour. Techniques for achieving this include the establishment of standard operating procedures and a monitoring of their implementation. This leads, on the one hand, to the intended consequence of reliable *individual action* which is *defensible* (3). On the other hand, however, for the reasons described above, there is the unintended effect of *rigid behaviour* (4) unsuited to dynamic conditions. Officials fail to respond to the peculiarities of individual cases and the *amount of difficulty with clients* (5) grows. As performance suffers, management responds with an even greater stress on control and reliability. This tends to increase the *felt need for defensibility of individual action* (6). Thus there is a renewed *emphasis on reliability* (2), and the 'vicious circle' is complete.

Thee role of anxiety

Presthus (1979) has argued that 'anxiety is probably the most critical variable in organizational behavior'. The sheer size and impersonality of the modern corporation is largely to blame:

> Fear is always prevalent . . . even if you're the topman, even if you're hard, even if you do your job—there's always insecurity. You're always fearful of the big mistake (Terkel, 1972).

Several sources of anxiety can be identified. Although they overlap, it is convenient to consider the main ones separately.

Fear of superiors When things go wrong, blame can always be attached to those who have violated the regulations whether they are responsible or not.

Afraid of this possibility, bureaucrats frequently choose to apply rules to the letter, even when discretion is called for:

> Bureaucratic superiors cannot generally censure a subordinate for following official regulations exactly, regardless of how inefficient or ridiculous such action may be in a particular case . . . feelings of dependency on superiors and anxiety over their reactions engender ritualistic tendencies (Blau and Meyer, 1971).

Fear of specialists Managers in bureaucracies find themselves increasingly reliant upon specialists for the achievement of goals. The specialists, who may be subordinates, have to be trusted to apply skills properly which are often little understood by others in the organization. Thompson (1961) points out that the anxieties which managers suffer as a result may lead to an exaggerated need to control and a consequent tendency towards ritualism. The problem is compounded by the fact that insecure superiors invariably generate pressures on those who are accountable to them, hence the creation of more anxiety among subordinates with the attendant behavioural consequences.

Fear of inadequacy Bureaucrats may be acutely aware of their failings in performing certain tasks. For many, the resultant anxiety can be calmed by a ritual performance of more straightforward activities. This explains the often irrational resistance of officials to improvements in procedure; they prefer to cling to the old routines with their comfortable familiarity (Blau and Meyer, 1971).

Fear of uncertainty The main anxiety of many bureaucrats stems from their uncertainty about how to behave. They are afraid of being caught in error and losing their jobs or at least being shunted off into isolated and unpleasant positions. Presthus (1979) described people afflicted in this way as 'indifferents'. Commitment to the organization is low and their most significant rewards are obtained away from work. Their main defence is 'going along' with the system: following the rules and documenting that they have done so, avoiding risks, offloading responsibilities and, on occasion, doing nothing (Benveniste, 1977).

Fear of failure Another kind of anxiety is associated with the pursuit of career success. Presthus (1979) has identified what he calls the 'upward mobiles' whose big fear is failure. Their anxiety, according to Thompson (1961), is like Calvinism in that it creates doubt as to who is 'chosen'. As with Calvinism, this doubt can be reduced by excessive activity, a businesslike demeanour and conformity. Their middle-class upbringing has taught them that conformity is a means to status and power, the ends which they value most.

Kanter (1977), in her study of an American industrial supply corporation, confirms the 'rules mindedness' of those who seek power. The rule book becomes a 'power tool' since it is the one thing over which superiors can be guaranteed to give their backing. This applies especially to officials who, though lacking significant power, hold managerial responsibility. To secure their position or impress superiors, they sacrifice subordinates' freedom for a desire to play safe and 'get it right'. Thus ritualistic conformity from subordinates is all important. Proper form rather than a good outcome is the main concern.

In search of the ritualists

In what kind of organization is the bureaucratic personality most prevalent? To begin to answer this question it is necessary to understand what bureaucracy really means. Its modern technical definition derives mainly from Weber's (1947) classic description. For him, bureaucracy in its ideal form is characterized by a hierarchical authority structure, specialist functions, strict separation of work from non-work activities, and control by written rules. Recruitment is on the basis of technical qualifications, and the formal requirements of the job are clearly distinguished from the qualities of the person who does it.

It seems logical to suggest that an organization is bureaucratized to the extent that it resembles Weber's archetype. Attempts at assessing bureaucratization have invariably revealed two fundamental dimensions of organization structure: the degree to which rules are formalized, procedures standardized and jobs specialized and the extent to which authority is centralized (Pugh and Hickson, 1976). A number of investigators (e.g. Child, 1972) have shown that these have a negative relationship with each other. This is not to say that there is a strict tendency for activities always to become more structured as authority is less concentrated, or vice versa. But it does indicate that bureaucracy in its purest form, as described by Weber, is likely to be structured and decentralized; once behaviour has been programmed through rules, standard procedures and job descriptions, decision-making can be delegated to lower levels with confidence.

What is surprising is the fact that research studies have consistently shown that this model is exemplified not by public-sector administrative organizations as popularly imagined, but by large industrial corporations in the private sector (Pugh and Hickson, 1976). So much for the idea that civil-service and local-government departments are the very epitome of bureaucracy in Weber's terms. The evidence suggests that, if anything, they represent its antithesis, relying on direct management of subordinates rather than structuring to achieve control.

The implication is that the bureaucratic personality seems more likely to be encountered in the administrative sections of big business than anywhere else. This is borne out by the author's own findings (Allinson, 1984, 1986). Over 300 employees at all job levels of six differently structured organizations were questioned about their 'bureaucratic orientation' (an index of bureaucratic personality) and job satisfaction. Questions relating to bureaucratic orientation concerned willingness to comply with commands, preference for impersonal work relationships, acceptance of rules and regulations and need for security provided by conformity. Questions relating to job satisfaction asked employees how well they liked their job, how much of the time they felt satisfied with it, whether or not they would consider changing it for another and how they thought their satisfaction compared with that of others. The results were consistent and interesting.

First, employees in large industrial bureaucracies (structured and decentralized) had a higher bureaucratic orientation than those in the other organizations. Second, the relationship of bureaucratic orientation with age and length of service was stronger in the industrial companies than elsewhere, suggesting the particular socializing effect of that kind of work environment. Third, employees in local-government departments (unstructured and centralized) had a lower bureaucratic orientation than those in the other organizations. And finally, the rate of increase in job satisfaction with bureaucratic orientation was higher in the industrial bureaucracies, and lower in local government, than anywhere else.

Looking ahead   Despite predictions of its demise, bureaucracy continues to flourish. More flexible structures have had to be adopted under volatile conditions, but organizing along the lines of Weber's model still appears to bring the best results for the large-scale operation in a relatively stable environment. The fact remains that:

> Bureaucracy is a form of organization superior to all others we know or can hope to afford in the near and middle future; the chances of doing away with it or changing it are probably nonexistent in the West in this century (Perrow, 1972).

So the bureaucratic personality seems unlikely to disappear completely. As long as organizations seek to regulate behaviour through formal rules and standard procedures, the excesses described by Merton will probably persist to some degree.

It is important, however, that the problem is not exaggerated. By no means are all bureaucrats ritualists. Many are notable for their innovation and creativity (Blau and Meyer, 1971; Williams, Sjoberg and Sjoberg, 1980) while others, especially those of a neurotic disposition, are more likely to resist formal rules or rebel against them (Thompson, 1961; Presthus, 1979). Furthermore, there may be ways in which the effects of the bureaucratic personality can be reduced or even eliminated.

One possibility is that modern methods of alleviating occupational stress and anxiety will strike at its very roots. Another is that organizations may, through appropriate training, re-socialize employees so that they are able to understand better the purpose of regulations, properly use their discretion and develop a willingness to treat each individual case on its merits. In conclusion, therefore, it seems reasonable to suggest that while the bureaucratic personality may represent an unfortunate side-effect of bureaucracy, it does not in itself justify the denigration or wholesale rejection of that mode of organization.

References   Acar, W. and K. E. Aupperle (1984) 'Bureaucracy as organizational pathology', *Systems Research* **1**, 157–66.

Allinson, C. W. (1984) *Bureaucratic Personality and Organization Structure*, Gower, Aldershot.

Allinson, C. W. (1986) 'The industrial bureaucrat', *Journal of General Management* **11**, 47–55.

Benveniste, G. (1977) *Bureaucracy*, Boyd and Fraser, San Francisco.

Berlew, D. E. and D. T. Hall (1966) 'The socialization of managers: effects of expectations on performance', *Administrative Science Quarterly*, **11**, 207–23.

Blau, P. M. and M. W. Meyer (1971) *Bureaucracy in Modern Society*, 2nd edn., Random House, New York.

Child, J. (1972) 'Organization structure and strategies of control: a replication of the Aston study', *Administrative Science Quarterly*, **17**, 163–77.

Jones, G. R. (1983) 'Psychological orientation and the process of organizational socialization: an interactionist perspective', *Academy of Management Review*, **8**, 464–74.

Kanter, R. M. (1977) *Men and Women of the Corporation*, Basic Books, New York.

Kohn, M. L. and C. Schooler (1983) *Work and Personality: An Inquiry into the Impact of Social Stratification*, Ablex, Norwood, New Jersey.

Kolb, D. A. and M. S. Plovnick (1977) 'The experiential learning theory of career development', in J. Van Maanen (ed.), *Organizational Careers: Some New Perspectives*, Wiley, New York, 65–87.

March, J. G. and H. A. Simon (1958) *Organizations*, Wiley, New York.

Merton, R. K. (1940) 'Bureaucratic structure and personality', *Social Forces*, **18**, 560–8.

Perrow, C. (1972) *Complex Organizations: A Critical Essay*, Scott, Foresman, Glenview, Ill.

Presthus, R. (1979) *The Organizational Society*, rev. edn., Macmillan, London.

Pugh, D. S. and D. J. Hickson (eds.), (1976) *Organizational Structure in its Context: The Aston Programme 1*, Saxon House, Westmead.

Terkel, S. (1974) *Working*, Wildwood, London.

Thompson, V. A. (1961) *Modern Organization*, Knopf, New York.

Van Maanen, J. and E. H. Schein (1979) 'Toward a theory of organizational socialization', in B. M. Staw (ed.), *Research in Organizational Behavior*, **1**, JAI Press, Greenwich, Conn., 209–64.

Weber, M. (1947) *The Theory of Social and Economic Organization*, A. M. Henderson and T. Parsons (eds.), Free Press, Glenview, Ill.

Williams, N. M., G. Sjoberg and A. F. Sjoberg (1980) 'The bureaucratic personality: an alternative view', *Journal of Applied Behavioral Science*, **16**, 389–405.

How people learn in organizations

Silvia Gherardi, Davide Nicolini and Francesca Odella

Learning as a social process

It is quite common, both among the general public and academics, to think of learning as a form of acquisition of knowledge and to relate it to the notion of instruction and training.

From this perspective, learning amounts essentially to the acquisition of the data, the facts, and the practical wisdom accumulated by all the generations that have preceded us. This knowledge is 'out there', stored as some form of memory (usually books), and the main effort of the learner is to acquire it and to store it in the proper compartment of his or her mind.

To a certain extent, when learning is thought of in this way it is equated to eating: knowledge is food for the mind, and the learner seeks to find the right or necessary sort of food and ingest it (consume it).

Learning therefore mostly takes place during our early development, as we move through schooling, instruction, and training. People usually receive their training at the end of their educational careers. Training is thus considered to be a specific and goal-oriented form of education which provides newcomers with the knowledge they require to perform their roles in some organization appropriately. Training also intervenes later, if for some reason (updating existing knowledge, retraining for a new job), new learning is necessary. Generally speaking, in this case training takes the form of a supplementary dose of instruction and schooling.

Although this conception of learning may seem quite reasonable, it is a highly reductive account of how people learn in organizations, in at least two ways: it implies that learning is an achievement, and it gives the idea that learning and acting are two very distinct and separate domains.

First, the traditional equation between learning, training and instruction suggests that the time for learning and the time for working are quite separate, and that the former precedes the latter. Learning is thus regarded as a preparation for something else, and something which ends when the expected goal is achieved.

Matters appear differently, however, if we take a broader perspective and treat learning as the historical production, transformation and change of people. Seen from this point of view, learning never ends, for our identities, both as individuals and as members of organizations, are constantly changing. In fact, not only youth but adulthood too is characterized by a succession of periods of stability and change both in personality and in socio-cultural identity. What sociologists call secondary socialization is a continuous process of learning new ways to interact with others and to act in the world. For many adults, indeed, the main context of their evolution, and one of the strongest forces shaping it, is the organization for which they work and in which they spend a large part of their lives.

Examination of a person's work experience shows that learning is a never-ending process. Three typical stages are customarily identified in organizational socialization:

1 anticipatory socialization relative to the task of becoming a new member of the occupational community;
2 the encounter with the organization, at which stage the newcomer begins to understand the context in which she or he has entered;
3 change and acquisition, at which stage the person has become an insider (Porter, Lawler and Hackman, 1975).

These three phases correspond to major restructurings in the professional and life trajectories of managers which require them to re-learn a great many things—not only in their workplaces but also in their lives as a whole. These phases, of course, recur repeatedly (the first ones, especially, may occur several times), but in a different form on each occasion. Although more experience is gained as the years pass, there is always a new horizon ahead. Conceived within this broader context, training and instruction seem much less momentous than in the traditional account, and they are very distinct from the lifelong process of learning.

The traditional view of learning is that it is separate from—and to some extent opposed to—everyday behaviour in the organization. According to the conventional wisdom, not only do we learn only in certain periods of our lives, but our learning is restricted to specific occasions, such as when we take a course, or read a book, or watch an instructional video. However, this is an inaccurate description of what actually happens in practice. Studying and instruction are indeeed important, but learning is deeply rooted in our everyday activities as well. Most of the knowledge that distinguishes an expert from a novice is learned on a day-to-day basis by acting and reflecting, that is, by thinking about what one is doing and why, and talking about it with others. Formal training and instruction are in fact relatively modern institutions, while organizations, both formal and informal, are probably as old as mankind.

Finally, the view of learning as a totally individual activity, like eating, is misleading. Learning is very different from 'ingesting' items of organizational knowledge: learning is a social process, and it is better defined as the process whereby someone becomes a competent member of a group carrying out specific tasks. Among many other things, organizations are places in which people and groups constantly negotiate the meaning of actions, of situations, and even of material artefacts (Gherardi, 1995). Those who act in organizations participate in and contribute to a small world which is socially and culturally structured and constantly reconstituted by the activities of all those who belong to it. Any cognitive activity can only be pursued within, and through, this social and cultural network. Knowledge resides neither in the head nor in books. To know is in some sense to participate with the requisite competence in a complex web of relations among people and among their activities.

Communities of practice as the context and medium of learning in organizations

Learning within organizations is always a social process, the goal of which is to discover what to do, when to do it, how to do it according to routines and using specific artefacts, and then how to give reasonable account of why it was done. Learning, moreover, takes place among others and through others.

Hutchins (1993) offers a vivid example of how a complex cognitive task like navigating a ship through a crowded harbour is a joint endeavour, one that is not attributable to any particular individual, and he stresses the related social character of learning. He shows that the cognition necessary for this collective and co-operative task is unevenly distributed among the members of the team, and that it is deeply rooted in the situation. Take, for example, the task of calculating the position of the vessel. Although this requires mathematical computation, it is very different activity from 'solving a problem in a maths test', and it requires much more than the simple ability to crank numbers. Calculating the ship's position involves listening selectively to the information provided by the prospectors, rapidly deciding whether the data are both valid and useful, asking the appropriate questions in order to prevent and/or correct mistakes, and a number of other 'cognitive' activities involved in the peculiar practical context. Quartermasters learn their job through others and among others when they become part of a group of people acting together to achieve a specific goal. According to some authors, this type of learning is not related to the specific task of navigating a vessel but is a ubiquitous form of learning in organizations.

Lave and Wenger (1991) analyse apprenticeship as a social form of learning. They propose that learning is a context-based process and call this form of learning experience 'Legitimate Peripheral Participation'. In their interpretation learning at work is a special type of social activity associated with gradual participation in a community of practice. From the viewpoint of legitimate peripheral participation, learning essentially involves becoming an 'insider.' Learners do not receive or construct abstract, 'objective,' individual knowledge; rather, they learn to function in a community.

A community of practices is the grouping of people who belong to the same occupational group and who in their common experience of work create a culture, a language and rites, as well as practical routines, technical knowledge and coping strategies—all aspects which can be summed up in the word 'practices'. When entering an organization newcomers commit themselves to achieving mastery of all the community's practices, and their ability to learn will develop in parallel with an ability to perform tasks and to acquire the social structure of work within that specific community. Learners acquire the community's subjective viewpoint and learn to speak its language. Learners do not acquire explicit, formal 'expert knowledge', but the embodied ability to behave as community members. (Brown and Duguid, 1991)

Consider the example of a professional musician. The occupational career of a musician involves playing—usually only for few months or a year—in an orchestra, an ensemble, or a smaller group. Most of his or her work time is spent improving his or her musical rapport with new colleagues and a new conductor. Being a musician thus implies learning how to adapt personal characteristics and professional competence to different organizational situations. Instrumental skill and musical knowledge are not enough to become a real musician, since relational and situated competence are of primary importance in definition of the collective goal of playing together.

If newcomers are to be able to work with others, they will need to learn how to organize their own behaviour so that it produces competent performance. This, however, is not accomplished through individual training. It instead requires active participant observation of the interactions that take place among the members of their community. The quartermaster novices described by Hutchins learn through supervised interaction both how to use artefacts (either symbolic, such as maps and language, or material, such as tools) and how to relate to others in order to perform the collective task of navigating. Movement through the system with increasing expertise gives rise to a pattern of overlapping expertise, with knowledge of the entry level tasks 'more redundantly represented and the knowledge of expert level tasks least redundantly represented' (Hutchins, 1993). This is well illustrated by the route followed by novice quartermasters as they develop into fully accredited experts. They are first given responsibility for guiding a large vessel safely out of a crowded harbour. They then progress from minor and less critical sub-tasks, dependent on directions given by other members, to critical tasks requiring autonomy of decision and initiative. Understanding each activity simultaneously involves understanding how and when it depends on others, and how and when others in their turn depend on it to do their own jobs. Therefore systems like apprenticeship schemes are ways of reproducing part of the culture of a community of practice, and of giving newcomers a global vision of their own and of their community's practices and functions within an organization. Learning activity displays a distinctive pattern. Learners, as peripheral participants, can develop a view of what the whole enterprise is about, and what there is to be learned. Learning itself is an improvised practice: a learning 'curriculum' unfolds in opportunities for engagement in practice. It is not specified as a set of dictates for proper practices (Lave and Wenger, 1991).

Accordingly, it is important to note that to achieve full participation in a community its members must enjoy legitimacy to act; they must occupy a stable position in the social organization and exert control over organizational resources. The division of labour in the social context of work therefore plays a major role in establishing the forms of participation and of reproduction of knowledge permitted to newcomers. The 'transparency' of the socio-political organization of practices, in particular, is one of the conditions that legitimate participation by the newcomer as a future member of the community.

Active observation is crucial: learners who are highly motivated to become members of the community of practice will try to acquire professional expertise by watching their mentors or more expert colleagues. In fact, they will often try to 'steal (extort)' the secrets of practice by carefully observing the actions of competent others. Weick and Roberts (1993) discuss the importance of 'heedfulness', a term which they use to describe a set of qualities of acting conducive to high performance and learning. The capacity to induce and to sustain heedful action is a key feature of learning in organizations.

Focusing on the importance of heedful observation helps to clarify the notion of learning by imitation and by experimentation. When we say that somebody learns by imitation, we mean that he or she is making an effort to reproduce someone else's performance successfully by applying all his or her practical cognition, and by re-interpreting every clue about how to do things acquired from previous observations. Experimenting, especially in practical activity, involves putting learning to work, testing one's ability to achieve an outcome. The capacity to attain a result, or to ascertain whatever has gone wrong, is deeply rooted in all cognition.

Another fundamental aspect of the organizational expertise that is transferred implicitly, often in the form of informal hints, is the 'map' of who knows what in the organization. When people do something collectively, they establish interdependencies which also involve collective memory processes. In other words, people who work together create a 'transactive' memory system complete with differentiated responsibility for remembering experience, (Wegner, 1987). Knowledge is distributed among members of the group, and their behaviour may be spontaneously or tacitly activated. Learning the domains of expertise of particular members (that is, the location of the right source of information) becomes a crucial source of knowledge for competent behaviour among others. This form of social 'metacognition' becomes more and more important as the number of people involved in the collective undertaking increases.

The community shapes technical skills, the performance of tasks, the organization of activities, the proper use of routines, and the management of strategies; at the same time, the community lays down the guidelines for social competence in relationships with the community's other members. In this set of practices, formal or canonical aspects of the work activity have the same importance as informal or practical ones—as shown by studies of the training of police recruits (McNulty, 1994) and of service technicians (Orr, 1993). Police recruits must learn standardized work routines—for example, how to book prisoners and how to conduct inspections—as well as strategies for coping with the uncertainty of their work. Storytelling, examples of critical cases among colleagues, generate 'commonsense knowledge' which equips recruits with a general understanding of their future work. Narratives by police officers stress the primary importance of developing an active relationship with the work context, and of recognizing unusual and deviant features in people, situations and the physical environment. Experienced police officers talk about their skill at detecting unusual aspects in reported situations and about the strategies they use to solve problems. They provide examples which have the implicit purpose of showing novices how to think and behave as accredited police officers. Stories in this context serve to instruct novices about how the uncertainty in their work can be overcome by means of individual and organizational strategies.

Storytelling as a source of knowledge is also reported by Orr (1993) in his description of the community of practice of service technicians. Strategies to cope with unpredictable machines and difficult clients are coded and transmitted among service technicians in the form of 'war stories' and practical recipes of 'how to manage'. This latter example may suggest that learning is better understood if it is conceived as an active and intentional process. A community's organizational style and culture thus not only equips people with practical and formal knowledge of work; it also suggests what they should learn, how they should discriminate among different aspects of their jobs, what they should care about and what they should ignore, and finally how they construct their vision of the work. This view of learning is opposed to the conventional account that learning in adulthood is only a form of training, and that workplace innovation only involves the use of advanced high technology. On the contrary, learning and innovation are more closely linked than might appear, and the closeness of this relationship is due to the co-presence of practical and formal knowledge within communities and work groups.

Brown and Duguid (1991) have studied innovation processes in communities of practice in order to shed light on the relationships between working and learning on the job. They find that organizations rarely recognize the importance of this interlinking between work, learning and innovation. Organizations incrementally standardize work practices and thereby prevent communities from developing *ad hoc* strategies with which to deal with specific problems. Conversely, focusing on communities of practice may give rise to a new conception of learning in organizations and a different perspective on the concept of learning itself.

Although training, as a specific form of education, is widely used to prepare novices for their future work, it may not provide them with the kind of expertise and organizational insight that they really need. Lave and Wenger argue that training courses only give people an opportunity to gain competence in performing as a member of a group of trainees, and in forming relationships with their fellow trainees and teachers. Training thus does not teach work as a social situated activity, and the learning is consequently unrealistic. By contrast, full participation in the real work setting—either as an apprentice or a newcomer—gives people a perspective on learning which does not have strictly defined boundaries on using skills, information, and performance styles; a perspective which gives greatest priority to innovation and flexibility in the workplace

The ways in which people learn in organizations

The forms and mechanisms of learning have been described and conceptualized in numerous ways in the specialized literature. Although detailed discussion of the subject is beyond the scope of this brief survey, certain aspects of special relevance to understanding of how people learn in organizations nevertheless warrant mention.

Levels of learning

Among the several classifications of learning employed by organization studies, Bateson's discussion of levels of learning has aroused such great interest that it is worth describing in some detail. Bateson sought to impose order on the different ways in which behavioural scientists conceive learning, regardless of whether they were studying humans, animals or machines. For Bateson, a mistaken action can be called an 'error' only if it provides us with feedback of use for future action. If we are able to take appropriate action and correct an error, then we may say that we have 'learned'. Bateson orders different forms of learning into a hierarchy of types of error and remedies for them. In order to correct an error of a particular type, we must learn about it, that is, we must move one step up in the hierarchy, (Bateson, 1972).

Learning 0 is the simplest form of learning, that is, the ability to recognize things. For example, we say that 'I learned it was noon because my watch beeped' although there is little feedback or change for the future involved. Though very important, this form of learning takes place mostly unconsciously. It is in fact closely connected with the process of socialization within a practice that was described above, and it simply amounts to learning how to see things as they are.

Learning 1 involves a change in Learning 0 and occurs when there is a change of response to the same situation. It is what we usually call the learning of new behaviour. This is the kind of learning commonly described by experimental psychologists, and it corresponds to a change in the specificity of the response within a particular set of alternatives. In other words, learning at level 1 involves finding an alternative way to respond to the same 'problem'. Note that this conception of learning implies that actors segment the course of events into contexts that enable them to recognize two situations as alike or different. However, the contexts people use to give order to the world are usually implicit until a breakdown—that is, something highly unusual or deeply disturbing—calls them into question.

Learning 2 takes place at a higher logical level—where the shift is not among responses in the same set, but among sets of responses. In this case learning implies changing the set of alternatives used so far; that is, questioning the usual way in which experience is segmented, situations defined, and sense given to things. Learning 2 thus involves a change in the frame of reference and contextualization which creates an entirely new set of alternative actions. As Bateson notes, this is not an easy way to learn, because our ways of 'sense-making' are deeply entrenched and they tend to confirm.

Witchcraft provides a good example: the fact that a spell fails to have the expected effect is seldom a good reason for giving up belief in the power of magic—which would constitute an instance of Learning 2. On the contrary, its failure will probably be interpreted as stemming from some other more powerful and contrary magic force, which is an instance of Learning 1. This will confirm and validate the superstitious way of making sense of events, corroborating the original set of options.

Bateson also discusses Learning 3, which at the individual level corresponds to a profound change in the pattern that holds together the ways in which we give sense to and organize experience (Learning 2). These events are rare, and they resemble mystical experiences or conversions. Bateson's classification is attractive to those who study learning in organizations because it describes a number of features typical of organizational life.

For most of the time and in most of their activities, individuals and organizations rely on mental habits, on the taken-for-granted, on thinking-as-usual, on automatic functioning and on quasi-automatic decisions. This allows for considerable energy-saving and it is a strategy that usually works well in familiar situations. In unfamiliar, uncertain or ambiguous ones, however, it may prove disastrous. These other situations require a different level of awareness, active thought, reflexive activity, consciously controlled behaviour, a more systematic search for solutions and analysis of the situation. From quasi-automatic decisions, the person passes to decisions about the validity of the decision-making premises or to innovative decisions. Bateson's classification sheds considerable light on this transition, and explains why learning efforts in organizations are sometimes doomed to failure.

Argyris and Schön, for example, argue that in every organization there is a difference between what people say they do (exposed theory of action) and what they actually do (theory in use). When the members of an organization must respond to some change in the internal or external environment, they tend to adhere to the theory already in use. Accordingly, they will respond to a problem by choosing from habitual solutions. They will not question the validity of their customary way of making sense of what is wrong, and they will not challenge the extant set of norms, rules and ways of acting that generate those solutions. Argyris and Schön adopt Bateson's terminology to call this manner of reacting to change 'single loop learning'. However, responses of this kind are not always sufficient. If the problem is different in kind from those confronted in the past, a profound change in the very premises of action is required. Inquiry into the existing set of premises in order to resolve the breakdown and to establish a new frame of reference for action is called 'double loop learning' (Argyris and Schön, 1978). Failure to recognize that a Learning 2 process is necessary may be catastrophic, even for the most successful organizations. By applying the same solution over and over again, they engender a vicious circle whereby the more they act, the less they realize the true origin of the problem: their own behaviour.

Louis and Sutton (1991) describe the same phenomenon by drawing an analogy with a car gear-box. They propose the metaphor of the cognitive gear change to describe the sequential shift from automatic functioning, to perception and change of gear, to active functioning, to another change of gear and then a return to automatic. This change of gear is stimulated by novel situations, discrepancies, or explicit requests to think actively. For example, situations of this kind may arise for an individual following promotion or demotion, or when being assessed. For organizations, they may be a merger, a technological changeover, a critical incident, signs of decline or crisis. However, as well as these somewhat exceptional situations, it is important to stress the organizational activities which constitute—in their terms—an explicit request for active thought: personnel planning, monitoring of the environment, assessment of the organization's performance, planning in general.

Another line of inquiry has stressed the difference between reflection *in* action and reflection *on* action (Schön, 1983). Reflection *in* action is a way of changing our cognitive attitude toward what we are doing in order to look at it from a different angle. This often happens as action unfolds, and it does not require any form of codification, such as describing to ourselves what we are doing. Schön calls this process 'reflective conversation with the situation'. When practitioners reflect in action, he argues, they receive 'back talk' from the situation in which they are operating. This may induce them either to 'practise' their practice, that is, explore new ways of doing things, or to correct 'overlearning', that is, counteract the de-sensitization to differences inherent in each situation due to frequent repetition (a case in point being a doctor who examines too many patients). In both cases, Schön argues, good practitioners are able to learn through tacit conversation with their own practice.

Reflection *on* action can instead be described as the effort to 'move' outside ourselves or our situation in order to provide a codified description of what we are doing. This, for example, happens when good performers of some practical activity (sports or the arts, for example), seek to describe their ability so that others may learn from them. The difficulties involved in this operation are demonstrated by the fact that after several unsuccessful attempts, the 'teacher' often reverts to a practical example, where the potential learners are required to apply what we earlier called 'heedful watching'. Those who have ever attended a performing arts class, or to a basket-ball court, will understand this point immediately.

The tacit-explicit dimension

The notion of cognitive gear shift points out the difference between tacit and explicit knowledge—another widely-used distinction between forms of learning in organizations.

The expression 'tacit knowledge' was coined by Polanyi (1958) to refer to that stock of knowledge which we all possess although we are not aware of it. This is the practical knowledge that enables us to do things in our everyday life, in our professions, and which makes most of us competent actors in an amazing variety of situations. Polanyi was wont to say that 'We know more than we can tell', implying that the formalized, codified knowledge transmittable through structured discourse is just the tip of an iceberg of practical cognition which can be communicated in a structured way only with great difficulty.

For example, learning to ski involves the memorization of complex patterns of behaviour which ensure balance and purposeful action. Once someone has learnt to ski they forget the analytical knowledge that predominated while they were learning, and practical knowledge becomes part of their stock-in-trade. Many work activities resemble skiing in that the original context and motives for learning them are forgotten. They turn into routines which are then handed on as 'the right way' to do things, thereby becoming part of thinking-as-usual.

The line of inquiry that studies these questions was begun by Alfred Schutz (1962). Since Schutz, a number of scholars in several fields, including organizational studies, have devoted considerable effort to analysis of practical cognition. The study of learning by novice quartermasters and police recruits, of communities of practice, as well as many of the issues discussed in the present reading, are instances of such research. More recently, Nonaka has advanced the idea that the interaction between tacit and explicit knowledge is a key factor in fostering learning and producing new knowledge in organizations. Nonaka stresses that this process, which he calls 'knowledge conversion', is a social process which is not restricted to individuals (Nonaka, 1994). Using the two dimensions of tacit and explicit, he singles out the four modes of knowledge conversion illustrated in Figure R6.1.

Figure R6.1
Nonaka's four modes of knowledge conversion

Source: Nonaka (1994).

According to Nonaka (1994), the first mode of knowledge conversion whereby tacit knowledge is transferred among individuals is 'socialization'. It is this kind of learning that takes place in the community of practice, and its basic feature—as already mentioned—is that it takes place without resorting to structured discourse. The conversion of tacit into explicit knowledge has been called 'externalization'. As yet we know very little about the mechanisms which render practice overt and available for conscious inspection.

Metaphors are especially effective devices for converting implicit into explicit knowledge. Nonaka also stresses the usefulness of analogies and reference patterns for the translation of the content of metaphorical 'images' into the rules of language and logic. As already mentioned, story-telling is a further powerful device with which to externalize implicit cognition. Stories and other forms of narrative (such as jokes and myths) are potent media with which to represent, store, promote or contest, forms of organizational behaviour and the value attached to them. Stories describe different ways of doing things, and they help people to communicate their expertise. At the same time, narratives highlight different styles of conduct and alternative ways of being at work, thereby rendering available to the attention and conversation of the members the set of values accepted by the community and its differences from other competing groups within the organization.

The third mode of conversion is the combination of explicit knowledge. People combine and exchange what they know at meetings, by telephone calls, and other formal gatherings. For this purpose, what people know is usually written or recorded in some form, and then sorted, organized, classified and combined. Educational and training institutions promote this way of learning and creating new knowledge.

Finally, the fourth mode of conversion is internalization, that is, the conversion of explicit into tacit knowledge. The sources of internalization are familiar to us all: we learn in this way from books, lessons, training courses and from instruction in general; we also learn by internalizing rules, plans, instructions, and routines. As noted before, internalization has been sometimes mistakenly regarded as the only mechanism of learning; in fact, internalization requires some form of interpretation, and this is always socially mediated. So what we learn is always somehow related to when, where, and with whom we learned. In a sense, explicit and codified knowledge is *just a hint* to be understood in terms of our practical knowledge. Nonaka suggests that each form of conversion creates several occasions for learning and acquiring new knowledge. However, tacit and explicit knowledge are not, of course, separate entities, and their interplay is fundamental to the process of learning.

Learning in organizations can be portrayed as a spiral of knowledge acquisition whereby individual tacit knowledge is 'organizationally' amplified through the four modes of knowledge conversion, crystallized into routines, institutionalized by those in charge, and then circulated through the organization. This in turn has a backwash effect on the milieu of action of individuals and of communities of practice, starting the process all over again. This never-ending process is based on individual learning, but its characteristic pattern depends on the specific characteristics of the organization. It is consequently possible to talk both of learning in organizations and of organizational learning.

Organizational learning is a metaphor which combines two concepts—learning and organization—and enables exploration of the organization as if it were a subject which learns, which processes information, which reflects on experiences, which is endowed with a stock of knowledge, skills and expertise. It is a metaphor that *questions* the relationship between organization and knowledge, between organization and the social and cognitive processing of knowledge, between organizational action and organizational thought.

Knowledge is today a vital problem for all organizations because the production of goods and services increasingly involves knowledge; because new information technologies are 'knowledge intensive', and such knowledge has an extremely short life-span and is highly innovative; because flexibility is today the most valued of competences. In the post-industrial age, knowledge is a resource just as important as raw materials, economic and human resources, and so on, and may give an organization competitive advantage.

References   Argyris, C. and Schon D. A. (1978) *Organizational Learning*, Addison-Wesley, Cambridge.

Bateson, G. (1972) *Steps to an Ecology of Mind*, Ballantine Books, New York.

Brown, J. S. and P. Duguid (1991) 'Organizational Learning and Communities-of-Practice, toward a Unified View of Learning, Working and Innovation' *Organization Science*, **2** (1), 40–57.

Gherardi S. (1995) 'When Will He Say:' Today the Plates are Soft'? Management of Ambiguity and Situated Decision-Making' *Studies in Culture, Organization, and Societies*, **1** (1), 7–24.

Hutchins, E. (1993) 'Learning to Navigate', in S. Chaiklin and J. Lave (eds.), *Understanding Practice*, Cambridge University Press, New York.

Lave, J. and E. Wenger (1991) *Situated Learning: Legitimate Peripheral Participation*, Cambridge University Press, New York.

Louis, M. R. and R. Sutton (1991) 'Switching Cognitive Gears: From Habits of Mind to Active Thinking' *Human Relations* **44** (1), 55–76.

McNulty, E. W. (1994) 'Generating Commonsense Knowledge among Police Officers', *Symbolic Interaction*, **17** (3), 281–94.

Nonaka, I. (1994) 'Dynamic Theory of Organizational Knowledge Creation', *Organization Science*, **5** (1).

Orr J. (1993) 'Sharing Knowledge, Celebrating Identity: War Stories and Community Memory among Service Technicians', in D. S. Middleton and D. Edwards (eds.), *Collective Remembering: Memory in Society*, Sage, Beverly Hills.

Polanyi, M. (1958) *Personal Knowledge: Towards a Post-Critical Philosophy*, Routledge and Kegan, London.

Porter, L. W., E. E. Lawler and J. Hackman (1975) *Behavior in Organizations*, McGraw-Hill, New York.

Schon, D. A. (1983) *The Reflective Practitioner*, Basic Books, New York.

Schutz, A, (1962) *Collected Papers*, Nijhoff, The Hague.

Wegner, D. M. (1987) 'Transactive Memory: A Contemporary Analysis of the Group Mind' in B. Mullen and G. R. Goethals (eds.), *Theories of Group Behaviour*, Springer-Verlag, New York, 185–208.

Weick, K. E. and K. H. Roberts (1993) 'Collective Mind in Organizations: Heedful Interrelating on Flight Decks,' *Administrative Science Quarterly*, 358–78.

Lloyds TSB Group

Matt Hudson

This case study focuses upon one of the largest financial services retailers in the UK. Lloyds TSB Group was formed from the merger of Lloyds Bank Group and TSB Group. The case study focuses upon some of the people management implications from the merger and how the development of a competence framework, provided a valuable tool to assist the management of the business through these issues.

Background to Lloyds TSB Group

In November 1995 the shareholders of Lloyds Bank Group and TSB Group voted in favour of a proposed merger between the two organizations. The merger was approved by the High Court, and on 28 December 1995 Lloyds TSB Group was formed. The newly formed organization had a workforce of 82 000 staff, and by early 1997 had become the fifth biggest company in the UK, by market capitalization, larger than ICI, Sainsbury's and British Gas combined.

Lloyds TSB's governing objective

The overall objective of the new Group is to maximize shareholder value—by dividend increase and share price appreciation. In order to achieve this, the Bank's management team had to develop strategies to enable the business to benefit from the merger. Exploiting the synergy between the two businesses, and identifying and removing waste and duplication were key.

The merger process and competencies

As the process of merging departments began, it was recognized that in order to provide a fair and objective selection process, a set of common selection criteria, using a common competency vocabulary to describe HR requirements would be required. A 'merger menu' comprising a mixture of the Lloyds and TSB competencies was developed, along with processes to ensure that each candidate for a position in the new organization was assessed in a consistent and fair way.

Business issues

In common with most other financial service retailers, Lloyds TSB has responded to a series of internal and external factors, many of which were being pursued prior to the merger. These have led to significant change. These influences can be categorized as follows.

Customers

Customers are increasingly aware of financial products and services. Their expectations require banks and other players in the market to design, promote and deliver products and services in a more customer-focused way. In addition, customers demand higher levels of service and are less accepting of some of the traditional attitudes of banks and building societies.

Technology

Technology enables enormous enhancements in customer service, speed and quality. These advances also enable the effective use of available data about customer behaviour patterns and propensity to buy, to better meet their requirements. Additionally, these developments enable reductions in staffing levels and the centralization of many of the back office systems traditionally sited in branches.

Regulatory controls   Overall the market for financial services has seen deregulation. However, the activities of financial services sales staff have been the focus of ever increasing regulatory scrutiny. Quality of advice has become a key issue for all organizations in the market and the need for well structured and evaluated training has become critical for all. For some organizations the cost of this has become too burdensome—leading to withdrawal from the market.

Competition   The financial services market is overcrowded, leading to intense competition, particularly from new entrants who are able to establish themselves with lower network overheads and infrastructure. There is clear evidence of international companies moving into the UK market. Strategic mergers and the changing status of building societies to banks are common strategies. In order to survive, Financial service retailers need to gain competitive advantage through continuous innovation and by providing increasing competitive products and services. The contribution of staff and their relationships with their customer base are increasingly seen as sources of competitive advantage.

Shareholders   Like most publicly quoted organizations there is an increasing pressure from the city and shareholders to provide a greater return on investment. Although the market leaders can take a longer term view, there are pressures to take a short-termist view on long-term issues.

Staff   The financial services sector has been typified by downsizing over the last five years. This has been brought about largely due to improvements in business efficiency created through the increased use of technology, process reengineering, and reductions in the size of the branch networks.

Reflecting general trends throughout the UK, organizational structures are generally flatter, with spans of control increasing. An increased focus upon a broad role rather than a specific job typifies the approach adopted by most companies.

Staff need to develop a broader range of skills and competencies and to be prepared to undertake an increasingly broad range of responsibilities. The flexibility of the workforce is increasingly a key issue for large-scale employers, enabling the business to move staff into new areas of work, thereby reducing redundancy.

Unsurprisingly, these issues have impacted upon staff, providing a great challenge to the HR function. Staff attitude surveys and focus groups indicated the following issues:

- Uncertainty about the future
- Fear of losing job
- Fall out from the breaking of the psychological contract
- Fear of having the wrong skill set
- Lack of recognition from managers
- Lack of role clarity about: –
  - how to operate in new and changing roles

- the future and what it requires of them
- career prospects in a greatly changed business

Other strategic HR issues

In addition to the need to manage the reactions of staff to the merger and its implications, there was also a need to introduce new ways of working to support the major change programmes being planned by the business. These called for positive strategies to address the following:

- Requirement for enhanced performance from staff
- Need to harmonize and integrate the workforce, now made up from 'mixed' teams of TSB and Lloyds staff (especially in the functions)
- A vehicle to communicate the values of the business
- Definition and communication of a set of values to support the new culture for the merged business
- Creating a flexible workforce capable of rising to the challenges of the future
- Alignment of key HR policies, such as terms and conditions, recruitment and selection, performance management, training and development etc.

Competencies as an approach to helping the business

Background to competencies in Lloyds and TSB

Both Lloyds Bank and TSB Group had used competencies in the past. While the rationale and implementation had differed, both recognized that there was value to be gained from identifying and communicating those behaviours which could be linked to successful performance. Analysis of each company's approach to competencies led to the following conclusions:

1   There was a lack of understanding about what competencies were, and how they differed from skills, attitudes, experience and knowledge; and how they impacted upon overall performance on the job.
2   That the frameworks developed and used by each business reflected the old culture and approaches, and were generally developed using 'backward looking' techniques of competence profiling.
3   Each business had developed levels of behaviours which described different levels of each competence, these often led to confusion and, at times, manipulation (by linking the levels to grades).
4   An increasing recognition that the differentiating behaviours within the frameworks used were more related to the type of role performed than the grade or level within the organization at which it was performed.

Definition of competencies

Many staff within each business had failed to fully reap the benefits of competencies because they did not understand what 'a competence' was nor how it differed to skills, attitudes, traits, understanding and 'orientations'. This has been a general issue in which the HR community has succeeded in creating much confusion, and still cannot agree among itself a consistent and meaningful definition of competencies. In order to ensure clarity of communication and understanding, a decision was taken to redefine the meaning of the word 'competence'. A definition was therefore agreed:

> A competence is a group of 'effective behaviours' which have been clustered together in a way which is logical to the business.

Performance management discussions between line manager and job holder

Staff and line managers must engage in a meaningful discussion about the requirements of the job and the objectives which need to be achieved for successful performance. Competencies can assist in the following ways:

1   By discussing and agreeing not only the objectives, but which competencies and behaviours within each competence will be necessary

to achieve those objectives in the best way for the individual, and the business as a whole.

2   Line managers are able to structure their discussions and use the behaviours in the competencies as a vehicle for giving feedback ('I want to see you doing that more often').

3   When job holders are clear about the behaviours which need to be demonstrated in order to deliver successful performance, they are much more likely to demonstrate them in their work.

4   Misperceptions about the requirements of the role can be identified and action agreed about the way the role will be performed in the future.

Common language   Competencies provide a common language to describe performance. This enables business units around the business to gain a shared understanding of the capabilities of individual members of the workforce and for the workforce as a whole.

To communicate the values of the new business to bring about culture change   In a merger, where two cultures are being brought together, there is a need to rapidly understand what the expectations of the new business are. The merged bank developed a new sense of what is important, and a new perspective of the desired culture.

Creating a more flexible workforce   In order to meet the challenges of the future, the business needs to create a workforce which is more flexible and capable of reacting to changing requirements. An approach to gaining a better understanding of how that might affect Lloyds TSB is to divide the workforce into six role types:

- Customer service roles
- Sales roles
- People manager roles
- Business operations roles
- Specialist roles
- Strategic/leadership roles

All roles within the business can be assigned to one or possibly two of these role types see Figure CS1.1.

By gaining a greater understanding of the requirements of each of these role types for the future, and the differences and similarities between them, the business can develop strategies and processes to assist staff to develop within each of these roles and to be able to move between them more effectively.

Research was suggesting that behaviours for successful performance could be grouped in two ways. Those behaviours which all staff must demonstrate for the business to be effective and those which were driven by the additional needs of the role. This last point is important because until this point the business had generally worked upon the premise that 'levels' of competence were influenced primarily by complexity and seniority, rather than role type. By adopting a more 'inclusive' approach to categorization of behaviours, the framework would begin to break down some of the status/grade assumptions which had typified both organizations in the past. Having considered the ways in which the role types could be used to create a more flexible workforce, and break down some of the cultures of the past, it also became apparent that the role types approach could be used to review organizational design. Increasingly, trends show that organizational design can reflect groupings of similar competencies and skills, rather than similar disciplines and accountabilities.

Figure CS1.1
Role types and
organizational design

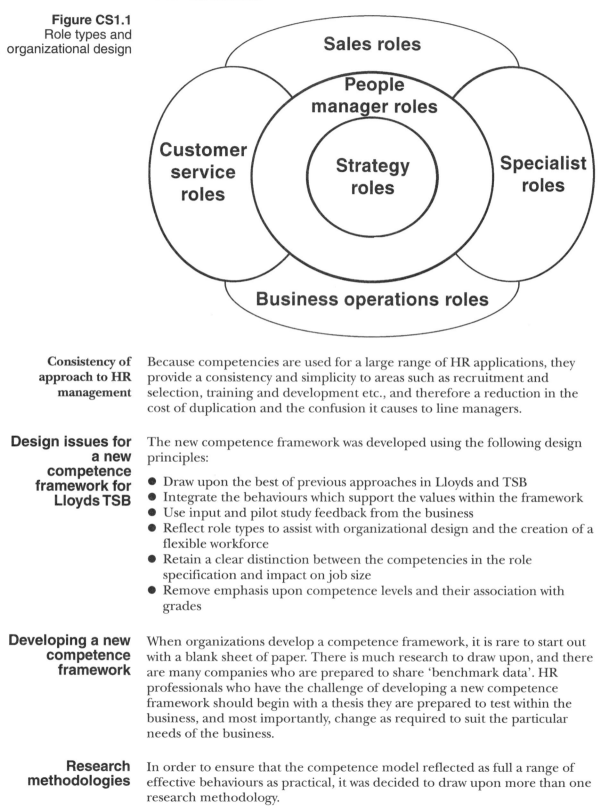

Consistency of approach to HR management

Because competencies are used for a large range of HR applications, they provide a consistency and simplicity to areas such as recruitment and selection, training and development etc., and therefore a reduction in the cost of duplication and the confusion it causes to line managers.

Design issues for a new competence framework for Lloyds TSB

The new competence framework was developed using the following design principles:

- Draw upon the best of previous approaches in Lloyds and TSB
- Integrate the behaviours which support the values within the framework
- Use input and pilot study feedback from the business
- Reflect role types to assist with organizational design and the creation of a flexible workforce
- Retain a clear distinction between the competencies in the role specification and impact on job size
- Remove emphasis upon competence levels and their association with grades

Developing a new competence framework

When organizations develop a competence framework, it is rare to start out with a blank sheet of paper. There is much research to draw upon, and there are many companies who are prepared to share 'benchmark data'. HR professionals who have the challenge of developing a new competence framework should begin with a thesis they are prepared to test within the business, and most importantly, change as required to suit the particular needs of the business.

Research methodologies

In order to ensure that the competence model reflected as full a range of effective behaviours as practical, it was decided to draw upon more than one research methodology.

Integration of existing frameworks

Both Lloyds Bank and TSB had, over the five years prior to the merger, developed their own competence frameworks. These frameworks had relied heavily on the Boyatzis (1982) approach to competencies but as a result of the merger failed to reflect the recent and anticipated changes in the business. Frameworks designed to develop high performance in the old businesses were not always necessary or desirable for the future. There were, however, some behaviours which would add value in the future, as they had done in the past.

Behavioural event interviewing (BEI)

These structured interviews and subsequent analysis of transcripts identified behaviours which could be clearly linked to superior performance. Job holders and line managers within the business were interviewed.

Repertory grid

Using groups and individuals from a range of business units, those factors and behaviours which were linked to effective performance and superior performance could be defined and isolated.

Critical incident interviewing

A more focused approach than BEI, these interviews provided invaluable data on specific areas of interest such as 'Bringing innovation to problem-solving and leading others'.

Benchmarking

This process had two perspectives:

1 looking at the competence models of other organizations to see how they phrased, grouped and assessed competencies;
2 looking at research data on competitor organizations to identify behaviours which Lloyds TSB needed to promote in order to 'stay one step ahead'.

National and internal training programmes

Analysis of the requirements for recognition in NVQs and other qualifications enabled a clear alignment between the language of NVQs and the new competence framework, with a view to offering vocational qualifications for the effective achievement of the requirements of the role, as set out in the role specification. This would remove the need for staff to 'translate' Lloyds TSB competencies into NVQ language, as well as making the qualifications more relevant to the job.

Interviews with training and development staff about organizational training needs (at a behavioural level) and the way that the most successful learners demonstrated their competence also provided a source of information.

Links to the business strategy

One of the critical success factors for any competence framework is whether it reflects and communicates the strategic direction of the business. Many traditional competence models and frameworks depend on historical data about successful performance and failure, thereby reducing the emphasis upon the future behaviours required of staff by the business. Discussions with senior executives and strategic planning consultants were used to identify aspects of the organization's strategic direction which could be reflected through behaviours in the framework.

Overview of the new competence framework

There are 16 competencies in total, and they are clustered into five key result areas (see Figure CS1.2):

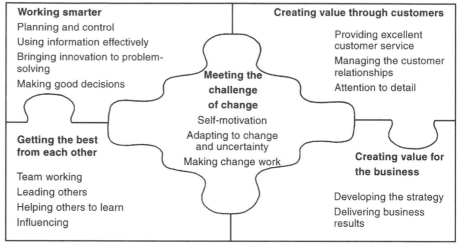

- Creating value through customers
- Creating value for the business
- Getting the best out of each other
- Working smarter
- Meeting the challenge of change

Each competence contains 'core behaviours' which apply to all roles within the business, regardless of an individual's position in the hierarchy. In addition to the core behaviours there are behaviours which relate to the type of role performed by the job holder. This is in recognition of the fact that different role types require the job holder to demonstrate different behaviours in order to be effective. For example, someone in a 'customer service' role type will need to demonstrate 'influencing skills' in a different way to a colleague in a 'sales' role type. See Figure CS1.3 for an example of a competence (team working) drawn from the framework.

The profiling process

For the implementation of competencies, there needs to be a vehicle for communication. In the case of Lloyds TSB, the most appropriate vehicle was the role specification which sets out the requirements of the job in terms of the purpose, accountabilities, performance measures, competence requirements, and technical skills. Identifying the right competencies for each role specification would require the following:

1   Structured job analysis to determine the type of role performed.
2   Selection of the key competencies for success (5–6 from the 16).
3   All core behaviours for each key competencies are drawn onto the competence profile.
4   Role type behaviours are analysed in the context of the job and those which are relevant to the job are included in the profile.
5   Where a job requires the holder to perform more than one role, then the selection of relevant behaviours from each of the relevant role types is allowed.

A note about job analysis

A quality approach to job analysis lies at the heart of almost all HR interventions. Without balanced data about what a role requires of the job holder and how that role is performed, both line managers and job holders are at a disadvantage in attempting to enhance performance. Generally, job

Figure CS1.3
What each
competence looks
like: Example extract
of competence
profile for customer
service officer role

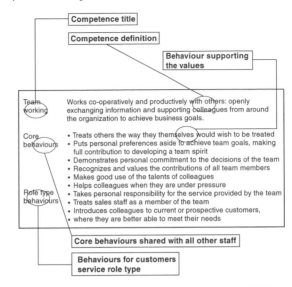

analysis is not seen as a particularly interesting aspect of HRM, and the
general skill levels in the HR community are relatively low. Being capable of
identifying and articulating the various components of a job is a skill which
places any member of an HR department at an advantage over less skilled
colleagues, and offers the potential to add real value to the business.

The key features of the new framework are:

● Core behaviours set out common standards and expectations which
everyone in the business must demonstrate. The behaviours within each of
the competencies reinforce the values of both the business and the brand.

● Using role types to enable job holders to understand the prime purpose
of their role. This emphasizes the business contribution of a role. By
understanding the type of role performed, job holders gain a clearer
understanding of the nature of their contribution to business success.
This moves the emphasis away from grade and towards value-added,
enabling the framework to apply to all roles.

● The framework applies to all jobs within the Lloyds TSB Group regardless of
grade or status. Many organizations have different models and frameworks
for different levels of staff and managers. The Lloyds TSB Framework is all
embracing and provides a continuity through all grade bands.

● The use of the competencies, primarily through the role specifications is
locally owned and driven, within guidelines to be established at the centre
to protect the integrity of framework.

**Relationship to
business issues**

Enhanced performance from staff throughout central services.   When job holders
know *what* is expected of them, and *how* they are expected to operate in a
role, they are more likely to be able to meet those requirements.
Accountabilities and objectives focus on *whats*, competencies focus on the
hows. By focusing upon those competencies which have a proven relationship
to performance, staff perform better and are more motivated.

Role clarity in an ever-changing work environment   The new framework enables
job holders and line managers to discuss and agree those behaviours which
are key to success in the role. By discussing the competencies in the profile,
the job holder prompts and receives feedback about their effectiveness. Line
managers can give and receive usable feedback about the behaviours which

they see demonstrated at work, and what they want to see done differently. This would be a two-way process, where both parties work together to identify the best way to demonstrate the competencies to enhance effectiveness.

A vehicle to communicate the values   The core behaviours in the framework are applicable to all job holders in central services, regardless of grade and role. The behaviours which support the business values, recently discussed at central services executive, are in the core behaviours. Line managers can therefore give feedback upon the demonstration of the values and additionally assess candidates in selection, development planning and performance management.

A process for creating a flexible workforce   By placing increasing emphasis upon the role types, the business is better placed to create a more flexible workforce through a deeper understanding of the differences and similarities between the role types.

Historically, the business had little data about the staff performing these role types, nor the inter-relationships between the six role types. Implementing the new framework, with the proposed measurement systems, enables the business to answer questions such as:

- Is the proportion of staff in service and sales roles increasing/decreasing? What strategies are required to drive this figure up?
- What are the capabilities of the workforce and where are their priority development needs?
- What new behaviours must business operations staff develop if required to move into Customer-facing service and sales roles?

Alignment of key HR policies   There is no proven link between the behaviours in historical frameworks and successful performance. Harmonization and integration of HR policies, processes and systems around a common language, accessible and understandable by all staff is the fulcrum of the HR strategy. It enables the business to maximize the cost benefits of a consistent and common approach to the following critical HR policies:

- Recruitment and selection—using the competencies as principal selection criteria.
- Training and development—focusing development expenditure on those areas which have the greatest impact on performance.
- Career management—enabling job holders and line managers to plan structured development around the requirements of roles for the future.
- Performance management—providing a key mechanism for feedback and performance improvement, both at an individual and process level.

Validation of the competence framework

There are several forms of validation, concurrent, predictive and so on. From the outset, it was considered as essential that the competence framework was validated to identify and articulate the links between the behaviours in the framework and performance. Other factors were to assist in gaining business commitment to implementation and to protect the business from the possibility of challenge.

Factors which might mean that a new competence framework is not validated include:

1   Face validity—the framework looks right on the face of it and therefore
    need not be validated. This is especially so where the competence
    framework is being introduced for the first time, and there is therefore
    greater urgency for implementation.
2   Cost—the cost associated with the validation exercise is high, although
    the resultant data provides a clear agenda for the HR function and assists
    in identifying implementation priorities.
3   Interference with the business—the process of validating competencies is
    intrusive; it must involve line managers and job holders and therefore
    take them away from normal business activities for a period of time.

Validation objectives   The draft framework was externally scrutinized in a validation study to identify:

- Whether the behaviours in the framework could be linked to effective
  performance;
- any behaviours which discriminated unfairly (gender or race-loaded
  language);
- any overlaps or duplication between the behaviours, competencies or key
  result areas.

The validation process   Using external consultants to advise and analyse results, the process was as
follows:

A series of 'benchmark roles' for each of the six role types were identified.
These roles typified each of the role type definitions for customer service,
sales, business operations, specialist, strategy roles and people managers.

A set of questionnaires were developed for each role type, using the
behaviours from the competence framework. The questionnaires asked job
holders for a self-assessment of which behaviours they demonstrated at work
and line managers for their assessment of the behaviours each job holder
demonstrated at work. The questionnaire also asked for a ranking of each
competence and an assessment of strengths and development needs.

Line managers were additionally asked to complete a further
questionnaire, assessing the performance of the job holder against a series
of criteria developed through a series of interviews. Thus the criteria for
successful performance for each role type was slightly different, but captured
essential data to differentiate performance in a way which had real meaning
to the business.

Questionnaires were sent to job holders and line managers who were
asked to complete them and return them to the advising consultants directly
to ensure confidentiality. Sufficient numbers of responses were received to
avoid the need for any statistical adjustment to the figures during analysis.
Data was fed into a computer which produced the following correlations:

1   Job holders' self-assessment of the behaviours they demonstrated and
    their line managers assessment of performance, and;
2   Line managers' assessment of the behaviours each job holder
    demonstrated and their assessment of the job holders' performance.

Results   Correlation tables were produced and confirmed that those staff who
demonstrated the behaviours in new framework are considered by line
managers to be the most successful against the agreed criteria for
performance. There were some areas where correlations were not significant
and these behaviours were reviewed and amended or deleted if they were
not considered key to future success.

There was some differences in response pattern between job holders and line managers; line managers using more of the assessment scales and job holders demonstrating a central tendency. The line managers' perspective was relied upon where there was a significant difference in perspective.

Overall correlations for all six role types ranged from .33 (Developing the Strategy) to .61 (Adapting to Change and Uncertainty). Only three of the 16 competencies had a correlation of less than .50. Correlations for individual role types averaged around the .6, with the specialist role type recording correlations between the competencies and performance of up to .92.

In addition to acceptable overall correlations with performance, it has been possible to use the data from the study, not only to identify those competencies which drive performance the most, but also to use the performance measures as a diagnostic for needs analysis. For example, if sales conversion rates were an issue for a particular population, by looking at those competencies and behaviours which correlate most strongly with conversion rates and develop these accordingly.

Other useful data produced by the study included:

- A comprehensive audit of the strengths and development needs of the business.
- The perspective of staff about the most and least important competencies to their roles.
- An appreciation of the extent to which job holders and line managers agreed about which behaviours and competencies were drivers of performance and where job holders saw little relationship between how they operated and their line managers' assessment of their performance. This gives a clear picture of the extent of 'role clarity' in the business, and enables HR to focus upon particular role types to help them to develop that understanding.

Getting buy-in

In any organization change is either impossible or made more precarious when it lacks commitment. In a large organization, the commitment of top managers is critical. It is they who set the agenda for the business and they who decide what the business objectives and priorities of each unit will be. If any implementation programme is to succeed, top managers need to be clear about:

1 the business benefits to their unit; in a language they understand;
2 the precise involvement of their staff and how much time it will take;
3 the overall resource that the programme will take up.

Another stakeholder group which is key to successful implementation is the HR community. When line managers cannot get consistent advice on an initiative, their faith in their advisers becomes suspect. The involvement of representatives from throughout the HR community ensured that they were kept informed of the development process and implementation plans, and had opportunities to contribute to the new framework and give local expertise in the development of implementation plans.

Other dependencies included

- Identifying local business priorities and issues, and demonstrating the business impact of the new competence framework in the context of those local needs.

- Clear and consistent policy upon the use of the competence framework to ensure that the integrity of the framework is protected through all its applications.
- Clear communications, explaining what was happening and why it was happening.
- Education and training for line managers, their staff and local HR who support them.

Summary

A competence model can provide the business with a powerful tool which can add value at both the strategic and operational levels. If it is properly developed and integrated with the future direction of the business as well as reflecting the current requirements, it can act as a key communication tool to changing behaviours and thereby enhancing performance.

By developing the Lloyds TSB Group competence framework from within the strategy and policy department of human resources, all the necessary links between high-level applications such as resourcing plans and organizational design could be integrated into the framework, while still enabling it to be used as an operational tool in such applications as recruitment and selection.

Questions

1 How might competencies add value to the business and address the issues outlined above?

2 A conscious decision was taken not to address the issue of competence-based pay. Do you feel that this was a missed opportunity? Given the situation in Lloyds TSB at the time, what factors would you have considered if you had to make that decision?

3 What are the risks and opportunities of conducting research with current role holders when developing a list of effective behaviours?

4 How would you plan and implement a programme in your organization?
- Who are the key stakeholders from whom you would need to gain early commitment?
- What would be their perspective?
- What business benefits can you identify, and how would you promote them?

Newton Ingredients

Richard Thorpe

Introduction

This case describes a highly successful company operating a continuous process plant. As competition has increased there has been a gradual move towards automation of many aspects of the work. The process is capital-intensive, with labour costs currently accounting for less than 5% of the total cost. However, it is recognized that the way in which labour is used will be crucial to maximizing the use of capital.

The company also recognize the important part that payment systems play in meeting its objectives—how, through design, they can not only ensure that employees produce the correct forms of effort, but also serve as important catalysts for change.

Newtons' Ingredients

Background of the company

Newton is a large, diversified, international company operating in the food industry. The group of companies of which Newton is a part has a turnover of £105m, £3m being contributed by the ingredients division. This contribution represents 2% of both turnover and cost.

The industry

The ingredients industry is fragmented, and although there are few direct competitors (the industry being oligopolistic) there is fierce competition, not only in relation to the price of existing products but also in terms of new market segments.

The products

Basically Newton has two types of product—baked and blended. Taken together they break down into 1500 individual products involving some 800 different ingredients, and they service some 2200 customers world-wide.

The processes

Both types of product require process technology of varying degrees of sophistication. The baked products, for example, require a fair amount of technical input from the operators, while the blended products need little technical intervention in the process and relatively unskilled labour is required.

The marketplace—change and uncertainty

Both types of products have enjoyed a stable, although steadily expanding, market share. In marketing terms it could be described as mature. The other manufacturers of the same types of commodity have begun to compete by expanding and fragmenting the product range.

The customer is essentially the retailer (i.e. someone making cakes or other food items). Branding is therefore unimportant, except for public-relations purposes. Emphasis is placed on price, quality and customer service.

A current requirement in order to remain competitive has been to push existing capacity to the limit of present resources, including people. With competition it is expected that volumes will decline and the upgrading of skills of machine-minders and technicians will become even more important.

To achieve this, staff at all levels will need to be both better trained and able to perform a much wider range of tasks, particularly when further technology is applied to existing processes.

Additional new market opportunities—baked products

The company has recently acquired a new, rapidly growing segment of the food ingredient market. Currently, it is the market leader with 70% of the market. Investment has already been made in new plant and there are other possibilities for expansion. A greenfield site has been acquired and there is the opportunity to develop completely new systems of plant operation and systems of remuneration. The latter, it is thought, would materially assist a move to more responsibility and flexibility on the part of the operatives.

Threats to blended products

There is a steadily growing demand for the blended products. However product quality is seen to be of paramount importance, with customer service a close second. The factor of the labour force is important in meeting these objectives, not because superior technical knowledge will improve the process but because it is felt that superior product knowledge will improve the quality. In this area of the business, automation is being increasingly applied to improve throughput; however increased throughput will not involve increased manpower. There is consequently a requirement for operatives to accept new skills and working practices if performance is to be improved.

Organization structure

The current organization is run on 'traditional' structured lines. Brief reporting lines are set out in Figure CS2.1. These include the factory manager, departmental managers, foremen, chargehands and mixers, classes 1 and 2.

Figure CS2.1
Traditional organizational structure

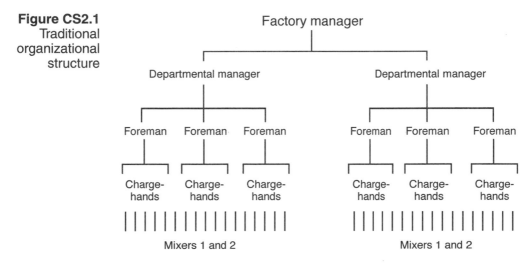

Motivation and manpower problems

The management recognized the following problems engendered by the 'traditional' structure:

● Brighter younger workers became frustrated. Once they had achieved mastery of their tasks, promotion could be slow. Many waited for 'dead men's' shoes.

- Senior managers often acted as 'gatekeepers' in the structure preventing junior employees from undertaking tasks for which they were perfectly capable. Delegation was not seen as a moral imperative and as a result junior employees became disillusioned. Failure of senior managers to develop subordinates was poor management practice, storing up problems for the future.
- In consequence, both managers and their subordinates underperformed. People were viewed as less important than roles, status and structure, with the result that there was inflexibility and a general reduction in the performance of the organization as a whole.

Union organization and affiliation

Working relationships with the unions were harmonious. Unions were strongly supported in the plant, with three unions representing the majority of the workforce (Table CS2.1).

Table CS2.1
Background to the payment system

Section of workforce	Union	Membership (%)
Manufacturing and warehousemen	USDOR	100
Drivers	T&G	100
Managers and ancillaries	M&F	52–60

The current senior management had begun to consider that the wage payment system was working against the changing priorities of the organization.

Employees were paid a fixed sum based on the demands of the job as set out in their job description. No system of job evaluation was used and differentials between job titles and responsibilities were purely on the basis of custom and practice, with differentials maintained or not as the case may be by the separate agreements made in the annual collective bargaining agreements.

No bonuses were paid although on various occasions in the past differentials had been altered by productivity bargaining agreements (mid-1960s) and time and attendance bonuses (1970s). These had long been consolidated. All that remained outside the basic wage figures were some short-shift payments.

The proposed new system—integrated pay

A radical plan has been proposed to alter completely the wage-payment system. It is hoped that the new system will promote two aspects of performance thought to be important for the company's continued success—flexibility and commitment. The basis of the system is flexible teamwork. Not only will multi-skilled teams work together, occasionally taking on a limited amount of each others' work, but they will also work flexibly as a whole. The new factory site is to be divided into a number of fairly large working areas. The group of workers in each area will be responsible for a discrete aspect of the process. Each group will include all current grades of employee and through a process of job evaluation it is hoped that all jobs will be accommodated into a single common wage structure. This structure with the hourly rate allotted to each grade is shown in Figure CS2.2.

Grade 1 is seen as a probationary grade. All new employees would be placed there for the first six months. Allocation to other grades would be strictly based on the range of testable skills which an employee can demonstrate that he or she has.

In order to attract employees to the new system the company would reduce the working week from 40 hours to $37\frac{1}{2}$ hours. It is considered that the effect would be to increase the average pay by 11% to all workers. Jobs falling outside the grades would be red-circled so that annual pay increases would eventually bring them into line.

Figure CS2.2
New organizational
structure

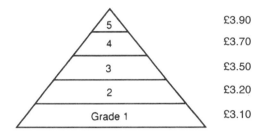

Perhaps the boldest aspect of the proposed new system is that employees would have to accept work at the same pay level in work specialisms outside their traditional discipline or skill. For this to be possible the company would guarantee to provide training in all personal and testable skills compatible with the proposed scheme. This should serve to prove the competence of employees to undertake the variety of work required.

Promotion through the grades will necessitate the demonstration of a wider range of skills, not only in their main discipline, but also to a limited extent in other disciplines. The aim is that ultimately employees will not only work flexibly within their own teams, but also with the overall group.

So, for example, Grade 1 workers in the manufacturing function will be expected to undertake a variety of manufacturing functions as well as a limited number of quality functions, such as sampling, and engineering functions, such as greasing (see Figure CS2.3, Employee A).

Figure CS2.3
Example of
functional flexibility

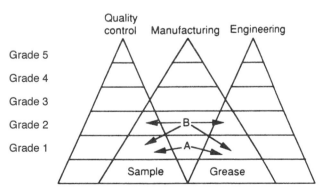

As individuals rise throughout the hierarchy, management would reserve the right to deploy them wherever they might be required provided they were qualified (sideways and down), regardless of their pay grade (see Figure CS2.3, Employee B). It would therefore be management's responsibility to achieve the maximum potential from their labour force. For the labour force, anyone would be free to advance up the grades provided their individual competence level can be increased. The company would be pledged to take individuals as far as the individuals can achieve and the responsibility thus placed on the company for training is recognized.

Questions   1   How might such a revolutionary new scheme be designed and
implemented so that it has the best possible chance of success? Design an
implementation plan.

2   What disadvantages do you foresee in the proposed new structure?
Comment on how you might alleviate or reduce any disadvantages.

3   In exactly what ways will the new system improve the motivation of
individuals and groups? Locate your discussion in theories of motivation.

Peter Dean[1]

Hugh Gunz

Building a career means taking some very difficult decisions. Careers involve choices (for instance about the subjects to study for a degree, the kind of job to take), and every choice constrains options later. The consequences of a bad decision may not become apparent until 10 or 20 years later, if ever.

There is never enough information, either. Jobs rarely turn out as expected, and what looks exciting now can lose its attractiveness as one gets more familiar with it or one's interests change. The fortunes of companies can change too. For instance, it's not uncommon for fast-growing, dynamic firms to lose their momentum and, in doing so, many of their jobs and opportunities for getting ahead.

Peter Dean toyed with the letter that had just come by the morning post and wondered what to do. It was nice to feel wanted, but just now he could do with being wanted by fewer people. If only, he reflected, there was some way of telling which of the four opportunities he was faced with would turn out best for him and his family. It wasn't the first time he'd contemplated changing directions in his career, but the older you got, the more hung on the decision. And people were pressing for answers.

Ignoring with some difficulty the domestic chaos of small children getting ready for school, he reviewed in his mind where he'd been and what he'd done.

Like many young people, Peter's first choice of a job had been a mistake. He'd left school without going to college, and, caught up with the excitement of computers, had been hired as a programmer by a plastics manufacturer. But a year of working on payrolls had taken the gloss off that one, and he'd left his job to go to college to study for a business degree. The course had been excellent, with plenty of opportunities to spend time working in a big engineering company nearby, and he'd come out realizing that he had the potential to get somewhere interesting.

He was hired by a division of a major multi-national, Stanton Industries. Stanton was a byword in the country for excellence: it was known as being a good company, well managed, and just getting hired by Stanton was an achievement. With such a reputation, the company could pick and choose whom it wanted. And it always made sure it picked young graduates with excellent grades and high recommendations.

His division, Norchem, made performance chemicals (chemicals which are sold to do a particular job rather than having a particular formula) for a number of industries, including textiles. Although much of the division's plant and equipment was very old, Norchem had a superb track record in the past for innovation. Its research and development facilities were excellent, and many of its scientists had achieved national and international reputations for their work.

Perhaps the most challenging problem Norchem's managers faced concerned its extremely complex product range. Approximately 3000 products were made by a sequence of batch processes, in chains of anything up to 12 separate stages. In addition, intermediate products could be sold as products in their own right, used as feedstock for another chain, or even fed back higher upstream in their own chain. This called for operations planning skills of a very high order, and the planners (normally science or engineering graduates from a plant operations background) occupied a key position in the organization.

As a business graduate, Peter was recruited into Norchem's marketing department. His first assignment involved market research and forecasting, and after two and a half years he was appointed product officer for a range of chemicals sold to the plastics industry. This meant co-ordinating the work of the sales organization (which reported through a different management structure), production operations, the central business planners, the technical support staff and the distribution department, and was an excellent training for his current job.

Then came a spell working for a very senior manager in a special task force examining the engineering, personnel, productivity management and other services provided to the central site of the division. He'd obviously got noticed as a result of these varied experiences, because after that he was sent to the Far East to help run Norchem's marketing and business development activities there.

This had been a marvellous time for him. He had been fascinated by the country to which he was posted, and had made great efforts to learn the language and absorb as much of the culture as he could. His job put him in contact with government as well as customers, giving him a superb overview of doing business in the country and introducing him to a great many people that most junior managers never have the chance to come near. The overseas posting lasted two and a half years. Now he was back home, in a more senior product management job. And, after three years in the post it was beginning to become clear that things weren't working out as well as he'd hoped. It wasn't necessarily his fault, he thought. In many ways, Norchem's past had caught up with it. Tied to a number of industries like textiles which had effectively moved overseas, Norchem was now competing with manufacturers in Third World countries and finding it very difficult. The age of much of the plant didn't help, and some of its most exciting innovations had been spun off as separate divisions within Stanton Industries. It was, in other words, an ageing cash cow, and its overhead structure was causing it to lose money heavily.

Norchem's top management was trying to stem the cash outflow. Plants had been closed, and the division now employed half the number of people it had some five years previously. Everyone kept saying that there was light at the end of the tunnel and that soon things would be looking up, but the light kept receding. And while the division was cutting staff, it was hard to see when the next promotion would come along. The word from his bosses was that yes, he was well thought of in the division, and he might eventually get to a senior level. But no-one was willing to say when this might happen, or even commit themselves to how likely it was. There didn't seem to be a chance of a move to another Stanton division, either.

Peter wasn't the only one who'd decided that maybe the time had come to look outside Norchem. He'd been interviewed by a number of smaller firms in the chemical industry, but most had said that he'd been too specialized in his job and they couldn't see how he would fit in with them. This had set him to thinking about what he really wanted to do with his life.

He'd always enjoyed teaching, and he loved business. Some years before, he'd been accepted by a major business school to study for a PhD, and when he approached them again he found that they were looking for research staff in the kind of areas of which he'd had experience. They were still keen to have him, and if he joined them there was a good possibility that after a couple of years, the experience he'd get would make him a good choice for their teaching staff. There were plenty of precedents for making a career move like this. He had friends who taught at business schools, and he was pretty sure not only that he'd find the work deeply satisfying, but that the flexibility of the academic life-style would give him more time to develop other sides of his life. His family was important to him, and he'd see a lot more of them too. Life, after all, wasn't just for work; one became increasingly aware of that as one aged.

But the salary would be nothing like what he'd been used to. And by now he had a comfortable house with a large mortgage, and two small children who needed feeding. His wife had trained as a physiotherapist, but had hated the work. For the last few years she had discovered a role and a talent for helping immigrant women learn the language of their new country, and, although immensely satisfying, this didn't pay much. It hadn't mattered while Peter earned his good Norchem salary, but if he joined the business school not only would they take a big cut in income, the appointment was only for two years in the first instance. What, they worried, would happen then? If Peter did succeed in joining the permanent teaching staff his salary would still not be very good. Would that be enough compensation for a job he expected that he'd find deeply satisfying? If he didn't, what would he be qualified for? Who would have him?

Two other opportunities had just come up. The first was with a major firm of management consultants, the second with a competitor of Stanton. Both offers had good and bad points.

The management consultants certainly paid well, and it was quite likely that if he joined them the experience he'd get would be valuable for the future. But management consulting means constantly being on the move. He knew from talking to consultants that one of the most frustrating features of the job was that no sooner you started getting interested in a client's problem, it would be time to move on to the next one. He didn't know how he'd like leading the rootless existence of the consultant, and especially so because it would mean being away from home, and his young family, so much.

The competitor's offer was a job in business development, working for the chief executive of the company. It, too, would pay well, and the company wasn't facing the same business problems as Norchem so his career prospects would probably be better. But to some extent at least, it was more of what he was already doing. And the company was the local subsidiary of a European firm well known for its highly ethnocentric style of management (you did as the Europeans told you). If he was to go far in the company he would have to learn the European language in question, and although his Far East experience had proved to him that he could adapt to different national cultures, he worried about how long it would take him to learn the language fluently enough to be fully accepted. It would also mean moving house, and that was not welcomed by his wife. She had built up good links with the local community in her role of teaching immigrant wives, and there was no sign that the place they would have to move to had the same opportunities. Most likely, she would have to start all over again, trying to build a new occupation and an interest for herself.

Peter was now approaching his mid-thirties. He knew that he wasn't going to have many more chances to make the sort of break he was being offered, and by the same token the decision he made now would, probably, irrevocably shape the rest of his career. Should he leave Norchem? The longer he stayed, the harder it would be to leave, but at least they knew him there and the chances were good that if the division's business position should turn around he'd do well. And if he left, which of the three options should he take? The various offers would not stay open for ever, either. At least two of his potential employers were getting impatient: the letter he'd just received was polite, but made it clear that he wasn't the only candidate for the job and that a decision was needed.

Note   1 Copyright © Hugh Gunz, 1988. The people, organizations and events in this case are real, although names have been changed to preserve confidentiality.

Questions   1 Prepare a short report advising Peter Dean which decisions to make.

2 Support your report with reference to the relevant literature, saying what points you would make and why.

3 Has Peter Dean thought of everything? If not, what other factors might influence the decision?

Part III
The Group

CHAPTER 8 Group behaviour

The group as the unit of analysis

In Parts I and II of this book we have so far been looking at the behaviour of individuals in organizations. The principles of scientific management, for example, were focused on the performance of individuals at work. The manager's task would be relatively straightforward if all behaviour in organizations could be treated on an individual basis. But this would be too simplistic to handle the complexity of most organizations. A great deal of management time, and that of other individuals in the organization, is spent in groups. Groups make recommendations; make decisions; inherit the decisions of other groups, and form, re-form and split up often in a relatively short time. We shall look at the different types of groups later in this chapter. For the moment, we need to be clear about certain aspects of behaviour which are common to all groups and which a manager must understand if poor performance, conflict, misunderstandings and bad communication are to be avoided.

Possibly the most fundamental lesson a manager must learn is that the behaviour patterns which occur within any group are directly related to its performance or its task achievement (Shaw, 1981). Groups which are badly managed, or which manage themselves badly, will be less effective in getting tasks accomplished and in making accurate and sensible decisions. Chapter 10 details how decision-making processes can be heavily influenced by the characteristics of a group and many other organizational processes can be similarly affected.

Small groups can be defined as two or more individuals who interact with one another and where there is a psychological interrelationship between them. There must be a significant level of interdependence between group members to the extent that members of the group perceive the group to be 'real' and to the extent that members can readily distinguish themselves from non-members (Alderfer, 1977). Within the group, members take on specific roles or tasks and these too are recognized by the group as a whole. Such roles build in expectations of behaviour from individuals and thus a certain measure of predictability can also emerge.

We can distinguish between formal groups and informal groups in organizations. *Formal groups* are designed and created around specific tasks. Membership is often assigned to individuals in an organization and they may serve the group for a specified length of time (for example, one year or six months). In general, formal groups would show up on the organization chart. They are mostly specified by functional differentiation. A standing committee is an example of a formal group. Most people in an organization are members of at least one formal group. It is through this that they achieve a formal role in the company.

Other kinds of formal groups are task groups which are rather more temporary than standing groups. Task groups form around a specific need at a particular point in time. Product development groups, some research groups and some marketing or sales teams are examples of task groups. Likert (1961) showed that often individuals could be members of many formal groups in an organization. Structurally, co-ordination between formal groups is achieved through 'linking pins' created by multiple membership. Figure 8.1 shows a typical linking-pin structure.

Figure 8.1
Multiple group membership through a 'linking-pin' structure

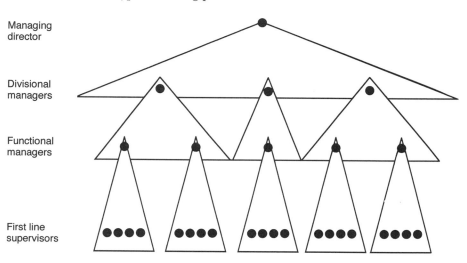

Managing director

Divisional managers

Functional managers

First line supervisors

Informal groups occur because organizations are social places as well as functional purposive structures. People like to talk to one another. The groups of friends which arise in this way, cross functional as well as hierarchical boundaries. Membership of informal groups is voluntary, although access into one of these groups can be difficult since such groups can quickly develop their own ways of doing things which provide barriers to entry and acceptability. This includes an implicit or explicit description of the kind of person who is acceptable to the group and who is not.

Informal groups are the focus of information-sharing, allow the testing out new ideas and schemes, act as sounding boards for all kinds of information and they can mobilize considerable resistance to formal schemes and plans. The weight of resistance is likely to increase to the extent that the informal group contains mostly co-workers from similar levels in the hierarchy. It is too easy to concentrate only on the negative side of informal groups. Much has been written about their resistance to reorganization schemes, new designs of jobs and the adoption of new technologies. However, the coherence and psychological solidarity that characterize informal groups can also be a great asset to the organization when management goals and those of the group are in line. If the informal group wants to streamline inventory processing or wants to improve product or service quality, then this is probably the fastest way of achieving these goals! It will certainly be quicker than the formal route. The management process, therefore, must take into account both types of groups when dealing with almost any aspect of organization.

Operating problems and opportunities of the group

Like individuals, groups develop and change over time. There are some predictable stages through which most groups will progress although the strict sequence of these stages may vary. The stages are:

1 *Forming* Testing by group members to try and determine acceptable behaviour and attitudes. Life in this stage of the group is mostly about taking and giving cues about expected behaviour.
2 *Storming* Identifies the pecking order of members in the group. A time of negotiation and sometimes outright conflict as power and status are allocated to individuals around the group. Group leaders tend to emerge at this stage although their tenure of office may be short-lived if the group continues to storm.
3 *Norming* This is the stage at which group rules are made. Tasks of the group are clear and are freely articulated by all group members. The group is developing norms.
4 *Performing* A mature group psychologically which will impart considerable effort into achieving goals and successful performance generally. Levels of within-group conflict are very low and further sub-grouping of specialisms is likely as the level of task flexibility increases.

Not all groups go through all stages. Each stage, however, has some overall implications for management styles which may be appropriate. For example, the process of storming can be avoided entirely by autocratic leadership styles. A group created by a hierarchically superior manager will be in no doubt about the question of who is boss. The feelings of cohesiveness which develop at the next stage (norming) are not likely to be always in line with what the autocratic manager initially intended and the group will assemble a position which is defensive or even antagonistic. This raises the question of whether an appropriate management style would be to let the group get on with its formation without much overt interference (with the benefit of ultimately achieving a cohesive and good performing group, balanced against the time cost of the group going through all its developmental stages).

Roles and role behaviour

The division of labour within any organization between its maintenance, its productive and other support functions necessitates the creation of *roles*. Put simply, roles ensure that the life of any organization is capable of outlasting its present sum total of individuals. Formal roles are created in organizations so that different individuals can be selected to carry out specified tasks. When a selection panel chooses an individual for a job in an organization, they are really matching what they know about that individual to a role description. Just as there can be formal and informal groups, so too are roles both formal and informal. Formal roles are those such as job descriptions, and task specifications. They can be clearly specified quite independently of any single individual. We talk of people holding 'office' in an organization when we refer to the role they currently perform. The organization is thus (in formal terms) a system of multiple roles.

Informal roles are those actions and behaviours of individuals which are not specified or expected by their formal role position. We all take on multiple roles in organizations as well as in the wider society. For example, how would you describe all the roles you undertake during a typical day? Your formal role might be production controller. You might also be fairly handy with computers and software because that is one of your hobbies. So an informal role might be that of fixer and possibly trainer for your group in regard to their personal computers. You might also be well experienced in the school of life and inter-personally sympathetic, so another informal role you might take on could be that of 'agony aunt' or counsellor to your organizational colleagues. In wider society, you will also occupy a number of formal and informal roles: wife, father, mother, friend, cricketer, golfer, squash player, do-it-yourself expert are examples. Together, these multiple roles are called a 'role set' (Katz and Kahn, 1978).

The application of role theory and the taking up of roles in groups has a long and disputed history in management science. As far back as 1936, Linton (1936) began to give primacy to the concept of role in social sciences and Parsons (1951) and Merton (1957) pronounced roles and role behaviour central to the understanding of action and structure in organizations. Others have argued that the concept of role is of little analytical or practical value (Bittner, 1965; Garfinkel, 1967; Goffman, 1956). The argument against roles hinges upon the difficulty of trying to understand human behaviour in organizations. To talk about roles is merely to impose a construct which is not 'real' in an objective sense. Behaviour is only understandable in the descriptions and the terminology of those individuals who do the behaving. It is argued that this has little to do with roles or role behaviour.

The implications of roles for the study of organizational behaviour cannot be ignored, however, despite the continuing academic debates. Roles are based upon expected behaviours and performances from individuals in the group. These multiple expectations form the basis of judgements (can this person do the job?) and the basis of appraisal and rewards (how well did the person occupy the role?). Gross (1968) has identified a list of roles which are most commonly taken on in a work group. It is not an exhaustive list, but it is instructive in that it gives illustrations of specific roles and their associated behaviours in the group. See how many in Table 8.1 you recognize from your last group meeting:

Multiple roles: conflict and ambiguity

An organization consists of sets of multiple roles all of which overlap in some form or other. Some roles will be directly related while others will only be tangential to one another. We examine the inter-relationships between groups in the next chapter. Here, we are concerned with the multiple roles which any one individual might occupy simultaneously and which can give rise to conflict and ambiguity. Multiple roles are not easy to manage either for the individual or for the manager of individuals in organizations. For example, multiple activities (that is, tasks) might comprise one role description. Alternatively, any organizational task may involve the individual taking on multiple roles. Finally, a single individual might be responsible for multiple tasks in the organization. The possible permutation of multiple roles, tasks and people is thus complex. However, the symptoms of things going wrong as a result of multiple roles are known as conflict and ambiguity.

Role conflict is heightened when multiple role expectations are mutually exclusive. That is, any attempt to fulfil one set of role expectations automatically makes satisfying other expectations difficult or impossible. There are four types of role conflict which occur in organizations (see Table 8.2.)

Table 8.1
Common roles in a
work group

Task-oriented individuals:	Those who predominantly try to get the job done and get some output from the group
People-oriented individuals:	Those who are concerned with inter-personal relationships in the group and who work hard to maintain a good social climate
No-sayers:	Those who consistently oppose most proposals, have thick skins and find fault with virtually everything
Yes-sayers:	Those who try to get round opposition, are enthusiastic and counter the no-sayers.
Regulars:	Those who are obviously accepted by the group. These are the 'in people' who accept and project the group's norms and values
Deviants:	Mavericks who depart from group values
Isolates:	'Lone wolves' who often depart even further from expected values and behaviour than the deviants
Newcomers:	New entrants to the group who need to be guided by others and who are expected to be seen but not heard.
Old timers:	Those who have been in the group for a long time and who know the ropes
Climbers:	Individuals who are commonly expected to get ahead often on the basis of assumed potential rather than any concrete demonstration of ability
Cosmopolitans:	Group members who view themselves as part of a wider professional or cultural community and who often consider the group and its members inferior to this wider community.
Locals:	Those who are firmly rooted in the group and in the organizational community

Role conflict is a serious issue for both organizations and for individuals. Most evidence on role conflict is unambiguous. The greater is the level of conflict, the less effective is the organization overall and the less satisfied are the individuals within it (see Mitchell and Larson, 1987 who discuss the extensive study carried out by Fisher and Gitelson, 1983).

One of the aspects of reorganization which is frequently overlooked is that any form of structural change in an organization will bring with it different levels and intensities of role conflict. Structural change may reduce some existing conflicts, but it may equally create new role expectations which are incompatible. Since reorganization appears to be a common response by managers to a range of organizational difficulties (falling market share, lack of profitability, feelings of stagnation and human resource problems) the implications that this is likely to have for creating conflicts should not be dismissed lightly. Future performance may not be as good as expected (Hickson *et al.*, 1986).

Role ambiguity is more simple to identify than role conflict. It describes the situation where an individual is unsure what to do when they occupy a role (Katz and Kahn, 1978). There can be two aspects to this ambiguity, the means and the ends. An individual can be unsure what is expected or which

Table 8.2
Types of role conflict

Type of role conflict	Description
Intra-sender role conflict	Occurs when your boss tells you to do two or more things which are impossible. For example, you might be asked to give a job top priority and be told simultaneously not to neglect any other task. Obviously, doing one task will be at the expense of the other. Conflict occurs because you have to decide what to do in the knowledge that one or more jobs will be neglected and the task allocated will not be fully accomplished.
Inter-sender role conflict	Occurs when two or more people in your role set send messages which conflict. You cannot meet both sets of expectations. This is a common managerial problem. Conflicting demands might be from sales functions to produce multiple products or variants to satisfy customer demand versus demands from production functions to stick to one or two product variants to smooth the production process and inventory processing
Inter-role conflict	Occurs when a single person occupies multiple roles. Fulfilling one role automatically obviates the other. In organizations, managers frequently experience role conflict in this way. They may be expected to make decisions which are for the good of the organization overall, and at the same time, be expected by their subordinates to make decisions and fight for the good of the department. Both are likely to be incompatible, just as conflicts between being a full-time mother and a full-time manager cannot easily be resolved
Person–role conflict	Occurs when the person and the expected behaviours of the role do not coincide. For example, you might be recruited to a position in which the expected role behaviour is to adopt an aloof, distant and aggressive management style. If this conflicts with your own feelings about how other people in the organization should be treated then conflict will occur. Many of us look to our 'principles' to sort out this conflict, by which we mean what we feel fundamentally is right. Many resignations and requests for transfers are directly related to this conflict.

tasks are to be achieved (the ends). Equally, there can be ambiguity over how to achieve tasks, even though they may be specified quite clearly (the means). Selection and promotion procedures in organizations can inadvertently increase levels of role ambiguity. If the aim is to retain a key individual, for example, by creating a new post or by promotion, it is unlikely that anyone in the organization including the role occupant will have a clear idea of what is expected. An organization facing rapid and far-reaching changes will also create an environment of high role ambiguity for its staff.

Since both role conflict and ambiguity have deleterious consequences for both organizational and individual performance, it is important that they are recognized and managed effectively. This is more complex than simply identifying the problem and trying to remove the ambiguity or conflict. The confounding factors are:

1 Position in hierarchy
2 The design of jobs
3 Variable abilities of the individual in their ability to handle conflict and ambiguity.

Research indicates that role conflict is most often experienced by more junior managers and in other relatively lower positions in the firm (McClelland, 1985). Conversely, role ambiguity is likely to increase at more senior levels of management. Senior management tasks simply cannot be broken down into specific and identifiable features which would obviate ambiguity. In many respects, a definition of the key elements of senior management tasks would place role ambiguity at centre stage. Selection of senior managers is often based upon the predicted ability of the role occupant to handle (even welcome) ambiguity.

Role conflict and ambiguity can create a situation which individuals find stressful (see Chapter 4). However, just as in the studies of stress, the perception of conflict and ambiguity will differ between individuals. Some individuals can handle quite high levels of conflict and ambiguity and feel at ease in their organizational position. Others suffer quite marked degrees of stress because they do not enjoy, and possibly cannot cope with, the levels of ambiguity and conflict (Cooper and Marshall, 1976). Trying to match individual characteristics with the ability to cope with conflict and ambiguity has been the focus of empirical research. Those individuals with a high need to achieve, for example, have been identified as those who experience most difficulty with role ambiguity (McClelland, 1985). Ambiguity frustrates the clear identification of factors which will lead to the fulfilment of their achieving goals. On the other hand, extroverts appear to feel quite at home in the same situation.

Even though the relationships between personality variables and perceived ease with role conflict and ambiguity are persuasive, they are only partially useful. They ignore the dynamic context of organizational life. Individuals change as they progress through organizations and as they get older. The ability to handle problems encountered through role changes also. It is likely that an individual's ability to handle conflict and ambiguity increases positively with experience but only to a point. After that, as maturity sets in, the ability may reduce. Since different individuals will reach such a hypothetical maturity point at different rates, matching individual characteristics and role conflict and ambiguity becomes tenuous.

Training in handling situations which exhibit conflict and ambiguity can also help individuals to cope better with existing levels and even actively to seek such positions. Managers also may benefit from training in role conflict and ambiguity even though they may not experience it themselves (or are able to cope with it 'naturally'). This is because it is all too easy to equate poor performance with specific individuals or aspects of personality rather than with characteristics of the role. The person gets blamed, not the role. An understanding of why conflict and ambiguity can arise, often from seemingly unrelated decisions, can be of immense help in alleviating problems.

Role conflicts and inter-nationalization

The above concepts of role can be viewed in an international context, especially since many teams either operate internationally or consist of members from different nations. The factors which create role stress can be triggered or heightened by working internationally. For example, the very concept of working in teams is a highly 'Western' idea. Some cultures indicate a preference to a more hierarchical management structure in which each team member has a well-defined role (Peterson, 1995). If the concept of work teams is Western-centric (Trompenaars, 1993; Hampden-Turner and Trompenaars, 1995) so, too, are some of the management 'tools' which are natural to Western teams (such as management by objectives) but which can be extremely divisive in an international context. Furthermore, the desire for speedy decision-making, a feature of many Western culture teams, sits ill-at-ease (for example) with its polar extreme, the Japanese 'ringi' system of decision-making where proposals are circulated to interested parties until a consensus is achieved.

Peterson (1995) along with 22 other researchers around the world, conducted a study into role conflict in 21 different countries. They looked at organizational, demographic and country-specific factors. The conclusions were that: 'Role stress varies substantially more by country than by demographic and organizational factors' (Peterson, 1995). Overall, managers working in teams from those countries with a high 'power distance' (see Reading 14) reported the greatest levels of role stress. These countries include Brazil, Portugal and some Far Eastern countries in the developing world.

Western middle managers overall felt they had a workload which was manageable. They felt able to cope. They were, however, not always sure exactly how to go about doing it. Middle managers in non-Western countries would appear to know their roles more clearly, but feel they cannot fulfil all their roles since they have too much work to do. Peterson, (1995) does point out that the Western/non-Western split is not exact. Mexico, a Latin country and Indonesia in the Far East are certainly hierarchical, but respondents gave little evidence of role stress. Even within the Western world there can be significant differences in role stressors. Hampden-Turner and Trompenaars (1995) for example, describe how many Swedish managers are role stressed when they meet in groups with North American managers. They found that the North American way to engage in small-talk, present a highly polished sales pitch and talk about quality and performance of the product, for example, contrasted with the Swedish approach. Swedish managers generally preferred less small-talk, tended to mistrust sales pitches and felt that the product should speak for itself in terms of reliability and quality.

Organizations working internationally, using teams which often comprise individuals from different nations, face these problems continually. What are they doing to try and relieve role conflict and stress? The following seem to be the main approaches:

1 Use the global brand to unite and force people to bury their cultural differences under the potency of the brand (examples of this are McDonalds and Coca-Cola).
2 Use training and development to reduce role stress before the teams meet and are formed. This prior training takes time (it is estimated that putting a global team together in this way takes three times as long as a purely national team) but seems effective once in place. It avoids individuals confronting cultural differences head-on and encountering

role stress (Intel is an example of a company which invests heavily in this kind of pre-team training).

3   Reduce the time spent by the team in face-to-face discussion by increasing the use of technology (using Lotus Notes and video-conferencing instead, for example). Companies such as SmithKline Beecham and Price Waterhouse are advocates of this approach.

4   Use cultural sensitivity training. As organizations become increasingly affected by cultural divergence, there is a greater need to encourage employees to be aware of our 'cultural' assumptions and how they might be interpreted by others. Although there are many forms of such sensitivity training, they usually touch upon topics such as:

   a   awareness of cultural difference;
   b   behavioural differences;
   c   potential situations due to the interaction of different cultural assumptions; and
   d   developing techniques which avert the more obvious 'faux-pas'.

Socialization and the pressure to conform in groups

Anyone who has ever joined a group will have experienced pressures to conform and will have undergone a process of socialization. All social groups develop norms about expected behaviours from group members and they can exert considerable pressure upon new members to conform. The word conformity is important here, because it emphasizes the rather one-way nature of the change process which occurs. The group expects a certain kind of behaviour. The new member conforms by changing his or her earlier preferences to those of the group.

If any one is in doubt about the strength of the pressure to conform in groups, try arguing for a position which you know is counter to that held by the rest of the group. You will be subjected to the most intense pressure to conform. *You* should change and not the group. Leavitt (1972) has identified some discrete stages which occur in the above scenario of the group and its individual 'deviant':

1   *Reason*   The group attempts to question the 'data base' of the deviant. What evidence do you have for your position? At this stage, the group appears reasonable and rational in its behaviour.

2   *Seduction*   The group now tries to appeal to loyalty values. You're a valued member of this team, they say. We've been through a lot together, so why are you going against us now? The group is trying to get the deviant to see sense (its sense).

3   *Iron fist is revealed*   The group attempts to beat submission out of the deviant. They gang up on him or her. They shout, they harass and harangue and they disbelieve any further data revealed by the deviant.

4   *Amputation*   If the deviant can withstand the first three stages, then continued deviance will result in the group excommunicating him or her. They will no longer be held as a valued member of the team. This, of course, has tremendous implications for a group which meets regularly with the same members. The next time the group meets, the deviant will start by being perceived as hostile no matter what the topic and the group will be suspicious of all behaviour.

The potency of group pressure can be found in the classic study of Solomon Asch (1951). Stanley Milgram's (1974) empirical work also revealed a strong tendency for individuals to conform because the concept of obedience is ingrained in us from a very early age. The intrusion of authority into teamwork is starkly shown by Milgram. The study by Asch demonstrates the power of a group to elicit *conformity* of opinion and judgement among its members. Milgram's study illustrates the power of *obedience* in achieving conformity. Each study is described briefly in the next sections.

The Asch experiment in conformity

The Asch experiment took place in a laboratory setting. In the laboratory was a group of six subjects (college students). All were shown drawings of lines and were asked in turn to comment on the relative length of each. For example, they were asked which of the lines drawn in Figure 8.2 was the same length as line 'A'.

Figure 8.2
The Asch experiment in conformity

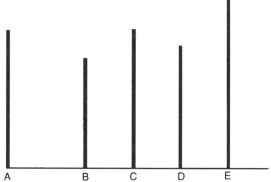

In the experiment, Asch had engineered who was in the group. Really, there was only one volunteer. The confederates and the one volunteer then said which line was the longest, the next longest and so on. At the first session, all group members correctly identified the lines. At a second session, the confederates consistently gave an incorrect answer. They would say, within hearing of the true volunteer, that a line blatantly shorter than 'A' was equal to it in length! In 32% of cases, the volunteer went along with this opinion despite initially showing hesitancy because the answer was obviously wrong. It seemed to be important to achieve unanimity of opinion from the group. Some volunteers did resist group pressure although the film record of the study shows how obviously uncomfortable and hesitant many of them felt in this.

In a further study, Asch demonstrated that if the volunteer had an 'ally' whereby one of the confederates consistently defied the group and gave the correct answer, the ability of the volunteer to withstand group pressure was greatly increased. Now the 'deviant' was no longer alone, the potency of group pressure was substantially eroded. The Asch experiment is important and relevant to today's managers for it shows what can happen in any group given a task to make a decision on data which are absolute by any standards of common sense. Given that most organizational problems are not so well defined, group pressure on conformity to feelings, hunches and other subjective data is greatly increased. Further pressures on conformity are also produced if the group is one which meets regularly and considers a range of issues (see Chapter 10).

Compliance and conformity

While compliance and conformity will produce the same end result (obedience to group pressure) it is important to distinguish between them.

Compliance differs from conformity in that it reflects conformity through ulterior motives (such as the desire to please the boss, pragmatism—you are new and the rest of the group are long serving—or the recognition of greater power bases in the group). Asch's study revealed three ways in which individuals conformed to, or complied with, group pressure:

1 *Distortion of perception* Individuals in the group are aware that the group is 'wrong' but they suppress their disagreement while the group is in session. Later, they believe the group was correct after all. Here is obedience through *compliance followed by conformity* (although this kind of conformity happens outside the confines of the group meeting, it can occur as the same group subsequently meets on separate issues).
2 *Distortion of judgement* Individuals think the group is correct and that they must be wrong. Any doubts they may have are extinguished during the process of the group meeting. This is obedience *solely through conformity*.
3 *Distortion of action* Individuals are aware that the group is 'wrong'. However, they suppress their deviation from the prevailing opinion. They never subsequently believe that the group was correct. This is *obedience solely through compliance.*

Asch's experiments indicated that distortion of judgement was the major reason for obedience. In other words, individuals tend to conform more than they tend to comply. While this is a surprising finding in a laboratory experiment, it is likely that in work organizations such factors as different hierarchical levels in a group will increase the tendency for individuals to comply rather than to conform. Compliance is thus the recognition of strong power bases (such as the chairperson who is the most senior manager) and compliance may be largely because of political or pragmatic motives (see Chapter 11).

The Milgram studies of obedience to authority

Even the most democratic organizations rely ultimately upon one set of persons following the directions of another group because they are perceived to have the *authority* to give that direction. Managers have to rely on their staff following their directions. If this were not so, organizations would become chaotic places which would never achieve any targets or goals. Most of us recognize authority (although it eludes precise definition) and readily react to it when we think its exercise is reasonable. Of course, the definition of what is reasonable is also not amenable to precise definition, although it is worth noting that the basis of the British and many other legal systems is founded upon the judgement of what a 'reasonable' person would have done in a particular set of circumstances.

In wider society, too, there is a rule system based upon the acknowledgement of authority. Driving on the public highway requires that drivers and pedestrians follow rules laid down by another authority. The majority of us follow those rules since they allow traffic to flow relatively smoothly and are designed to avoid accidents and collisions. We also talk of 'blind obedience' to authority and of 'authoritarian regimes' wherein the populace of a country are subjected to extremes of dictat. Here, we are making value judgements about the appropriate exercise of authority.

Milgram wanted to show that individuals are socialized to obey. In a group, this tendency can induce people to obey and carry out tasks which, outside the group, would be considered evil or malicious. One of Milgram's intentions was to demonstrate why so many soldiers in the Second World

War had apparently followed without question the orders of their officers and inflicted horrendous torture upon prisoners. Such barbarism, said Milgram, could largely be explained by group pressure.

The study consisted of volunteers who took part in a learning experiment. The experiment took place in the early 1960s. Forty adult males from a wide range of social and economic backgrounds were paid to volunteer to be subjects in the experiment. They were told that they were part of an experiment in learning, education and punishment. Each volunteer was then asked to assist another (who was actually a confederate) to learn sets of word pairs. Both individuals faced each other divided by a thick glass screen much as you would find in most recording studios, so that communication between the two was only possible by microphone and loudspeaker.

In front of the volunteer was a machine which administered electric shocks to the 'learner'. On hearing a wrong answer, the volunteer was to administer an electric shock to the learner in order to assist learning by a small punishment. A correct answer resulted in no electric shock being given. The voltage of the shock varied on a scale which ran between 15 and 450 volts. Each time the learner gave a wrong answer, the voltage was to increase to the next higher voltage and so on. The voltage scale was labelled clearly from 'slight shock' through 'extreme intensity shock' to 'XXX'.

As the voltages increased, the learner would protest about the pain being inflicted and that he no longer wanted to take part in the experiment. The volunteer was told to continue by the researcher running the experiment. This continued until severe electric shocks were given. It needed the volunteer to protest four times to the researcher for the experiment to be abandoned. Screams of pain and sometimes ominous silences were clearly audible by the volunteer each time a severe shock was administered. The results indicated that:

1 65% of the volunteers administered the maximum severity electric shock. This represented 26 out of 40 volunteers.
2 Most volunteers, when pressed to continue by the researcher, exhibited signs of tension and stress such as nervous laughter and trembling. Nevertheless, they continued often on the cajoling of the researcher who insisted that the experiment would be spoiled if they did not continue.
3 At the end of the experiment, all volunteers were told the true nature of the research and that in fact no electric shocks had been administered.
4 The extremely high percentage of conformity by the volunteers gives very strong indications that individuals will obey those they consider to be authoritative and responsible. Even in the case where obvious pain was being inflicted on another individual, the tendency was dominantly to follow directions which came from the source of authority.

Since the time of the Milgram study, virtually no further replications or similar studies have been conducted (although at the time, the Milgram studies were replicated many times in different countries with almost identical results to the original). Concern for ethics in social science research have precluded recent replications. Whether differences in the propensity toward obeying authority exist between different nations or in different periods in history is debatable. However, the number of mass atrocities in wider society (such as those in Uganda, Bosnia etc.) and mass devotion to group causes (such as the Moonies and the mass suicide pact of the religious group 'The People's Temple' in Jonestown, Guyana in 1978) lend substantial support to the broad applicability of Milgram's findings. Led by the Reverend Jim Jones in 1978, an estimated 912 of his 'People's Temple' followers died by taking cyanide or apparently shooting themselves. In 1993, another religious leader, David Koresh of the Branch Davidians, seemingly persuaded over 80 individuals to commit suicide at the Mt. Carmel religious centre in the US. This became known as the Waco massacre. Koresh was able to assert his authority apparently by demonizing the opposition (in this case the FBI and the Department of Public Safety) to gain a collective view under his leadership that all outside the group were the enemy. His authority was secured. Obedience was complete.

In organizations, group structures can impose authority and legitimacy upon member individuals in the same way that authority can be used or abused by managers more senior in the hierarchy. The dangers in not recognizing the potency of conformity and obedience to authority are two-fold. First, authority can be abused or misused. Second, individuals will feel pressured to follow the directions of that authority irrespective of whether such actions would be considered immoral or questionable in the wider context. Within organizations, there is great potential for the abuse of authority both by groups and individuals. Recognition of this by both the authority figure and the recipient can act as some kind of counterweight, although it is unlikely completely to rule out immoral acts in business, political and social organizations.

Team-building

This approach has been popular in the management development literature for some years as a way of getting individuals to think positively about groups and to avoid some of the pitfalls of compliance, conflict and conformity outlined in this chapter. The practical application of team-building techniques has gained significant momentum over the past few years. There are many books and articles dealing with this subject. Three of the leading exponents of team-building are Belbin, (1997) and Katzenbach and Smith (1992). Belbin (1997) places teams in the context of the 'modern job'. He argues that jobs themselves need to change first by getting rid of the straitjackets of job specifications and role definitions. Once achieved, work can be reclassified (he distinguished between tasks and responsibilities) and teams can then be formed around this new vision. Teams take a firm from the individual competencies of its members to excellence and continued flexibility. Not surprisingly, Belbin focuses on the importance of team roles in this study which draws on his earlier work (described in Chapter 10).

Katzenbach and Smith (1992) studied over 50 different teams in 30 organizations. Like Belbin, they emphasize that team-building begins first with an assessment of individual performance and competencies which can then be built into team structures. These individual competencies are *technical or functional expertise, problem-solving skills* and *good inter-personal skills*. Successful teams are small; usually less than 10 members. The small size of the team facilitates communication and effective problem-solving. Their model of team-building is dynamic in that reinforcing cycles are incorporated into team processes. These serve either to identify when a team can continue to grow and sustain high performance, or when the team has peaked and it is time for a change in which the team may be permanently disbanded.

Summary

When looking at groups rather than individuals in organizations, we recognize that group behaviour has its own set of issues which need to be recognized and managed. In particular, the notion of roles is central to understanding the operating problems of groups and the difficulties that individuals can encounter in participating in organizational groups. Roles can cause severe conflict and can create high levels of ambiguity for individuals.

Groups also exert a great deal of influence over constituent members. They can be considered greater than the sum total of their parts, as if they had a life of their own. This is most prevalent in group norms and in socialization processes. New and existing members of groups will consistently be required to conform to the collective norms and expectations of the group. Those who refuse become deviants who are given a few chances to come back into the fold but who are excommunicated if they continue their deviance.

The pressure to conform or *comply* (and thus the intense difficulty in resisting) to group authority and group norms is immense. Both the experiments by Asch (1951) and by Milgram (1974) are powerful landmarks which bear witness to the levels of obedience to authority and to group pressure. Moral and ideological commitment by individuals can also be subverted by group pressure which can persuade individuals to conform to certain aspects of behaviour they would consider unthinkable in another context. Thus the abuse of this pressure by individuals in organizations is a constant threat. Illegal acts such as deception and deliberate deceit can occur (Staw and Swajowski, 1975) as well as self-interested actions by managers such as insider trading and other illegal financial dealings.

References

Alderfer, C. P. (1977) 'Group and inter-group relations', in J. R. Hackman and J. L. Suttle (eds.), *Improving Life at Work*, Goodyear, Santa Monica, Calif.

Asch, S. E. (1951) 'Effects of group pressure upon the modification and distortion of judgement', in H. Guetzkow (ed.), *Groups, Leadership And Men*, Carnegie Press, New York.

Belbin, J. M. (1997) *Changing the Way We Work*, Butterworth-Heinemann, Oxford.

Bittner, E. (1965) 'The concept of organization', *Social Research*, **32**, 239–55.

Cooper, C. L., and J. Marshall (1976) 'Occupational sources of stress: a review of the literature relating to coronary heart disease and mental health', *Journal Of Occupational Psychology*, **49**, 11–28.

Fisher, C. D. and R. Gitelson (1983) 'A meta-analysis of the correlates of role conflict and ambiguity', *Journal Of Applied Psychology*, **68**, 320–33.

Garfinkel, H. (1967) *Studies In Ethnomethodology*, Prentice-Hall, New York.

Goffman, E. (1956) *The Presentation Of Self In Everyday Life*, Edinburgh University Press, Edinburgh.

Gross, B. M. (1968) *Organizations and Their Managing*, Free Press, New York.

Hampden-Turner, C. M. and F. Trompenaars (1995) *The Seven Cultures of Capitalism*, Piaktus, London.

Hickson, D. J., R. J. Butler, D. Cray, G. R. Mallory and D. C. Wilson (1986) *Top Decisions: Strategic Decision Making In Organizations*, Jossey-Bass, San Francisco and Blackwell, Oxford.

Katz, D. and R. L. Kahn (1978) *The Social Psychology Of Organizations*, 2nd edn., Wiley, New York.

Katzenbach, J. R. and D. K. Smith (1992) *The Wisdom of Teams: Creating the High Performance Organization*, Harvard Business School Press, Harvard.

Leavitt, H. (1972) *Managerial Psychology: An Introduction To Individuals, Pairs And Groups In Organizations*, 3rd edn., University Of Chicago Press, Chicago and London.

Likert, R. (1961) *New Patterns of Management*. McGraw-Hill, New York.

Linton, R. (1936) *The Study Of Man*, Appleton-Century, New York.

McClelland, D. C. (1985) *Human Motivation*, Scott, Foresman, Glenview, Ill.

Merton R. K. (1957) *Social Theory And Social Structure*, Free Press, New York.

Milgram, S. (1974) *Obedience And Authority*, Tavistock, London.

Mitchell, T. R., and J. R. Larson, Jr. (1987) *People In Organizations: An Introduction To Organizational Behaviour*, McGraw-Hill, New York.

Parsons, T. (1951) *The Social System*, Free Press, New York.

Peterson, M. F. (1995) 'Role conflict, ambiguity and overload: a 21-nation study', *Academy of Management Journal*, **38** (2), 429–52.

Shaw, M. E. (1981) *Group Dynamics*, 3rd edn., McGraw-Hill, New York.

Staw, B. and E. Swajowski (1975) 'The scarcity-munificence component of organizational environments and the commission of illegal acts', *Administrative Science Quarterly*, **20** (3), 345–54.

Trompenaars, F. (1993) *Riding the Waves of Culture*, Economist Books, London.

CHAPTER 9 Inter-group behaviour

Multiple groups as the unit of analysis

Understanding behaviour within any one group can be a significant aid to the management process. However, most organizations consist of multiple groups each of which interacts with another in order to achieve common organizational tasks. The kinds of behaviours which occur between groups are very different from those which occur within them. They have their own dynamic and their own characteristics which require a different set of management skills to handle them.

Organizations consist of multiple groups each of which is interdependent. This interdependence can take a number of specific forms. It can be *sequential, pooled* or *reciprocal* (Thompson, 1967). Each form of interdependence has implications for the nature of the interaction between the various groups and for the management of this interaction.

Sequential inter-dependence

Describes where one group always initiates action for subsequent groups. For example, in an assembly line, production groups initiate action for other groups such as the paintshop or the trim assembly. The production line is the most pure example of sequential interdependence in organizations. The output of group A becomes the input of group B and so on until the last group is reached. The output of this last group (or set of groups) is the final product of the organization (see Figure 9.1).

Figure 9.1
Sequential interdependence

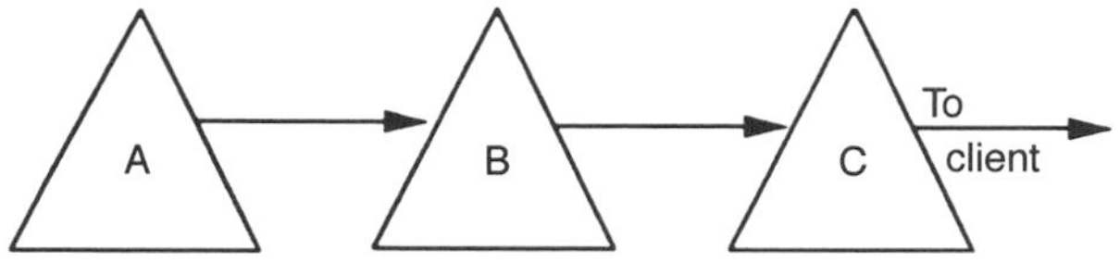

Pooled inter-dependence

Occurs when two or more groups carry out their tasks independently. The output of these groups is then co-ordinated by another group (or set of groups) before final output is produced. In some organizations such as universities, pooled interdependence is commonplace and a relatively enduring feature of organizational life. In other organizations, such as manufacturing firms, pooled interdependence often occurs at specific times in the production cycle or during the development of new products where research, design and piloting can go on without being linked in to the rest of the organization (such as finance and quality control). Figure 9.2 illustrates a simple form of pooled interdependence.

Figure 9.2
Pooled
interdependence

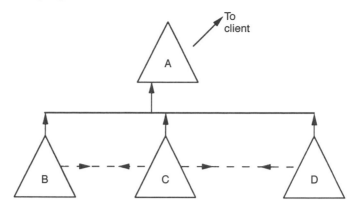

Reciprocal inter-dependence

This is the most highly interlinked relationship between groups. The output of one or more groups is passed to and fro between a number of groups until final output is achieved. Some hospitals work on this principle as well as some firms in the high technology industries. Figure 9.3 depicts the arrangement of reciprocal interdependence.

Figure 9.3
Reciprocal
interdependence

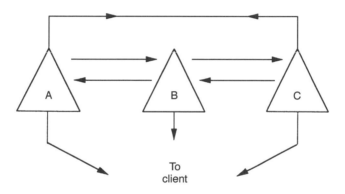

Each of these forms of interlinking between groups has a fundamental impact upon the need for high levels of mutual assistance, information gathering and availability, agreement and compliance between groups, feedback and general co-ordination. The management task is to ensure maximum effectiveness in inter-group co-ordination whatever the nature of their interdependence. This is confounded by a number of factors, the net result of which can make inter-group relations problematic, hostile and unco-operative.

This is not always the case, however. Miller (1976) has noted that certain types of interdependence can effectively act as a self-regulating influence on inter-group activities and promote effective and efficient functioning. For example, high reciprocal interdependence between groups coupled with an inability to distinguish precisely between individual group contribution and a reward system which is equally broad, will tend to unite groups in a common purpose (Katzenbach and Smith, 1992). On the other hand, where groups are required to interact intensively, yet are not bound up in common reward or joint problem-solving activities, the propensity for them to conflict or compete is significantly increased (Dutton and Walton, 1966). Since organizations can never achieve the ideal of total self-regulation between groups, the management task becomes one of handling inter-group competition and conflict. The first step to achieving this, is to understand the nature of conflict and competition. There are a number of identifiable factors and stages through which conflicting groups progress. We examine these in the following section.

Inter-group competition and conflict

Even if it is a largely subconscious activity, a great deal of managerial time will be spent organizing and achieving coherence among different parts of the organization. Even fairly common and seemingly innocuous managerial techniques can backfire and fail because of the severity of inter-group competition. The following example gives an illustration:

> In a large British financial services organization, recovery of debts and poor repayments on outstanding loans was big business. Nearly one in ten loans to individuals resulted in poor repayment. Since the financial services industry is extremely competitive, each organization is both trying to extend the amount of credit it allocates as well as trying to achieve efficient recovery of bad debts. Successful competitive performance comes from securing effective repayments from debtors.
>
> The organization had a number of teams of debt collecting clerks all of whom reported to a manager of the section. At first, all clerks were organized on an individual basis. Each one dealt with a set number of clients who were in arrears with repayments. The level of success in securing repayments began to fall. So the manager of the section divided his clerks into four groups, appointed one supervisor per group and, because he had read his management text books, installed a system of management by objectives (MBO), a common enough system which had worked previously.
>
> Now, groups were assessed on their performance. Every month, the group which had the best performance (measured by debts repaid) received a cash bonus. Initially, debt repayment levels got better. Then, the level slid back to its original point and gradually began to worsen. The problem turned out to be that the manager of the section did not recognize that each of the groups was increasingly in competition with the others and that levels of inter-group conflict were extremely high.
>
> Individual clerks would now work to achieve the cash bonus for their group. They would contact a much greater number of clients than before, trying to secure a repayment. This led to a situation where clerks would contact a client who would secure a repayment for a single month without having much regard to whether that client continued payment. There were high levels of competition between group members to secure clients who would pay up for a single month and poaching of each others' clients became common.
>
> Of course, some groups were better at this than others, and one group consistently won the cash bonus. The other groups became disenchanted and ceased working as hard as they had done previously. The net result was a feeling of extreme hostility between group members (where none had occurred before) coupled with an increase in debt levels to the organization. Clients were only being asked to repay for one month to secure performance figures for the clerks. Subsequent payments were of secondary importance. Given the high number of clients who were in debt, clerks could 'shop around' different individuals to achieve repayment.

Thus, setting up a seemingly effective management system can result in the creation of inter-group competition and conflict which actually reduces performance rather than enhances it (as in the example above). We discuss at what levels conflict becomes dysfunctional later in this chapter. For the present, we try to define conflict before we elaborate on its management.

Attempting a definition is difficult enough. Some common themes are identifiable, however.

1 Conflict exists only insofar as it is perceived by the parties it is deemed to concern. If a person or a group is unaware of the conflict, they generally

agree that no conflict exists. Others in the organization may suggest that there is conflict between two parties who themselves do not perceive this.

2 There must be evidence of overt or covert opposition or blockage to particular stances adopted by various individuals or groups in the organization.

3 There must be two or more parties whose interests or goals appear to be incompatible.

Traditional management approaches to conflict

For many managers, the assumption is that all conflict in their organization is bad. It detracts from the efficient functioning of the organization. Conflict becomes described in terms of *violence, destruction* or *irrationality*. Since conflict is assumed to result in ineffective and inefficient organization, 'good' managers aimed to avoid it altogether. Avoidance of conflict thus becomes the major role of managerial responsibilities. This traditional philosophy, that agreement is good and that conflict is bad, still holds true in many organizations today.

This is hardly surprising if we examine some of the values which are prevalent in our developed societies. From early schooling we have all been encouraged to 'get along with others and to avoid conflict even if you do not like them' and domestic life most likely reinforced this philosophy. In national philosophies, the anti-conflict message is strong. America and Britain are often described as peace-loving nations no matter what their actions might imply, since they buy offensive weapons and act aggressively toward other countries in the name of peace-keeping and defence. Even the language-in-use in the example below shows the discrepancies between groups. Taken from UN and US forces' description of the Gulf War in 1991, they are the 'we' in the following:

We have	They have
Army, Navy and Air Force	A war machine
Reporting guidelines	Censorship
Press briefings	Propaganda
We	*They*
Suppress	Destroy
Eliminate	Kill
Neutralize	Kill
Decapitate	Kill
We launch	*They launch*
First strikes	Sneak missile attacks
Pre-emptively	Without provocation
Our men are	*Their men are*
Boys, lads	Troops, hordes

Source: Wilson (1992)

Much of the management literature which deals with conflict takes a particular orientation to it. Conflict should be resolved. That is the manager's job. Part of the salary is 'combat pay' for attending to all the aggravation the manager faces in the process of conflict resolution. This is particularly true of the literature which sprung up around and developed from the human relations school (see Chapter 2).

The interactionist management approach to conflict

This management approach says that conflict management and conflict resolution are not the same thing. Certain levels of conflict are seen as a good thing in the organization. Managers should encourage the occurrence of some conflict in their organizations. Of course, beyond a certain level, conflict does become destructive or dysfunctional, but up to that point conflict is good for helping stimulate creativity and encourage innovation.

- It keeps the organization on its toes.
- It avoids the organization getting too routinized and its members becoming apathetic to change.
- It results in better decisions since ready-made solutions are not immediately applied unquestioningly to problems. There is the possibility of collecting a greater number and diversity of alternatives.
- It provides a forum for all members of the organization to be self-critical, and to be critical of the organization as a whole.

The main characteristics of the traditional and the interactionist management approaches are summarised in Table 9.1.

Table 9.1
Traditional and interactionist models of conflict

Traditional	Interactionists
Conflict is avoidable	Conflict is inevitable
Conflict is caused by troublemakers, prima donnas and boat rockers	Conflict is determined by structural factors such as the physical shape or the hierarchical design of an organization, the design of a career structure or the nature of a class system
Managerial forms of authority tend to emphasize of the rational elements, e.g. going through the appropriate channels or sticking to the rules	Conflict is seen as integral to the nature of organizational change
Allocation of blame to scapegoats is accepted as inevitable	A particular level of conflicts is optimal, Individuals are not blamed or engaging in conflict

Figure 9.4 shows the relationship between levels of conflict and organizational performance.

Figure 9.4
Organizational performance and conflict

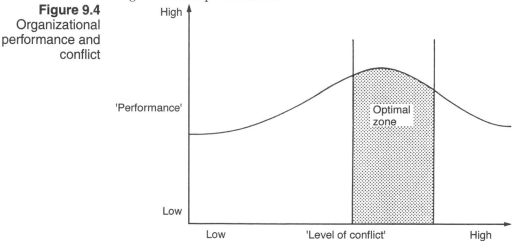

Of course, defining the level at which conflict is optimal is an extremely difficult task, but it is safe to say that most of us would feel distinctly uncomfortable in organizations with very high levels of conflict. Equally, many of us would feel bored and unfulfilled in organizations which had little or no inter-group conflict in them. They would be very bland places indeed. There is, therefore, a large safety margin in between these two extremes.

This feeling of comfort with certain levels of conflict is dependent upon assuming the archetypal 'reasonable person'. It is unlikely, however, that all organizations are staffed with such reasonable people.

Managing inter-group conflict

Most inter-group conflict is a product of organizational structure (Daft, 1995). Managing conflict requires the identification of the underlying and predictable structural causes before attending to particular groups or individuals who are only a part of the structural jigsaw puzzle. We have seen already how various configurations of interdependence can heighten or contain inter-group conflict. The following is a well-known experiment which describes inter-group conflict and shows how the levels of conflict can be managed by paying attention to structural variables rather than inter-personal ones. It also shows how conflict can be managed into becoming co-operation.

The Sherif and Sherif studies of inter-group conflict

A study conducted by the psychologists Muzafar and Carolyn Sherif (1953) in North America consisted of a series of experiments relating to group formation, group conflict and co-operation. They tell us a great deal about conflict and its origins in organizational structure.

The experiment

Summer camps for boys were the setting. This was so that sample conditions could be controlled and reproduced exactly in the future. The groups were informal and comprised boys previously unacquainted prior to the experiment. All the boys came from similar socio-economic backgrounds. They were all healthy, well-adjusted and from white, Protestant, middle-class homes. Experimental situations were kept life-like by choosing activities characteristic of such camps (such as making camp and canoeing) but usually requiring obstacles to be overcome first. Data collection methods were disguised or made a natural part of the setting. Several methods were used at all the stages so that results could be cross-validated.

The experiment was designed to be in three stages of one week each. The stages for the whole experiment comprised:

Stage 1 Group formation
Stage 2 The development of conflict between the groups
Stage 3 The reduction of conflict and the development of co-operation.

Stage 1: Group formation This was characterized by the formation of group norms and status and role relations. Leaders and their assistants emerged. As the groups established themselves, rituals, nicknames, group names and secret symbols were adopted.

Stage 2: Inter-group conflict Now, there were activities where only one group could achieve an outcome at the expense of all the other groups. Games were played such as tug-of-war and baseball. This created animosity between the groups (inter-group conflict). The level of conflict was sufficiently high that a boy who previously nominated another a 'best friend' rating (in another group) now gave him a negative rating. The effect of inter-group conflict was to increase the solidarity, co-operativeness and morale within each group.

Stage 3: Co-operation   At first, events were introduced which required the groups to meet for pleasant contacts such as the sharing in prizes or other benefits. There was no need for the groups to be interdependent or to compete. However, these events heightened conflict rather than reduced it. Further hostilities ensued between the groups.

Activities which required mutual assistance between groups were then introduced. These 'superordinate goals' were extremely appealing to both groups but necessitated their co-operation if they were to achieve their goal. For example, a lorry was to go for food, but it 'broke down'. Everyone was hungry, so the groups had to work together and pool resources to get the lorry started (for example, some rope, some cables, tools, etc). At the end of this week, the groups became increasingly friendly and positive ratings began to develop across group lines. Best friends once again were found frequently between individuals in different groups.

Conclusions to be drawn out of the Sherif study

1 The occurrence of conflict is not solely attributable to the characteristics of individuals. It arises under given structural conditions. The fact that individuals within the groups are 'well-adjusted' and otherwise normal appears not to matter.
2 Co-operative and democratic procedures created within any one group are not transferable directly to inter-group relations.
3 Solidarity within a group is most pronounced when conflict between groups is at its highest.
4 Interaction between rival groups in pleasant circumstances does not itself eliminate conflict.
5 Interaction between groups toward a commonly desired superordinate goal helps to create good relations between groups. This needs to occur more than just once to secure co-operation out of previous conflict. A sense of teamwork is thus created toward a common goal. Katzenbach and Smith (1992) have argued that it is possible to create just one such sense of teamwork in a complex organization of thousands of people. The management task is one of identifying superordinate goals at which the majority of these groups can aim and which they find broadly acceptable (Cyert and March, 1963).

The use of superordinate goals can be promoted by managers as a genuine attempt to achieve co-operation between groups. This will only be a successful strategy if:

1 The conflicting groups share the same goal.
2 Individuals are of equal status.
3 The goal is actually attained.

If not, the likely result is an increase in both conflict and mutual prejudices (for example, stereotyping members of the other group).

The second is that the use of superordinate goals can be an overtly manipulative ploy, aimed at serving the self-interest of the manager rather than solving any inter-group conflict. Machiavelli (1984) in *The Prince* knew this well. He argued that an effective manipulative strategy for handling internal dissent between factions within one nation was to go to war (or appear to do so) with another nation. The once divided country now became united in its hostility toward the supposedly hostile nation. Governmental policies toward the domestic population can be rather less than generous or even unfair, since the population will be willing to endure hardship in the face of external threat and pull together in a national effort. This aspect of handling conflict in organizations is covered in some detail by Kelly (1974), Jay (1967) and Daft (1995).

Another less obvious facet of the Sherif studies is that the 'Hawthorne Effect' has to be borne in mind, as it does in most experiments in managerial science. This effect describes how changes can occur in the experimental situation more because of the novelty of the enterprise and the desire by participants to please or achieve the goals of the researcher, and less because of the variables at play in the experiment, (see Adair, 1984 for an extended discussion of this effect).

Finally, it is too easy to identify the structural underpinnings of inter-group conflict and argue that a solution to any such inter-group problem is to change the structure of the organization. Most organizations have structural arrangements that are unlikely to be changed radically by any single or any group of managers. The re-structuring of a complex organization is usually a ponderous and a painful process and many managers would rather settle for handling dysfunctional conflict by 'finger-in-the-dyke' management rather than undergo the stresses and strains of structural change (see Miller and Friesen, 1984).

Miller and Friesen (1984) show that many firms display characteristics of makeshift changes to their structures, attending to the detail of the present day but neglecting to think more broadly about the nature of smooth, integrated inter-group relations. Many managers seemed to be willing to let bureaucracy take the blame for inter-group disharmonies. The firm had a structure, the structure had its rules and if groups disagreed with one another, the solution was to consult the rules or to create new ones to accommodate the present conflict. In an assessment of successful organizational performance, Miller and Friesen (1984) empirically supported the adoption of proactive and anticipatory strategies by managers. That is, they did not try and tackle problems such as dysfunctional levels of conflict between groups in a piecemeal fashion, but tried to avoid its occurrence in the first place by attention to the structural rather than personal causes of conflict in organizations.

Implementing strategies to handle inter-group conflict

In order to implement changes to reduce inter-group conflict when it occurs, first we have to identify the nature of the conflict. For example, it might fall into one or more of the following categories:

1 *Hierarchical conflict* For example, senior management versus middle management.
2 *Functional conflict* For example, work study versus personnel, or sales versus production.
3 *Professional versus functional conflict* For example, accountants versus production, or more complex conflicts for example between management, workforce and shop stewards.

4 *Management versus the shop floor* For example, management versus the
   workforce directly.
5 *Union versus union* For example, craft unions versus a general workers'
   union, or more general multiple union conflict.
6 *Management versus union* For example, management versus one or more
   trades' unions

Having established the locus of the conflict, it is then necessary to examine
the nature of the conflict. There are three broad types. Any inter-group conflict
can be one of these types. Over time, the nature of the conflict can change
from one to the other.

1 *A fight* The aim is to injure or destroy, subdue or drive away the
   perceived source of conflict by the group. One group wants to get rid of
   the other group/s permanently.
2 *A game* The source of conflict is accepted as being integral to the
   situation. Other conflicting groups are not exact mirror images of one
   another, fighting for scarce resources in an irreconcilable fashion.
   Compromise can be reached, although this will mean some groups
   appear to benefit more than others. The situation can be structured over
   time so that different groups benefit over a set time frame.
3 *A debate* The aim of all groups is to convince one another of their logic.
   This is not usually detrimental to organizational functioning since the
   aim is neither to destroy other groups nor to score points from them.

The nature of the conflict will determine to some extent the managerial
strategy for its resolution into functional levels. A debate, for example, will
possibly not need resolution at all. It probably represents around the ideal
level of conflict for securing good performance from groups. A game is
more likely to require managerial intervention. An assessment of the
structural context and the range of mutually acceptable compromise
positions by the groups would likely be a productive way of handling this
kind of conflict. A fight, on the other hand, needs instant attention
otherwise irreparable damage may be done both to the organization in
terms of loss of production, profits and personnel and in terms of
psychological damage inflicted upon group members. This can be one of the
prime causes of stress encountered by individuals in organizations (Albrecht,
1979; French, Caplan and Harrison, 1982).

Adapted from much of the literature on industrial relations, many current
managerial strategies toward handling inter-group conflict rely on one or
more of the following:

1 negotiation
2 mediation
3 arbitration

Negotiation   Disputing parties come together to determine the terms of the exchange
which will be acceptable to both parties. Essentially, negotiation is about the
quid pro quo which is acceptable to all parties. Negotiation tests the power
balance in an organization. It is conducted on a face-to-face basis and the
terms of the dispute are hammered out person to person.

Mediation   A third party is involved in trying to resolve the conflict between two
parties. This is a useful strategy to employ when face-to-face contact

(negotiation) has failed. Usually negotiation fails because in the process of testing the power balance, the parties become polarized into positions which preclude further face-to-face contact. There is no common ground whatsoever.

The mediator is usually able to keep contact between the factions and can effect neutral communication between them. But even this can go wrong or can be ineffective at resolving disputes. In this case, arbitration may be the next step.

Arbitration The dispute goes to a third party, but in this case, the third party has the power to formulate and implement a settlement which is binding on both parties. Arbitration can be compulsory by law. This is the kind of arbitration which trades unions often use when negotiations break down using other means of conflict resolution. Other kinds of arbitration are not legally necessary, but can be effected in organizations by voluntary agreement.

None of the above strategies will preclude the outbreak of further inter-group conflicts since the underlying structural causes are not changed. They have been shown to be successful, however, in a number of disputes so their efficacy is not to be dismissed lightly. In many cases, sufficient degrees of necessary structural change are either not possible or are too time-consuming, so other strategies have to be pursued. Thomas (1977) has outlined five possible strategies for handling conflict which build upon the rather stark negotiation, mediation and arbitration framework. These are shown in Table 9.2.

Table 9.2
Five conflict
management
strategies

Strategy	Useful when
Competition	• Other groups take advantage of non-competitive behaviour • Very quick decisions need to be made • The organization's survival is at stake
Collaboration	• The goal is to learn more information/skills • Commitment and consensus are needed above all else • Feelings and emotions need exploring
Avoidance	• An immediate decision is not needed • More information is required • There is no chance of winning in a competition • People are angry and need to cool down before they can talk and think rationally again
Accommodation	• Losses need minimizing • You discover you were wrong • The impact on other groups is more important than on your own • Credit is needed for future situations
Compromise	• The issue needs breaking down into manageable pieces • A temporary settlement is needed • Collaboration and/or competition do not work • When stalemate is achieved between groups of equal power

Source: adapted from Thomas (1977:487).

Summary

This chapter has highlighted the importance of understanding the behaviours which occur between groups in organizations. Since most complex firms cannot achieve the provision of goods or services without functional differentiation, certain interdependencies are inevitably created between groups. The nature of these interdependencies can vary. They can be sequential, pooled or reciprocally related, although many inter-group relations are complex mixtures of all three types. These interdependencies are the source of inter-group conflict, competition and co-operation.

Conflict between groups is usually much less attributable to the personalities who inhabit the group and much more related to the ways in which multiple groups are structured together. The nature of their interdependencies will give a clue to the likely levels of conflict between groups.

For most managers, effecting radical changes in the structure of their organizations is not a feasible proposition although fine-tuning within the limits of feasibility can reduce inter-group conflict markedly. Other strategies adopted rely on correctly identifying the source of the conflict, its nature and its intensity. With this information, resolution of intense conflicts can occur. Among these are the creation of superordinate goals to unite groups, the reduction of interdependence (where feasible), expanding the resource base (to avoid fighting for slices of a small cake), resorting to systems of problem-solving such as arbitration and mediation (Robbins, 1983).

All organizations seem to need a certain level of conflict within them to spur on performance and to provide the impetus for change and innovation. Without this driving force, most organizations would become stifled by becoming over-institutionalized and resistant to any form of change. Part of the management process is therefore to keep the balance between effective and ineffective levels of conflict. This is all the more difficult since there are no fixed guidelines to gauge the 'level' of conflict which is appropriate. Other factors such as the incidence of stress, feelings of discomfort, incidence of complaints and stereotyping behaviours have to serve as guides in this respect.

It is equally likely that a manager will be in a position where the creation rather than the reduction of inter-group conflict and competition might be required. Complacency and rigorous adherence to the *status quo* are typical contexts in which this might be necessary.

References

Adair, J. (1984) 'The Hawthorne Effect: a reconsideration of the methodological artifact', *Journal Of Applied Psychology*, **69**, 334–45.

Albrecht, K. (1979) *Stress and the Manager*, Prentice-Hall, Englewood Cliffs, New Jersey.

Cyert, R. and J. G. March (1963) *A Behavioural Theory of the Firm*, Prentice-Hall, Englewood Cliffs, New Jersey.

Daft, R. L. (1995) *Organization Theory and Design*, 5th edn., West, St. Paul Minn.

Dutton, J. M. and R. E. Walton (1966) 'Interdepartmental conflict and co-operation: two contrasting studies', *Human Organization*, **25**, 207–20.

French, J. R. P., R. D. Caplan, and R. V. Harrison (1982) *The Mechanism Of Job Stress And Strain*, Wiley, London.

Jay, A. (1967) *Management And Machiavelli*, Holt, New York.

Katzenbach, J. R. and D. K. Smith (1992) *The Wisdom of Teams: Creating the High-Performance Organization*, Harvard Business School Press, Harvard.

Kelly, J. (1974) *Organizational Behaviour*, Irwin, Illinios.

Machiavelli (1984) *The Prince*, New York: Bantam Classics.

Miller, D. and P. H. Friesen (1984) *Organizations: A Quantum View*, Prentice-Hall, Englewood Cliffs, New Jersey.

Miller, E. J. (ed.), (1976) *Task And Organization*, Wiley, New York.

Robbins, S. P. (1983) *Organization Theory: The Structure and Design of Organizations*, Prentice-Hall, Englewood Cliffs, New Jersey.

Sherif, M. and C. W. Sherif (1953) *Groups in Harmony and Tension*, Harper & Bros., New York.

Thomas, K. W. (1977) 'Toward multidimensional values in teaching: the example of conflict behaviours', *Academy Of Management Review*, **20** (2), 472–91.

Thompson, J. D. (1967) *Organizations In Action*, McGraw-Hill, New York.

Wilson, D. C. (1992) *A Strategy of Change: Concepts and Controversies in the Management of Change*, Routledge, London.

CHAPTER 10 Decision-making

Introduction

If any single task is central to the management function, decision-making would be the main activity of virtually all managers in all organizations. It is arguably this process which distinguishes managerial activity from that of other functional responsibilities and tasks in the organization.

At first sight, decision-making appears deceptively simple. To decide means to make up your mind by choosing among alternative courses of action. Such actions do not necessarily have to be concrete or tangible. One can decide to become a better or more educated and informed person. One can decide to eat a healthier diet sometime in the future.

In business organizations, managers do make decisions about tangible organizational problems. They make decisions about new products or new services. Managers decide upon the size and scope of existing operations and can choose to add to or subtract from these as conditions are deemed to suggest. Some of these decisions are taken regularly in organizations by individual managers. Other decision topics are taken by groups of them. Over time, organizations develop accustomed and predictable ways of making these decisions. This routinization of decision-making allows for shorthand ways of making decisions since many of the arguments and rationalizations can be encoded in very precise and predictable form. This is called 'programmed' decision-making (Simon, 1960).

Programming is evident, for example, in standard operating procedures or in the computerization of regularly occurring decisions or situations. Beyond these parameters or guidelines, however, there lies an almost infinite scope for how decisions are to be made. When choosing among alternatives is not guided by precedent or by standard procedure, the focus of managerial activity is centred upon managing the decision-making process and achieving a set of outcomes on which action can be taken.

One popular stereotype of the manager is that of creative, energetic individual decision-maker. While this may be true of some senior executives or the owners of small family businesses, most managers will find themselves most of the time involved with other managers discussing a wide range of decision topics. The role each individual manager plays in these group decisions will vary from topic to topic. Sometimes, the manager will be representing the collective feeling or viewpoint of his or her department. At other times, the manager will be called into a group (or may form one) because of specialist knowledge or because what is to be decided will have implications for most areas of the organization. In either case, the topics under discussion are usually beyond the scope of any one individual in the organization. A single manager would lack sufficient information, technical skill, or both, to make the decision alone.

We have already seen in Chapters 8 and 9 that groups of individuals can be characterized by a number of aspects which are specific to group rather than individual processes. Decision-making in groups is no exception. Not only do the overall group process characteristics arise, but also the act of trying to make a decision can result in very specific kinds of behaviours from group members. So much is this a recognized part of organizational life that a number of aphorisms have arisen around the topic of committees, working parties, boards of directors and other decision-making groups:

- 'A camel is a racehorse designed by a committee'.
- 'The best committee is a five-people group where four of them are absent'.
- 'A committee is a collection of the unfit appointed by the unwilling to perform the unnecessary'.

These humorous, but often all too accurate descriptions of decision processes in groups, find their grains of truth in what can happen in group decisions if not actively recognized and managed. They describe what happens when the decision process deviates for whatever reason from the rational or theoretically ideal process. This ideal process is called 'synoptic' by Lindblom (1959). It can be modelled thus:

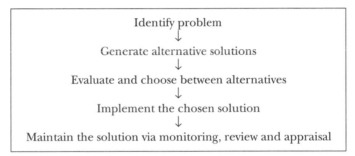

Identify problem
↓
Generate alternative solutions
↓
Evaluate and choose between alternatives
↓
Implement the chosen solution
↓
Maintain the solution via monitoring, review and appraisal

Humans make decisions trying to be rational but they rarely succeed in practice. They are *intended* to be rational. This is why Herbert Simon has made the distinction between economic man and administrative man. Economic man tries to maximize—that is, selects the best possible course open to him. Administrative man tries to achieve outcomes which are satisfactory and sufficient. Combining these two words together gives us the portmanteau word—*satisficing*—which is how Cyert and March (1963) describe the bulk of organizational decision-making activity.

Man cannot, or will not, spend time looking for optimal alternatives. Man is happy with and can only deal with gross simplifications and only a few limited variables at any one time. In business organizations, this means going for adequate rather than optimal market share—or going for sufficient rather than optimal profit.

Since humans are notoriously inefficient decision-makers in the above ways, this is why it makes sense to have at least some decisions in organizations programmed by standard procedures so that people are not making all decisions from scratch each time. People can and do make new or novel decisions, of course, but they are usually very bad at it when compared to the theoretically rational process.

The rational model appears accurate and robust, especially if we add in feedback loops to it at all the various stages in the process which is what occurs in computer modelling of decision processes. The problem is that the model assumes two things:

1 perfect knowledge
2 perfect rationality

Perfect knowledge implies that any one person or group of people making a decision have all the information available to them that they need and exactly when they want it. Perfect rationality means that once in possession of the information, the individual or the group will act in sequence, without prejudice, emotion, or without any of the characteristics of being 'human'. Of course, these are unrealistic expectations. In practice, a number of things can contribute to decisions in groups being rather less than rational both in terms of the process (what happens in the interactions between the group members) and the outcome (what the group eventually decides). We have highlighted three major areas, conformity, culture and power.

Conformity

Because groups tend to foster conformity behaviour (see Asch, 1955; Milgram, 1974; Leavitt, 1972), they equally put this pressure upon participants in decision-making. While it might appear useful to have a group comprising the same individuals meeting regularly on a number of topics (because they represent the whole organization, they free up time for others, they are considered 'good' judges and are fair-minded) the reverse is often true. The outcomes and processes of this group are likely to be defective in the following respects:

- Information is not actively sought beyond that which is to hand, or information is only partial or biased.
- Only a handful of alternatives are considered.
- Those alternatives which are considered are then only evaluated partially and some are not really evaluated at all.
- There is a strong tendency among the group members to keep things as they are and not to seek or recommend change.
- Once an outcome is reached, there is little or no consideration of planning for any other future contingencies which might occur.

Source: adapted from Janis and Mann (1977).

The appearance of this group from the outside is one of unanimity and it is this which often tempts other managers to leave the group alone by equating the group's ability to achieve consensus with its apparent effectiveness. This conformity is called 'groupthink' by Janis (1972). He describes groupthink as:

> a deterioration of mental efficiency, reality testing and moral judgement that is the result of in-group pressures.

Janis examined some very famous cases of decision-making by groups in world history. He looked at the decision to invade Cuba (Bay of Pigs), the attack on Pearl Harbor and the escalation of the Vietnam war. He concluded that all these decisions or events were characterized by the propensity of the group just to drift along. Such drift builds in false consensus in the group. Individuals who might feel that they disagree with the group's decision rarely voice that opinion inside the group.

Symptoms of groupthink

1 The group feels invulnerable. There is excessive optimism and risk-taking.
2 Warnings that things might be going awry are discounted by the group members in the name of rationality.
3 There is an unquestioned belief in the group's morality. The group will ignore questionable stances on moral or ethical issues.

4   Those who dare to oppose the group are called evil, weak, or stupid.
5   There is direct pressure on anyone who opposes the prevailing mood of
    the group.
6   Individuals in the group self-censor if they feel that they are deviating
    from group norms.
7   There is an illusion of unanimity. Silence is interpreted as consent.
8   There are often self-appointed people in the group who protect it from
    adverse information. These people are referred to as 'mindguards'.

Janis' work has important implications. All of the above can commonly occur
in committees or board meetings. Organizations can very quickly become
helpless, with managerial decisions drifting towards goals which are either
inappropriate or are left unquestioned. Once decline has set in through
groupthink, its reversal is tremendously difficult.

Risky shift decisions

Another group effect upon decision process is risky shift. This is the
tendency for individuals to accept higher levels of risk when taking decisions
in groups. Stoner (1968) found that there was a significant tendency for
groups to go for relatively risky but high pay-off decisions, while individuals
favour relatively safe decisions with moderate pay-offs. Thus, groups do not
represent the 'average' risk of their constituent individuals. One explanation
of risky shift is the diffusion of responsibility. You can blame it on the group
if things go wrong. Other explanations focus on the conformity effect of
group processes (like groupthink). If an individual favours moderate risk,
the group will take this as a base line and shift toward greater risks. The
reverse trend toward safe decisions can also occur.

Culture

There can also be conformity between group decision-making and overall
organizational culture. Meyer and Rowan (1977) and Mitchell, Rediker and
Beach (1986) show how images, values and ideas that are held *corporately* are
used as guidelines for decision-making. Organizations in which bold,
adventurous risk-taking is predominant will inevitably hold these cultural
attributes against any group decision outcome as a measure of its worth.
Decisions will be seen as good or as acceptable to the extent that they fit with
the prevailing cultural values of the organization.

Wilson *et al.*, (1986) also demonstrate that decision-making is 'bounded'
by what is considered organizationally legitimate or acceptable. This is
different to the fit of culture and decision criteria because it refers to the
rules and structures of organizations which are set up before
decision-making begins. As long as decision processes are in line with what is
prescribed in the organization, then decisions will be fairly trouble-free.
Even the most important, strategic decisions will be made fairly routinely.
This phenomenon has been described at length by Lukes (1974) and is
derived from earlier work by Schattsneider (1960) which refers to this
process as the 'mobilization of bias'.

Of course, decisions made by groups which conform to the bias of
organization may be effective and contribute to organizational success. This
in turn reinforces the rules and procedures by which decisions are made. On
the other hand, decisions may not yield such good results, but it is the
decision-makers themselves who are targeted as the source of failure and
rarely the overall system. Decision-making is likely to go on in the same old

way and thus contribute to an ever-increasing spiral of decline (Whetten, 1980).

Power

We shall deal with power as a separate topic in Chapter 11 of this book. Here, we shall just highlight some aspects of power as it relates to group decision-making.

Groups in organizations generally comprise individuals who come from various parts of the firm. They are likely to be from finance, from production, from sales and/or marketing and in a group they are all expected to agree on common organizational policy which should bring them equal benefits. Of course, this is not what happens in practice.

Each individual brings to the group his or her own perspective on how the problem should be solved. Each person views the organization they are in not as a global overall being, but from a very 'local' view which is essentially coloured by the particular department they are in. Sales managers will tend to see all organizational problems and opportunities from a sales point of view and production managers likewise from a production point of view. One will be interested in the sales volume aspects of any decision, while the other will focus on efficient and trouble-free inventory processing.

'Local rationalities' is the term given by Cyert and March (1963) for these often conflicting perspectives. Taken to an extreme, these conflicts can be disruptive and can lead eventually to organizational failure. Usually, it does not reach this level. This is because humans work on the principle of *satisficing*. We will accept what is satisfactory rather than go full out for exactly what we want. In this way, a level of compromise can be achieved between parties rather than total conflict. Achieving this compromise, however, can involve managers in the most intense political activity where achieving success in the political battles for power can seem more important than achieving an acceptable decision outcome (see Pettigrew, 1973; Wilson, 1982 for cases which vividly describe such processes).

Groups of managers also rarely try and solve all the pressing decision issues at once. This would be impossible given its complexity and the level of conflict it would generate. What happens in practice is that groups commit themselves to solving problems in sequence. First they try to satisfy market demand and then they try to keep production and stock levels smooth, for example.

Managers will also try to avoid making decisions with very long-term implications. A decision group would be unable to handle the complexity involved. Decision-making thus becomes an activity to solve pressing problems and not to discuss long-range strategies. This is called 'uncertainty avoidance' (Cyert and March, 1963).

Information search is generally only carried out in the face of a problem. It does not occur all the time. Search for information is motivated—it rarely occurs naturally. As we already know, search is also never optimal, since decision-makers satisfice. The search is also for recipes or solutions which have worked previously and which now look appropriate to the present problem.

The implications are that organizations will develop slowly and in piecemeal rather than radical steps since their decision-makers will tend to act reactively to demands and will seek solutions to their current problems by seeing what the group or the organization did in the past. Four major theories of decision process describe this. These are:

1 *Incrementalism,* or the science of muddling through (Lindblom, 1959 and Braybrooke and Lindblom, 1963).
2 *Garbage-can theory,* (Cohen *et al.,* 1972 and March and Olsen, 1976).
3 *Process typologies,* (Mintzberg *et al.,* 1976; Hickson *et al.,* 1986).
4 *Patterns of implementation* (Dean and Sharfman, 1996; Miller, 1997; Wilson *et al.,* 1996; Hickson *et al.,* 1997).

Incrementalism

According to Lindblom (1959) this is the way most decisions are handled in organizations most of the time. The history of actions in the past dominate current and future decisions. Only a limited number of alternatives are considered and decision outcomes are nearly always piecemeal steps forward from current practice. Lustick (1980) notes that even when problems arise which are so large that they cannot be tackled piecemeal, managers still attempt to muddle through by taking bits at a time and by relying on history for guidance and inspiration.

In a study of nine American firms, Quinn (1980) reinforced the finding that incrementalism was a dominant mode of process. He also suggested that perhaps incrementalism was a logical way forward for decision-makers and organizations, arguing that it was a useful recipe for achieving progressive change. The other side of incrementalism is that both managers and organizations will become locked in to particular frames of reference which are inherently conservative. Decisions will always be made, some even appearing quite efficient processes, but it may also be that the wrong set of decisions are being made and the organization is in danger of sliding incrementally out of business.

Garbage-can theory

First proposed by Cohen *et al.,* (1972), this theory argued that the linear, rational model of decision-making was both unrealistic and useless to practising managers. What happened instead, they argued, was that organizations were really collections of solutions. Solutions represent an individual's or, more likely, a group's view of what ought to be done in a given set of circumstances. These solutions were a product of organizational culture and the outcomes of previous decision processes. As soon as a fresh problem faced decision-makers, one of these preexisting solutions was attached to it. Organizations are thus:

> a collection of choices looking for problems . . . solutions looking for issues to which they might be the answer, and decision-makers looking for work. (Cohen *et al.,* 1972: 2).

The term garbage-can (or dustbin, to Anglicize the terminology) is a colourfully chosen symbol which describes the decision-making forum (for example, a committee) as a rubbish bin. Anything gets thrown in and any number of people can use the same or multiple rubbish bins. Trying to sort out the rubbish into a coherent whole is useless since its contents are initially unrelated anyway. The only way decisions are made, therefore, is by individuals or groups trying to get their preferred solution implemented. The key factor here is that chosen solutions are not necessarily logically connected to the current decision topic. They are merely stimulated by its occurrence.

March and Olsen (1976) have taken this analogy a stage further by suggesting that choices, ready-made solutions, the occurrence of problems, what information is wanted and who should make the decision are almost totally unconnected! That is, organizations are places in which groups and individuals have multiple and conflicting interests and goals. These are not pieced together in any 'rational' way. It may be, for example, that someone's view is proposed, accepted and implemented even if this is unrelated to prior discussions or information.

The picture is one of an organization which appears not to know what it is doing, for it is impossible to uncover any single strand of logic to decision processes. There are multiple garbage-cans into which multiple topics for decision are placed. There is, however, no apparent logic to who gets involved, who proposes solutions and which solution is eventually chosen. This situation is termed 'organizational anarchy' by March and Olsen (1976).

Process typologies

It is unlikely that 'organized anarchy' occurs in all organizations. Two large-scale empirical studies of decision-making suggest that only a handful of organizations might be like this and an even smaller handful of topics. In a study of 25 decision topics, Mintzberg *et al.*, (1976) found that quasi-linear processes were the norm in Canadian organizations. They were characterized by many interruptions (lack of information or political blocking) and many recycles, especially from phases of the process where alternatives were being considered and the nature of the problem came in for some redefinition. So, while processes are complicated, there does appear to be an attempt by decision-makers at achieving some linear sequences.

In the largest study of strategic decision-making so far, Hickson *et al.*, (1986) examined 150 cases of decision process in 30 UK organizations. Details of this study can be found later in this chapter and in Reading 7 by Professor David Hickson. It is sufficient to record here that all the decision processes could be described as characteristically, sporadic, fluid and constricted. Each process type is co-related to two factors, the level of Complexity facing decision-makers through a topic and the level of Political activity each arouses (see Figure 10.1).

Managing decision-making processes

The study of decision-making requires a detailed analysis on many levels, ranging from organizational to individual. Managing the process, therefore, is complex but not impossible. Empirical studies have demonstrated that there do seem to be patterns of process which are mediated by group and organizational factors as well as by the topic under scrutiny (for example, a reorganization topic or a new product decision).

Here, we differentiate between managing the group of individuals making the decision, and managing the more abstract processes of decisions at the organizational level.

Managing groups

Although groups do generally outperform individuals in decision-making (they are consistently less creative, however, see Van de Ven and Delbecq, 1974), the first question to answer is 'Do we need to resolve this problem by using a group, or would an individual be more effective?'

Research by Vroom and Yetton (1973) indicates that groups have clear advantages over individual decision-makers according to situation, time and leadership. When information is scarce, deadlines are medium-term, the nature of the problem is unclear and many individuals need to accept the

Figure 10.1
Three
decision-making
process types:
constricted, sporadic
and fluid

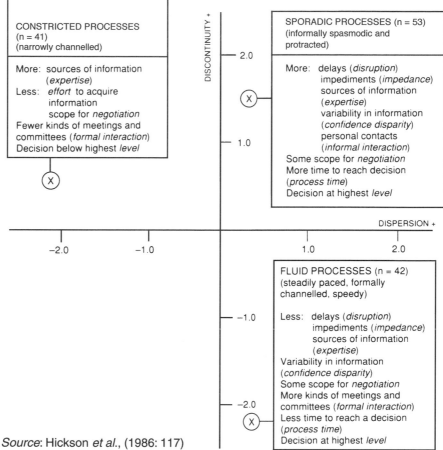

CONSTRICTED PROCESSES
(n = 41)
(narrowly channelled)

More: sources of information
     (*expertise*)
Less: *effort* to acquire
     information
     scope for *negotiation*
Fewer kinds of meetings and
committees (*formal interaction*)
Decision below highest *level*

SPORADIC PROCESSES (n = 53)
(informally spasmodic and
protracted)

More: delays (*disruption*)
     impediments (*impedance*)
     sources of information
     (*expertise*)
     variability in information
     (*confidence disparity*)
     personal contacts
     (*informal interaction*)
Some scope for *negotiation*
More time to reach decision
(*process time*)
Decision at highest *level*

DISCONTINUITY +

2.0

1.0

DISPERSION +

−2.0   −1.0   1.0   2.0

FLUID PROCESSES (n = 42)
(steadily paced, formally
channelled, speedy)

Less: delays (*disruption*)
     impediments (*impedance*)
     sources of information
     (*expertise*)
Variability in information
(*confidence disparity*)
Some scope for *negotiation*
More kinds of meetings and
committees (*formal interaction*)
Less time to reach a decision
(*process time*)
Decision at highest *level*

−1.0

−2.0

Source: Hickson *et al.*, (1986: 117)

decision outcome, groups are more effective and offer more advantages than
individuals. If the group also shares its leader's preferred outcomes, then the
group will be all the more effective.

Making groups work once they are together is another matter. There have
been a number of techniques introduced which attempt to do this, although
all have had limited success.

Brainstorming   Developed as far back as 1939 (see Osborn, 1963), this is still the most
prevalent use of groups by managers who are looking for a creative solution
or new ideas. Members of the group suggest ideas or solutions to the topic or
problem which immediately come to mind. They can be as innovative,
seemingly 'silly' or unrelated as people want. The aim of brainstorming is
thus to break through conventional thinking and, through creativity, chance
or serendipity, come up with a comparatively superior solution.
Unfortunately, the bulk of empirical research does not support claims of
superior creative performance from brainstorming groups. Individual
decision-makers are better (see Van de Ven and Delbecq, 1974).

Delphi   Introduced in the 1970s by the Rand Corporation, this method avoids
technique   face-to-face contact, but uses multiple ideas and inputs from individuals.

Anonymous suggestions are centrally recorded, members are sent each others' ideas and subsequently give their feedback. A centrally placed manager collects and recirculates written notes and ideas. These steps recycle until consensus is reached. The idea is to try and obtain all the benefits of a group decision (multiple ideas, suggestions, more expertise, and greater amounts of information) without also having the disadvantages of group processes (such as groupthink and inter-personal conflict). This technique is time-consuming and can feel artificial or forced to managers, but is more effective than brainstorming (Jewell and Reitz, 1981). It is not yet known to what extent the technique is more or less effective than using conventional face-to-face group decision-making. The nominal group technique is similar, except that individuals rank order the ideas of others in the 'group'. The decision is then made on the basis of the highest ranking idea.

Quality circles

Originally developed in North America and often mistakenly attributed to the Japanese, quality circles are groups of employees who meet together on company time (about a half day each month) to generate solutions to problems they face in the organization. They are designed to enable people to talk over problems they face in the organization (such as poor quality of some manufactured goods, or suggestions for improving production processing) and to discuss day-to-day difficulties which crop up from time to time. Originally designed to improve the quality of manufactured products, they are now extensively used to achieve participative decision-making throughout the entire firm. Results are mixed. Many quality circles end up being characterized by plenty of talk but little action on their ideas which are not taken up by others in the firm (see Lawler and Moreman, 1985).

Decision conferencing

Developed in the 1980s, decision conferencing originated first as an aid to making high technology decisions. It is a two-or three-day decision-making session in which 'owners' of a problem or set of problems participate. Different viewpoints of the participants are combined into a computer model which is generated on the spot by the group. The model then allows experimentation of the 'What if?' kind, to test the consequences of preferred courses of action.

Decision conferencing requires three specialist staff. A facilitator looks after the group processes that occur; an analyst looks after the computer modelling; and a recorder uses a projected word processor to highlight to the group the words it is using and to determine the central issues.

This technique can, of course, be used for all types of decision topic although it is obviously resource intensive. It is designed to handle decisions which are complex, over which there are different points of view already known and where the objective is to reach consensus. The group has support from other staff who feed in information. The decision process is deliberately phased (identify the problem, generate data, analyse data and discuss solution toward consensus) so that group members are clear where they are in the decision process (Rowe, Boulgarides and McGrath, 1984).

Overcoming groupthink

Specific techniques which have been developed to overcome groupthink are also worth mentioning since their efficacy extends into the central core of organizational life. As Furtado (1988: 43) states '. . . clearly defining a vision, getting the organization behind it, encouraging risk-taking and participative involvement of all the workforce are not incompatible with the basic management skills . . .' These are the very aims of earlier attempts by researchers to overcome the phenomenon of groupthink.

The manager must be sensitive to the various roles that can be played in any group decision. In any group, there are identifiable positions which individuals adopt during the decision-making process. For a 'balanced group' to allow full discussion and avoid some of the pitfalls of groupthink, all the following roles should be represented (Belbin, 1981):

1 *Chairman* The co-ordinator
2 *Team leader* the shaper: gives the process direction
3 *Innovator* creative thinker
4 *Monitor* the critical thinker
5 *Company worker* getting the task done for the firm
6 *Team worker* manages the inter-personal interaction in the group
7 *The Completer* keeps the team on its toes by always making reference to the end goal of the decision
8 *Resource investigator* keeps the team in touch with others in the organization

Over the years, Belbin has added various other roles, but the above gives the basic set of eight roles that underpin Belbin's approach. Individuals tend to adopt one or maybe two of these roles quite consistently. All these roles are necessary, so a well-balanced group will contain all roles. Note that this might mean individuals adopting more than two roles in a very small group.

Having identified the various roles at play in group decision-making, the manager can also take further steps to achieve commitment from members of decision-making groups. They are:

1 The leader encourages each member to be a critical evaluator.
2 The leader and the key members should be impartial in the early stages of the decision.
3 The same problem is assigned to outside groups who input their results.
4 Before a consensus is reached, each member tests proposals on subordinates and reports the results.
5 Outside members are invited in to challenge the views of key group members.
6 At every meeting, someone is assigned the role of devil's advocate.
7 Big groups are split into sub-groups to get more involvement and address any differences in the big group.
8 Explore and anticipate the actions of any rival groups.
9 After reaching consensus, hold a follow-up meeting to air any residual doubts or second thoughts.

Managing group decisions: summary

1 Look at the composition of the group. Who is in it and what roles do they take?
2 What is the nature of the problem to be solved?
3 What kind of decision quality do we want? An interim incremental step, or a radical shift decision?
4 Decision content and process must be examined together.

Placing the group in the context of the organization

Creating efficient and participative workgroups is a central part of the manager's task. Equally central is to recognize that all decisions by such groups are made in the wider context of the organization. As Hickson *et al.*, (1986) show, there appear to be three major kinds of process through which decisions will travel (sporadic, fluid and constricted), irrespective of organization type (public or private ownership, service or manufacturing firm), see Reading 7 by David Hickson.

Decisions also appear to be deliberate managerial strategies rather than the more chaotic model of decision anarchy proposed by Cohen *et al.*, (1972). Deliberation, however, does not always mean a smooth, rational process. We summarize in Table 10.1 the major aspects of the Hickson *et al.*, (1986) study.

Table 10.1
Major features of decision-making in organizations. The Bradford Studies

Type of process duration (Months)	Examples of typical decision topics	Mean
Sporadic	New products	22 months
	Location of headquarters or of plant	13 months
Fluid	Sources of inputs	6 months
	Major share issues	6 months
	Some reorganizations	13 months
	Some technology issues	20 months
Constricted	Budget decisions	10 months
	Some personnel issues	11 months
	Some domain issues	10 months
	Some service provision decisions	12 months

Source: adapted from Hickson *et al.*, (1986).

The bulk of decision processes take between 4 and 24 months to process through an organization. The sample mean for 150 cases was 12.4 months. Of course, there were some outliers. One decision took four years to get to the authorization stage, while another took only 2 months, which occurred in a public administration organization belying the stereotype that public bureaucracies are necessarily slower than their commercial counterparts.

Neither do committees slow down decision processes. Again this is counter-intuitive, but strongly supported by empirical evidence from all 150 cases of the Bradford Study. They take more individual time of the group members, but overall decisions taken through the committee or group route take no longer than those which are taken individually by managers. This highlights the point that it all depends which perspective you take when looking at decision-making.

If you were one of the managers in the decisions which used committees, you would say that they were time-consuming, lengthy processes which probably took up a lot of your valuable time when you could be more productive. Yet if you were to take an organizational perspective, those decisions take no longer in the long run, so by concentrating your management effort and channelling it into committees you were possibly saving yourself time on the same issue at subsequent stages. This may be especially true of implementation, which is covered in the next section.

Patterns of implementation

A great deal of work has been carried out on the processes of decision-making. Surprisingly little empirical research has been carried out into what the relationships might be (if any) between decision processes and ultimate outcomes or relative performance. Do process characteristics matter for a relatively successful outcome? Are there any relationships between process and outcomes of decisions? These are obvious questions to ask and difficult ones to answer.

First, the distinction between decision-making processes and implementation is contested by some researchers, arguing that the two may be interwoven over time rather than strictly sequential. Recent data indicate, however, that managers make an analytical distinction between process and implementation and there is a 'start' point of the process of implementation (Miller, 1997).

Second, establishing links between implementation and decision performance is not easy and the research described here is at the decision specific level of analysis. This is for a number of reasons. As Dean and Sharfman (1996) note, there are problems in establishing causal relationships in the light of the many exogenous factors influencing firm performance overall. Focusing on the decision level of analysis may permit a tighter link between process and outcomes (Dean and Sharfman, 1996: 371). In addition, the number of 'critical success factors', (Varadarajan and Ramanujam, 1990), as well as factors associated with failure (Hall, 1994; Valentin, 1994; Miller, 1994; Wilson *et al.*, 1996) is an ever-growing list of often disparate variables which currently defy synthesis.

At this decision level of analysis, Hickson *et al.*, (1997) identify two major characteristics of implementation which seem to be related to the success (or not) of decisions. From a sample of 55 cases examined over many years (ranging up to 15 years in some decisions), two distinct implementation patterns were identified. One pattern is characterized by the more *contextual* aspects of organization, in particular the extent to which both organizational culture and structure are 'receptive' or 'antagonistic' (Pettigrew and Whipp, 1991) to the implementation of the decision. A second pattern is characterized by the extent to which managers can *specify, assess and mobilize resources* to support the decision, including gaining the support or *backing* of the various stakeholders in the process. Some decisions follow one or both patterns. Almost invariably, these are the more successful decisions. Other decisions have no identifiable pattern on these factors. These are the less successful decisions. Success is measured here by both 'objective' measures such as profit and market success, the achievement of stated objectives as well as by managers' own perceptions of outcomes.

It is important to note that there is no direct relationship between achievement (success) and the implementation patterns followed. The context pattern results in decisions becoming more easily *prioritized* in the organization. The other pattern (resourcing and know-how) results in decisions being more *acceptable* to the stakeholders involved. Decisions which do follow the patterns stand a better chance of success since they are either prioritized or acceptable to stakeholders (or both). So we can identify when decisions are *positioned* for success. But there can be many a 'slip between cup and lip'. The main factors of the patterns are depicted in Figure 10.2.

Summary

Groups are essential mechanisms for making organizational decisions even though individual managers are often considered or consider themselves to

Figure 10.2
Positioning for
success: twin
patterns of
implementation and
decision performance

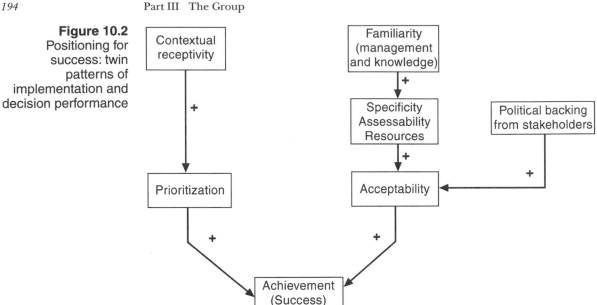

Source: Hickson *et al.*, (1997)

be effective decision-makers. When groups get together, some predictable group effects occur which, if not managed will detract from the efficacy of using groups to solve organizational problems.

The major group problem is that of conformity, which raises its head in a number of guises ranging from groupthink—where within the group there is excessive conformity to method and content of decision—to organizational culture, where there is pressure from outside the group to make decisions in such a way to fit in with what is considered acceptable by the wider organization.

Both individuals and groups are unable to achieve anything close to the rational model of decision-making. They invariably compromise because of:

● *Cognitive limits* on their capacity to process information.
● *Competing demands* from different parts of the organization which have to be met in order to achieve an outcome.

There are a number of techniques which can overcome some of the problems of group decision-making but none seem wholly effective. The most common, brainstorming, is the least effective of other possible techniques such as the Delphi method and its derivatives such as the nominal group, and decision conferencing.

Decision-making should also be considered from the organizational perspective. There are some predictions that can be made at this level. Ownership of the organization, for example, appears to make little difference to any aspect of the decision process. Most strategic decisions take on average 12 months from first idea to authorization. Committees do not slow things down at this level of analysis, although they do take more time in concentrated bouts from individual managers. Successful outcomes are more likely from decisions which are implemented with a view to gaining acceptability from stakeholders and which are clearly prioritized.

References

Asch, S. E. (1955) 'Studies of independence and conformity: A minority of one against unanimous majority', *Psychological Monographs*, **20**, (whole no. 416).

Belbin, R. M. (1981) *Management Teams: Why They Succeed or Fail*, Heinemann, London.

Braybrooke, D. and C. E. Lindblom (1963) *A Strategy of Decision*, Free Press, New York.

Cohen, M. D., J. G. March, and J. P. Olsen (1972) 'A garbage can model of organizational choice,' *Administrative Science Quarterly*, **17**, 1–25.

Cyert, R. and J. G. March (1963) *A Behavioral Theory of the Firm*, Prentice-Hall, Englewood Cliffs, New Jersey.

Dean, J. W. and M. P. Sharfman (1996) 'Does decision process matter? a study of strategic decision-making effectiveness', *Academy of Management Journal*, **39**, (2), 368–96.

Furtado, T. (1988) 'Training for a different management style', *Personnel Management*, March, 40–3.

Hall, G. (1994) 'Factors distinguishing survivors from failures among small firms in the UK construction sector', *Journal of Management Studies*, **31** (5), 737–60.

Hickson, D. J., R. J. Butler, D. Cray, G. R. Mallory, and D. C. Wilson (1986) *Top Decisions: Strategic Decision Making in Organizations*, Blackwell, Oxford, Jossey-Bass, San Francisco.

Hickson, D. J., S. Miller and D. C. Wilson (1997) 'Positioning for success: the implementation of strategic decisions', Working Paper, University of Warwick, UK.

Janis, I. L. (1972) *Victims of Groupthink: A Psychological Study of Foreign Policy Decisions and Fiascos*, Houghton-Mifflin, Boston.

Janis, I. L. and L. Mann (1977) *Decision Making*, Free Press, New York.

Jewell, L. N. and H. J. Reitz (1981) *Group Effectiveness in Organizations*, Scott, Foresman, Glenview, Illinios.

Lawler, (III) E. E. and S. A. Moreman (1985) 'Quality circles after the fad', *Harvard Business Review*, Jan–Feb, 65–71.

Leavitt, H. J. (1972) *Managerial Psychology*, 2nd edn., Chicago University Press, Chicago.

Lindblom, C. E. (1959) 'The science of muddling through', *Public Administration Review*, **xix**, (2), 79–88.

Lukes, S. (1974) *Power: A Radical View*, MacMillan, London.

Lustick, I. (1980) 'Explaining the variable utility of disjointed incrementalism', *American Political Science Review*, **74**, 342–53.

March, J. G. and J. P. Olsen (1976) *Ambiguity and Choice in Organizations*, Universitetsforlaget, Bergen.

Meyer, J. M., and B. Rowan (1977) 'Institutionalized organization: formal structures as myth and ceremony', *American Journal of Sociology*, **83** (2), 340–63.

Milgram, S. (1974) *Obedience and Authority*, Tavistock, London.

Miller, D. (1994) 'What happens after success: the perils of excellence', *Journal of Management Studies*, **31** (3), 325–58.

Miller, S. (1997) 'Implementing strategic decisions: four key success factors', *Organization Studies*, **18** (4), 577–602.

Mintzberg, H., D. Raisinghani and A. Theoret (1976) 'The structure of "unstructured" decision processes', *Administrative Science Quarterly*, **21**, 246–75.

Mitchell, T. R., K. J. Rediker and L. R. Beach (1986) 'Image theory and organizational decision-making', in H. P. Sims Jr. and D. A. Gioia (eds.), *The Thinking Organization: Dynamics of Organizational Social Cognition*, Jossey-Bass, San Francisco.

Osborn, A. F. (1963) *Applied Imagination: Principles and Procedures of Creative Thinking*, Scribner's, New York.

Pettigrew, A. M. (1973) *The Politics of Organisational Decision Making*, Tavistock, London.

Pettigrew, A. M. and R. Whipp (1991) *Managing Change for Competitive Success*, Blackwell, Oxford.

Quinn, J. B. (1980) *Strategies for Change: Logical Incrementalism*, Irwin, Homewood, Illinois.

Rowe, A. J., J. D. Boulgarides, and M. R. McGrath (1984) *Managerial Decision Making*, Science Research Associates, Chicago.

Schattsneider, E. E. (1960) *The Semi-Sovereign People: A Realists' View of Democracy in America*, Holt, Rinehart and Winston, New York.

Simon, H. A (1960) *The New Science of Management Decision*, Harper & Row, New York.

Stoner, J. (1968) 'Risky and cautious shifts in group decision: the influence of widely held values', *Journal of Experimental Social Psychology*, **4**, 442–59.

Van de Ven, A. H., and A. Delbecq (1974) 'The effectiveness of nominal, Delphi and interaction group decision-making processes', *Academy of Management Journal*, **17**, 605–32.

Valentin, E. K. (1994) 'Anatomy of a fatal business strategy', *Journal of Management Studies,* **31** (3), 359–82.

Varadarajan, P. R. and V. Ramanujam (1990) 'The corporate performance conundrum: a synthesis of current views and an extension', *Journal of Management Studies,* **27** (5), 463–83.

Vroom, V. H., and P. W. Yetton (1973) *Leadership and Decision Making,* University of Pittsburgh Press, Pittsburgh.

Whetten, D. (1980) 'Sources, responses and effects of organizational decline', in J. R. Kimberly and R. H. Miles (eds.), *The Organizational Life Cycle,* Jossey-Bass, San Francisco, 342–74.

Wilson, D. C. (1982) 'Electricity and resistance: a case study of innovation and politics', *Organization Studies,* **3** (2), 119–40.

Wilson, D. C., R. J. Butler, D. Cray, D. J. Hickson, and G. R. Mallory (1986) 'Breaking the bounds of organization in strategic decision-making', *Human Relations,* **39** (4), 309–31.

Wilson D. C., Hickson, D. J. and S. J. Miller (1996) 'How organizations can overbalance: decision over-reach as a cause for failure', *American Behavioral Scientist,* **39** (8), 995–1010.

Power and leadership in organizations

Introduction

Leadership in organizations concerns the exercise of power to some degree. As Shackleton (1995) notes, leaders can influence the behaviour of others directly or can do so through the context of a group or the wider organization. In Stogdill's (1974) marathon survey of over 3000 studies of leadership (some of which date back to his earlier work in the 1940s) the influence exerted by leaders over others emerges as a consistent pattern. However, leadership, power and position are not always equated with one another in any organization. It would be folly for any manager to assume that position in the hierarchy necessarily meant the commensurate possession of power and influence. Sometimes, seniority and power do go hand in hand. More often, power is also to be found elsewhere in the organization and, sometimes, in the most unexpected places.

First, we must decide exactly what power is. Its definition has caused some problems, since achieving an all-embracing, precise and workable, social scientific definition has proved elusive. All of us can recognize when power is exercised, especially when it is exercised against us! Defining where that power came from, or why our own power seems somehow *less* than that of our peers is not so easy. In this chapter, we shall use a broad but workable definition:

> Power is the ability of one social unit to influence the behaviour of another social unit and to achieve their preferred situation or outcomes.
>
> A social unit can be an individual, a group, an organization or a group of organizations.

Usually, the exercise of power occurs over specific issues, such as in decision-making processes where at its simplest one manager wants one outcome while another manager wants something very different. We could predict the likely outcome of this power struggle if the managers were of different levels of seniority and if we equated hierarchical position and power. We would say that one manager has the *authority* to exercise power over the other. As we shall see, authority is only one aspect of power and can be relatively impotent in relation to other bases (or sources) of power.

Before developing an analysis of power in organizations, this chapter will first examine leadership as one example of exercising influence in organizations.

Leadership: managing power and influence

Analysing the manager as leader is perhaps the most explicit recognition that a part of the management process concerns exercising power and influence. Of course, the management task overall is much wider than this in its scope. It contains many tasks which could be described as non-political (planning, thinking and co-ordinating, for example) although these too may have substantial elements of managing power within them.

The potency of the leader to influence other people and even whole organizations is a common theme which pervades the history of many industries. Based on the assumption that the ability to lead and influence was embodied in certain characteristics (or traits) of the individual, many key positions in government and in all kinds of organizations have been filled with dynamic, enthusiastic and arguably highly competent individuals. Certain traits defined effective leaders. Bryman (1992) has analysed charisma as one such leadership trait. For example, the appointments of Lord King as chairman of British Airways, Sir Iain Vallance as chairman of British Telecom, Percy Barnevik as chairman of Asea Brown Boveri and Helmut Maucher as Chairman of Nestlé were all examples of leadership positions appointed through a faith in traits which include charisma among others. Their successors are also likely to be appointed for the same trait.

Initial studies aimed at identifying significant and commonly-held traits in successful leaders all failed to come up with any conclusive evidence over what they were, or which were the most important. Nevertheless, some current selection criteria for senior management positions seem to reflect a prevailing belief in some traits. Examples include:

● The ability to solve problems and see how they fit into the wider scheme of things.
● A strong desire to achieve.
● Self-confident and self-disciplined.
● The ability to listen and to communicate effectively.
● Stability of emotion and a positive attitude toward other members of the organization, especially subordinates.
● Analytical and intelligent (but not *too* intelligent).

Direct links are often made in the popular business press between leaders who possess such traits and the success of their organizations. This linkage can also be seen in reverse, whereby a leader's traits are argued to be directly responsible for a firm going through difficult times. For example, after just over two years as chairman and chief executive of British Petroleum (BP), Robert Horton was forced to resign on 25 June 1992 by nine non-executive directors. They argued that his management style was at fault, being perhaps a little too abrasive (paradoxically, Horton's 'no-nonsense' style was one of the traits which landed him the job in the first place). He is currently chairman of Railtrack plc. Similarly, after reporting a significant loss for 1992 ($4.97 billion net loss) IBM non-executives were quick to remove John Akers as chief executive. He was allegedly too conservative, too ready to play safe and therefore averse to the risks that were arguably needed to restructure and reorganize the company. All this makes for good stories which link personalities with firms (Richard Branson *is* Virgin; Signor Agnelli *is* FIAT), but the causal links between traits and corporate success are too simple-minded and stand little scrutiny.

Contingency approaches to leadership began to uncover factors other than traits which had an impact not only on the leader and organizational performance, but also on the followers, especially their job performance and levels of satisfaction. Power exercised through leadership was argued to be mediated by a number of other characteristics. Key contingency researchers are Fiedler, Chemers and Mahar (1978), House (1971) and Vroom and Yetton (1973).

Contingency approaches to leadership

Fiedler's model of leadership effectiveness

Fiedler argued that leadership style could vary. The effectiveness of any work group was dependent upon achieving a *match between leadership style and context* (the situation in which leadership was exercised). He argued that certain situations determined the amount of control and influence open to the leader.

There were two measures which Fiedler used to assess the match between leadership style and situation. These were assumed similarity between opposites (ASO) and least preferred co-worker (LPC):

1 *ASO scale* meassured how similar were the most and the least preferred co-workers as perceived by leaders.
2 *LPC scale* measured the degree to which leaders favourably perceive their least preferred co-worker.

The idea was for respondents to think of all the individuals with whom they had worked, and to rank the persons who they perceived to be the most and least difficult to work with in terms of getting the job done. This was not to measure like or dislike of a person. It was to identify the person with whom accomplishing a task proved most difficult and most easy. The results from Fiedler's research indicated that the LPC scale was a significantly better predictor of match in leadership style than the ASO scale.

Three styles of leadership were identified:

Relationship-motivated (Human relations leadership style).	High similarity in ASO. A favourable co-worker description. LPC score above 64.
Task-directed (Hard-nosed leadership style)	Great difference in ASO. Unfavourable co-worker description. LPC score below 57.
Choice of task/relationship style	ASO does not distinguish. LPC lies between 58 and 63. Manager has to decide the type of blend between task and relationship-orientated styles.

Fiedler argued that the appropriate style of leadership could be predicted from ASO and LPC scores. To the extent that there was a match between situation and style, the effectiveness of the work group would be enhanced. There was no one best style, and neither the task-directed or relationship-motivated styles were 'better' than one another.

To put the LPC scores into a more complex contingency framework, Fiedler also assessed the amount of *control* available to a manager under particular situations. These 'situational variables' are:

1 *The leader–member relationship* the acceptability of the leader to the members of a group.
2 *The degree of structure in the task to be accomplished* whether everything is spelled out or is ambiguous.
3 *The degree of position power of the leader* whether the leader has formal authority endowed to him or her by virtue of position in the hierarchy.

A context of high favourability toward the leader would comprise, for example, being readily acceptable to the group; a task which is structured and unambiguous; coupled with a position of high formal authority. This would be a situation which was highly favourable to the leader since it allowed him or her a large degree of control. Matching favourability of context and leadership style, Fiedler found that the best match of style to situation was achieved where the task directed style was adopted under *both* favourable and unfavourable conditions, with the human relations style most effective in the mid-ranges of favourability (see Figure 11.1).

Figure 11.1
Style and situational context: Fiedler's effectiveness model

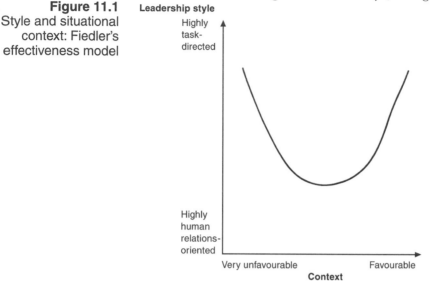

Fiedler's theory of leadership and influence may be summarised as follows:

1   Appropriate styles of leadership are contingent upon the degree of control pertaining to various situations.
2   The exercise of influence through leadership is likely to be most successful when there is a match between situation and style.
3   In the event of a mis-match, Fiedler suggests that it is easier to try and change the situation rather than to attempt to change style.

House's path-goal theory of leadership

Well-rooted in the contingency approach, House argues that the role of influence through leadership is to compensate for things lacking in the work context. Leaders are both more influential and more effective when they complement the context. He identifies four styles of leadership and three contingency variables:

1   *Leader directiveness*
    ● Letting subordinates know what is expected.
    ● Saying what should be done and how.
    ● Clearly defining the role of the leader.
    ● Maintaining standards of performance and work scheduling.
2   *Leader supportiveness*
    ● Being inter-personally aware of the needs of others.
    ● Treating group members as equals.
    ● Being friendly and approachable.
3   *Leader achievement-orientedness*
    ● Setting goals which are challenging.
    ● Continuously seeking performance improvements.
    ● Having a high degree of faith in others to perform to the best of their ability.
    ● Continually emphasizing the achievement of excellence.

4 *Leader participativeness*
- Consulting others regularly.
- Asking for suggestions and advice from others over specific decisions.
- Taking all suggestions into account when taking a decision.

Source: adapted from House and Mitchell (1974).

Each of the four styles is dependent upon three contingency variables, each of which has an impact on the effectiveness of the style employed. The three variables relate to the characteristics of subordinates. They are:

1 Whether subordinates are close-minded and rigid, or are open and flexible to how they operate.
2 Whether subordinates are internally or externally oriented. Internals believe broadly that any event is a consequence of their own actions. Externals believe that what happens to them is largely a matter of luck, chance or fate (Rotter, 1966).
3 The ability of subordinates to handle the current task and to develop and learn how to handle future tasks.

In general, House's results confirm those of Fiedler. Directiveness is positively related to subordinates' satisfactions and expectations when the task is ambiguous. The leader absorbs uncertainty for the group. The reverse is true when tasks are clear and well-defined. Supportiveness is an appropriate style for highly repetitive tasks, or those which are frustrating or physically unpleasant. Being one of the crowd helps to compensate for situational conditions. Achievement-orientedness is appropriate for groups who face non-repetitive tasks which are also ambiguous. This style is argued to maintain a constant striving for excellence in performance. Participativeness is appropriate in situations where the group comprises largely internally oriented individuals who are engaged in non-repetitive tasks.

Vroom and Yetton's normative theory of leadership effectiveness

Vroom and Yetton (1973) concentrate upon decision-making in their studies of leadership. They argue that leaders should be flexible and change their styles to match situations. This, of course, is the reverse of Fiedler's argument, who proposed that leadership style was less amenable to change than the situation.

Two criteria of decision effectiveness are used by Vroom and Yetton to indicate the kind of appropriate leadership style. These are decision *quality* and *acceptance*. The argument is that some decision topics are more directly related to performance from a work group than others. Those topics which centrally affect the working conditions and environment of a group (such as job design or responsibilities) should require the leader to adopt a participative decision process.

Where a decision is relatively peripheral to the concerns of a group, then the manager can adopt either an authoritative or participative style. It has little effect upon performance. Vroom and Yetton identified five alternative styles open to the manager. These are summarized in Table 11.1. The five styles range from autocratic to collaborative. As subordinate commitment to the decision increases, then the appropriate style should become more collaborative. This is based on the assumption that a decision even if technically correct can be blocked and caused to fail because of resistance from those who have to carry it out, or live with its results.

Table 11.1
Vroom and Yetton's
five decision styles

Autocratic styles
1   You solve the problem or make the decision yourself, using information available to you at the time
2   You obtain the information required from your subordinates, then decide yourself. You may or may not let your subordinates know the nature of the decision problem. Subordinates are treated solely as information givers, not as generators of alternative courses of action or of solutions

Consultative styles
1   You share the problem with subordinates on an individual basis. Having collected together their ideas and suggestions, you then make the decision yourself. This may or may not reflect subordinates' influence
2   You collect together subordinates as a group. They generate alternatives and suggest solutions in discussion with you. Then you make the decision individually (as above)

Collective or group style
1   You share the problem with a group of subordinates. Together you try and reach consensus on the problem and its solution. You act much as a chairperson of the group, not trying to influence the group to adopt your preferred solution. You are also willing to accept and to implement any solution which has the support of the entire group

Source: adapted from Vroom and Yetton (1973: 13).

Both Likert (1967) and Reddin (1970) offer similar models, arguing that autocratic power exercised through leadership is likely to result in poor performance and non-acceptance by others. Likert's results indicated that significantly greater levels of performance came from groups in which the power of the leader was articulated through a participative and democratic style.

Shortcomings of the contingency approaches to leadership

Shackleton (1995:38) summarizes the major critiques of the validity of contingency models. He argues that since many of the studies relied on the recall or self-reporting of respondents, the success or failure of decisions taken may well influence the judgement of respondents. Second, while leaders might prefer the styles outlined by the contingency models, subordinates tend to prefer predominantly participative approaches whatever the contingencies (Heilman *et al.*, 1984). Contingency models may, therefore, be more applicable to managers than to subordinates. Finally, it may be the leader's skill in *implementing* decisions which is more important, rather than the style of decision-making they choose. It is not what is done, it is the way in which it is done that matters (Tjosvold *et al.*, 1986).

Leadership, transformation and vision

Recent views of leadership have attempted to link the qualities of individual leaders with the ability to transform or provide a vision for the organization. Various words have been used to describe this approach (such as inspirational, transformational) but whatever the vocabulary, the key aspect of this perspective is on the link between the individual and the provision of a vision for the organization's future. Bennis (1994: 49) calls this 'visionary leadership'. The idea is that leaders develop a mental image of a possible (and desirable) future state for the organization. This may be vague, as in a dream, or may be quite precise. In either case, this image is the vision.

Leadership then becomes the process through which the vision is turned into action and realized.

Transformation is achieved since leadership provides the link between the present (known) and the future (unknown). Inspiration, too, is part of this process. Leaders who can envision the future must also inspire in all other individuals in the organization a sense of purpose, direction and importance so that they feel they contribute and make a difference. Those who subscribe to the transformational views of leadership argue that it is a universal principle of management equally applicable to football club managers, orchestra leaders and corporate executives. The aim is to achieve consensus of direction and goals throughout the organization. Without this, 'the most brilliant management strategy will fail' (Bennis, 1994: 52). The transformational view of leadership has gained considerable currency among some organizational thinkers and has had a direct impact on the work of scholars who deal with organizational learning and change (see Chapter 14).

One of the key problems with this way of viewing leadership is that a number of key assumptions are made and often treated as being unproblematic (Hampden-Turner, 1994). First, the accuracy of vision is central. What if leaders get the vision wrong, yet still inspire their 'followers' to implement the vision? Second, the approach rarely questions the ethics or morals of the leader's vision (which may be neither ethical nor moral) and, third, the approach relies heavily on the abilities and traits of key individuals to inspire and transform. The latter are scarce resources in human beings and are likely to be unrealistic expectations of the leaders of many organizations. Some authors claim that both the contingency and transformational approaches are both limiting and misleading. Instead, these authors suggest, we should concentrate on the wider context in which leaders operate to explain why they are effective or not. For convenience, these are classified together as 'contextual' approaches to leadership in the following section.

Contextual approaches to leadership

Hosking (1988) argues that the exercise of power through leadership is more complex than either simple trait models or complex contingency theories. She argues that to understand leadership completely, one must understand it as a negotiated process worked out between leader, group and situation. Hosking's reading (Reading 8) summarizes this argument succinctly. Any analysis of leadership should include 'people, processes, and contexts' (Hosking, 1988: 164).

Leavy and Wilson (1994) studied leadership in the historical context of organizations, tracing the history of four firms over a period of over 60 years. They found that leaders within these organizations (which included Irish Distillers Group, Golden Vale, Irish Sugar and a co-operative) were not solely agents of their own destiny but were fashioned by a host of factors external to the firm and its members. These included the state of technological development, the national and international trading environment, political and cultural policies as well as the history of the organization itself.

When examined over time, the contributions of various leaders in each organization were closely related to the socio-economic challenges facing their organizations during their tenure (Leavy and Wilson, 1994: 113). Leaders were tenants of time and of context. The study identified four distinct roles taken by leaders:

1 *Builders* Those who typically are founders of the organization, or who lead it in its early stages of development.
2 *Revitalizers* Leaders who try to inject new life into the strategies of the firm, but choosing not to change very much in terms of strategic direction for the firm.
3 *Turnarounders* Leaders who change strategy, structure and, sometimes, overall direction of the organization.
4 *Inheritors* Those whose major task is to implement the decisions of their predecessors.

In each organization, all four roles were identified as different leaders came and went. The roles adopted were dependent upon the stage in the life-cycle of the organization (the older the firm the more difficult it was to turn round and the more likely an inheritor would be the leader, for example), the characteristics of the industrial sector (upturn, stability or downturn) and the political economy of the nation state.

Finally, two further contextual factors permeate leadership perhaps more than any other aspect of management thinking. One is nationality. The other is gender. It is striking that the majority of studies of leadership treat the subject as if it were only applicable to men—and men from the USA or at least the Western European countries. We shall deal with the interplay of gender and national differences in more detail within Reading 14. However, it is worth noting at this stage that what constitutes 'good' leadership in the Western world is unlikely to be perceived in the same way in other countries. An example from political leadership in Japan makes the point. Open debate and criticism of one's leaders is not the done thing in Japan (in politics as well as in business). It is not surprising, therefore, that when Hiroshi Kumagai (a liberal democrat) verbally attacked the Prime Minister (Kiichi Miyazawa) in 1993 over his failure to stamp out corruption, he managed to shock and outrage the whole nation. Yet, in Brazil or in Italy such open debate and criticism would be encouraged and expected. We shall explore the reasons why this might be the case later in Part VII, but the question whether predominantly North American models of leadership can easily be translated across other national boundaries remains pertinent and, as yet, unresolved.

Fiona Wilson (1995) argues that leadership studies are almost exclusively concerned with males (Western males) and address a male-dominated agenda. She points out that Stogdill (1974) only uses the term 'men' when summarizing leadership. Wilson also emphasizes that as recently as the 1960s, women were seen as being temperamentally unfit for management since they were too emotional (Wilson, 1995: 155). The overlap between being a typical male and being a good leader was extremely strong. Men are more predisposed to viewing leadership as transactional. That is, they view their job as a series of transactions, trading rewards for services and transferring power and favour for good performance (Rosener, 1990). Vinnicombe (1987) showed that men tended to be more traditionalist in their leadership style (that is, they conformed to the above descriptions) but that women tended to be more visionary or predisposed toward change (catalysts). Women are better communicators, better at presenting information orally and are more co-operative than their male counterparts, yet the dominant trend in the literature on leadership has been to assume that the leader is male. As women become a more significant feature of the workplace (in number and in influence, see Chapter 1) this will have a marked effect on what is popularly considered to be a good leader. It may be time for a drastic re-think.

Understanding the nature of power in organizations

An initial framework for the study of the bases of power was described by French and Raven (1960). This represents something of a classic analysis of the sources of power. There are five key *bases* of power:

1 *Reward* To the extent that one individual has the capacity to reward another, and to the extent that this is recognized by both parties, then there is an imbalance of power. For example, if one manager has the capacity to promote, appraise or otherwise reward then he or she has this source of power.
2 *Coercive* If individual A has the capacity to operate sanctions or punishments against B for behaviour unwanted by A, then A has a coercive base of power. The giving of unpopular tasks, firing and reprimanding are all illustrations of this kind of power.
3 *Legitimate* To the extent that individual B feels that it is right for A to make a request then A has power over B. This is the concept of authority described earlier.
4 *Expert* If one manager perceives another to have key knowledge or specialized technical skill, then the 'expert' manager will have a significantly more potent source of power.
5 *Referent* To the extent that others in the organization wish to identify with a single individual, for example in leadership style, manner of dress, or manner of handling difficult clients, then that individual will have a substantial power base.

All of these can occur in a work organization and they are not necessarily correlated with seniority. The possession of all five power bases would make an individual very powerful indeed, so the bases are also additive. Some of the bases can occur outside formal organizations. Referent power can be seen in the relationship between a rock star and fans or sporting heros and their fans. Other bases can occur in family life, between parent and child for example. It is easy to see how reward and coercive power might operate in this context.

All this only begins the analysis of power. It is a necessary, but not sufficient description of what happens in organizations. There are a number of other factors which will contribute to or erode away a manager's power. Broadly, these can be found in organizational structure which is the subject of the next section.

Organizational structure
The operating environment of the organization

If we were to try and find where power lies in any organization, we would probably gain most insight by keeping structure and environment uppermost in our minds. For example, it is common managerial parlance to describe organizations as 'production-led' or as 'market-led'. This means that one differentiated part of the organization's functions has become dominant outside the scope of its own functional area. In a production-led company, we would predict that the production director would be more influential and more successful in achieving desired outcomes over a range of decisions than the sales director, even though hierarchy does not differentiate between their positions.

As Mangham (1986: 9–15) notes, this use of managerial language assumes and subsumes a number of aspects of power which are rarely made explicit in day-to-day managerial activity. The aim of this chapter is to uncover theses assumptions and identify sources of power.

Power and organizational structure

The most explicit and precise analysis of power through structure was outlined in by Hickson *et al.*,(1971). Termed a '*Strategic contingencies theory*' of power, it built upon and brought together a number of previous studies (see, for example, Emerson, 1962 and Crozier, 1964) into a self-contained and testable theory of power. To acquire power, individuals in organizations needed to be indispensable, in the right place at the right time and considered by others in the organization to be doing a critically important job. The formal theory is set out in Table 11.2.

Table 11.2
Strategic contingencies theory of power bases

Power source	Description
Coping with uncertainty	Specialization allows some departments or individuals to cope with ambiguous and unpredictable circumstances. They create certainty for others in the organization and are thus more influential and powerful.
Non-substitutable	Dependence of other parts of the organization on those which cope with uncertainty can be reduced if there are alternative sources of information or service. The power of any part of a firm is lessened if it can be substituted
Centrality	Being well-networked into the whole organization will confer power. This has two aspects: 1 *Pervasiveness* Where the number of links with other groups in the firm are many 2 *Immediacy* Where the cessation of activity by a person or a group would impede the workflow of the organization straight away

Just like French and Raven's bases of power, the three elements of strategic contingency theory are additive. The key single contingency is that of coping with uncertainty (see Hinings *et al.*, 1974 for an empirical test of this theory) followed in turn by immediacy, non-substitutability and pervasiveness. In the Canadian brewery studied by Hinings *et al.*, (1974) for example, the four departments of this firm were ranked in order thus, from greatest to least powerful over a range of key decisions:

Department	*Power (most = 4; least = 1)*
Production	4
Marketing	3
Engineers	2
Accounting	1

The production department was most powerful since brewing is a relatively simple process in Engineering terms. Once the plant is designed and running, the crucial aspect of the organization is its product which is in the hands of production (quality and quantity of output, coupled with the special, non-substitutable 'brewers' expertise).

The division of labour into specialized departments and sub-groups and their relative dependence upon one another to keep the organization viable is a persuasive argument in favour of analysing key contingencies. It is not in the interests of any of the parts of the organization to engage in behaviour which is destructive to the firm as a whole, since if it founders so do they. It is in sub-groups' interests to fight for their particular stake in the scarce resource allocation process which is the fact of life for most organizations. Those which are most contingently placed will have the loudest and more influential voice over all decisions and will have primary access to resources.

This kind of analysis gives only a partial analysis and flavour of the exercise of power. 'Most middle managers know only too well . . . that hunches, inspiration and politicking are often what gives a company its shape' (*The Economist*, July, 1988:68). In other words, it is the *individual* exercise of power, the process of exercising power, which is the key to its understanding. We look at these aspects in the next section.

The individual in the structure

Not surprisingly, power studies which have emphasized the case study method for its analysis have concentrated mostly on the role of the individual manager as fighter, as manipulator, as terrier in the system and as gallant knight to save the day against all odds. Not much here about strategic contingencies (see Pettigrew, 1973, 1985; Wilson, 1982). Yet a common contingent theme can be found at least in some of the more detailed studies of individual activities.

Control of information, through gatekeeping, through filtering between parties, through manipulation and deceit figures large in many cases. In Pettigrew's (1973) description of the decision by a retail firm to purchase a new computer, Kenny, the 'gatekeeper' who had access to computer suppliers and all associated information, was able to sway the final decision in whichever way he saw beneficial to himself. Wilson's (1982) study of a chemical manufacturing company which took the decision to generate its own supply of electricity and become independent of the central electricity generating board, also focused on the role of individual power processes. Alwyn, one of the key individuals in the process, and who got what he wanted via the final decision (promotion to managing director) again used information and data to his own advantage, keeping some back from general view and publicly questioning other peoples' data on the topic.

Later empirical studies seem to reinforce *the primacy of individual action* within the organizational structure, rather than structural configuration itself as a source of power. Kenny and Wilson (1984) studied 188 managers from 60 Australian organizations and found that managers ranked managerial expertise (knowledge of the system) and access to and control of information above the sub-unit contingency of coping with uncertainty. Distinguishing between person, position and sub-unit sources of power, the study revealed the relative importance of person and position over the importance of the manager's department to the organization in endowing power over a wide range of decisions. Factors studied were:

1 **Person-based**
- *Expertise* knowledge of technical process or equivalent
- *Managerial expertise* knowledge of the organization and people—'the system'
- *Personality* the ability to get on with and persuade others

2 **Position-based**
- Formal authority

- Access to and control over information
- Access to senior management and other senior staff

3   Sub-unit based
- The importance of the department to the organization (for example, coping with uncertainty, non-substitutable etc.)

Source: Kenny and Wilson (1984: 414).

Managers from this sample consistently ranked managerial expertise as the most important power base followed by access to and control over information. Sub-unit contingencies came third. These findings concur with many of the detailed case studies of power in organizations (see, for example, Pettigrew, 1973; Wilson, 1982). Hickson *et al.*, (1971) in proposing the contingencies' view also suggested that individual actions of managers may take primacy over structural contingencies.

Thus we are at a stage in the understanding of power where the individual manager is pivotal. The exercise of power is best seen first as the outcome of individual action and individual characteristics. If these are supported by favourable *structural* configurations the power base is increased significantly. Power is thus a blend of individual person-based factors, and particular configurations of structure in the organization.

This is useful but still insufficient for a full understanding of power in organizations. Even integrating the individual and organizational structure makes some unwarranted assumptions about the nature of organizations and individuals.

The environment and inter-organizational relations

The operating environment of the organization

As Mintzberg (1973) showed, a great deal of managerial activity is spent interacting and liaising with the managers of other organizations. This is no accident, nor is it representative of a desire by managers for more business lunches. It is reflecting the fact that no organization exists in a vacuum. Virtually all organizations have suppliers, customers, competitors, government agencies and a host of other organizations to deal with in the everyday pursuit of their business.

This complex interaction between organizations comprises the operating environment of any firm, and it also has the capacity to develop and sustain power relationships. As a first step, one could simply convert the factors of the strategic contingencies' model to apply to external organizations in contact. Contingencies then become analysable across the immediate operating environment of the firm. For example, a supplier which is non-substitutable from the perspective of the focal organization will be more powerful and will have potentially more say in what that organization does, than just one of many undifferentiated customers. Key customers who buy a lot of products or services are also likely to be more central than those who are small or only occasional customers.

Further analysis reveals that we can go beyond this important but over-simplified perspective. As Pfeffer and Salancik (1978) argued, the overall system of inter-organizational relations has its own dynamic. Linkages between external organizations and the focal firm can either be 'loose' or 'tight'. Whole networks of organizations can also be characterized as loosely or tightly coupled. It may be that only *some* and *not all* of the actions by a supplier, a government agency or a customer impinge upon the operation of the focal firm. The network of inter-organizational relations is thus loosely coupled.

On the other hand, a single firm can be 'paralysed' in its strategic actions by a tightly coupled network of organizations in contact. Butler *et al.*, (1977) distinguish between organizations which are almost completely held in check by outside interests and those which can extend their actions beyond their formal boundaries and themselves exert influence over customers, regulatory bodies and suppliers. Organizations which can extend their influence beyond their formal boundaries into their operating environment are very powerful indeed. This was achieved by Jaguar, the British motor car manufacturer, in the early 1980s. When plagued with an increasing number of component breakdowns in their cars, Jaguar insisted on their suppliers taking responsibility for quality control and component failure. The recent developments toward thinking in 'supply chains' (including the firm, its suppliers and customers as essentially one unit of analysis) emphasizes the importance of power and where one chooses to draw the boundary of an organization.

It would be tempting to account for differences in strategic autonomy by ownership. State owned organizations are likely to be far more constrained in their 'strategic choice' than those which are privately owned (Child, 1972). This is not the case. In a study of 30 British firms, Hickson *et al.*, (1986) found no evidence at all to support differentiation of power distribution on ownership or manufacturing or service criteria. Public and private, manufacturing and service organizations were not characterized by differences in external control.

The management task of addressing these power relations is thus the same in all organizations. There are a number of ways in which we can see organizations attempting to reduce the impact or the potency of external influences. The boards of many companies contain directors who also sit on the boards of other related companies. These interlocking directorates help smooth out dependencies. They can also present excellent opportunities for control by these directors (see Useem and McCormack, 1981). Used in this way, directors can use a number of organizations in the network to satisfy their own personal ambitions.

When the external control of organizations becomes too far balanced toward one or two external constituencies, then 'organizational drift' is a likely result. This process was described by Engwall (1978). Giving the example of a newspaper company, Engwall shows how the initial aims of the organization to be a fair, liberal and analytical newspaper were confounded when financial dependence on politically motivated external sources forced the editors of the newspaper to follow a particular political line.

Mintzberg (1983, 1984) also argues that the nature of the power balance in the operating environment (its 'configuration') will differ according to type of firm and its strategic history. For example, in a large mature firm it is likely that no single external interest has sufficient power to exert pressure on the managers in the focal organization. Such a configuration will hold until major changes in strategic direction occur (or are forced by demand or fiscal exigencies) and then the opportunity for a re-establishment of the power balance is created once more. This is one of the reasons why many large, mature organizations resist change to such a degree since the potential political threats to which they may become exposed are enormous (see Chapter 14).

Joint ventures are another way in which managers handle power imbalances in the wider environment and keep influence in check. The problem with this approach as Harrigan (1986) illustrates, is that all parties to a joint venture have to be convinced that there is at least an equal split of benefits to be obtained from entering the partnership. Since this is not always easy to demonstrate, the number of joint ventures is relatively low. There is also the suspicion that one party may hold about the other, that information detrimental to one party is being deliberately withheld by the other (see the next section).

Reciprocal trade agreements, representation of multiple firms in trade associations and verbal agreements on good business practice are other examples of managing the wider political environment. Even this level of analysis still misses some important aspects of the nature of power in organizations. We explore these in the next section.

Power beyond the individual, organizational structure and operating environments

Power can be exercised in far more subtle ways than the analysis currently reveals. So far, the analysis relies upon observing or accounting for the relative influence of managers (or organizations in the wider context) over decisions or organizational problems. At first sight this looks promising, especially if the spread of decision topics studied is representative of managerial reality. Certainly, studies by Hickson *et al.*, (1971, 1986), Tannenbaum (1968) and Hinings *et al.*, (1974) cover all the issues a manager is likely to meet in any organization. So it is not that the situation is unrepresentative.

Closer inspection reveals another side to power. It is not just overt influence over identifiable decisions which is an important indication of power. Those who influence what is *not* open to decision are at least of equal (and probably greater) power. These are the issues which are not debated in any wider managerial decision arena. They are called '*non-decisions*' (Bachrach and Baratz, 1970) and they can arise in a number of ways.

It is useful at this stage to distinguish two separate arguments. One is that *non-decisions arise because of limited participation opportunities in the decision-making process.* Senior management, for example, might take a particular view over the future strategic direction of the organization. In turn, this will involve substantial investment programmes, constant introduction of new or revised products, the nature of which has already been decided by the time middle management come to debate such issues. Because middle management did not participate in the initial decisions, any subsequent decisions they take will be framed in a particular context set outside their own control. A great many alternatives, therefore, are not open to debate. This process of power framing or context setting can be a deliberate action which can span across many levels in the organization. It is a fairly sophisticated version of 'agenda setting', something familiar to all managers who sit through committees and working groups.

Another form in which non-decisions can arise is less a deliberate strategy on the part of one group or individual and more *a product of the kind of organization in question and its history.* As Daudi (1986) notes, all power relations in organizations take place within a context that has characteristics and dynamics of its own. Over time, organizational customs and practices take on a life of their own and these can also shape power relations in any firm. Such customs and practices are the result of organizations coping with the uncertainty they face in their operating environment. Particular forms of interdependencies and reporting relationships develop, as well as particular degrees of centralization or decentralization, and formal or informal practice (see, for example, Pfeffer and Salancik, 1978 and Brooke, 1984). This develops over time and collects much in the same way as alluvial silt builds up along the course of a river. The effects on power relations are two-fold:

The creation of myth and ceremony

Argued in detail by Meyer and Rowan (1977), the creation of myth and ceremony means that the process of institutionalization effectively acts as an unrecognized control mechanism. Certain behaviours and practices are taken for granted or encouraged often without anyone reflecting on their efficacy or even why they are there in the first place. For example, organizations which have developed with the 'ceremony' of ensuring all functional managers kept within budgets which are strictly controlled outside their domain will produce predictable patterns of behaviour in their managers. All decision-making will be directed at keeping within the financial control procedures. Functions will become territorial, since the primary way to demonstrate managerial performance will be on financial data for the department or section (Burchell *et al.* 1980).

Other kinds of behaviour are inertia, resistance to change, the non-recognition of opportunities and the conviction that the organization is already doing things right. Pettigrew's (1985) case study of ICI showed graphically how the conceptions of senior management were constrained by the tremendous weight of institutionalization in the company. Certain alternatives were just not open to debate and it took an era of leadership from a very different perspective to break the mould and effect changes. The resistance which met John Harvey-Jones and his predecessors who tried to effect changes is a sobering illustration of the enormous strength of such institutionalized power.

The creation of knowledge elites

This is really the other side of the myth and ceremony argument. Power will accrue to those individuals who understand how the system works. Those who can accurately predict outcomes for a given set of circumstances in their firm are in a relatively more powerful position than their peers who cannot recognize cause and effect. Knowledge of the system has been illustrated in a number of case studies. In Pettigrew's (1973) study of a retail organization's computer purchase, Kenny recognized that his organization's system focused on the role of the 'gatekeeper'. Those who interfaced with external organizations (in this case, computer suppliers) could effectively control much of what subsequently happened within their own organization.

In Wilson's (1982) case study of a chemical company, Alwyn recognized that a decision taken against his interests could be re-opened by his subsequently casting doubt on the data produced to support the arguments. In an organization where the culture was to favour fast action on quantifiable data, undermining the empirical arguments was a sure route to ensuring continued debate which was what Alwyn wanted (see Mangham, 1986: Chapter 4).

In the exercise of upward influence, knowing how your boss operates, reasons, and thinks has been described in some detail. This kind of knowledge can foster or protect self-interest in subordinates. Knowing your boss's preferences on a set of issues enables effective screening mechanisms to be set up which operate in your self-interest. For example, you would only pass on certain kinds of information and withhold that which you knew would be detrimental to your interests. You might also pass information upward in a particular form, missing out some selected facts perhaps, or preserving ambiguity in the presentation of data allowing the boss to interpret them in whichever way was thought desirable (see Leavitt, 1972; Sayles, 1979; Gabarro and Kotter, 1980).

Post-modern approaches to power

Although the debates on power described so far represent varying levels of conceptual complexity, they are all 'modernist' theories in that they take structure, both organizational and social, as pivotal and assume a variety of relationships between various aspects of those factors. The ultimate aim of these modernist approaches is synthesis of knowledge to create a grand theory of organization (or a meta-theory). Recently, this modernist perspective has been challenged, especially in the area of power and organization. The debates between the modernists and the post-modernists are outside the scope of this book, but it is worth sketching here the approach of one of the most influential writers on power from the post-modern perspective, Michel Foucault. This will allow fruitful comparisons to be made between the approaches. Foucault is difficult to read in the original. Dreyfus and Rabinow (1982) and Burrell (1988) give more accessible descriptions of his approach. There are many other post-modern writers in organization theory, but the following summary of Foucault's approach should give a flavour for readers interested in investigating more fully this line of thought.

Michel Foucault was Professor of the History of Systems of Thought in Paris. He died in 1984 aged 57. Like most post-modern thinkers, he argued strongly against the idea of structuralist thinking and the goal of the meta-narrative. He studied only French organizations, most of which were non-mainstream in terms of business organizations (prisons and clinics). The real relevance for organization theory is that Foucault studied the concept of power as widely and as radically as probably any other author.

In particular, his explanations of why social institutions (which include all forms of organization) emerge, develop and sustain themselves are of relevance for management thought. Essentially, Foucault argues that knowledge is power but this knowledge is socially and individually constructed. Post-modern approaches to power try to go beyond individualism and structuralism. Foucault tried to re-think the concept of power by refuting the belief that an adequate theory of power can be encompassed by an analysis of structures, whether they are organizational or governmental. For Foucault, power is everywhere, at every strata in society and there is no differentiation in the 'potency' of power at any 'level' (although he refutes the notion of levels, of course). He has a radical view in the sense that he also sees power as equally bottom-up (he cites the family as an example of this) and top-down. He thus refutes Marxism and other institutionalized arguments for the understanding of power.

Foucault argues that power is a network of relationships which are connected by a variety of systems. These systems are, however, not random. They form a pattern of mechanisms, technologies, techniques and procedures. Foucault highlights the 'panopticon' as an example of a power system in which all seem willing participants and yet in which the panopticon gives knowledge and the capacity of surveillance to one set of individuals and not to another (the panopticon was a design by Jeremy Bentham in which the central core of an organization could view the rest of the staff but could not be observed themselves. It was initially a design for a prison). In this, Foucault predated many of the current debates in organization theory which argue that technology such as electronic mail and computer-based monitoring of tasks represent direct surveillance of workers by management. Of course, this technology was not available when Foucault was writing, but it was clear to him that it was coming. It was too simple, said Foucault, to take the above argument and apply a simple structural analysis that the dominant class have the capacity for surveillance and the oppressed do not. Power is relational. It is not something which can be gained and lost either within or outside a zero-sum game. Power is most evident in what people take to be most 'normal'. In organizations this can be such things as classification, ordering, distribution, definitions of activities, fixing of scales and rules or procedures.

Summary

Power can accrue to individuals in organizations in a number of ways, many of which do not lend themselves to direct empirical observation. Power is mostly a concept of action and, hence, its close association with leadership. It is a process which is acted out in a particular setting and what we usually see, or experience, as members of any organization are the effects of power being exercised and not the source of that power.

The sources or bases of power can result from the characteristics of individuals. More likely is that a combination of individual characteristics and the interrelationships which occur in complex organizations go toward explaining the locus of any individual or group influence. Extending the focus of the discussion further, we can view power as residing in networks of organizations and the managerial task becomes one of not only managing internal organizational processes, but also involves managing the wider environment of organizations in contact such as suppliers, customers, competitors and regulatory agencies.

Going beyond structural analyses of contingencies and coping with uncertainties, we uncover potentially more insidious sides to power. Those issues which are never recognized or which never come up for open debate really indicate that power is being exercised outside the arena of overt decision-making. There are a number of non-issues (non-decisions) which the very powerful can keep for themselves and which shape the subsequent choices of everyone else. Furthermore, power can be discovered in the everyday world of organizations—in the very ordinary day-to-day activities of organizing. Computers and databases may help remove piles of paper and may be less fallible than human systems, but they also provide the potential to be very efficient surveillance mechanisms whereby one set of individuals can observe and monitor the activities of another group. This group may not be even aware that it is being monitored and observed. To discover power at this level means we must analyse the history and the development of any organization as well as refer to the context in which it currently operates. This naturally makes the study of power in this depth extremely difficult. Nevertheless, the isolated cases of power and non-decisions which do exist demonstrate the potency of influence at this level and show that organizations can be the result of conscious political design rather than any other criteria such as efficiency, public good or utility.

References

Bachrach, P., and M. S. Baratz (1970) *Power And Poverty: Theory And Practice*, Oxford University Press, Oxford.

Bennis, W. (1994) Visionary Leadership, in W. Bennis, J. Parikh and R. Lessem (eds.), *Beyond Leadership: Balancing Economics, Ethics and Ecology*, Blackwell, Oxford.

Brooke, M. Z. (1984) *Centralization And Autonomy: A Study In Organizational Behaviour*, Holt, Rinehart and Winston, London.

Bryman, A. (1992) *Charisma And Leadership In Organizations*, Sage, London.

Burchell, S., C. Clubb, A. Hopwood, J. Hughes, and J. Nahapiet (1980) 'The role of accounting in organizations and society', *Accounting, Organizations And Society*, **5** (1), 5–27.

Burrell, W. G. (1988) 'Modernism, postmodernism and organisational analysis: the contribution of Michel Foucault', *Organization Studies*, **9** (2), 221–35.

Butler, R. J., D. J. Hickson, D. C. Wilson, and R. Axelsson (1977) Organizational power, politicking and paralysis', in M. Warner (ed.), *Organizational Choice And Constraint*, Sage, London.

Child, J. (1972) 'Organizational structure, environment and performance: the role of strategic choice', *Sociology*, **6** (1), 1–22.

Crozier, M. (1964) *The Bureaucratic Phenomenon*, Tavistock, London.

Daudi, P. (1986) *Power In The Organization: The Discourse Of Power In Managerial Practice*, Blackwell, Oxford.

Dreyfus, H. L. and P. Rabinow (1982) *Michel Foucault: Beyond Structuralism And Hermeneutics*, Harvester, Brighton.

Emerson, R. M. (1962) 'Power-dependence relations', *American Sociological Review*, **27** (1), 31–41.

Engwall, L. (1978) *Newspapers As Organizations*, Saxon House, Farnborough.

Fiedler, F. E., Chemers, M. M., and L. Mahar (1978) *The Leadership Match Concept*, Wiley, New Jersey.

French, J. R. P. [Jr.], and B. Raven (1960) 'The bases of social power', in D. Cartwright and A. F. Zander (eds.) *Group Dynamics*, 2nd edn., Row, Peterson, Evanston, Illinios.

Gabarro, J., and J. Kotter (1980) 'Managing your boss', *Harvard Business Review*, **58**, Jan–Feb., 92–100.

Hampden-Turner, C. (1994) 'Charting the corporate mind,' in W. Bennis, J. Parikh and R. Lessem (eds.) *Beyond Leadership: Balancing Economics, Ethics and Ecology*, Blackwell, Oxford.

Harrigan, K. R. (1986) *Managing For Joint Venture Success*, D. C. Heath, Lexington, Mass.

Heilman, M. E., Hornstein, H. A., Cage, J. H., and J. K. Herschlag (1984) 'Reactions to prescribed leader behavior as a function of the role perceived: the case of the vroom-yetton model', *Journal Of Applied Psychology*, **69**, 50–60.

Hickson, D. J., C. R. Hinings, C. A. Lee, R. E. Schneck, and J. M. Pennings (1971) 'A strategic contingencies' theory of intraorganizational power', *Administrative Science Quarterly*, **16** (2), 216–29.

Hickson, D. J., R. J. Butler, D. Cray, G. R. Mallory, and D. C. Wilson (1986) *Top Decisions: Strategic Decision Making In Organizations*, Blackwell, Oxford, Jossey-Bass, San Francisco.

Hinings, C. R., D. J. Hickson, J. M. Pennings, and R. E. Schneck (1974) 'Structural conditions of intraorganizational power', *Administrative Science Quarterly*, **19** (1), 22–44.

Hosking D. M. (1988) 'Organizing, leadership and skilful processes', *Journal Of Management Studies*, **25** (2), 147–66.

House, R. J., and T. R. Mitchell (1974) 'Path-goal theory of leadership', *Journal Of Contemporary Business*, Autumn, 81–97.

House, R. J. (1971) 'A path–goal theory of leader effectiveness', *Administrative Sciences Quarterly*, **16** (2), 321–38.

Kenny, G. K. and D. C. Wilson (1984) 'The interdepartmental influence of managers: individual and sub-unit perspectives', *Journal Of Management Studies*, **21** (4), 409–27.

Leavitt, H. (1972) *Managerial Psychology: An Introduction To Individuals, Pairs, And Groups In Organizations* 3rd edn., University Of Chicago Press, Chicago and London.

Leavy, B. and D. C. Wilson (1994) *Strategy And Leadership*, Routledge, London.

Likert, R. (1967) *The Human Organization*, McGraw-Hill, New York.

Mangham, I. L (1986) *Power And Performance In Organizations: An Exploration Of Executive Process*, Blackwell, Oxford.

Meyer, J. M. and B. Rowan (1977) *Institutionalised organization: formal structures as myth and ceremony*, *American Journal of Sociology*, **83** (2), 340–63.

Mintzberg, H. (1973) *The Nature Of Managerial Work*, Harper & Row, New York.

Mintzberg, H. (1983) *Power In And Around Organizations*, Prentice-Hall, Englewood Cliffs, N.J.

Mintzberg, H. (1984) 'Power and organizational life-cycles', *Academy Of Management Review*, April, 207–24.

Pettigrew, A. M. (1973) *The Politics Of Organisational Decision Making*, Tavistock, London.

Pettigrew, A. M. (1985) *The Awakening Giant: Continuity And Change In ICI*, Blackwell, Oxford.

Pfeffer, J. and G. R. Salancik (1978) *The External Control Of Organizations: A Resource Dependence Perspective*, Harper & Row, New York.

Reddin, W. J. (1970) *Managerial Effectiveness*, McGraw-Hill, New York.

Rosener, J. B. (1990) 'Ways women lead', *Harvard Business Review*, November–December, 119–25.

Rotter, J. B. (1966) 'Generalized expectancies for internal versus external control of reinforcement', *Psychological Monographs*, **609**, 80.

Sayles, L. (1979) *Leadership: What Effective Managers Really Do, And How They Do It*, McGraw-Hill, New York.

Shackleton, V. J. (1995) *Business Leadership*, Routledge, London.

Stogdill, R. M. (1974) *Handbook Of Leadership*, Free Press, New York.

Tanennbaum, A. S. (1968) *Control In Organizations*, McGraw-Hill, New York.

Tjosvold, D., Wedley W. C. and R. H. G. Field (1986) 'Constructive controversy, the Vroom-Yetton model and managerial decision-making', *Journal Of Occupational Behaviour*, **7**, 125–38.

Useem. M., and A. McCormack (1981) 'The dominant segment of the British business elite,' *Sociology*, **15**, 381–406.

Vinnicombe, S. (1987) 'What exactly are the differences in male and female working styles?', *Women In Management Review*, **3** (1), 13–21.

Vroom, V. H., and P. Yetton (1973) *Leadership And Decision Making*, University Of Pittsburgh Press, Pittsburgh.

Wilson, F. (1995) *Organizational Behaviour And Gender*, McGraw-Hill, London.

Wilson, (1982). 'Electricity and Resistance: A Case Study of Innovation and Politics', *Organization Studies*, **3**(2), 119–40.

Politics permeate

David J. Hickson

Politics permeate organizations because organizations are collections of people who have differing past experiences, differing current circumstances and therefore potentially differing interests. Each person is interested in sustaining or improving his or her own job and future prospects, his or her own department and its future, as well as that of the organization on which both job and department depend. One highly politicized view of organizations is that of Crozier and Friedberg (1980) who see them as '*ensemble des jeux*'—groups of players vying for position in organizational games of self-interest. It may be that such a definition reflects a cultural bias. American executives seem to find over-politicized situations distasteful (Lyles, 1987).

Notwithstanding national differences, the task of accommodating everyone's interests when something is being decided is, to some extent, a political one. The instant thought 'To whose advantage?' is evidence of the political sensitivity of the managerial world. People influence one another to make sure that others are aware of their needs and problems, to make their views known and to reach some degree of consensus. Politics in this sense need not and should not have a negative connotation (Dror and Romm, 1988).

The interests implicated

Once a matter does come up for decision, numerous participants are drawn in along the way. They embody numerous affected interests. Each matter for decision impinges upon an assortment of such interests. They give the process its political character. Some may be involved in most major decisions, others only in a few. Production departments and their equivalents in service organizations (such as the medical and nursing staff in hospitals or administrative sections in insurance companies) are almost always in on the action. As are sales and the finance people. Production, sales and finance, by whichever titles they may be known in different forms of organization, are a core trio through whose hands most big decisions must pass. Others involved in many decisions are government departments and agencies, and suppliers, both of these form outside the organization itself. Personnel, research, purchasing and maintenance functions are drawn in on some decisions.

This assortment of interests coming in at one stage and exiting at another stage of the process of moving towards a decision has been called the 'decision-set' of interests (Hickson *et al.*, 1986). Some of them appear many times while a particular decision is being taken, other only once.

For those wishing to influence the course of events, the timing of the part they play can be crucial. Everyone cannot attend to everything at once. Timing when to join in and when to speak up requires political judgement. It has been suggested that even though most of the action takes place during the middle phase of a decision-making process, it is especially vital to influence the start and the finish (Heller *et al.*, 1987).

Influential interests

Pfeffer and Salancik (1978) see organizations as 'markets for influence and control'. As each interested party has something to gain and something to give, influence is created in the constant exchanges between them. In a study of British manufacturing and service organizations, trades unions influenced decisions on organization-wide personnel regrading and reallocation proposals but not decisions on investments in new technology (despite the effects these eventually may have upon their members). Customers influenced decisions on new products but not decisions on supplies of money (raising capital) or raw materials. Accounting departments influenced corporate budgets and plans but not decisions on new services where relatively little financial expenditure was required. Research or design departments influenced decisions on new products but not takeover bids, and so on (Hickson *et al.*, 1986:138).

Those internal units which exercise the greatest influence do so by influencing a range of matters not only within their own spheres but beyond that in matters that would be thought to be the primary concerns of other specialist units. Research conducted among small Canadian breweries (Hinings *et al.*, 1974) found that the production departments (the most influential of the departments) strongly influenced: (1) marketing and product packaging (primary concern of the sales departments); (2) capital budgets and personnel training (primary concerns of the small accounting-cum-personnel departments) as well as decisions on production volume, quality and efficiency within their own realm.

The set of interest units involved in the process of making a decision contains some heavyweights and lightweights. Some are involved in most decision-making and when involved are strongly influential—the heavyweights. Some are rarely involved and even if involved do not count for much—the lightweights. Then there are those who, although rarely involved, do have quite a say on those occasions when they come in, and those who although often involved have little say nevertheless. Those four groups are shown in Table R7.1. They are from the 1021 internal and external units named as having each been involved in one or more of the 150 cases of decision-making in the 30 organizations studied by Hickson *et al.*, (1986).

Table R7.1
Heavyweights and lightweight interest units

	Involvements infrequently	Involvements frequently
Influential infrequently	**Fringe lightweights** Trade unions Competitors Purchasing Maintenance personnel, etc.	**External lightweights** Auditors, trade associations, shareholders Government departments and agencies Suppliers
Influential frequently	**Fringe heavyweights** Customers, clients Research, design Liaison and claims	**Internal heavyweights** Production 'workflow' Sales, marketing Accounting, Divisions

Source: Hickson *et al.*, (1986)

The heavyweights are all internal, namely production and its equivalents in service organizations, sales and accounting (and other control departments such as inspection), and also large divisions where an organization has a divisional rather than a function form. The lightweights include purchasing, maintenance, and personnel as well as external interests such as unions and competitors. Unions were not invited to take part in decision-making nor did they seek to do so lest managerial entanglement should compromise their position. Occasionally, they would have a say on the bigger personnel grading issues, but mostly their role was to attempt to protect their members from disadvantage after the decisions had been taken (Wilson *et al.*, 1982). Competitors are important for the strategy of an organization, of course, but they were taken account of more through considering customers or clients.

Customers had substantial influence on decisions regarding new products, technology, and market-related matters such as distribution and prices. As such matters were only a minority of total strategic decisions, they were not often concerned in decision-making. Nor were research and design departments, though they were influential on matters within their own sphere. The liaison and claims category covers sections within local government and insurance companies, for example. Top right in Table R7.1 comes a group of interests all of which are external, including financial auditors, trade associations, shareholders, national and local government in all its forms, and suppliers. These become involved in many decision-making processes, but do not have much influence even so.

Solutions precede decisions

During the period it may take to reach a decision, many of those involved in the discussions will form their own ideas regarding the appropriate outcome. They are ides that are likely to have been in their minds long before the particular matter for decision took shape, even if only dimly so. Someone may have felt that co-ordination would be improved if several departments were merged, especially if this enhanced their own career chances. Someone else has recently become convinced that the company's future lies in overseas markets. Hence when a decision-making process gets underway, those involved bring a wide array of preconceived 'solutions'. Perhaps what they want may not fit into what this decision is about, but if not it may do so next time. Hence the notion of such a process as a 'garbage can' into which tumble streams of problems while participants dump in their many ready-made solutions (March and Olsen, 1976). When solutions coincide with problems that fit them, a decision is possible.

This reverses the conventional view of decision-making. Instead of an orderly process moving towards a decision, the decision is seen as 'uncoupled' from the process. This explains some of the peculiarities of the process. People do things for reasons other than making a decision. They fight for the right to participate, and then do not bother to do so. They ignore information already there, call for more, and then ignore that too. In service organizations, in particular in universities and hospitals, the process can itself be as important as the decision. Success tends to be judged more by who took part than in whether the means are available to implement a decision once taken (Rodrigues, 1980). How a decision is made can be more important than whether it is carried out.

As different 'solutions' surface during the process, there is potential for conflict. A production director and his supporters want equipment purchased, the purchasing director and those who think like him argue that money would be better put to other uses (Wilson, 1982). The production director's 'solution' comes from his long-term inclinations as an engineer to find the answer to a problem in new or better technology, whereas the purchasing director typifies his self-image as a champion of wise spending. Such views do not go away with the resolving of this particular controversy. They will remain to be voiced during other decision-making processes. So in each process there is only 'quasi-resolution of conflict' (Cyert and March, 1963), not real resolution.

The reasons for influence

Some individuals or groups have more influence than others in putting forward 'solutions' and knocking others. This results from a combination of factors which provide greater 'control of strategic contingencies' (Hickson *et al.*, 1971). By virtue of a position in the organization, others become dependent upon them and susceptible to their influence. Three reasons for this are: (1) if a department or other grouping within an organization is central to the workflows between sub-units (so the work of others waits upon what it does); (2) when its work is non-substitutable (no one else either inside or outside the organization can do what it does); and (3) when what it does effectively reduces the overall level of uncertainty felt within the organization.

In the Canadian breweries illustration (Hinings *et al.*, 1974), the production units were in every case the most influential because they coped with the main uncertainty. Markets were predictable and closely regulated by government, down to the details of advertising, distribution, sales territories and numbers of sales staff; the technology of heating and cooling liquid and passing it from vessel to vessel was simple and stable; accounting was little more than routine bookkeeping. But the quality of the hops was not under control. It varied seasonally and year to year. Thus the quality of what went into the bottles, and therefore the reputation on which all else rested, depended on the skill of the brewers in blending so as to produce a uniform output from a non-uniform input.

Crozier (1964) noticed the same phenomenon in tobacco factories in France where engineers coped with the only uncertainty in an otherwise routinized situation—the breaking down of the machinery, and wielded corresponding influence. In Israel, Cohen and Lachman (1988) found the same phenomenon in health-care clinics where the professional standing of the physicians was not sufficient of itself for predominant influence. Only by coping with primary uncertainties did they emerge as the most influential group in a clinic.

With varying influence, executives in the higher echelons of organizations strive to make what they can of the social pressures of decision-making. They may be successful, as in the story of the turn-round of Imperial Chemical Industries from a downward to an upward spiral (Pettigrew, 1985). They may fail, as the managers of a textile company whose decisions were studied by Hickson *et al.*, (1986) did when they decided to resist a takeover but were unable to prevent it.

The most political processes

The overall characters of the processes differ a great deal. The making of one strategic decision may be a most political affair, the next much less so, a third least political of all. This does not denote their importance. All will be strategic with costly and far-reaching consequences, yet some will be more political than others. The processes most likely to be politically charged have been termed 'sporadic', those less so 'constricted' those least so 'fluid' (Hickson *et al.*, 1986; Cray *et al.*, 1988).

Sporadic processes

These are most likely to be highly politically charged as they concern particularly 'weighty and controversial' matters (Hickson *et al.*, 1986: 174). These are matters with potentially serious consequences, drawing in a multiplicity of information and views from numerous departments and external sources. Many of those involved have interests which come from differing objectives. In short, such a matter is diversely involving, contentious, with external influences, from which come its political nature. Typical examples would be decisions on novel new products and on takeover bids.

What happens then is an 'informally spasmodic and protracted' process (see Chapter 10) swirling with activity. Comparatively more of the action takes place informally around the office desk or over lunch, and less in arranged meetings of committees and the like. There are flurries of action between delays, rather than smooth movement, and all this tends to take longer than otherwise. The politics of it demand time and attention.

For example, the management of a British nationalized industry had to decide what to do about a firm that was a large purchaser of its products (Hickson *et al.*, 1986: 118). A situation arose where either the firm might go out of business or it might be bought by other interested parties. The firm itself hoped for an injection of capital to revive it, but the local authorities were opposed to any expansion on ecological grounds. Here was a vital matter which involved not only internal departments but a range of powerful external bodies whose interests had to be accommodated. Spasms of work to produce and agree upon forecasts of cost and output, and prepare proposals to the other organizations concerned and appraise their counter-proposals, were broken by pauses as their next moves were awaited. After 18 months of careful negotiations the board decided to take a one-third share in its customer firm. A tricky, political process came to an end.

A constricted process

This is likely to be less politically loaded. It will probably concern a relatively 'normal and recurrent' matter that has some familiarity about it. Something similar has been dealt with before, and the way in which it will be handled is widely understood and accepted. Its consequences do not concern everyone, and in particular they do not implicate external interests. If strong influences have to be reckoned with they will be from inside the organization. In short, such a matter is comparatively well known, with consequences that are more limited, influenced by internal interests only.

So usually the process can be held within bounds. The matter moves along a 'narrowly channelled' course without too many interests becoming directly involved all at once since those concerned 'know the form' and they allow it to proceed as usual. Appropriate departmental experts contribute, but there is a minimum of committee work as most things can be settled informally. The process stays within accustomed channels around a central figure, such as a financial director or a managing director who may be able to conclude the decision without reference to any higher authority.

Yet there can be political undercurrents, always liable to surge to the surface and divert the flow of events in a sporadic direction. A corporate plan or budget is a good example. It can be prepared from the information used for the previous annual plan or budget, departments putting in their sectional estimates as usual with no need to go further for information nor anyone outside taking an interest in the decision. At the same time a plan or budget is a latent statement of the pattern of power which no one can afford to lose out. It is politically delicate.

An example of another kind was a decision to modernize an insurance company. On the surface, it was a commitment to update and centralize data processing for the main line of business, vehicle insurance. But its underlying significance was much greater. The company had been taken over by a larger firm and its management feared obliteration by the new owners. They set out to defend the company by demonstrating that it was such a good profit-earner that it would be best left undisturbed. Their decision to rationalize administration and organization was a political move to this end.

Fluid processes   Least politically prone are *fluid processes* since they are unlikely to encounter controversy. Most often they focus on 'unusual but non-controversial' matters. Although the consequences will be widely felt they are not likely to be as serious as those of the weighty kind of question which excites a sporadic process. Moreover, fewer interests are implicated, and their objectives are compatible. Influence is evenly spread, no one interest having sufficient influence to attempt to push its proposals forward in a way that could arouse controversy and resistance. In short, though such a matter can be quite novel and have diffuse consequences, it is not excessively serious or contentious. So it is unlikely to be dealt with in a relatively smooth 'steadily paced, formally channelled, speedy' way.

For example, the management of a retail financial services supplier was pursuing an expansionist strategy. The question arose whether they should take this as far as offering current-account facilities in direct competition to the clearing banks or continue with merely paying out cash to depositors in person. The decision-making was straightforward. It revolved around the deliberations of a special managerial working committee set up to consider the matter. They met regularly to collate and assess information on costs and competition, and a year later, the main board accepted its recommendation to take the risk. It was a smooth committee-co-ordinated process.

Interests, influence, and the resulting politics are, then, the very stuff of decision-making in organizations. How else could it be when organizations are made up of so many people with diverse viewpoints and are surrounded by so many others who have a stake in what they do? Highly politically charged matters, the sort which energize sporadic processes, arise most often in manufacturing and in publicly owned organizations (Hickson *et al.*, 1986). But evidence suggests that they arise sooner or later in every kind of organization. Managers are constantly making and remaking the decisions that shape the future of an organization. What they decide is shaped by interests within and without, and subsequent events may change what they intend to happen. Nevertheless, most of the time they are more in control than anyone else is, and their decisions affect not only their own lives but the lives of many others.

References

Cohen, I. and R. Lachman (1988) 'The generality of the strategic contingencies approach to subunit power', *Organization Studies*, **9**, 371–91.

Cray, D., G. R. Mallory, R. J. Butler, D. J. Hickson and D. C. Wilson (1988) 'Sporadic fluid and constricted processes: three types of strategic decision-making in organizations', *Journal of Management Studies*, **25** (1), 13–39.

Crozier, M. (1964) *The Bureaucratic Phenomenon*, Tavistock, London.

Crozier, M. and E. Friedberg (1980) *Actors and Systems*, University of Chicago Press, Chicago.

Cyert, R. M. and J. G. March (1963) *A Behavioural Theory of the Firm*, Prentice Hall, Englewood Cliffs, New Jersey.

Dror, Y. and T. Romm (1988) 'Politics in organizations and its perception within the organization', *Organization Studies*, **9** (2), 165–80.

Heller, F., P. Drenth, P. Koopman and V. Rus (1987) *Decisions in Organizations: A Three Country Longitudinal Study*, Wiley, New York.

Hickson, D. J., R. J. Butler, D. Cray, G. R. Mallory and D. C. Wilson (1986) *Top Decisions: Strategic Decision-Making in Organizations*, Blackwell, Oxford; Jossey-Bass, San Francisco.

Hickson, D. J., C. R. Hinings, C. A. Lee, R. E. Schneck and J. M. Pennings (1971) 'A strategic contingencies' theory of intra-organizational power', *Administrative Science Quarterly*, **16** (2), 216–29.

Hinings, C. R., D. J. Hickson, J. M. Pennings and R. E. Schneck (1974) 'Structural conditions of intraorganizational power', *Administrative Science Quarterly* **19** (1), 22–44.

Lyles, M. (1987) 'Defining strategic problems: subjective criteria of executives', *Organization Studies*, **8** (3), 263–80.

March, J. G. and J. P. Olsen (1976) *Ambiguity and Choice in Organizations*, Universitesforlaget, Oslo and Tromso.

Pettigrew, A. (1985) *The Awakening Giant*, Blackwell, Oxford.

Pfeffer, J. and G. R. Salancik (1978) *The External Control of Organizations: A Resolute Dependence Perspective*, Harper & Row, London.

Rodrigues, S. B. (1980) 'Processes of successful managerial decision-making in organizations', PhD Thesis, University of Bradford, Yorkshire.

Wilson, D. C. (1982) 'Electricity and resistance: a case study of innovation and politics', *Organization Studies*, **3** (2), 119–40.

Wilson, D. C., R. J. Butler, D. Cray, D. J. Hickson and G. R. Mallory (1982) 'The limits of trade union power in organizational decision-making', *British Journal of Industrial Relations*, **20** (3), 322–41.

READING 8

Leadership processes

Dian-Marie Hosking

Introduction

'Leadership' has returned to the boutique of management fashion. Leaders again are celebrated. Attention has shifted from junior managers, to chief executives (CEOs), and consequently, from groups 'in' organizations, to organizations as 'wholes'. No longer are we called on to abandon the concept of leadership as unhelpful. Instead, tributes are trumpeted to the designers of 'excellence': organizations are treated as designer goods, more or less effectively fashioned by CEOs who have learned 'human handling skills' (Bennis and Nanus, 1985) or learned how to motivate through 'beautiful values' (Peters and Waterman, 1982).

The purpose of this reading is not to review the vast literatures on leadership thorough treatments of this kind may be found elsewhere (Bryman, 1986; Smith and Peterson, 1988). Rather, the intention is to indicate what a truly *social-psychological perspective* must look like and why. Arguments are also laid out for a model in which the concepts of leadership and organizations are integrated using the concept of skill; a more detailed description can be found in Hosking and Morley (1988).

Leadership is argued to be central to the dynamics of organizations (Hosking, 1983; Hosking and Morley, 1988). The concept of 'organization' is here being used as a verb, not a noun, as is more usual. Few have attempted to develop the concept of 'organizing' as an alternative for the concept of organization. Work of this kind has much to recommend it.

It will be argued that the skills of leadership are the skills of organizing: the concept of *skill* will be offered as a way of integrating the analysis of leadership and organization. The skills are claimed to be those implicated in the processes of *political decision-making*, very broadly defined. Processes of this sort are viewed as fundamental to the creation and maintenance of social order within and between groups. Broadly speaking, a perspective is adopted in which leadership processes are understood to define and implement understandings concerning the status quo, or rather, potential changes which imply either losses or gains for a given group (see Chapter 11).

It should be said that the model is intended to facilitate analysis of leadership and organization regardless of whether there are appointed managers, contracts of employment, or a written charter. So, for example, it has been employed to analyse more or less effective strategies for organizing women's groups (Brown and Hosking, 1986), and the 'domestic portfolio' of tasks (Hosking, 1989), as well as design teams, and chief executive action (Hosking and Mann, 1988).

The model is intended to be neither predictive, nor causal. It is offered as an 'appreciation', emphasizing the crucial ways in which organization is a matter, not just of 'fact', but also, value. Leadership and organization are infused with value. To understand this requires knowing something of the skills involved.

Contexts of leadership: managers and managerial processes

A great deal of 'leadership' research has concentrated on managers: on persons charged, through formal appointment, with responsibility for the work of others. Such persons have been deemed to be leaders on the grounds of their appointed responsibilities; alternatively, they are assumed to meet some analytical criterion such as being the prime source of influence over the work of others (e.g. Hosking, 1981).

This said, leadership typically has been abstracted from the broader context of managerial work and organizing activity. It was partly through an examination of the literatures on managerial work that the 'organizing skills' model emerged. These will be reviewed briefly to show what is important for the understanding of leadership.

Managerial work: activities, contacts and content

Studies of managerial work can broadly be summarized under three headings: activities, contacts, and content.

Managerial activities

There exists a long tradition of studies designed to document the 'observable' aspects of what managers do. Through methods such as diary completion, and activity sampling, there has emerged a picture of what seems to be typical. It seems clear that any attempt seriously to discuss leadership in the context of management has to recognize that 'live action', usually face-to-face, is the norm; quiet reflection, and solitary action is relatively rare (Mintzberg, 1973; Whitely, 1984).

Live action is very significant, but not for the reasons commonly supposed. The model shortly to be outlined emphasizes that leadership is effected through 'live action', or more precisely, through social relationships; relationships are a basic resource in the definition, negotiation, and implementation of strategy.

Contacts

Managers have very large contact networks (Kotter, 1982; Stewart, 1976). These may be (a) authority relationships as might be formalized by an organization chart; (b) 'lateral' contacts, where neither has formal authority over the other; and (c) contact may be with someone 'outside' the manager's own workplace. The extent and significance of non-authority relations (b) and (c) has largely been ignored. It is these that suggest networking (rather than hierarchy), negotiations and exchange (rather than authority) are central to organizing processes and leadership. The model shortly to be outlined argues that leadership is more effective in protecting and promoting particular values and projects when *relationships* are used as medium for strategic action (Grieco and Hosking, 1987; Brown and Hosking, 1986).

Content

Authors such as Stewart, and Mintzberg, have written of their attempts to get at the 'content' of managerial behaviour. They have remarked on the difficulties involved in getting at the 'deep structure' and purposes of activities. The interest is in understanding what is 'going on' at a 'deeper level' when, for example, a manager is on the phone, participating in an unplanned meeting, or extending a network of contacts.

The kinds of questions that might be posed include: what is being learned and why; what knowledge bases are being drawn on, and contributed to; what are the essential human competences implicated in such activity; are the activities strategic, and if so, in pursuit of whose values and whose active interests (projects)? Questions such as these focus on the strategic aspects of *social* processes and their interrelated *cognitive* and *political* elements; questions such as these have seldom been asked; they are addressed in the 'organizing skills' model.

Implications

What we know about managerial activities and contacts suggests the need further to investigate social processes—interactions and relationships— particularly their strategic and negotiated qualities. The prevalence of social action should be taken, not as evidence of the absence of planning, but rather, as the context of 'cognition'. The processes of social action are recognized as the means by which individuals seek to protect their values and promote their projects. Similarly, the processes of leadership, management, and organization, can be 'joined' and 'ordered' through influence, in relation to value.

Contexts of leadership: organization

It is relatively uncontroversial to suggest that the concept of organization implies the following three elements. First, people must be 'included'—or some subset of their values, knowledge, and actions repertoires (Lewin, 1951). Second, organization implies relationships which have cognitive, social and political aspects. Third, relationships will show a degree of stability such that actions and interactions can be grounded in 'explanations' of the past, and anticipations of the future.

Writings on organization can broadly be distinguished but two traditions. These emphasize: on the one hand, organization as a noun—as a state, entity, or 'condition'; and on the other, organization as a verb—as activity and process (see Hosking, 1988).

There is a need for increased attention to organization as a verb. Such an approach offers a general framework for the study of organizing, whether or not the actors are legally contracted to the same, or indeed any, employer. What is important is that organizing is performed in interrelated social, cognitive, and political processes. The processes (a) reflect and effect differing values and interests; (b) reflect and create interdependence and inequalities of influence; (c) require leadership to facilitate their flexibility and effective long-term promotion of core values.

Leaders and leadership

Three elements seem common to most definitions of leadership. *First,* leadership is a fundamentally social phenomenon, and some form of social interaction, usually face-to-face, is required. *Second,* leadership has the effect of structuring activities and relationships. *Third,* to be defined as a *leader,* a participant must be perceived as salient, relative to others: in particular, they will be recognized as of higher status in terms of their contributions to influence.

Person or process

The bulk of research claimed to concern leadership has, in fact, focused on appointed officials—managers and the like. The approach has largely been 'top-down', attention being directed to those role occupants who are either assumed to be active in leadership processes, or who are assumed to meet some other conceptual requirement. As a result, a considerable portion of research has investigated *leaders'* characteristics, leadership being treated as though it were one.

In contrast, a 'bottom-up' approach does not conflate the concepts of leaders and leadership. Leadership *processes* are the focus of interest, leaders being identified as those who make especially salient contributions. This is the approach advocated here. Leadership acts are contributed by participants who 'influence their fellows more than they are influenced by them' (Gibb, 1969: 212). However, to be defined as leadership acts, it is essential that such influence is acceptable. Leaders are defined as those who 'consistently make effective contributions to social order, and who are expected and perceived to do so' (Hosking and Morley, 1988).

It is for these reasons that leadership here is claimed as a certain kind of 'organizing' activity. When leadership is defined in this way it implies: first, that leaders may or may not be appointed officials; second, that there may be one or more of them; third, that they can be identified only through the analysis of leadership processes; and last, that leadership processes, like organizing processes, cannot usefully be restricted within the arbitrary bounds of 'formal' organizations.

Physical and social realities

Those who have focused on leaders, and leadership as a personal characteristic, have paid little attention to the social realities of leaders or those with whom they interact. 'Situational' and 'organizational' characteristics have generally been treated as contextual variables, independent of the activities and sense-making of participants. This approach has dominated work on leadership, just as it has dominated work on organizations. This reflects in a person–situation split which treats: leaders as entities; leadership as their relatively unbounded acts; and contexts as conditions independent of participants' cognitive–social processes.

An emphasis on social realities directs attention to the sense-making activities of *all* participants; indeed, this is how leaders are identified. Sense-making identifies: acts which influence social constructions; those perceived to make the most consistent and significant contributions; and why they are perceived to do so.

Unitary or pluralist perspective

The unitary approach minimizes differences in values and interests as they might exist between groups 'within' an organization. When investigating leadership contributions such differences cannot be ignored (Hosking, 1984). Values and interests cannot be ignored for the reason that they are central to participants' constructions of their social order and the terms on which they will 'do business'.

A pluralist approach recognizes that political processes are endemic to leadership. Leadership is a political matter for the reason that participants differ in their projects and in their influence. Leadership is political for the reason that some values are likely to be promoted at the expense of others.

Choices and constraints

A bottom-up approach makes no assumptions about who necessarily exercises choice, or who are necessarily constrained: leaders are identified by the effects of their acts, not by the fact of their appointment. Leadership is considered as a process in which social order is negotiated, sometimes tacitly, and sometimes explicitly. Those who achieve most influence in the course of negotiations, who do so most consistently, and who come to be expected and perceived to do so, are defined as leaders.

Leadership processes: summary

Leaders emerge in the course of political decision processes: These 'organizing processes' involve the collective negotiation of social order, including recipes for action, and the terms of exchange. To have any degree of permanence, social order must be flexible to the degree that relatively enduring changes can be both created and handled. This is a 'dilemma' intrinsic to all social organization (Brown and Hosking, 1986). It is a dilemma because an 'uncommitted potentiality for change' (Bateson, 1972) must be achieved without sacrificing stability sufficient for participants to experience a sense of identity and continuity. There are various ways of trying to reconcile these conflicting demands, however, only some are effective in the longer term (Weick, 1979: 217). The handling of this dilemma is what leadership is all about. The processes required to achieve this must be very skilful indeed.

Leadership, skill, and the negotiation of order

It is now possible to outline an integrative model which combines these findings about management, leadership, and organization. Such a model requires adequate concepts of participants, processes, and contexts theorized in terms which are commensurate with the model.

Decision-making processes

The skills of leadership are the skills of complex decision-making. Decision-making is understood to begin when one or more participants conclude that the status quo is changing, is likely to change, or is in need of change, and takes action on that basis. Actual and potential changes are interpreted in relation to values and interests, and in relation to beliefs about causal connections. Changes may be interpreted as either 'threats' or 'opportunities', that is, as potential losses or gains in relation to particular projects.

Decision-making is complex when the consequences of a given course of action or policy are unclear. It is complex to the extent that some consequences seem desirable while others do not. It is complex when it is political: when participants disagree about 'the value at stake, the weight to be given to them, and the resolution of major uncertainties' (Steinbruner, 1974: 18). The skills in decision-making can be discussed using the terms summarized in Figure R8.1. Through their 'networking' actors effect the 'core processes' of search, interpretation, influence and choice. In so doing, they both build and mobilize 'knowledge bases' and other resources for influence. Through these processes, the 'core problems' of the social order are organized in relation to 'value'. Figure R8.1 shows each element to be connected with each other element. This is consistent with the argument that relations between persons and contexts are 'two'-way.

Networking, core processes, and core problems

Decision-makers may be more or less active in making social contacts and in building relationships. They may do so within their social order, and with persons 'outside' it. Social contacts provide information, sponsorship, and other resources, depending on factors such as the strength of direct and indirect relationships, and whether the participants share the same sense of social order.

'Networking' is a major organizing activity which may make all the difference to whether or not changes in the status quo are understood and handled. Networking may be performed by only a few, or by many participants in organizing. Networking has strategic implications, whether or not it is practised consciously. Leadership processes are more likely to be skilful when one or more participants is active in networking with those on whom the interests of the order most depend.

Figure R8.1
Schematic
representation of
organizing processes

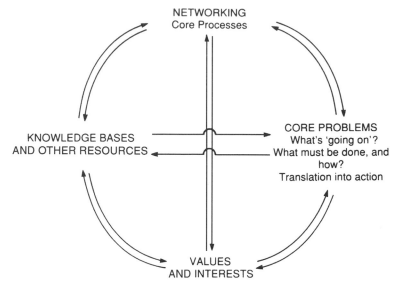

Through networking participants: (a) build up their knowledge bases, (b) understand the processes through which they can promote their values and interests; and (c) translate their understanding into action. Through these processes, they handle the 'core problems' of working out what is going on, what can and must be done, and how to implement these understandings.

Networking and knowledge

Networking is the social vehicle for cognition. 'Cognition' is a generic term used to refer to the totality of processes which affect appreciations of the 'outside' world, and the ways these are represented (Forgas, 1983). Networking is a more or less continuous process of building and implementing what recently has become known as 'practical intelligence' (Sternberg and Wagner, 1986). If managers, or indeed anyone else, learns the 'how' and 'why' of organizing and leadership, they do so, not by 'academic' means (Scribner, 1986) but through the social processes of networking.

Networking contributes to knowledge building through its relationship with 'ordinary seeing' (Neisser, 1976). In moving around, participants are less likely to distort, deny, or remain unaware of contradictions (Nisbett and Ross, 1980; Steinbruner, 1974). Networking reduces the likelihood of inflexible, categorical judgements, and by facilitating the recognition and accommodation of change, facilitates social learning (Figure R18.1).

Skilful organizing is a matter of getting the 'right' description of changes in the status quo. Given the arguments about the social construction of realities, 'right' does not have to mean 'real'. Instead, views about what is right are judgements that a particular description is reasonable, sensible, and agreeable. By 'moving around', participants can float ideas and get feedback to help them determine what agreements will work and which will be acceptable (Huff, 1984).

Some people 'move around' more than others; what is more, some are better than others in networking with those on whom they are, or could be, dependent. Similarly, groups differ in the degree to which one or more participants are active in these ways, and are expected to be so (Brown and Hosking, 1986).

Networking and influence

Networking helps to achieve influence, both within the social order, and with those 'outside'. Whether inside or 'outside' the group, relationships provide the medium for achieving direct and indirect influence, that is, for structuring the interpretations and choices of those on whom the values and interests of the group depend.

One of the ways in which influence is achieved follows from reasons already given: networking facilitates the development of 'knowledge bases'. Through networking 'information' is invested with value; it is in these processes that leadership is evidenced, since leadership acts are those which most influence what information is used and how. When particular individuals consistently make contributions of this kind, and are expected to do so, the term 'leader' is appropriate. For these reasons, leaders have a major impact on the creation of 'social knowledge' (Trujillo, 1983).

Networking, negotiation, and exchange

Negotiation characterizes relationships because: *different people sponsor different 'scripts'*, and influence has to be acceptable. Some participants are more influential than others because they know what, why and how to negotiate. Generally, negotiation characterizes processes within and between groups so that understandings are built and translated into action. These are organizing processes in which particular acts achieve influence and come to be associated with particular individuals, e.g. leaders emerge.

Organizing processes are processes of *exchange*. The term 'exchange' here is used broadly to include fairly tangible resources of the sort emphasized in *economic* perspectives, and in discussion of 'translational leadership' (Burns, 1978). However, importance is also attached to *symbolic* resources as contributed by acts which give meaning and perspective to events. A major reason why participants gain power in a system of relationships is because others come to rely on them for contributions of this kind. It seems to be popular to exclude such processes from the range of the exchange concept, defining them as something unusual, as 'transformational leadership' (Burns, 1978). However, the more general concept of exchange is essential for the understanding of leadership and organizing of long-term relationships and to the understanding of 'flexible' social order.

Knowledge bases

The processes developing and sharing knowledge has also been called 'organizational learning' (see Shrivastava, 1983). Those who are active in networking are more likely to be skilled 'perceivers' and skilled in the achievement of influence. What follows is a description of the knowledge bases they build and deploy.

Threats and opportunities

Those active in networking have more than one account of events and are more likely to understand which issues require action. They also will have a better understanding of these issues as potential threats and opportunities. When threats and opportunities are skilfully handled, the values and interests of the group are more likely to be protected and promoted.

Capacities and demands

Skill lies in the use of 'efficient strategies' to link the '*demands*' of tasks with the '*capacities*' of performers (Welford, 1980). 'Demands' are core problems: 'capacities' are resources, which are limited. These limitations have important implications for understanding threats and opportunities, and for mobilizing relationships to achieve influence.

'Efficient strategies' are likely to be more consistently practised by those who are active in networking. This is because they have more diverse and/or accurate 'scripts', but also they have built relationships within which they can negotiate acceptance of their influence. 'Demands' are met through the development and mobilisation of capacities, that is, network resources.

Dilemmas

Dilemmas are endemic to the process of complex decision-making and, therefore, to organizational processes. Dilemmas make decision-making difficult, and often stressful. They characterize situations of choice whereby selection of policy—concerning means or ends—rules out an alternative, and in so doing, *leaves a problem unresolved.*

Perhaps the most fundamental dilemma is that which underlies the achievement of 'flexible social order'. The dilemma is how to achieve a degree of order which is *sufficient* for core problems to continue to be solved, while at the same time *not too much*—perpetuating a rigid way of doing things as they have always been done.

Other kinds of knowledge

A number of authors have noted the extent and significance of knowledge bases in achieving effective organization. For example, certain general managers have been observed to be 'incredibly knowledgeable' about various aspects of their business (Kotter, 1982: 126). In particular, they have been found to have a high degree of 'organizational familiarity' and 'industry familiarity' (Gupta, 1984). Knowledge bases of this kind are an essential feature of flexible social orders.

What is important here is that the relevant knowledge is both *available* and *able to be mobilized.* Those most active in networking are most likely to contribute to, and make sense of, the network's knowledge bases, to have the relationships which will facilitate their mobilization and, therefore, to be most consistently influential in the structuring of social order. It is in this sense that leaders contribute most to skilful leadership processes.

Summary

Substantial literatures are to be found on 'leadership' and 'organization'; these literatures are almost entirely independent of each other. The concepts can, and should, be theorized in relation to one another. A model has been described which does just this. It is believed to represent a truly social psychological approach; combining arguments about persons, processes and contexts. This has been achieved through taking the view that leadership cannot be abstracted from the organizational processes of which it is a part. The study of leadership, properly conceived, is the study of the processes in which flexible social order is negotiated and practised so as to protect and promote the values and interests in which it is grounded. The skills here described are endemic to these processes such that if they are at a low level, the social order will be unlikely to survive long. Equally, to the extent that organizing processes reflect high levels of these skills, the values and interests of the social order are likely to be protected and promoted. To the extent that particular participants are expected and perceived to make consistent, influential, contributions, it is argued that leaders are to make especially important contributions to skilful organizing.

References

Bateson, G. (1972) *Steps to an Ecology of Mind*, Intertext, London.

Bennis, W. and B. Nanus (1985) *Leaders: Strategies for Taking Charge*. Harper & Row, New York.

Brown, H. and D. Hosking (1986) 'Distributed leadership and skilled performance as successful organization in social movements'. *Human Relations*, **39** (1), 65–79.

Bryman, A. (1986) *Leadership and Organizations*, RKP, London.

Burns, J. (1978) *Leadership*, Harper & Row, New York.

Forgas, J. P. (1983) 'Social skills and the perception of interaction episodes', *British Journal of Clinical Psychology*, **22**, 195–207.

Gibb, C. (1969) 'Leadership', in G. Lindzey and E. Aronson (eds), *Handbook of Social Psychology*, **4**, 2nd, Addison-Wesley, Mass.

Grieco, M. S. and D. M. Hosking (1987) 'Networking, exchange and skill', *International Studies of Management and Organization*, XVII, No. 1, 75–87.

Gupta, A. (1984) 'Contingency linkages between strategy and general manager characteristics: a conceptual examination', *Academy of Management Review*, **9**, 299–412.

Hosking, D. M. (1981) 'A Critical Evaluation of Fiedler's Contingency Hypothesis', *Progress in Applied Social Psychology*, **1**, G. Stephenson and J. Davis (eds), Wiley, New York.

Hosking, D. M. (1983) 'Leadership skills and organizational forms: the management of uncertainty', Paper Presented to the Sixth EGOS Colloquin, Florence.

Hosking, D. M. (1984) 'On paradigms and pigs', in J. Hunt, D. Hosking, C. Schriesheim and R. Stewart (eds), *Leaders and Managers: International Perspectives on Managerial Behaviour and Leadership*, Pergamon, Oxford.

Hosking, D. M. (1988) Organizing, Leadership and Skilful Process, *Journal of Management Studies*, **25** (2), 147–66.

Hosking, D. M. (1989) 'Organizing the domestic portfolio', in M. Grieco, L. Pickup and R. Whipp, *Gender, Transport and Employment*, Gower, Aldershot.

Hosking, D. M. and L. Mann (1988) 'The Organizing Skills of CEO's: A strategic Decision-Making Perspective', XXIV International Congress of Psychology, Sydney, Australia, August.

Hosking, D. M. and I. E. Morley (1988) 'The skills of leadership', in J. G. Hunt, R. Baliga, P. Dachler and G. Shriesheim, *Emerging Leadership Vistas*, Arlington Heights, Lexington, Mass.

Huff, A. (1984) 'Situation interpretation, leader behaviour, and effectiveness', in J. Hunt, D. Hosking, D. Schriesheim and R. Stewart (eds), *Leaders and Managers: International Perspectives on Managerial Behaviour and Leadership*, Pergamon, Oxford.

Kotter, J. (1982) The General Manager, Free Press, London.

Lewin, K. (1951) *Field Theory in Social Science*, Harper & Row, New York.

Mintzberg, H. (1973) *The Nature of Managerial Work*, Harper & Row, New York.

Neisser, U. (1976) *Cognition and Reality*, Freeman, San Francisco.

Nisbett, R. and L. Ross (1980) *Human Inference: Strategies and Shortcomings of Social Judgement*, Prentice Hall, Englewood Cliffs, New Jersey.

Peters, T. J. and R. H. Waterman, Jr. (1982) *In Search of Excellence: Lessons from America's Best Run Companies*, Harper & Row, New York.

Pugh, S. and I. E. Morley (1988) *Total Design*, University of Strathclyde, Monograph.

Scribner, S. (1986) 'Thinking in action: some characteristics of practical thought', in R. J. Sternberg and R. K. Wagner (eds), *Practical Intelligence: Nature of Origins of Competence in the Everyday World*, Cambridge University Press, Cambridge.

Shrivastava, P. (1983) 'A typology of organizational learning systems', *Journal of Management Studies*, **20**, 7–28.

Smith, P. B. and M. F. Peterson (1988) *Leadership, Organizations, and Culture*, Sage, London.

Steinbruner, J. (1974) 'The cybernetic theory of decision', Princeton University Press, New Jersey.

Sternberg, R. J. and R. K. Wagner (1986) *Practical Intelligence: Nature and Origins of Competence in the Everyday World*, Cambridge University Press, Cambridge.

Stewart, R. (1976) *Contrasts in Management*, McGraw-Hill, New York.

Trujillo, N. (1983) 'Performing Mintzberg's roles: the nature of managerial communication', in L. Putman and M. Pacanowsky (eds) *Communication in Organizations: An Interpretive Approach*, Sage, London.

Vickers, G. (1968) *Value Systems and Social Process*, Tavistock Publications, London.

Weick, K. (1979) *The Social Psychology of Organizing*, Addison-Wesley, Mass.

Welford, A. (1980) 'The concept of skill and its application to social performance' in W. Singleton, P. Spurgeon and R. Stammers (eds), *The Analysis of Social Skill*, Plenum Press, London.

Whitely, W. (1984) 'An exploratory study of managers reactions to properties of verbal communication', *Personal Psychology*, **33**, 77–89.

The Thoul plant

David Coghlan

The Thoul plant is a 30-year old plant which manufactures pharmaceutical supplies. It has a workforce of about 250 people comprising operators, fitters, electricians, managerial and administrative staff. It operates a 24-hour shift system. The plant is part of a multi-national company whose headquarters are in the USA. Prior to the late 1980s the plant was under the direct management of a sister plant in another city in the same country. In many respects the plant could be described as being a traditional plant from the 1950s and 1960s. There was a strong trade union culture with militant relationships between unions and management around changes in work practices. Job demarcation was clearly defined. There were strong subcultures between fitters, electricians and grades of operators within the workforce. Front-line management style was autocratic and confrontive. The plant was perceived as being old, sleepy and inefficient. To close it would have been costly.

Under a company reorganization in the late 1980s the plant's reporting relationship was changed. Instead of being directly under its sister plant, it reported to a European group headquarters in Germany. A new manager from outside the country was appointed to turn the plant into a more efficient operation in three years. This new plant manager was well-versed in organization development (OD) and committed himself to transforming the culture of the plant as means to its survival and profitability. He had a commitment to treat people better and move away from the old style of management. He wanted to foster good industrial relations and maintain the role of the trade unions. A total organizational approach was adopted. A total quality (TQ) programme was initiated and a movement towards achieving an ISO 9000 qualification was begun. The plant manager initiated team briefings and business updates. There was considerable investment in technological skills development. Technicians were sent on courses and visited corporate headquarters to learn the latest technology. Trade union officials were given the opportunity to attend courses in trade union studies. As well as the groups which had been set up to deal with the total quality issues, interdisciplinary task forces were used to solve problems. In these groups, electricians, fitters, operators and engineers met to solve technical problems.

To support the total quality management (TQM) programme, the plant manager realized that a change in the culture and mindset of the employees was pivotal to the renewal of the plant. This was articulated as a movement from 'control to commitment' (a term adopted from a well-known *Harvard Business Review* article of the same title by Richard Walton). Accordingly, investment in supervisory skills and team-building was initiated. An OD consultant was hired to conduct some coaching skills and team-building workshops.

In the supervisory skills workshops the focus was on developing listening skills. What emerged in the workshops was that when there was a problem the supervisors' natural tendency was to adopt a disciplinary mode of dealing with a subordinate. Accordingly, many situations tended to escalate. Through the workshops supervisors learned to 'ask before telling' and found that by adopting an enquiring and listening mode they could facilitate the resolution of problems more expeditiously and maintain good working relationships with subordinates, rather than initiating a disciplinary approach and creating unnecessary inter-personal tension.

Day-long team-building workshops were held with the plant management team, the production teams' supervisors, the quality control team and the administrative services team over an 18-month period. Each workshop focused on:

1   the team's goals—what they were, how they were decided;
2   the team's procedures in allocating the work to achieve the goals;
3   the team process—how information was communicated among the team members, its meetings and how they were conducted, how the team solved problems and made decisions, how conflict was managed and how the team leader exercised his or her role, and;
4   the relationships between the members. Focus was also given to relationships and workflow issues with other teams.

For some of the teams these workshops were the first time they had been afforded the opportunity to take time off-site to discuss and review team-based issues. In the initial stages of the team-building sessions the teams tended to generate engineering hit lists, that is, engineering issues they needed to resolve, and slipped easily into discussing these. Through the interventions of the process consultant they began to learn how to review *team process* issues and develop a sense of team. They reviewed procedures for problem identification and resolution and set up processes whereby procedures and roles could be reviewed. They worked on their perceptions of their role as team members and as supervisors of others. As supervisors they began to realize that they needed to initiate building a sense of team with their own shifts. This involved a re-thinking of the role of the supervisor. Between team-building sessions with the consultant some teams set goals which they did not keep and, so in reviewing, learned to review how it was that some things did not get done.

The plant's management team had its own particular agenda which was concerned with the development of the business plan and the constant focus on process through the organization. Communication of what was happening, building a team culture and redefining the role of the supervisors were critical issues. As each of its members was a leader of another team, the team-building sessions afforded the opportunity for them to learn about team process so as to model it in their own teams. They reflected on the way the plant manager facilitated their development and the effect it was having on them in terms of their sense of confidence in building teams with their subordinates.

Over the 18 months the OD consultant held two team-building sessions with each team, six months apart, conducted workshops for all supervisors and managers on 'managing change', 'leading a team' and 'managing meetings'. At the end of the period, the human resources manager reported that while some progress was evident, there were still issues outstanding. He reflected that the follow-up team-building sessions had not moved the teams on as the management had hoped. Development needed to happen more quickly than the employees perceived. There was a good deal of denial about the seriousness of the problems relating to the plant's future and so there was a lack of a sense of urgency in achieving the terms of the business plan. There was a need for a significant development of cross-functional awareness and co-operation.

Questions

1   What were the significant behavioural elements which were perceived by the plant manager as hindrances to the effective implementation of developing technology and the total quality programme? What needed to happen to deal with these elements?

2   What did the OD programme aim to achieve? How did it go about meeting the issues you have identified in your answer to Question 1?

3   If you were the plant manager what would you do now?

Software writing team

Terry Thornley

The software team's project

The project was concerned with the development of a management planning system. The system held large amounts of financial and accounting data and used COBOL programs to access and dissect the data in order to adapt it and produce reports. The users ran the system interactively from a terminal receiving output either to the terminal or as hard copy. The system had proved very popular within the company and had become a potentially viable commercial product.

The project had been running for about two years under the control of the system designer. Various people had worked on it but the team concerned in the research had been together for approximately 18 months. The project had been developed in 'releases' and was in fact completed at the time of writing. New releases were concerned with improvements and amendments aimed at making the product of the project more flexible and improving its general capability. As the demand for the product increased it grew too large to be controlled by the team. More forward planning and direction was needed. Control was passing from the team to individuals higher up in the organization.

Team members

The project leader, for analysis and design, was Caroline. She was also the troubleshooter and spent quite a lot of time with the users in London. The rest of the time she was mainly with the rest of the team in the North of the UK. She was the only permanent company employee in the team. Elizabeth was originally employed as a contract programmer/analyst but took over as team leader when the person originally appointed as team leader proved unsuccessful. Her appointment was made by Caroline. Andrew and Peter were contract programmers. Both were appointed by Caroline. Janet was the industrial trainee who joined the team when the previous trainee left to go back to college.

The five people identified above formed the software team. Above them were Stuart and Alan, who were concerned with forward planning and the general progression of the project. Alan was subordinate to Stuart and was supposed to be the link between the team and Stuart. This presented few problems for most of the life of the project because Stuart was an absent external manager, leaving Caroline as *de facto* manager. In the months immediately prior to the research, however, Stuart had started to play a larger part in the management of the project—a development that was strongly resented by the team.

In the early stages of the project Sally and June were employed as home programmers. The women worked at home, part-time, so it took longer for their programs to be completed. Consequently, they were always behind the rest of the team and communication between them and the team was not very good. Their mode of work did not fit in with that of the team and their level of commitment seemed lower. After they had completed an initial batch of work Caroline terminated their employment, which met with the approval of the rest of the team.

The internal organization of the team

The members of the team did not enter it with predetermined responsibilities. They entered as programmers or programmer/analysts and little was known of the industrial trainee's abilities. The allocation of tasks occurred partly through Caroline's assessment of the strengths and weaknesses of the team members and partly through negotiation and mutual agreement:

> We all sat down and agreed about the splitting of the work. It's the same sort of idea when new work comes in—we talk about it and ideas are thrown around until there is a volunteer or someone is volunteered!

Although this had led to the allocation of tasks to specific individuals such allocations were not seen as final. Tasks could be reallocated depending on workloads and timescales.

The level of standardization of tasks and procedures in the team had largely been determined by the members themselves. For example, they had their own programming standards which they applied as experienced professionals. Where it was felt necessary, such as the ordering of stationery and manuals, standard routines were used. In other areas, however, such as complaints about the computer service, standard procedures were not maintained. On the whole, few rules and standards had been imposed on the team by the larger organization.

There was little emphasis on formalization within the team. For example, program designs were usually agreed verbally rather than programmers being issued with specific instructions. Each contractor had a formal contract with the organization but the work he or she did bore little relationship to the job description associated with the post. Caroline did not have a job description: 'I don't exist!' There was little formal communication with higher management in the form of rules and regulations but the team communicated formally through memoranda with individuals and departments concerned with the project. Communication between the members of the team was largely verbal.

A formal hierarchy existed to the extent that Caroline was in charge of the project and Elizabeth was team leader but there were few signs of superior/subordinate relationships in the day-to-day activities of the team. Authority largely resided with the individual who possessed the requisite skill, knowledge and expertise.

Leadership of the team

Caroline acted as the leader of the team. Although Elizabeth was designated team leader she largely played a passive role, being seen by the other members as Caroline's deputy. Elizabeth filled an enabling role, for example, performing liaison and co-ordinative duties, though she also held the team together on a day-to-day basis.

Caroline was the driving force behind the project and the team. She was very committed to the project and was acknowledged as a hard worker:

She wants to develop a very high standard product.

She had a good understanding of the strengths and weaknesses of the individuals in the team and had helped to shape their roles, though she expected roles to change in a dynamic way and viewed the process of reformulation of tasks, etc. as being a matter of negotiation between members of the team rather than direction by her. Similarly, she imposed few controls on the team with regard to either work or general behaviour.

Caroline was the designer of the systems and as such led the team at a general technical level. She often worked with individual members on the solution of problems. She had a high level of technical expertise but not always in the same areas as individual team members. Caroline's main impact on the level of the team's performance was through her ability to motivate by example:

She makes you stay and work when normally you would have gone home.

Although payment was made for overtime working, many hours of overtime were worked which were not claimed for. The working of unpaid overtime had, in fact, become an established norm of behaviour. All the team had great respect for Caroline and were very loyal to her:

There is a loyalty to her—she has earned it. She makes the project work. She brought us together. She has drive, energy and ability and an excellent circle of contacts.

I wouldn't have renewed my contract if it hadn't been for her. I still don't want to let her down even though I don't like the situation with the new management.

She is very good at judging character and attitudes. She chose a very good team.

She is easy to work with—good-tempered when you make silly mistakes. She just doesn't leave you with the manual—she takes time to help you.

Caroline had a very participative approach to decision-making. She kept the team informed of developments and looked to them for advice and help. Decision-making was largely a team effort, based on discussion and a frank exchange of views.

The social activities and task activities of the team

The team was sited in an office which contained two other people. The terminal room, which was an extension to the office, was used by other staff. So, although there was communication with other staff, the most frequent opportunities for communication were with team members. Caroline, when not dealing with users, spent most of her time with the team. The close proximity of the members of the team to each other and their common interest in the project had led to the emergence of a task and a social system to which all the team belonged.

As a task group, the members of the team worked well together. This cohesion appeared to be partly a function of Caroline's leadership style, partly because they found the work interesting and fulfilling and partly because they considered themselves to be 'professionals' and expected high standards of performance from each other:

We all work hard—you wouldn't be able to get away with not pulling your weight, unlike some teams I've worked with.

The team was highly task-orientated. Each member filled in Fiedler's Least Preferred Co-Worker questionnaire (which gives a measure of task orientation) and achieved low scores (the lower the score, the higher the task orientation). Another indicator of task orientation was the team's reaction to the person who filled the team leader role in the early stages of the project and to the two home programmers. The leader could not keep pace with the group nor provide the support which was needed. He did not fit into the fast-moving task system:

> Whatever he did he was always lagging behind—he was pedestrian.

Similarly, the two home programmers were seen as falling below the standard of performance required by the group:

> They just weren't organized enough. They worked two days a week always out of phase. They needed to be able to take twice as long as everyone else over a task and because they did not work with us they needed an organized environment. In the end we just couldn't give it to them and because we couldn't plan forward to give them a buffer they had to go.

The social system had emerged through the team working together and through their common concern for the project—the task system. There was a good, friendly atmosphere, with frequent interaction and communication. All the members of the team got on well with each other and socialized during working hours. Social practices had emerged such as doing the crossword in the paper every day and going to the pub on special occasions such as birthdays. Work was often the topic of conversation, however, during social activities.

Caroline was the leader of both the task and the social system. When she was present both social and task activities took place around her. The social relationships were invaluable to the achievement of task activities:

> You enjoy what you are doing so you get on with it.

The atmosphere was also conducive to learning and development and there was little feeling of competition between members:

> Everyone helps you, nobody tries to put you down.

Generally speaking, the social system was not as important as the task system to the members of the team. Although each member expressed disappointment at the prospect of the team eventually splitting up, they took the view that transient relationships were inevitable in contracting work. However, they expressed great satisfaction from working with people for whom there was liking and respect stemming from shared commitment to a common task:

> It's a good working environment—the people are friendly yet know when to back off. Everyone is interested and helps with problems.

> It is good experience—it will be a bit of a shock when it ends, but it will. That's how it goes in this business.

Although the team had a large degree of autonomy there was obviously a need for contact with other groups and individuals. Most of the contacts were maintained by Caroline. These included contact with administration, typists, higher management and the computer service. It was very important that the team remained on good terms with the operations staff. If there were problems on the operations side the service could be lost for long periods. The computer was located near London, which further complicated this aspect of communications. Elizabeth had fewer contacts but her contribution was nevertheless important, especially her contact with other technical staff. There was strong competition for their services, and as a result, Elizabeth had to be resolute in her demands but tactful and diplomatic when her requests for help were turned down.

The team's performance and effectiveness

The life of the project had three distinct stages. The first stage was essentially concerned with the selection, assessment and organization of the team by the project leader, Caroline. She was very task-orientated and recruited people whom she thought would have a similar orientation. She knew Andrew and Peter had this quality from their work on other projects. The other members of the team were selected on the basis of their performance at interview. During the first six months three personnel were replaced. Caroline actually had a budget for six contractors but chose what she considered were high-quality staff rather than spread the money over six workers at lower quality.

Caroline's relationship with higher management at this point was an autonomous one. She was given the brief and the budget and allowed to make decisions and allocate resources in the way she thought best. For example, hard decisions such as the removal of staff were not avoided, with the result that a hard-working, able team was established.

In the second stage the product was developed and put into operation. During this stage the team again worked in an autonomous way, with control largely being in Caroline's hands. She in turn adopted a democratic and participative style of leadership.

The members of the team were asked if they thought they were effective. Their responses fell into two categories. One set of responses concerned methodological problems associated with the measurement of effectiveness. The other set produced a number of indicators of the concept. Four indicators of effectiveness were identified by the team:

1 Was the team staying within its budget?
2 Were deadlines being met?
3 Was the product of a high quality?
4 Were the users happy?

The cost of the project was quite small in relation to many other projects run by the firm. Money had always been available when needed and overtime had always been freely allowed. Caroline thought the project had stayed within budget but acknowledged the subjective nature of the determination of a budget figure and the assessment of variations from it:

> If people want something they will pay for it.

Subjective judgement also caused problems regarding the team's assessment of their ability to keep to deadlines:

> When originally deciding, one doesn't always see everything that has to be done. All knowledge is not there and one has to learn.

> There have always been problems reaching release dates but that's part and parcel of any job.

> We wouldn't manage if we only worked normal hours, but I don't think we are expected to go home at five with everyone else.

The team also pointed to the fact that failure to meet deadlines was often due to factors outside their control:

We have continual problems with the computer. We should have gone live yesterday but we hadn't got a service at all.

It's the second time we've been shifted to a new computer these last few months. The management doesn't seem to consider the implications and repercussions of what they do. It's wasted us days and made meeting the deadlines impossible.

The lack of secretarial services has caused us no end of problems. All our specifications and documents are in my handwriting and no one can read them! Reissues take months to do properly. Handwritten texts get so thick that photocopying becomes a problem—it's a ridiculous situation.

The team did acknowledge, however, that they themselves were partly the cause of some of the delays:

We are not particularly efficient. I think of things afterwards and have to backtrack. We've had our criticisms when we were late. I suppose most of the internal things could be controlled—we change our minds too much, but then who can design a perfect system and methods? We are a development team not robots and we are trying to innovate.

Stuart says I don't control the project properly. I don't do proper designs and I don't know exactly what is going on all the time, but I think what we are trying to achieve is more important—it's like that in other departments.

The members of the team were quite strong in their belief that they were producing what the users wanted:

It's the only project I've worked on where the users think it is wonderful and the developers are never satisfied?

I'm sure our users think we are effective. They get more help, support, information and assistance out of us than they do anyone else—we are their favourite people!

We might be late in getting a release out of the door but once it was gone we don't expect to see it again. We don't wait for the users to find errors—we find them ourselves!

We don't get dragged in at three in the morning.

A number of the responses to the questions of effectiveness were of a general nature:

We need a better designer but I don't think there is one in the firm. I'm not a professional designer. I try my best but someone else could do it better. I have all the good ideas but I can't write good specifications. Luckily I've got a very perceptive team!

Yes, we are effective but we are against the grain—that's why we are always in trouble. We are told that we need analysts and proper specifications but we short-cut all that. We could do with an overall structure, but if we can work straight from the users' needs we don't need separate analysts.

It is the company's big new baby. There are queues both inside and outside waiting for it. Mind you, it is our main user who has sold it. He has got a lot staked in it—he designed it by telling me what he wanted.

The third stage of the project was concerned with the product's further development and expansion. Higher management decided that it would be necessary to put the project into the wider organizational structure of the firm. This was achieved by appointing Stuart project leader over Caroline. The decision was greeted with dismay, resentment and anxiety by the team. They realized that more planning and management were needed but did not like Stuart's leadership style nor his intentions to make sweeping changes in the membership of the team. Additionally, they were professionally concerned that the standards of the product would be lowered and its future threatened by its exposure to the various political machinations of the organization:

> Stuart isn't interested in the project and the software product—it is going to cause problems.

> Stuart wants to move the project to a site where there is notoriously little care over standards and performance. Others could do the job as well as we can once they got used to it but it seems that there is little interest in doing a good job—it's a shame but it is the typical attitude. He will tie up the package and let it stagnate.

> No wonder this company is in such a mess, nobody can see beyond internal power politics.

> That's what's so good about this project. It hasn't got tangled up in the politics and power struggles up 'til now. Once a project does it is doomed. So many good ideas and money-makers have been suffocated.

> It's a potentially big money-maker, especially as we could sell hardware to run it on, but it will not be taken to its full potential because the guys at the top haven't got the same aims.

> Until recently we had no visible management. We have now been assigned to new management and they are taking an active and interfering role. Decisions have been thrust upon us.

> He [Stuart] seems to take notice and be on your side then goes behind your back.

> Stuart will not back up the team. He just harasses everybody.

> He [Stuart] doesn't care about not getting things done. If he can account for being 18 months late and not be blamed then he is an effective manager. He isn't interested in making the right decisions—as long as he is seen to be making the right decisions by his superiors.

The morale of the team fell in the third stage. This appeared to have an adverse affect on the members' motivation to work:

> We now don't work as hard or as single-mindedly. Our direction and purpose has been lost. Left alone we would have progressed much further, but there's nothing we can do. We will all be out of the picture soon anyway.

> We would have worked much better if people had just backed off. So many people have jumped on the bandwagon and are telling us what to do that we are getting nowhere and won't unless those that stay with it have got enough push to cut out the garbage.

The third stage of the project had only just begun at the time of writing but there had already been a marked change in the attitude and behaviour of the team. In terms of the dimensions of organizational climate, the following changes had occurred.

The task structure had become more pronounced and the direction and control of activities had increased. Rewards and punishments were now seen to be more related to organizational politics than to the development of the product. Centralization had increased, with decision-making passing from the team to the new project leader. The emphasis on achievement had fallen. There had been a noticeable increase in the level of stress in the team. The team members were still open with each other but there was resentment, suspicion and distrust of the new project leader. The morale and status of the team had fallen. Feedback from the users had started to fall and the feedback from the management was viewed with suspicion. There was still a desire to achieve the project's goals but the team saw these changing and being replaced by political goals.

(This case was prepared by Dr Terry Thornley, Principal Lecturer in Management Studies, Huddersfield Polytechnic, and is based on a study undertaken by Elizabeth Beddall, a fourth-year student on the Polytechnic's BA Computing in Business Course. The case is not designed to illustrate either the effective or ineffective management of a team but as a basis for analysis and discussion.)

Questions

1   What can Stuart do to alleviate some of the problems the team is facing? What actions would you recommend he take and why?

2   How would you have managed the software team in its early stages to prevent the negative aspects occurring as described in the case?

Jet Propulsion PLC—Part I

Richard J. Butler

Introduction

In principle, a jet (or gas turbine) engine is simple. It consists of a multi-stage fan (the compressor) which accelerates a large volume of air rearwards at high velocity thereby generating a forward thrust, according to Newton's law stating that every action has an equal but opposite reaction.

Turbines, connected by a shaft, drive the compressor; energy to drive the turbine is injected into the air stream by burning fuel at high temperatures in combustion chambers which further accelerates the air stream rearward. The whole is contained in a series of casings to make a kind of tube.

Manufacturing a jet engine is complex. Stresses are high due to high rotational speeds (30 000 revs per minute), temperatures and pressures. Weight has to be minimized and there is a constant search for new materials to cope with these conditions. The cost of failure is very high both in terms of money and human life.

Consequently safety and quality standards and checks have to be written in to every stage of research, design and manufacture and closely adhered to. Materials have to be inspected and major components identified by serial numbers throughout manufacture and their working lives. This allows a life history to be developed so that components can be replaced after so many operating hours or, if there is a failure, a component can be traced back throughout its stages of manufacture.

Engines (as with aircraft) have to be approved by the Air Regulations Board (ARB) for civil planes, or the Air Investigation Department (AID) for military planes. These government agencies have resident on-site engineers who have powers of access to the whole organization for inspection purposes.

Complexity also derives from the need to match a basic engine type to customer specifications. Here the customer usually means a combination of airframe manufacturer (Boeing, Douglas, BAC, etc.) and the final purchaser of the aircraft, either an airline or a government. Every engine type has to be adapted to a particular airframe and every aircraft is often adapted to purchaser needs. In general this means that major components are made for a particular order rather than for a general inventory from which components are taken for mass assembly. Batches of components then have to be tracked throughout manufacture and tied to a final engine order for assembly.

There is also a constant search for improved materials, ways of improving performance and ways of manufacture. When a new engine type is introduced it will provide a number of innovations (materials, etc.) which may require learning of new manufacturing techniques.

The organization of production

The major components of an engine are the blades (turbine and compressor), shafts, discs (for turbines and compressors), gears, casings (the main framework of an engine). Each of these are manufactured in self-contained shops within the area known as main works. There is also a separate forge, stores, and heat treatment area; assembly is carried out at another site. Each of these components presents special problems of manufacture.

The blade shop is one such self-contained manufacturing unit. Each compressor and turbine stage may require up to 100 blades of a particular size and design, there being perhaps 3 or 4 turbine stages and 9 or 10 compressor stages in an engine. There are 5 current basic engine types but spare parts have to be made for any gas turbine engine ever made by the company. Further, the blades required for a basic engine type can vary on certain features according to the specific customer order.

Manufacture starts with bought-in forgings and castings from one of two main suppliers. Inspection of these forgings is carried out on a 100% basis by the manufacturer to tight standards and using approved methods laid down by Jet Propulsion. These manufacturers are frequently visited by the purchasing superintendent for blades who has responsibility to ensure the required quality level.

Blades travel round the blade shop in batches through a fixed sequence of operations. Critical operations are the machining of the aerofoil sections and 'roots' for fixing blades into the discs. Batch sizes are usually about 100–200. One hundred percent inspection is carried out at each operation. A batch number enables quality to link a particular component back to a batch of forgings. This identity remains with a blade throughout its operating life.

The blade shop has 4 production foremen and 200 operators. There is also the purchasing superintendent, a production controller (whose job it is to ensure that production keeps to schedule; he has one assistant) and a quality superintendent who manages the 20 inspectors and has responsibility for ensuring quality standards. This requires frequent liaison with design (on another site), purchasing, production control and foremen.

These managers have a dual reporting responsibility. They are functionally responsible, respectively, to a procurement manager, product controller and quality controller for the whole works. These managers are in turn responsible to a works manager. There is also a line of responsibility to the blade shop manager. This arrangement is replicated across the other production shops (discs, shafts, gears, casings). Each shop operates as a cost centre.

There is a further grouping of other production works managers and various research, design and development groups who report to directors. At the works level there are also a number of central staff groupings, personnel, accounts and administration.

The organization is supposed to work as follows. The production plan comes down from the order book through the production director. Here, there is broad agreement, in discussion with works managers and production controllers, as to what is made where and what is bought in. This overall production plan is broken down at the works level to a production schedule on a week-by-week basis for each production shop. This production schedule becomes the plan for a shop manager who then has to assess requisite resources, labour, machines, tooling, jigs and fixtures, etc. It is his responsibility to plan for these resources, to produce cost estimates: on a week-by-week basis he is held responsible for so many units of (in the case of the blade shop) specific blades, or shafts, gears, etc., for the other shops.

For the blade shop this production plan ultimately results in batches of forgings arriving to be made into specific finished blades for delivery to a finished component stores which is a temporary holding place for components on the way to assembly. Production control's job within the shop is to develop a route card detailing the specific operation each batch has to encounter and to set a schedule. This has to be done in discussion with the shop manager, foremen, purchasing (who have to ensure the supply of materials) and quality (who have to advise on any possible hold-ups due to quality standards).

All shop managers in the works have an early Monday morning meeting with the works manager, works production controller and works purchasing and quality managers to plan the week's production. Following this meeting, the blade shop manager meets his superintendents to plan the week's production within his shop. On Thursday morning, these meetings are repeated, but in reverse order, as the shop manager meets his superintendents to find out any hold-ups and then attends a works production meeting in which snags are discussed across the works.

Within the blade shop all components follow approximately the same sequence. Machines have to be adapted and set to different sized components, usually using jigs and fixtures which are located on to machines. Blade production is not yet a precise technology, however, especially in the final stages. The aerofoil section is checked but often has to be slightly altered to remove high spots. This is done by hand polishing. The extent to which this has to be done frequently causes disruptions which can only be sorted out by the superintendents getting together in a huddle on the shop floor and hammering out a problem. This is always done against the knowledge that there is a production schedule to be met.

Problems often come to light if a batch fails inspection at a particular stage of production. Why this has happened is not usually immediately obvious. It may be operator error, a fault with the machine, an incorrect instruction given to an operator, a faulty forging or tolerances which cannot be met. To solve problems like this needs a team effort between shop management. However, they often have to go outside the shop to resolve these problems. Quality may need to discuss tolerances with design, production control may need to re-examine their production plan, purchasing may need to discuss a batch with suppliers. These discussions may often involve the functional managers for quality, production control and purchasing if a problem threatens to disrupt the overall production plan. If the blade shop is having particular problems over producing for a particular engine, adjustments to the production schedule may have to be made, but this can only be done at the works-manager level. If disruptions become sufficiently severe to threaten the engine-building programmes, this can only be resolved at the next level up, the director level.

Problems of this severity are rare; generally problems are resolved by discussion within the relevant shop with some advice sought from outside. Production problems often come down to the need to resolve a tension between what design want and what production can routinely achieve.

When tolerances stated on engineering drawings are exceeded, components can be accepted through the official 'concession' system instead of being scrapped. A concession is a granting of permission to pass jobs outside these tolerances and requires approval of engineering design (perhaps more than one department), production, quality and AID or ARB. There is an official form, giving a concession number for this which gives details of the deviations and requires signatures from the appropriate interests. Copies of these forms are filed and the concession number is tied to the particular batch or even specific component in the case of larger components. If problems become apparent in service the concession may be referred to and it is important that the proper procedure is adhered to. Gaining a concession can often be an involved procedure. Production may pressure for quick passing of a batch to make up their schedule but design may be hesitant on the grounds that the performance and even safety of the engine may be affected. AID and ARB likewise may impose stringent restrictions upon the granting of concessions. Spontaneous meetings of design, quality, production control, purchasing, a foreman and perhaps the shop manager would often gather around a batch of components on the shop floor to see if a batch could be passed.

Questions

1 Draw an organization chart showing line relationships in solid lines, functional relationships in broken lines.

2 How would you describe the technology of the blade shop?

3 Describe the organization of production in terms of the main interdependencies. Where are the main reciprocal interdependencies located and why?

4 What is the difference in relationship between the functional superintendent in the blade shop and the shop managers and between the superintendents and their functional managers? What role do the functional managers play?

5 Can you predict some possible problems with this type of organization?

Jet Propulsion PLC—Part II

Richard J. Butler

Day-to-day operating problems in the blade shop at Jet Propulsion were generally worked out in discussions between the superintendent and the foremen, sometimes drawing upon the shop manager and functional heads to resolve conflicts. Variability in production arose because of variability in blades needed for particular engine orders and because the production processes, especially as regards the aerofoil section, were far from perfect.

Quite frequently, however, a problem would turn into a major crisis having ramifications beyond the blade shop. John Barker, the quality-control superintendent, always found himself at the centre of these crises. Quality occupied a rather uncomfortable position between design and production. For production, the weekly schedule was the 'Bible'; foremen were harassed by production control and eventually the shop manager, Uriah Humperdinck, for unfulfilled quotas. For design, engineering specifications and drawings were the 'Bible'; if they agreed to wider tolerances an engine could fail to achieve performance on test before dispatch to a customer. In pursuing a concession John Barker was sometimes pushed by production who wanted to achieve their schedule. His credibility as a good engineer was at stake with design if he tried too hard to gain a concession from design. Quality's role was to adjudicate in these disputes; this required an understanding of production processes and of the design requirements of engines and a considerable amount of tact and diplomacy.

One such crisis illustrates this problem well. John Barker was in his office one Thursday afternoon, reading some material sent to him by his boss, Cyril Smith, the quality control manager for the works. The material concerned a conference on non-destructive testing techniques the following week. Cyril had suggested that John attend since he was becoming the works expert on the subject.

The door burst open and there was Bert Buster, the production control superintendent for the blade shop.

'That blooming fusspot inspector of yours, Tony Tinker, has failed a whole batch of blades at final inspection again. These are a rush job needed tomorrow by assembly for the Saudi order. Humperdinck will have my hide if these are not through—and yours and your damn Tinker.'

'Here we go again,' thought John. After being in the blade shop for a year he could by now always recognize a first-rate crisis brewing. They went to find the inspector to investigate. True enough, every blade of a batch of 200 was no less than one thousandth of an inch (one 'thou') undersize on a tolerance of 5 thou for the aerofoil section. Many were out by 5 thou, i.e.10 thou less than the specified dimension.

'They are definitely outside the limits,' said John, looking at the inspection limit.

'I want those through today,' demanded Bert. 'I'm going to get Humperdinck.'

While Bert stormed off, John asked Tony Tinker to remeasure the blades. Then John saw Buster and Humperdinck approaching at a rapid pace. Humperdinck took one look at the inspection record, turned to John with a charming smile, and said: 'Not too bad, eh lad. We can get those through the boffins can't we? Just you go up to design now and explain—they'll understand.'

John said that most of the blades appeared too seriously at fault and in no way would design wear it.

Humperdinck's smile vanished. 'I need those, otherwise I'll be eating you for breakfast,' he snapped. 'See to it, and report to me at 5.30.' He walked off.

Both Buster and Uriah Humperdinck were long-service employees of vast experience in their own empires, who had worked their way up from the shop floor. Uriah was a large, bald man in his fifties with a stentorian, booming voice which could be heard across the noise of machinery. He struck fear into any young engineer. On the surface he showed a contempt for graduate 'whizzkids and boffins' as he called them, although John had noted that both his sons had gone to Cambridge. One had to be very careful and sure of one's facts before crossing Uriah Humperdinck.

John noted that it was now three o'clock. He phoned Charlie Butterworth, his main link man in design. Over the past year John had managed to gain quite a lot of respect among the design team dealing with blades as somebody who understood the problems of getting an engine to the required performance. John knew that a certain proportion of blades would be accepted outside the tolerances, but errors were cumulative and too high a proportion of blades with the wrong aerofoil section would reduce performance. At the limit, safety could be jeopardized since an engine with compressor stages not matching properly would 'stall'. This meant that a turbulent airflow could be caused and eventually blades could snap off and wreck the engine. In an extreme case, blades could burst through the engine casing and endanger the aircraft. News of an air crash anywhere in the world would immediately create interest in Jet Propulsion. Questions asked would be: was the aircraft fitted with air engines? was the crash a result of engine failure? Every engineer and inspector appreciated that failure in service could eventually be traced back to what they were doing many years previously.

When Charlie heard the numbers of blades involved he whistled and said, 'No way—we let on some under-tolerance blades on that engine only last week as a concession, as you know. Already that engine is going to be struggling.' John had expected this answer so did not argue, but asked that Charlie might come to the blade shop to see for himself.

'I'm not sure what good that will do,' said Charlie, but reluctantly agreed.

By the time Charlie arrived, Tony Tinker had completed the remeasuring. It was now 3.45. The picture had not substantially changed. 'I don't see what I can do,' said Charlie. 'I checked before coming down. We are already to our limit on fitting and of tolerance blades. Anyway, there's no possibility of accepting blades 10 thou under.' John noted that about one-third of the batch were badly outside the tolerances; two-thirds were only 2 thou outside. So he asked if this two-thirds might be acceptable. 'Now you're putting pressure on me,' said Charlie. 'You know better than that, John. You've seen how performance can be affected. We're also getting near the stall limit. I don't like it and it won't do you any good if you're seen to side with production.' John knew there was no joy to be had here and for the moment did not pressurize any more.

John thought he should let Cyril Smith know about the situation; things were looking bleak. Next he contacted the quality superintendent on assembly, Ralph Debenham. 'You know that Saudi order, what's the position on that?' he asked.

'It's urgent and they're short of blades,' said Ralph. 'Are there any spare around?' asked John. Ralph promised to have a look. The time was 4.45. He knew there would be no news from that quarter before he was due to see Humperdinck. He prepared himself.

'Well, lad, have you got 'em?' was Uriah's greeting. He received the news stonily. 'I'll get Pat Childs [works manager] in on this,' he said. 'We'd better get Cyril as well.' Uriah knew the limits of bluster and had quietened down.

There followed a meeting in Uriah's office of John, Uriah, Bert Buster, Pat Childs and Cyril Smith. John outlined the engineering problems and his discussion with design. Bert outlined the seriousness of the hold-up in production. Pat Childs asked a few questions. John told him about his enquiry to assembly.

By now it was six o'clock and Pat said there was nothing more they could do that day. He asked that John should follow up his enquiries with assembly and have further discussions with design first thing in the morning. Bert should find out if any work in progress in the blade shop could be adapted or speeded up to replace the faulty batch. They were all to reconvene next morning at 10.30 in Uriah Humperdinck's office. Pat concluded by stressing the importance of the Saudi Arabian order to the company.

'We've been wanting to get our engines fitted for the Saudi Arabian air force. The Americans have had their own way there for too long,' he said. 'This will have to go to Harvey King [managing director] if there is any hiccup,' he concluded.

John was in his office in the blade shop by 7.45 next morning when the production operators started. He wanted to check the inspection figures and get some more precise breakdown of the measurements. He was now working on the theory that design might be able to accept some of the blades that were only a small margin outside tolerance. Maybe some other blades could be brought to light from other sources.

He also had a word with Bert Buster to see what progress he had made in finding suitable material on the shop floor. Although Bert was a bit abrupt this morning, John and Bert usually got on quite well; Bert was beginning to accept that John knew something about production.

At 8.30 he contacted Ralph Debenham at assembly. The news was that there were about 250 blades of the same type awaiting fitment in another engine not due for delivery for another two months. He now contacted Charlie Butterworth and asked if it would be possible to take 50 of the least faulty blades from the batch which were all only one thou beyond tolerance. This would give the requisite 250 blades. Charlie said he would look into it and arrange to meet John in assembly at 9.15.

There they consulted the inspection record of the blades awaiting fitment to the other engine and found that they were all well within tolerances. Charlie said he would consult his colleagues to judge the effect on performance.

It was now time to attend the meeting in Uriah Humperdinck's office. Harvey King was also there. John emphasized the possibility that design might accept 50 of the faulty batch if they could be mixed with 200 from the batch in assembly. There was concern that this would then make the other engine late, but Bert Buster reported that there were probably sufficient of this blade type as work in progress to make this unlikely. At last a solution was appearing on the horizon.

Shortly after this, design phoned to say that 50 of the faulty blades within one thou tolerance could be mixed with some of the other batch of blades. A concession was written out and accepted by all parties. Assembly had been held up for one day. The engine eventually passed its running test.

Questions

1 Analyse the way in which this decision was made, how information was used and influence exerted.

2 Would you call this effective decision-making? Is there anything that might improve it?

Part IV
The Organization

Organizational structure

Introduction Probably the most immediate and accessible way to describe any formal organizations is to outline its structure. For the student of organizations, knowledge of its structure is indispensable as a first step to understanding the processes which occur within it. When asked to describe their organization, managers will frequently sketch out an organization chart to show how their organization 'works.'

They do not really mean this is how the organization functions. That would be too simplistic. The organization chart merely gives some tangible evidence of who reports to whom, how many levels of senior, middle and junior management there are in the firm and how the whole organization is assembled together. The chart gives the formal authority and communications structure of the organization. It tells you very little about the informal processes which occur within any organization. Nevertheless, an understanding of organizational structure is fundamental for both the manager and the student of organization, for structure can cast its influence in a number of key areas. Problems with organizational structure, such as might be found in an inappropriate design for example, are likely to be major problems for the organization.

This chapter is chiefly about the structure and design of formal organizations. We may define structure as:

> **The established pattern of relationships between the component parts of an organization, outlining both communication, control and authority patterns. Structure distinguishes the parts of an organization and delineates the relationship between them**

The level of analysis has moved on from Part III (which looked at multiple groups as its focus) to looking at organizations as entities in themselves. When talking about organizational structure in this chapter, we are generally going to be describing a unit which *is* the whole organization.

There are antecedents for examining organizational structure in both individual and group levels of analysis. From the earlier parts of this book, we know that the classical school of management theory was closely concerned with job design, administrative efficiency and overall structure (Taylor, 1911; Gilbreth, 1908; Urwick, 1943). Equally, the human relations school of management theory had something to say about appropriate structures for effective performance from organizations (Mayo, 1949; Roethlisberger and Dickson, 1939). Essentially, the argument was that organizations should be structured around the needs and desires of its individuals. If these needs were 'blocked' through the adoption of a particular structure, then the structure should change. In this way, greater levels of sustained commitment were argued to be achieved from individuals.

The problem with both the classical and the human relations approaches to organizational structure was that the links between organizational performance and preferred structure remained tenuous and ambiguous. For example, Blain (1964) demonstrated that there was no simple causal relation between limiting the spans of control of managers as proposed by Graicunas (see Urwick, 1943) and effectiveness. Other tenets of the classical school were equally shown to be questionable in securing effective performance from organizations. The aims of these researchers of the 1930s and 1940s to try and identify universal organizational structures which were effective were not realized.

Later work, beginning in the late 1950s and developing rapidly through the 1960s stressed that the adoption of a particular structure by an organization was no accident. Appropriate structures all depended on a number of identifiable factors such as size of the organization, what kind of technology it used, and whether it was in stable or unpredictable market conditions. This approach has been classified by Lupton (1971) and many others as the '*contingency*' approach to organizational structure and design.

Contingency approaches to organizational structure
Differentiation and integration

Unlike the classical and human relations schools, contingency theorists argued that there was no one best way of structuring an organization. It all depends on circumstances, they said. In order to narrow this approach down a little, we have selected those aspects of structure from a wide literature base which appear to occur most frequently and which seem to have commonalities between them. The first distinction to be made along these lines is between *differentiation* and *integration*.

Differentiation	**Vertical**	The extent to which an organization is divided into specific levels of decision-making authority.
	Horizontal	The extent to which overall tasks are performed in specialized task units across the organization.
Integration	**Vertical**	The extent to which there is co-ordination and control in the organizational hierarchy.
	Horizontal	The extent to which there are co-ordination and control procedures across different levels of the organization.

Both differentiation and integration are keynote factors in any understanding of organizational structure. Before we see how they are argued to vary with situational factors, it is necessary to expand each concept a little further.

Both concepts can be regarded from the vertical or the horizontal perspectives. Vertical simply means viewing how much variation of each occurs at different levels hierarchically in the organization. Horizontal refers to variation across the organization at the same hierarchical level. Vertical and horizontal differentiation is self-explanatory, but integration can be both vertical and horizontal because in the majority of organizations ownership, formal authority and ultimate responsiblity tend to be located at the top of the hierarchy.

Problems in vertical integration can be resolved by resorting to power endowed by the formal authority of senior position (see Chapter 11). Achieving problem-free horizontal integration is less easy since no formal authority can force it to work. Many organizations design elaborate integration procedures to cope with this situation. These include management information systems, networked databases, the creation of liaison roles between functions, decision conferencing (see Chapter 10) and other operating procedures. It is by no means certain that implementing such procedures leads necessarily to effective integration (Galbraith, 1973).

Differentiation A manager who lets decisions be made away from his or her authority at lower levels in the hierarchy is creating vertical differentiation. Of course, recall of this decision-making authority by senior management alone would result in lower levels of vertical differentiation. Therefore, we could look solely at the *number of levels* that occur within an organization as an indicator of differentiation. This would give us a guide, but it would not tell us *how decentralized* decision-making authority is in that firm. Both measures are required to provide an index of vertical differentiation (see Figure 12.1).

Integration Integration is closely linked with differentiation. An organization which is highly differentiated will obviously need a greater number and intensity of integration mechanisms. Generally, three contingencies impact upon integration and differentiation. These are:

Figure 12.1
Tall and flat organization structures
(a) Tall structure with high vertical differentiation,
(b) Flat structure with low differentiation

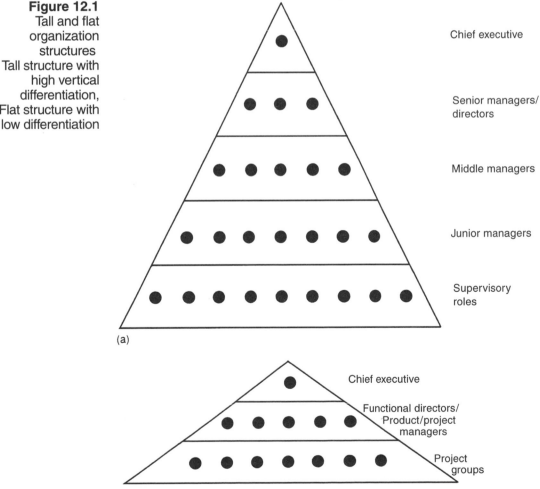

Size of Organization   As long as organizations remain small, there is really little need for large levels of differentiation and little consequent need for complex or sophisticated integration devices. As organizations grow, the need to differentiate and to set up integration procedures becomes a greater priority. The organization is no longer under the control of one person or group of persons. It is also likely that the number of product or service lines will have expanded, each requiring its own mini-organization internally to cope with operating conditions for each product or service.

Technology   The kind of technology (or technologies) employed by an organization will also affect the extent of possible integration and differentiation. In modern manufacturing processes, such as in car design and manufacture for example, integration by computer networks has become relatively commonplace. The number of different units which go into car design and manufacture may be very large indeed, resulting in a relatively high degree of horizontal differentiation. To change levels of both integration and differentiation would bring with it implications for the manufacturing process. So, to this extent, integration and differentiation are contingent upon technology.

Environment   The nature of the organizational environment also will have a contingent effect upon differentiation and integration. We shall discuss environments more fully in Chapter 17. For the moment, the greater the complexity of the operating environment of the firm, the greater is the need for a highly differentiated organizational structure. That is, where an organization faces a large number of different demands from its immediate environment, then it is appropriate to adopt a differentiated structure with specialist sub-units to cope with these demands.

In a pioneering study relating demands of the environment to organizational structure, Burns and Stalker (1961) identified two extreme types of combinations of differentiation and integration. These are:

Mechanistic structures   Typically with a great number of tasks broken down into functional specializations, clear and formal definitions of duties and responsibilities, a precise hierarchy and levels of formal authority, information flowing up the organization chart and decisions filtering down. The continued development and survival of these organizations rests on the assumption that sets of rules and procedures outlast the life-span of individual human beings. Thus, each well-defined role in the mechanistic structure can be filled with a number of different individuals.

Organic structures   Tasks are not so precisely defined with relatively little functional specialization, flexible definitions of duties and responsibilities, information and decisions flowing across and up and down the organization. The continued development and survival of these organizations lies in the continual development of ideas and innovations rather than in the formality of the structure itself.

Burns and Stalker studied the adaptation processes of English and Scottish organizations from the beginnings of the Second World War to the late 1950s. A number of British firms had been successful since the taking up of defence contract work for the government, requiring the adoption of new technologies and the close interlinking of scientific research and organizational practice. These firms were both successful and had adopted an organic structure. Scottish firms had not entered this market. They were largely concentrated in heavy industries based on iron and coal. By the end of the Second World War, the British government tried to persuade selected Scottish firms to join the new electronics industry which was expanding, rather than persist in heavy industry which was declining.

According to Burns and Stalker, the majority of the Scottish firms which did take up the new challenge retained their 'old' mechanistic structures rather than adopt the more organic structures of their English counterparts. They all failed to be profitable and many were forced into irreversible decline.

Thus, firms which face changeable and unforeseen circumstances are best suited to cope with this environment by adopting an organic structure. Similarly, firms facing routine demands which are predictable should adopt a more mechanistic structure to be effective. In a later study conducted in North America, Lawrence and Lorsch (1967) appeared to confirm Burns and Stalker's earlier findings. There seemed strong evidence to suggest that an appropriate organizational structure could be divined from looking at the characteristics of the immediate environment of the firm. The more stable the environment, the more mechanistic the structure should be (and vice versa). It should be noted that this relationship between environment and structure has come in for a lot of criticism and many of the explanations for organizational successes are laid at the door of political manoeuvrings by governments, rather than be attributed to appropriate structural design (see Hughes, 1985, for example).

However, the findings by Lawrence and Lorsch (1967) and the current experiences of British organizations suggests that Burns and Stalker's findings may be broadly true after all. Organizations such as the BMW-Rover Group, Philips, the TI Group and Glaxo Holdings have consistently put into practice organic, flexible, structures and have survived and thrived in difficult and turbulent environments. All these organizations were previously mechanistic and all faced extreme threats to their survival when markets and operating environments experienced dramatic change in the 1980s and 1990s. They survived arguably because they had flexible structures in place which could adapt to and cope with extreme changes. The remaining two important contingent factors, size and technology have had a wealth of studies devoted to them to assess their relative influence upon organizational structure. The work of Joan Woodward and the Aston School are the keynote British studies here. We look at each in the next sections.

Technology and organizational structure

Joan Woodward's (1965) research represents one of the first systematic studies of organization carried out in Britain. Like many scientific studies, the key findings that technology and structure were closely related emerged almost by chance.

Together with a team of researchers from South-east Essex Technical College, Woodward tried to verify that a certain kind of organizational structure or style of management was universally the most effective. The influence of the classical and human relations schools can be seen at work here, assuming that there must be one best way to organize. Woodward's sample of organizations studies was impressive. She covered 91% of all firms in South-east Essex which employed a hundred people or more. In this way, a large spread of organizational types and sizes were examined, although engineering, chemical and electronic firms were better represented than others. Using interviews, documentary data such as company records and observation techniques, the research examined the success of the firm related to:

1   Market share, the corporate vision of chief executives, and financial strategies.
2   Style of management. For example, was it formal, associated with specific task descriptions and duties?
3   The number of levels in the hierarchy, the relative size of the administrative component of the firm and the average span of control of managers.
4   The kind of manufacturing process used by the firm (its technology).

Finding initially no common patterns in the data, Woodward continued to reanalyse the large and unique data base at her disposal. It was not until she had reduced the number of categories of organizations in the sample to three, based upon their *complexity of production processes*, that the relationships between organizational structure and technology emerged. From this, she argued that *the complexity of the production process determined the structural characteristics of the firm*.

Woodward's three categories of production process were: unit or small batch; large batch and mass production; and process production.

Unit or small batch production   Production is designed to handle different customer requirements. Such processes typically produce custom-made goods or specialized equipment. Predictability and control over the production process are low. The key department or sub-unit is product development.

Mass or large batch production   Production is designed to handle volume output with production runs of over a week. Examples include assembly lines and large bakeries. Because the majority of the production process is standardized, control and predictability are much greater than in unit production. The key department or sub-unit is production.

Process production   Production processes are organized on a continuous basis, unlike a production line which can be stopped intermittently. Procedures are both standardised and repetitive. Control and predictability are at their highest with marketing as the key function. Examples of firms with process production are, chemical manufacture, oil refining and some pharmaceutical firms.

The primary relationships between the three production process types and structural variation are shown in Figure 12.2.

Technological predictability   Charles Perrow (1967), examined the same questions as Woodward. He, too, came to the conclusion that technology was a key determinant of organizational structure. One obvious omission from Woodward's work was that it only covered a dominantly manufacturing set of technologies. As this kind of manufacturing technology became substituted by other technologies (micro-chips, computer-aided manufacture and design, artificial intelligence systems and so on) the relevance of Woodward's work declined.

Perrow argued that new and emerging technologies could be analysed along a simple dimension. It was *the extent to which the technology was predictable*

Figure 12.2
Structure and
technology: a
summary of
Woodward's findings

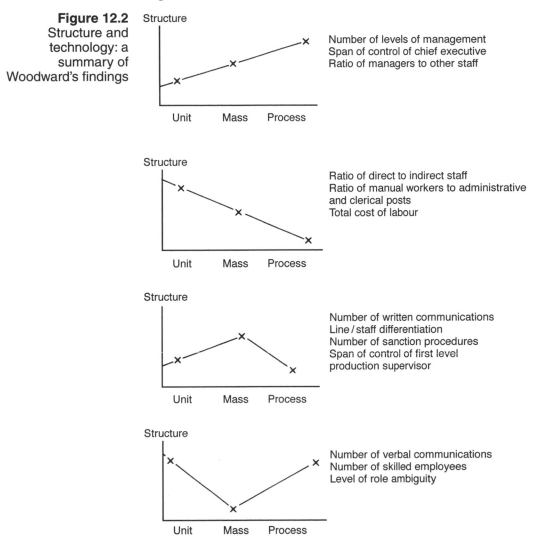

Structure

Number of levels of management
Span of control of chief executive
Ratio of managers to other staff

Unit   Mass   Process

Structure

Ratio of direct to indirect staff
Ratio of manual workers to administrative
and clerical posts
Total cost of labour

Unit   Mass   Process

Structure

Number of written communications
Line / staff differentiation
Number of sanction procedures
Span of control of first level
production supervisor

Unit   Mass   Process

Structure

Number of verbal communications
Number of skilled employees
Level of role ambiguity

Unit   Mass   Process

which was the key factor in assessing the impact of technology on
organizational structure, rather than complexity. The second dimension
concerns the nature of the search process when exceptions do arise (see
Table 12.1).

Table 12.1
Perrow's
classification of
technologies

Problem/solution search processes	Few exceptions	Many exceptions
Well defined and analysable problems	Routine	Engineering
Problems are ill defined and difficult to analyse	Craft	Non-routine

The routine quality of a firm's technology determined how many specialist
roles were needed to handle events which were unpredictable or which
needed constant monitoring. This is the case with many manufacturing firms
which use mass production, assembly-line methods and many standardized
service outlets, such as fast-food chains. At the non-routine end of the

spectrum are firms which specialize in research and development work, or which adopt and adapt technologies which are still developing, such as aerospace industries, some firms in nuclear technologies, modern architecture firms and some predominantly computer-based firms such as design and financial services organizations.

Perrow's classification of technologies is summarized in Table 12.1. Some technologies present greater problems than others if things go wrong or there is a breakdown. Even getting a common level of understanding of how the manufacturing process works is extremely difficult if you cannot see, feel or touch it! More routine technologies permit more bureaucratic organizational structures to be employed. The reverse is true for firms with non-routine, ill-defined technologies. They need structural flexibility to cope with the demands made by using such complex technologies and to accommodate the fast pace of change and development which usually goes hand in hand with modern technologies.

It was not until the 1980s that Perrow shed some empirical light on his typology of technology, although other researchers had used his model and had produced a high level of support for it. One such study was by Hage and Aiken (1969), who found that the more routine the task, the more decision-making is centralized and vice versa.

Perrow (1984) looked at the occurrence of disasters or accidents in organizations, arguing that one seemingly common factor was the mismatch between organizational structure and technology in use. Among many of the examples he describes, possibly the best known is that of the horrific explosion in the Union Carbide chemical plant in Bhopal, India. Not suprisingly, the firm had grown over the years into a highly structured, mechanistic organization. Technology in the meantime had moved on from the early days of chemical manufacture. Organizational structure remained the same.

When a fault occurred in the Bhopal plant, it was not immediately noticed since the specialization of roles coupled with the remoteness of the manufacturing process (control at a distance, located at a console, and heavy reliance on automatic safety checks) did not bargain for the need for inter-role communication (as in the organic structure). When a switch was accidentally thrown which had the effect of giving a false 'all systems OK' reading, role specialization was such that there was no facility for checking this, even though there were signs that something was amiss. By the time that the problem was recognized it was too late. No individual had the capacity to stop the inevitable explosion which ensued, causing widespread and long-term chemical damage to human and plant life. Organizational structure and technology in use were mismatched according to Perrow. In this case, the results were far worse than the loss of effective organizational performance which is inevitably associated with inappropriate organizational structures.

Later work on disasters has supported Perrow's arguments. Alexander (1996) describes the bursting of a gas pipeline in New Jersey in March 1994. This was the first time an urban area had experienced a large-scale gas escape. Alexander (1996) argues that the structure of the firm (Texas Eastern Transmission Company) was traditional and inflexible, unable to cope with the technological demands of gas transmission. Structure and technology were incongruent. Similarly, Greening and Johnson (1996) argue that highly interactive, tightly coupled and high-risk technologies can spell disaster for the bureaucratic, inflexible structure. They argue that one of the results of bureaucratic structuring is a cadre of top-level managers incapable of dealing with disasters (or of preventing them). Greening and Johnson (1996) advocate the formation of flexible, cross-functional top management teams which rotate regularly and, perhaps a little in extreme, advocate dialectical inquiry at top management levels.

Size and organizational structure
The Aston studies

Although based in the 1960s, the research conducted at the University of Aston, Birmingham, England still has a strong influence over current research and managerial practice. The research did two things. It identified the basic dimensions of organizational structure and looked at what factors were important 'in influencing the structure and functioning of an organization' (Pugh *et al.*, 1969: 91). In a study of 46 organizations in the Birmingham area, ranging from family-owned firms to large manufacturing and service organizations, six initial dimensions of structure were identified:

1 *Specialization*   The number of different specialist roles in an organization and their distribution.
2 *Standardization*   The number of regularly occurring procedures which are supported by bureaucratic procedures of invariable rules and processes.
3 *Formalization*   The number of written rules, procedures, instructions and communications.
4 *Centralization*   Where authority lies in the hierarchy to make decisions that have an impact for the whole organization.
5 *Configuration*   The width and the height of the role structure. Height describes the number of roles from the lowest-paid worker to the chief executive. Width describes the reporting relationships of roles. For example, the number of people reporting directly to a supervisor, other managers and the chief executive.
6 *Traditionalism*   Often forgotten by many researchers, this dimension predates much of the work which was to follow on organizational climate and culture (see Chapter 13). It examined how many procedures in the firm were standardized but not written down.

Since some of the above dimensions were found to be interrelated, four major features of organizational structure were identified as separate features:

1 *Structuring of activities*   The extent to which there is formal regulation of the roles of individuals. It includes some aspects of specialization, formalization, standardization and span of control.
2 *Concentration of authority*   To what extent the authority for decision-making rests in bodies outside the organization (for example, headquarters in a divisional organization) and is centralized at the higher levels within it.
3 *Line control of the workflow*   To what extent throughputs were controlled directly by line management as opposed to standard procedures or recording processes of staff functions.
4 *Supportive component*   The relative size of administrative and other non-workflow personnel.

The key aspect of technology examined by the Aston group was *workflow integration* which measured the extent to which operations were continuous, automated and in a fixed sequence (Hickson *et al.*, 1969). Workflow refers to the production and distribution of outputs. Manufacturing firms showed much greater levels of workflow integration than service organizations. Also, the more the technology was automated, continuous and in a fixed sequence the more likely it was that the structure of the firm would be mechanistic. It would have, for example, highly specialized and differentiated roles, a large number of standard procedures and a high percentage of staff (non-workflow) employees. These results concur with the findings of Woodward and Perrow. However, the Aston group also showed that *organizational size* appeared to have a strong relationship with organizational structure.

In larger organizations (measured by the total number of employees) the impact of technology on organizational structure was less. It was rather the size of the organization which seemed to create some structural imperatives for organizational design. Larger organizations were more specialized and formalized. They were also relatively decentralized. Increased size seemed to increase the likelihood of recurrent events and predictable decision problems. Thus, standardization becomes almost inevitable. Many other researchers have conducted supportive studies of the size/structure relationship (see Blau and Schoenherr, 1971; Child and Mansfield, 1972; Meyer, 1972).

There has been some discussion of the direction of the size/structure relationship. For example, it is possible that rather than size causing structure, the relationship is the other way around. Organizations become large because their structure predisposes them to grow. Aldrich (1972) presents this alternative interpretation. However, Meyer's (1972) study, conducted over time to allow for causal inferences to be made, supports the finding that size causes structure (and not the other way round). The practical implications here are that size and structure are closely interrelated. Equally, unless active steps are taken to manage organization design specifically, the firm will become bureaucratic in structure as it grows in size. This may be a good thing in environments which are stable and predictable, but in rapidly changing contexts it may result in an inflexible, bureaucratic dinosaur of an organization, efficient for yesterday's business and ill-equipped for current operations.

In smaller firms, the Aston group found that technology had a substantial impact upon structure along the lines Woodward had suggested. Finally, those parts of the organization which were immediately impinged upon by the production process were more likely to be designed along the lines of the technological imperative suggested by Woodward and Perrow.

A further set of studies on organizational structure needs mention here, for they are both very different in tenor and tone from any studies which have preceded them. They also have important implications for managers who must look to what their organization is doing strategically if they are to understand the appropriateness of structure.

The link between strategy and structure

Although we shall discuss some aspects of strategy later in this book (see Chapter 18), here we shall concentrate on the relationships between organizational strategy and its structure. Chandler (1962) was one of the pioneers in forging the link between strategy and structure. He defined strategy as:

> the determination of the basic long-term goals and objectives of an enterprise, and the adoption of courses of action and the allocation of resources necessary for carrying out these goals.
>
> (Chandler, 1962: 13).

A business historian, Chandler was one of the first analysts to examine the structure of organizations over time in order to see what factors affected structure and in which causal sequence. In his study of nearly one hundred American firms (such as DuPont, Standard Oil and Sears), he found a consistent pattern:

● The structure of an organization was related to its strategy.
● Structural adaptation always seemed to follow the pursuit of a chosen strategy.
● Thus, over time, structure follows strategy.

Nearly all firms in the sample began as centralized bureaucracies offering limited product lines. As they grew, in line with increasing demand for their products, each firm changed its structure dramatically. They bought suppliers (vertical integration), they increased the number of different sources of supply and they began to diversify their product range. To cope with this, they created a *divisionalized structure* instead of the former centralized bureaucracy (see Figure 12.3). So common were these patterns that Chandler asserted:

> growth without structural adjustment can lead only to economic inefficiency. Unless new structures are developed to meet new administrative needs . . . the technological, financial, and personnel economies of growth and size cannot be realized.
>
> (Chandler, 1962: 16).

Further studies appeared to confirm that structure follows strategy, and those firms which expand and do not progress toward more decentralized and ultimately divisionalized structures risk almost certain inefficiencies in economic performance (see Stopford and Wells, 1972; Rumelt, 1974). A similar study to Chandler's was conducted in Britain by Channon (1973). He also found support for the structure follows strategy thesis. The only major difference between British and American firms appeared to be that managers in British firms were more reluctant to decentralize to the same extent as their North American counterparts. It was common to find

Figure 12.3
A 'typical'
divisionalized
structure

1 Overall policy and financial control are from centralized headquarters. This facilitates corporate integration across the wide range of products and services provided by the divisions

2 At the division level, each is treated as a profit centre in its own right. Each will have a chief executive and its own administrative support systems

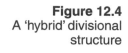

Figure 12.4
A 'hybrid' divisional
structure

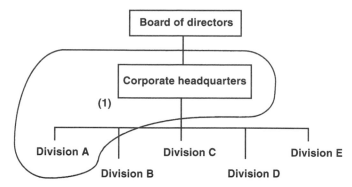

1 The 'hybrid' refers to the relation between headquarters and one of the divisions.
   This division will be in the same business area which was pursued prior to
   divisionalization. It is not unusual for the division to account for up to 80% of total
   business

structural progression to the divisionalized form, but often one division
would be carrying on a closely related business to the original firm and
could account for up to 80% of total business. These structures were termed
'hybrids' and were argued to be less efficient than a fully decentralized
divisional structure (see Figure 12.4).

Other studies of strategy and structure were to reveal that while structure
virtually always follows strategy, managers do have a limited choice in the
kind of structures they adopt. Child (1972) called this area of discretion
'strategic choice'. The argument was that some structural adaptation must
occur if changes in strategy are to be fully effective, but the nature of the
adaptation allows for some level of choice away from the purely
divisionalized form (see Mintzberg, 1979: Miller and Friesen, 1984). This
means that managers can choose a particular configuration of structural
forms such as planning systems, level of computerized support, level of
decentralization, spans of control and degree of formalization to suit
particular operating and environmental conditions. These are described in
more detail in Part V of this book.

Summary

When we try to describe any organization, we inevitably make an attempt to
describe its structure. By itself, knowing how to describe structure in the
terminology of management science is a useful start, but not particularly
edifying for the student or the practising manager. The key to understanding
structural elements in organizations lies in the research by the Aston
researchers, who gave us the analytical factors to describe structures as
formalized, specialized and so on.
   The real contributions of research into organizational structure, however,
are to be found in the attempts to relate appropriate structural forms to
identifiable operating conditions of the firm. This was attempted by the
Aston researchers and many others who, if nothing else, revealed that
structure was most likely related to multi-variate phenomena. The major
established relationships are with:

1 *Types of technology* (a large category covering the work of Woodward and
   Perrow);

2 *Size* of organization;

3 *Strategy* pursued by the organization (for example, a consistent strategy of growth is best served by adopting a structure which is decentralized and divisionalized in a multi-product company).

One problem is that all the different elements of the research on structure are virtually incompatible, so any additive knowledge is difficult to achieve. Perrow's use and definitions of technology for example are not completely compatible with those of Woodward. We do know, however, that technology, size and strategy are going to have fundamental implications for the success or failure of a firm and that adopting changes in organizational structure can bolster the probability of success or can exacerbate failure.

References

Aldrich, H. E. (1972) 'Technology and organizational structure: a re-examination of the findings of the Aston group', *Administrative Science Quarterly*, March, 26–43.

Alexander, C. B. (1996) 'Planning for disaster', *American Gas*, **78** (2), 24–7.

Blain, I. (1964) *Structure In Management*, National Institute For Industrial Psychology, London.

Blau, P. and R. A. Schoenherr (1971) *The Structure of Organizations*, Basic Books, New York.

Burns, T. and G. M. Stalker (1961) *The Management of Innovation*, Tavistock, London.

Chandler, A. E., Jr. (1962) *Strategy and Structure: Chapters in the History of the American Industrial Enterprise*, MIT Press, Cambridge, Mass.

Channon, D. (1973) *Strategy and Structure in the British Enterprise*, Harvard University Press, Boston, Mass.

Child, J. and R. Mansfield (1972) 'Technology, size and organization structure', *Sociology*, Sept., 369–93.

Child, J. (1972) 'Organizational structure, environment and performance: the role of strategic choice', *Sociology*, Jan., 1–22.

Galbraith, J. R. (1973) *Designing Complex Organizations*, Addison-Wesley, Reading, Mass.

Gilbreth, F. B. (1908) *Field System*, Myron C. Clark, New York and Chicago.

Greening, D. W. and R. A. Johnson (1996) 'Do managers and strategies matter? A study in crisis', *Journal of Management Studies*, **33** (1), 25–51.

Hage, J. and M. Aiken (1969) 'Routine technology, social structure and organizational goals', *Administrative Science Quarterly*, **14**, 366–77.

Hickson, D. J., D. S. Pugh and D. C. Pheysey (1969) 'Operations technology and organizational structure: an empirical reappraisal', *Administrative Science Quarterly*, **14** (2), 378–98.

Hughes, M. (1985) Debureaucratization and private interest government: the British state and economic development policy, in W. Streeck and P. C. Schmitter (eds.), *Private Interest Government: Beyond Market And State*, Sage, London.

Lawrence, P. R. and J. W. Lorsch (1967) *Organization And Environment*, Harvard University Press, Cambridge, Mass.

Lupton, T. (1971) *Management and the Social Sciences*, Penguin, Harmondsworth.

Mayo, E. (1949) *Hawthorne and the Western Electric Company: The Social Problems of an Industrial Civilization*, Routledge, London.

Meyer, M. W. (1972) 'Size and the structure of organizations: a causal analysis', *American Sociological Review*, Aug., 434–41.

Miller, D. and P. H. Friesen (1984) *Organizations: A Quantum View*, Prentice-Hall, Englewood Cliffs, New Jersey.

Mintzberg, H. (1979) *The Structuring of Organizations: A Synthesis of the Research*, Prentice-Hall, Englewood Cliffs, New Jersey.

Perrow, C. (1967) *Organizational Analysis: A Sociological View*, Tavistock, London.

Perrow, C. (1984) *Normal Accidents: Living With High Risk Technologies*, Basic Books, New York.

Pugh, D. S., D. J. Hickson, C. R. Hinings and C. Turner (1969) 'The context of organizational structures', *Administrative Science Quarterly*, **14** (2), 378–98.

Roethlisberger, F. J. and W. J. Dickson (1939) *Management And The Worker*, Harvard University Press, Cambridge, Mass.

Rumelt, R. P. (1974) *Strategy, Structure And Economic Performance*, Harvard University Press, Cambridge, Mass.

Stopford, J. M. and L. T. Wells, Jr. (1972) *Managing the Multi-National Enterprise: Organization of the Firm and Ownership of the Subsidiaries*, Basic Books, New York.

Taylor, F. W. (1911) *Principles of Scientific Management*, Harper, New York.

Urwick, L. (1943) *The Elements of Administration*, Harper, New York.

Woodward, J. (1965) *Industrial Organization: Theory and Practice*, Oxford University Press, Oxford.

Organizational culture

Introduction

Although we may describe an organization by referring to its formal structure, it tells us little about what it feels like to work in such organizations. Such formal descriptions of organizations rarely capture the *essence* of life in the organization, what it feels like to be part of a large or small firm, what the other employees are like, what are the stories and the gossip, or what are the informal rules surrounding dress codes or having a sense of humour about the firm.

If a friend asks you to describe the new organization you have joined, it is highly likely that you will begin to describe the *culture* of the organization. You might say that the office appears friendly, your peers are approachable, no-one is pressurizing you for completion of your work, so long as the job gets done you can fill your work hours as you like, and the new firm has a pleasant 'feel' to it. People laugh and have a joke and the work gets done just the same. All of these aspects describe the culture of the organization. They are often intangible. You cannot see or touch culture, but you can describe its manifestations and its effects upon you as a member of the organization.

Anyone who has worked for, or been a member of a number of different organizations, will immediately recognize that the mix and type of cultures within them varies widely. We will feel happier in some cultures than others and we will each perform and contribute to the organization differently depending upon how 'at home' we feel. An organization in which all people feel that the culture is alien to them is unlikely to be staffed with willing and highly motivated individuals. Given the right opportunities, such staff are also more likely to leave to join organizations in which they feel more comfortable. So culture has some fundamental implications for both individual and corporate performance. We will address these issues later in this chapter and they are also discussed in Readings 9 and 10 at the end of Part IV. For the moment, we must try and identify more precisely the nature of culture in organizations.

What is organizational culture?

Edgar Schein (1992) describes the concept of culture and occupational communities as:

> A set of basic tacit assumptions about how the world is and ought to be that is shared by a set of people and determines their perceptions, thoughts, feelings and, to some degree, their overt behaviour.
>
> (Schein, 1992: 12)

An earlier definition, which also serves to show that the concept of culture has been with the discipline of organizational behaviour for some considerable time, comes from Elliot Jaques over 35 years ago. He describes the culture of the firm as:

> . . . its customary and traditional way of thinking and of doing things, which is shared to a greater or lesser degree by all members, and which the new members must learn and at least partially accept, in order to be accepted into the services of the firm.
>
> (Jaques, 1952: 251).

One problem with these definitions is that they can include virtually everything within an organization. Therefore, definitions of culture tend to be vague and all-embracing (although they can often sound plausible at the level of 'corporate speak'). Beyond the corporate image lies an intricate analytical web of approaches to organizational culture. Culture is embedded in the day-to-day lives of organizational members. Outlining a culture, therefore, means defining a pattern of formal and informal practices (such as organizational structure, norms, values, humour and rituals).

Schein (1992) has undertaken significant work in attempting to identify patterns which typify organizational cultures and sub-cultures. His approach is to assess the organization at three different levels of analysis as illustrated in Figure 13.1.

Figure 13.1
Schein's patterns typifying organizational cultures and sub-cultures

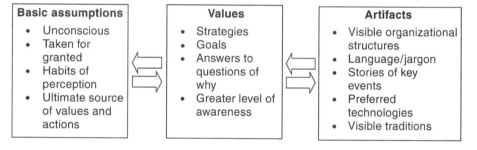

There are at least two broad dimensions along which we might first begin an analysis of such a broad definition (Wilson, 1992). The first concerns to what extent culture is viewed as tangible or intangible (culture is something that can be directly managed or is something deeper and more symbolic). The second concerns to what extent culture is viewed as an analytical construct or as an applicable variable (culture is understood as a set of symbols, subjective meaning, language and context, or is a set of identifiable factors which can be directly managed toward any given end). These are broad dimensions, of course, but they give us an insight into the wide range of perspectives we find in the copious literature on organizational culture. They also help us define it in more precise terms.

Risto (1990) provides a useful analysis, dividing organizational culture into two broad areas within organizational sociology. For Risto, culture is the structure of social action within an organization. This comprises:

1 *The structure of social organization* culture as reflected in the division of labour, the structure of roles and social networks.

2 *Symbols and codes of meaning* linguistic analysis, culture as ritual, meaning and language.

Culture as the structure of social organization

Martin (1992) draws on the structural ideas of differentiation and integration (see Chapter 12) in organizations to show how these can fashion the ways in which culture is viewed. The integration view emphasizes harmony and reinforcement of a strong culture throughout the organization. The differentiation view emphasizes the nature of sub-unit interests and a plurality of cultures within any single organization.

Strong, integrated cultures

Martin (1992) argues that integration perspective relies heavily on the creation of strong cultures at the top of an organization, with missions and objectives communicated down the hierarchy. A small but influential top management team sets the culture into which others are integrated and socialized. Typical of such mission statements are:

Yamaha	'Kill Honda'
Avis	'We try harder'
Federal Express	'Absolutely on time'
3M	'Traditional 3M margins'

These mission statements are intended as integrating devices within organizations. Individuals are expected to rally behind such battle cries. Anything which lies outside this predefined frame of reference is said to be counter-cultural and is to be discouraged. The integration perspective draws on the qualities of leadership (see Chapter 11) and control at senior management levels. In this way, 'strong' cultures can be achieved over time in theory, since counter-cultural behaviour is screened out (by failure to reward or by sanctions) and behaviour which 'fits' the prescribed culture is encouraged and communicated around the organization. This perspective has a relatively long history. Many authors have argued that getting an integrated organizational culture 'right' has widespread implications for both corporate success and for effective human resource management by achieving widespread commitment throughout staff to organizational goals and strategies.

The 'excellence' school

Beginning with Peters and Waterman (1982) and Kanter (1984) case evidence of successful companies was cited as supporting the link between strong organizational culture and financial success and sustainable competitive advantage (Porter, 1980). Peters and Waterman distilled the essence of corporate success into eight areas, all of which stem from getting the culture 'right'. Table 13.1 lists these eight attributes.

Kanter (1984) similarly argued that there were combinations of cultural factors which predisposed an organization to be able to cope more easily with changes, and which secured current and future successes. Broadly, she concluded from a study of both successful and less successful companies that sustainable success stemmed from an organizational culture which favoured corporate entrepreneurship coupled with heavy investment in human resources. For example, the value system of an organization should be committed to promoting people early in order to stretch them (ready for the next job), providing easily available seed capital for projects suggested by

Table 13.1
The core of
excellence: Peters
and Waterman's
eight basic attributes
of success

1	Bias for action	Getting on with it. The organization is not paralyzed by analysis. Managers think about decisions then get on with implementing them
2	Close to the customer	Learning from clients. Key concepts are quality, service and reliability
3	Autonomy and entrepreneurship	Foster many leaders and innovators throughout the organization
4	Productivity through people	The labour force is the root of quality and productivity. We/they attitudes are dysfunctional
5	Hands-on, value driven	Top management keeps in touch with all areas of organization. An emphasis on managing by walking about
6	Stick to the knitting	The odds for excellent performance seem to favour those organizations which stay close to the businesses they know
7	Simple form, lean staff	Keep structure simple and top management levels lean
8	Simultaneous loose–tight properties	Organizations are both centralized and decentralized. Autonomy and product development are decentralized. Core values are centralized

individuals throughout the organization, and rewarding the *attempt* at innovation rather than its subsequent success or failure.

Schwartz and Davies (1981) and Silverzweig and Allen (1976) have also produced empirical evidence from companies in North America which seems to suggest that intergated cultural configurations support and sustain success. They concur with all of Peters and Waterman's factors adding a ninth which emphasizes the importance of creating a culture which favours experimentation to which all staff are committed. In this way, innovations can be tested, tried out in the organization and experienced. Where this leads to improved performance, the experiment can then be incorporated into the organization in the knowledge that staff have already experienced the 'new' culture and are committed to it. It should be said that empirical support for this type of cultural integration is, at best, mixed. Almost a third of the Peters and Waterman sample firms experienced severe financial problems despite their strong integrated cultures (for example, IBM and Disney). Wilson (1992) summarized the major criticisms that have been levelled at the integrative approach of Peters and Waterman (see Table 13.2).

The role of culture in mergers and acquisitions

Another area in which more recent attempts to integrate organizational culture have been made is in mergers and acquisitions. Particularly where mergers involve the integration of organizations from different countries, an overriding concern has been to create and maintain a homogeneous and integrative culture. Olie (1994) notes that this usually entails making decisions over making administrative practices, management styles and organizational structures compatible, as well as deciding the relative autonomy of the partners in the merger. Overall, the concern is to create one integrative and widely shared organizational culture. Again, the empirical evidence points to the difficulties in achieving such cultural

Table 13.2
Criticisms of the
'Excellence' School

Empirical issues	*Theoretical issues*
The failure of many excellent companies to sustain corporate success	Assumes a one best way of organizing
The availability of alternative explanations of success (such as monopoly position in the market)	Assumes a simple causal relationship between culture and performance
Mostly poor sampling among the studies, so it is not known to what extent the organizations are representative	Generally dominated by a top management view of organization
The virtual omission of key business sectors, such as petrochemicals, motor manufacturing, financial services etc	Lacks a well-argued theoretical basis, preferring to borrow selectively from other work

Source: Adapted from Wilson, 1992: 73

integration. As Mirvis (1992), and Vansina (1992) note, just over half of attempted mergers fail at the post-merger integration stage. They fail to develop a widely-shared integrative culture. One of the first bi-national mergers was in the steel sector between a Dutch and a German firm in 1967. In theory, the merger was to be complementary. The Dutch firm had a good coastal position, ideal for supply and distribution. The German firm was well established with a large local demand. The merger fell apart in 1982. First, the merger was opposed by German workers who feared a loss of control and participation in running the firm. German companies have labour representation whereas Dutch firms do not. Second, the key driver of the merger, a German vice-president died with no natural or willing successor. In 1975 world-wide demand for steel began to fall. Conflict increased as the organization reduced its labour force. Continued losses saw the company seek government aid which the German government was unwilling to give. Finally, the German firm sought collaboration with another German firm and the Dutch-German merger disintegrated. The failure of the organizations to develop an integrative and sustainable culture was a key feature in leading to the demise of this merger. According to many commentators (including many managers involved in mergers and acquisitions) this example is not unusual.

Cultural differentiation

Building on Cyert and March's (1963) notion of 'local rationality' (see Chapter 10) the differentiation approach to organizational culture emphasizes that individuals and groups have different interests, jobs and perspectives as well as different backgrounds and levels of expertise. The ways in which an organization is structured, for example, will determine how many different sub-units there are and what are the formal and informal relationships between them.

One of the most well-known examples of linking structural differentiation with organizational culture is by Handy (1986). His widely-known distinction between four typologies of organizational culture is firmly based in this approach, describing the division of labour, the structure of roles and social networks.

1 *Power cultures* are centrally controlled by a single individual or a group. Structurally, these cultures are depicted as a spider's web. The analogy is that of the all-powerful spider controlling the organizational structure (the web).
2 *Role cultures* are associated with bureaucratic structures in which processes are subject to formal rules, precedents and regulations.
3 *Task cultures* are linked to organizational structures which are centred around the task to be performed (for example, matrix structures) rather than around formal hierarchy and;
4 *Person cultures* allow a virtually structureless organization of professionals. (see Handy (1986) for a full description of each cultural stereotype).

Other differentiation perspectives focus less on organizational structure and more on the identities or backgrounds of individuals. This would include such aspects as gender and ethnicity (Martin, 1992) or the different meanings ascribed by individuals who work in different parts of the organization, or in different locations of a geographically dispersed firm (Alvesson and Berg, 1992). Function and level in hierarchy thus become indicators of sub-cultures. Trice and Beyer (1993) argue that sub-units in an organization develop such strong sub-cultures that they can almost immediately translate their culture to another organization without difficulty. They give the examples of occupational similarities which occur across organizations, such as accountants all being the same irrespective of the firm they work for, or computer programmers and information specialists being equally similar. The strength of occupational subcultures is vividly described by Terkel (1972). Describing the job of a Chicago bus driver in the late 1940s, one driver explains the symbolic pride of the uniform:

> Instead of wearing a dress suit on Sunday, (we'd) wear (our) uniforms because it was a prestige thing . . . I wore it on social occasions.

(Terkel, 1972: 275).

Describing the occupation of a business executive, again in North America, the respondent says:

> You have a nice plush lovely office to go to. You have a private secretary. You walk down the corridor and everybody bows and says, 'Good morning Mr Ross. How are you today?' As you go up the line, the executives will say, 'How is Mrs Ross?' Until you get to the higher executives. They'll say 'How is Nancy?' Here, you socialize, you know each other. Everybody plays the game.

(Terkel, 1972: 538)

Within organizations and outside them there is an accepted pattern, a norm of occupational practice and expected behaviour from a variety of occupational groups. Terkel describes over 50 occupations ranging from steelworkers to jazz musicians, executives and prostitutes. Each has its identifiable pattern of stories, rituals and behaviours. From this perspective, organizational culture can only be understood in terms of the ways in which this collection of subcultures interact.

Along the same lines, individuals are often members of groups which have an important influence over their beliefs and behaviour. Examples would be a trade union, where allegiances are strong and the orientation of the group directly impinges on work. However, sports clubs, political parties and social groups also exert a powerful influence over individual members to conform to their prevailing culture. Their impact is less direct on formal work organizations, but no less influential for the individuals involved.

The differentiation perspective on organizational culture rests firmly within the structural–functional view of organizations. Drawing upon the work of Parsons (1937), Durkheim (1984) put forward the argument that sub-groups within organizations and society would develop a collective consciousness. Translating this directly into the realm of organizations, Schwartz and Davis (1981: 33) reminded us that culture is the 'norms that powerfully shape the behaviour of individuals and groups in the organization'. Each sub-group will have different norms and display different behaviours.

To describe organizational culture, thus, means that we are describing a relatively enduring 'pattern of basic assumptions' (Schein, 1984) which act as parameters for the considered correct way to think, feel and act.

Culture as symbols and codes of meaning

Quite distinct from structural—functional analyses of organizational culture are more symbolic interpretations of its characteristics and the ways in which individuals in the organization think and act. For example, we could ask the following questions about any organization's culture:

1 What combinations of *obedience* and *individual initiative* are expected from staff?
2 Do *formal work hours* matter or does it only matter that the work gets done in time and not when it is done?
3 *Do committees control* the organization or are individuals relatively autonomous to make decisions?
4 What about *dress codes or personal eccentricities*? To what extent are these prescribed, normatively encouraged or controlled?
5 What about the *physical appearance* of the organization?
6 What sorts of behaviour is *rewarded* in this organization?
7 Do senior management tend to come from one particular *function or educational background*?
8 What behaviours can lead to *expulsion* from the organization?
9 Do employees *co-operate or feel in competition* with each other?

We could try to answer these questions from a structural point of view, but that would only be a partial analysis. People ascribe meaning to the visual, to the symbolic and the intangible features of an organization. For example, the open-plan offices of a new commercial or financial firm give us an immediate impression, a very different message from the separate office, 'closed door' office layout of the older, more traditional firm. This may or may not be accurate, but we will still form an impression. Similarly, individuals will form an impression of an organization from the ways in which its staff dress (smart suits or more casual, for example). It is impossible to cover all approaches to symbolic interpretations of organizational culture in this chapter. However, the main approaches can be broadly gathered together as common approaches; namely, images, language, ways of thinking and organizational myths and rituals.

Culture through images of organization

One of the most compelling views of organizations using the approach of images is described by Morgan (1986). In this analysis, Morgan argues that we all engage to some extent in appreciating the situation around us. As Morgan (1986: 12) says:

> Many of our conventional ideas about organization and management build on a small number of taken-for-granted images, especially mechanical and biological ones . . . our theories and explanations of organizational life are based on metaphors that lead us to see and understand organizations in distinctive yet partial ways

Morgan then develops this imagery to outline eight distinctive ways in which we might view organizations. They can be viewed as machines, organisms, brains, social structures, political systems, psychic prisons, self-producing systems and, finally, as systems of domination. Table 13.3 summarizes each image.

Each image represents one way of looking at organizations. Each perspective will colour the view of organizational culture and will determine to a large extent which features predominate or are held to be most important by individuals. The 'mind maps' of individuals thus constitute the dominant culture (Hampden-Turner, 1981).

Organizational culture and language

Bate (1984) and Pettigrew (1979) for example, both view organizational culture as essentially an interactive phenomenon. Individuals observe, mix within and interact with the world around them. Through this process, an individual can symbolize and attribute meaning to events and objects. This is the basis of the philosophy of interactionism (see, for example, Blumer, 1965). The dominant factor (and the most recognizable) in this interaction is that of language, both written and verbal.

Pettigrew (1979) argues that language embodies the most important and the most obvious way in which culture is transmitted within organizations. There are accepted ways of doing things in an organization, and its spirit, character and overall philosophy are captured in the language written in formal documents and spoken in its boardrooms, offices, corridors, and shop-floors. It is by means of this language that new individuals to the culture learn its 'rules'. They learn what fits in and what is considered heretical. Expressions of language can also be reinforced by rituals and procedures such as those which might accompany the installation of a new director or company chairman. There will be dinners and banquets, formal toasts, the informal interaction of party-goers. The language which emanates from such rituals is important, for it shapes the social architecture of the organizational as surely as any formal structure or design (see Deal and Kennedy, 1982; Trice and Beyer, 1984).

The development and persistence of organizational cultures via language depends upon the notion of collective sharing. Listeners to and tellers of organizational stories all create and maintain a language which is only fully understandable within the organizational context. This is very much in the tradition of bygone village stories and storytelling as an oral tradition of communication. It is also doubtful whether social and organizational scientists will be able to label precisely the vast variability of cultures created by this shared interaction of structure, meaning and language over time. Descriptions by individuals in organizations which outline the 'taken for granted' and 'common sense' views which prevail are possibly the best keys we have as yet to understanding and categorizing organizational cultures (Silverman, 1970).

Humour, as a specific aspect of language has been picked out for study by a number of authors, each arguing that it both reflects, reinforces and can provide strong resistance to prevailing organizational culture. Linstead (1985), Burawoy (1979), Collinson (1988) and Rodrigues and Collinson

Table 13.3
Morgan's images of
organizations

Image	Cultural attributes
Machine	Based on classical management theory. Division of labour and a scalar chain of authority. Rules and attempts at creating an *esprit de corps* predominate. Efficiency and the one-best-way of organizing are the key cultural characteristics
Organisms	Organizations as species, adapting to their environment. Human needs also emphasized by attending to the interdependence of technolgy, human and organizational needs. Organizations viewed as systems contingent on the environment in which they operate. Natural selection as the predominant culture, resulting in survival of the fittest as a motto
Brains	Organizations as information processing systems. Pattern and design as important features. Rationality and decision-making emphasis. Information, control and communication (cybernetics) and learning (organizational and individual) as primary cultural aspects
Social Structure	Society and nation as key influences on organizational culture. The idea of industrial societies as distinctive and ritualistic (e.g. Japan compared to Europe). Subcultures in organizations viewed as mini-societies. Culture as shaping and structuring reality for individuals
Political Systems	Culture driven by the political perceptions of individuals. The organization as a jungle, with 'eat or be eaten' behaviours. Organization is a sub-system of competing interests with conflict an inevitable part of life. Culture is the control of one sub-unit by another. Hidden agendas and a very male-oriented view of organization predominate
Psychic Prisons	The perceptions of individuals restricted, literally imprisoned by their own thoughts, beliefs and context in which they work and live. Culture as the maps of individual minds. Draws on psychological characterizations such as those by Freud and Jung as keys to understanding culture
Self-Producing Systems	Organizations are loops of interaction, patterning and form. Culture driven by statements of what the organization is and what it can be in the future. Culture thus becomes a fixed reference point especially for strategic planning
Systems of Domination	The dual faces of organizations namely achievement at the expense of exploitation of others (especially workers). Class structures reflected in organizational structures. The domination of one nation over another, reflected for example in the exploitation of riches and resources of one nation by another (as some multi-national organizations have operated). Dominant world views about business (e.g. North American) predominate and drive culture

(1995) all provide rich empirical evidence that humour and horseplay can maintain and reinforce culture as well as providing individuals with a form of resistance to it, such as by lampooning the behaviour of senior managers, or by creating jokes and cartoons in newsletters and other organizational communications. Czarniawska-Joerges and Jacobssen (1995) have combined this approach with that of action and theatre. In other words, we can view what happens in an organization very much as we would watch and analyse a stage play (Mangham and Overington, 1987). Using the example of *commedia dell'arte* (a little-known form of theatre from 16th century Italy), Czarniawska-Joerges and Jacobssen (1995) show how impression management, playing out politics and satirical humour are part of everyday organizational life. Like the *commedia dell'arte* play, in which participants wear masks and improvise their roles within an overall predetermined story line, all individuals in a modern organization play their parts. By ad-libbing and selecting various aspects of organization, selected issues can be given emphasis and possibly gain political backing from other 'actors' in the organization.

Ways of thinking and organizational culture

This perspective owes much to Schein (1985) who argued that culture is grounded in deeply held beliefs located in the subconscious of individuals. Because such beliefs have usually been held over long periods of time (throughout a lifetime's experience) they are difficult for people to identify and explain. Bloor and Dawson (1994: 276) concurred with this view, defining culture primarily as a 'patterned system of perceptions, meanings and beliefs'. They emphasize the importance of cognitive maps which all individuals possess. In joining a new organization, for example, people use these cognitive maps to understand and make predictions about what is going to happen and formulate appropriate responses. Such maps can be consciously held (and can thus be articulated) or might be sub-conscious (and thus difficult or impossible to articulate). Harris (1989) identifies four categories of these ways of thinking:

1 *Private internal* Individuals accumulate ways of thinking from past experience. These are privately held and may never surface consciously.
2 *Shared internal* Internally held beliefs which have been shown to be 'true' by checking them out with others in the organization.
3 *Private attributional* An individual's understanding of the values, beliefs and likely behaviours of others in the organization.
4 *Shared attributional* A shared understanding of others' values, beliefs and behaviours.

Bloor and Dawson (1994) argued that such ways of thinking helped establish things like a 'pecking order' in the organization and create common values. Taking professionals as an example, they showed that ways of thinking come not only from the individual's interaction with the organization, but also from prior experiences. In the case of professionals, this would include previous training, formal and informal interaction with peers, prior experience, membership of a professional association as well as on-the-job socialization. Professionals are an occupational group which develops specialized knowledge and has to apply such knowledge with discretion to a variety of clients. Doctors, lawyers, architects and consultants would be examples.

Organizational culture as myth and ritual

There are those researchers who argue that organizational culture is a product of both corporate and national history. Both have their strong rituals, myths and beliefs. Organizations are as they are because of the way they have developed over time and because of the way they have grown alongside the dominant ideologies and mores of their nation. Any organization thus becomes a reflection of the wider context in which it is (and, historically, has been) located. The beliefs, attitudes and values of individuals in organizations are thus little different from, and are supported by, the dominant belief systems of a wider national context. This continuity has been termed 'living history' by Malinowski (1945), and it has formed the framework for much recent research. In addition, individuals also learn stories and myths about their organization and some of its participants (Mitroff and Kilmann, 1976). New entrants into an organization have to learn about these organizational stories (which may or may not be true) as part of the process of socialization.

Organizations have many examples of rituals through which desired behaviours are achieved and some form of cultural commonality created. Initiation rites are obvious examples. New entrants into organizations are sometimes put through initiation rituals which, once completed, give legitimacy to the individual as a full member of the organization. The aim is to create strong bonding between individual and corporate values. Some initiations are more extreme than others. In the armed forces or the police service, for example, some initiations involve new entrants successfully going through some process which is personally degrading. Thus 'stripped' of any former identity, the individual then bonds closely with his or her colleagues helping maintain a common culture. Less obvious examples can be found in other organizations, although they are no less potent. For example, on the founder's (Ray Kroc) birthday, McDonalds' executives run the restaurants. It is called 'founder's day'. Unilever have an 'Oh be Joyful Day' when staff assemble to hear the annual results and celebrate. Many American organizations have ritual breakfast meetings. Other organizations have an early start–late finish ritual where managers are expected to be consistently early to work and return home late (very few studies have shown that such behaviour is actually effective, except perhaps in destroying family life for those involved). Other organizations have a drinking ritual, where heavy alcohol consumption coincides with management discussions and social bonding. Any who refuse to join in such rituals run the risk of being dubbed counter-cultural and suffer being marginalized or, in extreme cases, attempts at dismissal may be tried.

Other researchers emphasize the role of stories and myths in creating and perpetuating organizational culture. For example, Noon and Delbridge (1993) argue that gossip and storytelling are important aspects of culture. They argue that informal gossip in an organization can lead to the rapid creation of in-groups and out-groups and directly impacts upon values and attitudes of individuals. Gossip can act as a reinforcement of group beliefs or can be an indirect attack on the beliefs of others. They also argue that many organizations develop norms which pressure people to engage in gossip, since they are likely to be excluded if they do not play the game. Sub-cultures can question the prerogatives of other sub-cultures in organizations through gossip (for example, workers can maintain a degree of control or autonomy toward management). Noon and Delbridge (1993: 32) also argue that organizations need gossip since it plays:

> a vital role in group formation, regulation and perpetuation, so the removal of gossip from any social setting is not feasible unless there is a complete ban on all forms of communication.

Gabriel (1995) describes what he calls the 'unmanaged' aspects as being the key to understanding culture. These aspects include jokes, gossip, nicknames, stories and cartoons. He examined 400 stories which came from individuals in five organizations. Particularly interesting is where very different accounts of the same situation are given by different respondents. Meaning and value differ between individuals. Again, humour, fantasy and heroic tales populate these stories. From these perspectives, organizational culture is a mixture of intangible and unmanageable aspects of social organization. Human creativity and human agency create and reinforce culture. It has little to do with organizational design, strategy or structure from these perspectives.

Implications of organizational culture for organizations and management

The pervasive nature of organizational culture cannot be stressed too much. It is likely to affect virtually all aspects of organizational life. Because it is more often implicit in its articulation by members of an organization (rather than a set of explicit statements) managing the culture is both a difficult and imprecise task. Managing the culture requires that managers are relatively clear about the various cultures which exist in their organizations and can also decipher or interpret what others tell them about the culture.

Attempts to 'manage' culture must recognize that only a few of culture's many faces present themselves to direct managerial control. The other faces lie hidden and unobserved. To understand these aspects requires skills not normally in the realm of most managers (for example, anthropology or the social construction of reality). So it is not surprising that cultural change in any organization is hard to achieve in any depth (see Chapter 14).

Summary

We have seen that corporate culture is an all-embracing concept, highly complex but essential for a clear understanding of how most organizations operate both internally and toward their wider environment. We can view culture as:

1 *A control mechanism*   By making explicit what are the prevailing values, norms and vocabularies in the organization, managers can instigate powerful control over others by demarcating what are the acceptable and unacceptable ways in which things are done in their organization.

2 *Organizational history*   The context through which the organization has developed and progressed: the hallmarks of the past and the heavy hand of past actions over present beliefs, values and attitudes.

3 *Commitment to the firm and its values*   The process through which individuals are motivated and committed to the prevailing beliefs in the organization. Achieving commitment by getting individuals to incorporate the firm's value systems into their own personal beliefs.

4 *A recipe for success*   A presumed matching of corporate culture and strategic success: especially the argued ability of certain cultures to cope more easily with the change process in organizations.

5 *An anthropological analysis*   The organization as a mini-society, with myths, stories and rituals. Symbols and codes of meaning allow us to interpret how individuals view their organization.

Critics of the 'culture school' point out that many of the theories and assumptions are simplistic or are mutually exclusive (see Turner, 1986; Johnson, 1987; Young, 1989). One assumption is that culture is concerned primarily with corporate solidarity and common values. Another is concerned with corporate division into separate political factions. A further perspective would see myth, ritual and ceremony as important components of culture. However, common to all these views is that the cultural analysis of organizations enables the sets of meanings and interpretations of organizational events to be explored. Culture allows very convenient single interpretations of multiple events which, according to Weick (1979), are likely to have multiple causes including fate and chance.

Even though there is little solid empirical support for the link between organizational culture and performance, there are data which suggest that organizations can easily become locked into their respective culture (or set of cultures) whatever they may be. From this perspective, culture can become a significant barrier to organizational change. We approach the question of organizational change in Chapter 14.

References

Alvesson, M. and P. O. Berg (1992) *Corporate Culture and Organizational Symbolism*, De Gruyter, Berlin.

Bate, P. (1984) 'The impact of organizational culture on approaches to organizational problem solving', *Organization Studies*, **5** (1), 43–66.

Bloor, G. and P. Dawson (1994) 'Understanding Professional Culture in Organizational Context', *Organization Studies*, **15** (2), 275–95.

Blumer, H. (1965) 'Sociological implications of the thought of George Herbert Mead', *American Journal of Sociology*, **71**, 535–48.

Burawoy, M. (1979) *Manufacturing Consent*, Chicago University Press, Chicago.

Collinson, D. (1988) 'Engineering humour: masculinity, joking and conflict in shop-floor relations', *Organization Studies*, **9** (2), 181–99.

Cyert, R. and J. G. March (1963) *A Behavioural Theory of the Firm*, Prentice-Hall, Englewood Cliffs, New Jersey.

Czarniawska-Joerges, B. and B. Jacobssen (1995) 'Political organizations and commedia dell'arte', *Organization Studies*, **16** (3), 375–94.

Deal, T. E. and A. A. Kennedy (1982) *Corporate Cultures*, Addison-Wesley, Reading, MA.

Durkheim, E. (1984) *The Division of Labour in Society*, MacMillan, Basingstoke.

Gabriel, Y. (1995) 'The unmanaged organization: stories, fantasies and subjectivity', *Organization Studies*, **16** (3), 477–501.

Hampden-Turner, C. (1981) *Maps of the Mind*, MacMillan, New York.

Handy, C. B. (1986) *Understanding Organizations*, Penguin, Harmondsworth.

Harris, S. G. (1989) 'A schema-based perspective on organizational culture', *American Academy of Management Proceedings*, 178–82.

Jaques, E. (1952) *The Changing Culture of a Factory*, Tavistock, London.

Johnson, G. (1987) *Strategic Change and the Management Process*, Blackwell, Oxford.

Kanter, R. M. (1984) *The Change Masters: Corporate Entrepreneurs at Work*, Counterpoint, London.

Linstead, S. (1985) 'Jokers wild: the importance of humour in the maintenance of organizational culture', *The Sociological Review*, **33** (4), 741–67.

Malinowski, B. (1945) *The Dynamics of Culture Change*, Yale University Press, New Haven.

Mangham, I. and M. Overington (1987) *Organizations as Theatre: A Social Psychology of Dramatic Appearances*, Wiley, Chichester.

Martin, J. (1992) *Cultures in Organizations: Three Perspectives*, Oxford University Press, New York.

Mirvis, P. H. (1992) 'Merging of executive heart and mind in crisis management', *Centre for Organizational Studies*, Foundation Jose M. de Anzizu, Barcelona, **1**, 31–55.

Mitroff, I. I. and R. H. Kilmann (1976) 'On organization stories: an approach to the design and analysis of organizations through myths and stories', in R. H. Kilmann, L. R. Pondy and D. P. Slevin (eds.), *The Management of Organization Design: Strategies and Implementation*, North Holland, New York.

Morgan, G. (1986) *Images of Organization*, Sage, London.

Noon, M. and R. Delbridge (1993) 'News from behind my hand: gossip in organizations' *Organization Studies*, **14** (1), 23–36.

Olie, R. (1994) 'Shades of Culture and Institutions in International Mergers' *Organization Studies*, **15** (3), 381–405.

Parsons, T. (1937) *The Structure of Social Action*, Free Press, Chicago.

Peters, T. and R. Waterman Jr. (1982) *In Search of Excellence: Lessons from America's Best Run Companies*, Harper & Row, New York.

Pettigrew, A. M. (1979) 'On studying organizational cultures', *Administrative Science Quarterly*, **24** (2), 570–81.

Porter, M. E. (1980) *Competitive Strategy*, Free Press, New York.

Risto, H. (1990) 'Sociology as a discursive space—the coming age of a new orthodoxy?' *Acta Sociologica*, **33** (4), 443–56.

Rodrigues, S. and D. Collinson (1995) 'Having fun? Humour as resistance in Brazil', *Organization Studies*, **16** (5), 739–68.

Schein, E. (1992) *Organizational Culture and Leadership*, 2nd edn., Jossey-Bass, San Francisco.

Schein, E. (1984) 'Coming to a new awareness of organizational culture', *Sloan Management Review*, **25**, 3–16.

Schein, E. (1985) *Organizational Culture and Leadership*, Jossey-Bass, San Francisco.

Schwartz, H. and S. M. Davies (1981) 'Matching corporate culture and business strategy', *Organization Dynamics*, **2**, 30–49.

Silverman, D. (1970) *Theories of Organizations*, Heinemann, London.

Silverzweig, S. and R. F. Allen (1976) 'Changing the corporate culture', *Sloan Management Review*, **17** (3), 33–49.

Terkel, S. (1972) *Working*, Avon, New York.

Trice, H. M. and J. M. Beyer (1984) 'Studying organizational cultures through rites and ceremonials', *Academy of Management Review*, **9**, 653–69.

Trice, H. M. and J. M. Beyer (1993) *The Cultures of Work Organizations*, Prentice-Hall, Englewood Cliffs, New Jersey.

Turner, B. (1986) 'Sociological aspects of organizational symbolism', *Organization Studies*, **7** (1), 101–15.

Vansina, L. S. (1992) 'Mergers and acquisitions: strategic organizational change perspectives', *Centre for Organizational Studies*, Foundation Jose M. de Anzizu, Barcelona, **1**, 7–31.

Weick, K. (1979) *The Social Psychology of Organizing*, Addison-Wesley, Reading, Mass.

Wilson, D. C. (1992) *A Strategy of Change: Concepts and Controversies in the Management of Change*, Routledge, London.

Young, E. (1989) 'On the naming of the rose: interests and multiple meanings as elements of organizational culture', *Organization Studies*, **1** (2), 187–206.

Change in organizations

Introduction   In recent years there has been growing interest in the topic of organizational change. Whether or not organizations are facing greater pressures to change today than in earlier times is debatable. It is certain, however, that today's organizations face quite specific challenges. These include increasing internationalization (the introduction of the term 'globalization' to a business strategy), rapid advances in technology, uncertain political environments, faster product life-cycles, all supposedly achievable by organizations employing fewer people. A central topic of change for many organizations has been downsizing and delayering to try and achieve such efficiencies.

Competition from producers internationally has forced managers in domestic firms to re-assess the ways in which they organize. In technology, for example, fears that Japanese organizations might be 'doing it right' has prompted many European managers to study and copy their manufacturing processes, such as just-in-time (JIT) production sequencing and other forms of inventory processing. Coupled with these manufacturing changes has been an increased emphasis on product and service quality. Not only do manufactured products and service delivery need to be of the highest standard for firms to compete, but also management processes and human resource aspects of the organization also need to be as effective as possible. The ultimate intention is to design an organization which is effective and efficient today and is also flexible enough to change quickly and responsively to any future changes in its environment.

Socio-economic changes, especially in the role of the state, have also had a great impact on all organizations in the private, public and voluntary sectors. Across Europe there has been a substantial erosion of state support for each of these economic sectors in favour of a more individualistic or market-oriented approach (see Whitley 1992, 1994 for example). Today, individuals and organizations are masters and mistresses of their own fates. Recent years have seen an emphasis on survival and development based upon individual action and market-based competition.

It is not certain whether any of this represents a greater degree of change today than in previous decades. In the 1970s, for example, Alvin Toffler prophesied that 'Things are moving faster' and that to many there was a feeling that 'Change is out of control' (Toffler 1970: 27). The rapid industrialization at the turn of the century brought with it a whole host of changes focusing not only on the development of new technological processes for the emerging organizations, but also on the social and economic transformation of a previously rural-based community to an urban-based labour force. The introduction of the assembly line was another major change (Walker and Guest, 1952) and rapid advances in technology throughout the Second World War were soon making their impact in industrial organizations during the immediate post-war period.

The manager has always had to cope with and handle change. It is endemic to organizational life. Possibly the reason for the greater emphasis on managing change today lies in its increased pervasity into all aspects of our lives. Not only is technological change taking place, but also there are changes occurring at all levels of social and institutional practice. Personal values are questioned. Work is no longer a 'natural' part of individuals' lives. Managers are no longer accepted as 'natural' leaders. They have to earn and justify their position. And, at the bottom of all this, is the almost inevitable link between change and organizational survival. Those organizations which do not respond to the challenges and changes facing them are likely to become dinosaurs in the evolution of modern society. They will become old-fashioned, uneconomic and, ultimately, will close down, adding to perhaps already large unemployment figures.

Levels of organizational change

Change is too broad a topic to analyse without breaking it down into more manageable pieces. One way is to examine the content and the degree of change. Some changes will be of a greater order than others. They may affect the whole organization, or just part of it. They may require a total re-think in the products and services provided, or such changes may be essentially more of the same. Table 14.1 illustrates one way in which degrees of change may be classified.

Table 14.1
Degrees of organizational change

Type of change	Operational/ Strategic level	Characteristics
Status quo	Can be both operational and strategic	No change in current practice
Expanded reproduction	Mainly operational	Change involves producing more of the same (goods or services)
Evolutionary transition	Mainly strategic	Change occurs within existing parameters of the organization (e.g. change, but retain existing structure, technology, etc.)
Revolutionary transformation	Dominantly strategic	Change involves shifting or redefining existing parameters. Organizational structure and technology are likely to change, for example

Source: Wilson 1992: 20

Choosing not to change (that is, preserving the status quo) is always an option and is one that might be relatively trivial, or may be highly strategic. For example, deciding not to invest in new technology and sticking with existing forms of production could be a highly strategic decision, since opportunity costs of not being in the new technology or flexibility penalties may be incurred on future actions. Producing more of the same (expanded reproduction) will require decisions to be made about volume expansion, such as the number of employees and any extra space or building requirements. Overall, such changes are likely to be fairly operational and not involve managers in significant efforts to implement the change. Evolutionary transition is likely to take far more time and effort. Although the change is likely to be in line with the organization's core business, it will nevertheless involve significant investment of time, money and people. These will have to be accommodated using the same technology and within the existing structure of the organization.

Quinn (1980) and Taylor (1994) give some evidence that this kind of focused innovation stands a better chance of being successful. Largely this is because managers set targets which are difficult to achieve, but are perceived of as achievable. They work hard toward high-level targets. Taylor (1994) refers to these as 'stretch goals' and cites successful examples from Lloyds Bank, Rank Xerox, and the W.H. Smith Group. The reduction in uncertainty for others in the firm is also a key factor. Taylor (1994) describes Curteis Chains, a jewellery chain manufacturer and one of the fastest-growing firms in Britain. Continually stretching the firm, but keeping it within clear parameters and not trying to change everything all at once allowed this organization to become one of 3i's 'superleague' high-growth companies. Although the content of the change may be fairly radical, the processes through which change progressed at Curteis (and many other cases of transformation) are well-demarcated—building leaner and more flexible organization structures; reengineering key business processes; developing a culture of continuous improvement and the strategic management of human resources.

Revolutionary transformation is always strategic and virtually always high-risk. Such changes mean addressing key processes and structures simultaneously, as well as trying to instil a new culture and perhaps adopt a new technology. Managers will tend to attempt such a transformation in the face of crisis. Recently, however, some commentators have argued that transformation is a sure way to gain competitive advantage. For example, D'Aveni (1994) proposes that evolutionary transitions may be too slow for firms to gain any real advantage. He argues that competitive advantage is very short-term and distinctive competence has a finite life in most firms. To break out of the danger of firms locking themselves into the battlegrounds of today (and fighting in the wrong place when the competitive war has moved elsewhere), D'Aveni proposes rapid change to give the organization the advantages of rapid manoeuvre and shock action. This level of change is revolutionary transformation to achieve speed, surprise and manoeuvre. As yet, there is too little empirical evidence to say whether the strategic benefits outweigh the significant risks involved in revolutionary change. For those organizations which have succeeded in this way, however, the rewards have been substantial. Strebel (1995) calls revolutionary change the process of creating 'breakpoints'. Because managers find thinking radically difficult (since they are locked into the current frame of reference) Strebel shows that, often, breakpoints are created by outsiders, either new entrepreneurial activities, or unexpected competitors from other industries. As examples, he cites Nike in sports shoes, IKEA in furniture, Seiko in watches. Breakpoints can also come from within sectors:

> SMH with the Swatch has outpaced Seiko; the IBM PC changed the rules of the game on Apple; the Macintosh recaptured the high ground for Apple, and the IBM/Apple alliance may yet surprise Microsoft and Intel; Mercedes and BMW took over the high

end of the market from GM, the Toyota Lexus has displaced the Germans outside Europe, while the American Big Three make a comeback in the middle of the auto market

Strebel (1995: 11)

Whatever the degree and content of the change, its implementation can still pose large problems for organizations and their staff. To get people to accept and implement the new ways of doing things is neither a swift nor an easy task. We examine the difficulties of implementing change in the following sections.

Leading change

Despite the many heroic stories of leaders who have achieved substantial success in changing their organization from 'no-hoper' to 'world-class', it is somewhat frustrating to learn that there is no evidence of a set of universal rules for success (Pettigrew and Whipp, 1991). In a study of competitive change in a number of UK industries, Pettigrew and Whipp reported a number of similarities with regards to the process of leading major change initiatives. These are:

Primary features

1 Building a receptive context for change, legitimization
2 Creating a capability for change
3 Constructing the content and direction of change

Secondary mechanisms

4 Operationalizing the change agenda
5 Creating the critical mass for change within senior management
6 Communicating need for change and detailed requirements
7 Achieving and reinforcing success
8 Balance continuity and change
9 Sustaining coherence

Source: Pettigrew and Whipp, 1991: 106

Implementing organizational change

Putting change into place in any organization is likely to involve attention to most (if not all) levels of analysis. There will be issues to address at the individual, the group, the organizational and the societal levels (Pettigrew and Whipp, 1991). In addition, implementation itself can be thought through in advance (planned) or can take place in reaction to events as they occur both within and outside the organization (unplanned change). There is not enough space here to cover all aspects of planned and unplanned change strategies, but the major ones will be covered. First, we look at levels of analysis.

Change and the individual

Individuals create, maintain and allow change to happen. Organizations are incapable of initiating change although their features such as design and climate can sometimes block it, as we shall see later in this chapter. Change comes from people. It is the *how* of the change process. It is all too easy to equate the *what* of change (the goal or the target) with its implementation. Unless people are involved, committed and prepared to adapt and learn, objectives, plans and future desired states will be likely to founder on the rocks of resistance (which is often viewed as a negative response, but is one that can be quite legitimate where people are excluded or where commitment is deliberately not sought).

In many of the courses we have run for managers, a common response to the question of change is: 'Of course change is necessary: it's just that we can tell you who will resist any proposals before we even begin'. Here is the first fallacy. The tendency to stereotype or to articulate beliefs is not usually based upon any systematic analysis of the situation. Often it is guided by what happened in the past in similar circumstances or from folklore (what someone else in the organization said a certain individual or group would do). This *may* be accurate in present circumstances, but it is more likely to be full of inaccuracies. Resistance to change from an individual's perspective needs careful analysis, not glib prediction and stereotyping.

According to Kotter, Schlesinger and Sathe (1986), there are four common reasons for resistance to change from individuals. These are:

1 Self-interest
2 A lack of trust coupled with misunderstanding
3 Different viewpoints or assessments of the benefits of change
4 A low tolerance for change

They are based on *history* (what happened in the past in a similar situation), on *emotion* (how individuals feel about the proposed scenario) and *fact* (what individuals actually know about the change). Self-interest refers to the sense of loss that individuals feel they will encounter in future states of change and the actions they will take to avoid this happening. The feeling is that the aspects of the job they hold dear at present will be eroded or threatened under the new regime. The actions they take will be to try and 'block' the change, often by forming opposing camps or sections in the organization. They may argue that no-one really understands their concerns, that this is change just for the sake of it, that more analysis is required and so on. What they are doing is to act parochially and politically to defend their territory or to defend what they consider are their 'rights' in the organization (see Pettigrew, 1985 for an extended example of these kinds of resistance in Imperial Chemical Industries (ICI)).

A lack of trust can quite easily arise when the intentions of the proposed change are wrongly interpreted by one or more individuals. This can occur because mistrust exists already through previous experience, or can occur through a lack of effective communication. The initiator of the change may assume that others are aware of the details and the rationale for the proposal, but in reality they are probably only half-informed. Subsequent actions can become wrongly interpreted and resistance is inevitable. If there is a simple managerial maxim to be derived from this, it is that managing the change process needs a great deal of effort to secure a greater level and more effective communication throughout the organization (Plant, 1987).

Resistance to change is also inevitable when individuals perceive the situation in very different ways. Many managers assume that everyone in the organization sees the problem and their proposed solution in the same way. They also assume that everyone has the same level of access to the information which they have at their disposal. This is almost never true. Shop-floor workers, functional managers, people in other divisions of the company will all be privy to different sources of information. In turn, this will colour their view of the organization. Since people act on their perceptions (rather than on any rational set of 'facts') there will be a wide range of viewpoints toward a proposed change.

Some members of the organization will undoubtedly see the proposals as detrimental to their current position, others will be neutrally disposed and some will support them. Which group is 'correct' in their assessment is vital knowledge. It may be that the manager proposing the change is correct in their prediction of the likely benefits of the change. Resisting others who oppose the change is thus a good strategy to pursue. However, it may be that those resisting are in a position to predict more accurately the likely outcomes. This may even be based on information which the manager does not have.

In this case, standing up to resistance would not be an effective strategy. There are two difficulties which now become apparent. One is, how do we know in advance who has the most correct interpretation of likely outcomes? The other is that trying to fend off or block resistance is virtually always seen as a good thing for managers to do irrespective of who is right or wrong. That is part of their job and they get paid for handling the inevitable aggravation which ensues. Handling the first issue can only begin with increasing communication throughout the organization, but it also requires a great deal of further work to secure commitment to the change. The second problem is even harder to address since it requires a change in the way the organization is currently operating. It needs some degree of cultural change or shift. We shall deal with this in more detail later in the chapter.

A low tolerance for change means that some individuals who are less able than others to adapt to change and to new circumstances are likely to resist proposals for future changes irrespective of whether the change is likely to benefit them or not. As Drucker (1981) notes, the capacity for individuals to handle change is limited. This varies, of course, from person to person, but even the most receptive individual can easily reach the limits of their tolerance. Many managers talk of 'change fatigue' or describe the pattern of seemingly endless change as 'initiative-itis' as though it were some kind of organizational disease. Discussions we have had with many managers from the UK and Continental Europe revealed a particular dissatisfaction, for example, with the swings in centralization and decentralization of organizational structure. In addition, some individuals will resist any kind of change simply because they think that to support it would be to admit that their present position or viewpoint is wrong. They have a vested interest in maintaining the status quo.

Groups and implementing change

We have seen in Chapters 8, 9, and 10 the crucial importance of understanding and analysing group processes in organizations. Groups, too, can become formidable obstacles to achieving change. They can also be powerful promoters and supporters of the change process if they lend their weight to its promotion. Pettigrew (1985) showed this in his study of corporate change in ICI. It was not until a small group had mobilized itself around John Harvey-Jones and his proposals for change that any progress was made. Indeed, previous attempts to achieve the same kind and level of change had failed primarily because Lord Beeching, the proposer of the change had met solidly with group resistance from all the other directors.

Patterns of institutionalized behaviour in groups such as conformity to group pressure, 'groupthink' and obedience to authority figures in the group (Janis, 1972; Milgram, 1974) can also be powerful barriers to achieving change. Groups can develop extremely rigid patterns of behaviour which are not only difficult to change themselves, but which are also considered 'correct' by group members. Their way of doing things is the right way. Others in the organization are perceived by group members to be out of step with them if they choose to see things differently.

Organizations and implementing change

Moving to the organizational level of analysis we can immediately establish a link between the question of organizational culture (described in Chapter 13) and change. Just as patterns of behaviour in groups can block or enhance change, so too can the wider patterns of behaviour, values and beliefs prevalent in the organization overall (Hall, 1977). For example in bureaucracies, one of the noticeable features is the precision with which the most detailed aspects of organization are spelled out. Rules, regulations and procedures are mostly formalized by writing them down. This, of course, allows an organization to be extremely predictable. Promotion routes, entry points and salary scales are closely demarcated so that all members are clear of their place in the overall structure. There are documented plans for action in the face of most contingencies. Many organizations exhibit some aspects of bureaucratic cultures, especially if they have been in operation for along time. History can be a barrier to the implementation of change. For example, each time a new problem or contingency arose, rules and procedures were created to cope with them. This process continued until the organization became a very complex set of formal procedures. In a *perfectly stable environment*, these organizations are virtually unbeatable. There is a procedure for every eventuality. They will out-perform almost any other organization designed on different principles. Where there is significant and unpredictable change in the immediate environment these same organizations will display extreme agonies in trying to change and adapt. This is because they represent today's efficient solutions to yesterday's problems. They are not designed to change and adapt to new scenarios and solutions.

Changing the culture of an organization is one of the most difficult tasks facing all its constituent individuals. It is very much like trying to change all that you as an individual believe in, or have been brought up to believe in. To energize change requires an 'unfreezing' of the status quo, change to be effected, and a 'refreezing' or consolidation of the new state. This pattern was first identified by Kurt Lewin in 1951, and is still pertinent today. Lewin argued that organizations existed in a state of equilibrium which was not itself conducive to change. This equilibrium was the result of opposing forces which constantly acted upon the organization and its individuals. These were forces for change (driving forces) and forces against change (restraining forces). Figure 14.1 shows a typical set of these forces. Lewin called the process of balancing driving and restraining forces a '*quasi-stationary equilibrium*'. This is because a true equilibrium assumes that no change takes place at all given a perfect balance between opposing forces. In the world of organizations, of course, this is unrealistic. There is change happening all the time. The point is that the opposing pressures of driving and restraining forces will combine to constrain change to a minimum and mitigate against any degree of further and future changes.

In order to promote the right conditions for change there has to be an unfreezing of this situation. An imbalance must be created between the driving and restraining forces. This means removing restraint or fuelling driving forces. Lewin argued that there was an optimal way of configuring this process. First, the restraining forces should be attended to, and selectively removed. The driving forces will automatically push change

Figure 14.1
Lewin's equilibrium:
driving and
restraining forces for
organizational
change

Driving forces (forces for change)	*Restraining forces* (forces against change)
	From individuals
	• Fear of failure
	• Loss of status
• Changing markets	• Inertia (habit)
• Shorter product life-cycles	• Fear of the unknown
• Changing values toward work	• Loss of friends
• Internationalization	
• Global markets	*From organizations*
• Social transformations	• Strength of culture
• Increased competition	• Rigidity of structure
• New technology	• Sunk costs
	• Lack of resources
	• Contractual agreements
	• Strongly held beliefs and recipes for evaluating corporate activities

forward since removing the restraining forces has created an imbalance in the quasi-stationary equilibrium. Ideally, an increase in the number of driving forces or an increase in the potency of the existing set will achieve a greater degree of change. Refreezing the new situation is the final stage. This sequence is essential according to Lewin. If attention is first given to driving forces, then the result will be a commensurate increase in the number or the potency of restraining forces, and the status quo will remain. No change will occur.

Organizational culture and change

The prevailing culture of any organization can present a formidable challenge to those attempting to implement change. The sunk costs of individuals and groups in creating and maintaining the present culture are considerable. In order to achieve a significant shift in organizational culture most of the following key aspects of organization will have to be subject to change:

Changing the culture: key aspects of the organization

- *Balance of power* includes political imbalances between individuals, groups and at the organizational level.
- *Organizational structure* this will undoubtedly be designed around sustaining the present culture and not to accommodate new scenarios.
- *Management and leadership styles* these too will be a product of the culture which will have supported certain styles and screened out others.
- *Organizational history* antecedents of practice. If it worked in the past there is little reason to change it. Those who suggest change are considered to be abandoning tradition, flying in the face of history, or just plain heretical.

Changing organizational culture means achieving a significant and lasting change in the philosophy of management and the adoption of suitable and supportive organizational structures to consolidate and support the change. Not surprisingly, achieving cultural change is complex and difficult. The Lewinian model is attractive in its simplicity, but lacks analytical sophistication.

As Wilson (1992) and Miller and Friesen (1984) note, organizations can very easily become prisoners of their own cultures. They 'learn to become helpless' in the face of change (Bate, 1984). From a more dynamic perspective, organizations also tend toward more extreme forms of their existing culture. For example, organizations which are predominantly bureaucratic structures will tend to become more obviously bureaucratic in culture over time, while more task-oriented cultures will tend toward becoming more project-centred (Miller and Friesen, 1984). The task facing managers in these organizations is not to create conditions for change. This is happening all the time. The difficulty is in reversing or in changing the direction of the pattern of learned behaviours so that these can be implemented and become part of the new way of life for the organization.

Even seemingly small changes which are counter-cultural can be extremely difficult to achieve. For example, changing reward systems in an organization from those which give rewards for visible successes to those which also reward experimentation are relatively easy to design in theory. In practice, they are beset with difficulties. Even 'excellent' organizations such as the 3M Corporation described by Peters and Waterman (1982) finds it takes constant energy and managerial commitment to sustain a culture which encourages experimentation from all areas of the organization. Experimentation is done out of sight, away from the mainstream activities of the organization. Potentially innovating behaviour occurs in time 'borrowed' from the organization. This approach needs constant stimulation and support from the organizational context.

Where rewards are not based on trying out new ideas, or even developing them, but are solely focused on success, then the 3M approach will founder. Innovation is stifled through a fear of failure. An individual who has had one idea defined as a failure in public is unlikely to try again unless he or she is rewarded for the process of experimentation rather than just on results. This cultural 'rule' has become widely known in management parlance as the 'punishment culture'.

Contingency models of change

Rather than adopt a cultural perspective, many scholars have tried to establish links and patterns between change strategies and the context in which the firm operates. In particular, this has led to research which focuses on organizational structure, or on patterns in the processes of change themselves. The work of Chandler (1962) has become a standard in establishing the co-variance of strategy and structure (see Chapter 12). In this work, structure always follows strategy. The contingent relationships between strategy and structure have been assessed by many authors (for example, Miller and Friesen, 1984). In this type of work, strategy and structure are treated as categorical variables (one changes and then we notice a change in the other). Many management researchers have argued that this is insufficient because it loses the interplay of strategy and structure over time. The relationships may not be as simple as they look. Summarizing much of this approach, Amburgey and Dacin (1994) conducted their own study of 262 firms over a 28-year time period. They concluded that:

- strategy and structure are reciprocally interrelated over time;
- but strategy is a more important determinant of structure than structure is of strategy.

Source: Amburgey and Dacin, 1994: 1427.

This 'hierarchy' of contingent factors in strategic change has much support from many approaches to organization theory. The idea that strategy (the 'what' of change) is dominant can be found in Mintzberg's (1990) design school of strategic management and even in Ansoff's (1991) criticism of Mintzberg, he still sees strategy as the most important factor. Rumelt (1974) and Williamson (1985) suggest that once a strategy of growth is in place, the divisionalized structure will follow since it is economically the most efficient (reducing transactions costs) and also allows managers time to think and plan strategies for the division or business unit. Thinking in this way, managers then adopt a new 'what' of change. They think outside their current business; they grow their division and diversification occurs. Once diversified, structure begins to change from the divisional form (also known as the M-form) to the conglomerate, where related lines of business are put together. Even the 'population ecology' school of thought, essentially a survival of the fittest approach to organizational survival, regards strategy as the core feature of organizational change (Hannan and Freeman, 1984). Outside the design school approach, Mintzberg (1990) argued that strategy and structure were reciprocal:

> . . . Structure follows strategy as the left foot follows the right in walking . . . none takes precedence: each always precedes the other, and follows it, except when they move together, as the organization jumps to a new position.
>
> (Mintzberg, 1990: 183)

Other contingency approaches to organizational change have emphasized the process patterns of change over time. For example, Keats and Hitt (1988), Hoskisson and Johnson (1992) and Greenwood and Hinings (1988) have all argued that the strategy-structure debates were essentially flawed, since they fail to take into account the dynamics of the situation or the context in which the change is taking place (for example, type of firm, type of environment, level of competition, etc.). Greenwood and Hinings (1988) argued that change processes followed certain patterns (or tracks) depending upon the contextual conditions in which they occurred. They call these tracks 'archetypes'. Examples range from the linear transformations where all goes smoothly in a linear fashion, to 'aborted excursions' where the change effort is abandoned entirely.

At the societal level of analysis, change processes will be influenced to some extent by both the national cultural environment and the extent of international collaboration and trading between firms and countries. These topics are covered in greater detail in Chapters 20 and 21.

Planned and unplanned change processes

It is possible to distinguish between changes which are planned to try and achieve some specified future scenario (a vision or goal) and those which are unplanned processes (which can be reactions to changes in the organization's operating environment, or are changes which just seem to emerge). Both planned and unplanned change processes can range from simple increments to radical and perhaps revolutionary changes. The last 20 years have seen an increasing number of planned change programmes (beyond simply management by objectives) which are aimed at reducing the uncertainty inherent in unplanned changes and to provide a template for action throughout the organization. The proliferation of planned change programmes has been so great that this chapter can only outline some of the major approaches (see Wilson, 1992 for further reading).

Some of the key themes in planned change are covered in following paragraphs.

Many planned change programmes derive their essence from the control of manufacturing processes in order to reduce defects or sub-standard products. In manufacturing, the application of statistical process control (SPC) meant that manufacturing processes could be broken down into their component parts and a mathematical formula produced for the most efficient production runs and machine tolerances. This idea has been translated into the realm of human and organizational change. Programmes such as total quality management (TQM) and business process reengineering (BPR) are systematic and step-by-step approaches to change, largely based on SPC-type programming. Originally overseen by a quality department (sometimes specially set up) the desired changes were achieved by the completion of a series of pre-defined steps by employees. Maramonte (1996) describes how such planned changes can be incorporated (or indoctrinated?) into every employee. He cites the examples of Eastman Kodak and Motorola, which have abolished the original quality department and have imbued the quality concept in every employee. This is called 'invisible quality'. The results are argued to be improvements in quality, delivery, operating expenses, customer satisfaction and higher levels of innovation in research and development (R&D).

Other examples of planned change programmes involve trying to codify the process of implementation, once the direction of change has been established. Jacobs (1994) outlines a way of focusing and speeding up change processes. This involves working in 'real time' with very large groups of employees from the organization (instead of communicating or training people in smaller groups). Jacobs gives the examples of Ford (USA) and the Marriot hotel chain where large groups of up to 2000 people participate in a three-day programme to look at some specific change. In the Marriot case, it was focused on improving service but also contained some TQM tools and techniques. The idea is to build up a common vision or purpose so that individuals can be safely empowered (that is, they will act in the interests of the wider company). Stakeholders external to the firm can participate as well. The aim of this is to allow often competing interests to learn about others in the system of which they are a part. This 'real time' approach is based on a simple equation:

Dissatisfaction with the present $\times$ **future vision** $\times$ **first steps** $\rightarrow$ **lowered resistance to change**

The assumption is that there must be initially a level of dissatisfaction to act as the stimulus for change; there needs to be a clear articulation of the future (that is, what would 'better' look like?); there must be clear first steps to achieve change (may be small but must be specific). Multiplied together, these will overcome resistance to change. In this rather linear model, we can see similarities with the change equation of Lewin described earlier.

A further variant on planned change can be found in Scott-Morgan (1994). This is a programme for assessing failed change processes. The idea is that organizations can be viewed as a collection of written and unwritten rules. Once managers are aware of these rules, they can formalize their approach to change. Scott-Morgan describes this as a series of questions managers should ask themselves to achieve successful change:

- What motivates you?
- Who is important to you to achieve your ambitions?
- How do you impress your important contacts?
- How do you reach or contact those who can enable the change to occur?

Asking these questions will not only facilitate change, according to Scott-Morgan, but will also allow managers to counterpose the written rules against the unwritten rules (what actually happens). This can then expose the extent to which formal or informal organization is predominant. Scott-Morgan describes this facility as a diagnostic health check for any firm. The closer together the formal and the informal become, the healthier the organization. There is a recognition that there can be dysfunctional consequences from following the above 'rules'. For example, managers may change jobs rapidly which can result in cherry-picking (choosing only personally beneficial changes), fire-fighting (creating a 'problem' and then solving it to increase one's standing in the eyes of others) and a dilution of specialist expertise, where managers become predominantly generalists.

Problems in planned approaches to change

The momentum which has built up around planned or programmed approaches to change is large. TQM, BPR and patterning processes are a way of life for many organizations. Their attraction is obvious. They present ways of formalizing and codifying what are extremely messy and complex processes. They also appear more 'scientific' and 'rational' ways of dealing with fuzzy problems. Evidence of their efficacy, however, is mixed. First, there is still too little empirical support for the claims of programmed change. They work in some cases and not in others. We are uncertain whether programmes can be transferable across sectors. Can a quality programme designed for a manufacturing firm be just as easily applied without translation to a hospital or a public agency? Wilson (1992) and Egan (1996) detail many of the problems with these approaches. The main issues are:

- Needs a relatively healthy organization to start with. Failing firms rarely have the resources or the capacity to implement large programmes.
- Can become an end in itself, rather than a means to an end—many programmes rely on the completion of steps in a linear schedule of activities. The completion of the steps can be taken to mean that the organization has achieved the change and become a 'quality' organization, for example. Customers may think differently.
- Can become a programme into which virtually everything in the organization is put, 'it is not our functional problem, it's a quality problem'—is an often-heard phrase.

Planned change also involves the transference of knowledge or expertise from one source or another to the more general management of the organization. It is hardly surprising, therefore, that consultants and management 'gurus' have achieved prominence as change agents. We discuss the role of change agents in the next section.

Change agents

Change agents are the individuals or groups of individuals whose task is to effect the desired change. They can be internal or external to the organization. Internal change agents are usually employees of the organization, while external change agents are usually advisers or consultants. On any change programme, internal and external change agents can work together. The role of the change agent is to act as intermediary and as a spur to effecting change. This can range from complete collaboration with internal staff to adopting a role of absolute authority as the expert.

Internal change agents are almost always credible as 'experts' within their own organization. However, they also need a substantial power base in order to develop and sustain their efforts. Such political potency is often denied to the internal role. External change agents may have political credibility, but often lack the detailed knowledge of the organization which can undermine their role of 'expert'. Hesitation on the part of the external change agent over which route to take in the change effort can also lead to an undermining of expertise. Since the process of change rarely lends itself to precise mapping of future states, this problem is extremely common where external change agents are involved.

Difficulties in the role of external change agents

The majority of consultants (external agents) operate toward the *micro-level of change*. They are involved in specific 'one-shot' change efforts which are targeted at specific individuals or specific groups. This can range from management development training to T-groups and personal growth workshops. Quite often, these take place outside the premises of the organization in concentrated bursts of activity. Participants thus tend to view the whole experience as special or transitory and soon fall back into the old ways on return to their organization. Such change efforts are likely to have limitations in their scope and are likely to fade quickly.

Attempts at macro-level changes by external consultants are relatively rare. Two factors mitigate against macro level changes by external agents—power and complexity (Astley *et al.*, 1982). Inevitably, change will present real or imagined threats to the existing power structure of an organization. Resistance from those who perceive they will have some of their power eroded in the future desired state, will exert very strong resistance to the change. Often, access is required by the external agent at a level senior to the organization in question (the board of a company, or a governmental ministry) and this can present obvious problems since the consultant will rarely have been initially called in at this level.

Another factor is that external change agents are sometimes limited in the amount of access they have across the focal organization. It is quite common for access to be restricted to staff or human resource functions thus placing immediate limits on applicability and generalizeability. It also usually places severe budgetary limitations on the whole process.

External change agents are rarely presented with a well-specified problem to solve. The initial 'problem' itself can be spurious and misleading or, at best, only partially true. Consultants are also rarely called in by individuals from the focal organization. This could arouse accusations toward the individual of acting beyond their legitimate authority, being high-handed, or just plain incompetent. It could also raise suspicion by others in the organization as to the motives of calling in a change agent to a dysfunctional level.

Therefore, the problem facing the external change agent is really:

1   Ambiguous and ill-defined

2   The outcome of a process of group negotiation or consensus from within the focal organization.

There is no longer any clear point of ownership of the problems in the change process, and the external change agent has little chance of isolating and identifying specific, unambiguous issues. It is more likely that he or she will produce a set of further issues and problems rather than any solutions to current problems.

As we noted in Chapter 11, organizations cannot be considered in isolation from the political dimension of stakes and stake-holders, interests and interest groups. The change process is no stranger to the political arena. External change agents are often called in to bolster one side or the other in an internal political conflict. The change agent acts in a legitimating capacity to interests and issues in the focal organization.

It would be wrong, however, to assume that change through external change agents was never possible given the formidable array of problems outlined above. There are some distinct advantages to the role of external change agent which can contribute toward successful change programmes. External change agents can:

1   *Act as 'court jesters'* They can poke fun at practices in the organization which others, who are employed within it, cannot voice without fear of repercussions for themselves or their department.
2   *Act freely, since they are not tied to partisan politics*
3   *Gain access to a wider range of individuals and departments than is afforded members of the organization*
4   *Use a wider 'vocabulary' than most organizational members* They can express organizational events and processes in a new way, expressed in terms unfamiliar to those in the organization. This alone can be a powerful stimulant for promoting analytical thinking and a first step to unfreezing the status quo.
5   *Send information around the organization which would be impossible or prohibited to others*
6   *Avoid responsibility, to some extent, if things subsequently go wrong*

Significant organizational change is rarely achieved by external change agents alone. To ensure the greatest chance of success, internal and external change agents must work together. The creation of a special internal cross-functional team would be one way in which internal change agents could be organized. This team acts as an invaluable source of information for the external change agent. They are also a forum in which ideas can be piloted, discussed and subsequently spread to the rest of the organization. They will also need to have at least some access to powerful groups around the organization in order to mobilize support for their ideas.

The final step in this collaborative process between internal and external change agents is to cement the change, or to 'refreeze' it in Lewin's terminology. There are a number of ways of achieving this. The creation of a new set of terminology, or working vocabulary, can be very effective since it distinguishes a clear break from the 'old' and the 'new'. The old state of affairs cannot be described adequately using existing vocabulary. The changed state is thus not a case of what we used to do before (plus a few amendments). It is described and rationalized using new words, new phrases and with fresh aims. In this way, the change process is consolidated and the need for the external change agent dwindles to nothing. It now becomes the task of internal members of the organization to monitor the change and assess its efficacy in the light of current and future practice. Large firms, such as British Telecom, Nestlé and the Royal Dutch/Shell Group, create teams of internal consultants and change agents specifically to carry out the task of monitoring and suggesting future modifications to change processes.

Summary

The question of organizational change is central to all kinds of organizations. It is the way in which organizations thrive, grow and stabilize rather than wither and decline. Yet achieving change presents one of the most intransigent problems for both organizations and individuals.

Resistance to change seems endemic to both organizations and individuals. At the level of the organization, resistance is likely to come from accepted ways of doing things, the powerful hand of history ('we've always done this in the past . . . so why not now?') and sunk costs invested in strategic recipes toward their own sector of operations and toward other organizations. Individuals resist change for reasons of apprehension, possible loss of influence, a predisposition to stability and sheer conservatism.

References

Amburgey, T. L. and T. Dacin (1994) 'As the left foot follows the right? the dynamics of strategic and structural change', *The Academy of Management Journal*, **37** (6), 1427–52.

Ansoff, H. I. (1991) 'Critique of Henry Mintzberg's, "The Design School": Reconsidering the basic premises of strategic management', *Strategic Management Journal*, **13**, 463–466.

Astley, W. G., R. Axelsson, R. J. Butler, D. J. Hickson, and D. C. Wilson (1982) 'Complexity and Cleavage: dual explanations of strategic decision-making', *Journal of Management Studies*, **19** (4), 357–75.

Bate, P. (1984) 'The impact of organizational culture on approaches to organizational problem solving', *Organization Studies*, **5** (1), 43–66.

Chandler, A. D. Jr. (1962) *Strategy and Structure: Chapters in the History of the American Industrial Enterprise*, MIT Press, Cambridge, Mass.

D'Aveni, R. A. (1994) *Hypercompetition—Managing the Dynamics of Strategic Manoeuvring*, Free Press, New York.

Drucker, P. (1981) *Managing in Turbulent Times*, Pan, London.

Egan, C. (1996) *Creating Organizational Advantage*, Butterworth-Heinemann, Oxford.

Greenwood, R. and C. R. Hinings (1988) 'Organizational design types, tracks and the dynamics of strategic change', *Organization Studies*, **9** (2), 293–316.

Hall, R. H. (1977) *Organizations: Structure and Process*, 2nd edn., Prentice-Hall, Englewood Cliffs, New Jersey.

Hannan, M. T. and J. Freeman (1984) 'Structural inertia and organizational change', *American Sociological Review*, **49**, 149–164.

Hoskisson, R. E. and R. A. Johnson (1992) 'Corporate restructuring and strategic change: the effect on diversification strategy and R&D intensity', *Strategic Management Journal*, **13**, 625–634.

Jacobs, R. W. (1994) *Real Time Strategic Change*, Berrett-Koehler, San Francisco.

Janis, I. L. (1972) *Victims of Groupthink: A Psychological Study of Foreign Policy Decisions and Fiascos*, Houghton-Mifflin, Boston.

Keats, B. W. and M. A. Hitt (1988) 'A causal model of linkages among environmental dimensions, macro organizational characteristics, and performance', *The Academy of Management Journal*, **31**, 570–598.

Kotter, J. P., L. A. Schlesinger and V. Sathe (1986) *Organization: Text, Cases, and Readings on the Management of Organizational Design and Change*, 2nd edn., Irwin, Homewood, Illinois

Lewin, K. (1951) *Field Theory in Social Science*, Harper & Row, New York.

Maramonte, K. R. (1996) *Building the Invisible Quality Corporation: The Executive Guide to Transcending TQM*, Quorum Books, Westpoint, CT.

Milgram, S. (1974) *Obedience and Authority*, Tavistock, London.

Miller, D. and P. H. Friesen (1984) *Organizations: A Quantum View*, Prentice-Hall, Englewood Cliffs New Jersey.

Mintzberg, H. (1990) 'The design school: reconsidering the basic premises of strategic management', *Strategic Management Journal*, **11**, 171–195.

Peters, T. and R. Waterman Jr. (1982) *In Search of Excellence: Lessons from America's Best Run Companies*, Harper & Row, New York.

Pettigrew, A. M. (1985) *The Awakening Giant: Continuity and Change in ICI*, Blackwell, Oxford.

Pettigrew, A. M. and R. Whipp (1991) *Managing Change for Competitive Success*, Blackwell, Oxford.

Plant, R. (1987) *Managing Change and Making it Stick*, Fontana, London.

Quinn, J. B. (1980) *Strategies for Change: Logical Incrementalism*, Irwin, Homewood, Illinois.

Rumelt, R. (1974) *Strategy, Structure and Economic Performance*, Harvard University Press, Cambridge, Mass.

Scott-Morgan, P. (1994) *The Unwritten Rules of the Game*, McGraw-Hill, New York.

Strebel, P. (1995) 'Creating industry breakpoints: changing the rules of the game', *Long Range Planning*, **28** (2), 11–20.

Taylor, B. (1994) *Successful Change Strategies: Chief Executives in Action*, Director Books, London.

Toffler, A. (1970) *Future Shock*, Pan, London.

Walker, C. R. and R. H. Guest (1952) *The Man on the Assembly Line*, Harvard University Press, Cambridge, Mass.

Williamson, O. E. (1985) *The Economic Institutions of Capitalism: Firms, Markets and Relational Contracting*, MacMillan, Free Press, New York.

Wilson, D. C. (1992) *A Strategy of Change: Concepts and Controversies in the Management of Change*, Routledge, London.

CHAPTER 15 Alternative forms of organization

Using different means to achieve the same ends

It would only be a partial analysis to assume that we had covered all types of organizational structures in Chapter 12. Those we have already discussed can be broadly classified as variants on a theme of formal, functionally differentiated, bureaucratic organizational structures. They are designed to reinforce functional expertise, to maintain control using rules and regulations, with decision-making centralized at senior levels.

The structures we examine in this chapter are very different from functional organizations. They are a diverse group of organizational designs including matrix structures, voluntary and non-profit organizations, alliances and networks and other alternative organizational forms.

A point you might wish to bear in mind as you undertake this chapter is that it is essentially about how *structures* of organization differ. A related topic is the corresponding variations in how *work is undertaken* within organizations. For example, outsourcing, teleworking, short-term contracting are all important trends which relate to how individuals are employed. These topics will be dealt with in the final section of the book in which we examine some of the broad trends affecting work in the future.

Matrix organization structures

There is no precise definition of the matrix form of organization since, in practice, there are a number of variants. All matrix structures have a common theme, however. They are all traditional hierarchical structures which also have a formally recognized lateral dimension. That is, communication, authority, influence and control are structured as much laterally across the organization as they are vertically. Matrix organizations take the functional structure of traditional organization and superimpose a set of project areas or

Figure 15.1
A 'typical' matrix structure

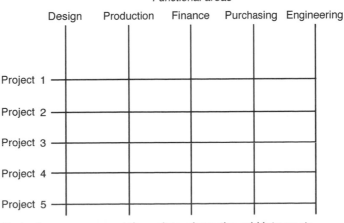

* Project groups occur at the points where the grid intersects
* Representatives from any function can be part of many project groups at the same time

business operations which cut laterally across the functions (Knight, 1976). Figure 15.1 depicts a typical matrix organization structure.

Functional areas are delineated vertically, while project operations or business areas cut across all functions laterally. The overall structure of a matrix organization thus resembles a 'cell' or a honeycomb. One key property of this kind of structure is that unity of command no longer applies. Individuals in the organization have two bosses. One will be the project team boss, and the other will be the functionally based manager. Both function and project thus produce authority figures.

Although we have used function and project as two dimensions of the matrix, other combinations can exist, such as national versus international responsibility in a multi-national firm, or between existing product profitability and new product innovation. The key to the matrix lies in its polarization of two dimensions creating a vertical and a horizontal information flow.

A number of well-known organizations are designed around the matrix principle. Many of these are North American, such as Monsanto Chemical, Texas Instruments and the 3M Corporation, but matrices are not confined to American practice. Asea Brown Boveri, British Petroleum, Fujitsu, and Christian Aid in the voluntary sector are also examples of matrix structures. Matrix structures can also be found widely throughout secondary and tertiary education organizations in Britain. Organizing into faculties, for example, represents the idea of a business area, while literacy schemes and introducing new technologies (such as information technology) in schools are examples of projects which span a number of functional areas.

The potential problems posed by individuals reporting to two managers simultaneously (such as divided loyalties, conflict and competition) can usually be reduced to manageable levels by segregating domains of authority. For example, project managers have authority over those members of the project team and functional managers retain authority over more general organizational areas such as promotion, appraisal and staffing. As Galbraith (1973; 1977) notes, matrix organizations are decentralized, horizontally differentiated structures, designed to combine the advantages of both functional and project forms of organization. But they can only achieve these aims if authority and responsibility are clearly differentiated and understood between function and project in the first place.

The benefits of functional differentiation are largely rooted in the efficient use of specialists. By grouping specialists together in functions (such as marketing, production, product development, or sales), clear economies of scale are achieved. The organization needs less specialists (who are expensive to employ) and clear areas of responsibility are demarcated. As we have noted in previous chapters, there are also disadvantages inherent in the functional structure. The most problematic lies in the development of 'local' interests (see Chapters 10 and 11). Functional goals and perspectives dominate wider organizational goals. Co-ordinating functions to work together, or to view the wider perspective becomes difficult to the extent that special liaison roles may have to be created. Matrix structures achieve, at least in theory, integration between functional specialists and multiple projects. In this respect they are *strategically flexible, open to change, and centred very much on the needs of their clients.*

It is rare, however, to find an organization which can be described wholly as a matrix. More frequently, only parts of an organization adopt the matrix form. It is common for certain activities such as research and development or marketing and sales staff to be organized along matrix lines while the rest of the organization is singularly functional. Broadly, the greater the extent of the matrix toward including the whole organization, the greater is the level of complexity in achieving integration between project areas and maintaining strategic direction and control of the organization overall (see Child, 1984; Hunt, 1986).

According to Davis and Lawrence (1977) there are specific conditions under which a matrix structure is appropriate. Implicit in their arguments (and those of Child, 1984, who is more explicit), in all other conditions, the matrix structure will be wholly inappropriate. Suitable conditions which favour a matrix structure are where:

1 There is an unambiguous need to act upon two key organizational areas simultaneously. This could be project and function; technical quality and product innovation; product manufacture and development of customer services.
2 External environmental pressures are high and conditions are turbulent. This increases the need for high levels of internal interdependence. It also has the secondary effect of creating a 'common enemy' for internal projects, and this acts as an integrating mechanism.
3 Technology in use does not involve substantial 'sunk costs'. That is, the overall technical characteristics of the organization are variable, flexible and usable in multiple sites. Thus, centralized computer integrative systems, for example, are likely to mitigate against the adoption of a matrix organization simply because they force centralized rather than dispersed integration.
4 It is apparent to the majority of organization members that multi-function, multi-skill linkages are both necessary and appropriate.
5 Part of this becoming apparent will rest with any obvious economies of scale which can be achieved through the shared use of people, skills and the development of project rather than functional culture.

According to Galbraith (1974), the matrix structure affords a number of strategic advantages to an organization. These are very much in line with the advantages claimed by Lawrence and Lorsch (1967) and Burns and Stalker (1961) for 'organic' organizational design. Because lateral communication and integration are increased in the matrix structure, the organization has the following advantages:

● *Strategically flexible* Information can be processed quickly and efficiently and difficult or rapidly changing environmental conditions can be analysed and responded to very rapidly.
● *High standards of technical excellence maintained* Since specialists interact frequently with both their own functional areas of knowledge as well as with other specialist knowledge domains, they maintain a state-of-the-art orientation to projects.
● *Clear differentiation between strategic and operating decisions* Top management is clearly charged with responsibility for strategic or policy decisions. Senior managers also have more time to concentrate on policy since they are no longer required to manage project teams or to oversee them closely. The financial and accounting systems of the organization are tailored to suit budgeting for projects and new products and services (rather than being functionally based). There are specific systems in place to support cost centres, profit centres, revenue and investment centres.

● *Enhanced aspects of social organization*   Motivation, commitment and personal development are enhanced. Individuals are not totally bound by status or level in the hierarchy. Project teams ensure that all who are members are there because they want to be and that all members will be able to have their views heard. Participation in the day-to-day running of the organization is also increased. Personal development is enhanced because working in project teams allows individuals to broaden their experience both in the technical sense as well as in the wider organizational perspective (that is, the broader aspects and implications of what is decided).

Source: Adapted from Galbraith, 1974; Knight, 1976

Disadvantages of matrix organization, apart from the obvious issue of individuals coping with dual authority, lie chiefly in the area of co-ordination. This covers both inter-personal co-ordination (learning how to work in groups, how to handle and live with conflict) and organizational co-ordination (administrative costs of integrating projects, ensuring efficient and effective communication). A further disadvantage can arise in conditions of resource scarcity. Where people or finance are no longer freely available throughout the organization, decisions have to be made about which projects will be supported and which projects will have to be put on ice for a while. Inevitably, this raises questions concerning exactly who makes these decisions between various projects as well as raises conflict and competition between project members themselves.

From a financial perspective, the creation of profit centres cannot be taken to be synonymous with a matrix structure. Individual profit centres can exist in the most centralized organizations. The key to financial co-ordination in the matrix is to allow managers as much leeway as possible in capital expenditure and sourcing of products and services (Horngren and Foster, 1987).

From a behavioural perspective, individuals must be able to handle role conflict and ambiguity as a natural part of everyday organizational life. They must become effective members of task groups. For many individuals who may be technical specialists used to working alone (or solely with a few other specialists in the same field) this can be a daunting prospect. A substantial amount of human resource investment in learning to work effectively in groups is required before matrix organization can realize its operating advantages over more mechanistic forms.

Global matrix structures

Daft (1995: 248) argues that the matrix structure can also work effectively for many multi-national corporations. The principle of achieving effective vertical and horizontal co-ordination simultaneously in the organizational structure can apply equally to multi-nationals. He argues that although communication is a little more difficult, given the geographical distances involved, the matrix can balance central versus decentralized decision-making tensions and can encourage the sharing of resources across the structure. Examples of organizations which operate global matrices include Virgin, Nestlé, General Electric and Asea Brown Boveri (ABB). ABB, for example, is the world's largest electrical engineering group. A $36 billion federation, ABB employs 217 000 people and owns some 1200 subsidiary companies in 140 countries. Based in Zurich, ABB is the largest single investor in Eastern Europe and the former Soviet Union. There is an international committee of top managers with 'country managers' reporting to them. This is the vertical axis of the matrix. On the horizontal axis are the business sectors into which ABB's products and services are arranged (nearly 70 sectors). The standardized working language is English, to aid communication.

Daft (1995) claims that it is the matrix structure which allows ABB to be the large and successful company it has become. Perhaps. But we should also not forget that Percy Barnevik, the organization's energetic president and chief executive from 1988–1996, spent a great deal of his time flying around and personally visiting all business sectors in all countries to spread the message of the ABB business philosophy. In addition, he created the ABB 'bible', a small document listing the corporate philosophy of ABB (it contains maxims such as 'Not to take action is the only non-acceptable behaviour'). So, global matrix ABB may be, but it is also a very tightly controlled and centralized organization at the same time. Kets de Vries (1996) also points to the same problem. Studying the contributions of Richard Branson (Virgin), Jack Welch (General Electric) and Percy Barnevik (ABB), he argues that these leaders have two roles—the architectural (organizational design) and the charismatic (personal leadership). The problem is differentiating between the relative effects of the two. Is it tight, often personal, control or the matrix structure which bring success?

Beyond the single organization: networks and alliances

Alternative structural designs can be found outside the strictures of the single organization. Economists such as Williamson (1991) argue that the only real advantage organizational design can give is relative efficiency and is concentrated on the transaction costs of organizing and co-ordinating activities. These are inevitably going to take a perspective beyond the single firm. The *transactions cost* approach takes the view that organizations survive largely because they have designed efficient ways of transacting with other organizations in their domain (such as suppliers and customers). The structural design perspective is thus that of the transaction, rather than the single organization. Organizations may integrate with their supplier, for example, if the cost of transactions is less than when they were separate organizations. Alternatively, organizations may outsource functions if it proves cheaper to transact externally rather than keep the function internally and accrue more expensive internal transaction costs (information technology departments seem particularly prone to being outsourced on this basis). The ideal structure for Williamson is one in which transaction costs are minimized. Like much economic theory, this approach takes a rather narrow view of appropriate structural design. It concentrates on the exchange of goods and services and ignores inter-organizational activities which rely on trust and social relationships.

Another approach to organizational structures is that of the network. Here, the perspective is that the single firm is engaged in a number of business relationships with other organizations. The total sum of these relationships is the network. According to Johanson and Mattsson (1992) the network can be analysed from different perspectives. A network can be viewed as:

- a set of connected relationships between individual actors;
- a structure governing the production system of an organization (that is, all internal activities in the firm);
- a way of viewing the position of firms in relation to one another in the network.

One of the basic building blocks of network analysis is the exchange relationship in which two actors are prepared to co-ordinated and develop interdependent resources that each controls. This exchange can, of course, be viewed at the organizational level of analysis just as readily. The network works as a circular structure. Through exchange, actors (individuals and organizations) learn about each other and begin to develop some trust in one another. Having established that trust, they then seek to develop their individual resources to increase overall productivity which, in turn, benefits the entire network. The overall network structure is characterized by high levels of resource dependency (firms are reliant on one another) sustained by trust. Any focal firm can have a position in one or many networks and each firm will have a different position in a network, ranging from a strong position where the majority of other firms are highly dependent on the focal firm, to a weaker position where the focal organization is heavily reliant itself on others. One way the concept of the network has been put into practice is through the creation of *supply chains.*

Supply chains

e pluribus, unum—
(many made one)

As the name suggests, supply chains comprise all those organizations which have to interact in order to get the product or the service to the customer. At its simplest, this would include the supplier, the focal organization and the customer. The structural arrangement would thus be focused on three organizations (one each of supplier, customer and focal organization). In practice, the supply chain is more complicated since there are usually multiples of each stage in the chain for any focal organization which will have multiple suppliers and customers. The theory of efficient structures is the same, however. The perspective taken to assess performance is that of the overall chain as one unit (hence the sub-title to this section). Taken together, efficient and effective relationships between the suppliers, the focal organization and the customer create a chain with unique and not easily substitutable properties. In terms of economic competition, barriers to entry are high for anyone else. Therefore the chain has a distinctive competence and can compete effectively, adding value along the way for each participant in the chain (the protest that it is solely the customer who benefits is only partially true).

This alternative lens highlights the obvious point that it is the nature of the relationships between the firms in the supply chain which will make it more or less efficient and effective. Like the network theories, these relationships depend on trust, mutual reciprocity and personal relationships as much as they do on price and quality of service or product. In a study of the automobile industry supply chains, Choi and Hartley (1996) found that successful and long-lived chains depended heavily on long-term co-operative relationships between members and that price was the least important selection criterion for choosing a supplier. *Trust, reliability* and *co-operation* were the most important factors. Typical supply chains can be found in supermarket chains (Tesco, Woolworths for example) and in manufacturing firms such as British Steel and Nissan Motors. Innovation and new product design can be a feature of supply chains as customer and supplier work together on a common problem. British Steel, for example, is working with Railtrack in the UK to produce the next generation of railway lines which will be technically better and easier to put in place. This kind of simultaneous design is only possible to this extent in a co-operative supply chain relationship.

Efficiencies in the supply chain are usually achieved by each organization being an efficient unit in its own right (using just-in-time (JIT) manufacturing processes, for example). Linked by efficient information networks and systems, the chain becomes an effective single unit. Simbari (1996) shows how the chain can also be used to synchronize demand from the customer (the demand chain) so that, ultimately, supply and demand can be synchronized. This is happening already in Volvo cars. Up to 1993 vehicle distribution was organized through its numerous sale companies and importers. The problem was that the customer could not always get the vehicle type and specification they wanted from stock. So, in 1994, Volvo set up a simultaneous supply/demand chain in which customers order the model they want and dealers transmit the orders directly to the Volvo factories. This eliminates sales companies holding stocks (effecting cost savings) and improves customer service at the same time.

Alliances between organizations

Organizations may adopt yet a further form of structuring their activities. They may choose to collaborate, or co-operate to achieve mutual benefits. Such co-operation may be temporary or permanent and may involve the bulk of organizational activities or just be concentrated on a single product or service. Such arrangements are generally known as alliances and include joint ventures, strategic alliances and the rather clichéd 'co-option' whereby firms which co-operate find they can compete more effectively than if they remained separate entities in competition with one another. Alliances are partnerships between organizations in which resources, capabilities and core competencies are combined to pursue mutual interests (Borys and Jemison, 1989; Forrest, 1992).

Alliances can occur for many reasons and each is a subject in its own right. In the limited space allowed here, alliances can be focused on *service* where organizations with a similar need get together in a consortium. Research and development (R&D) is an example, where organizations pool their resources in the expectation that each will individually benefit from the new product or service produced. Alliances can be *joint ventures* where a temporary joining of organizations occurs to form a new venture or create opportunities that did not exist for each individual organization. Joint ventures can also be used to block the competition or to benefit from economies of scale (airlines in particular benefit from this type of joint venture). Finally, alliances can be with *stake-holders* such as customers or suppliers. In this way, development, research, testing and the manufacture of a product can be shared across the stake-holders in the joint venture. Table 15.1 summarizes the advantages of alliances between organizations as a structural form.

Voluntary and non-profit organizations

As alternative forms of organization, voluntary and non-profit organizations are mostly absent from the concerns of most organizational analysis. Textbooks covering organizational behaviour rarely deal with these kinds of organizations other than perhaps to give them a passing mention as alternative forms of organization. Williamson and Ouchi (1981: 366) argue that such organizations are obscure, defy systematic analysis and cannot be studied easily by the conventional analytical tools of organizational analysis.

This is both surprising and not strictly true. First, voluntary organizations form a significant part of many economies in Britain and in Europe. In Britain alone, there are over 250 000 voluntary organizations, with a paid

Table 15.1
Main reasons for
strategic alliances

Risk reduction	Diversify product/service portfolio Share fixed costs Reduce capital costs Faster entry to competitive markets
Economies of scale	Larger volume means lower average cost Competencies of each partner are shared
Blocking competition	Defensive alliances to reduce competition Offensive alliances to increase barriers to entry
Regulations and expertise	Permitted to operate locally in foreign countries because of alliance with local partner Benefits from partner's know-how of local context
Integration	Access to distribution channels Access to technology, materials Benefit from strong brand of partner Access to expert labour

Source: adapted from Contractor (1986)

workforce of nearly 200 000 (and countless volunteers) disposing of an income of over £17 billion (Billis and Harris, 1996). Second, voluntary organizations have also been around for a long time. They are an established part of most economies, many with roots going back to the 11th and 12th centuries.

If we took a purely structural analysis of present day voluntary and non-profit organizations, we would see initially very little difference between them and their 'for-profit' cousins. Most voluntary organizations have functions, a hierarchy, a reporting structure and a communication and integrating network (although these may not be described in this language which is borrowed from business organization). In most other respects voluntary and non-profit organizations are very different. So what are these organizations, and how might we define them?

Definitions of these organizations are particularly imprecise given the broad spectrum of types which comprise voluntary and non-profit organizations. Any attempt at definition must also recognize that it is culturally bound. The following broad descriptions apply for Britain only. Both North America and the rest of Europe generally differ widely in their use of terminology.

1 In Britain, a voluntary organization is one which provides goods and services on a non-commercial basis. Revenue is sourced from donations and other gifts rather than from the sale of products. Well-known examples would be Oxfam, Mencap or the Royal National Lifeboat Institution. A considerable proportion of the labour force is voluntary and, hence, unpaid. The voluntary title is not lost if some of its members are paid or if the organization receives most of its funding through government agencies. Membership of the organization is not through inheritance, nor through family or society connections. Membership is not directly aimed at securing economic benefits for its members.
2 A non-profit organization is similar in many respects to a voluntary organization except that its aims are almost always explicitly aimed toward the economic or social betterment of its members. Examples include professional associations and labour unions. Membership is voluntary

and much of the work of the organization is carried out by volunteers in addition to full-time paid staff.

3   Not all voluntary organizations are legally constituted charities. Charitable status is endowed by the Charity Commission, an independent body which is charged with the task of ensuring that the activities of a voluntary organization conform with the laws of charitable trusts. Broadly, voluntary organizations which are political, or are pressure groups aimed at effecting changes in current practice, or are self-help groups, cannot be legally registered charities. The benefits of being a registered charity are discussed in detail in Chesterman (1979) and Wilson (1984). They include tangible benefits of fiscal advantage (charities can claim tax relief and rate relief) and less tangible benefits of organizational image (which appears legitimized by its inclusion on the charities' register).

The above organizations are quite distinct and specifically different from their commercial counterparts. For example, a key aspect of their survival rests on the contract each individual has with the organization. This is dependent on notions of altruism and self-help. Volunteers join an organization because they want to help others. Titmuss (1970) examined the motives of 3325 blood donors in Britain, asking them why they gave blood. The predominant category of responses cited altruism, a general desire to help people or society without seeking extrinsic reward for such help.

Many voluntary organizations act as 'brokers', relying on individuals giving money and services to the organization which are then translated into service provision for the needy, the elderly or the handicapped, for example. An extreme form of this kind of brokerage can be seen in an organization such as Oxfam which collects money from people in Britain and distributes its services in Third World countries. Donors thus rely on the organization being an 'honest broker', translating their resources efficiently and effectively into disaster relief.

These interrelationships between giver, organization and receiver have been described by Mauss (1954) and Titmuss as the *gift relationship*. It is this relationship which forms the foundation for the host of concerns which arise in voluntary and non-profit organizations and their management. Butler and Wilson (1989) and Wilson (1996) argue that the interdependencies of the gift relationship coupled with the concept of organizational membership based on voluntarism have brought two key areas into sharp focus. These are:

● The need to formulate strategies which place equal emphasis on gaining inputs as on providing services. Alongside this comes the need to adopt a more professional style of management, often based upon or copied from models in the commercial sector.
● A concern with organizational structure. In particular, a propensity to decentralize and to adopt a more project-centred or matrix structure. This is usually coupled with an attempt to change or to improve organizational image.

Managers of voluntary organizations face a vast number of interdependencies. They must simultaneously manage inputs, outputs and internal organization. This task is very different from managing the same activities in commercial organizations. First, there are very few instances of contracts with suppliers which are common in other forms of for-profit organization. Second, there are usually a vast number of suppliers ranging from thousands of individuals who put money into tins held by street collectors, to donations by corporate bodies such as government agencies or commercial firms. Both these factors make managing the external environment of the organization complex. Third, internal control is difficult to secure. Much of the labour force is voluntary and therefore not amenable to many of the leadership and motivation theories culled from commercial practice. Nor are precise job definitions, descriptions and other aspects of formalized organization wholly appropriate.

We can understand the complexities of managing voluntary and non-profit organizations if we examine first of all their position in the overall economy. As Butler (1983) suggests, the economy consists of a mix of three broad areas. These are:

1 *The market* Survives on the generation of surplus value. Revenue created primarily through the sale of goods and services and secondarily through various patterns of investment. Resources are allocated primarily by the price mechanism. This alerts entrepreneurial activity into selecting areas of provision of goods and services which are most profitable for them and to move away from less profitable areas.
2 *The statutory sector* Includes central and local government agencies. Survives primarily through revenue produced through various systems of taxation. Resources are primarily allocated by means of central planning. Some price mechanism may be used (such as in nationalized industries like the railways) but these are really pseudo-prices which are aimed at reducing the overall level of government subsidy.
3 *The voluntary sector* Includes registered charities and non-charities. Survives primarily through donations of time, money and other resources from thousands of individual donors and volunteers. Revenue also gained from some statutory grants and to a much less extent from commercial organizations. Charges for services are very rare. Some revenue raised through limited trading such as retail outlets or mail order services for Christmas cards and similar goods.

As a third way of providing services, the voluntary sector is becoming increasingly popular. One reason is that if a voluntary organization performs a function which was previously provided by the state, then this allows state spending to be allocated to other areas (or allows an overall reduction in state spending).

The management of voluntary organizations requires attention to a number of criteria. The gift relationship must be managed. At its simplest, this means some form of specialization in order to deal with securing inputs. More complex scenarios occur where funds come from government agencies or from commercial organizations which are earmarked for a particular purpose. Managers of voluntary organizations in receipt of such funds are now no longer benign recipients of altruistic behaviour. They have to manage a dependence relationship between giver and their organization (Pfeffer and Salancik, 1978). As the external environment changes, voluntary organizations will have to respond and adapt. This will mean managers spending some considerable time managing the political economy of the voluntary sector, liaising with government agencies, checking on the activities of competitor sister organizations and trying to secure a stable funding base. The 1990s saw the beginning of *contract culture* for voluntary organizations in Britain (this had started much earlier in North America) whereby their relationships with statutory bodies was essentially to bid for services and, if successful, are tied into quite specific contracts over the nature and type of service delivery. Managing the contract can take excessive amounts of management time. Lewis (1996) gives examples where up to 75% of a director's time is absorbed by running a contract.

As far as internal organization is concerned, pressure will be felt by managers in an attempt to increase efficiency, rationalize services, secure distinctive competence and generally to professionalize management of the organization (Handy, 1988; Wilson, 1996). Some key behavioural issues will have to be addressed in this process. For example, given the ideology of voluntarism which lies at the heart of voluntary and non-profit organizations, one would expect that decentralized structures with a minimum of hierarchy, formalization and standard procedures would be the norm.

To a large extent, decentralization has been a common feature, with organizations such as Christian Aid adopting a matrix structure. Others, such as Oxfam, have decentralized without reaching the stage of implementing a total matrix structure. Oxfam is a project organization. Other voluntary organizations such as the Royal National Institute for the Blind have recruited managers from commercial organizations as a deliberate strategy to 'import' the benefits of efficient commercial practice (see Butler and Wilson, 1989).

The overall need for precision in everything from job descriptions and responsibilities to standardized accounting procedures has not been a natural process of transition for organizations in the non-profit and voluntary sectors. For example, volunteers who feel that they do good job and who can expand their activities into a number of organizational activities, quite naturally resent the imposition of job demarcations. Historically, volunteers have been able to fit in where required and to expand or contract their role as necessary. Job descriptions and role responsibilities preclude this to a large extent.

The need for co-ordination in a decentralized organization has sometimes been overlooked. A danger here is one of creating a decentralized organization, comprising a set of different projects, but without the facility to integrate and co-ordinate the overall organization. The importation of managers from the commercial sector has done little to ameliorate these difficulties, since their message of professionalization equally clashes with the individualistic culture of most voluntary organizations. The culture itself presents a barrier to attempts at corporate integration.

In countries such as Britain where the role of the state has been consistently one of reducing the number of services offered and provided by statutory agencies, the strategic importance of the voluntary sector is likely to increase substantially. Data on income, level of investments and the number of voluntary organizations in operation support this view. In countries such as Sweden, where the activities of statutory agencies are, for the moment, far more comprehensive and complete, the need for a healthy, efficient voluntary sector is less pressing.

Where there is a demonstrable need for a strong voluntary sector, the pressures toward professionalization and achieving distinctive competence (as competition increases) are likely to result in the operation of fewer, larger charities. Those which cannot or will not change are likely not to gain long-term support and will thus find continued operation difficult or impossible.

Other alternative forms of organization

At the most extreme end of any centralized/decentralized continuum lie acephalous organizations. Quite literally, these are organizations without a head, without a leader, and without the necessary supporting structures to sustain either centralization or decentralization. Space limits us to little other than mentioning such organizations here. They are alternatives to hierarchies (heterarchies). Examples include the women's movement in Britain, some conservationist groups and peace movements. Some hippy communes, convoys and temporary social organizations (some festivals) could also be included as heterarchies.

In another view of 'alternative' organizations, Burrell (1997) argues against organization theory and many of its concepts of structure. He also rejects the linear structure of textbooks, writing one which is read front-to-back as well as back-to-front in an attempt to defy linearity. Burrell's (1997) main thesis is that organization theory has divorced itself from social theory. Therefore, what we profess in the name of organization theory is a partial and highly manipulative body of knowledge. It operates in the interests of management and the very conception of management itself is skewed. Since the Enlightenment, the creation of modern organization has been the product of exclusion of the non-literate, the non-affluent and the non-male (Burrell, 1997: 5). Management theory excludes, therefore, a whole range of human concerns which it effectively organizes 'out' of its domain. Whether the pre-modern, agrarian world that Burrell points toward can effect some rebalance is open to debate (he calls this nether world 'pandemonium'). What is certain is that when considering alternative forms of organization, it is always necessary to keep an open view about the likelihood of alternatives to the alternatives!

Summary

In this chapter we have looked at ways of structuring and designing organizations beyond the traditional, the formal, and the bureaucratic. We have also looked at moving the focus of designing organizations away from that of the single organization and widening the lens to include alliances and networks of firms as single units of analysis. Making organizations more project-centred and overlaying a lateral as well as a vertical dimension gives us the matrix structure. The fostering of a task culture and a project or matrix structure have been argued to create a flexible organization, capable of rapid and proactive change in the face of hostile or unpredictable environments.

Flexibility is also the keyword for describing voluntary organizations. Because of their position in the economy (relatively independent and non-profit seeking), these organizations can also adapt easily. Since they tend to be staffed with individuals who work through motives which are altruistic rather than instrumental or economic, motivating staff and achieving loyalty to the organization are less problematic.

All alternative forms of organization pose problems of achieving integration and co-ordination. Traditional systems of management and the application of well-worn management theories are unlikely to be effective. They are more likely to be counter-productive to effectiveness. These kinds of organization need very different styles of management if they are to succeed in the long term. Yet, there is always the pressure upon all 'alternative' structures to revert to traditional, formal bureaucratic structures. Once this has happened, the beliefs, ideologies and values of alternative organization will disappear. One challenge for the future will be to find new theories of management appropriate to alternative organizations; new theories which are not just borrowed and adapted from traditional management theory.

References

Billis, D. and M. Harris (eds.), (1996) *Voluntary Agencies: Challenges of Organisation and Management*, MacMillan, Basingstoke.

Borys, B. and D. B. Jemison (1989) 'Hybrid arrangements as strategic alliances: theoretical issues in organizational combinations', *Academy of Management Review*, **14**, 234–49.

Burns, T. and G. R. Stalker (1961) *The Management of Innovation*, Tavistock, London.

Burrell, W. G. (1997) *Pandemonium: Towards a Retro-Organization Theory*, Sage, London.

Butler, R. J. (1983) 'Control through markets, hierarchies and communes: a transactional approach to organizational analysis', in A. Francis, J. Turk and P. Willman (eds.), *Power, Efficiency and Institutions*, Heinemann, London.

Butler, R. J. and D. C. Wilson (1989) *Managing Voluntary and Non-Profit Organizations: Strategy And Structure*, Routledge, London,

Chesterman, M. (1979) *Charities, Trusts And Social Welfare*, Weidenfeld and Nicolson, London.

Child, J. (1984) *Organization: A Guide to Problems and Practice*, Harper & Row London.

Choi, T. Y. and J. L. Hartley (1996) 'An exploration of supplier selection practices across the supply chain', *Journal of Operations Management*, **14** (4), 333–43.

Contractor, F. J. (1986) 'International business: an alternative view', *International Marketing Review*, Spring, 74–85.

Daft, R. L. (1995) *Organization Theory and Design*, West, St. Paul, Minn.

Davis, S. M. and P. R. Lawrence (1977) *Matrix*, Addison-Wesley, Reading, Mass.

Forrest, J. E. (1992) 'Management aspects of strategic partnering', *Journal of General Management*, **17** (4), 25–40.

Galbraith, J. (1973) *Designing Complex Organizations*, Addison-Wesley, Reading, Mass.

Galbraith, J. R. (1974) 'Organizational design: an information processing view', *Interfaces*, **4**, 28–36.

Galbraith, J. K. (1977) 'Matrix organization design: how to combine functional and project forms', *Business Horizons*, 29–40.

Handy, C. B. (1988) *Understanding Voluntary Organizations*, Penguin, Harmondsworth.

Horngren, C. T. and G. Foster (1987) *Cost Accounting: A Managerial Perspective*, 6th edn., Prentice-Hall, Englewood Cliffs, New Jersey.

Hunt, J. (1986) *Managing People at Work: A Manager's Guide To Behaviour In Organizations*, McGraw-Hill, London.

Johanson, J. and L. G. Mattsson (1992) 'Network positions and strategic action', in B. Axelsson and G. Easton (eds.), *Industrial Networks: A New View of Reality*, Routledge, London.

Kets de Vries, M. (1996) 'Leaders who make a difference', *European Management Journal*, **14** (5), 486–93.

Knight, K. (1976) 'Matrix organizations: a review', *Journal of Management Studies*, **13** (2), 111–30.

Lawrence, P. and J. W. Lorsch (1967) *Organization And Environment*, Harvard University Press, Cambridge, Mass.

Lewis, J. (1996) 'What does contracting do to voluntary agencies?', in D. Billis and M. Harris (eds.), *Voluntary Agencies: Challenges of Organisation and Management*, MacMillan, Basingstoke.

Mauss, M. (1954) *The Gift*, Norton, New York.

Pfeffer, J. and G. R. Salancik (1978) *The External Control of Organizations: A Resource Dependence Perspective*, Harper & Row, New York.

Simbari, D. (1996) 'Competitive advantages', *Manufacturing Systems*, **14** (9), 92–6.

Titmuss, R. 1970) *The Gift Relationship: From Human Blood to Social Policy*, Penguin, Harmondsworth.

Williamson, O. E. and W. Ouchi (1981) 'The markets, hierarchies and visible hand perspectives', in A. H. Van De Ven and W. F. Joyce (eds.), *Perspectives On Organizational Design And Behaviour*, Wiley, New York.

Williamson, O. E. (1991) 'Strategizing, economizing and economic organization', *Strategic Management Journal*, **12**, 75–94.

Wilson, D. C. 1984) 'Charity law and the politics of regulation in the voluntary sector', *King's Counsel*, **34**, 36–41.

Wilson, D. C. (1996) 'How do voluntary agencies manage organisational change?', in D. Billis and M. Harris (eds.), *Voluntary Agencies: Challenges of Organisation and Management*, MacMillan, Basingstoke.

Is corporate culture manageable?

Andrew M. Pettigrew

Is corporate culture manageable? The straightforward answer to that question is—with the greatest difficulty! The more academic answer to the question depends on what is meant by corporate culture and management.

Let me be clear first of all what I mean by management, and in particular management process. Management is much more than just a process of analytical reasoning. A search through many of the basis textbooks in business strategy in the 1960s and 1970s gives the impression that the development of strategy is a rational analytical process. Seeing the process of management in such rational terms is not a helpful starting point for answering the question: is corporate culture manageable?

The rational approach to strategic management has tended to describe and prescribe techniques for identifying current strategy, analysing environments, resources, and gaps, revealing and assessing strategic alternatives, and choosing and implementing carefully analysed and well-thought-through outcomes. Depending on the author, explicitly or implicitly, the firm speaks with a unitary voice or can be composed of omnipotent, even heroic general managers or chief executives, looking at known and consistent preferences and assessing them with voluminous and presumably apposite information, which can be organized into clear input–output relationships.

More recently the empirical process research by authors such as Bower (1970), Pettigrew (1973; 1985a; 1985b), and Mintzberg (1978) has introduced a rather different and more realistic language for thinking about management processes of change. Strategic change is now to be viewed as a complex human process in which differential perception, quests for efficiency and power, visionary leadership skills, the vicariousness of chance, and subtle processes of additively building up a momentum of support for change, and then vigorously implementing change, all play their part.

If the process of management is conceived in such social and political terms, what is the working definition of corporate culture used to develop the arguments in this paper? Following Pettigrew (1979), Schein (1985), Barney (1986), and others, corporate culture is understood as a phenomenon which exists at a variety of different levels. At the deepest level, culture is thought of as the complex set of values, beliefs, and assumptions that define the ways in which a firm conducts its business. Such core beliefs and assumptions are, of course, manifested in the structures, systems, symbols, myths and patterns of reward inside the organization. The basic proposition of this reading is that it is rather easier to adjust the manifestations of culture than it is to change the core beliefs and assumptions within an organization. However, any practical strategy for changing corporate culture has to involve thought and action both at the level of core beliefs, and of the cultural manifestations of those core beliefs.

This reading has six parts. After this introduction, there is a section outlining the analytical framework used to understand processes of cultural change in organizations. There then follows a section which explores why corporate culture is so difficult to manage. The following section focuses on one of the central problems of strategic change, how to change the core beliefs of top decision-makers in the organization. We then move on to briefly describe some of the range of empirical studies going on at the Centre for Corporate Strategy and Change, University of Warwick, exploring the context, content, and processes of strategic change in a number of different firms in a variety of different sectors. This work is exemplified by brief reference to a completed study of Imperial Chemical Industries (Pettigrew, 1985a) and an on-going study of Jaguar Cars. The reading ends by cataloguing some of the key management tasks and mechanisms used to change corporate cultures.

Context, content and process in studying strategic change

Figure R9.1
Corporate culture and change: an analytical framework

In this writer's view, theoretically sound and practically useful research on strategic decision-making and change should involve the continuous interplay among ideas about the *context* of change, the *process* of change and the *content* of change, together with skill in regulating the relations among the three. Figure R9.1 outlines the broad analytical framework used at Warwick for guiding our empirical research.

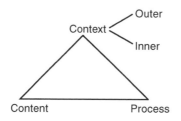

The starting point for this analysis of strategic change is the notion that formulating the content of any new strategy inevitably entails managing its context and process. Outer context refers to the social, economic, political and competitive environment in which the firm operates. Inner context refers to the structure, corporate culture and political context within the firm through which ideas for change have to proceed. Content refers to the particular areas of change under examination. Thus the firm may be seeking to change technology, manpower, products, geographical positioning, or indeed corporate culture. The process of change refers to the actions, reactions, and interactions from the various interested parties as they seek to move the firms from its present to its future state. Thus the *what* of change is encapsulated under the label content, much of the *why* of change is derived from an analysis of inner and outer context, and the *how* of change can be understood from an analysis of process.

One of the weaknesses of the existing literature on business strategy is its focus on the link between outer context and content. The singular and exclusive analytical concern with outer context and content has led to the planners' nightmare of the lack of acceptance of planning solutions. A major practical suggestion of this reading is that action to change the strategies and cultures of firm is much dependent on the ability not only to link the *what* of change to the outer context of the firm, but also to link and fashion such suggestions to the internal political and context of the firm, and to manage such connections through the firm by adroit considerations about the process of management.

Why is corporate culture difficult to manage?

Listed below are seven major factors which make corporate culture difficult to manage. These are:

1 the levels issue
2 the pervasiveness issue
3 the implicitness issue
4 the imprinting issue
5 the political issue
6 the plurality issue
7 the interdependence issue

Briefly put, the levels issue relates to the fact that corporate culture exists at a variety of different levels in the firm. Thus at the deepest level is refers to the beliefs and assumptions of people inside the organization both about the internal workings of the organization and the way the organization faces its external environment. As I have already suggested, it is rather more difficult to change the core beliefs and assumptions within the organization than it is to change some of the manifestations of culture in, for example, the organization's structure and systems.

The pervasiveness issue is a corollary of the points made above about different levels of culture. Culture is not only deep, it is also broad. Thus corporate culture refers not just to people, their relationships and beliefs; it also refers to their views about company products, structures, systems, corporate purpose, and modes of recruitment, socialization, and reward.

The implicitness issue pertains to the fact that much of corporate culture is taken for granted. It is remarkably difficult to change things which are implicitly part of people's thinking and behaviour, and are rarely brought out explicitly for consideration.

Imprinting draws attention to the deep historical roots of much of corporate culture. History weighs a very heavy hand in the present and future management of most corporations.

The political issue refers to the connections between corporate culture and the power distribution in the firm. Certain power groups in the organization have a vested interest in the beliefs and assumptions which may have primacy at any point in time in the firm's development. Those power groups are unlikely to be willing to discard those beliefs and assumptions without persistent and consistent challenge.

The plurality issue is a close cousin of politics and culture. Most firms do not just have a single corporate culture but at any point in time may have a variety of different sets of beliefs and assumptions—in effect of series of subcultures. Tension about the future development of the firm is often expressed in terms of the language and political positioning of these different subcultures.

Finally, the interdependency issue focuses on the fact that culture is interconnected not only with the politics of the firm, but also with the structure, systems, people and priorities of the firm. Between them the above seven issues make corporate culture remarkably difficult to manage, and certainly to change.

A key aspect of strategic change: changing the core beliefs of the top decision-makers

The point has been made that corporate culture exists at a variety of different levels in the firm. The deepest of these levels is the core beliefs and assumptions of the organization's top decision-makers. Such beliefs are obviously critical, for they not only define what key people perceive as is important in the organization's environment; such beliefs also help to determine areas for management attention, choice, and change within the firm. Studies by, for example, Grinyer and Spender (1979), Pettigrew (1985a), and Johnson (1987) all reveal the critical role of top management beliefs in inhibiting and facilitating change in the firm.

Research at the Centre for Corporate Strategy and Change at the University of Warwick is seeking to explore some of the key problems of strategy and change in private- and public-sector organizations in the UK. Longitudinal empirical studies are under way in firms in the automobile, merchant banking, publishing, engineering, commercial banking, office automation and computing and retailing sectors. A large empirical project has just begun in 8 of the 14 regions in the NHS in the UK. In this reading, the briefest reference can only be made to completed study of the long-term processes of strategic change in Imperical Chemicals Industries (ICI), and a study under way in Jaguar Cars.

The ICI study of strategic change

The ICI study of strategic change uses extensive high-level and longitudinal data to explore processes of strategic and operational change on the main board of ICI, and in ICI's four largest divisions over the period 1960–83. The full results of this study are now available in Pettigrew (1985a). Some of the key findings of the study relevant to the question: 'Is culture manageable?,' can be stated as follows:

1 Change in ICI did not occur as a continuous incremental process.
2 The pattern of change over a 25-year period in the company was for radical periods of change to occur at certain critical points in time. Such radical periods were interspersed with long periods of incremental adjustment. These radical periods featured changes in the core beliefs, structure and business strategy of ICI.
3 The timing of these radical packages of a change were associated with:
   (a) Real and constructed business crises. In other words, ICI made substantial changes only when it was in severe economic difficulties. The two great eras of change over the last two or three decades have been between 1960 and 1964 and between 1980 and 1986. A critical facet of these change periods was not only the association with business crisis but also the active strategies by the managers in ICI to construct a climate for change around these business crises. Mobilizing the context in order to provide the legitimacy and justification for change was a critical part of the process of managing change.
   (b) Such radical packages were also connected with changes in leadership and power in ICI. The era of change in the early 1960s was associated with the appearance of Paul Chambers, later Sir Paul Chambers, as Chairman of ICI. More recently John Harvey-Jones, now Sir John Harvey-Jones, has provided substantial change leadership in the company. Both Chambers and Harvey-Jones supplied quite different business leadership in the company. They were both men who had not spent their whole career in the ICI culture.

(c) Finally the timing of these radical packages of a change were much associated with the transformation in the beliefs of the top decision-makers in ICI.

A crucial finding in the ICI study relates to the sequencing in the pattern of change in the company. The sequencing of change did not follow the conventional wisdom of the business policy literature that changes in organizational structure should follow changes in business strategy. Rather the pattern of change in ICI was a complex mixture of adjustments of core beliefs of the top decision-makers, followed by changes in beliefs, and out of those changes in beliefs and structure began to emerge the new business strategy of the firm. If this pattern is clearly established in other case studies, it makes the issue of first challenging and then changing the core beliefs of the top decision-makers a critical factor in the theory and practice of managing strategic change.

For a discussion of how the ICI process of change occurred, see Pettigrew (1985a). In addition, the final section of this paper draws on the ICI case to reveal some of the key management tasks and mechanisms used to effect changes in corporate culture.

Changes in corporate culture in Jaguar Cars

In ICI the change problem was how to break down the core beliefs of the top decision-makers as ICI faced a rapidly changing external environment. As the old beliefs were questioned, so a new ideology was introduced by Harvey-Jones and others which emphasized a sharpening in market focus, a greater entrepreneurial emphasis to more decentralized units, a lessening of bureaucracy and central control, and a change in the mode and style of operation of the main board. These attempts at cultural change were linked to major changes in structure and manpower. The business strategy changes which emerged emphasized a move from heavy to speciality chemicals and a continuation of attempts to reposition ICI in North America and to move increasingly into the markets of the Pacific Basin.

Paradoxically, in Jaguar Cars the problem of cultural change has been the revival and revamping of an old culture in line with the business and competitive conditions of the 1980s. What the chairman and chief executive of Jaguar Cars, Sir John Egan, has attempted to do is best understood in relationship to the three main phases of Jaguar's development. These phases are the Lyons' era, 1920–72; the BL era, 1972–80; and the Egan era from 1980 onwards.

In broad terms the Jaguar culture under Lyons was one of the intense personal loyalty to 'Sir William' linked to a marked identification with a distinctive product ('grace, pace, space'). This culture also rested on a clear commitment to engineering excellence which was routinely expressed in a 'can do' mentality (for example, the meeting of exceptional project deadlines) which became famous within the industry. There was an absence of elaborate management control.

Under BL the strength of this culture and approach to building luxury and racing cars withered. As BL removed key functions (sales, purchasing) to central office or other plants, those who remained at Jaguar's main manufacturing plants concentrated on surviving a hostile corporate overload and a series of senior managers who did not respect the Jaguar culture.

John Egan, however, saw the Jaguar culture, albeit the remnants in 1980, as a vital resource in rebuilding the company. The chairman and other senior executives, as part of the process of establishing a 'stand-alone company', have attempted to revive and extend that culture which had all but died under BL. The chairman and board have demonstrated that the new stand-alone company was to be built on both the accepted qualities of the old Jaguar culture, together with an infusion of outside expertise (for example, university engineers, sales and marketing heads from Lotus).

The core beliefs of the newly created senior management were examined by Egan at an early stage in 1980 as part of his securing their total commitment to saving the company. Once that commitment was forthcoming it then became a question of reviewing the traditional features of adherence to engineering excellence and product loyalty on a wider basis, as well as extending those features to embrace the highest standards of competitiveness in quality, reliability and productivity recognized in the 1980s. In effect Jaguar decided they had to emulate Daimler-Benz.

Since 1980/81 the task of changing Jaguar's culture has centred on the inculcation of this commitment among middle management, workforce, suppliers, and contractors. This task is very much in progress but some important examples of structures and symbols within the company emerge. They include:

1 Regular US dealer visits to the major Jaguar manufacturing plants and confrontations with factory sections responsible for quality defects. These visits are backed-up by monthly dealer award schemes, and successful employees have their names put on a plaque in the reception area adjacent to the Queen's Awards to Industry which have been presented to Jaguar.
2 New contractoral relationships with suppliers are reinforced by an annual Jaguar award ceremony for the best performers, held at prestige locations in London.
3 The creation of weekly 'washing-up' meetings on the manufacturing tracks. These washing-up meetings tackle problems as they arise and are linked via parallel engineering meetings to the monthly board.
4 Many of these symptoms of cultural change have been recognized by outsiders. One city analyst connected with Jaguar observed that the new head of communications and corporate affairs is now 'more Jaguar than some of the people who have been there for 25 years'.

Changing corporate culture: key management tasks and mechanisms

The ICI, Jaguar, and related Warwick studies reveal the following factors as important in facilitating changes in corporate culture:

1 A receptive outer context, together with managerial skill in mobilizing that context in order to create an overall climate for change to occur.
2 Leadership behaviour either from individuals recently brought into the organization from outside, or from individuals who have been pushing for change from a powerful internal position for some time. Most of the cases of change reveal a very clear and consistent drive from the top.
3 The existence of inarticulate and imprecise visions from the agents of change at the very top.
4 The use of discrepant action by key figures in the new guard in order to raise the level of tension in the organization for change.
5 Using deviants and heretics, both external and internal to the organization in order to say the unsayable and think the unthinkable. External and internal consultants are regularly used for this purpose.

6   Releasing avenues and energy for change by moving people and portfolios.

7   Creating new meetings and other arenas where problems can be articulated and shares and energy focused around the need for change.

8   Altering the management process at the very top. A key aspect of this seems to be the need to change top management processes from being highly divisive in character to being much more coherent and cohesive.

9   Reinforcing any embryonic cultural shifts through closely matched structural changes, then strengthening such cultural and structural changes through the public use of the organization's reward systems.

10   Finding and using 'role models' who can through their own public behaviour display key aspects of the new culture. The identification of people who can 'walk and talk' seems to be a key aspect of making concrete and public the desire cultural changes. These role models of the new era also help the continuing reinforcement of change.

11   Carrying the message deep into the organization through the use of training and development strategies.

12   Transmitting the new beliefs and behaviour down into the organization by revamping employee communication mechanisms.

13   Finally there is the old-fashioned but critical need for persistence and patience. All of these studies of strategic change we are looking at emphasize the complexity and difficulty of effecting such changes, even where the change is eventually triggered by major environmental disturbances. Persistence and patience is critically important at the difficult stage of breaking down the core beliefs of the old guard, getting new problems sensed and articulated in the organization, developing a sense of concern that those problems are worthy or analytical and political attention, and then articulating the new order often through highly inarticulate and impressive visions of the future.

References

Barney, J. B. (1986) 'Organizational culture: can it be a source of sustained competitive advantage?' *Academy of Management Review* **11** (3), 656–65.

Bower, J. L. (1970) *Managing the Resource Allocation Process*, Harvard University Press, Cambridge, Mass.

Grinyer, P. H. and J. C. Spender (1979) 'Recipes, crises, and adaptation in mature businesses', *International Journal of Management and Organization*, **IX**, (3), 113–25.

Johnson, G. (1987) *The Process of Strategic Change: A Management Perspective*, Basil Blackwell, Oxford.

Mintzberg, H. (1978) 'Patterns in strategy formation', *Management Science*, **24**, 934–48.

Pettigrew, A. M. (1973) *The Politics of Organizational Decision-Making*, Tavistock, London.

Pettigrew, A. M. (1979) 'On Studying organizational cultures' *Administrative Science Quarterly*, **24**, 570–81.

Pettigrew, A. M. (1985a) *The Awakening Giant: Continuity and Change in ICI*, Basil Blackwell, Oxford.

Pettigrew, A. M. (1985b) 'Culture and politics in strategic decision-making and change' in J. M. Pennings (ed.), *Organizational Strategy and Change*, Jossey-Bass, San Francisco.

Schein, E. H. (1985) *Organizational Culture and Leadership*, Jossey-Bass, San Francisco.

Integrating organizational dynamics through organizational levels

David Coghlan

The common way of understanding organizations is to view them as systems. There are two ways in which organizations as systems can be understood. Organizations are open systems, that is, a set of interrelated elements which transform various inputs into desired outputs and which are influenced by their external environment (Katz and Kahn, 1978, Hanna, 1987). A second understanding of organizations as systems is the 'recursive' systems model which represents organizations as patterns of feedback loops—sequences of interaction which link and integrate elements of a system (Senge, 1990, Ballé, 1994, McCaughan and Palmer, 1994). In an organization there are dynamic interrelationships between its purposes, the formal structure, the technology, how employees are managed and rewarded, communications and the informal system of how employees feel about the organization, how they work together and how change is managed. The elements in the recursive systems approach are also open systems in that they are affected by their external environment.

Levels of complexity—individual, group, inter-group, organizational—are frequently used as frameworks for understanding organizational processes. Several essential points need to be made about the concept and usage of the term levels. First, the notion of levels must be distinguished from that of echelon (Rousseau, 1985). Echelon refers to position on a chain of command in an organization, such as worker, supervisor, manager, group manager and chief executive. The less common use of organizational levels as a construct in organizational behaviour, however, is descriptive of levels of complexity.

Rashford and Coghlan's four levels of organizational behaviour

Present levels in terms of how people participate in organizations and link them to provide a useful tool for the manager, consultant and teacher of organizational behaviour has been presented (Rashford and Coghlan 1994, Coghlan and Rashford, 1991). They distinguish four levels of behaviour in organizations—the individual, the face-to-face team, the inter-departmental group and the organizational. The first level (Level I) is the *bonding* relationship that the individual has with the organization and the organization with the individual. For the individual, this involves a utilization of membership and participation in the organization in order to meet personal life goals, while for management the core issue is to get a person committed to the goals, values and culture of the organization. The more complex approach to participation exists in establishing *effective working relationships in a face-to-face team* (Level II). An even more complex involvement exists in terms of the inter-departmental group type of interface where teams must be *co-ordinated* in order to achieve complex tasks and maintain a balance of power among competing political interest groups (Level III). Finally, the most complex, from the point of view of the individual, is the relationship of the total organization to its external environment in which other organizations are individual competitors, competing for scarce resources to produce similar products or services. The key task for any organization is its ability to *adapt* to environmental forces driving for change (Level IV).

Level I — individual

Individuals within the organization have life-tasks, needs and wishes which extend far beyond their participation in any given work setting. Each individual person struggles to find unique and personalized satisfactions in this regard. Management's perspective at the same point, however, is that individuals somehow belong to the organization in an appropriate psychological contract. When the tasks at this level are reasonably and adequately met, individuals can allow the organization and its goals be a source of personal goal motivation. Individuals will still retain their own individuality while 'belonging' to the organization. In contrast, the awareness and utilization of motivational techniques are the basic functions of management towards each individual in the organization in the hope that they will enhance growth and effectiveness. Therefore, management's ideal goal is to create a matching process in which people are able and encouraged to become involved, and find that the work situation develops them as human beings while the organization benefits from such an involvement.

In its essence, Level I focuses the issues inherent in individual–organizational relationships, human resource management, and career dynamics through naming the core task as bonding, for both the individual to the organization and the organization to the individual. Contemporary issues in this regard, such as part-time and contract workers, the impact of technology on work, benefit from being viewed in terms of the *bonding* task.

Organizational change typically means that individual employees have to change too (Clarke, 1994). Individuals may be required to change what they do or how they do it. It may be required of them to change their attitudes towards their work or some particular aspect of it. A consequence of this may be that an individual's sense of bonding to the changed or changing organization may be altered, either positively or negatively (Coghlan, 1993). An organizational change if not well managed may result in individuals feeling demotivated and alienated and exhibiting defensive behaviour. Organization development consultants may work with individuals' negative perception of the change, which may be located in a particular individual's personality or in how the change is introduced and managed. The change process may also suggest that it be useful for the consultant to work at facilitating individuals to identify and evaluate the dynamics of the life-cycle, the work-cycle and the family-cycle and place them in juxtaposition so that they can locate their career issues in the context of their lives. Individuals can be facilitated to take ownership of their lives and career and adopt positive coping responses to the tasks facing them. Furthermore, work with these individuals aims towards empowering them to suggest, initiate and promote change in the organization and reduce undesired stressful side effects. At the same time, work with managers enables them to reflect on and restructure managerial assumptions and behaviour towards their subordinates and colleagues (Argyris, 1990). Consultants in this situation are facilitating the individual employee and the manager to become more aware of their separate and mutual needs as persons within the organization as well as the needs of the organization. As organizational change involves individual and personal change, attention to the individual in the context of the wider systemic change is critical for the success of the change process.

Level II — face-to-face team

From the individual's perspective, entry into the work activity generally involves interfacing with other persons in clearly defined units. Face-to-face teams are typically formal groups and defined in terms of: face-to-face interaction, common objectives, psychological awareness of other members, and self-definition as a team with member–non member boundaries clearly defined. The issues for the face-to-face team are setting and achieving objectives, allocating the work to the members, while at the same time, maintaining co-operative relations among the members through how they work together and perform the team tasks necessary for effective co-operative action (Kolb, Rubin and McIntyre, 1984, Beckhard, 1985).

Level II issues encompass the dynamics of working teams and groups, whether as formal teams in an organization's hierarchy or as temporary committees or task forces in policy formulation or change management (Payne and Cooper, 1981).

The change agenda in an organization typically affects the work of teams. Teams may be set new goals and targets. They may have to work differently. The process of organizational change typically involves the change agenda being assessed and responded to by the permanent working teams in the organization's structure and by the involvement of temporary committees or task forces in solving problems, creating policy or generating commitment (Coghlan, 1994). Level II processes may occur in the permanent teams which are the basis of the structures of most organizations. In this context the long-term relationships among the members and the patterns of interaction which have become taken for granted and have become largely unnoticed can be a significant area of focus and intervention for the consultant. In the context of temporary groups, such as task forces or *ad hoc* committees, the consultant, as well as attending to issues of task achievement and interpersonal dynamics, needs also attend to how the task force relates to and is integrated into the structure and culture of the organization. One important aspect of the manager or consultant's work at this second level is to enable a team (whether a permanent team or a temporary task force) to build its team skills (Schein, 1988, Coghlan, 1994, Reddy, 1994).

Level III — inter-departmental group

From the team's point of view, to be effective and enter the organization's life is to work within a larger system. This third level can be made up of any number of face-to-face working teams which must function together to accomplish an inter-departmental purpose, such as manufacturing, sales, or marketing. This third level can have many different applications. For instance, it can refer to functional inter-departmental relations, strategic business units or national companies in a multi-national organization. In its operation, it needs to have critical information which passes beyond the boundaries of individual teams in order to implement programmes and projects at a range beyond their direct contact. In large organizations where size and distance dissolve immediate personal relationships, it is imperative that this third level functions well. From management's standpoint, the team's tasks within the overall group is to perform effectively in its own right, while at the same time have a clearly defined commitment to the inter-departmental group. When this third level is working effectively, the inter-departmental group is capable of obtaining information and converting it into decision processes, enabling the implementation of complex programmes or operations. The key task at this level is to map the flow of information and partially completed work from one team to another in order that the organization function as an integrated whole. Level III encompasses inter-team dynamics, industrial relations and the impact of information technology on organizational structure and processes.

The inter-departmental group is critical in an organizational change. As resources are re-allocated and technology and advanced information systems alter access to the flow of information, teams are required to communicate more effectively across functions and departments. Such a process may involve integral cultural change (Schein, 1992). Managers or consultants can enable the inter-departmental group to locate problems through the use of internal mapping. Internal mapping utilizes a process whereby individual heads of work units or team leaders are facilitated to plot the workflow through their section, and to do this in such a way that from the beginning of a work process to its finish, all the intermediate links between different functioning teams are plotted, and all the members of the group then have a chance to *jointly* take ownership of all the dysfunctional areas and proceed to work in small tasks forces in order to remedy the dysfunctions. Other interventions may occur through the search conference, where the inter-departmental group gather to view the past, present and future of the organization in order to create a shared future vision (Weisbord and Janov, 1995). Consultants may also facilitate situations in which inter-team tensions require resolution. This can be done by providing a safe environment in which inter-functional relations can be examined and discussed in a manner which enables protagonists to actively listen to one another and come to understand experiences and perspectives of teams other than their own.

Level IV—organizational

The fourth level is the organizational goals, policy and strategy level. It is the final fusion of all three levels together to form a working, cohesive organization. The organization's task is to have a unified corporate identity, to exist in a competitive environment by exchanging products or services in order to obtain much sought-after resources. Consequently, an organization needs to be capable of reflecting on its own strengths and weaknesses, as well as engaging in proactive relationships to determine and deal with the opportunities and threats from the external environment. The assessment of strengths, weaknesses, opportunities and threats result in a selection process which establishes programmes, services and products. These procedures aim at accomplishing the goals of the organization and adapting to external environmental demands. An awareness of the cultural assumptions which underlie any organization's policies, strategies, structures and behaviours contributes to the successful completion of the tasks at this level (Schein, 1992).

Level IV encompass the organizational focus on strategic planning and management and organizational change and development (Worley, Hitchin and Ross, 1996). A further dimension of this fourth level is the inter-organizational interface created through information technology. The networked organization is a consequence of the advances in information technology in creating the possibility of organizational interdependence. Issues of quality, service, cost and time act as driving forces for organizations to enter into forms of co-operation with their suppliers and customers through extensive communication networks, accessible databases and enhanced human performance workstations (Scott-Morton, 1991).

Inter-level dynamics

The Rashford and Coghlan framework contains an essential inter-level element in that each level has a dynamic relationship with each of the others. This relationship is grounded in systems dynamics, whereby the relationship each of the four levels has with the other three is systemic, with feedback loops forming a complex pattern of relationships (Senge, 1990; McCaughan and Palmer, 1994). In short, Level I issues affect Levels II, III and IV. Level II issues affect Levels I, III and IV, and Level III issues affect Levels I, II and IV: that is, the feedback loops work in both directions. In systemic terms, each of the four levels affects each of the other three. Dysfunctions on any of the four levels can cause dysfunctions on any of the other three levels.

An individual's level of stress can be expressed in dysfunctional behaviour in the team and affect a team's ability to function effectively, which in turn affects the individual's ability to cope and ultimately the bonding relationship with the organization. If a team is not functioning effectively, it can limit the inter-departmental group's effectiveness which may depend on the quality and timeliness of information, resources and partially completed work from that team. If the inter-departmental group's multiple activities are not co-ordinated, the organization's ability to survive and compete effectively may be affected.

While Rashford and Coghlan's framework of organizational levels focuses on levels as a notion of complexity rather than a position on the hierarchy of command, positioning on a chain of command has an impact on the functioning of the four levels. When an individual has a problem, the higher he or she is on the hierarchy the greater the impact is on the organization. The higher one is on the hierarchy or the more power a team has the greater the influence to bring about change. The inter-connectedness between positions on the hierarchy and levels of complexity exists in the role of the 'key' individual. The key individual is a general term to connote those whose role involves crossing boundaries from one sub-system to another (Likert, 1961). The team-leader, supervisor, manager and administrator crosses the boundary from his or her area of responsibility to those of other functions or higher management. This constitutes crossing boundaries within the hierarchy. At the same time, these individual are interacting in cross-level dynamics. They bring individual issues to a team, and team issues to the group. When an individual represents his or her own department to a broader function, he or she crosses from the team to the group level and the dynamic of that interaction may lead to a re-assessment of the individual level. Other cross-level interaction occurs in the 'gatekeeping' role (Allen, 1977; Ancona and Caldwell, 1988), whereby new information is brought into the team from the external environment. New information, especially disconfirming information, may cause the individual to be rejected by the team, thereby producing conflict in the team.

Levels in organizational change and development

The manager or organization development consultant can use the construct of the four levels as a diagnostic framework by being aware of the issues occurring at each level and how one level affects another, and be able to work with individuals, teams and inter-team groups to evaluate the effect of one level on another (Rashford and Coghlan, 1994). The process of moving a change through an organization—creating a vision of the changed state, planning interventions, building commitment and managing the transition (Beckhard and Harris, 1987)—requires a systemic view of the complex interrelationship and interdependence of the individual, the face-to-face team, the inter-departmental group and the organization (Rashford and Coghlan, 1994).

In this process of evaluating the impact of one level on another, the manager or consultant must take notice of the systemic nature of the relationship between each of the levels, that is to say, to construct how the relationship between one level and another works in both directions. An individual's sense of alienation from the team in which she works, not only affects her participation in the team and the team's work, but what happens in the team affects her sense of alienation. When relationships are viewed as systems, then there is no simple cause-and-effect linear chain. There is no direct line of blame. Each element in the system both causes and is caused by the other elements.

Conclusions

This reading introduced the notion of organizational levels, as descriptive of levels of complexity in organizational behaviour, as contrasted with levels of hierarchy. One particular framework of four organizational levels, Rashford and Coghlan, was presented and developed in order to provide a construct in which the interrelationship between individuals and an organization, the dynamics of the working teams of which they are members, the co-ordinating function of inter-team relationships and an organization's strategic endeavours can be viewed in a systemic framework, and how planned organizational change in a complex system moves through each level. Such a focus on inter-level dynamics is essential in order to understand and manage organizations.

References

Allen, T. J. (1977) *Managing the Flow of Technology*, MIT Press, Cambridge, Mass.

Ancona, D. and D. Caldwell (1988) 'Beyond Task and Maintenance: Defining External Relations in Groups', *Group & Organization Studies*, **13** (4), 468–94.

Argyris, C. (1990) *Overcoming Organizational Defenses*, Allyn & Bacon, Boston, Mass.

Ballé, M. (1994) *Managing with Systems Thinking*, McGraw-Hill, London.

Beckhard, R. (1985) 'Optimizing Team Building Efforts', in W. French, C. Bell, and R. Zawacki (eds.), *Organization Development: Theory, Practice and Research*, BPI, Houston, Texas.

Beckhard, R. and R. Harris (1987) *Organizational Transitions: Managing Complex Change*, 2nd edn, Addison-Wesley, Reading, Mass.

Clarke, L. (1994) *The Essence of Change*, Prentice-Hall, London.

Coghlan, D. (1993) 'A Person-Centred Approach to Dealing with Resistance to Change', *Leadership and Organization Development Journal*, **14** (4), 10–4.

Coghlan, D. (1994) 'Managing Organizational Change through Teams and Groups', *Leadership and Organization Development Journal*, **15** (2), 18–23.

Coghlan, D. and N. S. Rashford (1991) 'Developing Key Intervention Skills on Four Organizational Levels,' in J. D. Bigelow, (ed.), *Managerial Skills Explorations in Practical Knowledge*, Sage, Newbury Park, CA.

Hanna, D. (1987) *Designing Organizations for High Performance*, Addison-Wesley, Reading, Mass.

Katz, D. and R. Kahn (1978) *The Social Psychology of Organizations*, Wiley, New York.

Kolb, D., I. Rubin and J. McIntyre (1984) *Organizational Psychology: An Experiential Approach*, 4th edn, Prentice-Hall, Englewood Cliffs, New Jersey.

Likert, R. (1961) *New Patterns of Management*, McGraw-Hill, New York.

McCaughan, N. and B. Palmer (1994) *Systems Thinking for Harassed Managers*, Karnac, London.

Payne, R. and C. L. Cooper (1981) *Groups at Work*, Wiley, Chicester.

Rashford, N. S. and D. Coghlan (1994) *The Dynamics of Organizational Levels: a Change Framework for Managers and Consultants*, Addison-Wesley, Reading, Mass.

Reddy, W. B. (1994) *Intervention Skills: Process Consultation for Small Groups and Teams*, Pfeiffer, San Diego.

Rousseau, D. (1985) 'Issues of Level in Organizational Research: Multi-level and Cross-level Perspectives', in L. L. Cummings, and B. M. Staw eds.), *Research in Organizational Behaviour*, **7**, JAI Press, Greenwich, CN.

Schein, E. H. (1988) *Process Consultation, Volume 1: Its Role in Organization Development*, revised edn., Addison-Wesley, Reading, Mass.

Schein, E. H. (1992) *Organizational Culture and Leadership*, 2nd edn., Jossey-Bass, San Francisco.

Scott-Morton, M. (1991) *The Corporation of the 1990s: Information Technology and Organizational Transformation*, Oxford University Press, New York.

Senge, P. (1990) *The Fifth Discipline*, Doubleday, New York.

Weisbord, M. and S. Janov (1995) *Future Search*, Berrett-Koehler, San Francisco.

Worley, C., D. Hitchin, and W. Ross (1996) *Integrated Strategic Change*, Addison-Wesley, Reading, Mass.

Electronic Components Ltd[1]

Hugh Gunz

Introduction

Electronic Components Ltd (ECL) is typical of thousands of small-to-medium sized engineering companies in the UK. A wholly owned subsidiary of Intertron Ltd, a diversified multi-national manufacturing firm, it has a turnover of £20 million per annum and operates from four sites: its headquarters on the South Coast, two others in the UK and a fourth on the Continent (Figure CS7.1).

Although ECL is entirely profit-responsible under its managing director, Arnold Gresham, it is subject to strong central control from Intertron. The parent company's board must approve any capital expenditure above quite trivial sums, and it is not unknown, for instance, for Intertron's managing director to turn up in person without warning at some remote location demanding to know why stock levels are as high as they are.

Historically, ECL has been involved in the electronics entertainment industry. It designs and makes a particular range of components supplied under sub-contract to manufacturers of consumer electronics products. It has been very successful, with a high share of the UK market. The components themselves are specific to consumer electronics (CE) products. It has been the policy of ECL's customers, the UK manufacturers, not to make these particular components themselves, nor to standardize on their designs. ECL thus had a steady stream of orders coming in for components for many years, each order with its own specific requirements.

Within the UK each incoming order went first to the R&D laboratory, located on the headquarters site, whose job it was to turn the order into a set of working drawings and specifications for the production departments. Although the theoretical principles of the work were simple it had never proved possible to reduce the design work to a set of routine calculations; with each job there was always a large element of trial and error before an acceptable design was produced.

As well as this design work the R&D laboratory was responsible for providing a technical service to the production departments, chiefly

Figure CS7.1
ECL before reorganization

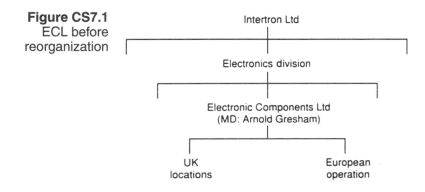

troubleshooting. This could at times become quite a significant part of the R&D workload, not least because the trial-and-error nature of the technology meant that when problems arose it could take no little skill and time to sort them out. The laboratory was not large, with 30–40 staff, and was often badly stretched to meet the conflicting demands of design and troubleshooting.

The UK R&D laboratory serviced all three UK production facilities, although most of its time was taken up with the one on the same site which was by far the largest. The European operation was self-contained, with its own R&D laboratory producing its own designs for its own production facility.

In the mid-1970s, however, ECL management became concerned at the company's almost total dependence on the CE market. Diversification was clearly needed, and Arnold Gresham set the objective of reducing the firm's dependence on CE to 50% within five years, while retaining its existing share of the CE business. Very soon ECL spotted an opportunity for using its existing technology in an entirely different sector of the domestic appliances market, and New Products group was set up within the R&D laboratory in order to build a range of products to exploit this.

By the mid-1980s ECL had succeeded in reducing its dependence on the CE business to 70% by adopting an aggressive 'first-to-market' strategy with its new product. It was realized from the outset that the company could not rely on patent protection in a new, fast-expanding market, so that it became vital that the R&D engineers developed new products as quickly as possible and that the process of putting them into production should be speedy and trouble-free. The self-contained European operation was in Mr Gresham's view conspicuously better at this, and he lost few opportunities to make the point to his local R&D staff.

With the UK CE manufacturing business coming under increasing threat from imports (chiefly Japanese) pressure on ECL's diversification programme progressively increased. In order to improve the effectiveness of the company's innovation programme, Mr Gresham reorganized the business functions, creating five executive posts reporting to him. Each of these was responsible for all activities within a given business function across all locations (Figure CS7.2).

The head of the UK R&D Department, Oliver Smith, was promoted to technical director, and his place was taken by a young, highly-successful manager called Simon Davies. A well-qualified engineer, Davies had not worked in R&D before, but had been moved between a number of locations of the parent company, Intertron, in order to develop him for eventual senior management posts.

Figure CS7.2
ECL after
reorganization

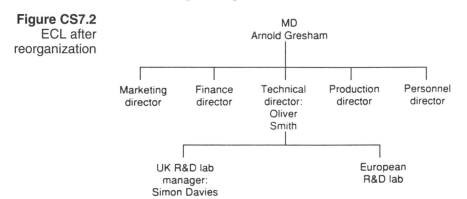

Meanwhile, the diversification programme was running into trouble. New products were taking too long to emerge from the R&D laboratory, in Mr Gresham's opinion. On more than one occasion he became exasperated at the engineers' tendency to continue to 'tinker about' with the design of a new product long after they had produced something which was in fact at the point where it could be manufactured and sold. He had been forced into arbitrarily stopping development of the products in question, telling the engineers that once the design was in production and earning cash they could carry on improving it to produce a Mark Two, which could supersede the first model. As a former production manager Mr Gresham was critical of the unrealistic view the R&D engineers took at the time they needed for their work, and was glad that Davies was making it his business to change this.

In this already difficult situation management became seriously alarmed to find that R&D engineers were beginning to leave the firm in large numbers. In one year alone turnover (excluding natural wastage) almost reached 25%, with serious consequences for the morale and work of the laboratory. Something had to be done if ECL's diversification programme was not to be seriously threatened.

Technical management's diagnosis of the situation

The technical director, Oliver Smith, and his successor as R&D manager, Simon Davies, were deeply worried by the high turnover among the R&D staff, although they could readily understand why it might have happened. Their explanation was as follows.

The parent company places tremendous stress on the financial performance of its subsidiaries, so that ECL feels itself under great pressure to be, in Mr Smith's words, a 'production-oriented cash generator'. This puts the laboratory under great pressure to provide a troubleshooting service as and when needed to the production department, generally seen as the key part of the company. Not only does this demand for service constantly interfere with the laboratory's work of developing new products, but it tends to devalue innovatory work in the eyes of everyone. As a result the engineers come to feel that their professional contribution has been downgraded by the company into merely that of the troubleshooter. This professional dissatisfaction is exacerbated by the nature of the main products (the CE components), which are subject to very tight design specifications. One component looks much like another, reinforcing the lack of innovative atmosphere in the laboratory. It is hard to feel that one's professional expertise is being put to good use under such circumstances.

The parent company holds a very tight control over ECL's capital investment programme. However Intertron's behaviour is sometimes apparently capricious, turning down plans to which it has previously agreed in principle and so increasing the general air of uncertainty in the company. A further manifestation of centralized control is rigid salary grades, which limit the material and status rewards management can give the engineers. With no freedom to award 'perks' for good performance there is reduced flexibility for motivating staff to work hard to respond to the changing demands on ECL. This situation is made more difficult to change by the insistence of the trades unions on job evaluation principles covering all grades. Sometimes the only way a good engineer can be paid more is by rewriting this job description, a lengthy, tedious and often unsuccessful procedure.

Finally, the engineers have no particularly exciting career prospects to compensate for these shortcomings. Unless they changed disciplines and ceased to be engineers there is no promotion route open for them other than laboratory line management, culminating in Mr Smith's job. The parent company does not, on the whole, regard engineering skills as transferable between its different businesses, cutting off another promotion route. When engineers go on Intertron courses and find out about attractive career opportunities elsewhere in the Group, they resent the implication that they are thought of as only capable of working in ECL and become suspicious that viable career possibilities are being deliberately withheld from them.

The best engineers are not prepared to put up with these conditions of work, and in due course leave. Their vacancies are filled by less able engineers, blocking the promotion paths for good junior staff, increasing the frustrations of the juniors and making it more likely that in turn they will leave as well.

Although salaries are low by comparison with other employers neither Mr Smith nor Mr Davies feel that this is a major factor. Bad business conditions mean that the labour market is very tight, and anyway, given the parent company's salary policies, there is nothing they can do about it.

The engineers' diagnosis of the situation

Many of the engineers disagreed with the views of top technical management concerning the importance of salary levels as a factor in the turnover of R&D engineers at ECL. The younger staff felt themselves particularly hard done by, and found that their only real chance of a rise was to leave for a better-paid job (so-called 'leap-frogging'). They did not seem to think that the labour market was nearly as tight as did their senior management. The more senior engineers did not feel the money problem nearly as acutely, and rarely gave it as an important reason for their (or their peers') leaving.

While the engineers resented the way they were treated by the production department, they found the engineering content of their work very satisfying. It provided variety and interest, and a change to work in a small, tightly knit organization where personal relationships were friendly and co-operative. Promotion prospects were not on the whole a serious concern. Apart from anything else, there was a widespread feeling that the technical expertise necessary to do Mr Smith's or Mr Davies's job took many years to acquire, and very few of the staff felt technically competent to manage at such a level.

The engineers were concerned about the commercial success of their designs. On one occasion Mr Smith had given a presentation to the laboratory staff on ECL's business plans, but although they had found this very interesting it had not been repeated. A constant source of irritation had always been the way in which projects would be stopped without anyone knowing why, and then perhaps restarted some months later just when people had forgotten where they had got to.

Their difficulties with the production department were put down largely to the ignorance of the production staff about what it took to develop a new product. This ignorance was amply demonstrated by the way in which, although production management complained about the speed at which the laboratory was able to work, they usually refused to allow production equipment to be used for essential test runs, claiming that this interfered with production schedules. What, the engineers asked, did the production department think they were going to be making in the future if they constantly prevented new products from being tested? The engineers agreed that the European operation was being held back because the advanced production techniques being proposed were completely ignored by UK production management.

The real problem, however, was nothing to do with these issues. For many years Mr Smith had run the laboratory in the style of, in his words, 'the involved engineer'. Deeply respected as an engineer among his staff, he kept closely in touch with staff at all levels and was always ready to discuss technical problems with them and provide advice when it was wanted. Although there was a line-management structure under Mr Smith, nobody put a great deal of emphasis on it. Good working relationships were based on a shared interest at all levels in the technical nature of the work, and engineers often referred back to the laboratory in those days as having a 'family atmosphere'.

When Simon Davies took over the management of the laboratory the atmosphere changed dramatically. As an outsider to the laboratory he came like a bolt from the blue, ordering a complete cleanout of everything that was not going to be used for the next six months—a job which stopped all other work for three days. Systems were tightened up, and communication, to everyone's consternation, became strictly through the line. Suddenly engineers found that the laboratory manager was not keeping in touch with them on their work. When he did, it was usually in formal meetings which he was usually too busy to be able to arrange at short notice. The same often applied when people wanted to see him about personnel matters. It became harder to find out what was going on: there seemed to be a much greater tendency to restrict information on a 'need-to-know' basis.

There were exceptions to this rule, however. Mr Davies took a particular interest in the work of the New Product group, and in one instance took over the role of project leader himself since there was no one else available. Unfortunately some events which flowed from this only increased the resentment of the laboratory staff at his managerial style, since at one point he used his authority to stop all other work going on in the drawing office in order to progress his project. Although he was well informed technically on the New Products work, it was clear, however, that on the CE component side of the laboratory's work his technical knowledge was comparatively weak. It was generally known that although he was seen by the company as a rising star, his previous job had been managing a routine testing laboratory, and his attempts to pick up technical know-how about CE components emphasized to the engineers a serious weakness in his ability to do his job effectively.

It was not long before resentment was beginning to build up. Another of Mr Davies's early moves had been to force out two engineers who, by common consent, were low performers. Although the staff agreed with the decision, it meant that other personnel changes he made were often interpreted as directed towards easing others out of the laboratory. His remoteness (by comparison with Mr Smith's style) exacerbated this problem. Other staff began to leave, and staff turnover began to climb dramatically. Looking back on events, both those who left and those who stayed agreed that a major reason for the resignations was the change in the way the laboratory was managed.

Note   1 The people and events in this case study are real, although names have
been altered to preserve confidentiality.

Questions   1 Comments on the apparent lack of success in achieving and sustaining
the change process of diversification. Were any parts of the change
agenda successful? Why?

2 To what extent do you think the diversification strategy was appropriate
to ECL's continued performance and operation in the engineering
industry? What are the relationships between strategy and structure in
this case? What other alternative strategies were open to ECL?

3 Explain why technical management and the engineers see the problems
differently. What could cause this? What are the most and least important
causal factors in your list?

4 You are called in as an external consultant. Detail your agenda for
handling the situation in ECL. How will you address, for example, high
labour turnover, lack of interfunctional knowledge and trust as well as the
different internal organizational cultures? What would be your strategy
for detailing proposed changes to Intertron Ltd?

Isracom Ltd[1]

Abraham R. Sagie

Meni Kaufman, the general manager of Isracom, a large Israeli company engaged in the communication equipment industry, considered the following suggestion. Samuel Winer, an organizational consultant, argued firmly that Isracom should adopt Total Quality Management (TQM). In a way, Kaufman expected this to be Winer's recommendation. The marketing considerations supported the suggested change. Also, no meaningful opposition could be expected from the shareholders. Nevertheless, he was unsure of how the workers' committee would respond. Recently, very poor work relations existed between the Isracom management and the employees' committee. Although Kaufman suspected that personal interests of the committee leaders rather than substantive reasons were causing these annoying work relations, he anticipated that the committee would stubbornly oppose *any* change proposed by the management. 'I don't know', he told Winer at last, 'what the workers' committee will require in exchange for the adoption of TQM. I shall summon a management meeting, and we will discuss your suggestions.'

Kaufman has been serving for five years as a general manager of Isracom. This period has seen a transition in the firm from stagnation to growth. Instead of only marketing imported American communication equipment inside Israel, the company had progressed to designing, developing, and producing its own products. At the time reported here, Isracom manufactured more than 20 different types of completely locally developed products, ranging from antennas to complex communication systems. In the last year, about 70% of Isracom's products were self-developed. In addition, the company continued to distribute imported high-tech communication systems from several major US and Japanese companies. The number of employees had increased from 800, five years ago, to the current number of 1200. Annual sales increased to more than $70 000 000, which implies an annual increase rate of about 15%. Finally, the export of Isracom products which constituted five years ago approximately 10% of the sales increased to more than 50%, especially to the USA and Western Europe. Yet, the strong competition in these markets required structural and functional changes in the R&D, production, and marketing departments that could be achieved by adopting TQM. Another problem was the company's troubling work relations. While the volume of sales had increased and the quality of products had improved, work relations had deteriorated over the last five years. 'It seems that the major topic in the firm that I have not managed to change', thought Meni Kaufman 'is work relations, the very thing that should urgently be changed. Now it has become the major obstacle in the path of any further improvement.'

The management meeting took place in the company's main offices in Tel-Aviv several days later. The general manager Kaufman and consultant Winer introduced to the board their recommendation to adopt TQM. They specified the advantages to the company stemming from this programme. In particular, they emphasized the policy of the US and some European governmental authorities to allow commercial contacts only with suppliers that can prove a quality-oriented management system. Surprisingly, although Kaufman and Winer's suggestion required a comprehensive and costly change in the organization, the directors raised no sincere doubts regarding its necessity. Somehow, all of the participants were ready for such a move. They inquired, however, what plans the general manager had regarding the TQM implementation. 'That is exactly the point,' Kaufman thought and added loudly: 'What are your suggestions?'

'I can start the programme tomorrow in my department' said Noah Rabinovitz, the engineering manager, 'I see no implementation problem. All we need is a clear and unambiguous announcement that we are moving to TQM.'

'I am not sure that it will be so easy', responded Sarah Levy, the personnel manager. 'As you all well know, employee involvement is an essential part of TQM and we must ensure the workers' support of this plan'.

'Just a minute', Moshe Kedar, the production manager, interrupted her, 'did you say "the workers" or "the workers' committee"?'

'What is the difference?' asked Rabinovitz 'I do not see any difference between both terms.'

Winer, the organizational consultant, seemed to agree with Kedar. 'These are two quite different bodies. Introducing TQM requires enriching the roles of all the workers, and involving each one in the making of work decisions relevant for his or her job. Every individual has a unique expertise and work knowledge that cannot be transmitted to any representative on the committee. Also, the control of the quality of the products and work processes is shared among all of the employees involved in these processes. They all should take part in the decision-making in order to guarantee a high level of quality. Thus, this is knowledge-based participation in work-related issues that is based on common interests of both employers and employees. This type of participation is quite different from involving the representatives of the workers, or more precisely, negotiating with them, on topics in which the interests of employers and employees can differ.'

Samuel Winer approached the blackboard, and drew up a three-column by two-row table. 'We distinguish between two types of groups: work teams versus the workers' committee, and between two types of change decisions: strategic, the "if" of the change, namely whether we should implement the TQM programme or not, versus tactical or operational decisions derived from the strategic one. The TQM tactical decisions are relevant only after an affirmative strategic decision is made. They include questions such as: "In which department will the programme start? What processes will be changed first? How, where, and when, will our workers be trained?" and so on.' Winer wrote 'work teams' and 'workers' committee' as headings of the fist two columns and 'strategic' and 'tactical' as titles of the two rows. 'Each one of the two types of decisions, the strategic and tactical, can be made by involving either work teams or the workers' committee', he said, clarifying his drawing.

'And what is the meaning of the third column?', asked Meni Kaufman.

'The third alternative is that neither the work teams nor the workers' committee will be involved in making decisions. This alternative can be applied to either the strategic decision, and/or to every tactical decision'. Winer wrote 'nobody' on the header of the table's third column (see

Figure CS8.1). 'Now, what we have to do is to consider separately each situation, or every cell in this table, and to address the following two questions: first, who will be involved in the strategic decision, if anyone at all is allowed to participate, and, second, who will be involved in the tactical decisions'.

Figure CS8.1
Employee participation in the various TQM decisions: Winer's initial table

Decision/Group	Work teams	Workers' committee	Nobody
Strategic			
Tactical			

'I do not like the idea that the workers' committee, or any other body outside this board, is needed to approve the TQM programme', argued Noah Rabinovitz, pointing at the title 'strategic' on the first row. 'It is our sole responsibility to make this decision. It is ridiculous to think that strategic decisions determining the fate of this company will be made by worker representatives who are looking after their own interests rather than those of Isracom. I can tell you both', he added while looking alternately at Sarah Levy, the personnel manager, and at Samuel Winer, the consultant, 'many stories of how workers' committees, in this company as well as in others, have defied excellent programmes for change suggested by management. Furthermore, there were some cases in which the committees resisted programmes attempting to improve the quality of the employees' working life! Very often the committee members are more interested in their own private interests than in the global interests of the larger body of employees they are supposed to be representing!'

'So, what do you suggest?', Sarah Levy asked the engineering manager, 'to totally ignore the workers' committee?'

'We can allow either the committee or the work teams to participate in these decisions that Samuel termed "tactical". I really don't care either way. However, the decision whether or not to initiate the TQM programme is this board's exclusive responsibility!' Rabinovitz glanced at the participants and continued, 'Just think what would happen here if the committee had a veto right and could cancel our plans, or what would happen if the price for its readiness to co-operate would be too high for us! How could we continue to manage this company?'

'I can't agree with you', responded Levy. 'Remember that we are talking about TQM and that employee involvement is a fundamental part of it. Notice also the workers' point of view. They feel, rightly or wrongly, that they have been treated unfairly during the last five years. When we needed them very much in order to move from stagnation to growth, they contributed their part. However, after the company succeeded to recover, they did not earn a fair share in this growth.' Sarah Levy looked around, seeking the support of her colleagues for her position. She continued: 'This plan will require a lot of effort from every worker. They will insist on being in the picture from the first moment on'.

'So, what do you suggest?' asked Rabinovitch coldly, 'to immediately discuss our new plan with the workers' committee? They will demand that we begin negotiating their wages immediately. But we already have a signed agreement with them! And what should we do afterwards? Pay more money during each successive phase of the implementation process?' Rabinovitch did not wait for an answer, but addressed the organizational consultant: 'Samuel, you expect four or five distinct phases in this process. Don't you?'

Samuel Winer nodded in agreement, but did not intervene in the dispute. Sarah Levy attempted to clarify her point: 'I did not mean to say that all, or even some, of the committee's demands should be met. Nevertheless, we should be aware of their claims.'

'We should listen to Sarah', agreed Winer, 'employee participation is really an important part of TQM. The workers are responsible for the quality of our products and work processes. So', he turned to Levy and pointed at the drawing on the blackboard, 'What are your suggestions with regards to the strategic and tactical decisions regarding the TQM proposal? Who has to be involved in each one of them?'

'The employees' committee, of course', Levy answered, 'It should take part in each decision, either strategic or tactical, if it is relevant to the interests of the entire group of the employees. In addition, we shall allow individual workers or groups to participate in making tactical decisions that are relevant to their jobs.'

The general manager listened carefully to Levy's suggestion, and then asked Moshe Kedar, the production manager: 'Moshe, what is your opinion?'

'Let's restate the points, suggested by either Sarah or Noah, that I can undoubtedly adopt', Kedar responded, 'Sarah correctly argued that if we are interested in TQM then we should apply employee participation. Noah warned that a negotiation with the employees' committee should be avoided because in most cases it implies a monetary compensation. He is also quite right. Should we repeat this type of participation during each successive phase of the implementation process, we will have to pay more money in each phase. I suggest, therefore, to totally neglect the employees' committee in the TQM-related decisions and to involve individuals or work teams in each decision. Independently of the TQM issue, the time for allowing the committee to participate in decision-making will be next year, as we shall then be negotiating an additional wage agreement'.

Kedar's colleagues attentively listened to his arguments. 'Very interesting', responded Meni Kaufman. 'Is there any other suggestion?' As no answer came from the participants, the general manager turned to Winer, the organizational consultant, and asked: 'What are your conclusions, Samuel?'

Winer preferred not to present his personal opinion. As the directors presented their views, he was taking notes. After Kedar finished his speech, Winer glanced at his notes and said: 'So far, we have heard three different approaches to the issue of the introduction of TQM in this company. More specifically, these views describe alternative ways of involving employee teams or their committee in the strategic or tactical decisions. Let's depict these suggestions on the blackboard.' Winer proceeded to the blackboard and

Figure CS8.2
Employee participation in the various TQM decisions: Rabinovitz's suggestion

Decision/Group	Work teams	Workers' committee	Nobody
Strategic			X
Tactical	X?	X?	

Note: X denotes that the group mentioned in the column should participate in the decision that appears in the relevant row.

Figure CS8.3
Employee participation in the various TQM decisions: Levy's suggestion

Decision/Group	Work teams	Workers' committee	Nobody
Strategic		X	
Tactical	X	X	

Figure CS8.4
Employee participation
in the various TQM
decisions: Kedar's
suggestion

Decision/Group	Work teams	Workers' committee	Nobody
Strategic	X		
Tactical	X		

represented the suggestions made by Noah Rabinovitz, Sarah Levy, and Moshe Kedar by means of three successive tables (see Figures CS8.2, CS8.3, CS8.4]).

'These suggestions substantively differ from each other', Kaufman, the general manager, said when Winer finished drawing the three tables. 'It remains for us', he added 'to carefully consider the different opinions and decide how to arrive at both types of the TQM decisions'.

Note

1 The names of the company and its managers have been changed in accordance with the management's request.

Questions

1 Suppose you are one of the Isracom directors. What would *your* suggestion be regarding employee participation in the strategic and tactical TQM decisions?

2 Based on your understanding of organizational structure, culture and change, can you define what are some of the dynamics which face Isracom?

3 What pre-conditions should exist in order that large scale change initiatives (like TQM) are implemented successfully?

A tale of two cultures

Allan H. Church

Organizational situation

In 1988, the chairmen of two large pharmaceutical companies, one headquartered in the USA and one in the UK, began transatlantic exploratory talks regarding the possible merger of their respective organizations. Both men were clear that given the highly competitive and fractured state of their industry and the acquisition and takeover mentality during the mid-to-late 1980s, more consolidation of the major players in the industry was required in order to remain viable competitive entities in the global marketplace. Having assessed their external environment, they concluded that only a 'friendly merger' would provide them with the ability and resources to become a world-class pharmaceuticals organization in the 1990s and beyond. Despite this agreement in principle, talks continued for another year while various financial issues and terms were explored and ultimately resolved. During the early spring of 1989, the merger was officially announced to the public. The actual process was completed by late July of that same year. As the chief financial officer (CFO) put it, 'Employees were greeted at their offices that morning with the message that they were now working for a new company.'

Clearly, the process of merging two different companies, particularly with two very distinct cultures (both organizational and to some extent national as well) is not as simple as saying to employees, 'Good morning and welcome to your new company.' The majority of the people involved do not simply stop what they have been doing and start a new job the morning of the announcement. Plans must be actively made to make the merger work. Everything should be geared to developing a new culture and new processes—in effect, a new way of doing business based on the best of both organizations. In doing so, as in any organizational change effort, attention must be equally split between focusing on the business indicators (e.g., financial performance and productivity) and on the people issues (e.g., needs and values, motivation, management behaviours). More and more practitioners are pointing to the lack of attention to the human details as being the major downfall in failed mergers, TQM efforts, and reengineering initiatives (Ludeman, 1992; Wellins and Murphy, 1995). Thus, an organizational survey based on the guiding framework of the Burke-Litwin (1992) model of organizational change and performance was proposed to help in the merger process. It was intended to serve three distinct purposes:

1 As a means of communicating to management and employees the desired vision, values and practices of the desired culture of the organization.
2 As a means of assessing the cultural and organizational strengths and weaknesses in order to target improvement and subsequent change efforts.
3 As the first 'measurement' comparison point in an ongoing change and development process.

The desired culture

Although there were clearly some similarities in the cultures of the two organizations, a 'new' culture was needed to facilitate effectively the integration of the US and UK entities. If one or the other were to achieve cultural dominance instead, then the merger would have failed; in essence, to produce a stronger entity it should be based on the strengths of both. The intent was to begin a longitudinal process of cultural change that would result in a truly global company for the future. After much exploration and debate among senior managers and work process teams, five core values were chosen to represent the direction and future of the company:

- *Performance*—challenge what people do, how they do it, and continuously strive to do it better.
- *Customers*—be responsible to customers, and think of all employees as internal customers serving the external customers in long supplier chain.
- *Innovation*—encourage, recognize and reward responsible risk-taking and innovative achievements.
- *People*—respect, encourage, develop and support employees as key to organizational success; attract and retain the very best and talented performers.
- *Integrity*—be absolutely honest and open in all dealings with internal and external customers, and suppliers; focus on maintaining consistency in word and deed at all levels.

Although these five values could apply to any organization, it is the process of making the choices and the accompanying commitment, ownership and implementation in day-to-day behaviours that is critical to the change process (for a more detailed description of the identification of these values and the accompanying leadership practices see Burke and Jackson, 1991).

The survey process

The importance of these values and the leadership and management behaviours associated with their implementation were reinforced with the use of a corporate-wide customized survey instrument containing 105 items derived from the application of the Burke-Litwin (Burke and Litwin, 1992) model framework to the existing conditions in the organization. All items were asked using a 1 to 5 extent-based Likert rating scale, where 1 = to a very small extent and 5 = to a very great extent. After initial pilot testing, the final version of the survey was administered to all levels of management across all locations around the world. The final document and accompanying cover letter from the chief executive officer (CEO) was translated into 10 different languages. In total, 73.4% (3584 returned of 4873 in population) responded to the survey.

Highlights of the results

Factor analyses revealed that, indeed, the data 'grouped' very closely to the Burke-Litwin model as initially intended (see Figure CS9.1).

Overall, the highest rated category based on the average item means was work unit climate ($M = 3.76$), suggesting that respondents apparently felt quite positive about their local work units and their colleagues, especially regarding co-operation. More specifically, the highest rated item among the total of 105 was 'I like the kind of work I do' ($M = 4.24$). Issues of individual motivation and the clarity of the stated business strategy—particularly about

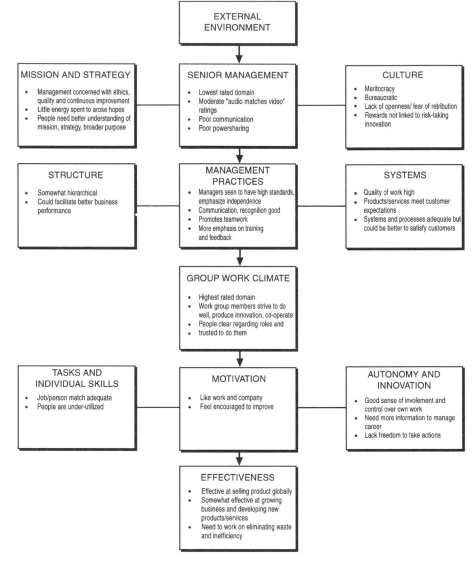

Figure CS9.1
Results of the corporate-wide survey of values, leadership and management behaviour based on the Burke-Litwin model

the importance of long-range planning for achieving success—also received high ratings across respondents.

Perhaps not surprisingly, aspects of the culture were rated the lowest along with perceptions of senior management. Overall, the culture was perceived to be:

● primarily a meritocracy (anyone who performs well could move ahead);
● too bureaucratic (e.g., having to go through channels) and highly political (who you know and what you say—or do not say—is important to one's career);
● risk averse and overly conforming to existing norms and ways of operating;
● insufficiently rewarding of innovation and creative achievement.

For example, the two items tied as the lowest rated ($M = 2.51$)—'People who take risks in this company are rewarded' and 'Senior management takes the time to talk informally with employees at my level' concerned these larger issues in the organization. The overly hierarchical and layered nature of the structure was also seen as a significant issue, particularly given the recent changes in reporting relationships and operations. And finally, the existing company systems and processes were not seen as being very helpful.

Modelling the results of the survey

Using a regression analysis, relationships were explored among each of the summary scores according to the Burke-Litwin model dimensions. A critical path to performance for this specific organization was identified that delineates the domains most directly related to (or most predictive of) organizational effectiveness. Based on these results it was clear that the selection, development, and appropriate assignment of people predicted more than any other dimensions the effectiveness of the organization. In other words, for this organization, full utilization of talent was critical to success. Additionally, the organizational systems, structure and management practices all contributed relatively equally to the process of utilizing people's talent and motivational energies. As anticipated, culture was found to have a major impact on these higher level variables (e.g., systems, structure and practices) as well. In addition, it was evident that the clarity and communication of the mission affected the efficiency and adequacy of the systems (policies and procedures) that were developed as well as management behaviour. Further, senior management's ability to 'walk the talk' and engage in open, two-way communication with employees impacted their perceptions of the organizational structure (the degree of hierarchy and policies).

Outcomes of the process

Based on the survey results that were reported back to organizational members in meetings with their respective managers, action steps and organization development efforts were planned in several critical areas including communication, mission, utilization of talent, risk-taking and people development. In some business areas, task forces were established to provide responses to various issues both at the corporate and the local levels. In conjunction with plans for more systemic changes to structures and processes in the organization, an initiative to deliver individual self and other feedback, and later full 360° feedback, (self, direct reports, peers, and supervisors) to all managers through various training programs and workshops was undertaken. This intervention was based on the notion that individual behaviourally-based feedback leads to enhanced managerial self-awareness which in turn leads to behaviour change and ultimately improved performance (Church, 1994). Over the course of three years this feedback process resulted in more than 2300 managers receiving ratings from their co-workers on specific management practices and leadership behaviours, based on the core values, that were seen as being critical for both (*a*) successful performance and (*b*) integration of the new culture.

Where is the company now? Just a few years after the merger, the $9 billion-plus company had moved from a ranking of 23 and 7 in the industry as separate entities to being the fifth largest competitor in the global health-care arena—a major accomplishment. Today this company continues to expand its business and compete effectively in the global health-care marketplace. The results of the second survey, about two years after the initial survey, administered this time to all employees in the organization, showed significant improvements in such areas as rewarding and celebrating achievements, utilizing people's skills and abilities, and being more customer-driven rather than profit-driven.

References

Burke, W. W. and P. Jackson, (1991) 'Making the SmithKline Beecham merger work,' *Human Resource Management*, **30**, 69–87.

Burke, W. W. and G. H. Litwin, (1992) 'A causal model of organizational performance and change,' *Journal of Management*, **18**, 523–545.

Church, A. H. (1994) 'Managerial self-awareness in high performing individuals in organizations,' *Dissertation Abstracts International*, **55–05B**, 2028, (University Microfilms No. AAI9427924).

Ludeman, K. (1992) 'Using employee surveys to revitalize TQM,' *Training*, **29** (12), 51–57.

Wellins, R. S., and J. S. Murphy, (1995) 'Reengineering: Plug into the human factor,' *Training and Development*, **49** (1), 33–37.

Questions

1   In 1998, the pharmaceutical industry was stunned by two events. First, the chief executives of Glaxo Wellcome and SmithKline Beecham, two of the world's largest pharmaceutical firms announced their intention to merge as 'equals'. The outcome of the merger would have been the largest pharmaceutical firm in the world. Within two weeks of the announcement, the merger was abruptly called off. Both sides stated that the reason was the failure of the two top management teams to agree on who would be the head of the merged operation. In your view, was this a sufficient reason given to shareholders to call off the merger? Why or why not?

2   Given the lessons of the merger in the case, alongside any other merger outcomes you may have found, develop a set of 'critical success factors' which might help senior management teams implement mergers more successfully.

Part V
The Environment

**Classifying organizational
environments**

Introduction

In this chapter we move away from a focus on the organization toward looking at the environment in which it operates. Previous chapters have outlined how managers scan and perceive the wider environment. Information from the external domain is filtered through both perceptive and cognitive processes by individual managers. They think differently; they see different things; and they act in different ways depending upon their interpretations.

This would seem at first sight to be a recipe for extreme complexity. The environment is all things to all individuals depending upon how they see it. Yet it is possible to classify parts of the environment of an organization, even if the distinctions between the parts are often blurred and overlap. Figure 16.1 outlines the major external factors which all organizations face.

Starting from the notion that the environment is everything that is external to an organization's formal boundary, we can split this undifferentiated definition into four broad categories (Jurkovich, 1974; Radford, 1978; Hitt, Ireland and Hoskisson, 1995):

Figure 16.1
The organizational
environment

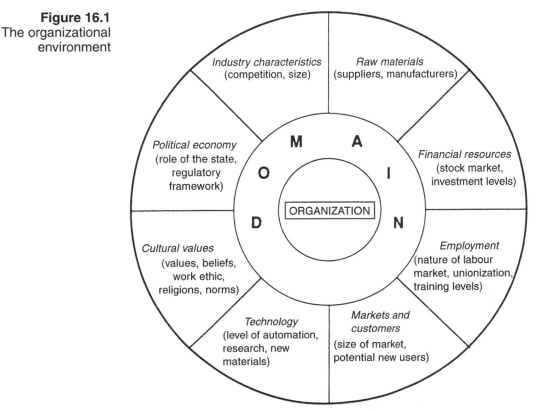

1   The general or societal environment
2   The specific or task environment
3   The inter-organizational environment
4   The political and economic Environment

The general or societal environment

The general environment facing organizations is characterized by a number of key elements which are separable analytically and which can have separate and different impacts upon organizations. The unifying theme is that they all affect all organizations all of the time.

Economic characteristics include the overall economy of a nation, the profile of ownership (public or private), the extent to which the economy is planned and centralized, levels of investment and consumption.

Technological characteristics include the level of advancement of knowledge and equipment in society (or in specific countries), and the rate of development and application of such knowledge.

Educational and cultural characteristics include the general literacy level of a country, the number of people with specialized knowledge or training, the beliefs, attitudes, values and norms of the country as well as its historical background.

Demographic and sociological characteristics include class structure and mobility, the nature of available human resources of working age, distributions throughout the general population of sex, age and geographical concentration and dispersion.

Natural resource characteristics include the availability of resources such as water, fuels, climate and topography.

The specific or task environment

This is the part of the general environment which directly concerns managers, since it impacts upon the decision-making, transformation processes and competitive performance of the organization (Porter, 1985; Grant, 1991). While the general environment is roughly the same for organizations in the same country or industrial sector, for example, the task environment of each is likely to differ widely.

The task environment comprises (typically) customers, suppliers, trades unions, government agencies and competitors. It can be quite large. Some organizations such as Hewlett Packard are in contact with around 5000 suppliers. Combine this with a large customer base, and the task environment becomes extremely large indeed. Thompson (1967) refers generally to this immediate environment as the 'organizational domain'. This domain not only describes the task environment but also refers to the relative emphasis placed by managers on its component parts. It describes the elements which allow managers to assess whether they defend, compete, or seek niches to offer their products and services.

Firms can be in the same industrial sector, but occupy distinctively different niches. For example, Rolls-Royce, Jaguar and Rover are all motor manufacturers, but their niche is self-evidently different. They have largely mutually exclusive customer bases and different groups of customers.

Changes in niche size, niche shape or emphasis will also mean commensurate changes in the task environment. The nature of dependencies and the sources of uncertainties will change quite markedly. Managers will then be faced with redefining the immediate environment and will begin to emphasize different sets of constraints and opportunities.

Direct competition in the environment has been summarized by Porter (1985) as the threat of new entrants, the power of suppliers and customers, the threat of product substitutes and the levels of rivalry among competitor organizations. These elements of the organization's task environment are likely to be powerful influencers of strategy and of ultimate success or failure. Where the threat of new entrants is small, suppliers and customers have little power (perhaps because they cannot access goods any other way) and the level of rivalry is small, then the firm will likely be competitive (according to Porter). Any changes in the environmental conditions of these 'five forces' will produce commensurate changes in competitive position of the firm. For example:

> General Steels, producers of small diameter steel tubing in the UK, had been profitable for over 20 years. They had moved from manufacturing rifle barrels in the Second World War to using the same tubing to supply gas in towns and cities across the country. One of the other profitable uses of this ex-rifle tubing was in fire sprinkler systems. When new or old buildings were equipped with fire sprinkler systems which ran across the ceilings of the building etc., they always used steel tubing. Never easy to fit (it needs threading and screwing together with sealing compounds to make a watertight joint) architects nevertheless specified steel tubing as the standard in new hotels, restaurants and other large public buildings. Industry dominance was high. Only steel could withstand temperatures of up to 1000°C. In 1992, a plastic was developed which would also withstand the same temperatures. Easy and light to handle, this plastic tubing was a push-fit assembly and was a fraction of the cost of steel. Almost overnight, product substitution (one of Porter's five forces of the task environment) had radically changed the competitive position of General Steels—in this case irreversibly.
>
> *Source*: D. Wilson, Warwick Business School.

Inter-organizational relations: networks

Rather than be viewed as a set of discrete factors or forces, the environment of many organizations can be viewed as being composed of networks of other organizations (see Chapter 15). Managing the task environment becomes more a process of handling inter-organizational relations than it does attending to its separate components (Evan, 1966; Axelsson and Easton, 1992). Management strategies toward handling this network are thus quite different in emphasis from those which deal with its separate parts. Thompson (1967) and Thompson and McEwen (1958) identified five strategies for managing the inter-organizational network:

1 *Contracting* Organizations can enter contracts with either suppliers or customers to reduce uncertainty. Fixed price supply contracts for 12 months would be an example. Agreeing to give money to a charity for a fixed period would be another example. Charities such as the Royal National Lifeboat Institution and the Royal National Institute for the Blind actively seek to secure this kind of funding rather than rely on unpredictable levels of income from individual donors. Irrespective of your opinion on how they cook them, McDonalds, the world-wide fast food chain, contracts for an entire crop of russet potatoes to ensure supply and quality.

2 *Co-opting* Managers may choose to absorb uncertainties by encompassing elements in the network. For example, inviting an environmental lobbyist or a merchant banker to sit on the board of your organization is likely to reduce resistance from environmentalists and could lead to easier access to money markets.

3 *Coalescing* A management strategy of combination. Joint action through pricing agreements, market shares and joint ventures, etc. While mostly legal, some practices under this strategy such as unwritten reciprocity or price agreements can become highly illegal. They are nevertheless attractive strategies since they achieve stability, especially in concentrated industrial sectors.

4 *Use of third parties* Occurs when managers of one organization use the services of another organization to negotiate on their behalf. Professional and trade associations are obvious examples. Statutory regulations such as codes of practice in medical spheres are less obvious, since here the medical practitioners are effectively restricting entry and regulating competition via a third-party agreement with government agencies. Depending upon your ideological persuasion, you could view this as generally beneficial (it protects the interests of the consumer and maintains standards) or as untenable (it protects and sustains monopoly provision of goods and services).

5 *Advertising* Is successful when it gains differential advantage to one organization in the network. A good example of this is the generic term in the UK for the vacuum cleaner—the Hoover (and its associated verb 'to hoover') which comes from one manufacturer among many others. All vacuum cleaner manufacturers are said to make 'hoovers' however.

The political and economic environment

Under this category we refer to the constitutional, institutional and political context of the organization. The nature of national political organization, the devolution or centralization of power nationally and the nature of the economy (not forgetting laws which refer to taxation and corporate activities) will all colour both the task and the specific environments.

Many managers understandably have a difficult time responding to all the demands imposed by this aspect of the environment since they are both vague and, often, conflicting. For example:

On one hand . . .	*On the other . . .*
Government research agencies suggest weight-adding safety equipment for cars	The Department of Transport insists on lighter vehicle weight to conserve petrol
The Department of the Environment suggests restrictions in the use of pesticides	The Department of Agriculture promotes pesticides for agriculture and forestry
Occupational health and safety suggests keeping exposure to hazardous substances at the lowest possible level, short of bankrupting the company	Departments of the Environment and Trade suggest flexible standards taking cost and risk level into consideration

**The
'embeddedness'
of the
environment**

Recent analysts of the political and economic environment suggest that the immediate or task environment of the organization is 'emebedded' in the wider environment of the political and institutional systems (Granovetter, 1985; Gerlach, 1992; Whitley, 1992; Hollingsworth and Boyers, 1997). The argument is that wide differences in economic co-ordination and control are evident across societies. These are attributable to significant differences in state and financial systems as well as to the processes of industrialization. Taking the overall perspective of the interrelationships between organizations and their institutional context has become known as the 'business systems' approach (Whitley, 1992).

Of course the major changes at this level of analysis have been the changes from the socialist economy of the former Eastern European countries (for example, Hungary, Czechoslovakia, East Germany) to market economies Western European-style.

Institutionally, this brought about the democratization of the political system (multi-party elections were held for the first time) as well as the liberalization of markets with incentives to import and export. Managers had to cope with the loss of state support of economic activities and the co-ordination of trade. They also lost a number of key customers, since former Eastern European products were not attractive in the West.

The impact of the institutional environments have been different in these former Eastern European countries. Where the legacy of the state socialist control was strong (as in the former USSR) then transformation to Western markets and technologies has been slow and painful. Where state control was either less (or more decentralized in any case) then transitions were a little easier. Countries such as Hungary already had a degree of decentralization in place under state socialism and many firms were already involved in OECD (Organization for Economic Co-operation and Development) markets (Whitley and Czaban, 1997). Those which were not, however, are unattractive to potential Western purchasers or to Western markets and may survive by cost cutting and delayering. Those which succeed in attracting foreign ownership or control will, of course, have access to greater skills knowledge and technology.

While Hungary shows one aspect of 'embeddedness', Soulsby and Clark (1996) identify another aspect in the former state enterprises of the Czech Republic. Here, the transitions have been less smooth, especially since many managers seem cynical toward Western management knowledge and draw upon managerial knowledge from the pre-1989 era. This is not necessarily a problem but it makes for a potent mixture of competing management approaches, many derived from being embedded in the Czech socialist context. Managers are working in an environment which demands market values but which is trapped and ensnared in its own history of the previous system. As Soulsby and Clark (1996: 238) point out, the transition from state socialism to capitalism was not a sudden 'flip'. It was, and still is, a slow incremental change process.

Other aspects of embeddedness are revealed. For example, most managers in former state socialist organizations would be (and many still are) unfamiliar with the everyday jargon of the Western manager or MBA graduate. The 'Porterian' vocabulary of product substitution and the threat of new entrants were more than just a foreign language. They were foreign concepts. So, too, was terminology associated with strategic change such as changing organizational cultures.

The enormity of these changes and the potency of institutional embeddedness is dramatically outlined by Child and Czegledy (1996). Changes in the former Eastern Europe mean that a combined population of over 400 million people and their histories will have to be changed radically. The pace of these changes has been more rapid than many comparable changes such as those in China or Cuba. The immense tasks of acquiring both foreign investment and management learning have been rather sudden, although there are exceptions such as the case of Hungary described above where transitions had been in place since the 1960s. As Child and Czegledy note, this will indeed be one of the world's greatest living experiments.

Of course, the notion of embeddedness does not solely apply to Eastern European organizations and their managers. It is just that the transition from state socialism to capitalism highlights institutionalism in stark relief. But Western firms are equally embedded in the taken-for-granted norms of behaviour of competition and market exchange. So much so, that the commercial model of organization (market-based) has become a dominant role model for all organized activities in other sectors ranging from hospitals and welfare institutions to voluntary and non-profit organizations. The market mechanism has become the 'one best way' of the 1990s and, perhaps, sadly is reminiscent of Taylor's enthusiasm (and short-sightedness) of the early part of this century.

Corporate social responsibility (CSR)

Over the past century, business organizations have emerged as major actors. They are politically potent, important economically and are, therefore, key agents of stability and social change. Thus, organizations also have a responsibility to the wider environment of which they are a part and in which they have an influence in the rate and direction of change.

Changes will be both for the good and the worse, depending upon your perspective. Perhaps as a previously skilled worker, you would not welcome the rapid advent of computer-controlled machines which have changed your job from operator to that of 'baby-sitter' for the machine. Customers who now receive better quality and more consistent products from the new technology would welcome the same change. Equally, those who now find themselves under the scrutiny of electronic data (from stored credit ratings to visual surveillance at work and elsewhere) may question the ethics of using electronic technology, although the level of violence in towns is falling since the installation of video cameras (Lyon, 1994).

The key to analysing such diametrically opposed views lies in the notion of control. If organizations have the power to effect changes of huge proportions, then what are the mechanisms by which control is achieved? Who monitors and checks corporate progress? Who decides? Regulations, laws and standards all play their part, of course, but recently there has been a move to alerting managers of all types of organizations to the idea of corporate social responsibility (CSR). The most obvious transgressions of CSR occur when an organization is publicly criticized for its actions. Examples would include the Brent Spar issue (Shell) and the debate over the best way to dispose of oil platforms and Ford Motor Company's decision to continue to produce the Pinto car despite evidence that its petrol tank was so located that it would buckle and split almost immediately even if subjected to a small impact. CSR is largely concerned with organizations' responses to longer-term issues such as pollution, employment discrimination, health, education, product and occupational safety. Not surprisingly, there have emerged many different views on the topic of CSR.

Arguments against CSR

The origins of the arguments against organizations embracing CSR originate with Adam Smith's economic doctrine of profit maximization (Friedman, 1970). The argument is that organizations perform a social good when they improve efficiency and reduce costs to maximize profits. Despite this being self-interested, profit-maximizing behaviour, managers do contribute to society by reducing costs and prices so that the consumer benefits in the long run. Frederick (1987) argues that if organizations were to engage in CSR, then this would impose hidden costs on society and create artificial and unequal costs among competitors. The free hand of the market would be constrained and society would be the loser since it would ultimately foot the bill.

Another argument against CSR is proposed by Stone (1975) who questions the competencies of managers in this domain. Managers are in place to ensure that production and the economics of business are carried out efficiently. They do not have the necessary expertise to engage in wider social issues and decisions. Davis (1973) extends this reasoning to suggest that pursuing CSR would dilute an organization's primary purpose (profit maximization) and that businesses already have enough economic and technological power, so why give them an opportunity to wield extra influence in society? These arguments echo Levitt's (1958:47) earlier view that 'Welfare and society are not the corporations' business . . . its business is making money, not sweet music'. A normative view of the place of the welfare state permeates these arguments, summarized as the belief that business should be concerned with increasing profits and reducing costs so that government can be left to care for the general welfare.

In support of CSR

Carroll (1993) supports CSR arguing that socially responsible actions by business lead to increased corporate responsiveness and, in turn, lead to improved social performance and productivity. A society which is satisfied with the ways in which business is carried out, will naturally have fewer public criticisms of organizations' current strategies, but will insist on increasingly higher standards of social responsibility from all organizations. Since social problems are in part created by the rise of large corporations, then they have a social and moral obligation to CSR. The two concepts of social contract and moral agency underpin much of the philosophy of CSR.

CSR is a commitment by managers to a wider range of responsibilities than to shareholders and to corporate and labour laws (Carroll, 1981; Jones, 1980). Managers are required to conform to the latter, but are not required to conform or contribute to any wider social values. In particular, CSR focuses on an organization's ethical and discretionary responsibilities. Ethical responsibilities include fairness to customers and employees, honesty and integrity in all dealings, and a responsibility to ensure that the general public are kept informed about corporate issues and developments. Discretionary responsibilities include providing monies for charities (often for urban renewal where previous generations of industry have left their marks and scars), supporting training programmes for the long-term unemployed, as well as protecting degradation of the natural environment and helping in its renewal.

Carroll (1979) argues that CSR may be viewed as having three important dimensions for any organization. First, organizations must be 'socially responsive'. That is, they are created by and sustained by society. There is, therefore, a reciprocal expectation that organizations will always be socially responsive to society's needs and values. Second, this responsiveness can be categorized into economic, legal, ethical and discretionary elements. Third, the topics of CSR for any business focus on consumerism, the environment, discrimination, product safety, occupational safety and shareholders.

Currently, CSR is a relatively ill-defined area. This is because the social issues agenda is subject to rapid change; does not apply to all organizations equally; and is often a confusing mixture of legal requirements and moral responsibilities. Dalton and Cosier (1982) for example, outline four types of organizational activities:

1 legal and responsible acts,
2 legal but irresponsible acts,
3 illegal but responsible acts and;
4 illegal and irresponsible acts.

Lawyers can deal with the legality/illegality dimension, but the definition of responsibility remains problematic and contested. For example, it is not clear whether responsibility is a global concept applying to all organizations, or is more specific (to certain sectors, for example). A chemical manufacturer is likely to be pressured to conform to some notion of environmental protection, yet it is by no means clear that such conformity applies so directly to a bank or an insurance company.

The debates over CSR will continue. However, the notion of corporate responsibility is gaining momentum, particularly in the emerging field of corporate citizenship. Drucker (1993) argues that citizenship is about the rights and duties of organizations as members of a particular country (in much the same way as individual citizens) and that citizenship means active commitment (not simply compliance). The influences which are making organizations consider their levels of citizenship largely come from the emergence of campaigning non-government organizations. The result is that organizations have been forced to consider their image and reputation in the market place. Good corporate citizenship rests on understanding and managing an organization's influences on and with the rest of society in a way which minimizes the negative consequences and maximizes the positive. Elkington (1997) terms this the 'triple bottom line', covering economic, environmental and social performance of an organization. The argument is that sustainable economic performance is dependent upon successful environmental and social performance (rather than the other way round).

Marsden and Andriof (1998) summarize some of the stances being taken by organizations toward being good citizens. For example, in countering social exclusion in 10 different countries, leading companies such as British Telecom, Carlsberg-Tetley, Volkswagen and Zanussi are involved in direct employment schemes for excluded groups, training programmes, business start-up support and consortium approaches toward urban renewal. As reasons given by the companies for their involvement in these activities, they are (in rank order of frequency of mention): employee morale and recruitment; reputation and community involvement; investing in a sustainable business environment; taking an ethical leadership stand and immediate financial benefits. The Council of Economic Priorities (part of the International Chamber of Commerce) has an accreditation board with representatives from organizations such as Reebok, Toys R Us, Sainsbury's, the Body Shop and Amnesty International. The Council has agreed a global standard for ethical sourcing, known currently as SA 8000.

Finally, the role of managerial or industrial expertise as the primary source of CSR decision-making has been called into question by recent work on corporate citizenship. Marsden and Andriof (1998) recount the example of Shell's decision to dump the Brent Spar floating oil structure in the deep Atlantic. Opposed by Greenpeace, Shell's president (C.A.J. Herkstroter) said:

> We took decisions which in retrospect were mistakes. We now realise that alone we could never have hoped to reach the right approach . . . in essence we were somewhat slow in understanding that environmentalist groups, consumer groups and so on were tending to acquire authority. Meanwhile, those groups we were used to dealing with (e.g. government and industry organizations) were tending to lose authority.
>
> *Source:* Marsden and Andriof, 1998: 17)

It is clearly not enough for organizations to do solely what their experts judge to be correct, even when there is government or legal support. A wider range of information, based on the idea of a wide range of stake-holders, is more appropriate. Debates such as these lead naturally into a consideration not only of corporate citizenship, but also of the ecological environment and organizational actions. These are discussed in the next section.

The ecological environment

The ecological environment is one which has emerged over the last decade or so and seems to be gaining ground since a number of commentators have begun to link long-term business success with a 'green' environmental stance by organizations. Before this link was made, the 'greens' were often associated with being a fringe concern of 'real' businesses. The green movement was stereotyped as being largely populated by ex-hippies and associated with aggressive acts toward profitable businesses, for example, Greenpeace toward fishing grounds and Shell's oil storage structure policies (described above) alongside 'Swampy' and his tunnelling colleagues protesting in 1997 about proposed urban road and airport runway developments in the UK.

The ecological environment is becoming an important issue for many businesses. The establishment of an international standard of 'green-ness' (ISO 14001) which is third-party assessed, has seen organizations begin to scramble to become accredited. Ford Motor Company is one of the first, setting up a process of the global standardization of environmental systems and processes in production. Others will follow, so long as ISO 14001 is seen to provide an extra competitive edge, very much in the same way that ISO 9000 (total quality) was utilized to differentiate organizations in the early 1990s. Many organizations have adopted pro-environmental strategies. There are too many to describe here, but Table 16.1 gives some diverse examples from around the world.

In addition to those organizations shown in Table 16.1, there is a growing number of paper and card recycling companies and a number of greeting card, office paper and container firms which use mostly or solely recycled products. Xerox, for example, not only uses recycled paper for copiers and printers but also recycles its photocopying machines, choosing to refurbish them and only replace necessary parts before returning them to the customer as a 'new' machine. British Nuclear Fuels Ltd (BNFL) has discovered a way to recycle some nuclear waste and recycle it to produce new nuclear energy. In the food retail business, Sainsbury's has decided to support organic foods and is pressurizing its suppliers to switch to organic farming methods. Tesco, in reply, is offering organic fruit and vegetables at the same price as its other fruit and vegetables. The potential market in food retail for green produce is huge. In other markets, demand from customers seems substantial. In Japan, for example, the market for green products overall is running at 15 trillion yen. This is about the same as the entire domestic vehicle production industry in Japan.

Table 16.1
Organizations taking a pro-environmental stance

Organization	'Green' strategies
Interplan (Germany)	Developed the micro-eco car (1996) which is easy and cheap to build and is 100% recyclable
Elf (France)	The first to use a low-emission gas burner in a shore area. The silent, enclosed gas burner burns up to 1.5 million m^3 of gas per day
Union Carbide (US)	Has developed a non-ionic surfactant for the treatment of water which is entirely pollution-free
Berlin Local Government (Germany)	Has authorized a regular bicycle-rickshaw service in the city centre as an alternative to cars and taxis
Chichibu Onodo (Japan)	This company makes cement out of 75% recycled material, including old pinball machines, tyres and scrap plastic and wood

This would seem good news for the pro-environmentalists. Businesses and governments seem to be taking green issues seriously. Academics researchers, however, have thrown doubt over the extent to which environmentalism has penetrated business in general and the extent to which it will only be sustained as policy so long as it is profitable. Cynical? Maybe, but the data seem to support the cynics, so far. At the individual level of analysis, Taft (1998) demonstrates the difficulties encountered by the green consumer in society. In a novel study, Taft experiences what it is to be a green consumer on the average shopping trip. He spends some weeks being totally green and then spends the next few weeks being unconcerned about being green, and compares the situations using a personal diary method. He shows the intense pressures exerted against being green for the individual. It is difficult to ride a bicycle to shopping malls. They are designed for the car. Anyone who has tried to walk in North American shopping malls will recognize the difficulties. Green, organic produce is difficult to find and sloppy or confusing labelling confounds choice. Supermarkets ensure that all customers are channelled past certain products, especially those which appeal to impulse purchases and to children. According to Taft (1998), none of these are green products.

Lave and Matthews (1996) studied 54 American companies which had publicly expressed concerns for the environment and ecology. Respondents were asked what they would do if non-toxic substitutes were available for the toxic products they currently used. The only problem was that the non-toxic products cost more. 66% of companies said they would only use the non-toxic products if the increase in production costs stayed below .1%, 33% said they would tolerate a 1% rise in production costs and only two companies said they would go to a 5% increase (but certainly no further).

Leisten (1996) argues that some material, such as plastic containers, are not recyclable. Yet manufacturers insist on producing them and, in some cases, coding them with obscure logos which give the impression that the plastic container is recyclable. Because of this, the Plastics Task Force in Berkeley, California, has decided against establishing plastic collection (from refuse) for recycling since it will increase the use of plastic containers if consumers think they can be recycled.

Montuori and Pursurer (1996) take a different approach. They argue that managers are the biggest barrier to establishing a pro-environmental strategy. This is because most managers think only in the short term, and are extremely focused on just their own organization. They do not understand systems theory (see Chapter 18) and the wider implications their actions may have. They feel, therefore, that the impact of their organization on wider society is minimal. Education is the only solution.

Johnson (1996) and Lober (1996) take a related view at the organizational levels of analysis. They argue that pro-environmental strategies are largely 'bolt-on' additions to the overall company portfolio. This is unlikely to result in an integrated approach to organizational strategy and that green issues will always be seen as something firms have to consider, view as expensive and perhaps unnecessary and graft environmentalism onto existing corporate plans. Lober (1996) argues that pro-environmental issues are mostly only considered in parts of organizations (such as in certain functions, or in certain internal processes, or in connection with selected stake-holders) but rarely overall. He suggests establishing an index of 'corporate green-ness' which will cut across organizational goals, system resources, internal processes such as decision-making and the various stake-holders internal and external to the organization. Until this is the case, Lober argues that it is unlikely for pro-environmental concerns to be at the centre of concern for organizations.

Summary

This chapter has attempted briefly to categorize and to classify the various environments which face the managers of all organizations. Broadly falling into two categories, there are very general environments which reflect widely held societal norms and values, and very specific, task-related, environments which are very much focused at the level of the individual firm.

Beyond the firm and the forces of competition are a more systemic view of networks and business systems. In these perspectives, managers had to try and exert some control over their environment by managing the network rather than attend to individual factors (such as one customer, or the prevailing fiscal conditions). Business systems show how the firm itself is embedded in wider society and that the relationship between societal factors and organizational factors is important. The emergence of the former Eastern European countries from socialism to capitalism is a good example of the relative influence of macro-economic policies and societal values.

Finally, corporate social responsibility and concern for the environment introduced the idea that managing the environment included a wider brief than just achieving profitability and accountability. Questions of ethics and voluntary actions toward the wider community could legitimately be thought of as management's brief in coping with the environment.

References

Axelsson, B. and G. Easton (1992) *Industrial Networks: A New View of Reality*, Routledge, London.

Carroll, A. B. (1979) 'A three-dimensional conceptual model of corporate performance', *Academy of Management Review*, **4**, 497–505.

Carroll, A. B. (1981) *Business And Society: Managing Corporate Social Responsibility*, Little, Brown & Co., Boston, Mass.

Carroll, A. B. (1993) *Business and Society: Ethics and Stakeholder Management*, South-Western, Cincinnati, Ohio.

Child, J. and A. P. Czegledy (1996) 'Managerial learning in the transformation of Eastern Europe: some key issues', *Organization Studies*, **17** (2), 167–79.

Dalton, D. R. and R. A. Cosier (1982) 'The four faces of social responsibility', *Business Horizons*, **25** (3), 19–27.

Davis, K. (1973) 'The case for and against business assumptions of social responsibilities', *Academy of Management Journal*, **16**, 312–22.

Drucker, P. (1993) *Post-Capitalist Society*, Butterworth-Heinemann, Oxford.

Elkington, J. (1997) *Cannibals with Forks: The Triple Bottom Line of 21st Century Business*, Clapstone, Oxford.

Evan, W. M. (1966) 'The organization set: toward a theory of interorganizational relations', in J. D. Thompson (ed.), *Approaches To Organizational Design*, Pittsburgh University Press, Pittsburgh.

Frederick, W. C. (1987) 'Theories of corporate social performance', in S. P. Sheti and C. Falbe (eds.), *Business and Society: Dimensions of Conflict and Co-operation*, Lexington Books, New York.

Friedman, M. (1970) 'The social responsibility of business is to increase its profits', *New York Time Magazine*, September, 32–33.

Gerlach, M. (1992) *Alliance Capitalism*, University of California, Berkeley, CA.

Granovetter, M. (1985) 'Economic action and social structure: the problem of embeddedness', *American Journal of Sociology*, **91** (3), 481–510.

Grant, R. M. (1991) *Contemporary Strategy Analysis*, Blackwell, Oxford.

Hitt, M. A., R. D. Ireland and R. E. Hoskisson (1995) *Strategic Management: Competitiveness and Globalization*, West, St Paul, Minn.

Hollingsworth, R. and R. Boyers (1997) (eds.), *Comparing Capitalisms: The Embeddedness of Institutions*, Cambridge University Press, Cambridge.

Johnson, P. C. (1996) 'Developments of an ecological conscience: is ecocentrism a prerequisite?' *Academy of Management Review*, **21** (3), 607–11.

Jones, T. M. (1980) 'Corporate social responsibility revisited, redefined', *California Management Review*, Spring, 59–60.

Jurkovich, R. (1974) 'A core typology of organizational environments', *Administrative Science Quarterly*, **19** (3), 380–94.

Lave, L. and H. S. Matthews (1996) 'It's easier to say green than be green', *Technology Review*, **99** (8), 68–9.

Leisten, D. (1996) 'To collect or not to collect plastics is the question', *World Wastes*, **39** (10), 8–9.

Levitt, T. (1958) The Danger of Social Responsibility, *Harvard Business Review* **36** (5), 41–50.

Lober, D. J. (1996) 'Evaluating the environmental performance of corporations', *Journal of Management Issues*, **8** (2), 184–205.

Lyon, D. (1994) *The Electronic Eye*, Polity Press, Cambridge.

Marsden, C. And J. Andriof (1998) 'Towards an understanding of corporate citizenship and how to influence it', working paper, *University of Warwick Business School*, Corporate Citizenship Unit, Centre for Corporate Strategy and Change, Coventry, UK.

Montuori, A. and R. E. Pursurer (1996) 'Complexity, epistemology and ecology', *Academy of Management Review*, **21** (4), 918–20.

Porter, M. E. (1985) *Competitive Advantage: Creating and Sustaining Superior Performance*, Free Press, New York.

Radford, K. J. (1978) 'Some initial specifications for a strategic information system', *The International Journal Of Management Sciences*, **6** (2), 139–44.

Soulsby, A. and E. Clark (1996) 'The emergence of post-communist management in the Czech Republic', *Organization Studies*, **17** (2), 227–47.

Stone, Christopher D. (1975) *Where the Law Ends: the Social Control of Corporate Behaviour*, Harper Colophon, New York.

Taft, K. (1998) *The Politics of the Green Consumer*, Unpublished PhD Thesis, University of Warwick, UK

Thompson, J. D. and W. J. McEwen (1958) 'Organizational goals and environments: goal-setting as an interaction process', *American Sociological Review*, February, 23–31.

Thompson, J. D. (1967) *Organizations In Action*, McGraw-Hill, New York.

Whitley, R. and L. Czaban (1997) 'Institutional transformation and enterprise change in an emergent capitalist economy', *Organization Studies*, (forthcoming).

Whitley, R. (1992) (edn.), *European Business Systems*, Sage, London.

CHAPTER 17 Understanding organizational systems

Introduction

We have seen in Chapter 12 how many authors argued the idea of organization–environment fit. Authors such as Burns and Stalker (1961) and Lawrence and Lorsch (1967) constructed contingency models of organizational design. The arguments that mechanistic structures seemed appropriate in relatively stable and predictable environments, and that organic structures were more effective in environments which are rapidly changing and are unpredictable, were empirically based, deterministic and seductively simple.

Recently, however, there has been a growing body of disquiet over the simplicity of this contingent 'fit' between structure and environment. Child (1972, 1997) for example suggests that environmental characteristics do not wholly fashion organizational structures. Managers have 'strategic choices' within certain limits to carve out their own organizational designs and processes irrespective of environmental characteristics. Other authors such as Astley and Van de Ven (1983), Hrebiniak and Joyce (1985) and Schreyogg (1980) have argued that factors other than environmental determinism must be taken into account when studying organizational design, performance and survival. These include subjective managerial perceptions, the ways in which perceptions are modelled (and interpreted) and the relative weights that can be given to strategic choice and other environmental factors.

While these debates have focused upon the interaction of environment and the firm, other researchers have argued that this is an inappropriate level of analysis for examining the questions of organizational survival, adaptation and performance. These authors argue that to understand such processes we have to shift our perspective to one of viewing *the dynamics of environment–organization relations as a system*. Based on general systems theory, many theories and empirical studies have emerged the most influential of which include *systems theory, population ecology, life-cycle* and the *chaos theory* perspectives. We discuss each in this chapter.

Systems theory

Systems theory, originally a theory of organism survival and adaptation in the biological sciences, has proved a very powerful analytical construct in the study of organizations. Put very simply, systems theory says that:

> **In any organization, the multitude of parts and processes are so interrelated and so interdependent that a small change in one part necessitates changes and adaptations in other parts.**

Systems can be closed or open. Examples of closed system models can be found in early theories of organizational behaviour, such as those of the Scientific Management or Human Relations Schools (Taylor, 1911, Mayo, 1949). In closed systems, only the interdependent parts of a single organization were considered. The focus was very much upon the internal workings of the firm. Job design, management roles and group behaviour were assumed to be themselves related, but to be independent of outside influences. It was assumed that there was one best way of organizing efficiently and effectively and this could be achieved by concentrating on the microcosm of the single organization in isolation.

The open systems approach views any one organization as an interdependent piece of a much larger whole. Its actions and characteristics are no longer just determined by the aspirations of its managers and founders, but by a wider environment with which the firm interacts. Common interactions occur between an organization and its suppliers, its customers and its peer organizations, sometimes on a daily basis. These actions and interactions form a pattern, the nature of which will impact upon internal organizational design and functioning (Katz and Kahn, 1966). Other external interactions are more remote but none the less significant. Government agencies, trade associations, banks and other nations all have some kind of input to any organization and are sometimes recipients of its outputs in the form of goods or services. This is the wider context in which the organization operates.

It is the patterning of these linkages and interdependencies which gave rise to open systems theory. Based around the three aspects of *Inputs–Throughputs–Outputs*, open systems theory is able to identify key aspects and principles of the system itself. Figure 17.1 gives an idea of how we might draw a map of an organization in an open system.

Given that the focal organization is the part of the system which effects the throughputs (transformation of raw material into goods or services) and that inputs and the output domain are external to it, then the open system is deemed to have the following properties:

Figure 17.1
The basic open
system's map

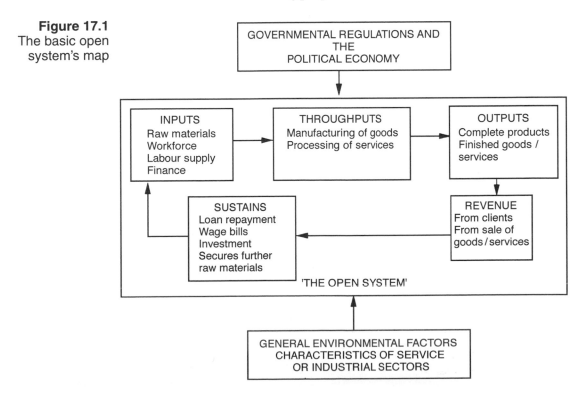

1 *Equifinality* Organizations and their managers have a choice over the design of internal organization. There is no one best way of doing things. There are multiple, different ways to achieve the same goal. In closed systems, the same initial variables lead to the same end result. In open systems no such assumptions are made.

2 *Negative entropy* Entropy is the predisposition of objects to decay and to disintegrate (such as a car, or a building or other structure). In an open system, this tendency is halted or sometimes reversed (hence the term negative entropy). Organizations import more resources from their environment than they expend in producing outputs. They can 'store' energy in much the same way as some animals survive periods of lean food supply by some form of hoarding.

3 *Steady state* The balance between inputs, outputs and throughputs is characterized by always being in steady state. This is not a true equilibrium, for the steady state itself is subject to movement, but the balance of the exchanges taking place in the system remains steady.

4 *Cycles and patterns* The open system itself is cyclical. Reciprocal patterns can be identified. The most obvious is where the revenue from the sale of goods (outputs) is used to purchase further inputs. This would represent a single loop cycle. More complex cycles can occur where single loops interact, or where tangential factors come into the equation. Nevertheless, the open system itself remains open to identifying patterns (however complex) and is cyclical.

Source: von Bertalanffy, 1956; Emery and Trist, 1960.

The open systems model has two benefits for the analysis of organizations:

● It allows for explanation of variance which occurs *within* the firm to be explained by factors which lie *outside* it.
● It facilitates the comparison of very different types of organization, since all organizations are argued to operate within an open system. This perspective gives us a *common denominator*, the language and *means of comparison*.

Understanding organizations as systems has become the basis for a number of other studies which take the properties of the open system as given and subsequently seek to explain other factors such as organizational survival, adaptation and transformation.

Populations of organizations
Population ecology models

Over long time-frames, the number of firms in a population initially grows slowly, then increases quickly to a maximum density and then declines before stabilizing to a lower level (Hannan and Freeman, 1977; Lomi and Larsen, 1996). These models combine elements of environmental determinism with open systems theory. Population ecology models argue that organizational survival is akin to 'Darwinism' wherein extreme demands from the environment can result in the demise of 'weaker' organizations and 'select out stronger, more dominant organizational forms' (Bedeian, 1987: 9). Aldrich (1979) is a leading supporter of the population ecology model. He has done a great deal to refine its analytical approach and to apply its theories to a variety of organizational types such as voluntary associations, trade associations, public and other social agencies (Aldrich, 1986). He writes:

> From the population perspective, the distribution of organizational forms at any time is a result of three processes: the creation or birth of new organizations, the

disappearance of existing organizations (through death, merger, bankruptcy, or whatever), and the transformation of existing organizations into new forms.

(Aldrich, 1986: 72).

Organizational survival is dependent upon achieving and sustaining a position within the general population of organizations. According to Carroll (1985), Hannan and Freeman (1977) and Harrigan (1985) this is achieved by examining (*a*) environmental niches and (*b*) organizational strategies.

Niches are characterized by the constellation of resources which impinge upon organizational action. Some resources (or, rather, lack of them) constrain action: others encourage and support action. Populations of organizations exist within each type of niche in a way similar to that described by Porter (1980) in his description of 'strategic groups'. These are groups of organizations within one industry or industrial sector which, faced with similar niches, adapt and adopt strategies at the level of the individual firm based upon the actions of others in the same domain. In the terminology of Grinyer and Spender (1979) such strategic responses are best described as 'recipes' which are shared throughout the sector.

Niches can be wide or narrow. Niche width (or narrowness) is determined by the combination of general resources and factors specific to a particular industrial sector, such as business cycles, product cycles, rates of innovation, union policies, the general economy, government policies and regulations and fiscal trends.

Populations of organizations which have a broad environmental niche width are those which are generalists. They can transform or reproduce themselves with relative ease since they have a tolerance for handling changing conditions and for being able to handle competitors. Specialist organizations are those which have a narrow niche. These organizations thrive in environments which are stable and which change slowly and predictably. They have specific resource requirements and usually have tightly defined markets. They also can build in to their structure a great deal of flexibility which also helps in the process of smooth adaptation to changing circumstances so long as change is neither too radical nor unpredictable.

Populations of organizations which are generalists are likely to find survival more difficult in environments which are stable. This is because they have to build in slack resources to cope with the broad niche and to fend off competition. These organizations are more likely to survive long term by continually transforming and by entering new populations and environmental states.

Organizational strategies For a given population of organizations, the pursuit of certain strategies by some organizations in the niche can upset the equilibrium of the wider open system. These strategies are characterized by either more efficient use of the existing resource base or by exploiting new aspects of the niche (usually by exploiting and acting upon information to which other organizations in the population are not yet privy). Such strategies create temporary disequilibrium, which can lead to competitive advantage for the organization.

Aldrich (1986) proposed three areas of strategy where any single organization could achieve advantage over the others in its population. The first occurs through the entrepreneurial spirit of managers which is unlikely to be distributed evenly throughout organizations in the population. Actions by entrepreneurs in one organization can lead to 'first mover' advantages, particularly if this entails the identification of new and unique products and services. The extent to which first movers remain in disequilibrium with other organizations depends, of course, on how quickly (or whether) these actions can be copied.

The second strategy occurs through the particular mix of structure, processes and people in any organization which can give it a unique character of culture. So long as this remains inimitable, the organization should enjoy competitive advantage. A third strategy focuses on technology. Where a firm can employ technological innovations not available to others the firm will be in an advantageous position in the population. If success ensues from using this technology, then managers are likely to build on this, developing the technology so that other organizations find it difficult or impossible to catch up.

Although Hannan and Freeman (1989) may be viewed as the leading proponents of Malthusian-Darwinism in population ecology models, it is worth noting that other researchers have identified the less deterministic side of the model. Usher and Evans (1996), for example, argue that Darwinism only applies when taking the organization as the unit of analysis in a population. If the *competencies* of the organization are taken into account, then 'Lamarckian' change is possible. Usher and Evans (1996: 1435) argue that, for example, the failure of an individual retail outlet of an oil company can be viewed as deterministic within the population, but only at the unit level of analysis. When viewed from the perspective of the larger, parent organization, this represents change and renewal, involving adaptation and renewal of competencies at the level of the multi-national.

Organizational life-cycles

The life-cycle provides a framework for studying the sequential patterns of birth, transformation and death in organizations (Kimberly and Miles, 1980). It is argued that all organizations go through a relatively predictable pattern of stages throughout their life-cycles. Just like products, organizations have life-cycles too. There are four broad stages in the organizational life-cycle:

1 Entrepreneurial
2 Collective
3 Formalization
4 Elaboration

The entrepreneurial stage

This is the first stage of any organization's life. The first tasks to be achieved are those of creating a service or a product and surviving in the chosen domain of operations. Usually, the creators of this organization are entrepreneurs for whom the organization is their complete focus of attention. They work long hours, do most jobs in the organization and set the climate and the culture.

If this first stage is successful, the organization will grow. The pressing need now comes from the increased number of employees in the organization since they require managerial direction and the organization needs someone to handle the general issues of management. It is unusual for the initial entrepreneurs to be skilled in general management, so the immediate problem is one of deciding either to limit growth and remain small (but risk being unable to sustain competition) or to grow and recruit professional managers.

The collective stage

Assuming the successful recruitment of professional managers, the organization enters the collective stage. The organization begins to take 'shape'. Departments and functions begin to be defined and the division of labour is the dominant theme. The culture may still largely be one of the collective (see Chapters 13 and 15) and individuals are likely to feel committed to the organization and the goals of its managers. The professional managers recruited tend to be strong, often dominant leaders, who have a clear vision where the organization should be heading.

As the organization continues to grow and to carve out with more precision its strategic niche, the need for management control and delegation arises. Strong leaders still want to lead. But the organization has begun to establish its position and consolidating how internal tasks are allocated and who has responsibility and autonomy to carry them out becomes pre-eminent.

The formalization stage

Here, we see the implementation of both control and information and communication systems. Communication and control become more formal. There is a division made explicit between the tasks of top management—to make strategic decisions and to implement policy—and lower level managers, who are charged with carrying out and overseeing operational decisions.

A whole system of co-ordination and control emerges, including salary structures, reward and incentive schemes, number of levels in the hierarchy, reporting relationships and levels of discretion and autonomy for lower level managers. The organization continues to grow, but more slowly. Structurally, it begins to resemble a bureaucracy, with pronounced functional specialization and differentiation. Toward the end of this stage, the organization can become over-burdened by the process of bureaucratization and the need for the structure to be 'freed up' becomes pressing. Retention of key staff is important. They are likely to leave the organization if they feel hemmed in, or impotent to influence or participate in wider organizational goals. One factor which contributes to this lies in the mechanism of formal control by management of roles (rather than individuals) which is characteristic of organizations in this stage of the life-cycle.

The elaboration stage

This is the stage during which the problems of over-formalization are addressed and solutions sought. The organization may have begun to 'plateau' in terms of growth and performance and may even show the first stages of decline. Managers used to handling bureaucratic structures and processes usually have to learn new skills or to unearth long forgotten notions of teamwork, self-assessment and problem confrontation. This stage of renewal can occur as soon as after 10 years of operation, but more usually takes around 15 to 20 years, during which time a number of other 'cures' may also have taken place such as the rapid turnover and replacement of senior managers (Greiner, 1972).

The idea of the life-cycle is also useful for drawing together some of the key management processes such as human resource management, power and decision-making processes. At each stage in the life-cycle, the profile of management concerns will alter in the relative emphasis a manager needs to

Table 17.1
Three stages of the
organizational
life-style: likely profile
of selected factors in
organizational
behaviour put on each. Table 17.1 summarize some of these differences. To avoid over-complication, the table distinguishes three phases in the life-cycle corresponding to growth, stability and decline.

The life-cycle concept has gained support from a number of researchers and practitioners over recent years. The Institute of Management Accountants (IMA) is recommending a life-cycle perspective to all its member organizations. Following a study conducted by IMA in North America, it was found that more successful firms consistently conducted a

	Growth	Stability	Decline
Strategy	Competitive and innovative	Emphasis on consolidation. Aimed at securing efficiency or securing change through planned increments	Nearly always *reactive* There is a strong tendency towards co-operation with other organizations in an attempt to secure stability. This can lead to serious organizational drift
Human resources	Focus on key individuals who have brought success	Focus on the *role* rather than upon the individual. Selection and appraisal schemes designed accordingly to accommodate role fulfilment	The focus returns very much towards the individual and not the role. Identification of 'problem' individuals (those who are assumed to have contributed to the decline) can lead to persecution. There is a tendency to sharpen stereotypes in the organization and to use these as justification for action
Power balance	Internal coalition very strong in relation to external coalition. Focus on the 'strong' few who are leading success. The organization 'enacts' its environment and tends towards niche management	Much less dominance internally. External interests play a large part in shaping decisions. There can be high levels of conflict between those in the organization who want to preserve the status quo and those who want to achieve change. This can bring with it the danger of slipping into decline through managing the politics rather than the organization	Usually externally dominated. Internal power is weak. Different parts of the organization begin to accrue power. Administration can become extremely Administration can become extremely powerful especially if its task is to monitor decline
Leadership	Style of leaders is determined largely by that which has brought success. There is general acknowledgement of this in the organization. Little attempt by individuals to try and change leaders' style. The only real alternative is to move organization if dissatisfied	Tends to be bound up with role description and behaviour expected. Style determined either by organizational culture, or by expected behaviours from sub-groups (especially in bureaucracies)	Becomes crucial. Key people who can aid recovery and who can be effective when turnaround occurs must be retained. This is a real problem, since these are the very people most likely to 'jump ship' when decline begins. Style must be contingent on both group and individual needs

Table 17.1 (cont.)

	Growth	Stability	Decline
Motivation	Usually through resource acquisition which heralds better times ahead (certainty) or through team spirit, peer-group pressure and general group conformity	Might not appear to be a problem. A sense of no news is good news! Motivation cannot just be assumed. It needs active management in order to keep existing staff levels constant. Care must be taken not to demotivate staff through the pursuit of efficiency which can bring with it the need for pruning and/or role change/ redefinition	Declining morale. Conflict increases. Need for change increases. Individuals resist change. Must avoid leaving motivation until the onset of crisis. It's too late then!

life-cycle analysis of products, services and activities at all stages in the life-cycle. They also found a positive correlation with life-cycle analysis and effective decision analysis. Spekman *et al.*, (1996) found the organizational life-cycle to be important in determining the success (or lack of it) in international alliances. They found that managers traditionally spend too much time on the question of forming the alliance and too little time on managing the process issues of keeping the alliance going over time. Success in international alliances depended to a large extent on the individual firms being at the same stage in the organizational life-cycle. Finally, Cyert and Kumar (1996) argue that there is always a balance between organizations continually searching for 'pay-off related' information or knowledge and their effective internal adaptation to it. They identify that the relative importance of information search versus internal adaptation change over the life-cycle of an organization, where information search becomes critical at the early and late stages of the cycle.

Non-linear systems: chaos theory

All of the previous systemic perspectives (open, population and life-cycle) are characterized by being both linear and sequential. Borrowed from Physics, chaos theory takes a completely different view, while remaining systemic in its focus. Chaos describes an irregular pattern of behaviour generated by non-linear feedback rules commonly found in nature or society (Stacey, 1993). The argument is that organizations are subjected both to forces of stability and instability which pushes them toward chaos. When in a chaotic domain, organizations are likely to exhibit properties of chaotic systems (Thietart and Forgues, 1995). In the long term, it becomes impossible to predict future results from what happened in the past. There is little or no determinism. In the short term, it may sometimes be possible to predict behaviour since time lags in the system mean that the consequences of small changes take time to accrue and take effect.

The example given by Stacey (1993) is that by heating a gas which emits no light at low temperatures, one can produce light (in this case a laser beam). At different points in the process, the system of atoms display different characteristics. At the low temperature they are in a particular order. At a slightly higher temperature, they become randomly ordered and chaotic. At a higher temperature still, the atoms suddenly realign themselves into a different pattern and light is emitted. This symmetry is both different from the original symmetry and could not be predicted from it in the first place.

Practical implementations of chaos theory are rare. Glass (1996) argues that chaos theories and non-linear systems are all right for the scientist, but too complex and rarefied for direct practical application. He does, however indicate that self-reinforcing *virtuous* and *vicious* spirals (a component part of chaos theory) have potential application.

Virtuous circle   For example, in the retail food war between Tesco and Sainsbury's in the UK, Tesco has embarked upon a virtuous circle. Whereas the previous market leader, Sainsbury's, diversified into various activities such as Homebase (DIY) and set up stores in North America, Tesco concentrated on its core business of food retailing. It could therefore commit more resources to stores, their layout and their activities. Sainsbury's were unable to compete. Tesco became market leader.

Vicious circle   For example in a manufacturing firm which needs to be more profitable, a common reaction is to cut costs. Savings may most easily be made by extending the time intervals when manufacturing plant is maintained and serviced. As a result, quality of the product suffers and the scrap rate increases. Profits fall again. Cost cutting is the answer and plant maintenance looks a logical target . . .

There have been very few studies as yet on the impact of chaos theory on managers. Stacey (1993) gives some general guidelines without being too specific, arguing that managers might make some sort of order out of the chaos if they follow these guidelines. They are:

- Allow teams to create leadership by their inherent self-organizing and self-policing behaviours. Managers should adopt a 'hands-off' policy and see what happens.
- Appreciate the use of power to dampen or amplify system effects. Key points are to ensure that rebellion and perceptions of submission are avoided.
- Provoke and maintain multiple cultures in the firm so that mavericks and deviants can ensure that a monolithic culture does not easily develop.
- Develop and nurture group learning skills.
- Create and maintain organizational slack so that the above changes can be invested in seriously and with commitment.

Torbet (1996) represents one of the few studies to try and link managers, chaos theory and organizational performance. The study of organizational leaders identified six cases of what Torbet calls 'transformational' leadership. This is where leaders had effected radical and successful changes. They ranged from leaders in the World Bank to an artist. Torbet found a positive relationship between these leaders' ability to think in ways consistent with chaos theory and successful transformational change. The application of chaos theory may be most useful in this area of the managerial role, which we deal with in the next section.

Boundary spanning as a managerial activity

Systems' theories provide us with a picture which is useful for understanding how organizations interact with their environments. A danger is that they can present an overly deterministic picture of the management process. We already know that managers have a strategic choice in the way they interpret their environment and implement decisions (Child, 1972, 1997). It is through the process of strategy formulation that managers, at least in part, can exert reciprocal influences on the environment. Strategies have an impact.

One of the key ways in which managers can achieve reciprocal impact on the environment occurs through boundary spanning activities. Boundary spanning refers to the role which sits astride the environment–organizational interface. It is a role, therefore, at 'the edge' of an organization. The role links and co-ordinates central parts of the organization, the 'technical core' (Thompson, 1967) with parts of the external environment (see Figure 17.2).

Figure 17.2
Monitoring and representing the organization: boundary spanning roles

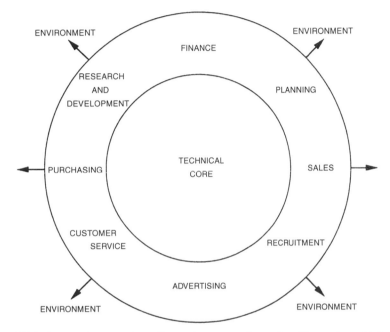

* This figure shows *external* boundary spanning roles. Examples of *internal* boundary spanning roles are: liason departments, product group managers and some personnel departments.

There are two key functions for boundary spanning roles. The first is to *monitor the environment*, detect changes which are occurring and feed these into the organization. The second role is one of *representation* (Jemison, 1984). Monitoring protects the technical core of the organization. Production units, for example, do not have to worry about factors other than production. Any information they need about what technologies competitors are using, or developments in the field can be fed to them by the boundary spanning roles. They are thus protected from many influences and from multiple sets of often conflicting information, which might otherwise impinge upon their ability to carry out their central task.

The representative task is primarily one of sending information about the organization out into the environment and thus influencing others' perceptions. Individuals in this role act as the public face of the organization. Many outsiders form strong opinions about the nature of the organization on the basis of what its representatives do and say. Organizational *image* is created and maintained by this role. In theory, the role has the capacity to influence the characteristics of the immediate external environment. Other individuals and organizations can be influenced in the way they perceive the organization and thus are likely to modify their behaviour toward it accordingly. In practice, the representative role often works this way. It can also spill over into 'impression management' in which representation is more a characteristic of the individual in the role. It can be, therefore, deceptive, misleading, calculated or dishonest (Goffman, 1959). Our interest here is to show that via this role, the organization can exert reciprocal influence on the external environment. It thus becomes an important part of the strategic management process, since strategic plans are likely to be formulated on the basis of the character of environmental–organizational linkages. This is the process of environmental scanning and monitoring.

Scanning

Scanning is the process of information search in the immediate environment. The search is for opportunities and threats which may accrue from major changes which are occurring in the wider context. Changes in government policies (both fiscal and legislative) and changes in public tastes (such as anti-smoking, anti-pollution, pro-safety and swings of fashion) all provide information for the formulation of organizational strategy.

Their accurate and effective targeting is essential information for any strategic plan. It can lead to the prevention of over-bureaucratization in the life-cycle, for example, by ensuring that the organization does not become 'prematurely ossified and possibly no longer matched with (its) environment' (Aldrich and Herker, 1977: 219).

Monitoring

This aspect of the role deals with tracking environmental contingencies which are already known to managers in the organization. This activity is essential in helping to formulate plans based upon forecasting future scenarios for products and services (Adams, 1976).

It is also important to note that monitoring (and to a lesser extent, scanning) do not operate solely at the input side of the systems' models. These roles also protect the organization at the output side. They monitor the characteristics of both source and sink environments. Examples are protecting the organization from producing and selling products which might have unintended harmful side effects, from excessive and avoidable pollution, and from generally acting in a way which would be held corporately irresponsible.

Summary

In this chapter, we have introduced a general model for examining and understanding organization–environment relations and exchanges. This model, the open systems perspective, allows us to analyse the particular processes though which organizations survive and grow in relation to their wider domain. The theory argues that the biological metaphor of the organization as an organism, constantly importing energy from its environment and exporting energy back into the environment, is both appropriate and useful.

The opposing view is presented by chaos theory, which argues that organizations operate in environments which can be characterized as non-linear systems. Thus very little can be inferred about the future from past actions. Yet, there are patterns at certain levels of analysis. As Stacey (1993) argues, snowflakes falling from the sky will be modified in shape and size by minute changes in temperature and air quality. We can never predict, therefore, the shape or size of snowflakes on the ground. What we do know, is that snowflakes will fall to the ground.

The utility of adopting any systemic perspective lies in allowing the very general comparison of all organizational types (public or private ownership; manufacturing or service; large or small). These variables of organization simply do not apply at this level of analysis. According to systems' theories, all organizations attempt to achieve an equilibrium or a balance between imports and exports.

Systems' theories are seductive in their generality and their seeming certainty about what will happen to all organizations. While they are useful analytical tools, they tend to portray the manager as powerless to do anything other than capitulate to the demands of the wider environment. Of course, this is not the case. The strategic management of an organization is a blend of environmental determinism and proactive managerial action. It is almost never just one or the other which is the engine of strategic change. Defining what is deterministic and what is open to choice is sometimes impossible since managerial actions can combine both forces simultaneously. It is important, however, at this stage to recognize this dualism for it provides the platform for an understanding of organizational strategies which is the subject of Chapter 18.

References

Adams, J. S. (1976) 'The structure and dynamics of behaviour in organization boundary roles', in M. D. Dunnette (ed.), *The Handbook of Industrial and Organizational Psychology*, Rand-MacNally, Chicago.

Aldrich, H. and D. Herker (1977) 'Boundary spanning roles and organization structure', *Academy Of Management Review*, **2**, 217–30.

Aldrich, H. (1986) *Population Perspectives on Organizations* (in collaboration with E. Auster, U. Staber and C. Zimmer) *Acta Universitatis Upsaliensis*, Uppsala, Sweden.

Aldrich, H. (1979) *Organizations And Environments*, Prentice-Hall, Englewood Cliffs, New Jersey.

Astley, W. G. and A. Van De Ven (1983) 'Central perspectives and debates in organization theory', *Administrative Science Quarterly*, **28**, 245–73.

Bedeian, H. (1987) 'Organization theory: current controversies, issues and directions', in C. L. Cooper and I. T. Robertson (eds.), *International Review of Industrial and Organizational Psychology*, Wiley, New York.

Burns, T. and G. M. Stalker (1961) *The Management Of Innovation*, Tavistock, London.

Carroll G. R. (1985) 'Concentration and specialization: dynamics of niche width in populations of organizations', *American Journal Of Sociology*, **90**, 1262–83.

Child, J. (1997) 'Strategic choice in the analysis of action, structure, organization and environment: retrospect and prospect', *Organization Studies*, **18** (1), 43–76.

Child, J. (1972) 'Organizational structures, environments and performance: the role of strategic choice', *Sociology*, **6**, 1–22.

Cyert, R. M. and P. Kumar (1996) 'Economizing by firms through learning and adaptation', *Journal of Economic Behaviour and Organization*, **29** (2), 211–31.

Emery, F. E. and E. L. Trist (1960) 'Socio-Technical Systems,' in *Management Sciences Models and Techniques*, **2**, Pergamon, London.

Glass, N. (1996) 'Chaos, non-linear systems and day-to-day management', *European Management Journal*, **14** (1), 98–106.

Goffman, E. (1959) *The Presentation of Self In Everyday Life*, Doubleday, New York.

Greiner, L. (1972) 'Evolution and revolution as organizations grow', *Harvard Business Review*, **50**, 37–46.

Grinyer, P. and J. C. Spender (1979) 'Recipes, crises and adaptation in mature businesses', *International Studies of Management and Organization*, **9** (3), 113–33.

Hannan, M. T. and J. Freeman (1977) 'The population ecology of organizations', *Sociology*, **82**, 929–64.

Hannan, M. T. and J. Freeman (1989) *Organizational Ecology*, Harvard University Press, Cambridge, Mass.

Harrigan, K. R. (1985) *Strategies For Vertical Integration*, Lexington Books, New York.

Hrebiniak, L. G. and W. F. Joyce (1985) 'Organizational adaptation: strategic choice and environmental determinism', *Administrative Science Quarterly*, **30**, 336–49.

Jemison, D. B. (1984) 'The importance of boundary spanning roles in strategic decision-making', *Journal Of Management Studies*, **21** (1), 131–52.

Katz, D. and R. L. Kahn (1966) *The Social Psychology Of Organizations*, Wiley, New York.

Kimberly, J. R. and R. H. Miles (and associates) (1980) The *Organizational Life-Cycle*, Jossey-Bass, San Francisco.

Lawrence, P. R. and J. W. Lorsch (1967) *Organization And Environment: Managing Differentiation And Integration*, Irwin, Homewood, Illinois.

Lomi, A. and E. R. Larsen (1996) 'Interacting locally and evolving globally, a computational approach to the dynamics of organizational populations', *American Management Journal*, **39** (4), 1287–321.

Mayo, E. (1949) *Hawthorne and the Western Electric Company: The Social Problems of an Industrial Civilization*, Routledge, London.

Porter, M. E. (1980) *Competitive Strategy*, Free Press, New York.

Schreyogg, G. (1980) 'Contingency and choice in organization theory', *Organization Studies*, **1**, 305–26.

Spekman, R. E., Isabella, L. A., MacAvoy, T. C. and T. Forbes (1996) 'Creating strategic alliances which endure', *Long-Range Planning*, **29** (3), 346–57.

Stacey, R. D. (1993) *Strategic Management and Organizational Dynamics*, Pitman, London.

Taylor, F. W. (1911) *Principles Of Scientific Management*, Harper, New York.

Thietart, R. A. and B. Forgues (1995) 'Chaos theory and organization', *Organization Science*, **6** (1), 19–31.

Thompson, J. D. (1967) *Organizations In Action*, McGraw-Hill, New York.

Torbet, W. R. (1996) 'The "chaotic" action awareness of transformational leaders', *International Journal of Public Administration*, **19** (6), 911–39.

Usher, J. M. and M. G. Evans (1996) 'Life and death along gasoline alley: Darwinian and Lamarckian processes in a differentiating population', *American Management Journal*, **39** (4), 1428–66.

Von Bertalanffy, L. (1956) 'General systems theory', in *General Systems, Yearbook Of The Society For The Advancement Of General Systems Theory*, **1**, 1–10.

Environments and managerial action: strategy and process

Introduction

In the Chapter 17 we described how the environment impacts upon organizations and their managers and concluded that the environment was not all deterministic. Managers and organizations have a choice about the ways in which they respond to and interact with their environments. In this chapter, we explore this scope for purposive action, *strategy*, in greater detail. There are many definitions of strategy, but most agree on the following features. Strategic decisions:

- are novel in their own right, or have an element of novelty to the organization;
- are organization-wide in their consequences;
- are the stated future goals of senior management in the organization;
- set precedents, which subsequent decisions are likely to follow;
- are usually resource costly (time, money and people).

Source: adapted from Wilson (1980:12)

Dror (1968) describes strategy as the 'major guidelines for action, directed at the future', while Chandler (1962: 13) defines strategy as:

> The determination of the basic long-term goals and objectives of an enterprise, and the adoption of courses of action and the allocation of resources necessary for carrying out these goals.

Useful though these definitions are, they give the distinct impression of almost total managerial control over strategy. As Ohmae (1982) observes, it is as if strategy belonged to some 'gold-plated' strategic planning department. While strategic decisions may be thought of as 'big' decisions, they may not always come about as a direct result of managerial action (nor environmental determinism). They 'emerge' as a pattern one can see retrospectively in a number of decisions made over time in an organization. This distinction between deliberate and emergent strategies has been well-documented by Mintzberg and Waters (1985).

Deliberate and emergent strategies

Mintzberg and Waters (1985) distinguish between:

- *Deliberate strategies* which are realized as intended
- *Emergent strategies* which are patterns or consistencies realized in the absence of, or despite, managerial intentions.

The polar extremes of deliberate and emergent strategies allow for many variants in between. Some strategies may be planned in a rough, macro-outline way, but without any detailed precision. Indeed, Andrews (1987) argues that precisely planned and detailed intended strategies are often little more than financial planning statements. Most strategies, as opposed to financial plans, tend to be emergent. Of course, strategies may

Figure 18.1
Deliberate and
emergent strategies

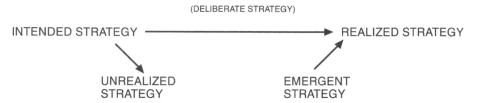

be realized or unrealized. Figure 18.1 shows the simple elements of the
Mintzberg and Waters (1985) continuum.

A strategy which is perfectly deliberate means that there must be an
absolute level of precision in the organization, shared by all and the strategy
must be implemented precisely as intended. This gives virtually no room for
environmental influences, or the environment must have been totally
predictable. At the other end of the scale, a totally emergent strategy means
that there must be some order which can be reconstructed (a pattern) in the
absence of any intentions. Both would seem extreme and unlikely to occur
in practice, but Mintzberg and Waters found otherwise. For example, they
argue that the decision over the escalation of war in Vietnam (taken by
Lyndon Johnson in 1965) was put into place in great detail by military
planners. It was a planned, deliberate strategy, maintained until 1968 when it

Table 18.1
Types of deliberate
and emergent
processes (from
most deliberate to
most emergent)

Process	Characteristics
Planned	Leaders in authority formulate plans, elaborate them as budgets, schedules, forecasts creating a 'surprise free' implementation plan. Those outside the planning process are allowed to act, but not think or plan beyond that
Entrepreneurial	Less precision in planning, but controlled by one person (entrepreneur) who imposes the concept on others. The vision can be changed, but only by the entrepreneur
Ideological	Collective vision in which a group exhibits such clear patterns of behaviour that a realized strategy can be identified
Umbrella	Less direct control from individuals or groups. Leaders set general guidelines for action and/or behaviour and let others manoeuvre within these boundaries
Process	Instead of setting guidelines, leaders influence the process of strategy-making (duration, discontinuity, recycles) but leave the content of strategy to others
Unconnected	One part of the organization (a sub-unit) is able to realize its own strategies independently of (and sometimes in opposition to) umbrella guidelines
Consensus	Very little (if any) prior intention. Individuals and groups converge on the same theme so that it becomes pervasive in the organization, obviating the need for any central direction or control
Imposed	Strategies imposed from outside the organization, forcing the organization into a pattern of actions regardless of any central controls

Source: adapted from Mintzberg and Waters (1985)

became clear that it was not achieving the intended results. Table 18.1 gives the variants of strategy processes identified by Mintzberg and Waters.

The Mintzberg and Waters approach allows us to characterize strategy processes in an organization. Such processes may apply to a single strategy in the firm or to all its various decisions (Hickson *et al.*, 1997). Other approaches have taken the organization overall as the single unit of analysis and have characterized 'its' strategy toward the environment in the form of a typology (Miles and Snow, 1978; Miller and Friesen, 1984).

The Miles and Snow typology is based upon empirical research in 87 organizations (manufacturing, service, public, non-profit and for profit). The research derived *patterns* of strategy adopted by various organizations. The patterns included characteristics of organizational competencies, structures and processes. The typology of Miller and Friesen is based upon 52 firms and is explicitly linked to organizational performance (to identify archetypes of successful and unsuccessful firms).

Snow and Hrebiniak (1980) later took the Miles and Snow typology and related it to organizational performance. First, we examine the work of Miles and Snow (1978) and Snow and Hrebiniak (1980).

Strategy and organizational domain

This approach to organizational strategy argues that all organizations are faced broadly with three problems which come from their immediate environment (domain) and from their position in the life-cycle (see Chapter 17). These domain-related problems are:

1 entrepreneurial problems
2 engineering problems
3 administrative problems

In general, the more mature an organization along its life-cycle, the more its managers will have to cope with all the above problems simultaneously. For analytical convenience, we describe each in turn, however.

Entrepreneurial problems Describe the processes through which an organization gradually develops a firm portfolio of goods and services coupled with a clear indication of target markets or market segments. For the organization in the initial phases of its life-cycle, this usually means shaping and refining the broad entrepreneurial vision of its founders into something more precise. In more mature organizations, these entrepreneurial problems are those which define the organization clearly in a particular product or market niche, but which also can constrain subsequent innovative changes or modifications to overall strategies.

Engineering problems Concern selecting the appropriate technology in order to achieve efficiency in the process of inputs, throughputs and outputs. Many manufacturing organizations have installed extensive (and expensive) technological solutions to achieving manufacturing efficiency. For example, many car manufacturing plants have installed a computer-integrated engineering system, which monitors and controls virtually everything from initial drawings to 'body-in-white' (the assembled, but unpainted car body). Separate plants which are located at some distance from one another can also be integrated in this way.

Of course, these solutions can also act as constraints to change should any factors of either organization or its domain shift markedly. Organizations can thus become locked in to their particular technology, which may be efficient in itself, but if the outputs it produces are aimed at the wrong market or are otherwise inappropriate, the organization risks sliding efficiently out of business.

Administrative problems Are those which focus on achieving stability for the organization. In order to make strategic decisions, managers require some level of predictability. Solving administrative problems allows this to happen. Reducing uncertainty is a key aspect here (Cyert and March, 1963; Thompson, 1967). The establishment of contracts with suppliers and customers, and the use of standard operating and control procedures internally are examples of reducing uncertainty. For organizations at an early stage in their life-cycle, the installation of an administrative system would represent a strategic response to the problems posed by domain uncertainty. More mature organizations must ensure that their internal processes are effectively monitored and controlled, but that equally, these do not become dominant and ingrained so as to preclude future changes.

Miles and Snow (1978) developed four categories of strategic responses to the above domain issues. These strategies represent attempts to co-ordinate

Table 18.2
Miles and Snow's
four strategic types

Domain defenders	This strategy is one where management attempts to locate the organization in a stable niche. It is aimed at sealing off part of the market to secure a stable and predictable domain. Products and services are limited both in scope and in number but are aimed to be of consistently higher quality than those of competitor organizations. Organizational growth through more intensive market penetration is preferred to diversification. In the league of organizations, these are the consistent 'home players'.
Domain prospectors	This strategy allows failures as well as successes to be part of the strategic portfolio. The organization is usually operating in a broad domain for services and products, but managers are willing to experiment in an attempt to be first-to-market with new or revised products. Managers are early responders to changes which occur in the domain. Market entry is nearly always swift, though not necessarily sustainable in all areas.
Domain analysers	This strategy is aimed at concentrating on a limited range of products and services. Nevertheless, the strategy is a mixture of both defender and prospector, combining the efficient concentration of market operation with an open mind toward pursuing market opportunities which might prove to be profitable. It is a 'balanced' strategy, although one which is difficult to sustain in rapidly changing environments
Domain reactors	This is not really a strategy at all in the strictest sense, since the organization is pulled this way and that by changes in its environment. There appears to be no consistent stance toward products and services or toward markets. These organizations are almost totally reactive in their strategies, unwilling to take risks or to exploit opportunities

a response to all domain problems, engineering, entrepreneurial and administrative. Empirical research identified four broad strategies, *defenders, prospectors, analysers* and *reactors*. The brief characteristics of each strategy are described in Table 18.2.

Domain defenders   Achieving stability is the response of top management in these organizations when faced with any entrepreneurial demands from their domains. There is a deliberate setting of parameters in order to seal off sections of the market. As a corollary, a great deal of effort is put into achieving efficient inventory processing. Technology is often the key to sustaining success, since it is aimed at producing and supporting a limited number of products or services. These, in turn, are sustained in the marketplace by means of their image of prestige, quality, exclusivity or all three.

Typical defender 'industries' according to Snow and Hrebiniak's (1980) study are motorcar production, airlines and plastics manufacturers. Consistently strong in the functions of general management and financial management, as well as being heavily biased toward production specialists, these organizations are structurally 'mechanistic' (Burns and Stalker, 1961) and strategically constrained. This is not surprising, since they all operate within industries which have relatively high set-up costs for manufacturing. Once established, the 'natural' tendency when faced with changes in the domain (such as increased competition, or greater numbers of foreign imports) is to look toward making the organization more efficient, keeping products relatively stable or as incremental additions to an existing range.

Domain prospectors   Prospecting is a relative term. It characterizes those organizations which, in a given industry, pursue a more dynamic and outward-looking strategy than others. While the defender is quite at home in a stable and predictable environment, the prospector consistently finds and exploits new markets, products and domains. Internally, the organization is constantly subject to change as some product lines flourish and others wither. This does not stop managers constantly trying to locate the organization in new areas. Failure and success are both at home in this dynamic strategy.

Snow and Hrebiniak (1980) show that organizations pursuing the prospector strategy are almost the reverse of defenders. In prospectors, technology is flexible. It is often embedded in people rather than in machines. There are also likely to be multiple levels and types of technology in the same firm. Structurally, these firms are often represented by a matrix or a project-based structure (see Handy, 1986). Domain prospectors also need to build into their structures plenty of environmental scanning departments or individuals. To thrive, these organizations rely on the accurate input of data concerning trends, changes and events in their domain. In terms of recruitment and selection, this means that such organizations may have to recruit individuals who currently appear not to fit with 'today's' business, but who have the potential to seek out and develop the business areas of tomorrow.

The matrix structure provides a good basis for securing the essential flexibility which these organizations require. Both strategies of stability and new ventures occur simultaneously. Innovation and entrepreneurial strategies will have primacy. Administration in these organizations operates in the role of facilitator and support system rather than in the role of controller (as in defenders). Strong departments tend to be general management, product development and research units. It is here that the organization has distinctive competencies.

Domain analysers

Organizations pursuing this strategy fall analytically between defenders and prospectors. This strategy is also a combination of some factors of both defenders and prospectors. The primary characteristic of analyser organizations is one of maintaining stability and at the same time being geared up for change. This parallels the 'loose–tight' orientation identified in Peters and Waterman's (1982) high-performing companies such as 3M, Disney and McDonalds. According to Miles and Snow (1978), domain analysers define their entrepreneurial problems as how to maintain a stable product and customer base while simultaneously identifying and exploiting new market opportunities.

Analysers tend to play safe. They are rarely first movers. Imitation or slight modification of what prospectors have done previously is the norm. In this way, the strategic risks are lessened, but then so too are the potential rewards of being first to market. Snow and Hrebiniak's (1980) study revealed two important characteristics of analysers. First, only 50 of 247 managers said that their organization pursued an analyser strategy. This is the least well represented category of the four strategic types. Second, the structures of analysers were extremely mixed. No single department (or group of them) was dominant, or contributed unambiguously to the distinctive competence of the firm (Selznick, 1957). The only consistent pattern found in the study was the high ranking of the finance function by respondents in all analyser organizations as contributing to success and continued good performance. It is likely that this reflects the centrality of finance in an organization which has to be both stable and flexible. Finance allows some measure of decision criteria to be examined when assessing competing bids for new projects, for example, and thus can act as a powerful control mechanism (see Burchell *et al.*, 1980; Jones, 1986).

Domain reactors

The key difference between reactors and the former three strategic types is that the reactor is never proactive in formulating strategies. The other three types can be either reactive or proactive. As their name implies, reactors spend most of their strategic life responding to one environmental change after another. As a result, they are strategically defined from without rather than from within. Reactors often lack a clearly defined and articulated strategy within the ranks of their top management. We saw in the previous chapter how this situation might occur in an organization which is approaching maturity in its life-cycle (Kimberly and Miles, 1980). Having gone through a period of growth, led by a forceful entrepreneurial spirit (one person or a group), the organization enters a strategic void if the initial leaders leave or move on, and are not replaced with managers of equal or similar skills. It can sometimes be impossible for a new top manager to brought in from outside the organization, to achieve a sense of strategic unity and purpose, particularly if his or her brief is to consolidate the previous eras of change and dynamism.

Decline can readily set in to reactor organizations. This is particularly evident in cases where management concerns focus largely on maintaining a particular configuration of organizational structure, to the neglect of scanning the immediate environment for changes, opportunities and trends. This can result in structural efficiency internally, but produce a structure which is largely inconsistent with the demands of the operating environment. The organization becomes ineffective and decline soon sets in unless quite radical changes occur to both strategy and structure.

Linking strategy and organizational performance

The work of Miller and Friesen (1984) follows and develops the themes outlined above of achieving fit or congruence between strategy, structure and environment. They argue that organizational performance is inextricably linked to the extent to which there is a match between these three factors. Many other authors have also pointed to this as the key aspect of organizing at the strategic level (see, for example, Chandler, 1962; Rumelt, 1974; Pettigrew, 1987; McKiernan, 1993).

Miller and Friesen (1984) attempt to forge a link between patterns of strategy and organizational performance (measured in terms of growth in profits and sales as well as return on equity in relation to competitor organizations). Their study covered 81 organizations, 52 of which were eventually selected to produce a comparison between successful and unsuccessful companies. Tables 18.3 and 18.4 summarize the major findings.

Tables 18.3 and 18.4 show the 10 archetypes of strategy and their relationship with organizational success. There are some obvious parallels with these archetypes and those outlined earlier by Miles and Snow (1978). For example, assertive strategies equate with domain prospectors. Incremental strategies equate with analysers, and grafting and groping strategies reflect the domain reactor.

Miller and Friesen's work, however, tells us that the interrelationships between environment, structure and strategy are not simple. They are multivariate and equifinal. That is, many different combinations can lead ultimately to organizational success. There are some patterns nonetheless which deserve mention since they fit the overall picture we have built up in

Table 18.3 Summary of successful organizations strategy, structure and environment

Strategy	Structure	Environment
ADAPTIVE	Functional and monolithic with co-ordination by a strong leader	Firm adapts to environment. Power on a par with competition
ASSERTIVE	Functional, differentiated and integrated	Adaptive, but in the lead of competitors
EXTRA-POLATING	Hierarchical, control by committees, functional technocratic	Proactive toward domain. Dominates competitors
INCREMENTAL	Decentralized, differentiated but with an elaborate and formal committee structure	Adaptive. Follows competitors
EXPANSION	Divisionalized, controlled from central HQ. Elaborate and formal collaborative mechanisms	Selects domain by process of diversification and aquisition
NICHE	Functional, centralized	Creates a new segment within domain

Source: Miller and Friesen (1984: 98)

Table 18.4
Summary of
unsuccessful
organizations:
strategy, structure
and environment

Strategy	Structure	Environment
OVER-EXTENSION	Divisionalized, centralized, differentiated, not integrated	Select environment via aquisitions
ULTRA-CONSERVATIVE	Bureaucratic, mechanistic, formal monolithic, with centralized controls	Mostly ignore the environment
MUDDLE THROUGH	Leaderless. Extremely decentralized, unco-ordinated and fragmented. Political. divisionalized	Each division has a different and unique relationship with the environment
GRAFTING AND GROPING	Functional, centralized with few resources, differentiated	Adapt to the environment in a piecemeal way

Source: Miller and Friesen (1984: 102)

this section of the book. Wensley (1997) supports the multivariate argument. In this case, however, he argues that the complexity of factors which are deemed to account for success in organizations lead us to a point where it is almost impossible in a single study to account for more than 10% of the variation in business performance. This is despite using large samples of firms such as those in the Profit Impact of Marketing Strategy (PIMS) studies. Wensley also mentions the problem in much research on organizational success of being unable to provide a 'control' group of failures to secure comparative and well-anchored research. Miller and Friesen's work is one exception of course, although more popular texts on success and performance, such as Peters and Waterman's (1982) studies of excellence, only reported studies of successful companies. They also only studied firms at one particular moment in their corporate history. Miller's later work in 1990 shows how studying firms in multiple time periods is important, since success in one time period will not always ensure high performance in another. So-called 'excellent' organizations in one time period can bring about their downfall in the next. He calls this the Icarus paradox.

The Icarus paradox: the failure of success

Miller (1990) argued that it was ironic that in the case of many successful firms, the seeds were already sown for their demise. Icarus flew too close to the sun in the Greek myth and his artificial wax wings melted. He plunged down to the Aegean sea, to his death. In the same way, organizations which become too complacent, too adventurous and too prone to indulging in excesses following success, can also plunge to their death. According to Miller (1990) there are four identifiable 'trajectories' of decline:

1 *The focusing trajectory* Where quality-driven craftsmen are driven to become tinkerers. Firm become obsessed with a monocultural technocratic attention to detail. These organizations alienate their customers with perfect (to the organization), but irrelevant (to the customer) offerings.

2 *The venturing trajectory* This is where growth-driven entrepreneurial builders and their companies turn into impulsive greed imperialists who overtax their resources by expanding helter-skelter into businesses they

know nothing about. In the terminology of Wilson *et al.*, (1996) they 'over-reach' themselves and eventually find it impossible to reverse or retract the process.

3 *The inventing trajectory* This occurs when previously ordinary functions such as R&D departments change to become a bunch of Utopian escapists run by a cult of chaos-loving scientists who squander resources in the pursuit of hopelessly grand and futuristic inventions.

4 *The decoupling trajectory* Transforms organizations which have excellent marketing skills, well-known brand names and broad markets into rather sales-oriented firms (to the exclusion of all else). The result is an organization which produce a stale and disjointed line of 'me too' products and services.

Miller includes some famous organizational names which have undergone one or more of the above trajectories, citing Apple Computers, IBM, Proctor & Gamble and Caterpillar Tractor among many others. In another example, Miller shows how Harold Geneen, the initially successful chief executive officer of ITT, was unable to prevent a doomed *venturing trajectory* once a corporate culture of growth by acquisition had set in. This led to the buying of over 100 companies. Such a large and diverse group of companies defied even Geneen's control mechanisms (including sophisticated information systems and his own personal 'charisma'). On the latter point, it was rumoured that Geneen could pressure executives to be on the brink of tears. Nevertheless, failure of the company was the result, and Geneen's replacement (Rand Araskog) had to sell off over 100 units and reduce the workforce by 60% to restore profitability.

Miller (1990) lists many reasons which act behind the scenes in organizations to lead them down the routes of failure trajectories. The following are synopsis of the major reasons:

1 *Leadership traps* Where success reinforces 'bad habits' in leaders by encouraging them to stick to their tried and tested strategic recipes. These might not work in a new context. Even worse, leaders may develop to become conceited and obstinate, isolating both themselves from the organization and their organizations from their markets.

2 *Power and politics* Success gives some managers increased power (see Chapter 11). These managers in turn become barriers to subsequent changes. They are more likely to protect the status quo and amplify prevailing strategies.

3 *Structural memories* Organizations are prey to the heavy hands of history. They develop routines and memories over time. These can be formalized into systems and programmes. Strategies can become driven by routine, informed by history rather than addressing the current demands of the context.

Strong individual leaders can lead to both success and failure

Strong, entrepreneurial leaders can succeed. We have ample evidence from firms which have turned round and escaped from the jaws of decline due to the tireless efforts of individual leaders. Much popular management theory is concerned with descriptions of chief executives who exhibit strong leadership qualities and quite literally lead their organizations from the front. These include familiar names such as Sam Walton, founder of Wal-Mart (which in 1993 had the greatest market value added in the US economy); Jack Welch and General Electric; John Harvey-Jones and ICI;

Richard Branson and Virgin, and Roberto Goizueta's Coca-Cola empire. As a proportion of organizational success stories, however, such high-profile individual leaders are relatively rare.

They can also lead to a strategy which will 'over-extend' the organization (see Table 18.3) with rapid growth followed perhaps by divisionalization, but which is uncontrolled or simply in the wrong strategic direction.

Decision-making is focused on the individual entrepreneur. Individual strategic decision processes are likely to be risky, impulsive and sporadic (Hickson *et al.*, 1986). There is no counterweight to the dominant power of the individual leader. The powerful chief executive remains unchecked by perhaps more cautious managers. So long as the decisions made by the leader are successful, the organization will survive. A series of false moves could secure organizational demise. There is an obvious parallel here with the 'power culture' described in Handy (1986) and outlined in Chapter 13 of this book.

We can also see that organizations themselves can be dynamic and innovative, populated by creative managers with multiple projects and ideas on the go all the time. Yet, a dominant leader (who is conservative and anti-risk) in these kinds of organizations will stifle innovation by 'constricting' decision-making processes (Hickson *et al.*, 1986). All major decisions will be made effectively by one person despite the potential corporate creativity over which he or she presides. Large, well-known companies can be blighted by such leaders with equal ease to their smaller, more domestic counterparts. For example, in 1993 George Fisher was appointed chief executive of Eastman Kodak. Nothing surprising, so far, but he was the first outsider to run the company for a 160 years! Up to that time, the company had been run by insiders, all of whom saw the company in the same way and all of whom viewed the advent of digital technology in photography as a threat (from Fuji). They ran the company down to a point when Eastman Kodak was sustaining losses of $1.5 billion on sales of $16 billion. Fisher broke the constricted leadership pattern. Using digital technolgy as an opportunity to focus Kodak's business, he turned the company round so that in 1996 profits were $1.5 billion on sales of $16.4 billion.

In a long-term study of the effects of leadership on organizational performance, Leavy and Wilson (1994) found that the impact and the influence of the environment of the firm was equally important as strong, individual leaders. Macro-economic conditions, the operating environment of the organization, as well as the kinds of technology-in-use were equally influential factors in organizational performance. This led Leavy and Wilson (1994) to conclude that time and context were important factors. While some leaders could revitalize or turn their organizations around, all leaders were tenants of time and context. This long-term study (over three decades) meant that only four organizations could be studied. Yet, even in larger sample sizes, it seems that the influence of leaders as being individually responsible for organizational success is limited. They can also be responsible for failure. In a study of 55 cases of strategy implementation in UK organizations, Hickson *et al.*, (1997) found that only nine cases revealed the influence of strong, individual leadership in bringing about enhanced organizational performance. Of these nine cases, four were taken to the extremes of failure where the strategies failed altogether. In two of these failure cases, the whole organization was jeopardized and eventually went out of business, or was taken over.

Summary

There are no simple, easy answers to the question of fit between environment, structure and strategy, but it appears there are general patterns. We have attempted to draw together these themes. The reader must be cautioned however. Relatively small sample sizes for research; investigations conducted mainly in North America and at different periods of history, all raise a number of question marks over the validity of these findings in multiple contexts. The 10% rule may indeed be true. We cannot and should not expect to account for more than 10% of the variance in strategy, structure and environment interrelationships. Equally, do these findings hold true for companies emerging out of what was formerly socialist Eastern Europe and firms in the Far and Middle East, for example? We address the questions of international perspectives in the following chapters.

References

Andrews, K. R. (1987) *The Concept of Corporate Strategy*, 3rd edn, Irwin, Homewood, Illinois.

Burchell, S., Clubb, C. Hopwood, A. G, and J. Hughes (1980) 'The roles of accounting in organizations and society', *Accounting, Organizations And Society*, **5** (1), 5–27.

Burns, T. and G. R. Stalker (1961) *The Management Of Innovation*, Tavistock, London.

Chandler, A. D. Jr. (1962) *Strategy And Structure: Chapters In The History Of The American Industrial Enterprise*, MIT Press, Cambridge, Mass.

Cyert, R. and J. G. March (1963) *A Behavioural Theory Of The Firm*, Prentice-Hall, Englewood Cliffs, New Jersey.

Dror, Y. (1968) *Public Policy Re-examined*, Chandler Publishing Co., San Francisco.

Handy, C. B. (1986) *Understanding Organizations*, Penguin, Harmondsworth.

Hickson, D. J., R. J. Butler, D. Cray, G. R. Mallory, and D. C. Wilson (1986) *Top Decisions: Strategic Decision Making In Organizations*, Blackwell, Oxford, Jossey-Bass, San Francisco.

Hickson, D. J., S. Miller, and D. C. Wilson (1997) 'Organizational decision-making and success', *Working Paper*, University of Warwick Business School.

Jones, C. S. (1986) 'Organizational change and the function of accounting', *Journal Of Business Finance And Accounting*, **13** (3), 283–310.

Kimberly, J. R. and R. H. Miles (and associates) (1980) *The Organizational Life Cycle*, Jossey-Bass, San Francisco.

Leavy, B. and D. C. Wilson (1994) *Strategy and Leadership*, Routledge, London.

McKiernan, P. (1993) *A Strategy of Growth*, Routledge, London.

Miles, R. E. and C. C. Snow (1978) *Organizational Strategy, Structure And Process*, McGraw-Hill, New York.

Miller, D. (1990) *The Icarus Paradox: How Excellent Companies Can Bring About Their Own Downfall*, Harper Business, New York.

Miller, D. and P. H. Friesen (1984) *Organizations: A Quantum View*, Prentice-Hall, Englewood Cliffs, New Jersey.

Mintzberg, H. and J. A. Waters (1985) 'Of strategies deliberate and emergent', *Strategic Management Journal*, July/Sept 257–72.

Ohmae, K. (1982) *The Mind of the Strategist*, McGraw-Hill, New York.

Peters, T. and R. Waterman Jr. (1982) *In Search Of Excellence: Lessons From America's Best Run Companies*, Harper & Row, New York.

Pettigrew, A. M. (ed.), (1987) *The Management Of Strategic Change*, Blackwell, Oxford.

Rumelt, R. P. (1974) *Strategy, Structure And Economic Performance*, Harvard University Press, Cambridge, Mass.

Selznick, P. (1957) *Leadership In Administration*, Harper & Row, New York.

Snow, C. C. and L. R. Hrebiniak (1980) 'Strategy, distinctive competence and organizational performance', *Administrative Science Quarterly*, **25** (2), 317–36.

Thompson, J. D. (1967) *Organizations In Action*, McGraw-Hill, New York.

Wensley, R. (1997) 'Explaining success: the rule of ten percent and the example of market share', *Business Strategy Review*, **8** (1), 63–70.

Wilson, D. C. (1980) *Organizational Strategy*, PhD, Thesis, University Of Bradford Management Centre.

Wilson, D. C., Hickson, D. J. and S. Miller (1996) 'How organizations can overbalance: decision overreach as a reason for failure', *American Behavioural Scientist*, **39** (8), 995–1010.

A flat pyramid: a symbolic processing of organizational structure

Mats Alvesson[1]

Introduction

This reading discusses organizational structure using a medium-sized Swedish computing consultant company, Enator, as an example. Special attention is paid to the corporate hierarchy and management's attempt to control different representations of the hierarchy. Organizational structure is first examined from a conventional, 'objectivist' perspective but is later analysed as 'meaning patterns' and 'interpretative schemes' for the existing social structures. Structures are viewed as symbolic patterns whose meanings must be interpreted.

Organizational structure

Traditionally, organizational structure has been thought to have exerted a decisive influence on the functioning of the organization. However, how the organizational structure should be understood is far from self-evident, as this reading illustrates. Organizational structure is usually defined as the sum of the ways in which work tasks are distributed among different units and roles, and how tasks and roles are formally co-ordinated. In other words, organizational structure is a result of the division of labour and the authority hierarchy (see Chapter 12).

In the appropriate 'positivist' spirit, many organizational researchers have tried to measure these variables in the last two decades, and they have attempted to study a correlation with each other and with other key dimensions (organizational size, corporate strategy, technology and the organizational environment, for example, Robbins (1983) and Veen (1984) give an overview of literature). This research has not succeeded in providing many surprising results (see the main interrelationships in Chapter 12). As Miller and Mintzberg (1983) claim, the fundamental weakness of the analytical, variable-correlating research approach in organizational research, as in much other social scientific work, has been an excessive interest in testing simple, limited relationships rather than searching for, or constructing, richer patterns based on deeper insights. Miller and Mintzberg proposed that research should focus on configurations, that is, clusters of attributes that are internally consistent and that correspond to actual organizational patterns.

Mintzberg's (1983) five configurations are the simple structure, the machine bureaucracy, the professional bureaucracy, the divisional organization, and the adhocracy. Enator fits the adhocracy configuration relatively well, but it also has features of the simple structure, the professional bureaucracy, and the divisionalized structure. The characteristic feature of the adhocracy is that it combines personnel in different project teams to deal with specific tasks in a given period. Teams largely comprise specialists who supply innovative solutions. Project groups are formed and dissolved, depending on the nature of the task concerned. It is usually impossible to formalize and standardize the work. Mutual adaption between the members of the project groups, largely based on informal communication, is the main co-ordination mechanism.

Enator: a case study

Enator employs around 500 people in the computer consulting business. It was studied using 35 interviews with managers and employees, plus about three weeks of participatory observation (in 1987). The full case study, including a number of aspects that do not involve organizational structure, is reported in Alvesson (1989). Enator was founded in 1977 by three individuals whose business concept was to combine computer and management know-how and to offer consultant services in the computer area. The market for such services, as for computer consultant services in general, has expanded dramatically and Enator has been extremely successful. This has led to high profits and a good reputation.

The company is primarily based in Sweden, but about one-third of its staff work in foreign subsidiaries located in six European countries. Enator has exploited the corporate subsidiary form and is a group with more than 20 subsidiaries. However, several Enator subsidiaries only employ one or two people (although one has 50 employees). Enator has three types of subsidiary companies: companies oriented toward a certain product (service) located at the head office near Stockholm, local companies in Sweden, and subsidiaries abroad. The first is either concerned with administrative computer consultancy involving assistance to users (banks, the distributive trade, etc.) in computer development projects, or in offering technical services to assist manufacturing industry in the development of products that include a computer element. The regional and foreign companies offer a wide range of consultancy services. All the Swedish companies form part of Enator Sweden AB, which was established in 1986 primarily to co-ordinate marketing in Sweden.

Consultancy projects

In most cases, the consulting project is organized within a particular subsidiary. This means that the project only employs staff from this company. This normally applies to assignments involving only one person or where only a limited number of consultants are concerned. The consultancy project may employ only one person for a few weeks, or dozens of staff may be involved for several years. Sometimes the company (subsidiary) employs consultants from other Enator companies. This may be because the subsidiary requires a given specialist competence or lacks the capacity to handle the assignment, or another subsidiary may need the work (its consultants have nothing to do). Major projects involve many subsidiaries, since a company with less than 50 employees does not have sufficient personnel to staff a project requiring 8–10 people (as well as handling other assignments). Staff employed on the project are then subordinated to the 'project' subsidiary. Consultants may be employed by a company for which they do not work directly, when the project they are assigned to belongs to another subsidiary.

These consultants have two bosses in principle: the manager of their own company and the project management of the company awarded the project. This is a typical matrix organization (see Chapter 15).

> What I sell is flexibility. The ability to absorb knowledge and apply it. I can rapidly work out of the context, see it in abstract terms, understand the customer's problems and do something about them (consultant).

Projects are undertaken in close co-operation with the customer company. The work usually takes place totally within the framework of the customer's organization so that the consultant/project group has much closer contact with the customer company than with its own:

> After one or two years with the customer we know them better that we know Enator (consultant).

Enator's organizational structure

Enator's organization is simple (as described above) and, also complex in terms of the degree of horizontal, vertical, and geographic differentiation. A simple organization has a limited division of labour and is localized to a single place. A complex organization has several hierarchical levels, a high degree of specialization between units, and is located in several geographic places (Robbins, 1983). In addition, uniformity may be contrasted with multiplicity in terms of criteria for the grouping of various tasks and roles in units, the changeablity of the organization (which is linked to some extent with the market situation), and the range of products (services). Thus, complexity increases with a multiplicity of (complex) products, external pressures for change, and the degree of hierarchical, vertical, and geographic division of labour.

The Enator group is characterized by a mixed picture of differing companies and organizational forms because operations have developed very rapidly, and corporate strategies in this industry are sometimes a question of catching emerging opportunities, etc, Enator seems to be fairly typical in this industry. One of its colleagues, Programmator, has an even more complicated structure (Sveiby and Risling, 1986). Such an organizational structure may limit management's opportunities of establishing effective control. However, in the growth area in which Enator has found itself, this has clearly not been regarded as a major problem.

An important aspect of Enator's corporate strategy is growth while retaining the advantages of small-scale operations. The limit of 50 staff members for each company has been established as a compromise between two contradictory principles: market orientation and organizational/ personnel orientation. From the marketing point of view, it is probably not desirable to split up operations into a number of separate companies. Customers often work with several different areas of Enator's operations and they are not interested in being faced with several different companies. They prefer to deal with one Enator, which can give them everything they require. From a marketing point of view, it is also probably most fruitful to present Enator as one company, so that the marketing aspect favours a single large company.

On the other hand, personnel and organizational criteria tend to favour a small number of employees in each basic unit. Small-scale operations facilitate a pleasant atmosphere, group loyalty, a feeling of common interests, and effective management without a hierarchical emphasis. The fewer the number of consultants involved, the easier it is for the subsidiary's managing director to provide support, co-ordination and personnel development. The relatively small groups that characterize the company also facilitate flexibility and the acceptance of responsibility. Enator is a flat, informal and non-hierarchical firm. There are only three hierarchical levels:

managing director, subsidiary manager, and consultant. Flatness is emphasized in annual reports, interviews, and introductory courses for new employees. As with many other youthful companies in 'high-tech' industries, there is a desire to preserve a certain degree of equality (Kanter, 1983). But all is not quite so simple. Despite the apparent absence of formally appointed managers at other levels, such leadership functions do exist. One subsidiary manager describes the situation as follows:

> We don't really appoint managers. But of course we have an informal hierarchy. This is quite natural because otherwise things wouldn't work. But those who have quite a lot of authority have done so because they have created a position. They haven't been appointed by me. People have to create a 'platform.' You are not appointed to anything, you have to create it. We don't have any career paths in the consulting business traditionally. But of course there are careers that are based on authority and platforms.

In professional organizations, formal position is often less important than professional competence. This implies that influence and prestige are linked with competence in specific areas—and this does not always follow formal organizational structures (Mills, 1980; Sveiby and Risling, 1986). The formal—informal dimensions are not always adequate. The subsidiary manager quoted above, who said that no formal superiors were appointed, said five minutes later that:

> There is a management group in the company that is official. People know who's in the group. There isn't really any appointed deputy. But actually there is. I have stated that X is the number two. There is a deputy managing director and a management group. But apart from that, things are very flat.

In the larger companies, there is normally what is known as a 'Number Two' who holds overall responsibility together with the company's managing director. One or two other people are also included in the management group, perhaps a salesman or a person with combined consulting and marketing responsibility.

Thus, the companies have a deputy manager *de facto*. It might be possible to regard the rhetoric of the flat structure as an attempt to deceive people. But a lack of formal positions and titles does indicate a certain de-emphasis of the hierarchy in Enator subsidiaries, and it means that the 'second man' cannot totally and formally represent his or her superior in relationships with the staff.

Subsidiary managers have established positions clearly superior to those of other employees, but totally differently from what would be the case if the subsidiaries were departments or units in a division. A subsidiary manager describes the position as follows:

> Each company can really only handle one true leader. That's in the nature of the structure. Managing director lunches and other conferences for managing directors are arranged. Those who are one rung lower on the ladder feel that they are not part of this privileged circle.

The same person felt that his position before he became managing director of a subsidiary was as follows:

> If you presented important ideas it was to your own managing director, and if he passed on these ideas they were virtually his ideas.

As Eriksson (1986) observes, it is not only the number of rungs on the organizational hierarchy that are significant, but also how far apart the rungs are placed. The Enator project organization—which is supposed to function in line with the fundamental model describing the company in terms of how projects are conducted—also means that the hierarchical dimensions receives some additional emphasis. Apart from having project members and project leaders, there is also a superior level that is termed the project head. (The subsidiary manager or the deputy subsidiary manager sometimes has this function.) This practice does not seem to be particularly common in other companies in the industry. While the project leader has technical responsibility for the project, the project head has overall responsibility for quality, customer contacts, etc. Thus, there are often three formal hierarchical levels in a project. However, the project organizational form is rarely mentioned in interviews and in official corporate documents, such as the annual report. Nor do management representatives or consultants mention the project organization form.

Enator's history

Enator's history provides a clue to understanding these contradictions. An employee who has worked with Enator almost since the start disappointedly commented:

> If you look at the company culture and think about what people said at the beginning and how things have turned out . . . They always said that we should have as low profile a hierarchy as possible. And in a way that's what's been achieved, since every subsidiary company has a managing director. But actually the real hierarchy doesn't look like that. The hierarchy is just as overpowering as in any other ordinary company, almost at least. You have a manager for Sweden, a foreign manager, a global manager, and a board.

> And the owners—there were three originally—they put some life into the whole operation. But nowadays it is not like that. Who the hell meets the owners today? You see a glimpse of them going past occasionally. You don't meet Enator's managing director particularly often either. (consultant)

The establishment of a company group—Pronator—which is superior to Enator and of which Enator is a part, supports this view. Enator's companies in Sweden are subsidiaries of Enator Sweden AB, which in turn is a subsidiary of Enator AB, which is a sub-group within Pronator. The founder of Enator made so much money that other companies were bought and formed into a large corporate group (Pronator), which is now owned and managed by Enator's founders.

The quotation serves to illustrate two points. One is the importance of key persons in emphasizing or weakening hierarchies. The founders appear to have (had) some ability in de-emphasizing the feeling of a formal hierarchy through their personal style of management. They were successful in persuading everyone to feel a sense of participation in operations and to see the company as a whole, by providing information about what was happening in different corners of the company. The founders were also successful in appearing to be relaxed in their positions, avoiding prestige and distance, etc. Nonetheless, decisions were undeniably taken by the founders, and their power position was not in question. The company's early successes can be seen as a result of this ability to combine strong control with good cohesion.

Of course, such a style of management is closely connected with the size of organization, but is not purely determined by it. Given a certain size and a certain formal structure, social circumstances can reinforce or weaken the feeling of (formal) hierarchy. On the whole, corporate management and subsidiary managers also seem to have the ability to regulate the relationship between hierarchy and cohesion and, in some way, to de-emphasize consistently the special status of the 'big bosses'. One way of achieving this is by using such expressions ironically and by requiring subsidiary managers to participate in different types of social activities outside working hours. This encourages informality and reduces the hierarchical element at work as well (Ouchi, 1981). It is hardly possible to realize in full the flat organizational form with 500 employees (as opposed to only a few dozen staff). Ideals and reality are not wholly in conflict—on the contrary, flatness is something that is aimed at and exists—but it is easy to identify obvious deviations from the original ideological purity.

Organizational structure from the cultural perspective

From cultural (and symbolic) perspectives, organizational structure is not regarded as an 'objective' phenomenon with virtually physical characteristics. Instead, it is viewed as a symbolic system (Geertz, 1973; Smircich, 1983). Organizational structure must be interpreted. For example, the status of subsidiary managing directors and the process of establishing subsidiary companies acquires a different meaning from a symbolic perspective. According to the 1986 annual report, Enator had 22 managing directors altogether (all men), half of whom are only in charge of themselves or a handful of individuals. Understanding the significance of the managing director's status is crucial in comprehending Enator's organizational hierarchy. Generally speaking, in Sweden the title 'managing director' has several different meanings besides the strictly legal and formal implications: the title denotes authority, responsibility, independence, and superiority. It is also associated with status and prestige. Its status may also be regarded as a symbol of action: activity, the ability to take actions, initiative, involvement, and hard work. With a more restricted policy on creating subsidiaries and hence managing director positions, the titles that in many cases replaced 'managing director', for example, director (without the 'managing' prefix), department manager, or sales manager, were associated much less with the above characteristics.

The symbolic significance of managing directors is not identical internally or externally. Despite customers' interest in the provision of different services by a *single* Enator rather than by a set of companies with differing names or orientations, the managing director function is clearly considered to have benefits when dealing with external relations. It may have a door-opening function in the outside world, and the managing director title makes it easier for subsidiary managers to function as salesmen. The considerable number of managing directors is emphasized in the extensive and expensive annual reports. In the 1985 edition, for example, photographs of all managing directors were presented and they were given the opportunity to answer 10 questions about their company's situation, future, etc. In the same report, however, only Enator's managing director and the national managing directors were given the opportunity to describe their operations and future prospects. These eight managing directors appeared in enlarged pictures, occupying a half-page per person. Managing directors (plus a couple of representatives of the executive staff) appeared on a large photograph at the end of the annual report—a charming colour photograph in which the gentlemen appeared in their winter coats against a snowy background. The caption reads: 'Some of the leading executives in the Enator group meeting at the base of Kebnekaise mountain for free discussions about the company's orientation.' Kebnekaise is Sweden's highest mountain.

The considerable number of managing directors seems to imply that the company is top-heavy and dominated by directors. But the significance of managing directorship in Enator differs somewhat from Swedish norms in general and also with respect to relationships with customers and external interested parties. Enator's informal and familiar tradition implies that the status of managing director and formal titles should not be taken too seriously in connection with social relationships within the organization.

Although the absence of managerial authority tend to be less prominent than traditionally believed this does not preclude even further deviations by companies like Enator (that is, adhocracies) from a 'systematic-bureaucratic' management style (Mintzberg, 1975). Many Enator employees refer to the managing director as a sparring partner, that is, someone who functions as a partner in high-level discussions about projects and project problems. Apart from this, the subsidiary managers' most important function is probably to attract assignments, that is, to be a salesman. The symbolic significance of managing director status at Enator denotes superiority, independence, responsibility and initiative. These attributes are de-emphasized and supplemented—but not replaced by—concepts such as 'discussion partner' and 'one of the boys.'

Internally, Enator's management must clarify how managing director status should be interpreted and evaluated in the framework of the corporate collective. Managing director status varies in accordance with the context, rather than being a predetermined, rigid interpretation. In social terms, the managing director is on friendly terms with his staff, but in financial and economic terms, he is nonetheless responsible and must take major decisions.

Organizational structure in this respect is a question of a structuring process in which the interpretive system is developed, partly based on the influence of Enator's management, and partly on more random and external organizational foundations (Ranson, Hinings and Greenwood, 1980). Organizational design is just as much a question of establishing a given approach and certain evaluations of positions and relationships between these (formal) organizational structures as it is a question of the construction and structuring of (formal) positions, units, roles and relationships among them.

Understanding structure also requires consideration of contextual circumstances, primarily market situation and societal values. These contribute both to determining the purely formal elements in the organization, by creating external expectations and associations as to the symbolic value of managing-director status, for example, and also by influencing the members of the organization's 'cultural' preparedness to allocate a specific significance to managing-director status. Since Enator is also internally based on the symbolic values attributed to the managerial role in several respects, while it is also in some respects in conflict with the corporate ideology, it appears logical that the company makes considerable efforts to influence exactly how staff should interpret managerial status within the company in various situations. Thus, an important aspect of local culture (corporate culture) is understanding the precise significance of managing-director status in the company.

Another fundamental aspect of the company's structure that cannot be understood without giving the organizational members' definitions a central role is the 'flat hierarchy.' We may, for example, use the following quotation, which is interpreted as objective and unambiguous: '(Enator has) a very "flat" organization and is a company that is unusually informal. The pyramid has been broad and low, and the hierarchy is virtually non-existent' (Enator's managing director in the 1986 annual report, p.3).

From this perspective, one might just as well end up with twice as many hierarchical levels (for example, consultant, project leader, project head, subsidiary managing director, Sweden's managing director, and Enator's managing director) rather than the three basic hierarchical levels of consultant, subsidiary managing director, and Enator managing director. Neither of these two conclusions is '*more true*' then the other. The conflict in meaning does indicate that in many cases it is misleading to use the pyramid's unambiguous physical form as a concept that can capture social interaction patterns in organizations. *Formal organizational structures attain their real consequences via the interpretations and meanings the employees give them.* If collective consciousness says that the organization is basically flat and unhierarchical, this means more for the real functioning of the organization than some objective empirical measure. The flat organization may be regarded as of symbolic importance. It indicates an attempt to achieve cohesion among the personnel, to create a feeling of belonging and a 'we-sense'. Flatness symbolizes proximity, informality and free communication. Hierarchy and top-steered organizations represent the opposite. The top-steered organization provides a 'misleading' map of the organizational reality that it should represent, according to Enator's founder, management, and personnel.

Naturally, the 'cultural interpretation' is not totally independent of formal structures and action patterns. Nor is the cultural level a mechanical reflection of the social level. The organizational structure may be regarded on the basis of three dimensions: infrastructure, socio-structure, and superstructure (Fombrun, 1986). Thus, the superstructure (the cultural level) is in parallel with the material and formal aspects (that is, the infra-and socio-structures) and contributes to determining the organization's actual social pattern. However, the relationship between the various structural aspects is far from harmonious, as proponents of dialectical and dynamic organizational theories have emphasized (Fombrun, 1986; Benson, 1977). Potential discrepancies and contradictions have been pointed out in the discussion of the corporate and managing director structure in Enator.

As dialectically minded organizational researchers point out, there is no reason to assume that convergence and harmony are 'natural' and 'normal,' while regarding tendencies to divergence and contradiction as something strange. Divergence and contradiction must be regarded as something central since: 'Equilibrium structures . . . are at best fleeting moments in a dynamic process of structuring . . .' Fombrun (1986).

It might be imagined that social structures at Enator—including the formal organizational hierarchy—will develop so that a clearer discrepancy or conflict between the social structures and the cultural level will characterize the company. This would be the case if the latter does not change in harmony with the former (a 'culture lag'). Tendencies toward such a contradiction between the 'actual' organizational structure (that is, the action patterns and social practices) and how the organization is interpreted can be traced at Enator. The relationship between the socio-structural and the cultural factors is not without tension—anything else would be strange. 'Small-scale operations' as an organizational symbol can hardly be unaffected by a development that has caused the company to evolve from being a closely knit Swedish company with one hundred employees to an international corporate group with five times the staff in a mere five years. This is clearly illustrated by the quotation in the section on 'Enator's history' above.

Despite the weakening of symbolic values, 'small-scale' operations nonetheless function as a clear symbol for the organization, even if the meaning of 'small-scale' is probably subject to a process of continuous reinterpretation. As Enator continues to grow and acquire the character of a major international corporate group, dramatic changes are probably required to the cultural level of interpretation (the pattern of meaning, the superstructure), if clear conflicts between the small scale and the flat ideology, on the one hand, and the infra- and socio-structures, on the other, are to be avoided.

Conclusion

Enator's structure can best be understood in the sense that it shows different faces in different situations and to different groups. Subsidiary managing director status, the core of the corporate hierarchy, must also be understood from an organizational-symbolic perspective. Externally, involving customer contact, it is a question of emphasizing high status. Internally, this is less important. For corporate control, the idea (to a large extent realized) is that free flows of communication between levels and considerable opportunities for competence-based influence that is independent of formal status should be favoured. However, the managing director's formal position undoubtedly has considerable importance, and corporate hierarchy is not simply 'flat'. In social contexts, the hierarchy is heavily de-emphasized, and friendship between managers and colleagues is stressed instead. The different hierarchical elements are not totally divorced from each other, but interact as the formal hierarchy heavily overlaps the socially constructed hierarchy. The 'flatness ideology' and values that emphasize informality, equality, together with considerable efforts to establish a 'fun atmosphere' and feelings of belonging, soften the impact of formal hierarchy.

Considerable efforts to reproduce these patterns of meanings and values and to maintain social practices that comply with them, have not hindered the emergence of contradictions between this cultural level and the socio-structural level. Among other things, these contradictions are the result of the fact that the socio-structural level is more immediately influenced by increasing corporate size and by hierarchical differentiation.

Note

1 Adapted by permission Alvesson (1990: 5–23)

References

Alvesson, M. (1989) *Ledning av kunskapsföretag* (Management of Knowledge-Based Company). Norstedts, Stockholm.

Alvesson, M. (1990) 'A Flat Pyramid: A Symbolic Processing of Organizational Structure', International Studies of Management and Organizationl Structure', *International Studies of Management and Organization*, **19** (4), 5–23.

Benson, J. K. (1977) 'Organizations: A Dilalectical View', *Administrative Science Quarterly*, **22**, 1–21

Eriksson, A. H. (1986) *Service. Kultur. Förändring: Ny organisationslära I facklig belysning*

(Service, Culture, Change: New Organization Theory in a Union Perspective).
Tjänstemännens centrala organisation, Stockholm.

Fombrun, C. (1986) 'Structural Dynamics within and between Organizations',
Administrative Science Quarterly, **31**, 403–21

Geertz, C. (1973) *The Interpretation of Culture*, Basic Books, New York.

Kanter, R. M. (1983) *The Change Masters*, Unwin, London.

Mintzberg, H. (1983) *Structure in Fives*, Prentice-Hall, Englewood Cliffs, New Jersey.

Mintzberg, H. (1975) 'The Managers's Job, Folklore and Fact', *Harvard Business Review*,
July/August, 49–61

Mills, P. K. *et al.*, (1980) 'Flexiform. A Model for Professional Service Organization',
Academy of Management Review, **8**, 118–31.

Miller, D. and H. Mintzberg (1983) 'The Case of Configuration', in G. Morgan (ed.),
Beyond Method, Beverley Hills, Sage, CA.

Ouchi, W. G. (1981) *Theory Z*. Addison-Wesley, Reading, Mass.

Ranson, S., C. R. Hinings, and R. Greenwood (1980) 'The Structuring of Organizational
Structure', *Administrative Science Quarterly*, **25**, 1–17

Robbins, S. R. (1983) *Organization Theory*, Prentice-Hall, Englewood Cliffs, New Jersey.

Smircich, L. (1983) 'Concepts of Culture and Organizational Analysis', *Administrative
Science Quarterly*, **28**, 339–58.

Sveiby, K. E. and A. Risling (1986) *Kunskapsföretaget* (The Knowledge-Based Company),
Liber, Malmö.

Veen, P. (1984) 'Characteristics of Organization', in P. J. Drenth *et al.*, (eds.), *Handbook of
Work and Organizational Psychology*, **2**, Wiley, Chichester.

The older employee in the organization: a managerial and a developmental problem

J. G. Boerlijst and B. I. J. M. van der Heijden

The interest in the contribution of the older worker in the organization is growing. It seems to be connected with the economic climate and the situation in the labour market. In periods of increasing prosperity and full employment, such as the post-war period up to around 1965, the older skilled and unskilled worker was in demand. At that time, themes such as functional age, further training/retraining and task changes were studied against this background (Belbin and Shimmin, 1964; Griew; 1964; Munnichs, 1966; Munnichs, Dirken, Dohmen and Thierry, 1986). In this period, schemes were even set up to offer older employees work *after* retirement on a voluntary basis (Boerlijst-Bosch, 1962).

Subsequently, with the ebbing of the period of boom, interest in the added value of older, skilled and unskilled employees declined rapidly. They were no longer in great demand or even welcome on the labour market. Increasing international competition, hectic market developments and the need for drastic organizational, economic and technological modifications and innovations forced companies and organizations to face the possibility of rapidly increasing obsolescence of knowledge on the part of management and workers (Dubin, 1971; Dalton and Thompson, 1971; Kaufman, 1974, 1975). In this period the theme of 'survival, renewal and rejuvenation' of the organization came to the fore and was then never to disappear from the scene. Personnel play a crucial role in this theme. The human activities and qualities needed for survival and renewal have never been systematically studied, presumably being thought self-evident and trivial. In business and in management literature, the view is held that salvation is to be sought in 'creativity', 'innovative ability', 'elan', 'decisiveness', 'flexibility' or qualities of similar purport, more often attributed to younger than to older workers. Those lacking in these qualities to any degree are not wanted. Older workers tend to be labelled 'less capable', 'less efficient', 'slower on the uptake' and so on (Rosen and Jerdee, 1976; Stagner, 1985: 789; Boerlijst, van der Heijden and Van Assen, 1994). The question as to whether this is a 'valid' attribution in the sense that *under all circumstances* younger people are supposedly more creative etc., than comparable older colleagues is difficult to investigate. Double-blind psychological experiments would have to be conducted to exclude the possibility of *self-fulfilling prophecies*. However, these are scarcely feasible in everyday business practice.

However, more important is the question how the employability of the older worker can be guaranteed. The above-mentioned study of Boerlijst, van der Heijden and Van Assen (1994) concerning individual employees of age 40 plus considers this subject. The study was done in 10 different Dutch work organizations: Shell, AKZO, PTT Telecom, IBM, Unilever Research,

DSM Research, DHV, Heidemij, De Nederlandsche Bank and the Directorate-General 'Management and Personnel Policy' of the Dutch Home Office. The main question was to find out what the over-40s contribute to the organization, and what they will contribute in the future. Further questions like: 'What can be said about the resilience and versality of the over-40s?' and 'Do this resilience and versatility decline as employees grow older?' were asked. After investigating the contribution of the older worker, light was shed on the question whether the management was able to exert a positive influence on the qualities of the older employee, and if so, what methods it can employ.

The questions, in different forms and variations, were put not to the over-40s themselves but to their immediate superiors. The main point of interest were the standpoints and the opinions of managers on these matters. The superior is considered to be one of the best sources of information on individual personnel in a company. The supervisor is the one who can optimize the quality of the functioning of the employees in his or her department. He or she plays a crucial role by allocating the so-called management activities. The management activities are intended to monitor the tasks and the functions of the individuals and to stimulate their development.

As we were particularly interested in the consequences of growing older, we have made a comparison of three successive over-40s age groups, namely 'juniors', 'mediors[1]' and 'seniors', active at middle or higher levels of functioning within their respective organizations (see Table R12.1). In every organization we tried to gather information about 100 employees, evenly spread over the ages of 40 and over, active at least on a middle level of functioning or in a middle management position. Besides these two conditions there were no further sampling restrictions, that is, sampling could be done on a random basis.[2] For this study we combined the available data of all 10 participant organizations. Since some of them did not succeed in getting 100 protocols and there were no prescriptions made about the division between the two function levels, the available sample totalled 738, and it comprised less employees on the middle functioning level (N (middle) = 308) than on higher one (N (higher) = 430).

Table R12.1
Comparison of over-40 age groups in organizations

Age group		Middle-level function	Higher-level function
juniors	40–46 years	N = 100	N = 161
mediors	47–52 years	N = 91	N = 148
seniors	53 years and older	N = 117	N = 121

The reason why we have restricted ourselves to the over-40s with functions at a middle and higher level is the following. Looking for data which can be generalized for application in the future, we made allowance for the possibility that the present over-40s, particularly the mediors and seniors, will be difficult to compare, on one point at least, with the over-40s who will be populating our companies in 20 years' time. Until 20 years ago simple functions and simple tasks were dominant in most work organizations. As a consequence the bulk of over-40s in our existing workforce has a rather low level of education. As the complexity and level of difficulty of future functions will on average be higher than it is now, we have every reason to expect that the average educational level of the over-40s will likewise have undergone a sharp rise by the year 2010.

When analysing the study data, we made a distinction between employees at middle function levels and employees at higher levels. The contributions made by the over-40s with an intermediate vocational background are generally of a different nature than those who function at a higher academic level. In this connection, we were particularly interested in whether management makes a significant distinction between the two levels, for example in the evaluation of their functions and their functioning. In addition to this, we investigated whether there is any difference in the management's approach to and treatment of these two categories.

The 10 organizations participating in the study occupy a prominent position in the Netherlands, but they do not, of course, offer a representative picture of the Dutch business community as a whole. Our impression is, however, that there are certain relationships within the personnel sphere of activities which are found to operate in virtually the same manner in every company, possibly in the one case to a greater extent than in the other. For this reason we saw no objection to combining the observations on the over-40s and their executive management in the ten companies into one whole. This, then, allowed us to test, with a fairly large margin of certainty, certain consequences we had previously formulated on the over-40 ageing process against their reality content. In so doing, we chiefly made use of an ANOVA design.

The central themes in our study were:

- How does the value of the functions occupied by over-40s functioning on intermediate and higher levels in the organization develop as they grow older?
- How do the quality of the functioning of these over-40s and the influence which they exert inside and outside the organization develop?
- What can be said about their mobility in the sense of transitions to other functions?
- To what extent and in what field do they participate in training and development programmes?

As already stated, we were particularly interested in the extent to which certain management activities can stimulate the development of the over-40s in these fields. In this reading, a few *highlights* are mentioned.

Successively the following topics are discussed:

1 The utility and the learning value of the function;
2 The quality of functioning;
3 Mobility;
4 Training and development.

The utility and the learning value of the function

We have assigned two value aspects to functions:

1 The value which the function has within the framework of the organization or, in a smaller context, the department in which the function is positioned. From now on we will designate this aspect as the '*utility value*' of the function for the organization or department respectively.
2 The value which the function has as nutrient for the employee's further development. This aspect will be termed the '*learning value*' of the function of the employee.

Figure R12.1 contains an oversight of the utility values of the functions exerted by the over-40s. Of every function level and of every age group it gives the percentage of those whose function is indispensable or rather essential for their organization.

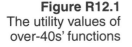

Figure R12.1
The utility values of
over-40s' functions

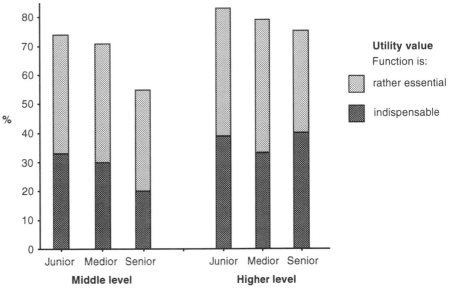

In general we can conclude from the research data that the utility value of the functions or positions held by the over-40s are by no means so badly off. Particularly on the higher level only a minority of these functions can be missed. With the increase in age, a slight decline in mean utility value is noticeable, but certainly not a dramatically large one. More important and problematic is the relatively low learning value of the functions for development of new expertise, especially at the middle level.

Figure R12.2
The learning values
of over-40s' functions

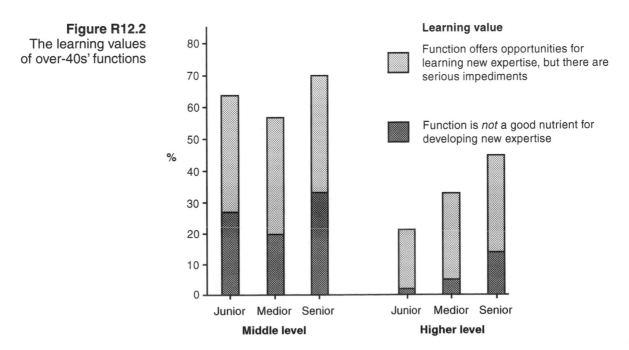

The percentage of employees with a functioning offering too few opportunities for acquiring new learning experiences and, more specifically, for learning new expertise, is higher at the middle level than in the higher functions (see Figure R12.2). At both levels the seniors are worse off than their younger colleagues. In a relatively large number of cases, the function does in principle offer opportunities for growth in expertise, but there are impediments or thwarting circumstances. Unfavourable working conditions and being allowed too little time to extend him or herself beyond the scope of the 'normal' work, tend to be to the disadvantage of many employees. In practice nothing more can then come of what might have been a development. Such 'impediments' occur more often at the middle level. This category also covers those cases of the employees themselves not taking advantage of the potential opportunities offered by their function. In their superior's opinion, they do not make any particular efforts themselves.

Facing the rapid technological changes it seems very important to maintain a continuous development of expertise. A lifelong stable career is far out of date and workers need to posses an enormous amount of flexibility. Nowadays, it is important to develop the capability to maintain a high level of performance under changing circumstances. This is also true (and must be learned and prepared for) for higher level jobs when a new workplace is found, also because of social change when one stays in the same place. This is why management and professionals should try to develop expertise as well as flexibility in the functioning of all workers.

While certain routines will be needed in every job, there is a growing need for people who are able to develop 'flexpertise' (van der Heijden and Boerlijst, 1996), the ability to maintain a certain amount of expertise under changing circumstances and in different situations. Lifelong learning implies developing the flexibility to learn new expertises and to enlarge the amount of circumstances and situations in which a person can maintain a certain standard of performance. When the organization has the disposal of 'flexperts' it can face the changing environment and the changing demands. The ageing of the population is not necessarily problematic when one keeps in mind that the key to success is a continuous attention to the development of this so-called 'flexpertise'; flexibility in combination with expertise.

The quality of functioning

Within the circle of top management of companies there is a widespread stereotypical opinion that the functioning of subordinates diminishes in quality as they grow older. On the other hand, findings from gerontological studies reveal that people who are not afflicted by any illness, handicap or stress, can continue to carry out their normal work for a long time without it undergoing any appreciable decline in quality (Munnichs and Uildriks, 1989).

It is not age, but it is the domain of activities which is the differentiating factor concerning the age-related changes in performance. In some fields ageing means that the larger amount of experience facilitates the solving of new problems encountered at work. In other domains, ageing means a decline in, for example, speed and quality of the workers' productivity. Overall, however, no clear evidence emerges of a universal age deficit in job performance, although older workers may be disadvantaged in particular kinds of jobs, for example, those requiring physical strength, speedy reactions, or close attention to visual detail. The range of performance variation is considerable, probably more so among older than younger workers, and in many cases older workers seem able to perform at least as well as, and sometimes better than, their younger employees (Davies *et al.*, 1991). Warr (1993) has compiled a veritable encyclopedia of available research results on the link between age and achievements in many kinds of fields and at various levels of work.

Figure R12.3
The quality of
over-40s' functions

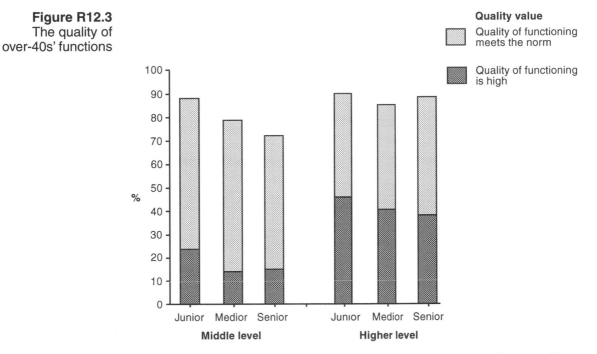

Our study shows that, as a rule, the quality of the functioning of the over-40s meets the norms set by their superiors (see Figure R12.3). This applies equally well to the effect or influence of the work performed by the over-40s inside and outside the organization. In so far as there are any age differences, these are not dramatically large. In some cases, the seniors, too, do no less well than their younger over-40 colleagues. There are, however, systematic differences between both function levels. Employees at the middle level on average achieve a slightly lower score than those at the higher level. Here too, however, one can state that it is not much lower. It can further be said that the work performed by the over-40s is mainly oriented to the employee's own organization. In general, it has a greater effect within the organization.

Mobility
- *Remaining very mobile* These employees have performed their present function for less than three years.
- *Remaining mobile* These employees have performed their present function for three to six years and . . . will probably change functions in the next five years.
- *Becoming mobile* These employees have performed their present function for seven years or longer.
- *Becoming immobile* These employees have performed their present function for less than three years.
- *Remaining immobile* These employees have performed their present function for three to six years.
- *Remaining very immobile* These employees have performed their present function for seven years or longer and . . . will probably *not* change functions in the next five years.

Figure R12.4
The mobility of
over-40s in
organizations

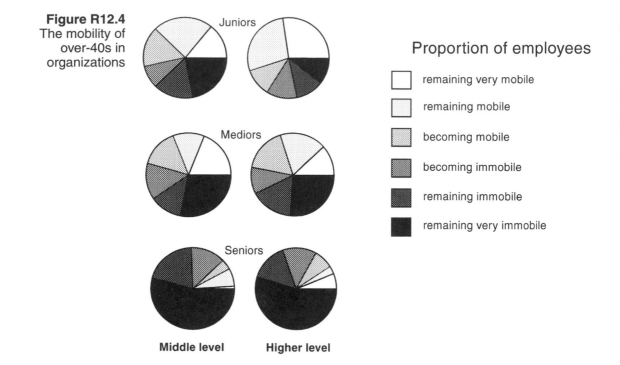

Figure R12.4 shows that *functional* mobility, meaning the transition to another position or function, by employees at the middle or higher levels of large- to medium-sized companies sharply declines from their 40th year onwards. Seven out of every eight employees over 50 have been in their present position for longer than seven years. Furthermore, in their superiors' opinion, they will no longer be employable elsewhere in the foreseeable future, either outside their own organization or within it. Among the younger over-40s, those between 40 and 46, the same applies to one in eight at the higher functioning level and two in eight at the middle level. This difference demonstrates the intensity and the speed at which older employees become set in their ways. In any case, it transpires that in the superiors' expectations, the perceived mobility and the employability of the over-40s studied is confined to a transition to functions 'close to home'. In other words: to functions within the employee's own department or organizational unit, and in the area of his or her own familiar expertise.

Remember the learning value of the function. It appears that for the over-40s at middle and higher functioning levels, the 'learning value' of their function is often minimal, which is probably the result of the fact that many people have performed this function for years on end without any drastic changes in their tasks, responsibilities or working environment. More highly educated over-40s are often over-specialized in the function area which they are familiar with, but the majority fail to measure up in other areas of skills and expertise. Thijssen (1992) has also observed this phenomenon, which he terms 'concentration of experiences', at lower function levels.

Training and development

In our study we have been able to ascertain that certain management activities help to promote the utility value of the functions as well as the quality and influence of the functioning of the over-40s. This is irrespective of the age and level of functioning of the over-40s concerned. On the other hand, we see that such activities are often not forthcoming, especially in the case of the seniors. In addition, these activities are often much less frequently allocated to the middle level than to the higher level. This form of relative neglect appears on all kinds of fronts, including in the area of the stimulation of training and development.

Without training and development, one will not get very far. In the business community, they occupy an increasingly more important position. Schools and other external vocational training courses are increasingly less able to turn out professional practitioners who are, comparatively soon after their arrival and without too many extras, capable of being productive and effective in a working environment. Moreover, business dynamics requires prompt adjustments to new developments and targets, and switching to new areas of know-how and experience. For employees in the organization this means that they cannot look forward to a more-or-less predictable working career from their school desks right up to retirement. Nowadays everyone should allow for the considerable likelihood of there being drastic changes of course in his or her own career. Companies should provide facilities for this, whether they like it or not. Retraining and in-service courses are both indispensible and unavoidable.

The costs of training and development programmes are high. It is entirely understandable that the management of work organizations feels little inclined to invest in these if there is no certainty of sufficient yield. There are very few training programmes for which the revenue begins to flow in, as it were, the day after their completion. More usually a great deal of time is involved, certainly in the case of training programmes in complex and new areas of knowledge.

The starting point and the duration of a training and development course during a career are not neutral issues for management or for the employees in question either. The time still remaining for the recovery of the costs of investment in individual training and the efforts involved, are critical factors in the consideration as to whether to start or not. It is not likely that people will be overkeen to offer new training perspectives to employees with retirement in sight. Moreover, the seniors concerned will most likely not be highly motivated to start on a new and possibly tricky training course if no personal or commercial profit can be expected.

The current practice of early retirement schemes probably does nothing to improve the situation. It is obvious that such provisions will result in employees being 'written-off' for further training sooner rather than later. In short, we may expect that seniors will be given less opportunity to follow training and development courses and that they themselves will deploy fewer initiatives than their younger colleagues.

There are also counterforces. If seniors occupy a function which is of vital importance for the company and which would soon devalue if they did not 'keep up-to-date' or 'keep pace with the times', then it is obvious that training and development courses will be embarked on after all and the argument of 'cost recovery' will be less relevant. Let us see whether these expectations are confirmed by the study data. We will stay close to home by at first limiting ourselves to training and development courses in the field in which the employee currently functions: his or her 'own' territory. In Figure R12.5 we have recorded the data relating to one recent time-period (1990–1991), assuming that even superiors who have known their subordinates for a relatively short period have provided reliable information on this[3].

There are no differences between the middle and the higher level for the

Figure R12.5
Participation in training and development in over-40s' own field

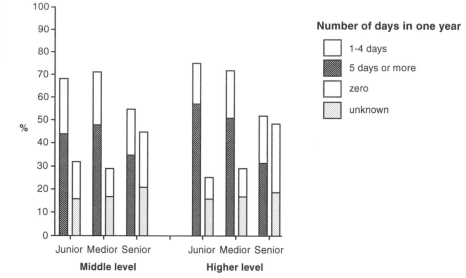

percentage of participation in training and development courses in one's own field. The proportion of rather longer courses is greater than that of the shorter ones. This, too, applies all the way across the board. There is, however, a gap between juniors and mediors on the one hand, and seniors on the other: the percentage of employees who have not followed any training or development course at all is significantly higher among the seniors and the share of longer courses is substantially lower than in the younger age categories.

If we examine this data over a longer period, we see that non-participation in courses is largely a phenomenon that is structurally person- (or function?-) related. Approximately 20% of the juniors and mediors and 25% of the seniors have never participated in any sort of training activity during the last five years. At the higher level, these 'structural' percentages are somewhat lower among juniors and mediors (10% and 15% respectively), but higher among the seniors (30%). All in all, we can ascertain that the older section of the over-40s are much less favoured with courses in their own field than the younger section. In the case of courses in a different field, the number of days involved is much smaller. At least 65% of the over-40s are not, or hardly ever, given (or take advantage of) the opportunity to do this.

Again in figure R12.6 there is no systematic difference between both function levels, and also there are no significant differences between the three age levels. The mean number of days spent on courses or training in a different function area is much lower than the number spent in the 'home area'. In so far as participation in such training programmes in another function area occurs at all, the mean number of days spent and the proportion of longer training courses are much lower than with courses in their own territory. We see, then, that training and development courses for the over-40s concentrate primarily on their own function area. There, as one grows older, participation in courses and such like decreases, as was our previous assumption. Courses in other function domains are only seldomly undertaken by over-40s in general.

The number of days per year that is devoted to further personal development of employees, not to function-oriented courses, is zero for over

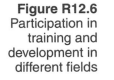

Figure R12.6
Participation in
training and
development in
different fields

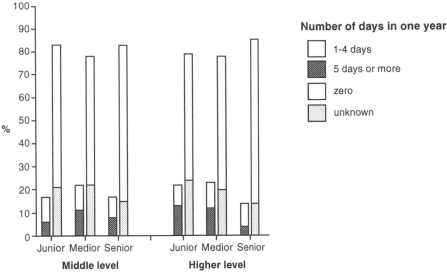

55% of employees. Only at the higher level can a decline be traced in the higher age groups. In general, the training courses in question are of shorter duration (see Figure R12.7).

From a comparison between the participation in training courses last year and the annual average for the past five years, we may conclude that whether or not to participate is to some degree person-related (or possibly function-related). (Figure R12.7) Anyone who acquires the taste, stays in the running. Anyone who makes no effort, will persevere in this. The annual number of days devoted to courses is also, to a certain extent, person-related. There are typical 'short' and 'long' course participants.[4] Moreover, the fact is that anyone taking part in training courses in his or her own function area is also given the opportunity or opts more often for training courses in a different area (which, as stated earlier, occur much less frequently).

Figure R12.7
Time devoted to
personal
development of
over-40s

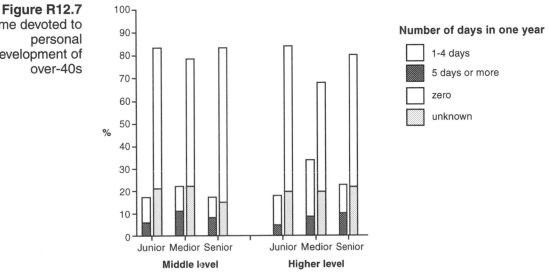

**General
conclusion
and evaluation**

From our study we conclude that working over-40s do not seem to have serious problems with their present function or position, insofar and as long as this function stays indispensable or essential for their organization. As a matter of fact, most over-40s *have* a rather essential function and have fulfilled this job for quite a long time. Besides, supervisors are of the opinion that most over-40s (seniors also) are performing quite satisfactorily.

However, when an over-40s function becomes obsolete or superfluous, chances that the person in question is at a loss are quite high, since most over-40s, seniors a lot more than juniors or mediors, are simply not equipped at all for other functions outside their own well-known territory. In other words, they lack the skills and expertise needed for other fields outside the immediate scope of their present job. They cannot be put in other positions without serious losses of time and money, and in that sense they are evaluated by their management as being immobile.

In this respect the organization of the work related to the age of the employee is very important. We can conclude that nowadays obsolescence and overcompensation are not compensated sufficiently by measures such as job rotation, training, etc. It is not all guaranteed that the older worker is capable to attain a level of functioning that is high enough. The attitudes of the management and the employees have to change in order to put into action more effective programmes, because there are many instances in which the positive potential of the older worker are usable (Sheppard, 1990; Dennis, 1988). The measures that are taken are too small and not suited to motivations and to the principles of learning by older adults (Thijssen, 1992).

An ongoing career development is possible when initiatives both from the management as well as from the employee him or herself are brought into action. A worker who has an increasing need for job security and a growing fear of obsolescence might be helped by updating old skills and learning new ones or by giving that person a role in 'mentoring' younger employees. But any organizational response to the needs of middle-aged people should occur with an awareness of the great diversity among individuals. Some will need change while others will need stability. Career development is a complex process influenced by many factors. Individual characteristics interact with social-environmental characteristics to shape the decisions of the person.

It is very important that the psychological research of adult learning starts paying attention to the question of how individuals learn expertise and develop work-related wisdom and which factors influence this development. When one knows more about the processes that take place when people become familiar with a certain field or domain of expertise and the factors that influence these processes, one can guide individual development (van der Heijden and Boerlijst, 1996).

Notes

1 'Medior' is a neologism, meaning something like 'more in the middle'.

2 We were not in the position to control the randomization process in great depth. Most sampling preparations were done by personnel departments. Although we do not have the impression that they intentionally violated the given sampling prescriptions, we cannot be sure of lack of any bias.

3 At the M-level the supervisors in question have a supervisory relationship of only two years or less with approximately 40% of the over-40s. At the H-level, this percentage is even higher: about 50%.

4 The correlations between the number of course days in the past year (1990–1991) reported by the supervisor and the yearly average for the past five years, both for training courses in one's own or in a different function area and for training courses geared to personal development are in the order of r =.40/.50.

References

Belbin, E. and S. Shimmin (1964) 'Training the middle aged for inspection work', *Occupational Psychology*, **38** (1), 49–57.

Boerlijst, J. G., B. I. J. M. Van der Heijden and A. Van Assen (1994) *Veertig-plussers in de onderneming* (Over-forties on the organization), 2nd edn, Van Gorcum, Amsterdam/Assen.

Boerlijst-Bosch, E. F. (1962) *Binnenkort met pensioen. Een onderzoek onder 60 aanstaande gepensioneerden*, Philips, Eindhoven.

Dalton, G. W. and P. H. Thompson (1971) 'Accelerating obsolescence of older engineers', *Harvard Business Review*, **4**, 57–67.

Davies, D. R., G. Matthews and C. S. K. Wong (1991) 'Ageing and work', in: C. L. Cooper and I. T. Robertson (eds.), *International Review of Industrial and Organizational Psychology*, **6**, Wiley, Chicester.

Dennis, H. (1988) *Fourteen steps in managing an ageing workforce*, D. C. Heath and Company, Lexington, Mass.

Dubin, S. S. (1971) *Professional obsolescence*, D. C. Heath and Company, Lexington, Mass.

Griew, S. (1964) *Job re-design*, OECD, Paris.

Kaufman, H. G. (1974) *Obsolescence and professional career development*, Amacom, New York.

Kaufman, H. G. (1975) *Career management: A guide to combating obsolescence*, IEEE Press, New York.

Munnichs, J. M. A. (1966) *Oudere werknemers, een verkennende studie*, Commissie Opvoering Produktiviteit/Sociaal-Economische Raad, Gravenhage.

Munnichs, J. M. A., J. M. Dirken, N. J. P. Dohmen, and H. Thierry (1986) *Leeftijd en bedrijfsbeleid*, **52**, NederlandseVereniging voor Bedrijfspsychologie, H. E. Stenfert Kroese, Leiden.

Munnichs, J. and G. Uildriks (1989) *Psychogerontologie: een inleidend leerboek over ouder worden, persoonlijkheid, zingeving, levensloop en tijd, sociale context, gezondheid en interventie*, Van Loghum Slaterus, Deventer.

Rosen, B. and T. H. Jerdee (1976) 'The nature of job-related stereotypes', *Journal of Applied Psychology*, **61**, 180–3.

Sheppard, H. L. (1990) *The future of older workers*, International Exchange Center on Gerontology, University of South Florida, Tampa, FL.

Stagner, R. (1985). 'Ageing in industry', in J. E. Birren, and K. W. Schaie (eds.), *Handbook of the psychology of ageing*, 2nd edn, 798–817, Prentice-Hall, Englewood Cliffs, New Jersey.

Thijssen, J. G. L. (1992) *Ervaringsconcentratie: Drempel voor kwalificatievernieuwing in de tweede loopbaanhelft, Gedrag en Organisatie, 5de jaargang*, **5**, 428–47.

van der Heijden, B. I. J. M. and J. G. Boerlijst (1996) *Life-long expertise development: goal of the nineties*, Proceedings of the Fifth Conference International Human Resource Management, June 24–28, San Diego, California.

Warr, P. (1993) 'Age and employment', in M. Dunnette, L. Hough and H. Triandis (eds.), *Handbook of Industrial and Organizational Psychology*, **4**, 485–550, Consulting Psychologists Press, Palo Alto.

Managing workforce diversity

Aminu Mamman

That almost every workplace is diverse is a fact few will dispute. What is in doubt however, is the ability of organizations and their members to cope with diversity. In spite of the potential benefits of diversity, it is common knowledge that many managers do not appreciate nor respect dissimilarity in needs, attitudes and behaviour of people in the workplace (Powell, 1993). As a result organizational structures, systems and practices do not take diversity into account (Copeland, 1988). Failure to know how to successfully manage diversity has forced some employers to avoid hiring minorities altogether (Jones, 1992). In line with the above observations, this reading suggests ways which employees can adjust to the growing diversity of the workforce. Also, how organizations can manage workforce diversity will be presented. Perhaps it is worth pointing out that, in this paper the term culture is used in its broadest sense to include norms, values and tradition, of a society as well as socio-psychological predisposition that can influence behaviour during interaction. This conceptualization is necessary given the definitions of diversity advanced here.

Definitions and concepts

In its basic form, diversity refers to the variety of gender, age, race and cultural backgrounds of employees in the workplace. There is growing realization however, that diversity encompasses various dimensions/characteristics of the workforce. For example, Taylor Cox, recently argued that:

> (*1*) diversity is a description of the total workforce not a name for members of minority groups: (*2*) diversity must be distinguished from related concepts such as affirmative action and race research while at the same time preserving the legitimacy of these topics: (*3*) diversity is best examined on multiple levels of analysis (Cox, 1994: 51).

Most recently McNerney (1994) argues that workforce diversity includes sexual orientation, physical (dis)ability, attitudes, work styles and functional roles. Similarly, Laudicina (1993) includes educational level and socio-economic status as some of the elements that constitutes workforce diversity. In the same vein, Jackson (1992) includes other categories of employees such as retirees and contract workers in his conceptualization of workforce diversity.

It is clear from the current conceptualizations that almost every workforce is diverse. However, not all managers are aware of the extent of diversity of their workforce nor its potential costs and benefits. Hence, commitment to managing diversity tends to vary across organizations (Cox and Blake, 1991). Jackson *et al.*, (1992) conceptualized organizational commitment to diversity in terms of the extent to which

1 contributions and interests of all stakeholders of the organization are

Figure R13.1
Key components of
managing diversity

**Meeting diverse,
needs of diverse workforce**
e.g.
- Familycare
- Work hours
- Accomodation
- Benefits and reward

CONTEXT

Valuing differences
e.g.
- Culture
- Race
- Age
- Gender
- (Dis)ability
- Psychological disposition
- Country of origin
- Work style
- Profession
- Employment contract
- Tenure

Developing structure,
culture, systems and
policies to accomodate
diversity

Benefits of
diversity

**Providing equal
opportunity for all**
e.g.
- Recruitment

CONTEXT

**Meeting diverse
needs of diverse workforce**
e.g.
- Familycare
- Work hours
- Accomodation
- Benefits and reward
- Selection
- Promotion
- Reward
- Placement
- Training

CONTEXT

reflected in the organization's mission, operations, and products or service,
2 the organization is committed to the removal of all forms of social
   oppression in the workplace,
3 diverse cultural and social groups actively participate in the decisions that
   shape the organization,
4 the organization is actively involved in eradicating all forms of social
   oppression in the wider community.

Managing diversity is about identifying and meeting the diverse needs of all
employees in the workforce. According to Jenner (1994), managing diversity
has three components. The first component concerns meeting employees'
quality of worklife needs, such as childcare, flexible work design and hours
of work. The second component relates to valuing differences such as race,
culture, gender, ability and age. The third component focuses on equal
opportunity in areas such as recruitment, training and promotion. Jenner's
conceptualization is illustrated in Figure R13.1.

Employee adjustment in a diverse workforce

Failure to adjust to the growing diversity of the workforce can result in conflict, low productivity, absenteeism and turnover. This section addresses some of the key socio-psychological factors that can influence employee adjustment in a diverse workforce.

It is widely agreed that the acquisition and use of knowledge can influence the process and outcome of social interaction (Gudykunst, 1988; Mendenhall, and Oddou, 1986). It has been argued that people process information through categorization which is, to a certain degree, culturally determined (Gertsen, 1990). Therefore experts argue that when people acquire knowledge of different cultures and social groups, the way they process and use information is likely to be effective during social interaction (Detweiler, 1975).

Implications for human resource management (HRM)

In a diverse workforce, knowledge of differences between and within groups will be useful during social interaction. Indeed even within the same culture, attitudes and behaviour between men and women and between old and young sometimes differ (Segall *et al.*, 1990). Apart from the acquisition of knowledge of national culture, knowledge of organizational culture and group norms can also enhance employee interaction adjustment. The significance of acquisition of knowledge has implications for training, recruitment and selection, job design and organizational structure. For example, organizations' training efforts should incorporate cross-cultural training and sensitivity training. Training programmes which focus on tasks and technical skills alone would be inadequate for organizations operating with diverse workforces. Given that workforce diversity has the potential of creating conflict and stress within the workforce, conflict resolution and stress management training should be a key part of the organization's training effort. As an incentive to encourage employees to acquire knowledge of others' culture, reward systems should recognize employee's ability to acquire knowledge of diverse groups. To exploit the benefits of diversity, job design should take into account the needs of the diverse workforce. To ensure better understanding of each other, experts argue that jobs should be designed to encourage interaction between diverse groups (Pettigrew and Martin, 1987). Organizational structure can enhance or hinder interaction of people in the workplace. Highly bureaucratic organizational structure is likely to limit face-to-face interaction given that people are less likely to use face-to-face methods of communication. The importance of knowledge of others' backgrounds has an implication for selection. For example, selection techniques and criteria should take into account a candidate's ability to accurately interpret other people's behaviour.

Rules governing social behaviour vary within and across social groups. Hence the significance of demonstrating 'socially appropriate' behaviour in a new setting has been advocated (Mendenhall and Oddou, 1986). Some of the behavioural dimensions that can enhance interaction adjustment as identified by researchers are:

1 The ability to establish inter-personal relationships. This consists of the ability to develop and maintain satisfying inter-personal relationships with 'strangers', accurately understand their feelings, effectively work with them, empathize and effectively deal with their different social customs;

2 The ability to effectively communicate. This includes the ability to enter into meaningful dialogue, initiate interaction and deal with

misunderstandings and inter-personal conflict and different communication styles (Hammer, 1987).

Workforce diversity would require employees to demonstrate appropriate behaviour relevant to the backgrounds of the diverse workforce. Rather than acquiring new values, a diverse employee could acquire new social skills for use in the work setting and discard them if need be (Furnham and Bochner, 1986). As already pointed out, acquisition of knowledge is not enough to guarantee effective functioning in a diverse workforce, therefore, training programmes should provide the opportunity to acquire the social skills necessary for interaction with people from diverse backgrounds. Role play on conflict resolution and intercultural conflict can help in developing social skills. Employees' prior experience with diverse workforces can be used as case studies during training. Organizations can encourage the acquisition of relevant social skills by rewarding employees who can demonstrate the ability to work with people from diverse backgrounds. Organizations can quicken the acquisition of social skills by organizing cultural and social activities. Here employees should be encouraged to interact and openly display their cultural heritage. It is very likely that not all employees will be keen to or capable of learning other people's culture. Such people can be assigned to jobs that do not require constant interaction with the diverse workforce or diverse customers.

Researchers argue that the acquisition and demonstration of socially appropriate skills should be complemented with the right attitude and personality (Brislin, 1981; Ruben, 1976). This is because strangers may face situations which will demand unique attitudes and traits. Among the personality and attitudinal factors are flexibility, self-confidence, self-efficacy, openness, motivation, orientation to knowledge, cultural empathy, openness to information and optimism.

Effective functioning in a diverse workforce will require employees to possess specific attitudes. For example, employees would need empathy to appreciate others' attitudes and behaviours. Without empathy, an employee is likely to misinterpret others' attitudes and behaviour. This can result in inter-personal conflict and psychological stress which may lead to low productivity, absenteeism and low turnover. Similarly, motivation to acquire knowledge of other people's background can quicken adjustment in a diverse work setting. Organizations can attempt to moderate employees' attitudes towards diversity through its training programmes and reward system. Employees should not be forced to change their attitudes but encouraged to moderate them and respect others' attitudes. Organizations can exploit the benefits of diversity by assigning employees to jobs that suit their personality rather than forcing them to change their personality to suit the job. This is based on the assumption that in most organizations there are enough jobs to suit a wide range of personalities. Indeed it can be argued that it may be easier to assign people to jobs that suit their personality than change people to suit the job. It is worth noting that the broader range of personality is likely to suit this age of discontinuous change and diverse clients. Indeed experts have already argued against organizational culture that puts too much emphasis on 'conformity to narrow attitude and behaviour'. This is because such behaviour can entrap the workforce in a mindset that can create resistance to change. Diversity of personalities could create a situation where the organization is not trapped in a mindset that hinders exploitation of opportunities.

People who have had prior experience in a foreign setting are more likely to find it easier to adjust to an unfamiliar environment than those who do not (Black *et al.*, 1991). Thus, employees' prior experience with workforce diversity can enhance their interaction adjustment. Similarly, an employee's tenure in the workplace could affect his or her interaction adjustment. This is because research indicates that adjustment in a new environment is influenced by the duration of stay in the new setting (Dodd, 1982). The longer one stays or is expected to stay in the new environment the more likely it would be that he or she will put an extra effort into learning to adjust to the environment (Dodd, 1982).

Given the potential benefits of experience, employees would need to acquire experience of interacting with people from diverse backgrounds. This can be acquired within and outside the workplace. An organization can ensure effective management of its diverse workforce by selecting applicants on the basis of technical skill as well as prior experience in working with a diverse workforce. And organizations can encourage employees to acquire the experience of dealing with people from diverse backgrounds within and outside the workplace. Recognizing and rewarding such experience can encourage employees to acquire more experience.

Given that certain categories of employees still experience negative stereotypes, prejudice and outright discrimination in the workplace, the next section recommends some strategies for interacting with people who may harbour negative attitudes toward an employee.

Dealing with stereotype, prejudice and discrimination in the workplace

Managing others' attitudes is based on

● uncertainty reduction theory,
● contact theory and
● organizational socialization literature. The theoretical background will be presented followed by the proposed strategies.

According to Gudykunst (1988) uncertainty reduction is a cognitive construct that relates to the capability of individuals to foresee and explain their own behaviour and that of others during social interaction. Uncertainty is caused by the lack of knowledge of each other, and this can lead to negative attitudes and behaviour. Hence, reducing uncertainty has been found to be central to intercultural effectiveness (Gudykunst, 1985; Witte, 1993).

According to Berger (1979), individuals use three strategies to reduce uncertainty about others. First, people use *passive* strategy to reduce uncertainty. This includes reading books, watching films and television, and observation in order to gain knowledge of the 'object' of uncertainty. Second, people use *active* strategy to reduce uncertainty. This strategy relies on asking others about the 'object' of uncertainty. Third, people use *interactive* strategy. This is when information about the 'object' is obtained through direct interaction with the 'object'. To Gudykunst (1988), reducing uncertainty would include correcting stereotypes, developing networks and favourable contacts, understanding and appreciating one's culture and that of others.

Implication   Lack of knowledge of others' backgrounds can lead to uncertainty and this may inspire negative attitudes and behaviour. Conversely, knowledge of others' backgrounds can reduce uncertainty and this may lead to accurate and positive stereotyping. Thus, acquisition of knowledge of others' attitudes and behaviour through various means, and attempting to use various methods to 'educate' others would improve employees' interaction adjustment in the workplace.

While uncertainty reduction theory lay emphasis on the *acquisition of knowledge* by all means (Berger, 1979), contact theory insists on the acquisition of knowledge through *direct contact* with the stranger. It is based on the idea that the more people get in contact with each other, the more they understand each other, this leads to gradual acceptance of differences between people. Hence, frequent contact has been argued to reduce negative perception and increase social acceptability (Dodd, 1982).

Implication   Sometimes, direct contact will be the only effective way to reduce uncertainty that may exist between diverse groups. For example, this may happen when one party has no other reliable source of knowledge about the other. Given that some groups may hold inaccurate stereotypes about an employee's background, and may be reluctant to take the initiative to learn more about his or her backgrounds, it will be helpful if the employee took the initiative to provide accurate information about his or her backgrounds through direct contact.

The literature on organizational socialization indicates that to be successful in adapting to the new environment an employee should either 'change' him or herself or the situation (Dawis and Lofquist, 1984). Nicholson (1984) proposed that organizational socialization tactics can take the form of:

● changing neither oneself or the situation (*replication*);
● changing self not the situation (*absorption*);
● changing the situation not self (*determination*);
● changing self and the situation (*exploration*).

Empirical evidence supports the above propositions. For example, writing on coping strategies for gay and lesbians in the workplace, Lucas and Kaplan (1994) note three strategies: First, the *staying in the closet strategy*. Here 'Closeted employees feel that they have no choice but to avoid talking about their personal life at the workplace for fear of giving themselves away'. Lucas and Kaplan (1994), suggest that such people often lie to protect themselves and often face ethical dilemmas which result in psychological stress. Second, the *coming out strategy*. Employees who adopt this strategy often reveal their sexuality in the same way heterosexuals do. According to Lucas and Kaplan, people who use this strategy feel empowered, honest, valued and connected. However, as the authors admit, this strategy is not without risk. Third, the *avoiding the issue strategy*. Employees who use this strategy avoid dealing with the issue. They tend to become vague, distant professionals who isolate themselves from close relationships with co-workers, team members, and mentors. 'Such people tend to be aloof at work, they steer clear of situations in which they might reveal the everyday information people typically share with co-workers. If they do participate in informal discussions, they try to redirect attention away from themselves' (Lucas and Kaplan, 1994: 37). Also, studies by Hall (1986, 1989) on the coping strategies of lesbians in an organizational setting supports Lucas and Kaplan's categorization (1994).

In a study of inter-racial dynamics between African-Americans and White Americans, Thomas (1993) found that the groups used two strategies for interaction: (*a*) denial and suppression and (*b*) direct engagement. In the former, the parties behave as if racial differences do not exist, while in the latter the parties openly discuss their racial differences. Thomas maintains that the effectiveness of the strategy will vary with the situation. In other words, both strategies can be appropriate when used contextually (for example, when both parties prefer to use an identical strategy).

Implication Managing others' attitudes and behaviour should be 'pragmatic' and 'evolutionary'. An employee would need to assess when it is appropriate to attempt to change others' attitudes and when to accommodate them. For example, carefully deciding on the stage of entry in the organization when it is appropriate to use a particular strategy would be essential.

The literature and propositions reviewed above can be summarized into three practical strategies.

Strategy One When faced with negative attitudes the employee should ignore them or try to avoid situations that may lead to experiencing such attitudes. This strategy is based on the assumption that there are situations when the employee cannot correct others' attitudes and behaviour, in the short term at least. For example, this can happen when the interaction between them is infrequent; others are not receptive to his or her 'overtures'; they hold inflexible attitudes that seems unlikely to change; he or she has no knowledge of the causes of others' attitudes. Indeed, research evidence indicates that 'suppression' of socio-biological identity during inter-racial interaction is one of the strategies used by employees at the workplace (Lucas and Kaplan, 1994; Thomas, 1993).

Strategy Two Rather than avoiding negative attitudes or ignoring them, an employee should attempt to take corrective action whenever he or she experiences this. Indeed, such an approach has been argued to be a prerequisite for personal growth and development (Hellriegel *et al.*, 1989). By attempting to correct others' attitudes, the employee is helping to reduce uncertainty on both sides. This is because negative stereotypes are likely to be inspired by misinformation. Therefore an employee should take advantage of responding to others' attitudes by 'educating' them through provision of information concerning his or her backgrounds. This strategy can be appropriate if the employee has passed the early stage of entry; he or she occupies a lower position; interaction with others is infrequent; others appear to be receptive to his or her 'overtures'; he or she has some knowledge of the causes of others' attitudes.

Strategy Three Here, an employee is expected to initiate interaction in order to know more about others' attitudes and encourage them to know more about his or her background. An employee should take advantage of this interaction to correct any misconception, misinformation and negative stereotyping by educating others through the provision of accurate information. A person's motivation to interact with others has been argued to be a significant determinant of reducing anxiety (that is, fear of negative consequences of ineffectiveness) (Gudykunst, 1988; Witte, 1993). Therefore, an employee's willingness and ability to initiate interaction with others should improve the chance of reducing anxiety.

Like the previous strategies, the outcome of this strategy could depend on factors such as: the frequency of interaction, the position of the employee in the organizational hierarchy, knowledge of the causes of

Table R13.1
Summary of the
strategies for
managing perception
of an employee's
backgrounds

others' attitudes, level of intimacy, stage of entry, willingness to discuss
issues pertaining to an employee's background (Asante and Davies, 1989;
Dodd, 1982; Kahn *et al.*, 1964; Thomas, 1993). If others are willing to
discuss issues pertaining to an employee's background, strategy three
could be the most effective of the three. Table R13.1 provides a summary
of the three strategies.

Strategy	Description	Central assumptions	Example of situations	Probable level of effectiveness
Strategy one	Ignoring or avoiding those who display negative attitudes	Given the situation, the employee cannot make meaningful impact on others' attitudes	• Inflexible attitudes of others • Low frequency of contact • At the early stage of entry • Low receptivity on the part of others • Employee occupies lower position • Lack of knowledge of the causes of others' attitudes • Low level of intimacy	Low–Average
Strategy Two	Responding to those who display negative attitudes	Given the situation, the employee should attempt to change others' attitudes by responding only	• Others appear receptive • Some knowledge of the causes of others' attitudes • Has passed the entry stage • Interaction is frequent • Moderate level of intimacy	Average–High
Strategy Three	Taking action before a negative attitude is experienced	Given the situation, the employee should not wait until confronted by negative attitudes	• Others are receptive • High level of intimacy • High frequency of interaction • Occupies higher position • Has passed the early stage of entry • Full knowledge of the causes of others' attitudes	High

Conclusion

Perhaps one of the major tasks for organizations today is to identify
appropriate human resource management practices that suit their diverse
workforce. This conclusion echoes suggestions put forward by experts on
how to manage workforce diversity.

It is widely agreed that an employee's interaction adjustment and
subsequent integration in a diverse workforce can be influenced by
organizational factors such as the policy on equal opportunity, sexual
harassment, diversity training, flexible working hours, job design,
organizational culture, workforce profile etc. (Cox, 1991; Offermann and
Armitage, 1993). For example, Kanter (1977, 1990) and Cox (1991) argue
that the composition of the workforce can influence employee integration
and adjustment. The fewer the number of diverse employees the more
difficult it would be to adjust. In other words, the more heterogenous the
workforce, the more likely a diverse employee would find someone 'similar
to him or her' in the organization that can provide a role model, social and
moral support.

Many organizations have found that the benefits of diversity can
depend on the extent to which they are committed to train their

workforce on the value of diversity. For example, training employees to cope with the growing diversity of the workforce has been found to improve employee adjustment (Jackson *et al.*, 1992; Smith, 1994; Tung, 1993). Some organizational cultures tend to have a preferred management style and 'ways of doing things' which inadvertently exclude certain categories of people (such as women) from occupying senior positions (Marshall, 1993). Harris (1994) argues that cultures that are stable provides fertile ground for developing an effective diversity programme. This is because diversity programmes require organizational change and change requires time and 'stability' to bear fruit. Harris argues that volatile culture is characterized by high turnover which is not conducive for developing effective diversity programmes.

Some commentators argue that many women find their working hours highly inflexible (Herr Van Nostrand, 1993; Symons, 1992). This view has been widely used to explain the high turnover rate and low career progression among women. It also partly explains the high percentage of women in part-time jobs. Many organizations have responded to this by developing flexible working hours. Other organizational initiatives that can relate to employee adjustment is the extent to which an organization is committed to the eradication of discrimination and harassment.

To be successful in operating with a diverse workforce, some organizations have to undergo major transformations. Already experts have prescribed ways in which this can be achieved (Cox and Blake, 1991; Harris, 1994; Jackson *et al.*, 1992). First, top management needs to give strong support and genuine commitment to diversity. Second, diversity training programmes should be a key feature of an organization's training programme. Third, data related to diversity should be collected and analysed regularly. This should include data on equal opportunities, turnover across all groups of employees, etc. Fourth, there should be a comprehensive assessment of organizational culture, human resource management systems, promotion and appraisal systems, etc. This should uncover any potential sources of bias which may inadvertently disadvantage certain groups of employees. Finally, monitoring the changes and evaluating the results. It is perhaps worth noting that unlike most organizational change, this change strikes at the heart of societal values and beliefs, therefore it has to be handled extremely carefully. Otherwise, the consequences are likely to be grave indeed. Already, some commentators are attributing the current 'backlash' against affirmative action in the USA to the failure to address the issue sensitively and effectively.

References

Asante, M. K. and A. Davis (1989) 'Encounters in the interracial workplace', in Asante, M. K. and W. B. Gudykunst (eds.), *Handbook of international and intercultural communication*, Sage Publications, 375. London.

Berger, C. R. (1979) 'Beyond initial interactions', in H. Giles and R. St. Clair (eds.), *Language and Social Psychology*, 122–44, Edward Arnold, London.

Black, J. S., M. Mendenhall and G. Oddou (1991) 'Toward a comprehensive model of International Adjustment: An Integration of Multiple Theoretical Perspective', *The Academy of Management Review*, **16** (2), April, 291–317.

Brislin, R. (1981) *Cross-cultural Encounters: Face-to-Face Interaction*, Pergamon Press, New York.

Copeland, L. (1988) 'Valuing workforce diversity', *Personnel Administrator*, Nov.

Cox, T. (1991) 'The multicultural organization', *Academy of Management Executive*, **5** (2), 34–47.

Cox, T. (1994) 'A comment on the language of diversity', *Organization*, **1** (1), 51–8.

Cox, T and S. Blake (1991) 'Managing cultural diversity: implications for organizational competitiveness', *Academy of Management Executive*, **5** (3), 45–56.

Dawis, R. V. and L. H. Lofquist (1984) *A Psychological theory of work adjustment*, University of Minnesota Press, Minneapolis.

Detweiler, R. (1975) 'On inferring the intensions of a person from another culture', *Journal of Personality*, **43**, 591–611.

Dodd, C. H. (1982) *Dynamics of Intercultural Communication*, Wm C. Brown, New York.

Furnham, A. and S. Bochner (1986) *Culture shock: Psychological reactions to unfamiliar environment*, Routledge, London.

Gertsen, M. C. (1990) 'Intercultural Competence and Expatriates', *The International Journal of Human Resource Management* **1** (3), Dec., 341–62.

Gudykunst, W. B. (1985) 'The influence of cultural similarity, type of relationships, and self-monitoring on uncertainty reduction processes', *Communication Monographs*, **52**, 203–17.

Gudykunst, W. B. (1988) 'Uncertainty and Anxiety', in Y. Y. Kim, and W. B. Gudykunst, (eds.), *Theories in Intercultural Communication*, Sage Publications, Newbury Park, CA. 123–56.

Hall, M. (1986) 'The lesbian corporate experience', *Journal of Homosexuality*, **12** (3/4), 59–75.

Hall, M. (1989) 'Private experiences in the public domain: lesbians in organizations', in J. Hearn; D. L. Sheppard, P. Tancred-Sheriff and G. Burrell (1989) (eds.), *The sexuality of organization*, Sage Publications, London, 125–38.

Hammer, M. R. (1987) 'Behavioural dimensions of intercultural effectives: a replication and extension', *International Journal of Intercultural Relations*, **11**, 65–88.

Harris, A. (1994) 'Breaking the glass ceiling for senior executives', *Human Resource Focus (HR Focus)*, March 1994, 1–5.

Hellriegel, D., J. W. Slocum, and R. W. Woodman (1989) *Organizational Behaviour*, 5th edn., West Publishing Company, New York.

Herr Van Nostrand, C. (1993) *Gender responsible leadership: Detecting bias implementing interventions*, Sage Publications, Newbury Park, CA.

Jackson, S. E. (1992) 'Team composition in organizational settings: Issues in managing an increasing diverse workforce', in S. Worchel. W. Wood. J. A. Simpson (eds.), *Group process and productivity*, Sage Publications, Newbury Park, CA.

Jackson, B., W. F. Lafasto, H. G. Schultz, and D. Kelley (1992) 'Diversity', *Human Resource Management*, Spring/Summer, **31** (1&2) 21–34.

Jenner, L. (1994) 'Diversity management: What does it mean?' *Human Resource Focus*, Jan., 9.

Jones, F. L. (1992) *Sex and ethnicity in the Australian Labour Market: the immigration experience*, Australian Bureau of Statistics (occasional paper). AGPS, Canberra.

Kahn, R. L., D. M. Wolfe, R. P. Quinn and J. D. Snock (1964) *Organizational Stress*, Wiley, New York.

Kanter, R. M. (1977) *Men and Women in the Corporation*, Basic Books, New York.

Kanter, R. M. (1990) 'Token Women in the corporation', in J. Heeren and M. Mason (eds.), *Sociology: Windows on Society*, Roxebury, Los Angeles.

Laudicina, E. V. (1993) 'Diversity and Productivity: Lessons from the corporate sector', *Public Productivity and Management Review*, **XVI** (1), Summer, 457–63.

Lucas, J. H. and M. G. Kaplan (1994) 'Unlocking the corporate closet', *Training and Development*, Jan., 35–8

Marshall, J. (1993) 'Organizational cultures and Women managers: Exploring the dynamics of resilience', *Applied Psychology: An International Review*, **42**, (4), 313–22.

McNerney, D. (1994) 'Competitive Advantage: Diverse Customers and Stakeholders', *Human Resource Focus*, June, 9–10.

Mendenhall, M. and G. Oddou (1986) 'Acculturation Profiles of Expatriates Managers: Implications for Cross-Cultural Training Programs', *Colombia Journal of World Business*, Winter, 73–9.

Nicholson, N. (1984) 'A theory of work role transitions', *Administrative Science Quarterly*, **29**, 172–91.

Offermann, L. R. and M. A. Armitage (1993) 'Stress and the Woman Manager: Sources, health outcomes, and interventions', in E. A. Fagenson (ed.), *Women in Management: Trends, Issues, and Challenges in Managerial Diversity*, Sage Publication, **25**, 131–61.

Pettigrew, T. F. and J. Martin (1987) 'Shaping the organizational context for Black American inclusion', *Journal of Social Issues* **43** (1), 41–78.

Powell, G. (1993) *Women and Men in Management*, 2nd edn, Sage Publications, Newbury Park, CA.

Ruben, B. D. (1976) 'Assessing communication competency for intercultural adaptation', *Group and Organizational Studies*, **1**, 334–54.

Segall, M. H., P. R. Dasen, J. W. Berry, Y. H. Poortinga (1990) *Human Behaviour in Global Perspective*, Pergamon Press, UK.

Smith, J. M. (1994) 'Sexual Orientation: Training can help to promote tolerance', *Human Resource Focus*, Jan., 12.

Symons, G. L. (1992) 'The glass ceiling is constructed over the gendered office', *Women in Management Review*, **7** (1), 18–22.

Thomas, D. A. (1993) 'Racial Dynamics in Cross-race Developmental Relationships', *Administrative Science Quarterly*, **38**, 169–94.

Tung, R. L. (1993) 'Managing Cross-National and Intra-National Diversity', *Human Resource Management*, Winter **32** (4), 461–77.

Witte, K. (1993) 'A theory of cognition and negative affect: extending Gudykunst and Hammer's theory of uncertainty and anxiety reduction', *International Journal of Intercultural Relations*, **17**, 197–215.

Pilkington

Ken Starkey and Alan McKinlay

Pilkington Brothers is one of the world's largest producers of glass and related products such as insulation material. The company entered the 1980s with a growing number of problems. Its privileged position of near-monopoly command of the glass market had been drastically eroded by competition, so much so that by the end of the 1970s its market share had dropped from a high of 80% to 50% of the UK glass business. It was also experiencing production-cost problems associated with inefficient and non-competitive working practices in its other core business—insulation material manufacture. 1980–82 saw two years of steady losses in the UK. Major readjustments were obviously necessary in management practices to meet changing market conditions and, because the company has lost the technological edge it once enjoyed with the elapsing of its float glass licensing rights, changes in working practices were also needed to make the most efficient use of a technology it now shared with its major competitors.

The company had to come to terms with the reality of new competition and the steady deterioration in its market share. Pilkington's problems reflected those of the British economy generally in a time of acute recession. Two major external forces have influenced the rate of change. The decline of the British motor industry has had major repercussions on its glass business and the loss of government financial support for home insulation programmes has profoundly affected the insulation business. The effects of the changes—in management strategy, structure, culture and in working practices—initiated in the first half of the 1980s are still working their way through the company but are already reflected in significant steps back to competitiveness. Improved results reflect the effects of cost reduction and productivity gains in traditional manufacturing areas due to rationalization and manpower reduction, cost cutting, and strict control on capital expenditure, limiting it to essential projects and working capital.

This has been achieved despite over-capacity in traditional markets, strong competition and the continuing depressed state of the building industry and the British car industry. In all business areas manufacturing capacity is now better matched to market demand. The focus of attention throughout the company is now on improving plant yields, plant utilization, and margins in highly competitive market environments.

Changes in work organization have been accompanied by major managerial changes. There has been significant reshaping of the Group both through acquisition and internal reorganization. This saw major changes of strategic direction in the diversification away from traditional products and markets and geographical diversification most notably into the USA. There have been important developments in the downstream side of the glass business with a new emphasis on value-added products as opposed to the previous concentration on flat glass. Business policy now aims at retaining two-thirds of the Group's activity in its core glass and insulation businesses while expanding new growth areas in electro-optical and ophthalmic glass.

A key element of the change process has been the attempt to inculcate a new managerial culture. One result of pre-1980s attitudes in management had been a high degree of bureaucratization and functionalization, the major dysfunctional consequence of which, in the markedly different market environment of the 1980s, was a lack of business focus. Managerial expertise was mainly concentrated on technical facets of the business—technical excellence for its own sake. Actual business expertise, in the 'entrepreneurial, cutting costs, getting things done' sense was low. The development of this expertise was a key element in the change strategy. The company emphasized the importance of a marketing focus—that making and selling are its 'life-blood'.

> Now the only way to get an edge on the competition is to emphasize the marketing end. But that is easier said than done if you have a company with a long tradition that based its success on operating complex plants. We almost need to grow a new breed of person.
>
> (*Financial Times*, 12 June 1985)

The company has become much more flexible to react quickly to customer requirements. This was reflected in a major restructuring of managerial responsibility with a reorganization of Group and board responsibilities and a new emphasis on decentralization. Operational and profit responsibility for budgeting, manufacturing, marketing, dividend policies and industrial relations was delegated to divisional chief executives. Most of the Group central committee structure was dismantled and decisions devolved to the operational level. Divisional reliance on the centre was minimized.

The need for cultural change was reflected in a major concern with personnel policy. The chairman, Antony Pilkington, emphasized the need to get 'our people situation right'. This was recognized as a business need. In its traditional operations Pilkington has always had a reputation for being a highly centralized company. In the 1980s centralization came to be associated with an over-reliance on the centre. A new departure was the decision to negotiate differently. New working practices negotiated at a greenfield site in the glass division could not be fitted into a central bargaining mould. Manning levels, for example, were to be very different to those in force at traditional plants. The principles underlying the negotiation of new working practices formed the basis of a change disseminated throughout the group. The central plank in all future negotiations was not to be the national agreement but an agreement based on the needs of particular sectors of the business analysed and responded to at the local level.

Personnel directors in the various divisions were offered a unique opportunity to make fundamental changes by negotiating according to their own particular market needs which were to be explained to their workforces in terms of that particular division's market position and not Pilkington Group's generally. The directive to divisional management from the board was that they relate whatever changes they thought necessary in work organization to their own particular business circumstances and not to the Group as a whole. The effort here was aimed at 'trying to break the culture thing they've had for years' (personnel director)—the recourse to the centre to solve all divisional problems and the reliance on central initiatives. For the Pilkington Board, the changes were associated with more realistic responses to market situations interpreted at the appropriate local level and also a different managerial culture, 'a different style of management, one in which the ball is pushed right down so that divisional managers became more accountable and responsible' (personnel director).

The company set itself the task of introducing innovations in working practices throughout the group. In particular, wage bargaining was decentralized. This decentralization initiative met with resistance from the unions. Despite prolonged negotiation and management's strong desire to negotiate the introduction of the new way of organizing resistance remained strong so that, ultimately, in 1983, decentralization of bargaining was imposed unilaterally over the unions' heads. An unintended consequence and major benefit of the prolonged negotiation and communication process involved in the attempt to arrive at agreement was that the understanding of the need for decentralization was accepted by the workforce despite union advice to the contrary. The main union argument against decentralization had been that it was a policy aimed at 'divide and rule'. The workforce, though, 'could see that they weren't just being divided or left. They could see the business starting to move away from them' (personnel manager) and consequently accepted the need for major changes. Key agents in the practice of implementation were line managers and shop stewards at site level who took responsibility for the negotiation and implementation of the new arrangements. Personnel managers took on the role of advisers, providing an enabling function, rather than an industrial-relations function.

The effects of this broader work reorganization can be clearly seen in the experiences of the Pilkington Insulation Division. What was exceptional here was the introduction of practices pioneered at a greenfield site into long-established factories with traditional working and pay-bargaining practices. Pilkington Insulation Division's business is predominantly UK-based principally because exporting insulation materials composed of trapped air is bad economics because it involves huge volumes for very little weight. The business is strongly affected, therefore, by the vagaries of the UK economy. There was rapid growth in the insulation market throughout the 1960s and 1970s with, at the end of the 1970s, an exponential scale of growth fuelled by the oil crisis arising from the policies of the OPEC cartel which caused energy costs to escalate. The UK government reacted with intervention in the insulation business by providing central grant aid for home insulation and, more important, finance for local authorities to embark on a major programme of insulation of local-authority properties. The insulation market at this time was characterized by under-capacity. Pilkington, as market leaders, sold their products at highly profitable prices.

In response to strong government pressure to expand capacity, a new plant was opened on the Ravenhead site. With such favourable market conditions two new UK competitors arrived in the market, setting up operations on greenfield sites, which meant that they had new working practices with low overheads and low-cost structures. But, in the short term, this did not pose a major threat to Pilkington.

However, in 1980, there was complete change around. As one senior manager put it: 'the world went mad'. The effects of oil-price stabilization and the deepening recession were exacerbated by a radical change in government policy. With the success of a Conservative government in the UK in the 1979 General Election the attitude to the public financing of energy conservation changed. Interventionism gave way to market forces. Grant aid was drastically reduced with the result that local authorities either dropped or greatly reduced their insulation programmes. The result was a massive slump in demand with huge overcapacity in the industry and heightened competition from the two new competitors who had to justify their high capital-intensive investments in terms of market share. Overcapacity, intense competition and a massive slump in demand led to intense downwards pressure on prices.

In 1979/80 the division made £20m in profit, almost doubling profits from the year before. Over the next 18 months it plunged to a dramatic loss of £12/13m. Standard responses aimed at reducing costs in energy and raw materials were implemented. Scope for these changes was soon exhausted. The next area to be examined was working practices. The fat times of the 1970s had bred overmanning to a large extent and a 'fairly soft' managerial approach. For instance, extensive demarcations had been allowed to develop with, in the craft area, large numbers of different mechanical trades without flexibility between them.

Three main measures were taken to reduce manufacturing costs: *capital investment* to transfer manually intensive processes on to continuous-process lines and investment in automatic handling technology; *rationalization* to bring capacity and costs more in line with the level of demand; and '*belt-tightening*' to reduce overmanning. At the main insulation works these measures led to a halving in numbers from 1800 to 900 over three years with the major reduction in the unskilled process workers. This rationalization was done by voluntary means.

These actions on manufacturing costs did not solve the division's problems. The issue turned out to be not just one of cost and capacity reduction. Major gains in this area were offset by a steady loss of market share. The company had tried to hold on to its market leadership posture and to keep prices high through marketing quality and service in an attempt to minimize the conflict in the industry so that competitors did not damage each other through a price-competition spiral. Its goal had been to keep prices stable rather than allowing them to drift down with competitive pressures. This strategy, in terms of market share, provided a marked failure. Pilkington market share fell from around 60% down to just over 40%, caused by the new competition establishing a position in the market, but also by competition generally exploiting the new market conditions to get share because Pilkington's were artificially trying to hold on to a high-price leadership posture.

1983 was a watershed for the division because it clearly could not go on losing market share to the extent it had been. The company decided that the only strategy still open was to exploit what impact it still had in the market and to engage in an outright price war. It adopted a much more aggressive marketing posture, the result of which was the beginning of an unrestricted price war. Prices fell by 30% in a six-month period in a high-asset industry with huge fixed costs. Finally prices stabilized when there was no longer a premium on undercutting. Pilkington market share started to pick up. The issue then became which company could support the lower prices best, which could adapt best to permanently lower realization from insulation manufacture.

Pilkington found that it was not them. Despite halving numbers employed, its sales revenue per employee was only £35 000 per year whereas its competitors' sales revenue per employee was between £55 000 and £65 000. It was clear that, despite all that had been accomplished in productivity, the company still had a long way to go in achieving efficiency.

The company's problems can be summarized as:

1 static-to-declining market demand, so no possibility of generating a bigger
   market;
2 unrelenting pressure on prices so that going for more share in an
   aggressive way was really just re-stimulating the price spiral;
3 £6 million of operating costs needed to achieve parity with its competitors
   and it had already pursued the obvious remedies open to it (capital
   investment, plant/process rationalization and belt-tightening). 'The only
   route left was a much more fundamental approach to people
   costs—structural solutions in other words, rather than simple trimming
   solutions' (personnel director).

The window of opportunity to introduce a fundamental restructuring of its
operations opened with the Pilkington Group decision to decentralize
collective bargaining. This presented the Division with a major opportunity
to overcome the inertia caused by central negotiations. The Division decided
to mount a major restructuring of jobs, working practices and rewards with
which to compete against companies that had all the advantages of
greenfield sites with highly efficient working practices and low-cost structures
in its own brownfield sites with their long-entrenched methods of working.

The broad objectives of the Insulation restructuring programme were: to
establish employment structures, systems and working practices aimed at
increased cost effectiveness in the use of human resources, based on a
stronger sense of site and business identity; to facilitate team-based
commitment to the objectives of the business and the elimination of artificial
divisions between employee groups; and to improve the quality of industrial
relations by changing attitudes.

The architecture for these changes was made up of: new job definitions to
enable optimum flexibility and mobility of employees; a single, integrated
pay structure for all employees below middle management based on
common job evaluation arrangements, participatively managed, and
multi-union negotiations on pay and conditions; a simple grading structure
with proper differentials and relativities. The basis for attitude change was to
be a commitment to a broad range of tasks in return for which the company
offered an annual salary without per occasion payments, harmonization of
terms and conditions, a pay structure that is simple to understand, common
to all groups and low on administration costs, computerized attendance
recording for all in order to support flexible working-time arrangements,
and a pay increase of 12%.

There were also three structural changes: fewer but bigger jobs with
greater responsibility and accountability; an emphasis on 'back to the line'
with fewer specialists; and fewer levels of accountability. 'Back to the line' was
critical as a means of reintroducing accountability for product quality and
for process conditions at the point of production and thus reducing the
need for indirect labour. It was also seen as a means of promoting individual
commitment. It also contributed to the overall goal of a leaner organization
with fewer levels and maximum flexibility and mobility of employees.

Flexibility was a key concept. It fell into three dimensions:

1 *Tackling the obvious* the development of mechanical/electrical craftsmen,
   the elimination of craftsmen's assistants and a simple three-level process
   structure (process operator, senior process operator and service
   attendant to replace the multiplicity of jobs;
2 *Addressing the not-so-obvious* the elimination of quality inspectors and the
   development of maintenance supervision to run the process to eliminate

on-line inspection and invest it back into the process operators, and the development of a multi-functional office structure (the introduction of an administrative job structure which transcends the functional specialism of such roles as supplies clerk, accounts clerk or salaries clerk);

3 *Enabling the future* the goal of a multi-disciplined process craftsman, the development of process workers in routine maintenance roles, using tools which had hitherto been the prerogative of craftsmen, and the elimination of craft supervision so that craftsmen become a self-supervising group.

The choice of implementation method for these new working practices is now seen as crucial in gaining acceptance for them by the workforce. The company saw itself faced with a choice:

> Whether to just whack an enormous package deal on the table, you know, Fawley, and recent versions of, or to actually do something more creative, to actually take our people and trade unions [and] sit round a table and develop the organizational changes and develop job structures as far as we could with them . . . we wanted people to open, to be open to the new structures. Perhaps most of all we wanted a process that was based on understanding business needs. If you say to somebody, 'Here's a package of changes and here's what you have to do and here's the extra money for them' you might well get them to do it but you don't get the understanding of why it's important. The understanding of why it was vital to us was the key for us . . . if we wanted to continue . . . and have it work and have it dynamic (personnel director).

The division entered into what it called its multi-union discussion plan. The focus of this centred upon the business plan rather than on changes in the forms of work organization that the company thought necessary. A major consultation exercise throughout the division focused on achieving cost competitiveness in enormous detail, so that a fundamental understanding of the economic problems was communicated to the workforce. The workforce gained an understanding of the necessary changes and the company gained outline agreement on a starting point for its change initiative and an objective.

Following this, discussions about the actual organization of work began. The unions were informed that the projected size of the workforce was to be around 600. Job structures were then analysed over a five-month period which included extensive discussion with the whole workforce. Job structure planning concentrated on the definition of the categories of jobs that the new principles of work organization required; 250 different jobs with their own job profiles were reduced to a final total of 60 new job definitions.

Having agreed a new framework the next stage was job analysis and job evaluation to flesh out the concept of the new work roles. Job-analysis teams were set up. They included one trade unionist and one manager responsible for translating the new job ideas into job definition in consultation with the shop-floor. In hindsight, these teams came to be construed as a vital element in affecting change. They 'preached the gospel, effectively selling this to the workforce and it was getting from the workforce a sense of realism too' (personnel director). Following this, job evaluation (also using multi-union-management teams and a team of management consultants) was used to match job to reward structures and create a new grading scheme. Between 7 and 8% of the workforce were actually members of the job-analysis teams or the job-evaluation panel and at various stages in this process the company stopped work to spend time (up to a week in total) briefing the whole workforce.

Payback was dramatic. Following the agreement in 1984, numbers reduced by the end of 1985 from 800 to 550. The target then was to reduce to 500 by the end of 1985/86. The actual reduction achieved was 470. Within 12 months there was recovery from £3.5m loss to £3.8 profit. A positive basis for future changes had also been established with the new negotiations structure providing a framework for ongoing change and establishing a style of operating and a receptivity to that form of involvement which the company believes will allow it to develop positive changes in the future. The process of implementation has forged a relationship with the workforce which is now far more aware of the impact of the organization's external environment. For labour there is the dual pay-off of enhanced job security and the extra pay that has accompanied the increase in productivity.

Questions

1   What were the environmental pressures affecting Pilkington?

2   Discuss the interrelationships between strategy, structure, culture and work organization that this case illustrates.

3   Discuss the changes in managerial orientation that changes in the company's external environment necessitated in Pilkington's search for renewed competitiveness.

4   What were the key elements of the company's strategy of getting 'its people situation right'?

5   Can you compare the changes at Pilkington to changes in other companies? What common features, if any, does such a comparison illuminate?

6   To what extent was change in corporate performance at Pilkington internally or externally determined?

Namibia Brewers Ltd

Karen Davies

Introduction

Namibia Brewers Ltd is an established firm, based in Namibia and selling its products throughout Botswana and South Africa. This brewery has decided to completely re-think its operating relationship with the local ecology and is reengineering itself to become a 100% environmentally friendly organization. Namibia Brewers Ltd is seen as one of the initial group of firms which have sought to position itself to take the ethical high ground as customers become increasingly aware of the costs of environmental damage.

Background to environmental concerns

Concern over environmental damage from manufacturing is not a new topic. The economist Thomas Malthus in his classic treatise *Essay on the Principle of Population* (1985) [1798] concluded that unless population was regulated, the misery of famine would become globally epidemic and eventually consume mankind. Malthus' view that poverty and famine were natural outcomes of population growth and food supply was not popular among social reformers who believed that with proper social structures and technological improvements, all the ills of mankind could be eradicated. Although Malthus' concepts were somewhat dire and ignored mankind's ability to use technologies to increase efficiency, similar soundings about the limits to our environment's ability to cope with inefficient economic growth are more frequent.

Damage to the environment has grown at an ever increasing rate during the 20th century. The statistics are worrisome. Over 70 species become extinct everyday. The average American produces twice his weight, daily, in waste. Deposits of oil, coal and gas are running low. Add to this that the global human population is predicted to rise to 8 billion by the year 2025 and some commentators suggest that the planet is fast moving towards 'environmental meltdown'.

The approach normally taken to protecting our environment is to look towards government to regulate on both a national and international level. Although this may have lead to some reduction in environmental damage, progress has been slow. Many argue that a rigid regulatory approach to such issues is not acceptable to the international business community and will be difficult to control and enforce.

At a corporate level, environmental lobbyists and pressure groups have been able to highlight selected organizations with poor environmental records. Although this process of negative publicity coupled with the threat of product boycotts has worked in a number of instances, many organizations faced with potentially large environmental problems are distancing themselves through subsidiary companies or possibly even 'outsourcing' the damaging components of their business portfolio. The late 1980s saw significant world-wide growth in concern among scientists, governments and consumers regarding a wide range of environmental and ecological issues such as pollution control, ozone depletion, recycling, renewable energy sources and waste management. The international community increasingly recognized these concerns and in 1987 the WCED Bruntland Report *Our Common Future*, put forward the first definition of what sustainable business development should mean. Bruntland defined sustainable development as 'development that meets the needs of the present without compromising the ability of future generations to meet their own needs'.

Original scepticism on the part of business leaders that consumers would not pay for the price of 'greening' products has been proved to some extent to be unfounded. However, despite the positive disposition the consumer public has towards environmentally friendly products, progress has been slow to develop products and manufacturing processes which are beneficial to the environment. During the 1980s and 1990s, some progress has been made. Most notably the pro-environment stance of the UK's Body Shop plc (cosmetics) and Belgium's Ecover, a manufacturer of environmentally friendly cleaning products, provide clear evidence of the consumer's interest in, and willingness to pay a premium for, what they perceive as environmentally friendly products.

Consumer power to affect industrial production, however, is not limited to specialist organizations who can exploit an environmental marketing niche. It has, in several areas, forced major changes in established technologies and industries. Increasingly tight legislation forced Imperial Chemical Industries (ICI) to seek an alternative to petroleum-based solvents for paints supplied to the automotive sector. A water-based substitute was developed and has in fact enabled ICI, in collaboration with Du Pont and PPG to make inroads into the US market where previously they had no share in this $1 billion market (Bonifant *et al.*, 1995).

Perhaps the most significant industrial and political effect of consumer interest in environmental issues has been the use of (CFCs) chloro-flouro carbons. Ozone-depleting agents, including CFCs, are used in such applications as solvents, refrigerants and degreasing agents. Approximately two billion pounds of CFCs were used annually in the mid-1980s. By the year 2000 all industrial countries have committed to their complete disuse.

Environmental progress

A surprising number of organizations have managed to exceed regulatory requirements and have even found that the search for new processes and technologies can result in economically attractive alternatives. For example, effective industrial cleaning chemicals have been derived as substitutes for CFCs from orange peel and canteloupe rinds!

Increasingly, research suggests that a more holistic approach to industrial processes is necessary to provide sustainable development while reducing the impact on the environment. This holistic approach encourages organizations to look at whole plant activities and pay increasing attention to the recovery and reuse of input materials and the by-products of the production processes. There is some evidence to suggest that such innovations in response to environmental pressure can lead to improved competitiveness.

At the simplest level there are a range of programmes that enable businesses to undertake actions that are basically economically sound and can help them audit and then reduce their impact on the environment.

Examples of such initiatives include Environmental Management and Audit Systems (EMAS) for which there is a British Standard, BS 7750 and an international equivalent ISO 14000 (Gray, Bebbington, 1995). These standards set a flexible framework for 'good' environmental management systems. Currently most companies view sustainability as an extension of such management systems. Environmental pragmatists would argue that such voluntary programmes are an invaluable step in the right direction. More strenuous ecologists believe that in isolation they are unlikely to be sufficient to encourage ecological change on the scale necessary for real sustainability.

Eco-organizations

Based on a need to develop answers to the problems of environmental damage due to economic growth, the concept of the eco-organization (Butler, 1996) has emerged. Essentially, an eco-organization has a core operating value of 100% environmental friendliness. The underlying principle is to create a 'closed-loop' manufacturing system by designing production facilities which eliminate waste products by re-using or recycling all raw materials. Ultimately, the ecological organizations will have 'cradle to grave' responsibility for products and services. This requires that an organization is responsible for minimizing the environmental impact from the extraction of raw materials through to the final disposal of a product when it reaches the end of its useful life.

In October 1992, Ecover, which made all of its products (laundry powder, dishwashing liquid, car wax, etc.) from natural soaps and renewable raw materials, opened a near-zero emissions factory in Belgium. This factory featured a grass roof to keep the plant cool in summer and warm in winter as well as a water-treatment system which ran on wind and solar energy. Gunter Pauli, former chief executive of Ecover, commented on what he saw as the key customer message from Ecover, 'We didn't sell, we educated. We didn't compete on price, we competed on emotion. We took products which were utterly devoid of excitement—who cares about laundry detergent—and made them something special.' Pauli continued, 'The heart of our message was our factory . . . we captured 6% of the Belgian detergent market in 18 months without spending a dime on advertising. Our factory didn't just supply cleaning products, it supplied education and entertainment. That's what people are looking for today. They want products that reflect their values, and they want a good story' (extract from Butler, 1996).

Namibia Brewers and the ZERI

Gunter Pauli left Ecover in 1994 and set up the Zero Emissions Research Initiative (ZERI)—a global network of scientists, business leaders and politicians who are working towards identifying commercial opportunities for zero-emissions technology and communicating its commercial benefits. In 1996, ZERI's budget was £7.5 million and Pauli is in the process of setting up a £30 million investment fund to underwrite investments in zero-emission factories.

The eco-brewery

Beer manufacture and consumption are increasing world-wide, in particular in the developing nations, and produce huge amounts of waste which are too costly to treat or dispose of. Namibia Brewers Ltd is seeking to become the first brewery in the world with a viable commercial-scale facility based on zero emissions technology. As an established brewery in Southern Africa,

Namibia Brewers already has a share of the premium, high-quality beer market in South Africa and Botswana with Windhoek Lager.

Brewing has four main outputs (aside from the beer):

1   solid waste, which is part protein and part fibre;
2   liquid waste—for one litre of beer you need about 10 litres of water;
3   carbon dioxide; and
4   heat.

The final two outputs are generated by the fermentation process. Research undertaken by ZERI found that by blending 40 different biochemical processes it is possible to reuse all of these outputs.

● The solid waste is broken down naturally by growing mushrooms on it to provide livestock feed. Additionally the protein can be extracted by introducing earthworms into the spent grain. This converts vegetable to animal protein and provides excellent chicken feed. The chickens and livestock then produce wastes which are primarily treated in a digester which produces biogas as fuel for the brewery.
● Liquid effluent provides the basis for growing algae in shallow basins by photosynthesis while producing oxygen during the day to provide the secondary treatment of solid waste by oxidation. The algae are then used for fish feed and the effluent itself provides a mineral-rich environment for plankton to flourish which provides a further source of feed for the fish.
● Waste heat is recovered and used to heat water for cleaning equipment and other purposes. This supplements the electricity generated from the biogas.
● A great deal of carbon dioxide is emitted during the brewing process and can be recovered for use in the brewery itself, or bottled under pressure and used for draught beer. The equipment for this is expensive for small breweries, so further research is underway to find less expensive alternatives.

The waste heat and bottled carbon dioxide outputs are re-processed by the brewery itself. The other recycling processes are carried out on small individual farms surrounding the brewery. Inevitably it remains the main purpose of the brewery to make beer for profit, so the recycling processes must also make a profit or the brewery would have no incentive to include them in their brewery operations.

This 'integrated biosystem' has already been successfully piloted in Fiji and further plants are planned for Tanzania. ZERI claims that this brewing/farming complex will produce seven times more food, fuel and fertilizer than a conventional operation and create four times as many jobs. The ability to design the complex eco-system that is Namibia Brewers was based on ZERI's ability to channel the interests of 4600 scientists participating in 60 different electronic conference groups. For example at Namibia Brewers, there was a mushroom group, an earthworm group, a methane gas group, etc. The principle was to draw upon the expertise of experts around the world to find creative organizational solutions to designing the eco-brewery.

Implications   Namibia Brewers Ltd is seen as the first full-scale attempt by ZERI to develop the eco-organization concept. The aim is to offer organizations the technologies and processes by licensing or franchizing to create their own ecologically sound businesses. Given the significant investments traditional organizations have sunk into their existing ecologically unfriendly manufacturing processes, it is likely that new competitors will emerge in selected markets to offer ecologically sound alternatives. These new organizations may have funds provided from the ZERI investment fund or from another of the growing number of 'green' investment funds (Roberts, 1997). Given their environmental ethos, such organizations may have less focus on short-term profits and more on long-term environmental benefits.

Judging from the Namibia Brewers experience, the eco-organizations will be less narrowly focused upon product specialization. They will strive to be 100% environmentally self-sustaining. From a marketing perspective, these firms may be hard for traditional firms to compete with. Ecover was able to compete effectively in the Belgian cleaning product market with higher prices and no advertising. As consumers become increasingly concerned about their environment, the price sensitivity of more expensive ecologically sound products may be overcome by consumers' desire to do something for future generations.

References

Butler, S. (1996) 'Green machine', *Fast Company*, **3**, July–August

Bonifant, B. C., M. B. Arnold, F. J. Long (1995) 'Gaining competitive advantage through environmental investments', *Business Horizons*, **38**, (4), July–August.

Bruntland Report (1987) *Our Common Future*, UN World Commission on Environment and Development, OUP, Oxford.

Gray, R. H., K. J. Bebbington, (1995) 'Sustainable development and accounting', The Centre for Social and Environmental Accounting Research, University of Dundee.

Malthus, T. R. (1985) 'Essay on the principle of population', Penguin English Library, Harmondsworth.

Roberts, P (1997) 'Ecotrust', *Fast Company*, **8**, April–May.

Questions

1   How sustainable is the eco-organizational format?

2   What sort of management style might Namibia Brewers need to adopt to balance environmental concerns with commercial practicalities?

3   How could the eco-organization model proposed by ZERI be transferred to other sectors? For example, banking or car manufacturing?

Part VI
International Management

European business environment

Introduction

In Chapter 16, we considered the variety of aspects which characterize the operating environment of organizations. In theory, the impact of environmental factors on how managers are expected to behave is easily understood. To some extent, we are all influenced by factors outside of our control. However, it becomes a significant challenge to assess how environmental changes might influence the organisations we work for and the way we interact with others. This chapter seeks to extrapolate upon significant prospective environmental changes and highlight some of the managerial and organizational issues which might emerge.

This book has been written with a European audience in mind. Consequently, we have focused this chapter on the impact of European integration upon our understanding of organizational behaviour. We are also conscious of our own ethnocentric perspective. Both authors have been raised within the Anglo-Saxon tradition of management education (one of us from the UK and the other from Canada), however we have both strived to explore our own operating assumptions and examine their relevance within different contexts in Western Europe, Eastern Europe and elsewhere. Our experience shows there is nothing like experience. Our own sensitivities and concerns about the relevance of established methods and models of organizational behaviour comes directly from getting personally involved in other cultures and contexts.

This chapter will examine some of the broad European contextual changes which are having an impact on the management function. In particular, we will use a well-established model for environmental scanning known as PEST analysis—political/legal, economic, social/demographic and technical—(Hitt *et al.*, 1995).

Why is Europe important?

This book is about how people and organizations react and interact. Therefore, it is sometimes difficult for readers to perceive why there should be a chapter on the European business environment. There are a number of different reasons.

● *American/Anglo Saxon management theories* Almost all of the major theories of organizational behaviour and structure have been derived from the legal structures, cultures and values of North America and the UK. It would be highly ethnocentric to believe that such theories and managerial practices are valid in different cultures and economic structures. Although more research work needs to be done, we must be sensitive to the differences which can exist and the impact they would have on how we understand and analyse organizations.

● *European diversity* Political differences, economic growth patterns, social variations and different languages all contribute to a Europe which is built on differences yet which also have to co-ordinate and co-operate to an increasing extent. Once again, the need for sensitivity and awareness of the challenges of the variations need to be considered.

● *On becoming 'European'* It would be an extraordinary situation if the entire population of Europe all wanted to proceed with European integration at exactly the same pace. Each one of us must determine how 'European' we wish to be and to evaluate where we might wish to retain our own national or cultural identities. This could have an impact on our working lives. We might choose to actively pursue job opportunities in other parts of Europe and to become one of the vanguard of Euro-managers. Alternatively, we might choose to work within the culture and environment we know and understand and to avoid as far as possible the cultural and economic dilemmas which will emerge from time-to-time.

● *Management education* Although we may believe we know what a manager is and does, it should come as no surprise to note that the content and process of training and accrediting managers differs widely across Europe. In Germany, management education has traditionally been seen as part of an individual's 'technical' training. In this way, the concept of specific management education is seen as somewhat novel. In France, management education has been more diverse with the *Grandes Ecoles* providing many of the business elite, with other management education institutions offering a range of qualifications. In the UK, management education was once largely dominated by accountancy training—although this is rapidly being overtaken by more general business studies and MBA programmes. In North America, the trend towards business degrees such as the MBA has been continuing for many years and may be reaching signs of maturity. The difficulty lies in determining what sort of education should the aspiring Euro-manager pursue? If you achieve a management qualification in one country, will it be seen as of any value or relevance in another? The European Foundation for Management Development (EFMD) is a group of business schools and other related bodies. Among other objectives, they hope to emerge as a quality overseer of management education throughout Europe. In 1997, the EFMD announced an initiative called EQUIS (European Quality Improvement System) with the objective of developing a 'quality level' for management education institutions throughout Europe.

European integration

The fitful progress of the countries which comprise the European Union (EU) towards ever more integration is a fascinating and somewhat agonizing story. The ultimate aim appears to be to create an integrated social, economic and political region. From its roots in the turmoil and aftermath of the Second World War, the trend towards greater European co-operation and harmonization has been slow but steady. Some of the key landmarks in the development of a 'single' Europe are listed in Table 19.1.

Initially, the development of the European Union worked on the principle of consensus among the member states. However, as the influence of European legislation began to have an impact on countries' own legislative agenda, progress slowed down. This situation reached a seeming impasse in 1993 with the unwillingness of the UK government to ratify the revised EEC Treaty due to objections with some of its components (the

Table 19.1
Key events in the EU

Year	Event
1952	Treaty of Paris signed by five European countries setting up the European Coal and Steel Community (ECSC)
1954	European Defence Community (EDC) treaty signed by all five ECSC members to set up a joint army and directly elected European Assembly—vetoed by French National Assembly
1958	Treaties of Rome signed to create the European Economic Community (EEC) and the European Atomic Energy Community (Euratom)
1967	The institutions of the ECSC, EEC and Euratom merged into the European Commission (EC). In addition, a single European Parliamentary Assembly was created, initially filled with government appointees
1979	Members of the European parliament directly elected by citizens of all Member States
1987	Single European Act was approved calling for the dismantling of all internal trade barriers and the creation of a Single European Market by 1992
1993	The European Union (EU) was officially established by the Maastricht treaty. This called for the creation of three institutions: • Common Foreign and Security Policy (CFSP); • Co-operation in the field of Justice and Home Affairs (JHA); and • Economic and Monetary Union with the goal of a single European currency by the beginning of the 21st century
1996	Intergovernmental Conference set up to promote the following: • making Europe more relevant to its citizens; • developing the EU infrastructure to prepare for an increase in Member States from Eastern Europe • increased development of a Common Foreign Policy and a European Security and Defence Policy

Social Chapter). As a solution, it was decided to offer—under very special circumstances only—an 'opt-out' clause for countries which are fundamentally unwilling to agree. The idea is that the 'opt-outs' would be able to reconsider the situation by observing the impact of the implementation throughout the rest of Europe and, hopefully, 'opt-in' at some future point.

The European Union itself is growing its membership steadily. The demise of the 'Iron Curtain' between Western and Eastern Europe has led to increasing pressure to include the newly democratizing states of the East into the European model. The membership of the EU is illustrated in Table 19.2.

PEST analysis
Political change

The European Union is the name of the umbrella organization through which its member states have agreed to channel its co-operative endeavours on matters ranging from foreign policy to currency union and to recognize each member states' national standards and accreditation in hundreds of areas including food and hygiene, police investigations, educational qualifications, etc.

The EU is renowned by some for its ability to draft complex and subtle legislation. This is a situation that probably has been created by the need to satisfy/placate the many diverse national/political/economic interests which

Table 19.2
Growth of EU
membership

Year	Enlargement	Countries
1952	Original ECSC membership	• Belgium • Germany (the five new Länder of the former GDR joined in 1991) • France • Italy • Luxembourg • Netherlands
1973	First enlargement	• Denmark • Republic of Ireland • UK • (Norwegians rejected membership)
1981	Second enlargement	• Greece
1986	Third enlargement	• Portugal • Spain
1995	Fourth enlargement	• Austria • Finland • Sweden • (Norwegians rejected membership)
?	Countries being considered for Fifth enlargement	• Bulgaria • Cyprus (in process already) • Czech Republic • Estonia • Hungary • Latvia • Lithuania • Malta (in process already) • Poland • Romania • Slovakia • Slovenia

are impacted by EU decisions. Legislation from the EU come in three 'strengths'. First, are Regulations which are equivalent to laws as passed by a member state. They must be implemented by EU members without intervention or modification.

Second, are the directives which are binding on members in terms of the Directive's stated goal or objective. However, each member has some discretion in how and when to achieve it. The rationale behind directives is that they recognizes the fact that each member has different legal systems which may require a different form of implementation. Directives must be transposed into statutes (laws) passed by each member within a certain specified time period or else risk some form of pressure being placed upon them by the EU and other members. For example, Hughes (1995) highlights the range of directives aimed at creating common health and safety standards across the EU. He predicts that these changes will have far-reaching implications on the cost base of organizations which are unaware of the proposals being considered. The third and final form of EU legislation are the decisions. These rulings do not have a general application on members although they are binding on those institutions and organizations to whom they are addressed.

Perhaps the most critical issue facing the EU in the 21st century will be the issue of enlargement of the membership to include former Soviet bloc countries. As can be seen from Table 19.2, many Eastern European countries are anxious to become EU members. The reasons are relatively simple. First, the loss of their traditional market (Russia and the other Soviet republics) has meant that these smaller nations must gain access to new export markets if they are to bring prosperity to their population. Becoming EU members will offer a large, free-trading market with a strong currency as an attractive inducement. From the existing EU members, there are two views. First, the pro-expansionists feel that the increased membership will create more growth within the EU and will provide jobs and income for all EU member states. Second, there are the expansion sceptics who feel that the equalization payments that will be payable to new members who require economic support will bankrupt the EU. It is likely that over time, many of the Eastern European states will be admitted. However, the process and duration of the membership process is unclear. Indeed, it may be possible that different 'levels' of membership are offered to appease those concerned about the costs of expansion.

Economic impact

The fundamental driving force behind the EU is the recognition among the member states that the free movement of goods and services among the countries is critical. It was very apparent that the inefficiency of having trade barriers between relatively small nations was harming all of the countries. Countries were able to pursue 'beggar-thy-neighbour' policies which served to inflict damage on the imports from other countries in return for enhancing your own—often inefficient—sectors. The introduction of the European Single Market (deemed to have been completed by 1 January 1993) has been something of an anticlimax. Forecasts at the time suggested that the result would be an additional two million jobs created in the EU and 4.5% growth within five years (Barnsley, 1995). Considerable barriers to free-trade remain (Barnsley, 1995) although many are invisible due to countries maintaining regulatory requirements. Such non-tariff barriers are much more difficult to identify and put pressure on the countries to alter than if tariffs were in place.

A global common market?

In addition to the movement towards dismantling economic barriers within the EU, the World Trade Organization (WTO) is seeking to undertake a similar objective on a global scale. The completion of the Uruguay round of GATT (General Agreement on Tariffs and Trade) negotiations in 1994 served to reduce the overall level of international tariffs and should boost long-term trade. Global trade liberalization is likely to proceed more slowly than within the EU. Economic protectionism at country level is still common.

EMU

Perhaps the most significant economic event associated with the EU is the move towards a common currency. European Monetary Union (EMU) will abolish borders for money: national currencies in all participating countries will be replaced with a single currency, the euro. For its proponents, the single currency will spare individuals and organizations the cost and effort of having to convert money. Were there to be a single currency, not only would exchange rate risk be eliminated, any pricing differences would become immediately apparent. One macro effect would be to force convergence in VAT rates; the micro equivalent would be a rapid harmonization in prices and an almost equally rapid shift in production to the lowest-cost production centres. If companies did not harmonize prices then arbitrage would do so; and the convergence of prices would mean that they could no longer 'carry' high-cost plants by imposing higher prices on those markets. Exporting industry will have to worry less about turbulence on the foreign exchange market. For banks and their customers, EMU will create a huge financial market.

The aim of EMU is to promote and advance the ideal of the European Single Market and the political unification of Europe. To this end, the participating countries will—for the first time—be merging important sphere of national identity such as monetary and exchange rate policy. The future European Central Bank (ECB) and the national central banks will be united in the European System of Central Banks (ESCB). Conditions governing participation, a fixed timetable and the structure of EMU were laid down in the 1991 'Treaty on European Union' (Maastricht Treaty). The countries of the European Union (EU) have given a binding undertaking under international law to join EMU by the beginning of 1999 at the latest, provided they fulfil the conditions. Only the UK and Denmark have an 'opt-in' clause.

The sceptical view is that the individual members will be unlikely or unwilling to meet the necessary convergence thresholds by the deadline and the process may be delayed indefinitely. Yet another perspective is that the movement to a single European currency is outdated. There are already indications that international electronic funds transfer systems such as Mondex (now part of MasterCard) and Visa may devise systems of exchange which offer global exchange at much lower costs than at present.

A common currency, however, will force convergence in other ways, for example, in pension provision. It would not be possible for one country to carry on with pensions paid largely on a pay-as-you-go basis, if other members of the currency union had funded schemes, a point which has great implications for stock markets in continental Europe (McRae, 1997)

Labour costs   As organizations operating within the EU adopt a more pan-European perspective, the issue of relative labour costs will undoubtedly become more critical. Although tariff and other artificial barriers to trade are being reduced, significant differences remain in the labour costs across the EU. Generally speaking, the first half of the 1990s was a period of relatively low inflation and growing unemployment across Europe. (Vardy and Hope, 1995). For example, during the period 1991–94, wage costs across the EU rose by only 1% (Vardy and Hope, 1995). As an indication of the variation in levels of pay across Europe, we quote from a survey undertaken by remuneration consultants Towers Perrin reporting on data as of April 1994 for four 'typical' job positions: a manufacturing employee, an accountant in industry, the HR director and the chief executive. To eliminate currency exchange differences, the information reported in Tables 19.3, 19.4, 19.5, 19.6 are in US dollars.

Social and demographic shifts   As we write this book, the emergence of the 'Euro-person' has yet to be reported. (Young, 1995). The EU is still very much a collection of diverse cultural, social and linguistic groups. As of the second half of the 1990s, it would appear that the 'European' as a recognizable social/cultural group is still some way off. From an organizational view, this creates complexity in terms of recruitment, selection, training, leadership styles, communication,

Table 19.3
Proportions of labour costs—manufacturing employee

		% of total labour costs		
	Base pay	Bonus	Perquisites	Contributions
Belgium	64	10	0	26
France	56	12	0	32
Germany	71	9	0	20
Italy	65	0	0	35
Netherlands	75	12	0	13
Spain	74	0	0	26
Sweden	72	1	0	27
Switzerland	82	7	0	11
UK	87	0	0	13

Source: Towers Perrin *1995 Annual Report on World-wide Renumeration*, cited in Vardy and Hope (1995)

Table 19.4
Proportions of labour costs—accountant

		% of total labour costs		
	Base pay	Bonus	Perquisites	Contributions
Belgium	63	10	0	27
France	61	7	0	32
Germany	71	9	0	20
Italy	64	0	0	36
Netherlands	76	12	0	12
Spain	75	0	0	25
Sweden	71	1	0	28
Switzerland	80	7	0	13
UK	70	3	12	15

Source: Towers Perrin *1995 Annual Report on World-wide Renumeration*, cited in Vardy and Hope (1995)

Table 19.5
Proportions of labour costs—human resource director

		% of total labour costs		
	Base pay	Bonus	Perquisites	Contributions
Belgium	47	17	7	29
France	47	11	15	27
Germany	69	12	5	14
Italy	56	7	5	32
Netherlands	60	17	9	14
Spain	68	9	7	16
Sweden	58	7	8	27
Switzerland	76	8	1	15
UK	59	6	17	18

Source: Towers Perrin *1995 Annual Report on World-wide Renumeration*, cited in Vardy and Hope (1995)

Table 19.6
Proportions of labour costs—chief executive officer

		% of total labour costs		
	Base pay	Bonus	Perquisites	Contributions
Belgium	44	20	6	30
France	44	14	19	23
Germany	63	16	6	15
Italy	53	13	8	26
Netherlands	56	23	7	14
Spain	63	13	11	13
Sweden	52	9	5	34
Switzerland	60	17	5	18
UK	50	8	21	21

Source: Towers Perrin *1995 Annual Report on World-wide Renumeration*, cited in Vardy and Hope (1995)

etc. A diverse workforce may, in fact, add cost rather quickly to an organization. Therefore, the costs and benefits of operating as a pan-European business needs to analysed carefully.

An important trend in the European labour force is the advancement of females into the workforce and, particularly, the higher status jobs in business and management. The EU has taken a lead in this area by legislation, in particular, via the Social Protocol which designed to enforce equal pay and opportunity (Hammond and Holton, 1991). The proportion of women in the European workforce has increased in every country of the EU with Denmark and the UK having the highest female participation rates (Denmark: 60.5% and UK: 50.8%). However, much of the increase of female participation in the workforce has been by accepting part-time or temporary work (Davidson and Cooper, 1993). One interesting development has been the increasing numbers of women entrepreneurs (see Table 19.7) It is possible that women are picking up on the advantages of becoming entrepreneurs such as: flexibility and control of the work/personal life balance as well as avoiding the potential gender discrimination of corporate employers.

Table 19.7 Women in management and business in the EU

Country[1]	Working females as a percentage of all			
	Managers	Middle managers	Senior managers	Entrepreneurs/ self-employed
UK	26	–	2	25
Eire	17.4	–	–	31.5
Denmark	11	10	5	–
Netherlands	13	18	–	24
Germany	6	–	–	17
France	25	44	4.6	16[2]
Belgium	–	12.5	5	–
Greece	14	–	8	14
Italy	–	–	3	25
Portugal	–	–	–	–
Spain	10	5	5	37

[1] Category definitions vary by country
[2] Head of firms with 10-plus employees
Source: Davidson and Cooper (1993: 13)

Labour flexibility   Greater workforce flexibility is an aim of the EU as well as the member states. Economists have indicated that a flexible workforce is a key element in improving the performance of an economy by allowing greater flexibility to adapt to changing market conditions (Commission of the European Communities, 1993) At its core, labour market flexibility is about the relative ease of hiring, relocating and firing of employees. The view of free-market economists was that government policies which restricted the freedom of employers to manage the size and composition of its workforce meant that the employers would be less willing to take on employees because of the potential additional hassle and costs of letting them go. Differences between countries can be quite significant. Within the EU, the UK appears to have much less government regulation in place restricting labour flexibility compared to other EU members (see Figure 19.1).

Technological factors   Although the initiative to create a united Europe has developed some internal momentum on a political level, another driving force behind

Figure 19.1
EU employers' perceptions of labour market flexibility

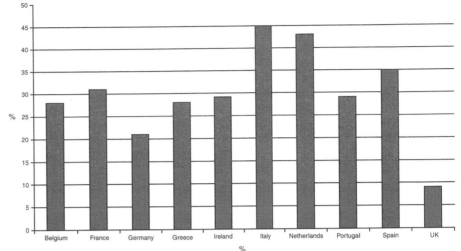

Source: European Commission, European Economy Report, 1991. Cited in *Employment Gazette*, February 1995. (103: 2: 63)

A percentage of employees thought that 'insufficient flexibility' in hiring and shedding labour was a very important reason for them not being able to employ more people.

further economic integration is technology. We would interpret technology to include not only advances in computers and telecommunications, but also in the physical distribution of goods and services.

For organizations based in the UK, the opening of the channel tunnel could be seen as a turning point. The flow of goods and people through the tunnel is increasing steadily. The concept of living in northern France and commuting into London on a fast express train is a reality. Similarly, for manufacturers in southern England, it has become cheaper and easier to move their products to France, Belgium and Holland than to Cardiff, Manchester and Glasgow. By radically transforming the ease of physical movement, the concept of a single market will become more real. Similarly, the extensive road and rail network criss-crossing Europe has improved due to the elimination of individual border-crossings. The realities of a vast and accessible market is encouraging organizations of all sizes to think on a European scale rather than within traditional national boundaries.

Yet another factor driving organizations towards a more European perspective is the advances in technology for audio, visual and data communication. The numbers of business 'road warriors' carrying digital mobile phones across Europe (and Eastern Europe) which link into the portable computers (for e-mails and faxes on the go) is growing rapidly. The availability of video and audio conferencing applications is also working to integrate customers, suppliers and colleagues across Europe and around the world. The traditional view of foreign markets as distant to reach, awkward to do business with and risky due to payment uncertainty is disappearing rapidly within Europe. Although language is still somewhat of a restriction, the increasing use of direct data exchange between computers even reduces such constraints to a minimum.

Personal impact of European integration

What will continuing European integration mean to you and to organizations you may be involved with? It is highly unlikely that it will mean nothing at all! Although somewhat speculative, some of the potential issues are covered in this section. We are sure that there will be many more as well!

Employer

It is likely that employers will be increasingly focused on the opportunities and threats which a single European market offers. Internally, employers may be more willing to promote and develop employees who are willing to move around Europe as their responsibility increases. It would be unlikely that all manufacturing, sales and administration are located within one single country. The key competency for such organizations may be the 'Euro-manager' (Calori and de Woot, 1995).

Colleagues

Individuals will need to be prepared to accept an increasingly heterogeneous set of work colleagues. Aside from cultural and linguistic differences, there will also be the geographic distance which separates work colleagues. The intimate '*tete à tete*' which characterized working teams may no longer be relevant or possible when you are dispersed throughout Europe. The rise of video conferences and telephone conference calls will substitute for face-to-face meetings. To overcome linguistic difficulties, there may be a greater reliance on written forms of communication to provide a record of what was agreed as well as further clarification. This may encourage greater levels of formalization in organizations than has recently been the case.

Customers

Cultural and linguistic diversity will also exist among the customer base. Aside from the cost of ensuring that sufficient numbers of staff speak other European languages, it may be that electronic forms of commerce are encouraged. For example, setting up Internet websites in a variety of languages and allowing customers to order goods and services via their computers may reduce the need for on-site language skills.

Mobility

As the spread of sites and markets fans out across Europe, it will become increasingly important to develop mobile European workers (Dück, 1994). The trend towards moving employees (particularly managers) around various locations will continue unabated and will offer even greater challenges for employees asked to uproot their families and move to new locations with different cultural and linguistic traditions.

Educational qualifications

Our ethnocentric assumptions about gathering the appropriate qualifications to enable us to pursue our chosen careers may be called into some question. The value of business study degrees and MBAs as a route to management positions in organizations may not be universally recognized. In other European countries, vocational qualifications and work-related training are more highly valued (Dück, 1994). In short, individuals will need to keep a close eye on which educational qualifications are likely to fit with career and life-style choices.

Summary

This chapter has sought to illustrate the potential impact of a single European community upon ourselves and our organizations. From an economic perspective, there are strong arguments regarding the benefits of European integration. Socially and culturally, the consensus is less clear.

Clearly more discussion and debate will take place over the coming years. The legislative changes being imposed on EU members is sometimes seen as obtrusive and unwanted—yet, they are a foundation of the requirement to create a common economic playing field. From a social and demographic perspective, the EU will operate as a heterogeneous and diverse state. Although there is much talk about the creation of the 'Euro-person', it is more likely to occur in small degrees rather than a full-scale convergence to a single cultural, social and linguistic perspective. No matter how sceptical one may be regarding the potential integration of European political and economic institutions, we all need to evaluate how it is likely to affect our working and personal lives. In much the same way as organizations need to assess the likely future scenarios and make strategic decisions, we as individuals are also being called upon to develop our own personal 'Euro-strategies' and implement them.

References

Barnsley, J. (1995) 'Free trade in Europe?' in A. Jolly and J. Reuvid, *European Business Handbook*, Kogan Page, London.

Calori, R. and P. de Woot (1995) *A European Management Model: Beyond Diversity*, Prentice-Hall, Englewood Cliffs, New Jersey.

Commission of the European Communities (1993) *Growth, Competitiveness, Employment: The Challenges and Ways Forward into the 21st Century*, European Union, Brussels.

Commission of the European Communities (1991) European Economy Report, in *Employment Gazette*, February 1995, **103**, (2), 63.

Davidson, M. J. and C. L. Cooper (1993) 'An Overview' in M. J. Davidson, and C. L. Coopers (eds.), *European Women in Business and Management*, Paul Chapman Publishing, London, 1–15.

Dück, T. (1994) '*Telcoms gemeinschaft und geselleschaft*' in T. Dück (ed.), *Liebedicht nicht sprecht*, de Gruyter, Berlin, 1–12.

Hammond, V. and V. Holton (1991) *A Balanced Workforce—Achieving Cultural Change for Women: A Comparative Study*, Ashridge Management College, Berkhamstead.

Hitt, M. A., R. D. Ireland and R. E. Hoskisson (1995) *Strategic Management: Competitiveness and Globalization*, West, St. Paul, Minnesota.

Hughes, P. (1995) 'European health and safety issues' in A. Jolly and J. Reuvid, *European Business Handbook*, Kogan Page, London.

McRae, H. (1996) 'EMU will force business to become more efficient', *The Independent*, 19 Nov.

Vardy, V. and G. Hope (1995) 'Employment costs in Europe' in A. Jolly and J. Reuvid, *European Business Handbook*, Kogan Page, London.

Young, M. (1995) 'Anyone seen a Europerson?' in A. Jolly and J. Reuvid, *European Business Handbook*, Kogan Page, London.

The national cultural environment

Introduction

The impact of national culture upon organizations is becoming of increasing concern for virtually all staff. Many single societies have become multicultural, and trade now regularly extends across a number of different countries. The advent of the single European market in the 1990s will also bring the question of national culture high on the agenda of managers around the world. So what is national culture? What is it like to work in a French or an Arab State organization? What are the similarities and differences to working in Britain, for example? How can managers cope with cross-national trade?

Identifying national cultures

To answer these questions really requires that the elements of national cultures are identified precisely giving us the means of comparison between countries. This is no easy task. Reading 14 by Geert Hofstede highlights one large study of some factors on which nations appear consistently to differ. Weinshall's, (1977) collection of papers on culture give an overview of the key issues. Some of the factors contributing to the national cultural environment of organizations are shown in Figure 20.1 (drawn generally from Hofstede, 1980; Tayeb, 1989).

Figure 20.1
The cultural environment of organizations

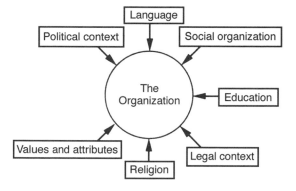

Convergence and divergence

There are two broad debates between researchers concerning the impact of national culture upon organizations. These deal with convergence and divergence (see Lammers and Hickson, 1979). The convergence view argues that organizations are becoming increasingly alike (in terms of structure, technology, levels of bureaucratization, etc). Thus, the context of business operates independently of national culture and predominates over it. The divergence view gives primacy to the differentiating effects of national culture (the residual effects of history, beliefs, values and attitudes held in each nation or society).

There is empirical support for both views, but there are no definitive studies which can strongly support one or the other. Of course, it is likely that both views are correct. Business pressures will certainly influence the common shaping of organizational structures and processes. Yet, such organizations are also staffed by individuals who hold very different beliefs, attitudes and values. These will obviously have an impact on motivation, satisfaction, group working and so on. Key differences in orientation toward time (linear clock time, or personal time), working (as a means to an end or as an end in itself), the accumulation of wealth (as a primary concern or not), and toward change (open to change or resistant) can be identified across different national cultures.

Many of the Aston researchers and their associates (see Chapter 12) conducted cross-national research using the variables of size, technology, formalization and specialization (see Hickson and McMillan, 1981). One conclusion of this work is that there appears to be a common industrial logic across different nations. Despite differences in political and ideological thought, organizations are converging around the common imperatives of economics, competition and technology (see Galbraith, 1967).

Other studies support divergence. They argue that organizational structures and processes are culture specific. Ruedi and Lawrence (1970) and Sorge and Warner (1986) conclude that national cultural factors specific to Germany accounted for differences between English and German organizations. These differences included education levels, (higher in Germany), power (German managers have a more significantly culturally ingrained view of organizations as authority structures), and autonomy (British managers experience more decentralization).

Categories of national cultures

Building on Hofstede's (1980) research, Ronen and Shenkar (1985) have produced a clustering of nations based upon certain commonalities in geographical position in the world, common language and similar religions. Table 20.1 summarises these results.

Since each category is based upon key cultural values and attitudes, we can predict that organizational behaviours generally should be more similar within categories than between them. A British manager would thus find not too much difficulty in recognizing and adapting to the structures and processes of firms in Ireland, New Zealand, Canada, etc. A more difficult cultural transition would be between managing in British and Colombian or Greek organizations.

One example of difficulties arising from cultural differences is provided by Giddy.

> The managers of one American firm tried to export the 'company picnic' idea into their Spanish subsidiary. On the day of the picnic, the US executives turned up dressed as cooks, and proceeded to serve the food to their Spanish employees. Far from creating a relaxed atmosphere, this merely embarrassed the Spanish workers. Instead of socializing with their superiors, the employees clung together uneasily and whenever an executive approached their table, everyone stood up. (Giddy, 1978: 102).

In societies which value and expect formal, authority relationships between individuals, informal management styles may be inappropriate as the illustration above indicates. Research also indicates that French managers view organizations as political networks, whose main purpose is to support the social order (and the prior distribution of power). North American managers view organizations as instrumental. They are designed primarily for task accomplishment (Laurent, 1983).

Table 20.1
Groupings of
national cultures
clustered by
language, geography
and religion

Anglo	Latin-European
Australia	France
Canada	Belgium
New Zealand	Italy
Ireland	Portugal
South Africa	Spain
USA	
UK	
Latin-American	*Far-Eastern*
Argentina	Malaysia
Venezuela	Hong Kong
Chile	Singapore
Mexico	Philippines
Peru	South Vietnam
Colombia	Indonesia
	Thailand
	Taiwan
Near-Eastern	*Germanic*
Turkey	Germany
Iran	Switzerland
Greece	Austria
Arab	*Nordic*
Bahrain	Sweden
United Arab Emirates	Denmark
Kuwait	Norway
Saudi Arabia	Finland
Oman	
Abu-Dhabi	
Unclassified	
Brazil	
Japan	
India	
Israel	

Source: Ronen and Shenkar (1985: 449)

Even within categories, there can be differences (which are of course not as great as those between categories). Ali and Al-Shakhis (1989) found significant differences in perceptions between 132 Saudi and 203 Iraqi managers. While both Arab cultures, Iraqi managers showed a greater predisposition to consensus, egalitarianism and humanistic beliefs. Saudi managers were found to be more individualistic:

> Iraqi managers believe more in hard work and independence, enjoy challenging work, and are more oriented toward teamwork and group success and the organization's collective norms. On the other hand, Saudi managers believe more in the free enterprise system, and that rich people should not exploit others and that workers should get a fair share and are more dubious about increasing leisure time.
>
> (Ali and Al-Shakhis, 1989: 177).

One of the countries not represented in Table 20.1 is the People's Republic of China. Partly this is because of the difficulty of classifying a country in which the whole context of the political economy has undergone massive changes in the last three decades. As Lansbury, Ng and McKern (1984) note,

China has swung violently and rapidly from extremely centralized control to highly decentralized anarchy.

In 1989 the world witnessed the Chinese government re-establish centralized control over what it considered to be overly-anarchistic student protesters. Violence and death were the result. It is thus difficult to classify China in terms of national culture other than to indicate its instability since the death of Chairman Mao. Warner (1986) indicated that China was likely to need massive investments in management training, professionalization and specialization. Largely it seemed these would be based on Western models of decentralization, apprenticeships, promotion and training. Following the events of 1989, it is unclear whether this will still take place.

Japan, unclassified in Table 20.1, is discussed in more detail in Part VII (see especially Chapter 24). In this chapter, the twin themes of language and religion which underpin the categorization in Table 20.1, are explored in more detail in the following sections.

Language

Language and national culture

While beliefs and attitudes form the basis of cultural differences, the first expression of national culture is found in language. Language can act as a mirror reflecting both the content and nature of the culture it represents. Despite attempts to create a universal language such as Esperanto, it seems unlikely to succeed until a universal culture is in place to support it. Language reflects the 'deep structure' of national culture.

There are over 3000 different languages in the world. Since the number of nations in the world numbers less than 200, it is obvious that culture, as reflected by language, rarely adheres to political boundaries. For example, it is estimated that in India alone some 1000 different languages are spoken. There are many countries which share the same official language. English, French and Spanish are the national languages in about 20 countries each. Arabic is the national language in a further dozen or so countries.

A common feature of linguistic diversity within a country is both cultural and political fragmentation. In many such countries, language bridges or *lingua francas* have been used to aid communication. In countries which have previously been controlled by a large colonial power, the colonists have usually imposed their own mother language as the bridge. For example, in India, it is English. In Zaire, it is French. In many former French and British colonies, the imperial language linked all parts of the country. Initially, few natives spoke the language. Gradually, it has become an important and widely spoken language. Such languages sometimes have a prestige value attached to them. English or French is often viewed as the language of higher education, economics and senior government.

Language and business

The wide variety in languages in the global economy present an enormous challenge to managers in organizations which wish to operate beyond their domestic markets. International business depends on communication and consists primarily of language. Every time a language barrier is crossed, a potential communication problem could result. To operate successfully in foreign cultures, effective communication must be achieved at virtually every level of analysis, the individual, the group, the organization and between societies.

As technology improves the speed of international communication, the ability to converse in a number of different languages becomes increasingly important. Within any large foreign subsidiary, parent company–subsidiary communications take place on a variety of levels (for example, the managing director, financial, marketing and technical staff).

Multi-national organizations have two options when deciding how to deal with this problem. First, they could put home-country nationals in key managerial positions. This strategy reduces the communication difficulties with the head office, but correspondingly may increase communication problems in the foreign subsidiaries. The second option relies upon local nationals assuming key managerial positions. The communication advantages within the foreign subsidiary must be viewed alongside the potential misunderstandings which can result from poor co-ordination between the head office and its various subsidiaries.

Communicating with a 'local' workforce requires a special understanding of the role of language. In many instances, this requires bilingual managers who can communicate between the subsidiary and its foreign owners. This situation is complicated by a workforce which may speak more than one language. In some African nations, where employees may be drawn from several tribes, a *lingua franca* may be used. In Canada, where there is some hostility between the French- and English-speaking segments of the population, both languages may have to be used appropriately. Because language reflects national culture, it may be impossible to find language equivalents for the particular terminology the firm wishes to introduce. For example, in many developing countries, to train an individual in such activities as computer operating requires some familiarity with English or French as a prerequisite.

A unique approach to overcoming this language barrier has been attempted by the Caterpillar Tractor Company. The company had been experiencing a problem with communicating its parts, service and repair manuals across the wide range of language areas in which their machinery operated. Local independent dealers and repair shops did not have the means to train their employees in the appropriate language skills as well as mechanical skills.

Caterpillar developed a simple system of printed communication called 'Caterpillar Fundamental English' (CFE). Essentially, CFE is one-way communication system which does not require the pronunciation of any words. Employees acquire an understanding of only 800 words, even though they may not be able to pronounce them properly. All words not necessary to service Caterpillar tractors are omitted. Over the past few years, several thousand individuals have taken the CFE course throughout the world.

This kind of simplification cannot be used when dealing with governments or customers for example. With customers, it is important that the seller can speak the customer's language fluently. Marketing across language groupings can require expensive and sometimes difficult changes to advertising, packaging and labelling. With governments, it is usually a matter of protocol which requires communication with foreign governments to be undertaken in their own national language. In the 70 or so nations where English, Spanish or French are the official languages, difficulties should not be insurmountable. However, in countries such as Saudi Arabia and Japan, it becomes much more important to employ local managers to represent the company's interests. Many organizations have discovered that it pays to hire the very best local people rather than attempt to provide bilingual foreign managers.

Only 10% of the world's population use English as their primary language. Despite this, English is currently the world's major language. The dominance of English was not solely the result of Imperialism. Although the English language would not have achieved its position if the British Empire had not been such a powerful trading nation in the 18th and 19th centuries, it was the rise of the US as a major world force which has further established English as an international language (Pei, 1965). The ubiquitous American tourist, films and television have spread the language much further than global conquest ever could. For instance:

- Around 700 million people use English as their second language.
- English is spoken, written and broadcast on every continent.
- About 75% of the world's post is written in English.
- One half of the world's newspapers are written in English.
- English is the language of over half of the world's radio stations.
- English is the most widely studied language in countries where it is not the native language
- SKF of Sweden and Philips of the Netherlands both have adopted English as an official company language.

Religion
Religion and national culture

Radcliffe-Brown, the British anthropologist, defined religion as 'an expression . . . of a sense of dependence on a power outside ourselves, a power of which we may speak as a spiritual or moral power' (Radcliffe-Brown, 1945). This potency of this belief system cannot fail to have been noticed virtually anywhere in the world. It has resulted, for example, in extensive 'hostage politics' particularly between Western Christian-based countries and Middle-Eastern Muslims; attempts on a global scale to ban the novel *The Satanic Verses* by Salman Rushdie (resulting in the author having to go into hiding following death threats); and violence within single countries which support a multi-racial, multi-religious population. In August 1989 Muslim extremists claimed the life of Lieutenant-Colonel William Higgins (videotaping his alleged hanging), threatened to execute another American hostage (Joseph Cicipio), and still hold other hostages from various Western nations. Within Britain, there were five consecutive weekends of violence in July 1989 with Muslims calling for the withdrawal of Rushdie's book and protesting about the failure of police to offer any kind of protection for racial and religious attacks. There are around one million Muslims in Britain and demonstrations can be sizeable (5000 in Bradford; 3000 in London in 1989). Such strong manifestations of religious beliefs are not confined to Muslims. Christians, Jews, Buddhists, Hindus all voice conflicting belief systems, often resulting in conflict and violence between and within nations.

The values and attitudes of religious belief systems shape individual behaviour. From the perspective of organizational behaviour, religion may be viewed as reinforcing the 'culture-bound' thesis. People behave differently and for different reasons because the values of their religion differ widely. We outline briefly below some of the core values and beliefs of some major religious groups.

Differences in Religious Beliefs

Five indicative religious belief systems are:

1 Animism
2 Hinduism
3 Buddhism
4 Islam
5 Christianity

The descriptions which follow are not intended to be comprehensive. Instead, the focus is to highlight some of the potential points of contact between religion and economic behaviour.

Animism

Major features include:

Ancestor Worship   The animist respects and fears ancestors and seeks to please and appease them. In practice, this means that the animist is encouraged to behave along traditional lines in order to please the ancestors. The effect of such beliefs is very strong conservatism and an overwhelming orientation towards maintaining traditional ways.

Spirit Worship   This goes beyond the respect given to ancestors. It attributes spiritual power not only to the departed, but also to non-human objects such as animals, trees and rocks. Magic is a key element of animism. It represents the 'science' through which unknown cause and effect relationships are made. In some developing countries, there have been marketing campaigns to introduce new products which either directly or indirectly imply that the possession of the products will give some sort of magical quality to the owner.

Taboos   Where belief in magic exists, there is usually a taboo against the use of an object or against engaging in a particular practice. Taboos are associated with almost every aspect of life (for example, childbearing, housebuilding and farming). Taboos also instil conservative values and traditional behaviour among its adherents.

Hinduism

No religion is more difficult to define than Hinduism. It has no recognized creed or dogma which can identify its followers. Despite such difficulties, there are some broad identifiable themes. First, though practices are important, statements of dogma are not. Second, Hinduism is an ethnic religion. Hindus are born, not made. Partly for this reason, Hinduism is almost exclusively identified with the Indian subcontinent. Third, Hinduism has existed for 4000 years largely through its ability to embrace rival philosophical beliefs, animist beliefs and a colourful mythology. Even today, there are elements of Christianity, Islam and Buddhism evident in some of the beliefs and practices of Hindus.

Some of the elements of Hinduism which have most impact upon organizational life are:

The Caste System   Though originating as a colour bar, it has gradually become tied with vocational/occupational restrictions. In total, there are some 3000 castes and sub-castes. *Varna* describes the national caste system; *jati* the localized systems. Membership in each caste is determined by birth. The word caste implies more than social class. It is more closely aligned to the European notion of 'species'. *Dharma* (duty) is the system of conduct appropriate to each caste. The caste hierarchy has been argued to be the main force in controlling the economy, in sustaining social structure (especially the constraints on women) and in being a major force against change (see Liddle and Joshi, 1986).

Baradari   Hindu ethics aim to uphold the preservation of the extended family unit. In economic terms, the strong family bonds have meant large numbers of family-owned and operated businesses, with organizational hierarchies based on family relationships. Such potential nepotism does not have the negative connotation which it has in the West.

Veneration of the Cow   Though there is some dispute, this is the one belief common to all Hindus. In practical terms, it means there is a total ban on the killing of cows. This has also meant that no animal husbandry can be effectively carried out.

Buddhism   Emerging out of Hindu beliefs in India, Buddhism is an international religion with a following in many countries, though particularly in South-East Asia and Japan. Buddhism is much easier to describe than Hinduism. Essentially, it was a reformation against Hinduism. One important practical difference between the two religions is that no caste system exists in Buddhism. The growth of the Buddhist religion is derived from its contemplative ethical system. Though it demands a high ethical standard of its adherents, there exists in Buddhism a greater sense of unity among its adherents than in many other religious groups. Essentially Buddhist beliefs focus on wantlessness and contemplation rather than upon consumption and work. It is an all-encompassing life-style involving spiritual, cultural and political identity.

Islam   Islam is the religion of about 500 million people in about 30 countries. Compared to many other religions, Islam has spread rapidly. One factor aiding this dissemination was the absence of racial discrimination. Islam actively promotes and practises the equality of every Muslim, regardless of race or colour. The term *Islam* is an Arabic verb meaning to submit. The word *Muslim* is the present participle of the same verb. The term *inshallah* means 'god willing'. This stems from the Muslim belief that everything, good or evil, proceeds directly from the divine will. Some aspects of Islam relevant to organizational behaviour include:

A ban on the payment of interest on loans   In some Muslim countries, interest payments are referred to as commissions to circumvent religious objections.

Religious Holidays   In Muslim countries, the normal weekend is Thursday afternoon and Friday. When combined with the Western weekends of Saturday and Sunday, this leaves only three and half days for business activity. In addition, the month-long celebration of *Ramadan*—involving fasting during daylight hours can cause dramatic drops in productivity.

Inshallah   In many Muslim countries, the view that nothing will happen unless Allah wills it makes it difficult for Western organizations to do business. For instance, insurance policies are seen by some Muslims as an attempt to defy Allah's will.

Christianity   The two major branches of Christianity—Catholicism and Protestantism—have both had a significant impact on economic life in areas where they have predominated. Within the Protestant sects, there was a downgrading in the role of the Church and the priest. The emphasis was placed upon the individual to be in charge of their own salvation. Consequently, individualism has become a major characteristic of Protestantism (Weber, 1952).

Weber was clear that individual entrepreneurs created capitalism, but that Protestantism was only one of many variables supporting this process. Thus, religion did not cause the economic structure of capitalism, but contributed to its continuity. Calvinism, for example, values method and rationality highly. A desire for efficiency encouraged accounting, controlled investment and general record keeping behaviours. In turn, this has arguably led to the development and the continuance of capitalist enterprises.

Within Christianity, it has been argued that the impact of its religious creed has been diminishing with respect to its social and economic significance. This process is called secularization (Wilson, 1966). Whether or not this is really occurring is open to debate since data are unreliable. Certainly the impact of Islam, Buddhism and Hinduism will continue to be a large influence in the area of cross-national trade and relations (Myrdal, 1968).

In addition to language and religion, two further aspects of cross-national analysis have a direct impact upon the study of organization behaviour. These are the political and legal contexts in which organizations operate.

The political context

For organizations operating internationally, the political context becomes an important variable. International organizations may operate in many, sometimes conflicting, political environments simultaneously. To operate in such conditions requires a heightened sensitivity by all staff toward political issues. In this section, four concepts are outlined briefly to illustrate the important implications of variations in political context. They are:

1 The nation-state
2 Nationalism
3 Business–Government relationships
4 Geopolitics

The nation-state

In its most simple form, a nation-state may be identified by its ability to exert political control over a discrete territory. A nation-state is thus a political unit which defines geographical boundaries, establishes citizenship requirements, controls the movement of goods and people across its borders, settles internal disputes and protects the nation against outsiders.

An alternative view identifies a nation-state in its social context. A nation can be said to exist in terms of its geography, history and culture. At least in theory, a nation can be identified as a community of individuals who share a common ethnic identity and history. However, many countries including Canada, Belgium, Nigeria and India do not meet such a definition particularly well. The borders of many nation-states indicate the degree of arbitrariness in assigning lines on a map to imply a common community of individuals.

The goals and objectives of nations are derived from their expressed national interests. Though the national interest may be used to imply a wide variety of objectives, there are at least five common themes:

1 Self-preservation is the prime goal of any state.
2 Security is of paramount concern and is exercised through efforts made at the minimization of threats to their continued existence.
3 In order to maintain the cohesive nature of a nation, attempts must be made to improve the collective well-being.
4 Nation-states seek prestige as a means of achieving recognition for their sovereignty.

5 Nations desire to increase their economic and political power relative to others.

Nationalism

Nationalism applies to individuals, not to nations. It is a state of mind in which the individual places loyalty to the nation-state, providing a basis for social and economic cohesion. Nationalism can range from rather mild feelings of 'belonging' to absolute and unswerving commitment and loyalty.

Current debates about the unification of Europe as a single market are beset with arguments based upon nationalism for example. Each nation appeals to its individuals to preserve what is 'typically' British, or 'typically French' and much time is spent by politicians assuring various populaces that nationalism will not disappear under the banner of the single market. Of course, nationalism at its extreme has figured large in the history of warfare.

Managers of organizations operating internationally ignore the potency of nationalism at their peril. Individuals in the host country can perceive expansionist moves by overseas organizations as threatening their national culture and will become defensive or aggressive toward the perceived threat.

In countries which have been formed as a consequence of some form of geographic division, nationalism can unite different tribes, racial origins and languages. In some instances, nationalism can serve as an ideological basis for behaviour. Governments commonly exhort their citizens to consider nationalism in their individual economic decisions (for example, 'Buy British' slogans for consumers).

Business–government relationships

The relationship between the state and business varies greatly between countries. At one extreme, the planned socialist economies do not distinguish between government and commercial enterprises. In the Western capitalist economies, the distinction is very clear. In between lie a wide range of possibilities. The nature of the interaction between state and enterprise colours the ways in which economic goals of the state are co-ordinated with organizational goals. For example, the close business–government relationship in Japan is credited with much of the success of the Japanese economy since the 1950s. It is also associated with the lack of economic development in China.

As the internationalization of business continues, the state–business relationship becomes important. Conflicting objectives can easily emerge between the multi-national company and the home and host country governments. For the host country, the placement of a multi-national company raises important issues of control over their economic destiny. The objectives of the multi-national firm and host state may differ considerably. For the multi-national company, the purpose of locating in a particular country lies in allocating and utilizing resources so as to maximize its competitive position on a global basis. The nation-state has a different view. Its interests lie in such concerns as domestic growth, employment, and social and economic stability. The two views are unlikely to coincide since that of the multi-national is largely exploitative, with economic benefits accruing to the home base without significantly contributing to the economic welfare of the host countries. There are exceptions of course, but in both directions. Some multi-nationals have arguably contributed to a decrease in overall welfare for the host nation. The case of Nestlé is a good but not unique example, where powdered baby formula milk with insufficient nutrients was used by mothers in the Third World, see Chapter 21 for details.

Geopolitics

So far, the assumption has been that of a simple two-country model, home and host country. Difficulties multiply when multi-national firms get caught up in international political issues which may involve many countries. For example, in the long-standing conflict in the Middle East between Israel and its Arab neighbours, many Arab countries have adopted a policy of boycotting those firms which have maintained a relationship with Israel or Israeli firms. Though many multi-nationals have gone to elaborate lengths to circumvent such political actions, it does raise complex legal and moral issues for the managers of multi-nationals. Many multi-nationals have been caught up in scandals of bribery, for example, where conduct considered ethical (or necessary) in the host country has contravened laws in the home country.

The need to understand the political context of host countries is an important issue. In response to such concerns, the field of 'political risk analysis' has emerged. Political change can be difficult to anticipate, particularly if little is known about the variety of host country contexts in which multi-nationals operate. For international investment decisions, the need to assess the potential political uncertainty of a country is crucial. These risks can arise out of the internal domestic political context as well as a result of international relationships. Results of political uncertainty include: restrictions on market shares, limits on the repatriation of profits and in extreme cases, expropriation.

Legal context

The laws of a society are one dimension of its culture. They are the rules established by authority, society, or custom. The laws of a nation are a manifestation of its attitudes and cultural norms, thus it is not surprising to find diversity among them. As societies differ in their attitudes towards the behaviour of individuals and institutions, then they will have different laws which regulate their behaviour. A common problem in international trade is that companies often do not understand key differences between legal systems. Briefly, three distinct bodies of law are relevant. They are:

1 Laws of Host Countries
2 International Law
3 Laws of Home Countries

Laws of host countries

Though it is safe to say that the laws of one nation will differ from the laws of any other nation, there is some similarity. The semblance between the various legal systems can be attributed to three factors. First, many laws are based on religious beliefs and practices. Consequently, countries with similar religious cultures would tend to reflect this in their legal codes. Second, the imperialist and colonial history of much of the modern world has served to impose a rough model of a legal system on the colonies. Such colonialism does not just derive from the more recent British and French colonial empires. The effects of the Roman Empire are still evident in those countries which use a codified set of laws. Third, the creation and recognition afforded to international law has mediated between differences among countries. As international law has grown from agreements between two or more countries, it implies an effort at reducing international legal difficulties. Nevertheless, sufficient differences exist in host country legal systems to make managing cross-national business an intricate and complex process.

International law   International law is different from the laws of nations for three reasons. First, there is no international legislative body which makes the laws. They exist solely through agreements, treaties and conventions between two or more nations. Second, there are relatively few ways in which international laws can be enforced. For example, the World Court may make rulings, but relies entirely on nation-states for enforcement. Third, the jurisdiction of international law covers only relations between nations. Topics covered include: international trade and investment, taxation, patents, the international flow of labour, etc.

Laws of home countries   A surprising number of domestic laws have an impact on the international operations of a firm. The concerns of government over the foreign activities of firms covers a wide range of issues. Three particular areas of concern can be highlighted. First, there is exporting. Many countries have restrictions. For example, the US has maintained a complete ban on trade with North Korea, Vietnam and Cuba among others. Controls also exist regarding the types of products which can be exported. For example, the US and its Western European allies maintain restrictions exist on the sale of products which use computer technology to the Soviet Union and its allies. A second area of concern to home country legislators lies in the area of potential monopolistic practices. For example, if a domestic company were to acquire a foreign competitor, it could be assumed that the domestic competitor may have lessened competition. A consequence could be a legal ruling to divest it of its holding to ensure the firm's market share does not rise disproportionately. The third area of influence of home country laws is in the area of taxation. The means by which foreign income is taxed can have serious consequences upon the economic viability of investing abroad. Tax incentives for exporters or reducing the taxes paid on foreign earnings can aid foreign investment.

Summary   Organizational behaviour can no longer assume homogeneity in organizational structures and processes. What happens in one firm in one country is likely to be very different from another. The key factor at play is national culture. Organizations and their constituent individuals reflect differences in national culture. Although difficult to define and to measure, national culture can be classified on a number of dimensions (such as tolerance for ambiguity among its people, preferences for individual or collective decision-making, or the pervasity of religious thought, for example).

Given the continued increase of international markets and trade, it seems a clearer understanding and analysis of national cultural differences and their impact upon organizational behaviour is necessary. As Roberts and Boyacigiller (1983) argue, key issues lie in the management of human resources, legal differences between countries, differential development rates of economies, the impact of new technologies, storage and retrieval of data and the general co-ordination and control of cross-national business.

References   Ali, A. and M. AL-Shakhis (1989) 'Managerial beliefs about work in two Arab States', *Organization Studies*, **10** (2), 169–86.

Galbraith, J. K. (1967) *The New Industrial State*, Hamilton, London.

Giddy, I. (1978) 'Social organization', in V. Terpstra (ed.), *Cultural Environment of International Business*, Southwestern, Cincinnati, Ohio.

Hickson, D. J. and C. J. McMillan (eds.), (1981) *Organization and Nation: The Aston Programme IV*, Gower, Farnborough.

Hofstede, G. (1980) 'Culture's Consequences', *International Differences in Work Related Values*, Sage Publications, London.

Lammers, C. J. and D. J. Hickson (eds.), (1979) *Organizations Alike and Unlike*, Routledge, London.

Lansbury, R., S. H. Ng, and B. McKern (1984) 'Management at the enterprise level in China', *Industrial Relations Journal*, **15**, 56–63.

Laurent, A. (1983) 'The cultural diversity of Western conceptions of management', *International Studies of Management and Organizations*, **13**, (1–2), 75–96.

Liddle, J. and R. Joshi (1986) *Daughters of Independence: Gender, Caste and Class in India*, Rutgers University Press, New Jersey and Zed Books, London.

Myrdal, G. (1968) *Asian Drama: An Inquiry into the Poverty of Nations*, Twentieth Century Fund, New York.

Pei, M. (1965) *The Story of Language*, J. B. Lippincot, Philadelphia.

Radcliffe-Brown, A. (1945) *Structure and Function in Primitive Society*, Free Press, New York.

Ronen, S. and O. Shenkar (1985) 'Clustering countries on attitudinal dimensions: A review and synthesis', *Academy of Management Review*, July, 445–54.

Ruedi, A. and P. R. Lawrence (1970) 'Organizations in two cultures', in J. W. Lorsch and P. R. Lawrence (eds.), *Studies in Organization Design*, Irwin-Dorsey, Homewood, Illinois.

Sorge, A. and M. Warner (1986) *Comparative Factory Organisation: An Anglo-German Comparison of Management and Manpower in Manufacturing*, WZB Publications, Wissenschaftszentrum, Berlin.

Tayeb, M. H. (1989) *Organisations and National Culture: A Comparative Analysis*, Sage Publications, London.

Warner, M. (1986) 'Managing human resources in China: an empirical study' *Organization Studies*, **7** (4), 353–66.

Weber, M. (1952) *The Protestant Ethic and the Spirit of Capitalism*, Allen & Unwin, London.

Weinshall, T. D. (ed.), (1977) *Culture and Management*, Penguin, Harmondsworth.

Wilson, B. (1966) *Religion in a Secular Society*, Watts and Co., London.

Managing the international organization

Introduction

There is little agreement or definition of what is and is not an international (or multi-national) organization. This difficulty is because there are many different types of organizations which operate, to some extent, across national boundaries (see Aharoni, 1971). In general, an international organization is one which operates directly managed investments in more than one country, has a number of foreign subsidiaries which employ a number of expatriate managers.

Though it is difficult to generalize, most companies which are considered international became so through a slow incremental process. Export orders received may have led to the licensing of a sales agency abroad. If successful, this then led to the creation of a dedicated foreign sales force, perhaps leading to foreign production sites and a divisional structure reflecting its global ambitions (see Chapter 12).

The international firm is likely to present very specific problems and opportunities from the perspective of organizational behaviour. Key (but not exhaustive) areas are:

1 Conflict between head office and subsidiaries.
2 Conflict within head office.
3 Conflict between the various subsidiaries and their host countries.
4 Communication difficulties between head office and subsidiaries (and between subsidiaries).
5 Appropriate human resource strategies to cope with the added complexity of international operations.

Conflict in the international firm

The international division

When domestic business firms begin developing regular business with foreign purchasers, a typical problem they face is a lack of management expertise in international matters. Their managements have not had any experience in operating under foreign conditions. The firm's managers have made their mark in the domestic setting. Conflict can occur at a number of levels. It is difficult for an organization to rectify this shortage of international skill in the short term. They cannot replace all their domestic managers by those more experienced in international business. Similarly, retraining the entire set of managers in a short period of time would also be expensive. The option which many firms adopt is to centralize all of the bits and pieces of international expertise that the firm does possess or can hire and to create a separate organizational unit in which to house it. From this 'international division' the scarce skills are then rationed out to the various operating divisions on the basis of their relative need.

Conflicts primarily occur over priorities in decision-making. Should production levels or sales volumes be the key criteria? How closely should the international division work with subsidiaries? Should head office decide corporate policy globally, or should the divisions (including the international division) have a say? How should resources be allocated across the organization and upon what criteria?

Decisions over structure

Decisions concerning organizational structure present a considerable challenge to the managers of international firms and they can also be the source of intense conflict. Do managers organize on product lines, or should the firm be structured largely according to its geographical markets? Should they create a separate international division to handle 'multi-national' problems centrally, or should decentralization be the hallmark of the operating subsidiaries? These are key questions which cannot always be easily resolved since mediating factors such as technology, maturity of the firm, specific global areas of operation and levels of competition will all confound apparently simple solutions.

Product structures

Firms which have adopted a product structure (where structure is designed around the portfolio of products) have generally done so due to the differing technologies associated with each product. Each division is required to master a significantly different product technology. In such a structure, management power is usually rooted in its knowledge of a technologically complex product. In product structures, an international division may cause difficulties since there is a tendency to regard the international division as a source of administrative expertise for handling letters of credit, invoices, customs duties, the translation of foreign documents, etc. The various product divisions tend to reserve all policy decisions pertaining to international operations for themselves. This reduces the influence of the international division's managers on overall strategies and policy decisions and inter-divisional conflict becomes inevitable.

Territorial structures

Companies which have structured themselves along territorial lines tend to lend primacy to policy decisions about markets rather than to considerations of technologies or specific products. This could be due to the relatively simple product technologies involved, the complexity of the markets, or both factors combined. In whichever case, the primary function of the line manager is to observe and develop the market.

The international division is essentially a variant of the territorial principle. Therefore, an international division will generally fit more easily into an organization structured along territorial lines than it would along product lines. Conflicts over policy are less likely, although questions of which subsidiaries get scarce resources will remain a source of friction.

Companies which have adopted such a geographically-based structure tend to share two characteristics (Prasad and Shety, 1976). First, the bulk of their sales revenue is derived from markets which all have similar end-uses for the goods produced. This minimizes the need for greater intensity of development, production and marketing expertise for particular product lines. Second, an understanding of local marketing requirements is critical to maintain demand for the products. In other words, though the product may require only minimal alterations to be suitable for particular markets (labelling, etc.) the techniques for penetrating local markets demand greater managerial attention.

Territorial structures can also be places of conflict. Because of the relative independence of the geographical groups, it is often difficult to transfer new ideas and experiences across territorial boundaries. Subsidiaries, once created, can become pressure groups for maintaining the status quo. This can result in conflicts between subsidiaries and head office, inter-subsidiary conflict, and conflict between the needs of production and markets. One typical example is the desire by the territorial management to have the products altered to correspond with their market requirements. This can affect the potential benefits of economies of scale by reducing the efficiency of the production processes.

Decisions over production

One solution to the conflicts described above is the decision to expand production capacity through facilities in other countries. International production facilities can be incorporated as part of either a territorial, a product-oriented structure or a mix of the two.

The decision to create an internationally dispersed range of production facilities marks a change of perspective for senior management. Rather than view foreign markets as adjuncts to domestic markets, foreign production capacity implies a decision to engage in international competition through the entire transformation process from raw materials to finished goods.

The challenge of international production facilities lies in the need to understand the implications of variations in the economic, social and political environment of the countries in which it produces goods as well as in those in which the products are sold. A lack of appreciation here can lead to intense conflict over raw materials, labour and capital. All these inputs can be scarce, variable in quality, and cost, as well as being difficult to procure. These differences can directly affect the transformation process through the choice of technology, the scale of operations, equipment, maintenance and manufacturing techniques.

Many firms which consider expanding their production facilities internationally do so because of potential cost savings either from raw materials or labour inputs. In particular, there has been a flow of production capacity to those countries which offer substantial savings on labour costs. Though such cost efficiencies can be attractive, they are in many cases outweighed by the supply conditions for the entire range of manufacturing inputs.

Many international firms which have chosen to locate production in developing countries for cost-saving reasons have found that the procurement of resources is one of their most critical problems (Brooke, 1984). In their efforts to manage production facilities, managers are frequently required to grapple with problems such as chronic late delivery of materials, high cost of raw materials, or shoddy quality. Other restrictions which can be imposed by the local government include: domestic content requirements and local procurement rules. By having to source their raw material requirements from within the host country, the manufacturer may not be able to take advantage of foreign-based potential suppliers who have achieved greater economies of scale. The potential for conflict at all levels in these cases is particularly high.

Communication problems in the international firm

The extent of global operations

The complexity of the structure of the international firm will have a marked effect on the ease or difficulty with which information is transmitted across the organization. However, it is difficult to determine precisely when an organization becomes truly 'international'. Managers of international organizations speak of 'degrees of multi-nationality', although quantifying this degree is almost impossible. An alternative approach is to consider the assumptions which lie beneath an organization's strategy. Perlmutter (1969) suggests that the key to understanding communication is to examine the relationships between headquarters and its international operations. Though they may never appear in pure form, four general types are proposed: ethnocentric, polycentric, regiocentric and geocentric. These are shown in Table 21.1.

Table 21.1
Four 'ideal types' of head office-subsidiary relationships

1   *Ethnocentric*
Focused on the home-country. Home-country nationals are considered superior in skill and performance to foreigners either at head office or in the subsidiaries. Performance criteria and decision rules are usually based on home-country standards and there is great resistance to any change.

2   *Polycentric*
The opposite of ethnocentricism. The assumption is that local people know what is best and can inform organizational strategy. Subsidiaries should be as local in identity and behaviour as possible. Structurally, a polycentric organization is similar to a loose confederation of quasi-independent subsidiaries.

3   *Regiocentric*
Managers are recruited, developed and assigned on a regional basis. An example would be an organizational structure which lumps together operations concentrating in European countries. The assumption underlying this approach is that greater economies of scale can be achieved than with a polycentric approach, but without resorting to the more centralized focus of an ethnocentric perspective.

4   *Geocentric*
Both head office and local subsidiaries see themselves as important parts of the global organizational entity. Such a world-wide approach considers subsidiaries neither as satellites nor as independent operations. Managerial efforts are directed towards increasing collaboration among subsidiaries and head office to establish universal standards as well as permissible local variations.

Communication difficulties

The levels of decentralization, the extent to which the international organization operates globally, and the structure of the firm will all create potential problems for communication. In extreme cases, head office can be unaware of critical information, or can misunderstand completely information coming from subsidiaries (Robock and Simmonds, 1983).

Despite the attractiveness of the geocentric perspective, it holds a number of difficulties in the added costs and efforts expended on communication. Managers tend to spend more time travelling between the various world-wide operations in order to train personnel, communicate objectives and achieve consensus. An associated communication cost is the relatively slow decision-making process associated with increased efforts to reach consensus. To make such an open system operate (see Chapter 18) also requires an adequate supply of managers at all levels who are sufficiently globally oriented to understand fully the dynamics of international business.

Communication in the ethnocentric perspective can suffer from both blinkered thinking and from the exercise of power. A truly global perspective is unlikely to be achieved since the views and experience of those with local operating conditions in international operations do not carry sufficient weight in head office strategic decision-making. Head office strategies become in danger of institutionalization, with the preclusion of certain attitudes and behaviours (see Chapter 11 on non-decision-making).

In polycentrics and regiocentrics, communication difficulties can arise from the duplication of effort between subsidiaries and from the inefficient use of head office experience (Heenan and Perlmutter, 1979).

Choosing an effective and efficient structure

There is no perfect organizational structure for undertaking international business. There are examples of successful companies which use a variety of the above organizational forms. Although there do not seem to be standard configuration requirements for multi-national organizations, the choice of organizational structure can be informed by considering a small number of key variables. Robock and Simmonds (1983) and Stopford and Wells (1972) have highlighted six broad factors which influence the choice of organizational structure:

1 Senior management perceptions regarding the relative importance of foreign and domestic markets both now and in the future.
2 The way in which the organization has evolved and the process by which it has become involved in international operations.
3 The nature of the organization's business and its competitive strategy.
4 The underlying philosophy and skills of the senior management of the organization.
5 The availability of sufficient numbers of internationally experienced managers.
6 The ability of the organization to undergo major structural changes.

All the above factors act as constraints in designing an 'ideal type' international organization in which host country and home country needs and values were balanced, and where levels of conflict were at a minimum, given effective communication channels. Many international organizations are prisoners of their own history. This can include the prevailing attitudes and beliefs of senior management as well as the characteristics of the foreign economies in which the organization operates (see Chapter 20).

Communication with local economies

So far, we have looked at communication strictly within the structure of the international firm. Of course, many communication difficulties arise from the interactions of firms with their local environments.

For the managers of an international organization, the relationships between the home country and the host country can be bewildering. The range of environmental factors faced by a manager of a foreign subsidiary does not normally fit with the established perceptual framework which was appropriate for head-office assignments. Managers of foreign subsidiaries are generally put in the role of go-between for the international company and the host country. The pressures arising from this role provide a formidable challenge given the often conflicting demands from home and host sources.

International organizations may provide a force for change in the host country's economy. This can occur through technology transfer, or more generally through economic and social development. This is particularly true in developing countries. Despite the potential benefits such development can bring, many host countries are concerned by the side effects of such foreign direct investment.

These can have a substantial impact on long-standing social networks as well as upon levels of environmental pollution, for example. The primary concern in many developing countries is the potential contribution international business can have on their economic, social and political development. To foreign firms, the attractiveness of doing business within a particular country may differ from the country's longer-term development goals.

To be successful over the long term, international companies must try to remain flexible to the differing requirements of the host country. The need to be flexible to national requirements can, in many instances, run counter to the company's desire to create a clear and consistent global strategy. Where the interests of the firm differ from the interests of the host country, conflict and poor communication will be the inevitable result (Doz, Bartlett and Prahalad, 1981). Two concrete examples of this lie in product image and in operations throughout developing countries.

Images, nationality and products

One issue which many international companies continually debate is whether it is best to create a local or a foreign image for their products. In some countries, imports from certain countries are seen as being of higher quality than domestic products. Consequently, advertisements for particular products in these markets may choose to accentuate the national origin of the product rather than the domestic source (Ronen, 1986).

The market perception of the goods from a particular country can vary significantly over time. For example, in the 1950s and 1960s, Japanese goods were perceived to be of poor quality and were characterized by low levels of technical innovation. The term 'Made in Japan' was used as an indication of cheap, but shoddy merchandise. By the late 1980s, the image of Japanese goods had changed completely. Japanese electronics producers such as Sony, Panasonic and Sharp have established international reputations for high-quality, innovative products. The turn-round by Japanese producers has been so successful that non-Japanese producers of electronic goods have taken to using 'Japanese' names to market their product.

Operating and communicating in developing countries

The relationship between multi-national companies and developing countries has sometimes become quite tense. There have been many occasions when the product strategies of some multi-nationals have placed them in direct confrontation with the governments involved. In Zambia, the government banned advertising for Fanta soft drinks after they discovered that mothers were weaning their children on the glamorous, but less than nutritious beverage. Another case involved the high pressure promotion of powdered baby milk formula in developing countries (Turner, 1974).

Although Nestlé of Switzerland are usually remembered in this context (the World Health Organization published a paper in 1974 called 'Nestlé Kills Babies'), other international firms were also involved. These included Borden, Cow & Gate, American Home Products and Glaxo among others. The firms were alleged to have sold powdered milk products to mothers in developing countries without providing sufficient instructions for their use. Small babies suffered health damage when mothers over-diluted the milk, or used unsterilized water which was all that was available. The milk provided none of the immunity found in natural mother's milk. High-pressure selling involved using radios, distributing free products via sales-people dressed in what looked like nurses' uniforms.

The problem for the international firms was a little more complex than this, however. Had they chosen not to sell to developing countries, criticism would also have inevitably followed. The sales promotion itself was expensive (given the difficulty of organizing such campaigns in poor countries) and this was reflected in a relatively highly priced product. The firms argued that the whole affair had been blown out of all proportion and that much benefit to health had occurred from using the milk (which was rarely voiced). Rectifying the situation was relatively easy, since mis-using the product was the prime cause of ill health rather than the product itself.

Nevertheless, the controversy over Nestlé's continued sale of the product stirred the emotions of many people and a number of boycotts of Nestlé products were mounted (Wall Street Journal, 1976).

Human resource issues in international organizations

Staffing international operations

International firms commonly categorize managers as 'locals' (that is, citizens of the country in which they are working) or 'expatriates' (non-citizens). Expatriates can be further sub-categorized as home-country or third-country nationals. Home-country nationals are citizens of the country where the firm has its head office. Third-country nationals are citizens of any other country. Simply at the level of who to choose (local or expatriate) to staff an organization, multiple factors have to be borne in mind. The major ones are listed below.

Knowledge of the local operating conditions Under ideal conditions, a firm should hire managers who understand the local environment as well as having the appropriate technical knowledge and business acumen. This combination is not always available. The trade-off which has to be made in terms of local knowledge or technical expertise will depend on a number of factors. The greater the difference in operating environment with the home country, the greater is the need to have managers skilled in local conditions. In contrast, where the need is great to maintain world-wide standards of production and close coherence to corporate directives, then it will be more critical to have in place a team of managers who are well-rehearsed in the usual methods of the firm. They act as preservers of corporate culture (Kotter, Schlesinger and Sathe, 1986).

Incentives to local personnel One of the arguments for giving preference to local personnel is that if incentives for advancement or increased pay are given, the potentially high turnover of skilled managerial personnel may be reduced. Another perspective is that the organization should only promote the best qualified people—regardless of national origin. Staffing with local managers can help promote a local image if this is sought. This can backfire, however, if the occasion should arise when local managers are no longer wanted or needed. There may be legal or social restrictions which could affect the firm's operations. The likelihood of such a situation arising could lead the organization to consider a risk-avoidance strategy of using predominantly expatriate managers.

Cost A strong argument for the use of local managers is the cost of transferring expatriate managers around the world. Aside from moving and settling-in expenses, many multi-national firms will purchase homes for their executives in order to ease the transition. In many cases, the executive's own furniture and household goods may be inappropriate for the new environment and will have to be put into storage.

Legal Restrictions   Every government has laws which favour employment of its own citizens. Such rules restrict foreign entry to take up employment. These restrictions are usually much more stringent at lesser-skilled jobs because unemployment rates are usually much higher. The process by which permission is obtained to import personnel can be very time-consuming, and delays of up to one year in obtaining the appropriate entry and permit requirements are not uncommon.

Control   One strategy used by many multi-national organizations to control their far-flung operations is by frequently transferring staff from head office to the foreign operations. The result is that those who have been 'acculturated' in the ways things are done in head office are likely to try and achieve the same procedures in the foreign subsidiaries (see Galbraith and Edstrom, 1976). Subsidiary benefits include the experience gained by those who are transferred around the world. Given the increased latitude of action given to managers of foreign subsidiaries, when these individuals are returned to head office, their managerial experience is much greater than those who remained at home.

Long-term Focus   Most multi-national organizations will transfer their personnel for only a few years to any particular subsidiary. Managers therefore tend to focus their attention on projects which will have a 'result' during their tenure. Though the satisfaction of seeing a successful result completed may be important to satisfy the personal advancement needs of the individual manager, it may not be best for overall corporate objectives. Employing local individuals as managers, who are expected to stay in-situ for longer periods, may facilitate a longer-term perspective on organizational objectives.

Management Development   Many multi-national organizations transfer their personnel through a variety of countries. One objective of this process is to train them in understanding the overall corporate system. Another benefit is their increased ability to adapt to differing social systems. By learning the means of managing in different, sometimes difficult environments, these managers are likely to be well prepared for ultimate corporate responsibility.

Global mobility of personnel

While nationality plays an important part in determining the staffing policies of foreign operations, there are other factors to consider. When moving across national cultures, there are countless variables which can affect the likely success and effectiveness of individual employees. Among these are:

Local prejudice   In some circumstances, individuals may have to be excluded from consideration for a particular cross-cultural assignment. This may have very little to do with the individual's aptitude for a particular job. For example, unlikely staffing policies would be a black manager operating in South Africa, a Jewish manager in Syria or a very young manager in Japan.

Technical competence   Multi-national companies must ensure that those awarded foreign assignments must be technically proficient in the tasks they are to be assigned. It is natural to expect that local employees may resent someone coming in from abroad, particularly if they feel that the newcomer can do the job no better than themselves. Managers also need to be able to adapt to local technical conditions. When moving to areas with different levels of economic and industrial development, the expatriate must be able to cope with often scaled-down plant and equipment, varying standards of productivity, a poor internal distribution system, and financial restrictions.

Repatriation Some of the difficulties encountered during repatriation are:

1 Financial—many of the benefits provided in foreign assignments are taken away on return;
2 Head office corporate structure—despite claims that assignments overseas will improve subsequent career prospects, this does not always occur. Returning expatriates can find their peers have been promoted while they were away and that they now have less autonomy in their current job; and
3 Personal re-acclimatization—the needed readjustment back to new schools and new life-styles after a long period away can be just as difficult as the initial move abroad.

Recruitment, selection and training

The most appropriate strategy for international organizations would seem to be one of staffing operations at all levels with 'truly' international managers. Recruitment should transcend nationality and the location of any specific job consideration. Very few organizations have been able to adopt this strategy, although some international companies such as Royal Dutch-Shell, Unilever and Nestlé have tried to develop an international cadre of managers.

The long-term success of any multi-national organization depends upon its ability to locate and tap sources of managerial manpower. One way of obtaining personnel for foreign operations is to buy an existing firm operating in the local markets and to use their stock of human resources. The difficulty in quickly attracting sufficient workers in foreign markets has been a major reason why many multi-national firms prefer to expand through acquisition rather than by setting up their own facilities from scratch (see Perlmutter and Heenan, 1974).

Recruitment For an international organization, the ideal employee is one who has:

1 a high level of expertise in the job required;
2 a good understanding of local operating conditions;
3 an ability to understand and fulfil head office demands.

Unfortunately, such individuals are seldom easy to find. Multi-nationals have devoted much effort to identifying suitable recruitment forums in which to select likely candidates. Many have made an effort to seek out foreign graduates of the major Western universities. The reasoning is that such recruits, who are familiar with Western ways, may wish to return to their home countries. A growing source of international management personnel has been the international business schools such as INSEAD and IMEDE. As the demand for multi-national managers increases, more business schools are becoming sensitive to these needs. This response to the demands of businesses can be seen in the increasing numbers of courses which relate to the international dimension of business studies.

Cross-cultural ability   The international transfer of personnel requires special qualities of intercultural flexibility if the move is to be a success. Unfortunately, many organizations are unable to accurately gauge the ability of their personnel to adapt to a different culture. As the needs of multi-national organizations have become more acute in the 1980s, more attention has been given to developing assessment procedures which purport to identify the likelihood of cross-cultural adaptability. Training consultancy organizations have emerged which provide such assessments as well as briefing courses for managers who are moving internationally. The large multi-national organizations such as Exxon and Mobil Oil have incorporated the assessment of a potential expatriate's family to try to identify potential problems in advance.

Training   Environmental training for an international assignment is an important part of the staffing process. An orientation programme which covers the country, its people, and its culture will facilitate the adjustment of an employee to a foreign environment. Living in a foreign country without adequate orientation may lead to 'culture shock'. To overcome this, multi-national companies provide training in language skills, along with a basic knowledge of the host country, its people and its culture. Aside from such rudimentary topics such as job characteristics, compensation and general information on housing, climate, education and health, a wide number of other issues must also be reviewed. These can include:

1 the mechanics of the relocation process;
2 foreign social structure;
3 communication links; and
4 personal and family security precautions.

Compensation   The compensation system of an international organization should effectively support the broad human resources objectives of the company. People performing relatively similar jobs in different countries may receive very different amounts and forms of compensation. These tend to reflect the diversity in productivity level of the countries involved, costs of living, tax rates, and the supply and demand of certain skills. International organizations must meet the local competitive labour market conditions or risk either not hiring sufficiently qualified people or incurring labour costs that are too high compared to the local competition. The issues which surround the international transfer of personnel are complex and sensitive. For example, if a French company transfers its British-based finance manager (who is earning £40 000 per year) to Italy (where the going rate is £49 000 per year) what should the salary be? Similarly, if the Italian-based finance manager was to be transferred to Britain, what salary should be offered? Non-monetary issues are also involved. In Britain, a holiday of four weeks per year may be the norm. In Italy, the holiday entitlement is likely to be six weeks. Similar questions also apply when considering fringe benefits such as pensions, health care, company car, etc.

To entice qualified managers to move abroad generally requires consideration of three components to the existing compensation package. First, there is the variation in cost-of-living between the countries. Second, is the need to align compensation packages with the equivalent job-status in the host country. If the status and compensation accorded particular skills or position in the host country is higher than back home, then the individual may feel maltreated if his or her compensation package is not upgraded accordingly. Third, is the issue of hardship allowances. In a foreign country certain brands of food and drink will not be available; the quality of children's schooling is likely to differ and television programmes will be in a 'foreign' language, etc. The amount of hardship allowance offered is dependent upon the perceived desirability of living in a particular location. Postings in cities like London, Paris, New York and Hong Kong arguably present less 'hardship' than in Lima, Nairobi and Riyadh, although there will be individual differences in preferred locations.

Comparative industrial relations

In every country in which it operates, the international organization must deal with its workers through some kind of systematic procedure. The relationship between the organization and its employees is determined by many variables. Two of the more important factors are the socio-political environment and trade union structure.

Whether or not a workforce is unionized, the organization must come to terms with the socio-political environment from which it draws its employees. One of the characteristics which distinguish national labour-management relations is how the two sides traditionally view each other. In societies where traditional delineations between labour and management remain strong, there may be relatively little effort towards co-operating to reach overall corporate objectives. This is particularly true if there is a marked class difference between management and labour. Many observers (see, for example Gallie, 1981) have argued that many of the labour difficulties in Britain are due to the perception among management and labour leaders that they are involved in a class struggle.

Trade union structure also varies by country. In some countries, unions may represent workers in many different companies (as in Britain). In other countries, unions may represent workers only in one company. In the US and Canada, trade unions tend to represent certain types of workers (coal miners, automobile workers, university academics) on a national basis. In Japan, a union typically represents all the workers in a particular company, with only very loose ties to any national body.

In other countries, a process of co-determination exists between management and labour. The concept of co-determination or Mitbestimmung (literally, having a voice in) is a process whereby management and labour jointly assume the responsibility for the determination of corporate policy. Co-determination was first introduced on a large scale in West Germany shortly after World War Two, when the steel and coal trade unions were given 50% representation on the industry boards. It proved to be popular and was subsequently extended to include all corporations with over 500 employees. Other countries in Europe and Scandinavia have also moved toward similarly 'democratic' procedures which are usually protected by government legislation.

Multi-national trade unions

As multi-national companies continue to grow and prosper, many trade unions have become concerned about the impact such a development may have on their ability to look after the interests of workers. The power of multi-national organizations to shift its operations from one country to another is seen as a highly effective strategy to reduce trade union bargaining power.

Trade unions also claim that the ability of the multi-national to use transfer pricing strategies for goods and services flowing between its various subsidiaries can also seriously affect labour negotiations. By portraying a misleading picture of profitability for a particular subsidiary, the firm can argue against local wage demands.

Yet another disadvantage of local trade unions when dealing with a multi-national is the tendency to decide on global relations policies at head office without regard to local issues and problems. The consequence is that local union negotiators will not be able to meet with the ultimate corporate decision-makers. It is exceptionally difficult for a trade union, which is confined to one country, to exert any influence on management that is located in a another country and which oversees operations in a number of other countries as well.

In response to these problems, many trade unions have been stressing the need to co-ordinate their action with their corresponding trade unions in other countries. These activities are aimed at building the strength and ability of the unions when confronting multi-national organizations. Such activities include an international exchange of information, international consultation and the co-ordination of policies and tactics.

Co-ordinated bargaining is also being sought by many trade unions. This would involve the simultaneous bargaining with all or most of a multi-national's subsidiaries (either throughout the world or in a given region). Trade unionists feel that such an arrangement would result in direct access to the top decision-makers in the multi-national organization and provide them with greater influence over decisions affecting employee relations.

Summary

Organizational behaviour concepts, originally developed in single country organizations, become especially relevant when applied to firms operating internationally. In particular, questions of organizational design, co-ordination and control take centre stage. Also in the spotlight, however, are the factors attributable to national differences in culture. These underpin the beliefs, attitudes and values of individuals within many of the subsidiaries of international firms. Differences here, between home and host country nationals can create tensions, misunderstandings and conflict.

In many respects, the problems facing international organizations are similar to those described in Chapter 13 when we examined corporate culture. Establishing a holistic culture (or a *modus vivendi*) for an international firm and its subsidiaries is the ultimate goal. This is both difficult to achieve and slow to develop. Other integrating devices are thus employed, including the careful selection and transfer of managers, designing around products, designing around markets and putting into place an explicit human resource strategy to cope with the challenges of international operations. It is assumed that business organizations will continue to develop an international focus, so these issues will become even more pressing as we enter the 21st century. We explore the challenges and opportunities of the future in Part VII.

References

Aharoni, Y. (1971) 'On the definition of a multi-national corporation', *Quarterly Review of Economics and Business*, Autumn, 27–37.

Brooke, M. Z. (1984) *Centralization and Autonomy: A Study in Organization Behaviour*, Holt, Rinehart & Winston, London.

Doz, Y. L., C. A. Bartlett and C. K. Prahalad (1981) 'Global competitive pressure and host country demands: managing tensions in MNCs' *California Management Review*, **23** (3), 72–84.

Galbraith, J. and A. Edstrom (1976) 'International transfer of managers: some important policy considerations', *Columbia Journal of World Business*, Summer, 100–12.

Gallie, D. (1981) 'Managerial strategies, the unions and the social integration of the workforce' In M. Zey-Ferrell and M. Aiken (eds.), *Complex Organizations: Critical Perspectives*, Scott, Foresman and Company, Glenview, Illinois.

Heenan, D. A. and H. Perlmutter (1979) *Multi-national Organization Development*, Addison-Wesley, Reading, MA.

Kotter, J. P., L. A. Schlesinger and V. Sathe (1986) *Organization: Text, Cases, and Readings on the Management of Organizational Design and Change*, 2nd edn, Irwin, Homewood, Illinois.

Perlmutter, H. and D. Heenan (1974) 'How multi-national should your managers be?' *Harvard Business Review*, Nov–Dec., 129.

Perlmutter, H. (1969) 'The tortuous evolution of the multi-national corporation' *Columbia Journal of World Business*, Jan–Feb., 9–18.

Prasad, S. B. and Y. K. Shety (1976) *An Introduction to Multi-national Management*, Prentice-Hall, Englewood Cliffs, New Jersey.

Robock, S. H. and K. Simmonds (1983) *International Business and Multi-national Enterprises*, 3rd edn, Prentice-Hall, Englewood Cliffs, New Jersey.

Ronen, S. (1986) *Comparative and Multi-national Management*, Wiley, New York.

Stopford, J. and L. T. Wells (1972) *Managing the Multi-national Enterprise*, Basic Books, New York.

Turner, L. (1974) 'There's no love lost between multi-nationals and the Third World', *Business and Society Review*, Autumn, 74.

Wall Street Journal (1976) 'Nestlé wins libel case, is ordered to revise some sales practices', 25 June, 30.

The cultural relativity of organizational practices and theories

Geert Hofstede

Introduction: management and national cultures

A key issue for organization science is the influence of national cultures on management. Twenty or even ten years ago, the existence of a relationship between management and national cultures was far from obvious to many, and it may not be obvious to everyone even now. In the 1950s and 1960s, the dominant belief, at least in Europe and the US, was that management was something universal. There were principles of sound management, which existed regardless of national environments. If national or local practice deviated from these principles, it was time to change local practice. In the future, the universality of sound management practices would lead to societies becoming more and more alike. This applied even to the poor countries of the Third World, which would become rich as well and would be managed just like the rich countries. Also, the difference between management in the First and Second World (capitalist and socialist) would disappear; in fact, under the surface they were thought to be a lot smaller than was officially recognized. This way of thinking, which dominated the 1950s and 1960s, is known as the 'convergence hypothesis'.

During the 1970s, the belief in the unavoidable convergence of management practices waned. It was too obviously in conflict with the reality we saw around us. At the same time supranational organizations like the European Common Market, which was founded very much on the convergence belief, had to recognize the stubbornness of national differences. Even within existing nations, regional differences became more rather than less accentuated. The Welsh, the Flemish, the Basques, the Bangladeshi, the Quebecois defended their own identity, and this was difficult to reconcile with a management philosophy of convergence. It slowly became clear that national and even regional cultures do matter for management. The national and regional differences are not disappearing; they are here to stay. In fact, these differences may become one of the most crucial problems for management—in particular for the management of multinational, multicultural organizations, whether public or private.

The importance of nationality

Nationality is important to management for at least three reasons. The first, very obviously, is political. Nations are political units, rooted in history, with their own institutions: forms of government, legal systems, educational systems, labour and employer's association systems. Not only do the formal institutions differ, but even if we could equalize them, the informal ways of using them differ. For example, formal law in France protects the rights of the individual against the state much better than formal law in Great Britain or Holland. However, few French citizens have ever won court cases against the state, whereas this happens quite regularly in Holland and Britain. Such informal political realities are quite resistant to change.

The second reason why nationality is important is sociological. Nationality or regionality has a symbolic value to citizens. We all derive part of our identity from it; it is part of the 'Who am I?'. The symbolic value of the fact of belonging to a nation or region has been and still is sufficient reason for people to go to war, when they feel their common identity to be threatened. National and regional differences are felt by people to be a reality—and therefore they are a reality.

The third reason why nationality is important is psychological. Our thinking is partly conditioned by national culture factors. This is an effect of early life experiences in the family and later educational experiences in schools and organizations, which are not the same across national borders. In a classroom, I can easily demonstrate the process of conditioning by experience. For this purpose I use an ambiguous picture: one that can be interpreted in two different ways. One such picture represents either an attractive young girl or an ugly old woman, depending on the way you look at it. In order to demonstrate the process of conditioning, I ask one half of the class to close their eyes. To the other half, I show for 5 seconds a slightly changed version of the picture, in which only the young girl can be seen. Then I ask the other half to close their eyes, and to the first half I show, also for 5 seconds, a version in which only the old woman can be seen. After this preparation, I show the ambiguous picture to everyone at the same time. The results are amazing: the vast majority of those 'conditioned' by seeing the young girl first, now see only the young girl in the ambiguous picture; and most of those 'conditioned' by seeing the old woman first can see only the old woman afterwards.

Mental programming

This very simple experiment shows that; as a teacher, I can in 5 seconds condition a randomly taken half of a class to see something else in a picture than would the other half. If this is so, how much stronger should the differences in perception of the same reality be between people who have been 'conditioned' by different educational and life experiences not for a mere 5 seconds, but for 20, 30, or 40 years? Through our experiences we become 'mentally programmed' to interpret new experiences in a certain way. My favourite definition of 'culture' is precisely that its essence is *collective mental programming*: it is that part of our conditioning that we share with other members of our nation, region, or group but not with members of other nations, regions, or groups.

Examples of differences in mental programming between members of different nations can be observed all around us. One source of difference is, of course, language and all that comes with it, but there is much more. In Europe, British people will form a neat queue whenever they have to wait; not so, the French. Dutch people will as a rule greet strangers when they enter a small, closed space like a railway compartment, doctor's waiting room, or lift; not so, the Belgians. Austrians will wait at a red pedestrian traffic light even when there is no traffic; not so the Dutch. Swiss tend to become very angry when somebody—say, a foreigner—makes a mistake in traffic; not so the Swedes. All these are part of an invisible set of mental programmes which belongs to these countries' national cultures.

Such cultural programmes are difficult to change, unless one detaches the individual from his or her culture. Within a nation or part of it, culture changes only slowly. This is the more so because what is in the minds of the people has also become crystallized in the institutions mentioned earlier: government, legal systems, educational systems, industrial relations systems, family structures, religious organizations, sports clubs, settlement patterns, literature, architecture, and even scientific theories. All these reflect traditions and common ways of thinking, which are rooted in the common culture but may be different for other cultures. The institutions constrain and reinforce the ways of thinking on which they are based. One well-known mechanism by which culturally determined ways of thinking perpetuate themselves is the self-fulfilling prophecy. If, for example, the belief is held that people from a certain minority are irresponsible, the institutions in such an environment will not admit these people into positions of responsibility; never being given responsibility, minority people will be unable to learn it, and very likely they will actually behave irresponsibly. So, everyone remains caught in the belief-including, probably, the minority of people themselves. Another example of the self-fulfilling prophecy: if the dominant way of thinking in a society is that all people are ultimately motivated by self-interest, those who do not pursue self-interest are considered as deviant. As it is unpleasant to be a deviant, most people in such an environment will justify whatever they want to do with some reference to self-interest, thereby reinforcing the dominant way of thinking. People in such a society cannot even imagine motives that cannot be reduced to self-interest.

National character

This reading is limited to national cultures, excluding cultural differences between groups within nations; such as, those based on regions, social classes, occupations, religion, age, sex, or even families. These differences in culture, within nations, of course, do exist, but for most nations we can still distinguish some ways of thinking that most inhabitants share and that we can consider part of their national culture or national character. National characters are more clearly distinguishable to foreigners than to the nationals themselves. When we live within a country, we do not discover what we have in common with our compatriots, only what makes us different from them.

Statements about national culture or national character smell of superficiality and false generalization. There are two reasons for this. First, there is no commonly accepted language to describe such a complex thing as a 'culture'. We meet the same problem if we want to describe someone's 'personality': we risk being subjective and superficial. In the case of 'personality', however, psychology has at least developed terms like intelligence, energy level, introversion–extroversion and emotional stability, to mention a few, which are more or less commonly understood. In the case of 'culture', such a scientific language does not exist. In the second place, statements about national character have often been based on impressions only, not on systematic study. Such statements can indeed be considered false generalizations.

A research project across 50 countries

My own research into national cultures was carried out between 1967 and 1978. It has attempted to meet the two objectives I just mentioned: to develop a commonly acceptable, well-defined, and empirically based terminology to describe cultures; and to use systematically collected data about a large number of cultures, rather than just impressions. I obtained these data more or less by accident. From 1967 to 1971 I worked as a psychologist on the international staff of a large multinational corporation. As part of my job I collected data on the employee's attitudes and values, by means of standardized paper-and-pencil questionnaires. Virtually all employees of the corporation were surveyed, from unskilled workers to research scientists in many countries around the globe. Then from 1971 to 1973 the surveys were repeated once more with the same group of employees. All in all the corporation collected over 116 000 questionnaires which were stored in a computerized data bank. For 40 countries, there were sufficient data for systematic analysis.

It soon appeared that those items in the questionnaires that dealt with employee values rather than attitudes showed remarkable and very stable differences between countries. By an attitude I mean the response to a question like 'How do you like your job?' or 'How do you like your boss?' By a value I mean answers to questions of whether people prefer one type of boss over another, or their choice of factors to describe an ideal job. Values indicate their desires, not their perceptions of what actually went on. These values, not the attitudes, reflect differences in mental programming and national character.

These differences, however, were always statistical in nature. Suppose people were asked whether they strongly agreed, agreed, were undecided, disagreed, or strongly disagreed with a certain value statement. In such a case we would not find that all employees in country A agreed and all in country B disagreed; instead we might find that 60% of the employees in country A agreed, while only 40% in country B agreed. Characterizing a national culture does not mean that every individual within that culture is mentally programmed in the same way. The national culture found is a kind of average pattern of beliefs and values, around which individuals in the country vary. For example, I found that, on average, Japanese have a greater desire for a strong authority than English; but some English have a greater desire for a strong authority than quite a few Japanese. In describing national cultures we refer to common elements within each nation, but we should not generalize to every individual within that nation.

In 1971 I went as a teacher to an international business school, where I asked the course participants, who were managers from many different countries, to answer the same values questions we used in the multinational corporation. The answers revealed the same type of pattern of differences between countries, showing that we were not dealing with a phenomenon particular to this one company. Then in my later research, from 1973 to 1979, at the European Institute for Advance Studies in Brussels, I looked for other studies comparing aspects of national character across countries. I found about 40 such studies comparing 5 or more countries which showed differences confirming the ones found in the multinational corporation. All this material together forms the basis for my book *Culture's Consequences* (Hofstede, 1980). Later, supplementary data became available for another 10 countries and 3 multi-country regions, thereby raising the total number of countries to 50 (Hofstede, 1983).

Four dimensions of national culture

My terminology for describing national cultures consists of four different criteria which I call 'dimensions' because they occur in nearly all possible combinations. They are largely independent of each other:

1   individualism versus collectivism;

2 large or small power distance;
3 strong or weak uncertainty avoidance; and
4 masculinity versus femininity.

The research data have allowed me to attribute to each of the 40 countries represented in the data bank of the multinational corporation an index value (between 0 and about 100) on each of these four dimensions.

The four dimensions were found through a combination of multivariate statistics (factor analysis) and theoretical reasoning. The cases analysed in the factor analysis were the 40 countries; the variables were the mean scores or answer percentages for the different value questions, as produced by the multinational corporation's employees within these countries. This factor analysis showed that 50% of the variance in answer patterns between countries on the value questions could be explained by three factors, corresponding to the dimensions 1 + 2, 3 and 4. Theoretical reasoning led to the further splitting of the first factor into two dimensions. The theoretical reasoning meant that each dimension should be conceptually linkable to some very fundamental problem in human societies, but a problem to which different societies have found different answers. These are the issues studied in primitive, nonliterate societies by cultural anthropologists, such as, the distribution of power, or the distribution of roles between the sexes. There is no reason why such issues should be relevant only for primitive societies.

Individualism–collectivism

The first dimension is labelled 'Individualism versus collectivism'. The fundamental issue involved in the relation between an individual and his or her fellow individuals. At one end of the scale we find societies in which the ties between individuals are very loose. Everybody is supposed to look after his or her own self-interest and maybe the interest of his or her immediate family. This is made possible by a large amount of freedom that such a society leaves individuals. At the other end of the scale we find societies in which the ties between individuals are very tight. People are born into collectivities or in-groups which may be their extended family (including grandparents, uncles, aunts, and so on), their tribe, or their village. Everybody is supposed to look after the interest of his or her in-group and to have no other opinions and beliefs than the opinions and beliefs in their in-group. In exchange, the in-group will protect them when they are in trouble. We see that both the individualist and the collectivist society are integrated wholes, but the individualist society is loosely integrated, and the collectivist society tightly integrated.

All 50 countries studied can be placed somewhere along the individualist-collectivist scale. On the basis of the answers obtained on the questionnaire in the multinational corporation, each country was given an individualism index score. The score is such that 100 represents a strong individualist society, and 0 a strongly collectivist society: all 50 countries are somewhere between these extremes.

It appears that the degree of individualism in a country is statistically related to that country's wealth. Figure R14.1 shows the list of countries used, and Figure R14.2 shows vertically the individualism index scores of the 50 countries and horizontally their wealth, expressed in their gross national product per capita at the time the surveys were taken (around 1970). We see evidence that wealthy countries are more individualist and poor countries more collectivist. Very individualist countries are the US, Great Britain, the

Figure R14.1
Cultural relativity

ARA	Arab countries (Egypt, Lebanon, Libya, Kuwait, Iraq, Saudi-Arabia, UAE)	JAM	Jamaica
		JPN	Japan
		KOR	South Korea
		MAL	Malaysia
ARG	Argentina	MEX	Mexico
AUL	Australia	NET	Netherlands
AUT	Austria	NOR	Norway
BEL	Belgium	NZL	New Zealand
BRA	Brazil	PAK	Pakistan
CAN	Canada	PAN	Panama
CHL	Chile	PER	Peru
COL	Colombia	PHI	Philippines
COS	Costa Rica	POR	Portugal
DEN	Denmark	SAF	South Africa
EAF	East Africa (Kenya, Ethiopia, Zambia)	SAL	Salvador
		SIN	Singapore
EQA	Equador	SPA	Spain
FIN	Finland	SWE	Sweden
FRA	France	SWI	Switzerland
GBR	Great Britain	TAI	Taiwan
GER	Germany	THA	Thailand
GRE	Greece	TUR	Turkey
GUA	Guatemala	URU	Uruguay
HOK	Hong Kong	USA	United States
IDO	Indonesia	VEN	Venezuela
IND	India	WAF	West Africa (Nigeria, Ghana, Sierra Leone)
IRA	Iran		
IRE	Ireland		
ISR	Israel	YUG	Yugoslavia
ITA	Italy		

Netherlands; very collectivist are Colombia, Pakistan, the Taiwan. In the middle we find Japan, India, Austria, and Spain.

Power distance

The second dimension is labelled 'Power distance'. The fundamental issue involved is how society deals with the fact that people are unequal. People are unequal in physical and intellectual capacities. Some societies let these inequalities grow over time into inequalities in power and wealth; the latter may become hereditary and no longer related to physical and intellectual capacities at all. Other societies try to play down inequalities in power and wealth as much as possible. Surely, no society has ever reached complete equality, because there are strong forces in society that perpetuate existing inequalities. All societies are unequal, but some are more unequal than others. This degree of inequality is measured by the power-distance scale, which also runs from 0 (small power distance) to 100 (large power distance).

In organizations, the level of power distance is related to the degree of centralization of authority and the degree of autocratic leadership. This relationship shows that centralization and autocratic leadership are rooted in the 'mental programming' of the members of a society, not only of those in power but also of those at the bottom of the power hierarchy. Societies in which power tends to be distributed unequally can remain so because this situation satisfies the psychological need for dependence of the people

Figure R14.2
The position of the 50 countries on their individualism index (IDV) versus their 1970 national wealth: individual index (IDV) versus 1970 national wealth (per capita GNP) for 50 countries

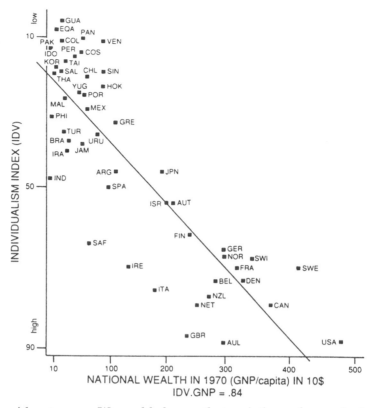

NATIONAL WEALTH IN 1970 (GNP/capita) IN 10$
IDV.GNP = .84

without power. We could also say that societies and organizations will be led as autocratically as their members will permit. The autocracy exists just as much in the members as in the leaders: the value systems of the two groups are usually complementary.

In Figure R14.3 power distance is plotted horizontally and individualism–collectivism vertically. The Phillipines, Venezuela, India, and others show large power distance index scores, but also France and Belgium score fairly high. Denmark, Israel, and Austria score low. We see that there is a global relationship between power distance and collectivism: collectivist countries always show large power distances, but individualist countries do not always show small power distances. The Latin European countries—France, Belgium, Italy, and Spain, plus marginally South Africa—show a combination of large power distances plus individualism. The other wealthy Western countries all combine smaller power distance with individualism. All poor countries are collectivist with larger power distances.

Uncertainty avoidance

The third dimension is labelled 'Uncertainty avoidance'. The fundamental issue involved here is how society deals with the fact that time runs only one way; that is, we are all caught in the reality of past, present and future, and we have to live with uncertainty because the future is unknown and always will be. Some societies socialize their members into accepting this uncertainty and not becoming upset but it. People in such societies will tend to accept each day as it comes. They will take risks rather easily. They will not work as hard. They will be relatively tolerant of behaviour and opinions different from their own because they do not feel threatened by them. Such societies can be called 'weak uncertainty avoidance' societies;

Figure R14.3
The position of the 50 countries on the power distance and individualism scales: A power distance × individualism–collectivism plot for 50 countries and three regions

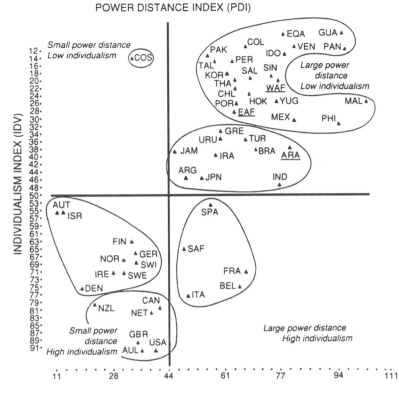

they are societies in which people have a natural tendency to feel relatively secure.

Other societies socialize their people into trying to beat the future. Because the future remains essentially unpredictable, in those societies there will be a higher level of anxiety in people, which becomes manifest in greater nervousness, emotionality, and aggressiveness. Such societies, called 'strong uncertainty-avoidance' societies, also have institutions that try to create security and avoid risk. We can create security in three ways. One is technology, in the broadest sense of the word. Through technology we protect ourselves from the risks of nature and war. We build houses, dikes, power stations, and ICBMs which are meant to give us a feeling of security. The second way of creating security is law, again in the broadest sense of the word. Through laws and all kinds of formal rules and institutions, we protect ourselves from the unpredictability of human behaviour. The proliferation of laws and rules implies an intolerance of deviant behaviours and opinions. Where laws cannot be made because the subject is too fuzzy, we can create a feeling of security by the nomination of experts. Experts are people whose word we accept as a kind of law because we assume them to be beyond uncertainty. The third way of creating a feeling of security is religion, once more in the broadest sense of the word. This sense includes secular religions and ideologies, such as Marxism, dogmatic capitalism, or movements that preach an escape into meditation. Even science is included. All human societies have their religions in some way or another. All religions, in some way, make uncertainty tolerable, because they all contain a message that is beyond uncertainty, that helps us to accept the uncertainty of today because we interpret experiences in terms of something bigger and more powerful that transcends personal reality. In strongly uncertainty-avoiding societies we find religions which claim absolute truth and which do not tolerate other religions. We also find in such societies scientific tradition looking for ultimate, absolute truths, as opposed to a more relativist, empiricist tradition in the weak uncertainty-avoidance societies.

The uncertainty-avoidance dimension, thus, implies a number of things, from aggressiveness to a need for absolute truth, that we do not usually consider as belonging together. They appear to belong together in the logic of culture patterns, but this logic differs from our own daily logic. Without research we would not have found that, on the level of societies, these things go together.

Figure R14.4 plots the uncertainty-avoidance index for 50 countries along the vertical axis, against the power-distance index of the horizontal axis. We find several clusters of countries. There is a large cluster of countries with strong uncertainty avoidance and large power distance. They are: all the Latin countries, both Latin European and Latin American; Mediterranean countries, such as, Yugoslavia, Greece, and Turkey; and Japan plus Korea.

Figure R14.4
The position of the 50 countries on the power distance and uncertainty avoidance scales: A power distance × uncertainty avoidance plot for 50 countries and three regions

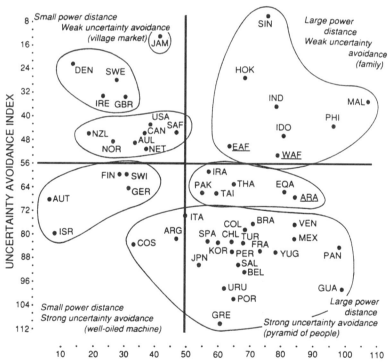

The Asian countries are found in two clusters with large power distance and medium to weak uncertainty avoidance. Then we find a cluster of German-speaking countries, including Israel and marginally Finland, combining small power distance with medium to strong uncertainty avoidance.

Both small power distance and weak uncertainty avoidance are found in Denmark, Sweden, Great Britain, and Ireland, while the Netherlands, US, Norway, and the other Anglo countries are in the middle.

Masculinity–femininity

The fourth dimension is labelled 'Masculinity versus femininity'. The fundamental issue involved is the division of roles between the sexes in society. All societies have to deal with the basic fact that one half of mankind is female and the other male. The only activities that are strictly determined by the sex of a person are those related to procreation. Men cannot have babies. Human societies, however, through the ages and around the globe, have also associated other roles to men only, or to women only. This is called social, rather than biological, sex role division.

All social-role divisions are more or less arbitrary, and what is seen as a typical task for men or for women can vary from one society to the other. We can classify societies on whether they try to minimize or to maximize the social sex role division. Some societies allow both men and women to take many different roles. Others make a sharp division between what men should do and what women should do. In this latter case, the distribution is always such that men take the more assertive and dominant roles and women the more service-oriented and caring roles. I have called those societies with a maximized social sex-role division 'Masculine' and those with a relatively small social sex-role division 'Feminine'. In masculine societies, the traditional masculine social values permeate the whole society—even the way of thinking of the women. These values include the importance of showing off, of performing, of achieving something visible, of making money, of 'big is beautiful'. In more feminine societies, the dominant values—for both men and women—are those more traditionally associated with the feminine role: not showing off, putting relationships with people before money, minding the quality of life and the preservation of the environment, helping others, in particular the weak, and 'small is beautiful'. In a masculine society, the public hero is the successful achiever, the superman. In a more feminine society, the public sympathy goes to the anti-hero, the underdog. Individual brilliance in a feminine society is suspect.

Following the procedure used for the other dimensions, each of the 50 countries was given an index score on the masculinity–femininity scale: a high score means a more masculine, a low score a more feminine country. Figure R14.5 plots the masculinity index score horizontally and the uncertainty avoidance index again vertically. The most masculine country is Japan; also quite masculine are the German-speaking countries: Germany, Austria, and Switzerland. Moderately masculine are a number of Latin countries, such as Venezuela, Mexico, and Italy; also the entire cluster of Anglo countries including some of their former colonies: India and the Philippines.

On the far end towards the feminine side we find the four Nordic countries and the Netherlands. Some Latin and Mediterranean countries like Yugoslavia, Chile, Portugal, Spain, and France are moderately feminine.

Some consequences for management theory and practice

The naïve assumption that management is the same or is becoming the same around the world is now tenable in view of these demonstrated differences in national cultures. Consider a few of the ideas about management which have been popularized in the Western literature in the past 15 years; in particular about leadership, about models of organization, and about motivation. These theories were almost without exception made in the US; in fact, the post-Second World War management literature is entirely US dominated. This reflects the economic importance of the US during this period, but culturally the US is just one country among all others, with its particular configuration of cultural values which differs from that of most other countries.

Figure R14.5
The position of the 50 countries on the uncertainty avoidance and masculinity scales: A masculinity–femininity × uncertainty avoidance plot for 50 countries and three regions

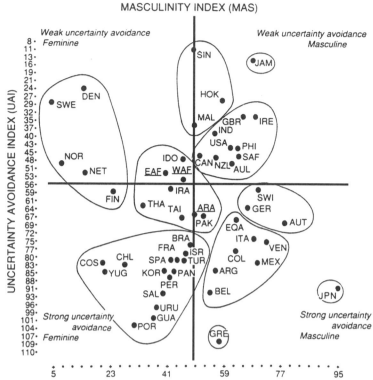

Leadership

The most relevant dimensions for leadership are individualism and power distance. Let us look at Figure R14.3 again. We find that the US in an extreme position on the individualism scale (50 out of 50) and just below average on the power distance scale (16 out of 50). What does the high individualism score mean? US leadership theories are about leading individuals based on the presumed needs of individuals who seek their ultimate self-interest. For example, the word 'duty', which implies obligations towards others or towards society, does not appear at all in the US leadership theories.

Leadership in a collectivist society—basically any Third World country—is a group phenomenon. A working group which is not the same as the natural in-group will have to be made into another in-group in order to be effective. People in these countries are able to bring considerable loyalty to their job, providing they feel that the employer returns the loyalty in the form of protection, just like their natural in-group does.

Let us now look at the power-distance dimensions, in terms of participative leadership. What does participative leadership US style mean?

Individual subordinates are allowed to participate in the leader's decisions, but these remain the leader's decisions; it is the leader who keeps the initiative. Management prerogatives are very important in the US. Let us remember that on power distance, the US is more or less in the middle zone. In countries with higher power distances—such as, many Third World countries, but also France and Belgium—individual subordinates as a rule do not want to participate. It is part of their expectations that leaders lead autocratically, and such subordinates will, in fact, by their own behaviour make it difficult for leaders to lead in any other way. There is very little participative leadership in France and Belgium. If the society is at the same time collectivist, however, there will be ways by which subordinates in a group can still influence the leader. This applies to all Asian countries.

Let us take some countries on the other side, however: Denmark, Sweden, or Israel. In this case, subordinates will not necessarily wait until their boss takes the initiative to let them participate. They will, for example, support forms of employee co-determination in which either individuals or groups can take initiatives towards management. In these cultures there are no management prerogatives that are automatically accepted; anything a boss does may be challenged by the subordinates. Management privileges in particular are much more easily accepted in US than in some of the very low power distance countries. A similar difference is found in the ratios between management compensation and subordinate compensation.

Organization

In organizations the decisive dimensions of culture are power distance and uncertainty avoidance. Organizations are devices to distribute power and they also serve to avoid uncertainty, to make things predictable. So let us look at Figure R14.4 again. My former colleague, Professor James Stevens from INSEAD, once gave the same description of an organizational problem to separate groups of French, West German, and British management students. The problem described a conflict between two departments. The students were asked to determine what was wrong and what should be done to resolve the problem. The French in majority referred the problem to the next higher authority level. The Germans suggested the setting of rules to resolve such problems in the future. The British wanted to improve communications between the two department heads, perhaps by some kind of human-relations training. My colleague concluded that the dominant underlying model of an organization for the French was a pyramid, a hierarchical structure held together by the unity of command (larger power distance) as well as by rules (strong uncertainty avoidance). The model for the Germans was a well-oiled machine; the exercise of personal command was largely unnecessary because the rules settled everything (strong uncertainty avoidance, but smaller power distance). The model for the British was a village market: no decisive hierarchy, flexible rules, and a resolution to problems by negotiating (small power distance and weak uncertainty avoidance). These models left one corner in the diagram of Figure R14.4 unexplained, but a discussion with an Indian colleague led me to believe that the underlying model of an organization for the Indians is the family: undisputed personal authority of the father-leader but few formal rules (large power distance and weak uncertainty avoidance). This should also apply in the Chinese culture city-states of Hong Kong and Singapore (see Figure R14.4).

The US is close to the centre of the diagram of Figure R14.4 and so are the Netherlands and Switzerland. This may explain something of the success of US, Dutch, and Swiss multi-nationals in operating in a variety of cultures; in the US literature and practice, all four models of organization—the pyramid, the well-oiled machine, the village market, and the family—can be found, but none of them can be considered dominant.

Motivation

The theories of motivation (what makes people act) and the practices of motivating people can both be related to the individualism–collectivism dimension. In the US the highest motivation is supposed to stem from the individuals' need to fulfil their obligations towards themselves. We find terms like 'self-actualization' and 'self-respect' on the top of the list of motivators. In a more collectivist society, however, people will try primarily to fulfil their obligations towards their in-group. This may be their family, but their collective loyalty may also be directed towards some larger unit: their enterprise, or their country. Such people do not seek self-actualization or self-respect, but they primarily seek 'face' in their relationships with in-group members. The importance of face as a motivator does not appear in the US motivation literature at all. The distinction between 'face' cultures and 'self-respect' cultures is similar to the distinction between 'shame' and 'guilt' cultures identified by the anthropologist Ruth Benedict (1974).

Other dimensions relevant to motivation are uncertainty avoidance and masculinity–femininity. Let us look at Figure R14.5 again. The dominant theme of the US literature of the past 20 years is that people are basically motivated by a desire to achieve something. We should, therefore, allow our people to achieve: give them a challenge, and enrich their jobs if they do not contain any challenge. The idea of 'achievement' and 'challenge', US style, implies two things: a willingness to take some risks (weak uncertainty avoidance) and a need to perform, to assert oneself (masculinity). It is therefore no wonder that in the diagram of Figure R14.5 we find the US in the weak uncertainty avoidance, masculine corner. It shares this position with the other Anglo countries. Let us take the case of some other countries, however: Japan or Germany. These are also masculine countries but with stronger uncertainty avoidance. This means that in these countries there is less willingness to take risks: security is a powerful motivator. People are very willing to perform if they are offered security in exchange. Interestingly, these security-seeking countries seem to have been doing better economically in the past 20 years than the risk-takers: but the management theories that tell us that risk-taking is a good thing were made in the US or Great Britain, not in Japan or Germany.

If we go to the other corner of Figure R14.5, we find the Netherlands, and the Nordic countries combining weak uncertainty avoidance with a more feminine value system. Here, the maintenance of good interpersonal relations is a strong motivator, and people frown at competition for performance. In these countries we meet a powerful interpersonal motivation which is missing in the US theories. There is striking difference in the forms of 'humanization of work' proposed in the US and in Sweden: a stress in the US on creating possibilities for individual performance, but a stress in Sweden on creating possibilities for interpersonal solidarity. In the fourth corner of Figure R14.5, we find both security and interpersonal motivation; Yugoslav worker self-management contains both elements. We are far away here from the motivation to achieve according to the US style.

Conclusion: the cultural relativity of management and organization practices and theories

Both management practitioners and management theorists over the past 80 years have been blind to the extent to which activities like 'management' and 'organizing' are culturally dependent. They are culturally dependent because managing and organizing do not consist of making or moving tangible objects, but of manipulating symbols which have meaning to the people who are managed or organized. Because the meaning which we associate with symbols is heavily affected by what we have learned in our family, in our school, in our work environment, and in our society, management and organization are penetrated with culture from the beginning to the end. Practice is usually wiser than theory, and if we see what effective organizations in different cultures have done, we recognize that their leaders have adapted foreign management ideas to local cultural conditions. This happened extremely effectively in Japan, where mainly US management theories were taken over but in an adapted form. This adaptation led to entirely new forms of practice which in the Japanese case were highly successful. An example is the quality control circle, originally based on US impulses but adapted to the Japanese uncertainty-avoiding, semicollectivism environment. The quality control circle has been so effective in Japan that now the Americans are bringing it back to the US; but it is doubtful whether most of its present US protagonists realize the role that Japanese educational and social conditions play in the ability of Japanese workers to function effectively in a quality control circle.

Not all other countries have been as fortunate as Japan in that a successful adaptation of American management theories and practices could take place. In Europe but even more often in Third World countries, foreign management methods and ideas were indiscriminately imported as part of 'technology transfer'. The evident failure of much of the international development assistance of the 1960s and 1970s is at least partly due to this lack of cultural sensitivity in the transfer of management ideas. It has caused enormous economic losses and human suffering. Free market capitalism as practised in the US, for example, is an idea which is deeply rooted historically and culturally in individualism. 'Everybody for himself' is supposed to lead to the highest common good, according to Adam Smith (1970) [1776]. If this idea is forced upon a traditionally collectivist society, it means that work organizations will be created which do not offer to employees the protection which they expect to get in exchange for their loyalty. The system itself in such a society breeds disloyal, irresponsible employees. Japan has not taken over this aspect of capitalism and has maintained a much higher level of protection of employees by their organization. Many US managers and politicians have great problems with recognizing that their type of capitalism is culturally unsuitable for a more collectivist society. It is for good cultural reasons that various forms of state capitalism or state socialism are tried in Third World countries.

Most present-day management theories are 'ethnocentric', that is, they take the cultural environment of the theorist for granted. What we need is more cultural sensitivity in management theories; we could call the result 'organizational anthropology' or 'management anthropology'. It is unlikely to be the product of one single country's intellectual effort; it needs by definition a synergy between ideas from different sources. The fact that no single country now enjoys a degree of economic dominance as the US once did will certainly help: economic power is all too often related to intellectual influence. In a world in which economic power is more widely spread, we can more easily hope to recognize truth coming from many sources. In this process, the contribution of Japanese and Chinese scholars, for example, will be vital, because they represent sources of practical wisdom and ideas which complement practices and ideas born in Europe and the US.

The convergence of management will never come. What we can bring about is an understanding of how the culture in which we grew up and which is dear to us affects our thinking differently from other people's thinking, and what this means for the transfer of management practices and theories. What this can also lead to is a better ability to manage intercultural negotiations and multicultural organizations like the United Nations, which are essential for the common survival of us all.

References

Benedict, R. (1974) *The Chrysanthemum and the Sword: Patterns of Japanese Culture*, 1st edn, 1946, New American Library, New York, 222.

Hofstede, G. (1980) *Culture's Consequences: International Differences in Work-Related Values*, Sage Publications, Beverly Hills/London.

Hofstede, G. (1983) 'Dimensions of national cultures in fifty countries and three regions'. J. Deregowski, S. Dziurawiec, and R. C. Annis (eds.), in *Expiscations in Cross-Cultural Psychology*, Swets and Zeitlinger, Lisse, Netherlands.

Smith, A. (1970) [1776] *The Wealth of Nations*, 1st edn, 1776, Penguin, Hardmondsworth.

National administrative heritages in borderless organizations

Roland Calori

The theory of convergence asserts that administrative science is supranational, it views all institutions as driven by a universal desire for efficiency that motivates them to adopt best administrative practices regardless of their societal context (Hickson *et al.*, 1974). Since the work of Bartlett and Ghoshal (1989), the 'transnational' form of organization tends to be considered as a model for companies involved in world-wide competition. The transnational organization is an asymmetrical 'integrated network' characterized by intense knowledge flows and socialization processes which are the 'physiology' and the 'psychology' of the organization (Bartlett and Ghoshal, 1989). But the authors also recognize the persistence of 'administrative heritages' at the level of a firm and at the level of a nation. A nationally bound administrative heritage can be seen as an observable manifestation of a national culture, this is the view of the culturalists (for instance, Hofstede, 1980). Institutional theory provides a deeper understanding of the phenomenon. Firms' administrative practices are influenced by the societal context in which they operate: this is known as the societal effect (Maurice *et al.*, 1980). National administrative heritages are shaped by national institutions, for instance the school and the institutions which organize financial and labour markets . . . (Whitley, 1992), they develop during the industrialization of the country (Chandler, 1990) and are passed from generation to generation through the educational system (Calori *et al.*, 1994).

International companies are confronted with different societal contexts, but the societal influence of the home country, in which they originated, may still be particularly strong. It may lead to ethnocentric attitudes (Perlmutter, 1969) and a lack of adaptation to different local contexts. Put differently, national administrative heritages may hinder the adoption of the transnational solution.

This reading aims at three complementary objectives:

1 describe differences in management practices across nations (that is, national administrative heritages) as perceived by top managers with extensive international experience,
2 analyze national administrative heritages and ethnocentric biases in the context of international acquisitions, and
3 discuss the convergence of management styles.

The reading provides some empirical evidence of the persistence of nationally bound administrative heritages *and* also argues that management practices tend to converge *slowly* in developed countries.

National administrative heritages in the triad

Being aware of the variety of management practices across countries is the first step in a learning process. This section compares management in the three zones of the Triad: the US, Japan and Europe, and the next section takes a closer view of management within Europe in order to understand its diversity. The arguments are grounded on unstructured interviews with 51 top managers in 40 large international companies established in 14 countries of Europe (including US and Japanese directors in charge of the European operations of their firms). The study was initiated by the European Round Table of Industrialists and achieved by the Groupe ESC Lyon, the detailed results have been published elsewhere (Calori and de Woot, 1994).

The American model

There is abundant literature comparing the North American and the Japanese models of management (see for instance, Ohmae, 1976; Pascale and Athos, 1981; Ouchi, 1981; Abbleglen and Stalk, 1985; Hamel and Prahalad, 1989; Albert, 1991; Thurow, 1992). Paradoxically the North American style became more apparent when its universality was questioned by the success of Japanese companies. Here we are more interested in the views of top managers with international experience than in the conclusions of the literature. Management in the United States is *oriented towards profit* and the satisfaction of shareholders, long-term strategies cannot overlook the constraint of short-term profits imposed by the stockmarket. *Competition* is seen as a major ethos of the American business system, perhaps due to the contrast with Europe and Japan where firms and markets are more protected. Competitiveness is a key concept in the North American enterprise. Competition goes hand in hand with *individualism* in the sense that the individual is responsible for his or her career and success, the relationship between the individual and the firm is contractual. Managers often move from one company to another and from one location to another. Entrepreneurship is typical of the American society, it is based on the three characteristics mentioned above: an orientation towards profit, competition and individualism. Finally, the Americans invented *professional management*, based on formalized methods and solid specialized training programmes. The American manager is a hero, equipped with an arsenal of techniques, written manuals and procedures on practically every issue. Competition and professionalism are the basic concepts of the MBA education programmes which permeate most developed countries (with the exception of Germany and Japan), and which has been heavily criticized for a few years by the Americans themselves.

The Japanese model

Top managers recognize their limited knowledge of the Japanese enterprise. However they suggest several key characteristics. Japanese firms are oriented towards *long-term growth*. Profitability is considered as a means towards the dominant goal: growth. The Japanese firm contributes to the economic power of Japan and the Japanese society is dedicated to the enterprise. Basically the Japanese society is consensual whereas the American society is contractual. Work relations are naturally based on *consensus* (or harmony: '*wa*') embedded in the collective culture: the group is more important than the individual. The core of the Japanese enterprise is the permanent worker group, decisions are taken in groups through formalized processes (known as '*nemawashi*' and '*ringi*'). Horizontal communication flows are organized between individuals from different functions in order to integrate the components of the firm. *Horizontal integration* generates synergies and facilitates technological transfers between business units. It is based on multi-functional career paths (internal rotation) and on-the-job training. The long-term orientation, consensual culture and integration processes go hand in hand with a great loyalty to the firm and a particular sense of hierarchy. The Japanese enterprise is hierarchical in the sense that individuals deeply respect the elder, more experienced members of the organization, but there are very few visible signs of hierarchy (such as individual offices and top-down decision processes) and middle managers do play key roles in building up decisions. Thirty years ago, Japanese products were not known for their quality. But the Japanese always cared about the satisfaction of customers' needs, they picked up some (US-made) quality control methods and invented quality circles. Indeed they built their world-wide competitiveness on the *search for superior quality.* This policy was backed up by tight inter-functional integration and naturally fitted their cultural background—heedfulness and perfectionism are entrenched in the Zen philosophy.

The ingredients of a European model

The idea that European firms may share some common characteristics that distinguish them from their Japanese or American counterparts is relatively new (Calori and de Woot, 1994; Henzler, 1992). Indeed, when one thinks about management in Europe, it is the image of diversity which dominates. The debate—homogeneity *or* heterogeneity—is useless, there is *both* unity and diversity across Europe, and the two perspectives complement each other. Top managers identified four common characteristics of management across (western) Europe: managing international diversity, internal negotiation, an orientation towards people, and a balance between extremes.

European managers have an ability to recognize diversity and a particular skill for *managing international diversity.* Because of the small size of their domestic markets, European firms have been forced to look outside at other different markets and their managers learned to deal with variety. European multi-nationals have a tendency to respect foreign cultures and to decentralize their international operations. But they are not so good at purely global strategies or at integrating diversity at the world level. They tend to integrate international operations through people (the mastery of foreign languages, international careers and training) more than through structures and procedures. Strategies tend to be negotiated between the headquarters and the foreign subsidiaries. Indeed *negotiation* is a typical European process. European firms have to negotiate with external stakeholders (the State, the EEC, the trade unions . . . even the Church sometimes) and management has less freedom of action that in the other zones of the Triad. But negotiation is also crucial within the organization, between the headquarters and the business units, between different levels of management and the employees. In Europe managers have to discuss, debate, negotiate and convince. Decision and implementation processes are more 'political' and less smooth than in the US and in Japan: 'You have to convince people in order to obtain their involvement'. European firms are *oriented towards people.* They fulfil social responsibilities, within a system which protects individuals (according to the managers in our study, even after 12 years of Thatcherism, the UK does not escape from this humanistic tradition). Also there is less conformism in European firms and 'quality of life' is generally preserved (flexible working hours, long holidays . . .). The dark side of the coin may be a tendency to individualism (as opposed to team spirit). Management in the US and management in Japan are often considered as two extremes on several characteristics, 'European firms are in-between' and *manage between extremes*. First there seems to be a better balance between complementary goals: profitability, growth and social responsiveness. Second, the relationship between the individual and the firm is a medium-term between the high Japanese loyalty and the high American independence. Also the European time-frame seems to fall between the US short-termism and the Japanese long-term perspective.

These European characteristics are probably rooted in the common history of Europe. Negotiation and the orientation towards people may be rooted in the tradition of dialectics and the blend of Christianity, humanism, and socialism. The attitude towards international diversity and the management between extremes may be the consequences of the very diversity of the European continent.

As demonstrated by Chandler (1990) in his comparison between the US, Germany and UK, the entry into a new socio-economic paradigm shapes administrative practices. As far as international management is concerned, the arguments developed by Nonaka (1990) explain the European tendency to respect diversity and the American-Japanese ability to implement purely global strategies. American firms initiated the first large wave of international investment in the 1950s, at a time when they were enjoying a very clear superiority over the rest of the world, hence their model of the multi-national dominated by the US headquarters. As for Japanese firms, they started to become international in the late 1960s and early 1970s. At that time, Japanese firms benefited from clear comparative advantages (low labour costs) which could be achieved through export strategies and centralized international operations. The same organization was also adequate when high quality strategies were developed. European firms started most of their international investments as the reconstruction period was ending, that is, in the mid-1960s. At that time they invested in other European countries in order to escape from their own narrow domestic markets. They were then confronted with the fragmentation of European industry structures and compelled to adapt to market diversity by favouring a local response type of strategy.

National administrative heritages develop in harmony with the broader societal context and the adaptation to new/foreign societal contexts may be problematic. For instance, top managers report the difficulties faced by North American executives in the political context of the European continent, where a stakeholder's approach is preferred (Turcq, 1994). To many Americans, European management appears to be 'chaotic' (which is not necessarily a bad thing when one considers the fad for 'Chaos management'). The Japanese subsidiaries in Europe seem to have difficulties in managing European managers and achieving a satisfactory integration of expatriates (Yoneyama, 1994; Hayashi, 1990). Europeans themselves do not yet master the diversity of management practices on their own continent.

European diversity

Several typologies of management systems in Europe have been suggested (see, for instance Hofstede, 1980; Laurent, 1983; Schneider and de Meyer, 1991; Albert, 1991; Simonet, 1992; Lessem and Neubauer, 1994) the problem is that they do not really fit with each other, as they are constructed on different and limited sets of variables. Here we present a segmentation of management styles in Western Europe based on top managers' synoptic perceptions of similarities and differences.

At a first level of segmentation the UK is considered as an exception in Western Europe. Management in the UK is somewhere between the American style and the continental style. The British, like the Americans, are more oriented towards short-term and quick financial profits than the other nationalities on the European continent. The British market has more of a trading nature than the rest of Europe, which has more of an investing nature. The economic and social policy under Thatcherism probably broadened the gap between the UK and continental Europe. However, the British share the European characteristics that we mentioned above and they differ from the Americans in three main respects: the British tradition of the manager as a 'gifted amateur' as compared to the American managerial professionalism, the low formalization of management in the UK, and the relatively low status of the managerial class in the British society as compared to the high status of business careers in the US.

At a second level of segmentation, continental Europe is split between the 'North' and the 'South'. The real invisible frontier between the North and the South may be the 'olive tree line' (which cuts France and Italy horizontally). However, considering the influence of religions, national educational systems and national policies, France and Italy are grouped in the Latin Catholic South. The South of Europe is characterized by more state intervention, more protectionism, more hierarchy in the firm, and management is more intuitive (some say 'chaotic'). The North of Europe is characterized by less state intervention, more liberalism, more participation in the firm and management is more 'organized'.

At a third level of segmentation, France is differentiated from other Latin countries. French firms combine intuition and formalization and the links between the state and the business community are tight and based on a management elite coming from the '*Grandes Ecoles*'. Also at a third level of segmentation, the northern group (which does not include the UK.) is split into three sub-groups: Germanic, Scandinavian countries, and 'small countries'. The German model (Germany and Austria) is characterized by several components: the system of co-determination (presence of workers' representatives on the board), the loyalty of employees who spend their career in a given firm which gives the priority to in-house training, the collective orientation of the workforce (team spirit and sense of discipline), the technical orientation and the specialization of managers (whereas the rest of Europe prefers a profile of 'generalist'), the long-term industrial orientation, and the stability of the shareholders among whom are the banks heavily involved in the industry.

Management in Scandinavia shares workers' participation with the German model, however it differentiates in being more oriented towards the quality of work life and less favourable to status differences between people. Also Scandinavian firms have been influenced by some aspects of the American style (for instance professionalism) which permeated through their foreign subsidiaries.

The 'small countries', the Netherlands, Switzerland, Belgium and Luxembourg also differentiate within the northern group. Because or thanks to their small size and history, they opened themselves to foreign countries and influences earlier and they are considered as the best illustration of a blend of practices, prefiguring European management.

Firms from small countries tend to have an international view of the business and their employees often speak foreign languages fluently. Pluralism is respected, there is a search of consensus built upon dialogue between the management and the works councils. Companies like Shell, Unilever (Anglo-Dutch for more than 50 years), Nestlé or Hoffmann-La Roche are the nearest to what one may call a European enterprise. Some managers also argue that such companies are close to the 'transnational' model suggested by Bartlett and Ghoshal (1989).

If Central and Eastern Europe were added to the picture, the diversity of administrative heritages would be even greater, at least during the transition phase in which most Eastern European companies are involved. Eastern European firms are now open to foreign influences. The future of their management paradigms will probably depend on the intensity and volume of interactions they will have with partners in other zones of the Triad. Indeed, in the case of Eastern Europe the (communist) administrative heritage seems to be refused. This exceptional situation suggests that the 'strength' of a national administrative heritage is proportional to the economic and social success of the nation.

International acquisitions are a particularly relevant phenomenon for studying administrative heritage. As Grant (1988) noted, individuals may not be as fully cognizant of their organization's administrative practices during periods of stability because the practices become a matter of routine. However, during the transition period following an acquisition the members of the two companies are confronted with a new set of practices that can cause them to develop a heightened awareness of their own practices and those of the other firm. In the next section we focus on a comparison between the integration mechanisms implemented by French, American and British firms involved in international acquisitions.

Administrative heritages and international acquisitions

A study conducted in 1991 provides empirical evidence of the persistence of national administrative heritages in the context of international acquisitions (Calori, Lubatkin and Very, 1994). The study first compared French companies with US companies when they acquire British firms. It showed that the French rely more on formal control of strategy and formal control of operations than the Americans. On the other hand the Americans seemed to rely more on the control of financial and human resources than the French. The American acquiring firms relied more on informal communication and co-operation (teamwork) than the French. These findings supported hypotheses derived from the 'culturalist' and the 'institutionalist' literature (Hofstede, 1980; Laurent, 1983; Gates and Egelhoff, 1986; d'Iribarne, 1989). British firms and US firms were compared as to the control mechanisms they exercise over (French) acquired firms. The Americans relied more on formal control by procedures (management control, budgeting and planning systems) than the British. Also the American managers tended to socialize more with the managers of the acquired firms and to involve themselves more than the British. These findings were in line with the culturalist and the institutionalist literature comparing the two countries (Hofstede, 1980; Chandler, 1990; Lawrence, 1993).

French, British and US acquiring firms do differ on several dimensions of the management of international operations—the centralization of strategic and operational decisions and the level of socialization, which are crucial to characterize the transnational organization (low centralization, high socialization). Clearly national administrative heritages seem to hinder the adoption of the transnational model.

The comparison between French acquiring firms and British acquiring firms provided a complementary empirical evidence (Calori, Lubatkin and Very, 1994). Comparing French domestic mergers with British domestic mergers showed that French buying firms exercise more control of strategy and operations than their British counterparts. This finding was confirmed when comparing French and British international mergers.

Such results were in line with the culturalist and institutionalist literature (Horovitz, 1980; Hofstede, 1980; Laurent, 1983; Elias, 1975; Noiriel, 1992). Comparing French domestic and French international acquisitions showed that French buying firms exercise *more* strategic and operational control when they acquire a *foreign* firm. Also in their international mergers the French appeared to socialize *more* than in their domestic mergers. Comparing British domestic and international mergers showed that British firms exercise *less* structural control (integration into existing divisions) and *less* control of human and financial resources when they acquire a *foreign* firm. Also when they are involved in international acquisitions, British firms socialize *less* than in their domestic mergers. The 'hands-off' attitude of the British contrasts with the 'hands-on' attitude of the French in international acquisitions.

These results are surprising in two ways. First, it seems that the national administrative heritage is even stronger when a firm merges across borders (as if managers would respond to uncertainty and newness with their most familiar routines). Second, the different attitudes of the French and the British towards socialization *with foreigners* call for explanations that can be found in a historical institutional analysis of the two countries (Calori, Lubatkin and Very, 1994). A historical institutional analysis shows that France and Great Britain differed in the administration of their colonial empires (Guillaume, 1994) and in their experience with immigrant populations (Tribalat, 1991). The 'assimilation' policy of the French can be traced back to the philosophy of Rousseau (*'Du Contrat Social'*, 1762), and the 'preservation' policy of the British can be traced back to Locke (*'A Letter Concerning Toleration'*, 1689; *'Two Treatises of Civil Government'*, 1690).

We argue that political ethos developed during the history of a nation are transmitted to the enterprises from generation to generation through the educational system (the school, the family and the Church). Educational programmes are designed at the national level and their national bounds perpetuate an ethnocentric view of the world. Primary socialization shapes cognitive structures (Berger and Luckmann, 1966) within the bounds of the home country. The work experiences that managers may have in other societies are processes of secondary socialization, in which the past is the reference for the interpretation of the present, and the interpretation of the present is always consistent with the past. Indeed, a national administrative heritage can be conceptualized as an explicit and implicit collective knowledge. We have presented some empirical evidence of the persistence of national administrative heritage in international settings. The problem with such knowledge is that it may not fit with new foreign societal contexts.

Ethnocentric biases and learning from the best foreign practices

Ethnocentric biases and cognitive rigidity often are unconscious. Managers who have to cope with international complexities should first be aware of their biases at the individual, the organizational and the national levels. In order to raise awareness, differences should be elicited *and* explained by a historical analysis. The question of the relevance of a given administrative heritage in a given new societal/organizational context should only come afterwards. Some empirical studies show that the answer is not so simple, put differently, national administrative heritages are not necessarily *bad* in international settings, and international differences do not always produce (cultural or administrative) clashes. First, managers may be more effective when they follow the ways they are most familiar with. Second, some new management practices may appear attractive to foreign managers. Turning back to the study of international acquisitions that we reported in the previous section: foreign managers may dislike the French tendency to centralize decisions and the British tendency to reduce socialization with foreigners. Indeed, excessive centralization and insufficient socialization appeared to be counter-productive in international acquisitions (Calori, Lubatkin and Very, 1994). On the other hand a complementary analysis of the same database showed that the French managers (in acquired firms) are attracted by the participative and co-operative culture of American buying firms and that both French and British managers are attracted by the objectiveness of the appraisal and reward systems implemented by North American companies. Put differently it is (administrative/cultural) preference that matters, not difference (Very, Lubatkin and Calori, 1993). Managers and workers in a given country may be *attracted* by some foreign practices and *stressed* by some other.

The recent attraction for western management practices in Eastern European companies is an extreme manifestation of this phenomenon which has been explained by the anthropological theory of 'social movements' and the psychological theory of 'procedural justice' (David, 1977). We interviewed top managers on these issues (Calori and de Woot, 1994), most of them agreed on the crucial importance of *learning from the best practices abroad*. Such a universalistic ethos may be explained by the shock produced by the Japanese competition in the 1980s and by the success of benchmarking at the beginning of the 1990s. Managers in large international companies acknowledge that the gap between the three zones of the Triad is narrowing. First, national institutions tend to converge or be replaced by regional institutions (as in the case of the European Union) and second, most importantly, multi-national companies actively transfer the best management practices across borders. The combination of these two globalization forces tend to reduce the societal effect (in the terms used by Mueller, 1994).

More precisely, North American companies and Japanese companies tend to become more locally responsive in their international operations and to balance their policies (that is, two characteristics of the European administrative heritage). Some managers are also tempted by the European tradition of long holidays. European managers recognize that they should learn entrepreneurship from the US and focus on the satisfaction of customers' needs in the way the Japanese and the Americans do. Both European and US companies try to catch up with the Japanese in the management of quality and the multi-functional horizontal integration of their firms (witness the current success of reengineering in the occidental business world). The challenge is to *re-invent* the best foreign practices so that they fit the cultural context of the receiving country. The Japanese quality circles adapted to the Japanese group culture had to be turned into total quality management (a top-down occidental concept) in order to be effective in western companies. In the same vein, reengineering is the western (top-down, quick-fix) version of the Japanese horizontal organization. Such adaptations are required because the cultural context does not change so quickly.

The very diversity of management practices within Europe is seen as an opportunity of reciprocal learning. Each national/regional administrative heritage can bring something to the community: the British—their sense of profit and their liberal world-wide vision of business; Southern Europe—some sense of chaos and intuitive management and the ability to conduct large-scale industrial projects; Northern Europe—participative systems of management, a zeal for quality and manufacturing skills; and the 'small countries'—their sense of dialogue and their international skills.

Achieving international knowledge flows is more difficult than rationalizing product flows, it cannot be done without some international rotation of managers and it takes time before new routines are adopted. Large international companies are the most active in this process of international convergence. Since the end of the 1980s some business schools have also tried to educate future transnational managers. However the *roots* of the administrative heritage—primary and secondary education, are still solidly planted in national ground. For these reasons the international convergence of management practices is very slow, particularly for these practices which touch the cultural foundations of a society and remain implicit. For years ahead managers will still be confronted with the diversity of management systems world-wide. They should be able to manage such variety if they are aware of differences and, at least, tolerate them.

References

Abbleglen, J. G. and G. Stalk (1985) *Kaisha, The Japanese Corporation*, Basic Books, New York.

Albert, M. (1991) *Capitalisme contre Capitalisme*, Editions du Seuil, Paris.

Bartlett, C. A. and S. Ghoshal (1989) *Managing Across Borders, The Transnational Solution*, Harvard Business School Press, Boston, Mass.

Berger and Luckmann (1966) *The Social Construction of Reality*, Pelican, London.

Calori, R. and P. de Woot (1994) *A European Management Model, Beyond Diversity*, Prentice-Hall, London.

Calori, R., M. Lubatkin and P. Very (1994). 'Control Mechanisms in Cross-border Acquisitions: An International Comparison', *Organization Studies*, **15** (3), 361–79.

Chandler, A. D. (1990) *Scale and Scope, The Dynamics of Industrial Capitalism*, The Belknap Press of Harvard University Press, Cambridge, Mass.

D'Iribarne, P. (1989) *La Logique de l'Honneur, gestion des entreprises et traditions nationales*, Editions du Seuil, Paris.

David, K. (1977) 'Epilogue: what shall we mean by changing identities?', *The New Wind: Changing Identities in South Asia*, K. David (ed.), in the series, *World Anthropology: Proceedings of the Ninth International Congress of Anthropological and Ethnological Sciences*, Mouton, The Hague.

Elias, N. (1975) *La Dynamique de l'Occident*, Calmann Levy, Paris.

Gates, S. and W. Egelhoff (1986) 'Centralization in headquarters-subsidiary relationships', *Journal of International Business Studies*, Summer, 71–93.

Grant, R. (1988) 'On dominant logic, relatedness, and the link between diversity and performance', *Strategic Management Journal*, **9**, 639–42.

Guillaume, P. (1994) *Le Monde Colonial XIXème-XXème siècle*, 2nd edn, Armand Colin, Paris.

Hamel, G. and C. K. Prahalad (1989) 'Strategic Intent', *Harvard Business Review*, May–June, 63–76.

Hayashi, K. (1990) *Global Kigyo No Kaigai Genchika Senryaku*, PHP Kenkyujo, Tokyo.

Henzler, H. (1992) 'La Renaissance de l'Eurocapitalisme', *Harvard l'Expansion*, Hiver, 48–59.

Hickson, D. J., C. R. Hinings, C. J. McMillan and J. P. Schwitter (1974) 'The culture-free context of organization structure', *Sociology*, **8**, 59–80.

Hofstede, G. (1980) *Culture's consequences: International differences in work-related values*, Sage Publications, London.

Horovitz, J. H. (1980) *Top Management Control in Europe*, MacMillan, London.

Laurent, A. (1983) 'The cultural diversity of Western conceptions of management', *International Studies of Management and Organization*, **XIII**, 1–2, 75–96.

Lawrence, P. (1993) 'Through a glass darkly: towards a characterization of British Management', paper presented at the Professions and Management in Britain Conference, University of Stirling, Scotland.

Lessem, R. and F. Neubauer (1994) *European Management Systems, towards unity out of cultural diversity*, McGraw-Hill, London.

Maurice, M., A. Sorge and M. Warner (1980) 'Societal differences in organizing manufacturing units: a comparison of France, West Germany and Great Britain', *Organization Studies*, **1/1**, 59–86.

Mueller, F. (1994) 'Societal Effect, Organizational Effect and Globalization' *Organization Studies*, **15/3**, 407–428.

Noiriel, G. (1992) *Population, immigration et identité nationale en France, XIXème-XXème siècle*, Hachette, Paris.

Nonaka, I. (1990) 'Managing globalization as a self-renewing process: experiences of Japanese MNCs', in C. A. Bartlett, Y. Doz and G. Hedlund (eds.), *Managing the Global Firm*, Routledge, New York. 69–94.

Ohmae, K. (1976) *The Mind of the Strategist: The Art of Japanese Business*, McGraw-Hill, New York.

Ouchi, W. A. (1981) *Theory Z: How American Business Can Meet the Japanese Challenge*, Addison-Wesley, Reading, Mass.

Pascale, R. T. and A. G. Athos (1981) *The Art of Japanese Management*, Warner Books, New York.

Perlmutter, H. (1969) 'The tortuous evolution of the multi-national corporation', *Columbia Journal of World Business*, **4**, 9–18.

Schneider, S. C. and A. de Meyer (1991) 'Interpreting and responding to strategic issues: the impact of national culture', *Strategic Management Journal*, **12**, 307–20.

Simonet, J. (1992) *Pratiques du Management en Europe, gérer les différences au quotidien*, Les Editions d'Organisation, Paris.

Thurow, L. (1992) *Head to Head*, Morrow, New York.

Tribalat, M. (1991) 'Cent ans d'immigration, Etrangers d'hier, Français d'aujourd'hui. Apports démographiques, dynamique familiale et économique de l'immigration étrangère', INED, *Travaux et Documents*, **131**, P.U.F.

Turcq, D. (1994) 'Is there a US company management style in Europe?', in R. Calori and P. de Woot (eds.), *A European Management Model, Beyond Diversity*, Prentice-Hall, London, 82–111.

Very, P., M. Lubatkin and R. Calori (1993). 'A Cross-National Assessment of Acculturative Stress in Recent European Mergers', Paper presented at the Academy of Management Conference, Atlanta.

Whitley, R. (1992 (edn.), *European Business Systems, Firms and Markets in their National Contexts*, Sage Publications, London.

Yoneyama, E. (1994) 'Japanese subsidiaries: strengths and weaknesses', in R. Calori and P. de Woot (eds.), *A European Management Model, Beyond Diversity*, Prentice-Hall, London, 112–32.

A day in the life of Aleksei Ustinov[1]

Philippe Le Comte and Stanislav V. Shekshnia

The working day did not begin with pleasant news. The first thing that Aleksei Ustinov, human resources (HR) manager for RosAmTrust, a Moscow-based Soviet-American joint venture, saw at his table was a memo he had sent to the general manager, George Nixon, a couple of days earlier. The memo came back with the brief handwritten comment: 'Aleksei, we are in business, not in business school and I need facts, not your emotions. GN.'

Aleksei felt disappointed, since he had been proud of his memo, a 22-page document. When George asked him to prepare a summary of recent developments in the area of human resources, Aleksei thought it would be an excellent chance to do something important for the company and to show off his managerial capabilities. He had been in his position for only a month and was keen to prove he was suited for the job. He decided he would not only describe the current state of affairs in his memo, but would also share with George his vision of what management in all areas should do, not just in the area of human resources, in order to bring excellence to RosAmTrust.

Before joining the company, Aleksei Ustinov had very little business experience. He graduated from the Moscow Institute of International Relations, then worked for some time in a research institute. When perestroika opened opportunities for private business development, he joined a Soviet-Finnish joint venture as assistant manager. After six months with that company, Aleksei was hired for the recently created RosAmTrust. His first assignment was to attend a six-week management development programme at Arkansas State University in the US. Upon completion of the programme, he became a human resource manager for the 200-employee joint venture that manufactured and serviced cutting and grinding equipment for the mining industry.

Working on his memo to George Nixon, Aleksei had tried to use all his previous experience to come up with a comprehensive plan for continuous improvement. He had looked up his notes from the management seminar, consulted his favourite management book, Peters and Waterman's *In Search of Excellence*, put in long hours and prepared a document which he thought would create a silent revolution at RosAmTrust. In 20 pages, complete with diagrams, Aleksei had developed his vision of the company and provided George with detailed advice on how to achieve this vision. The last two pages were devoted to the problem George had originally raised—recent developments in the human resources area.

Now, re-reading George's memo, Aleksei realized that George hadn't even seen that part—his pencilled notes stopped at the second page. 'I put much time and effort into this, and yet he has not even bothered to read it,' Aleksei fumed, frustrated and angry. 'I should go and see George immediately.' He reached for the phone, but remembered that he was scheduled to attend a meeting which had already started five minutes earlier. Postponing his conversation with George, Aleksei hurried to the meeting.

The meeting had been called by the manufacturing manager, Konstantin Bobrov, who wanted to discuss some problems concerning technology transfer with representatives of the American partner. Aleksei did not think he needed to attend such meetings, but he did not want to argue with Bobrov, who was well known for his stubbornness. When Ustinov entered the meeting room, he saw that the meeting had not yet started, even though all the participants were present. RosAmTrust's interpreter had called in sick that morning, and Bobrov was not able to find a replacement for him. As Bobrov explained to Aleksei, his secretary was trying to make arrangements with another interpreter who sometimes worked for RosAmTrust.

The situation was critical—the two Americans were smiling, but did not understand what was going on around them, nor why the meeting had not begun on time. Bobrov looked for help. Aleksei understood that, in order to save the meeting, something had to be done immediately. He spoke English and had even attended an American university, but he knew he was not good at simultaneous translation and did not like to do it. However, this time he decided to start translating himself.

The meeting began with Bobrov who explained that a $2 million machine, shipped two months earlier from the US and installed at RosAmTrust's factory, frequently broke down, and even when it worked correctly, did so at one-third the productivity initially anticipated. Bobrov wanted to know the reasons, and questioned the reliability of the suppliers. When one of the Americans suggested that they should speak with some workers to find out the real symptoms of the malfunctioning, Bobrov could not control his emotions any longer. He lost his temper and argued that some workers were supposed to work and they did, while suppliers were supposed to provide reliable equipment and yet they didn't. Aleksei translated the phrase in a less insulting form, but the visitors felt hurt anyway. They invited Bobrov to visit the factory immediately to assess the situation. Bobrov said that he had more important things to do, but would send one of his engineers with them to the factory. It was decided to resume the meeting upon their return.

Leaving the meeting room, Ustinov realized that he had almost missed another meeting with Ron Johnson, the marketing manager who had asked him to come by. Ron was a dynamic young fellow with lots of creative ideas, and Aleksei always liked to spend time with him. That day, Ron wanted to talk about hiring a new assistant for the marketing department. He had identified a candidate himself through personal connections and asked Aleksei to interview her. During the interview, Aleksei had been very impressed by the young woman's analytical and foreign-language skills, as well as by her desire to work hard and make a lot of money. He had communicated his impression back to Ron, who was very enthusiastic about his prospective new employee.

Ron explained why he had wanted to see Aleksei: Natasha, the candidate for the job, had called him the night before and explained her difficult situation. She had received a formal job offer from another company and had to give an answer by the following morning. She indicated that she would rather work for RosAmTrust, but since she had received no offer from them, she was going to accept the other offer. Ron was very disappointed with the news and wanted Aleksei to act immediately.

'We have to make her an offer today, Aleksei, otherwise we are going to lose her. We have to act fast.'

'But she hasn't had an interview with George yet. How can we make her an offer without his approval?'

'Well, you know how George interviews people: "How are you? What's going on? Thank you, good-bye". He has never rejected any candidate we put forward, has he?'

'No, but company policy . . .'

'Come on, Aleksei, company policy should be flexible. We have to make her an offer today. You probably don't remember, but three months ago I found an excellent administrative assistant—a woman who spoke three languages and typed like a machine. But George was travelling and had no time to interview her for three weeks. Remember what happened? She went to work for a German company.'

'Well, at least, we should tell George about it.'

'I've already tried, but he's out of the office for the rest of the day. Why don't you draft an offer and I'll sign it. If we read it to her over the phone tonight, she would be working for RosAmTrust in a week. If not, she is gone forever.'

'We can't do it, Ron. Hiring decisions are made only by the general manager, but in this case we haven't even told him about it.'

'Aleksei, you know better than I do that George just rubber-stamps your decisions. He's too busy to hire every marketing assistant himself.'

Aleksei was confused. He felt that he should not violate existing policy, and yet Ron had a sound argument. This young woman would be an excellent resource for their company, and it would be a shame to lose her. What should be done? How should the situation be handled correctly? Aleksei knew that he had to make a decision, but he did not know what the right decision was. However, when Ron said that he would take full responsibility for breaking company rules in this case, Aleksei readily agreed and went to his office to prepare the offer.

At lunch, which Aleksei always ate in RosAmTrust's small cafeteria, he saw Leonid Grechko, his colleague from the factory. Grechko had come to the office for a meeting and had decided to take advantage of the excellent food served in the cafeteria. They had been talking for a while when Grechko asked if Aleksei had heard about an accident in the factory three days earlier. Ustinov was taken completely by surprise, since he had not received any reports about it. Grechko explained that Nikita Suslov, a recently hired production worker, had deeply cut his finger while handling heavy metal sheets. The injury was serious and would keep him off work for at least 10 days.

Aleksei was upset about the accident itself, as well as the fact that it had not been reported to him. To find out more about it, he called the factory and spoke with a foreman of Suslov's team. The foreman confirmed the accident and explained that the injury was serious because Suslov had not been wearing gloves and had handled the sheets himself, thus violating procedures recommended during the mandatory training programme for new employees. Aleksei wanted to know more about what kind of training Suslov had received. He called the factory training manager and found out that no training whatsoever had been provided to Suslov, and even his hiring was unknown to the training manager. When he asked about what kind of training was scheduled for that position, Aleksei learned that none had been

planned at all, since hiring for that job had not been forecast at the time
they had developed a training plan and distributed it to all departments.

Aleksei sat back for a while and realized that the situation he had to
report to the factory manager was far from satisfactory. He felt that safety
was not a concern for most RosAmTrust managers, and that
inter-departmental and inter-personal communication should be
substantially improved. But how could he do it?

Later in the afternoon, Bobrov called Aleksei and said that he needed to
send three workers to the US for training. That request was another surprise
for Ustinov, since the training Bobrov requested was not in the training plan
he had prepared and distributed to all departments the previous week.
When he tried to explain it to Bobrov, the latter exploded and said that he
did not need a human resources manager who could not organize the kind
of training he wanted. It turned out that the problems with the newly
installed equipment were caused mainly by the inadequate skills of workers,
who had not received any preliminary training. To improve the situation, the
representatives of the American partner had suggested that the workers be
sent to the US for three weeks' training at one of the partner's factories.
Now Bobrov demanded that Aleksei organize the trip to take place in two
weeks' time.

After Bobrov angrily hung up, Aleksei remained still for some time. He
thought about his unpleasant day—his memo had provoked a very negative
reaction from his boss, he had just broken a company policy, and a person at
his same job level had spoken to him as if he were a school boy. Actually, the
last thing was not new at all: Bobrov, a heavy man in his late fifties, was often
rude to Aleksei and other younger employees. Moreover, he openly
expressed his low opinion of the human resources function, calling it, 'An
overseas toy, which will never work on hard Russian soil.' Once Aleksei had
tried to argue with Bobrov, but the latter had not even wanted to listen to
him, saying that Aleksei would have to work another 20 years before they
could work on any serious matters together.

Remembering all the unpleasant things Bobrov had done to him, Aleksei
could not think about the training request without getting upset. 'He badly
needs this training. If the machines don't work properly, Bobrov is in big
trouble. But this training has not been planned, so I have every right to say
"no" to him. If that's what I decide to do, it will be a good lesson to Bobrov.
Perhaps then he will learn to respect the human resources function and
younger people.' Thinking along these lines, Ustinov prepared a formal
memo to Konstantin Bobrov saying that the requested training could not be
organized until the following year, since it was not in the training plan for
the current year.

After finishing the memo, Aleksei looked at his watch and realized that
the working day was almost over, but he still had many things to do. 'Well, I
will have to stay late again,' he thought, and turned to the pile of paper
sitting on his desk. The papers were materials for a presentation Ustinov was
preparing for the next board of directors meeting. As a new company,
RosAmTrust was in the process of developing its operations, building up its
staff and creating internal systems. One of the systems to be created was a
compensation system, and George Nixon had asked Aleksei to develop a
proposal for a compensation policy for the joint venture. Ustinov was really
enthusiastic about the project and worked hard to complete it successfully.
Based on what he had learned at the management programme in the US, he
had come up with a plan which he thought would meet company needs. The

central idea was to attract the most capable people to the joint venture and motivate them to perform at their best. Staffed with a skilled and strongly motivated workforce, RosAmTrust could achieve excellent financial results to benefit both shareholders and employees. To ensure effective recruitment, the company should become a market leader in salary levels, recruit nationwide and provide benefits people had enjoyed at their previous companies.

As for the internal salary structure, Ustinov thought that RosAmTrust should adopt a system he had learned about in the US, 'pay-for-knowledge,' whereby employees are paid according to the skills they possess, rather than the relative worth of their current jobs. That system, thought Aleksei, would promote education and motivate employees to acquire new skills that RosAmTrust badly needed. To Aleksei, the concept seemed well developed; however, he was having a hard time supporting his ideas with numbers. In the highly inflationary and rapidly changing Russian economic environment, it was almost impossible to collect any reliable data about the labour market. So when Aleksei thought about market leadership in salaries, he really did not know what it represented in hard numbers.

After thinking things over, Ustinov went back to his papers. The previous night he had received a memo from the Siberian branch of RosAmTrust. The general manager of the branch reported salaries for the last month which were three times higher on average than those of employees based in Moscow. That was quite a puzzle—how to deal with such regional differences, while maintaining a national salary structure that Aleksei himself favoured.

The sound of the telephone ringing interrupted Aleksei's thoughts. George's secretary was on the line. A huge truck with equipment from Western Europe had just arrived at RosAmTrust's warehouse located 20 km away. However, no one except the security guard was there. The truck driver called the office and asked what he should do, threatening to turn back with his cargo if it was not unloaded that night. The secretary asked Ustinov to make a decision since he was the most senior manager in the office at that moment.

Note   1 The names of the organizations and employees have been changed to preserve confidentiality.

Questions   1 In what ways is Aleksei Ustinov's day different from the typical HR manager in a well-established Western company?

2 What underlying factors are causing problems for Aleksei Ustinov? Do you think they are culturally specific to FSU (former Soviet Union) countries? What factors do you suspect might be culturally derived?

3 What advice might you give Aleksei Ustinov in order to increase his overall effectiveness in the company?

4 How might a Western firm similar to RosAmTrust cope with the challenges they might face in a different environment such as Russia? What suggestions might you offer?

Bodegas Torres[1]

José Maria de Anzizu and Oriol Amat

At the wine-tasting at the 'International Wine Challenge 1993' held in England, 450 experts judged more than 6000 wines from all over the world. The results could not have been better for Bodegas Torres who obtained a gold medal for their white wine Milmanda 1991; a silver medal for their red wine Gran Coronas 1987 and another three wines received a bronze medal: Vina Esmeralda 1992, Gran Sangre de Toro 1988 and Sangre de Toro 1990. Torres was the Spanish *bodega* which obtained most prizes.

Some years ago, in 1979 to be exact, Gran Coronas from the same company was the winner, against all odds, of the 'Great Wine Marathon' held in Paris and organized by the prestigious *Gault Millau* magazine, in which 330 wines from 33 different countries participated. These prizes—along with the constant increase in sales in over 80 countries—served to confirm once again the appreciation on the part of the distributors and consumers, of a medium-sized Catalan company which continued to stand out by means of an excellent price–quality relationship in its products and which continued emphasizing creativity, innovation, and even originality.

Moreover, this time was particularly interesting, and, to a certain extent, delicate. On the one hand, Miguel Torres S.A. was competing in a market which was becoming more and more globalized and competitive along with companies, some of which were owned by multi-nationals, and others, by families with a long tradition and specialization in a specific segment of the wine market. On the other hand, Miguel Torres Carbo, owner and manager of the company since before the Spanish Civil War (1936–1939), had died in 1991 and many observers were wondering whether his heirs would be capable of maintaining 'the Torres business' in the privileged place which it occupied.

Like many other Spanish companies, in 1993 Miguel Torres S.A. was in full 'transition' period between a way of managing and organizing which could be considered 'traditional', at least in Catalonia during the decades of the 1960s to the 1980s, and another 'advanced' way which was emerging in the successful companies of the 1990s. This transition involved having to change focus and policies on a strategic level and, at the same time, put into practice changes or adaptations in the structural and organizational systems. As was to a certain extent normal in the history of the company, none of these changes took place in a 'revolutionary' or drastic way, but rather by taking the opinions of family members and professionals into account and making decisions step by step without running unnecessary risks.

This case attempts to summarize the situation of the company at the end of 1993 and to make clear some of the conflicting or particularly important areas, with a view to the future in order to facilitate internal discussion and for later use in teaching institutions.

Historical background

Bodegas Torres was founded in 1870 by the brothers Jaime and Miguel Torres, although the family had been cultivating its own vineyards since the 17th century. The company distinguished itself from the outset by innovation, quality and the priority it gave to commercial aspects. In this sense, it is interesting to emphasize the importance of the exportation of Torres wines in bulk to America and especially to Cuba.

Jaime and Miguel died in 1906 and 1910 respectively and were succeeded by Juan, Miguel's son, who began distilling wines to produce brandies and, in addition, had to run the company in difficult years due to the world economic crisis. Juan died in 1932 and was succeeded in the ownership and management of the company by his son Miguel, then aged 21. He had a degree in chemistry and was about to complete his pharmacy studies. Miguel Torres Carbo made up for his initial lack of experience by a total dedication to the company and an inborn commercial intuition. His wife, Margarita Riera, worked closely with him from the beginning of the new phase, and especially after the Spanish Civil War, when Miguel and Margarita had to begin again in order to resuscitate a company which had been reduced practically to ruins.

During the 1950s, 1960s and 1970s, Miguel Torres made several decisions which fashioned the growth and development of Bodegas Torres until it was one of the main wine-producing and export companies in Catalonia and in Spain. Among these decisions were: beginning to sell bottled wine instead of in bulk as was the norm then in the Penedes; reviewing the structure of its own commercial network in Spain and a network of distributors in the major countries; investments in Chile and the US; the adoption of a conservative policy and re-investment of profits in the financial aspect; and, in particular, the direction he gave to the training of his children: Juan Maria, Miguel Agustin and Marimar. It was Miguel Agustin, with a degree in oenology and viticulture from the French University of Dijon, who introduced foreign varieties to Spain, which were developed very successfully in the Penedes, and who gradually took charge of the management of the company during the last years of Miguel's life.

The company at the end of 1993

Miguel Agustin Torres became the main shareholder of the Spanish mother company in May 1991, as well as of the Chilean company, and his brother and sister—Juan Maria and Marimar—owned the rest of the shares. In the North American company, 'Marimar Torres Estate', Marimar owned the majority of shares and was in turn responsible for the operative management. The three children, along with their mother Margarita and some of the main executives, formed the Administrative Council which met quarterly in order to examine the most important matters, such as decisions on investment; the relation between different companies in the group; profit-sharing, etc. Some external consultants attended certain meetings.

By the time of his father's death, Miguel Agustin Torres had taken over the Presidency of the Council and general management, continuing, as before, to pay special attention to the production aspect. His brother, Juan Maria, collaborated in several of the company's activities, especially in representative activities at a high level—an important area in a company like Torres. All members of the family had their role in specific markets, collaborating with the person in charge of that market, as, for instance, with Miguel Agustin Torres' wife, Waltraud, in the management of the German market, as well as her participation in the design area.

Strategy   On a strategic level some ideas had been introduced and developed over the past years which were gradually influencing the dynamics and the day-to-day results. One of these was the introduction of high quality wines at a relatively higher price ('pagos', equivalent to the French 'cru') with which it was hoped to gradually change the image of 'an acceptable quality wine at a moderate price' which some brands had in certain countries (as, for instance, 'Sangre de Toro'). Another aspect was the increase in the presence of company products in less 'traditional' foreign markets, such as the Scandinavian countries, Japan, Australia, South Africa, etc. Commercialization and distribution aspects were increasingly important as they were considered to be one of the most strategically significant medium-term factors in the beverage sector. On the other hand, the company had acquired a large amount of land in order to plant vineyards and produce their own grapes without having to resort to buying them from third parties (except for a certain percentage) as many wine companies have to do. The importance of the research department should also be pointed out: it is connected to universities and wine-studying centres all over the world, thus allowing very rapid adaptation to the most advantageous developments and, in turn, their own applied research which is presented periodically at congresses and international meetings. For instance, at the moment of writing this case, research was being undertaken, together with the chemistry department at Tarragona University, on the 'Relationship between geographical origin and chemical composition of wood for oak barrels'.

Overseas operations   In the US, operations are run by Marimar Torres, sister of Miguel Agustin Torres, who moved to the US in 1975. Marimar added her dedication, perseverance and enthusiasm to the quality of the Torres products: 10 years later sales had multiplied ten-fold. In 1986, Marimar undertook the project of planting a vineyard in Sonoma Green Valley, near San Francisco, and received advice from Miguel Agustin on the development of the plantation which had an exceptional density: 5000 vines per hectare, over four times the traditional planting frame in California. According to Marimar Torres 'The experiments of our technicians in Spain prove that, despite the fact that the amount of grapes is lower, this way the vines live longer and they develop more delicate aromas, greater concentration and better balance'. The first 'Marimar Torres Estate' wine was a 1989 barrel-fermented Chardonnay, which was extraordinarily well received by wine critics in North America and Europe. The 1992 Pinot Noir was bottled in August 1993 and will be released for sale in 1994.

In 1979, Don Miguel Torres had acquired a well-known bodega in Chile and had placed his son, Miguel Agustin, in charge of its reorganization and future development so that the could acquire an initial experience at general management level. Miguel Agustin introduced modern oenological technology for the first time in Chile, successfully—which was totally unexpected for many people there. In 1993, Sociedad Vinicola Miguel Torres S.A. (Curico, Chile) was directed by Juan Campas, who has a degree in business administration from ESADE, Barcelona. He was one of the first young graduates to join Miguel Torres S.A. at the beginning of the 1980s. The Chilean company produced and sold five different varietals: whites, roses and reds of high quality, as well as a sparkling wine produced by the '*méthode champenois*'. Export sales were run by the sales team (Exports) from the Spanish mother company.

Table CS13.1
Economic data

	1989	1990	1991	1992	1993
Miguel Torres, S.A. (Vilafranca del Penedes, Barcelona)					
Total sales (m[1]cases)	1945	1920	1922	1955	1990
Total exports (m.cases)	505	620	565	652	665
Investment (m.ptas)	307	303	318	405	507
Staff	287	290	309	310	305
Hectares			900	900	940
Sociedad Vinicola Miguel Torres, S.A. (Chile)					
Production (m.bottles)			1250	1250	1250
Exports (m.bottles)			600	600	600
Staff			50	55	55
Hectares			230	230	230
Caliame (California)					
Production (m.bottles)				96	110
Staff			5	5	5
Hectares			22.5	22.5	22.5

[1]m = millions

Table CS13.1 provides some economic data for the Spanish, North American and Chilean companies.

Internal affairs

On an internal level, over the past two years the company had been trying to accommodate the organization and its structure to the demands of an increasingly competitive and changing environment. The various family members continued to play a very important role in the representative, and in some cases, operative, aspects of the company's life, but the complexity of the business made it necessary for more collaboration and responsibility on the part of professionals who were assigned important tasks in different areas. Many of these professionals had begun their activities in the company when young and had acquired experience and knowledge through their responsibilities in the daily operation; others, who had joined the company five years before or less, had a university degree or similar and had gradually been filling important posts in areas such as marketing, export sales, etc. Despite the fact that, in the selection process, the possibility of a candidate's adaptation to the company's culture was taken into account, on many occasions the adaptation process of young professionals, in particular those who had no work exprience, presented some difficulties. This was understandable in a company which attributed a large part of its success to factors such as innovation, intuition and hard, constant work with no 'fixed' working timetable by the family and all those who had achieved a position of responsibility over the years. In one executive's opinion, 'In the past, when we joined the company we went through different departments before taking on a specific responsibility. Sometimes I notice this process is missing in some of the executives who have been incorporated recently. They take on responsibilities and give their opinion without having enough knowledge of the company. We didn't have the opportunity for training: there was no time for that. And now they say we are behind the times . . .'. And one of the university graduates who joined the company in recent years reflected a point of view which is quite common among the youngest group of executives: 'The company has to become more professional although this does not mean that all executives should have MBAs or be university graduates. The time of huge gross margins is over. Management now has to be much more refined as a result of world competition. On the other hand, the Torres family is an indispensable asset for the company'.

The organization was restructured in 1991—and caused differing reactions, not all of them positive. For instance, in the words of one of the main directors: 'The organization restructuring was confusing. It was too ambiguous and this generated a certain amount of tension'. Although the new structure was meant to represent the functions and levels of responsibility of the main executives it could hardly replace the range of personal and work interrelations between the owner and employees in the different levels and departments which had developed over the years in an informal, and on some occasions, conflicting, way.

In 1991, a two-day meeting was held with some 20 or 30 main executives in order to deal with change in the company and to confront the various points of view. Everybody agreed that this meeting, the first in the company's history, was interesting and productive. The executives got together in small groups and gave their opinions on the main subjects of interest, with a view to the future. A similar meeting was being considered to strike a balance between what has been achieved since the previous meeting and to deal with several short-and medium-term matters of interest. Among these is the need to achieve greater and better communications between the different areas, given that lately, with the increase in delegating by general management, executives have been acquiring a greater degree of responsibility and should improve co-ordination among themselves. In one executive's opinion, 'There is a lack of communication between executives in the different departments and some responsibilities have not been clearly defined. We get together in meetings, but perhaps something more is necessary. The departments are much too closed in on themselves'.

The functional areas

The Spanish company at present has 303 employees, the Chilean company has 55 and the Californian company has 7. The Spanish company is divided into several functional areas: production, administration, commercial, human resources and—very recently—organization and systems.

The production department comprising the vineyards, wine production and bottling, is composed of relatively young people, in many instances with university degrees, who form a well-complemented team with a wide delegation of responsibilities on an individual level. Both wine and brandy production are divided into sections according to the different stages of the production cycle, from vinification (or distillation in the case of brandy) to bottling. They are supported by the maintenance, quality control and administration areas.

In 1992, Miguel Torres S.A. produced nearly two million cases in Vilafranca del Penedes, of which 630 000 were destined for export. A considerable part of the grapes was obtained from their own land. The company owns 930 hectares for vine cultivation. Production in the US and Chile, in the same year, amounted to almost one and a half million bottles, of which a little under a million were exported. The total number of hectares owned by the company in these countries is 252.

As regards costs, it is interesting to bear in mind grape prices on a world level. At this moment, the price of a kilo of grapes of the same variety is almost double the price in the Penedes than in Chile or

Australia, and it is also more expensive than the average price in California or Southern France. This is due to the reduced size of the properties, insufficient mechanization and the absence of irrigation, as it is not legally permitted.

The administrative–financial department is made up of professionals who have worked in the company for many years and are well integrated. It includes the following sections: accounting (general accounting and dealing with external auditors), treasury (in charge of the collecting and making of payments, relations between credit organizations and treasury) and management control (calculation of costs and producing and controlling budgets).

Due to the self-financing policy followed for years, the company's debt level is very low in spite of the large investments made. An updated system of management control, using responsibility centres, is currently being established.

The human resources department is in charge of the selection and training of personnel as well as the payroll. In recent years, continuous training, by means of agreements with external centres and the collaboration of consultants for internal courses, has acquired great importance. Periodically, sessions are organized on 'total quality', for executives and middle managers, led by experts on the subject.

The organization and systems department was created at the beginning of 1993 and is in charge of the computer section, interdepartmental co-ordination and internal auditing. It collaborates very closely with the economic-financial department in order to provide adequate information for management control.

The marketing department is made up of the following sections: domestic sales (with six area managers and its own network of sales force covering the whole national territory); exports (with four area managers and administrative staff); public relations (which organizes visits to the company's installations and runs the press office) as well as marketing in the true sense. This department had evolved over the years and in 1993 was in a full re-structuring phase in order to adapt to changes in the sales and distribution systems, both in Spain and in other countries. One of the company's characteristics is that it can reach any domestic customer directly without going through the distributors. Most sales staff are exclusive.

The area responsible for studying the development of the different products on the market had recently become more important and made recommendations on communication, price, and strategies to be followed in each case. It was made up of a small group of young professionals who had previous experience in the sector of consumer products.

The design committee was created shortly before the death of Don Miguel Torres Carbo. It is managed by Juan Maria Torres and works closely with the marketing department. This committee is concerned with the design of new products, labels, cases, etc, as well as the creation of sales and promotional material.

The President-Director-General's point of view

Miguel Agustin Torres is at present 52 years old and began working with the company prior to starting his university degree, at the age of 21. At his father's suggestion, he studied at the French University of Dijon and immediately after, he joined the company's technical or production area.

His father, Don Miguel, did not accept any interference in commercial and administrative decisions but did, however, have a great respect for his son Miguel Agustin's capability as an oenologist and as the person responsible for the production process. Miguel Agustin introduced and developed in Spain, with remarkable success, grape varieties from other wine regions in various parts of the world and played a key role in the growth of Bodegas Torres during the 1970s and 1980s. At the same time, he became very active as a writer and researcher in wine-related subjects and continued his studies and contacts with the best wine technicians in the sector from all over the world. At a general management level, it was he who took charge of Torres-Chile ever since the acquisition of the estate in Chile in 1979. During the latter years of his father's life, he gradually took over responsibility for other areas of the company so that when don Miguel died, the company continued running smoothly without upheavals and with a stability rare in similar cases. Over the two years which have followed Don Miguel's death, Miguel Agustin has been adapting the traditional strategy and structure of Bodegas Torres to his own ideas and management style.

Below are some of his views on certain subjects.

On the sector

We have seen very significant changes in our sector in recent years. After an almost total domination by France, good expansion has been started by other European countries. Italy in first place, and Spain up to a certain point, have overcome the image of 'cheap' wine or 'plonk', as it is sometimes called. Wines have also arrived from the 'New World': Australia, New Zealand, Chile, South Africa, California, etc. These wines have gradually acquired large shares of the market, especially in specific countries such as the UK, the US and Scandinavia.

There is also a change in the consumers' attitude: they no longer accept old attitudes, such as French wine is the only good wine. It seems what they are looking for is a good price–quality relationship. They try to test, experiment, etc. And in this sense, wines from the 'New World' can offer them something very interesting: a reference point—for instance, Chardonnay or Cabernet Sauvignon—and good quality, regardless of the traditionally known 'Appellation of Origin'. All this under the auspices of a brand with an adequate guarantee. And this works well, at least in the medium-price range, as it has not yet reached the higher range. This has been a major change.

Spain—and in particular the Penedes—is in an intermediate or mixed situation. As regards production, we are closer to the 'New World' policies. Brands continue playing a very important role and have not entered the atomization offering of the production areas, as in the French case. In addition, we had the good idea of planting varieties in the Penedes known all over the world: Chardonnay, Cabernet Sauvignon, Pinot Noir, etc. In this respect, we have one of the most considerable offers in the world as we also have local varieties. Another company, Jean Leon, pioneered the introduction of Cabernet Sauvignon and Chardonnay. Torres subsequently introduced a significant amount of these, and many other, varieties.

Regarding distribution, we have seen the phenomenon of multi-nationals realizing that the wine business was not as profitable as they thought and so they have been gradually drawing out of it. In the 1980s they used to buy bodegas, now they are selling them. In some cases they have concentrated on distribution. The wine business involves much investment and generates little profit. One has to invest in stocks, vineyards, etc. If we are talking about profits on sales, that is acceptable. But it is very low on invested capital. It could even make you want to give up!

Some months ago, at a course at IMD in Lausanne, we looked at several cases of big companies and I suggested an example that if a chocolate company had to buy land, plant it, wait four years until the product grew and then harvest it, then keep it in cellars for two years, etc., they would probably not be interested. The same thing would happen with the big tobacco companies. Large wine companies which have abandoned production are Seagram, for instance, Coca-Cola, which had a bodega in California, etc. Even Benetton went into Gonzalez Byass and has now drawn out. This is a prevailing trend.

On the family business

In connection with the above, I feel the family business is beneficial in the wine trade for many reasons. Because employees receive much more personal and direct treatment and they have a much higher level of motivation and collaboration than in big companies, either with public or shared ownership. Because there is dedication and a kind of fondness for the product which is shared by all members of the family and collaborators. Because of the love of quality, because the family business is not a great sharer-out of profits, but uses a Spartan philosophy of re-investment, thinking of future generations. It does not look for short-term profits like others. From a the consumers' point of view, they like to know who made the wine, which gives them confidence.

It is interesting to note that we have begun an association between 12 'wine families' ('*Primum familiae vini*') to which the most important wine-related families in Europe and one from the US (Mondavi) will belong. There are companies from France, Italy, Portugal, from Spain, Torres and Vega Sicilia. All of a very high level. They have to be prestigious companies, with family members at the head of the business, with a thorough knowledge of vineyards, wine, marketing, etc. There are large, medium-sized and small companies in this association. It is important that the family brings its philosophy to the wine company, for example, concerning wine-making. A bodega is a little like a restaurant: you become a customer because you like it, because it is well-run, you like the image, the wine, the people, the overall 'feeling', etc.

On professionals

There must be a balance, without doubt. When my father began in the 1940s, he did almost everything himself. Nowadays that would be impossible. There have to be professionals to delegate to, but who accept the family's philosophy.

A few days ago a friend was telling me that I travel too much. I replied that at that time one executive was in Brussels negotiating an important agreement, another was in the US, a third was in France with the distributor. I was here. I think that, little by little, we are seeing the fruits of having selected young managers over the past 10 years and several of them now occupy highly responsible posts, together with other people who have been in the company longer. For some time, the main executives have been meeting, without me, in order to discuss the most important day-to-day matters and to ensure proper co-ordination between departments. This allows me to have more time for representative tasks and to maintain permanent contact with what is happening in the world, both on a production as well as on a consumer level.

Factors for Torres' success

I will say something which is not new but for me is fundamental: work. To work with confidence, with dedication, with love. There is no secret. Spending hours doing things as you like them to be done. That is what is important. Doing a little better than the rest. Like the case mentioned in the book, *Wealth and Poverty* by George Gilder, Ronald Reagan's adviser, about the immigrant who arrived in Chicago and started up a fruit business. Everyone thought it would fail. But he always did something more than the others. He opened sooner, closed later, made home deliveries, etc. And things went very well for him.

Torres is a brand which gives confidence. The consumer knows that it is of high quality and a reasonable price. When you travel for instance, if you order our wines in restaurants in any country in the world, you will possibly find them. The 'wine families',

I mentioned before, want this: consumers to be able to find our wines in any country and so always be sure of what they are buying.

The future of the company

On a short-term level, and after the changes of the past years, we are in a phase of consolidating the company, 'digesting' the payment of inheritance taxes. We cannot, at this moment, think of great expansionist ideas or investments in other countries, but rather are concentrating on consolidating what we already have. In fact, Chile has already been self-sufficient since 1985 and generates profits which are re-invested. The Californian winery has already produced several years of a Chardonnay of excellent quality. We should advance in the idea not of increasing sales volume but increasing the sales of the higher quality wines. As regards production, we have made enormous investments in land and plantations over the past 10 years and are now starting to reap the fruits of this. We have very high quality wines which will improve our average prices and allow us to concentrate more than we have been able to, up to now, on better sales in the range of high quality wines, which I referred to above. As regards brandy, we should also proceed along these lines of quality. The Miguel Torres brandy is successfully exported and we have projects for other high range brandies, a market in which we are present although with little participation. Concerning variety, Torres Import, a company within the group, has been concentrating for two years on food products only (preserves, Belgian biscuits, 'marrons', luxury soaps, etc.) which are sold in delicatessens. And we are not ruling out other projects.

Regarding the role of the various family members, it is logical that in some cases this gradually becomes more representative, with less involvement in the day-to-day running. Formerly, for instance, each member of the family was responsible for a country, including my mother. Now, with the exception of my brother Juan Maria, who is directly in charge of two countries in order to follow the market trend, the other countries are controlled by professionals. However, the family members certainly play an outstanding representative role and visit specific countries.

For instance, my wife Waltraud visits Germany regularly in order to complement the task of the person in charge of that market, in agreement with him. On a representative and advisory level, the task carried out by my mother, Margarita, is also very important. My sister, Marimar, for her part, maintains regular contact with Vilafranca as well as her task of promoting our products in the US as the main shareholder and person responsible for the Californian company.

His role as Director-General

In any case, whenever one has adequate training, I think that the top management post in a company such as ours should be held by a member of the family. For my part, I feel directly responsible for the great strategical directions we take. I indicate the company's general objectives, in accordance with the guidelines of our Family Council and make a periodical follow-up of the management process. The departments work well and have been accepting the changes in the new organization chart, but management teams cannot be improvised: they are built and take shape over time and with daily experience. Our organization chart is already quite complete but there are still some aspects to be improved.

Note

1 This case was written with the support of the Centre for Organizational Studies, IESE, Barcelona.

Questions

1 What are the organizational challenges facing Bodegas Torres in fulfilling its growth strategy?

2 Can the structure and culture of Bodegas Torres function effectively across national boundaries?

Rus Build: joint venture[1]

Sheila M. Puffer and Iurii I. Ekaterinoslavskii

Rus Build is a joint venture (JV) between Fredericks Construction, Inc. and the Gribov Engineering Institute. The JV is engaged in three lines of business in Russia and abroad:

1 marketing of products in the construction industry,
2 management of large-scale construction projects, and
3 design and delivery of management training programs.

The company was founded in 1989 at the initiative of a professor at the Gribov Engineering Institute who learned, through one of his students studying abroad, of an American firm that was seeking a joint venture partner in the (then) USSR. The professor arranged a meeting with John Fredericks, president of Fredericks Construction, Inc. and several colleagues the professor worked with at the engineering institute. The process of creating the joint venture took three and a half months from the time of signing the protocol of intentions to application for registration with the USSR Ministry of Finance. Registration of the joint venture took two weeks.

Structure of the joint venture

Initially ownership of the JV was shared equally by the two partners. The Russians' investment consisted of a 25 000 roubles ($40 000 at the official rate at the time), 400 m^2 of office space, and four hotel rooms. The Americans' investment consisted of approximately $50 000 in hard currency and office equipment. The original board of directors comprised of four Russians and three Americans. The chairman of the board was Russian, the general director, American. On the Russian side were the director of the construction engineering institute, two professors who had extensive experience in the construction industry, and the marketing director who was an expert in supply issues. The Russians each had one vote on the board. On the American side were John Fredericks who had two votes, as well as his wife, Joanne, and his brother, Herman, who each had one vote. Thus, there were four votes on the Russian side, and four on the American side. In lieu of a salary, the members of the board of directors were entitled to 1000 roubles twice a year in a profit-sharing plan.

Four departments were formed: construction projects (i.e., buildings), ecological projects to clean up factories that polluted the environment, special construction projects (e.g., insulating subway systems to prevent water seepage), and management training programmes. Several administrative services were organized to operate the joint venture: planning and book-keeping, a secretariat, business services (in charge of travel arrangements), and communications. Operations were managed by a marketing director (who was also the deputy general director), a technical director, and a commercial (business) director. At the outset the JV employed more than 25 people.

Issues faced by the joint venture
Setting up the office

The Russian partner provided the facilities and supervised the necessary renovations. Office equipment including telephones, a photocopier and a fax machine were installed. Given the great shortage of suitable office space, it was crucial for the Russian partner to provide the facilities and for the American partner to provide the office equipment.

Hiring qualified staff

One of the early challenges was hiring qualified staff. Although the members of the board of directors had considerable experience in the technical aspects of managing large construction projects, they lacked experience in entrepreneurship and international business. Since few Russians possessed such knowledge, it was also difficult to find managers with the skills needed to run an international joint venture. For example, finding an accountant was difficult because very few Russian accountants had experience in managing hard currency and most were unfamiliar with the accounting systems and practices used in the West. The board of directors hired Russian nationals whom they knew personally, and these individuals then recommended others to be hired. No personnel testing was conducted or formalized selection procedures used.

The chief operating officer was also the marketing director of the JV and a professor at the Gribov Institute. He knew the construction sector well, was well connected, energetic, capable, and a risk-taker. His weakness was his lack of management knowledge. The technical director, a restrained, cautious individual, had a strong technical background. The commercial director was dynamic and a thoughtful decision-maker, but risk averse. The accountant, was well qualified, 'kept them honest,' and got along well with people. There was also an executive administrative support staff. The intensity of the work and the hours were much greater than in jobs in the state sector, but the personnel were highly motivated to perform at this more demanding level. They were attracted by the opportunity to work in a foreign firm, to learn how to do business in a market economy, and to have greater autonomy over their jobs. Additionally there was potential for significant monetary rewards relative to what they could earn in Russian organizations.

The role of the board of directors

The members of the board of directors typically spent two or three days a month performing their functions related to the JV. Communication between the American and Russian board members was by telephone and fax. Initially the board tended to rubber-stamp the recommendations proposed by management. The JV was just getting on its feet and they accepted virtually any client just to get started. However, after eight months, two of the Russian members of the board of directors threatened to quit because they objected to the 'irresponsible behaviour' of John Fredericks and the poor analysis of potential clients which had resulted in unprofitable contracts. The board also had difficulty defining its roles and responsibilities. It became overly involved in operational decisions that should have been left to the management. The board needed to learn to set the strategy for the enterprise and take a long-term view.

Building a client base

Another challenge for the JV was to find projects backed by foreign investors to enable the enterprise to earn hard currency. At first it seemed that it would be easy to find construction projects because of the great demand in the USSR. The partners thought that they would have the luxury of choosing among projects proposed by both American and Soviet clients. However, most of the projects turned out to be either not feasible or not serious. In addition, the instability of the political situation and the inconvertibility of the rouble deterred Western companies from investing. Therefore, in the first year of operation construction projects were not a source of income. The easiest way for the JV to make a profit (including hard currency) at that time was in its other line of business—conducting training programmes and seminars on business management and technology. The JV offered courses which resulted from the contacts of board members based on their personal reputation.

Major problems arose as a result of the JV's failure to engage in any systematic analysis of potential clients' seriousness and their ability to pay. This approach to accepting contracts was particularly evident in the case of a client who wanted to hire Rus Build to build a 35 million rouble hotel complex. The two parties engaged in lengthy negotiations, drew up construction plans, and held receptions to celebrate the deal with the minister and other officials from the industrial ministry that was to approve the project. At the last minute, after much time and effort had been spent, Rus Build learned that there was no financing for the project and the contract was cancelled.

Developing a relationship with the foreign partner

Although John Fredericks was the general director of Rus Build, the Russian partners felt he was minimally involved in developing strategy and overseeing operations. He appeared to do little to help the JV and failed to fulfill the promises he made when the JV was formed. For instance, he had promised to find American investors who would back the JV, as well as clients who would pay for the JV's services in hard currency. He had also promised to provide his expertise in construction project management. None of these promises was fulfilled to a significant extent. Instead, Fredericks engaged in a series of activities that the Russian partner felt actually undermined the JV. For example, he used the JV's office in Moscow to set up another unrelated business. Furthermore, he tarnished the reputation of the JV and drove away a potential client by overpromising a commitment that the JV could not fulfill. On another occasion, when one of the Russian board members went to the US in the Spring of 1990 to visit Fredericks' company, Fredericks failed to disclose that his business had gone bankrupt. Instead, Fredericks took him to his wife's company in an attempt to show that all was well. Fredericks' credibility with his Russian partners deteriorated further when he failed on two occasions to put up his share of the initial investment on time.

Adding new partners

In light of their disillusionment and disappointment with their initial foreign partner, the board of directors decided to search for a new partner and gradually 'ease out' Fredericks and his family members. First they tried to get a Finnish company to become a partner, but it was bought by another Finnish firm. They then invited an American company, Midwest Tek, to become a third partner based on the recommendation of a Russian who was familiar with the company. Midwest Tek took a wait-and-see attitude and asked for financial data on the JV. When Midwest Tek finally agreed, John Fredericks, the original American partner, said he was against it. At that point the Russian partners had lost faith in Fredericks. The JV was successful by then, so they simply made Midwest Tek a third partner and hoped that Fredericks would not interfere with the JV. To further complicate matters, it was difficult for even the Russian members of the board of directors to agree to accept a third partner. To make the decision, the vote had to be unanimous. However, one of the Russians initially refused to go along with the idea. He could provide no concrete data to support his view; he simply had a 'gut feeling' that it was not appropriate to have a third partner. Eventually, the other Russian board members convinced him otherwise and the company joined forces with Midwest Tek. The new partner was given two votes. John Fredericks' ownership was reduced to one vote, and his wife and brother were given no votes. Thus, the Russian side retained four votes, but the Americans had only three votes.

As a result of the addition of a new partner, the board decided it needed to restructure the JV and divided it into three separate businesses. It later added a fourth business when it joined forces with an existing Soviet-Japanese firm. In this way the JV became a *de facto* association of unrelated businesses rather than a unified business. It was an umbrella organization in which there were general accounts and sub-accounts for each of the four businesses.

Building a team

Another shortcoming of the JV was the failure to engage in team building. The greatest organizational weakness was that there was little horizontal communication or integration among the businesses. There was insufficient co-ordination of functions. Each functional department tried to conduct its affairs as an autonomous unit, which resulted in inefficient operations and poor management such as the duplication of various centralized services. In effect, the manager of each business built his own 'empire' and had his own staff in functional areas such as finance and marketing.

Prospects for the future

In spite of organizational problems and the lack of managerial skills, by the end of the first year the JV was engaged in 28 projects and had a staff of 70. They had developed strong contacts with potential foreign clients and were engaged in projects throughout the USSR. Sales for the first year were 3 million roubles. Profits amounted to 400 000 roubles, including $50 000 in hard currency. The JV projected 20 million roubles in sales for the second year, with profits of 1.5 million roubles, including $400 000 in hard currency. Rus Build had plans to emphasize construction and consulting, and to build construction projects in the West to earn hard currency.

There are many competitors to Rus Build. A formidable one is the state construction organization in the former USSR which employs 35 000 people. The management training field is also filled with many competitors. Rus Build believes that its competitive advantages are timeliness, price, and an entrepreneurial attitude. (An example of the latter is a profitable deal they made to sell Vietnamese wood to Israel.) Rus Build planned to expand operations throughout the former USSR and hoped to broaden the range of products and services it offered. Changes in government policies could be a major determinant of the JV's success.

Conclusion

Rus Build was one of the first joint ventures with foreign partners that became operational in the former USSR. The Russian participants, while experts in their own fields, had no experience in starting a business and had few precedents to follow. In their eagerness to take advantage of newly available opportunities to do business in a fledgling market economy, the partners of Rus Build functioned in a trial-and-error fashion and, in essence, 'felt their way' toward the market economy.

Note   1   The identities of the organization and individuals are disguised.

Questions   1   Identify the range of problems faced by Rus-Build? Why were they encountered? What could have been done to limit the problems?

2   What would be some of the key success factors for a foreign firm considering a strategic alliance in Russia?

3   What are the advantages and disadvantages of the creation of a joint venture in a developing market?

Part VII
Managing in the Future

The new worker

Introduction

How different is the future likely to be from the past? This chapter is about the outer boundaries of the future. If we believe that the future will be pretty much like the past, then much of this chapter's content will be, hopefully, interesting but irrelevant. On the other hand, if we perceive there will be some fundamental changes to how we work, why we work and where we work, then this chapter (and Chapters 23 and 24) become critical to our understanding of organizations.

This chapter considers some of the potential changes to how we, as individuals, might view work in the future. In so doing, we will need to challenge some assumptions about much of our understanding of organizational behaviour.

Values and attitudes towards work

The meaning of work is changing constantly. To the ancient Greeks and Romans, work was associated with drudgery. To the Calvinists, work was regarded as an act of religious salvation. From this view, the Protestant work ethic was derived. The reason for the Protestant label is simply because it was derived from the dogma followed by the Reformation movement which ultimately created the Protestant church. This much-discussed work ethic defined work as important, virtuous and a source of dignity. Work was seen as inherently good and should be continued even if the individual's financial position did not require it (Weber, 1976). The potency of the work ethic varies both over time within populations and between different populations (see Chapter 20).

How hard must we work?

In 1851, the average British worker had to work for 200 000 hours over his or her lifetime to pay for all of their physical, medical and social requirements. By 1971, this halved to 100 000 hours (47 hours per week for 47 weeks per year for 47 years) (Handy, 1989). By 1986, male employment had fallen to 86 000 hours over the average male lifetime. One forecast is that this it will fall to 70 000 hours by 2001 (Armstrong, 1984). The remainder of our time is being spent on a variety of activities: staying in education longer, on government-sponsored training schemes, being unemployed, married housewives who do not work outside the home, or individuals who are retired (and live longer) (Sparrow and Hiltrop, 1994)

The concept of more non-work time itself has become well-accepted. The long working hours of previous generations has evolved into a five-day, and perhaps even a compressed four-day working week. Currently, many European trade unions are pressing for a standard 35-hour working week. In addition, more people are opting to choose part-time work opportunities or job-sharing. This is particularly evident among women—partly out of choice and partly due to job inequalities (Sparrow and Hiltrop, 1994).

Strictly, the distinction is not between work and leisure, since working mothers who job share and work flexitime will look after the home and family at other times. This is work of course, but occurs away from the formal place of employment and statistically does not count. Research undertaken at Hewlett Packard in the US in 1995 has shown that of their employees who have dual income spouses, both spouses work about the same number of hours per week (50 hours per week). However, women spend an additional 33 hours per week engaged in household or childcare activities compared to only 19 hours for their male equivalents. (Platt, 1997) To organizations, the net result is the same. They will have to cope with very different attitudes toward work and non-work activities. Workers are likely to see working in formal organizations as only a part of their total lives. Expanding vacation times and paid sabbaticals are all part of the increasing amounts of time people can devote to non-work activities.

Working and not working: the social divide

There is a potentially very large problem looming on the horizon. If we can envisage a future where organizations are capable of producing all the goods and services which are required with a workforce of only 75% of those able to work—what happens to the other 25%? This remaining quarter of the population available for work would have, in theory, the opportunity to do whatever leisure activities they wanted. However, this situation raises important questions about such a society:

1   How should the unemployed 25% obtain their 'title to consumption', that is, money?
2   If their input is truly not required by society's economic apparatus, should the provision of unemployment benefits be seen as degrading?
3   What alternatives are there to providing support?
4   How should the decisions be made concerning who is in formal employment and who is not?
5   If a substantial proportion of the population continues to want to work, and continues to be excluded from this activity, why should they continue to support the existing economic and social system?

Revolt and anarchy could be the outcome of a process which is primarily aimed at increasing general welfare and promoting fairness. To make such a future society work, societal values will have to change substantially.

Despite an increase in potential non-work time, it has not all become 'leisure time'. Instead, many people have chosen to 'give back' their free time in exchange for higher earnings and an ability to become more consumerist (Sparrow and Hiltrop, 1994). Of course, this can only apply to the 'haves'—those who have some form of employment and therefore have either the money to indulge in increased leisure time or have the skills and knowledge to 'give back' their free time. The divided society this will create will be a difficult place in which to live (for both the haves and the have-nots).

Because of the increased emphasis on knowledge and education as prerequisites for employment, anyone who is unemployed is likely to become unemployable in a very short time. The long-term unemployed will pose a strong threat to the rest of employed society. Crime, especially the theft of high-value goods, is likely to rise. Such goods can easily be sold and disposed of without trace. The 'haves' are likely to be insured (at very high costs) and so will be able to replace their sophisticated electronic products (but probably not older items of considerable worth or sentimental value). What will 'leisure time' mean for the long-term unemployed? It certainly will not be the same kind of leisure time as that indulged in by the working population. Those who work will be able to afford the kind of 'integrated' entertainment that we can see already emerging in developed Western countries (leisure centres, where multiple varieties of entertainment are offered under the same roof ranging from indoor skiing to ten-pin bowling and multiple cinemas). Such entertainment centres are likely to become the domain of the privileged only.

Yet the privileged will suffer in a different way. This is speculation, of course, but the following scenario is quite believable (and has some evidence already to support it).

- The working population will become increasingly 'ghettoized'. They will tend to go only to those places deemed safe or which are policed to be safe (by a privatized security force, of course).
- Towns and cities will reflect this ghettoization to an even greater extent. Those employed will live in only one or two selected parts of town (or village) and the rest of the town will be populated by the long-term unemployed. Between these two groups will be a no-go area.
- The working population will need protection from the theft and violence perpetrated upon them out of sheer frustration by the long-term unemployed. Such protection will take many forms. Higher insurance policies have already been mentioned. Cars will become more expensive as increasingly sophisticated immobilization equipment is fitted to ward off theft. Suburbs where the 'haves' live will probably need protection. This might include guards, patrols and high fences as well as identification checks and electronic surveillance of all kinds.
- Those earning higher salaries will buy their own protection in different ways. The next 15 years will see major changes in the demographic structure of the population. By 2010, 20% of the population in Europe will be over 65 years old. This major consumer group will have their own savings and investments which for many will comprise significant wealth in the form of equity in houses and high levels of income from specific pension schemes. Those with high equity will be able to borrow easily and they will have high levels of disposable income.
- Since 'intelligence' is the valued future asset base of the individual (Handy, 1995), education will become a highly differentiated service. Elite schools and universities will cater for the *creme de la creme* and employers will select primarily from this pool of graduates.
- Intelligence (or knowledge) will become fast-moving commodities, however. Many of the currently employed could find themselves rapidly joining the unemployed as their state of knowledge becomes redundant or irrelevant to an organization's needs.
- Since organizations will not expect allegiance to them (knowledge workers have greater allegiance to their work than to the organization—see later in this chapter) they will have little hesitation in firing individuals at all levels who do not meet their required knowledge expectations. Companies will feel justified in 'bleeding dry' the knowledge base of individuals and then getting rid of them, since they know that they can easily recruit a new batch of employees who possess 'new' knowledge. Those sacked run the risk of having to cross the no-go area in their town and join the unemployed.
- Loneliness and isolation will increase both in the workplace and out of it.

Researchers in the United States have detected a decline in the prevalence of the work ethic over the past 20 years, at least in the male population. Among female workers, there are more conflicts with other equally important ethics: for example, the homemaker ethic or the mothering ethic (Walker, Tausky and Oliver, 1976). In Sweden, high levels of absenteeism have been attributed to the erosion of the work ethic, since workers appear to 'go sick' with increasing frequency. They prefer to absent themselves from work, even though Swedes have fewer working hours per week than almost any other nation [less than the 35 hours per week currently sought by unions across Europe]. According to Lennart Sunden, deputy managing director of Electrolux, 'A belief in work has deteriorated among the young' (*Financial Times*, 30th August, 1989).

In the future, the term work might become difficult to define. For some individuals, technology and more flexible work patterns could allow them to take on work which they otherwise would not be able to do. For example, technology can offer individuals a greater opportunity to work when and where they wish (Bridges, 1995). Similarly, with some technological assistance, workers with disabilities can now assume jobs which might not otherwise have been possible. Many firms are offering selected employees the opportunity to work from their homes (Bridges, 1995).

Work could take on many different meanings. For some, it will be something they never experience. For others, work will be Tayloristic drudgery by which they get paid sufficiently to carry on with their lives. Or, work may be an activity undertaken when necessary to provide the resources to do something else. The movement to use temporary or contract workers by many organizations has created a group of workers who have learned to benefit from this. By working for six months and then, taking time off to travel, go back to their studies, or simply try something else, people are living their lives as a 'portfolio' of experiences (Handy, 1995). In this way, work assumes a somewhat less onerous part of the individual's life—it becomes a means to achieve something else rather than the central activity of their adult life. Assuming we are discussing those who are employed, then what will the future hold?

What might motivate employees?

In Chapter 5 we highlighted some of the key debates regarding motivation theories. It is possible that the factors which motivate people to undertake a task will also change. Fritz (1996) highlights the key components of the re-think which might have to take place:

Table 22.1
Changes in motivation and reward structures

If people were motivated by	. . . the organization would need to reward them through:
Money	Compensation
Power	Position/budgets
Professional identity	Freedom of choice
Fear of negative	Control
Ideals/personal values	Concepts
Symbols	Awards
Job satisfaction	Interesting work
Job security	Continuity
Challenge	Change
Interaction with others	Work teams
Individual contribution	Independence
Career advancement	Opportunity

Source: adapted from Fritz (1996: 235)

One conclusion which emerges out of this approach is the need for organizations to become much more flexible in providing the right context for motivation for each employee. To many HR directors and managers the thought of individual redesign of the working environment may not be welcome. However, it does not avoid the issue that they may not be attracting the very best employees available because of the historic structures and practices in place in the organization.

What might the job have to offer?

As part of the educational process in our society, individuals are taught to anticipate a relatively high degree of choice in how they manage their lives. Unfortunately, most organizations have not been structured to allow them the freedoms or alternatives which they may have expected. In itself, this is a very complex, emotive issue. A variety of organizational factors impinge on this: job content, supervision styles, motivation and control systems, formal rules and structures, etc. If workers have been conditioned to expect considerable freedom in their lives, it is not surprising that they are disillusioned, spending great amounts of their time in an organization which explicitly seeks to control or to de-skill their knowledge. Reading 17 by Martin Corbett discusses how new automated technologies can reduce workers' skill requirements to those of machine-minding. In a challenging book, Cooley (1987) also argues that technology will play the largest part in shaping future expectations of work. He draws a pessimistic view of a future which de-skills and demotes workers to drones in the service of automated technologies thereby losing a great deal of craft and innovative skills.

The accepted practice within organizations is to break down what has to be done into small 'chunks' which we traditionally call 'jobs'. These defined tasks are then codified (job descriptions) and ranked within the organization in terms of reward, power, status, etc. However, the need for organizational flexibility and the decline in employee loyalty has meant that the definition of 'the job' might have to change. As Bridges points out:

> The reality we face is much more troubling, for what is disappearing is not just a certain number of jobs or jobs in certain industries, or jobs in some part of the country . . . What is disappearing is the very thing itself: the job.

Leaving aside the issues of whether the job as a defined set of activities will continue for much longer, we must also consider our own reasons why we might wish to work for an organization. Tulgan (1996) identified four common features which characterized what younger workers were looking for (see Table 22.2):

Table 22.2
What young workers seek: four common features

Factor	Concern
Belonging	Is this a team where I can make a meaningful contribution?
Learning	Do I have sufficient access to information?
Entrepreneurship	Is there room in my work to define problems, develop solutions at my own pace, and produce my own results?
Security	Am I able to monitor the success rate of my performance, my status at work, and my return on investment?

Source: adapted from Tulgan (1996)

The implication is that the in-built assumptions of organizations about how to organize employees and how to encourage them to undertake the required tasks may need to be reconsidered (Sellers, 1994).

It is hard to imagine many jobs which are not being influenced by technology. For example, a high-quality service function like the traditional secretarial/personal assistant role to a senior manager has been fundamentally altered. Answering telephones is now undertaken by voice-mail systems. Intra-organizational communication is conducted by electronic mail (email) and intranets. Video conferencing is reducing the need to travel and co-ordinate movements with others. Networked personal scheduling software allows others to check our diaries and place in it meetings, events and tasks. When we do travel, mobile phones and portable computers allow us to function by doing much the same activities as we would in the office. Indeed, the office itself may be our car, our home or a telecottage (*The Independent*, 1993). Training and education can now be delivered over the Internet at a time and place convenient to each individual. It would seem that a grasp of technology and its utility will form part of any job we undertake.

The potential de-skilling of work due to technology is a point that has already been made. The other side of the argument is that it can also be liberating (Sorohan, 1994). One study reported that telecommuters (those working away from their office) experienced less stress than those working in an office environment (Trent, Smith and Wood, 1994). Other studies report higher morale among teleworkers possibly due to their ability to control their own working time (Hartstein and Schulman, 1996)

A market research study conducted in the US indicated that the number of employees who telecommute to work has risen from 2.4 million in 1990 to 7.6 million by 1995 and is forecast to rise to 11 million by 2000. (McNerney, 1995). However, working remotely may not suit everyone. O'Connell (1996) highlights eight attributes which were common in successful telecommuters:

- familiar and comfortable with the job itself
- self-motivated with a strong work ethic
- disciplined and skilled in self-management
- an effective communicator
- adaptable and able to compromise
- knowledgeable about organizational procedures
- technically self-sufficient
- results-oriented

How will we relate to our colleagues?

For most of us, a large part of our working lives involve working in teams or small groups to accomplish defined activities. The ability of team members to get along and work together is an often unstated but vital part of completing tasks on time. Much of the research cited in Chapters 8 and 9 on group and inter-group behaviour assumes a physical closeness, that is, regular, frequent and often informal interactions. We look to others in our teams for guidance on the task itself, on hints about the organization itself, and indications as to appropriate sorts of behaviours. In return, we usually offer some sort of loyalty and camaraderie with the other team members. In some cases, this can be quite a close-knit community which includes social outings, in other cases, it can remain formal and professional. Irrespective of the 'climate' within your team, the future may dramatically alter our understanding of teams and their relevance.

As already mentioned, telecommuting will reduce the need to see other members of the teams as regularly as we might have done in the past. This may be compensated by an increase in other forms of communication. For example, email allows individuals to communicate almost instantaneously with others anywhere in the world. By addressing the email to any number of recipients, everyone can be kept up-to-date and informed as to what is going on. The downside of this use of email is the huge rise in the number of messages you can receive which are of little or no relevance (Stahl, 1995). Some organizations have recognized this email overload problem by restricting its emailing system to just two 'deliveries' per day (Stahl, 1995). Kawasaki (1995) offers some email etiquette for users:

- Do not send a file unless the recipient wants it and expects it.
- Describe the topic of the message in the subject area.
- Never write all in capital letters—it is considered the electronic version of shouting.
- When replying to someone else's email, only quote relevant text. There is no need to send the whole document back to them.
- Use carbon copies (cc) or blind carbon copies (bcc) sparingly—who really needs to know?
- Never create or forward chain-letter email.
- Message unto others as you would have them message unto you.

Our definition of a work team may also have to change. Team members may be widely dispersed geographically and indeed may be working for other organizations. In addition, our own career patterns may mean that we work on a variety of different projects or tasks with many different teams. The result is a decline in a sense of team identity and support. Because we might feel less personal loyalty to other team members, we might offer less support than in the past. Similarly, we may not receive much support or guidance from others as they do not feel part of the team either.

The knowledge worker

Advances in technology are changing the way we work (see Reading 16 by Chris Barnett and Reading 17 Martin Corbett). Beyond this, one result has been the continuing increase in demand for what has become known as 'the knowledge worker' (Drucker, 1977).

Traditionally, workers have been stereotyped into two broad classifications: white-collar and blue-collar. Over the past 30 years, the proportion of white-collar workers has grown rapidly. However, the changing workplace has caused the knowledge worker to emerge which, though more closely aligned to white-collar working environments, also includes activities formerly undertaken by blue-collar workers. Included in this group are engineers, computer programmers, accountants, teachers and nurses. The value of such employees does not lie in their manual dexterity. It lies in their ability to apply their knowledge to specific situations. They tailor their skills to the context of the job, which is likely to be highly varied. Such employees are flexible and knowledgeable. It is their ability to collect information, integrate it with what they already know, and incorporate this new information in new and often innovative ways, that make such individuals highly valued by employers.

Though one might think that managing such individuals would be easy—given the challenge and rewards associated with their jobs, many organizations have found it difficult to retain such valued employees. The problem lies in the old-fashioned human resource strategies still practised by many organizations. As a throwback to the days when managers had to dominate their workers through fear (of being sacked), organizations have found it difficult to cope with individuals who, if disillusioned with one employer, can get another job elsewhere relatively easily. In general, knowledge workers tend to prefer far more open operating environments and consequently resent traditional styles of control. Their specialized knowledge is usually so highly in demand that their tolerance of an unfavourable working atmosphere can afford to be slight.

Though it is difficult to generalize, knowledge workers tend to be achievement-oriented. They also prefer working environments which provide adequate recognition for their achievements. Among their personal goals, knowledge workers aspire to growth and personal satisfaction which are derived from challenging tasks. Data from a number of studies suggest that the following human resource strategies are favoured by this section of the labour force (see Sisson, 1989).

1 *Regular feedback*   Knowledge workers prefer to operate in an environment which shares information about their organization and how their job relates to the whole.
2 *Management by objectives*   By jointly developing goals and objectives with knowledge workers, and then following them up with supportive control and recognition, knowledge workers are more likely to remain committed to their role.
3 *Eliminating unnecessary activities*   Most organizations tend to restrict individual action through the use of meetings, reports and paperwork. It is important for managers to be aware of how such activities may impede the work of knowledge workers and to seek ways of reducing them.
4 *Challenging work*   Knowledge workers stand a greater chance of leaving from boredom if they are under-employed. Managers of such individuals therefore must ensure a constant supply of challenging, non-routine work activities.
5 *Opportunities for creativity*   Aside from providing challenging work, knowledge workers also prefer to see their work as creative. Therefore, some latitude has to be built in which allows individuality to emerge.
6 *Averting low morale*   For most organizations, the investment made in attracting and training knowledge workers is substantial. If problems which lead to low morale are not caused early enough, valuable human resources may leave the organization—seriously threatening the organization's competitive position.
7 *Careful selection and placement*   To get the most out of knowledge workers, organizations must seek to match the most appropriate people with particular jobs. Any mismatch is likely to result in low morale and high employee turnover.

Summary

The future holds immense challenges for human resource management. Attitudes toward work itself, toward working hours and toward the place of work in the wider social context are changing. Such perceptions differ significantly between countries such as Italy, France or Britain, despite their geographical proximity.

The composition of the labour force is also not stable over time. Demographic trends mean that the profile of available labour will be very different in the 21st century compared with the past. In particular, the number of available young people will be severely reduced. Technological advances have de-skilled (and removed) some jobs as well as enhancing others and have created a range of new knowledge-based occupations. There is a severe risk of creating a massively divided society based on those who have work and those who have little chance of ever finding any work. Increased crime, violence and social ghettoization will be the likely result.

Strategies to cope with these changes are varied and will be discussed in the Chapters 23 and 24. Whether or not such strategies are successful, only time will tell. It is certain, however, that organizations which do not confront the issues of the new worker in the future are unlikely to survive very long. It would seem that sustaining a competitive edge in the future will depend as much upon successful human resource management as upon product or service innovations.

We have expressed a view in this chapter that such strategies for dealing with the future will require changes both to the nature of the manager and managerial activities, and to the design and rationale of organizations. We explore these questions in the following chapters.

References

Armstrong, P. J. (1984) 'Work, rest or play? Changes in time spent at work', in P. Marstrand (edn.), *New technology and the future of work and skills*, Francis Pinter, London.

Bridges, W. (1994) 'The end of the job', *Fortune*, Sept., **19**, 62–74.

Bridges, W. (1995) *Job Shift*, Addison-Wesley, Boston, Mass.

Cooley, M. (1987) *Architect or Bee? The Human Price of Technology*, Hogarth Press, London.

Drucker, P. F. (1977) *People and Performance: The Best of Peter Drucker on Management*, Harper & Row, New York.

Fritz, R. (1996) *Corporate Tides: The Inescapable Laws of Organizational Structure*, Berrett-Koehler Publishing, New York.

Handy, C. (1989) *The Future of Work*, Blackwell, Oxford.

Handy, C. (1995) *The Empty Raincoat: Making Sense of the Future*, Arrow Books, London.

Hartstein, B. A. and M. L. Schulman (1996) 'Telecommuting—The new workplace of the 90s', *Employee Relations Law Journal*, **21** (4), 179–88.

Kawasaki, G. (1995) 'The rules of email,' *MacWorld*, **12** (10), Oct., 286.

McNerney, D. J. (1995) 'Telecommuting: An idea whose time has come', *HR Focus*, **72** (11), 1–4.

O'Connell, S. E. (1996) 'The virtual workplace moves at warp speed', *HR Magazine*, **41** (3), 50–3.

Platt, L. (1997) 'Employee work-life balance: The competitive advantage' in F. Hesselbein, M. Goldsmith and R. Beckhard (eds.), *The Organization of the Future*, Jossey-Bass, San Francisco.

Sellers, P. (1994) 'Don't call me a slacker', *Fortune*, Dec., 12, 181–96.

Sisson, K. (ed.), (1989) *Personnel Management in Britain*, Blackwell, Oxford.

Sorohan, E. G. (1994) 'Telecommuting takes off', *Training & Development*, **48** (9), 9–11.

Sparrow, P. and J. M. Hiltrop (1994) *European Human Resource Management in Transition*, Prentice-Hall, London.

Stahl, S. (1995) 'Fighting email glut' *Information Week*, **551**, Oct., 30, 40.

The Independent, (1993) 'Computer group aims to keep work at a distance', April 24, 4.

Trent, J. T., A. L. Smith and D. L. Wood (1994) 'Stress and social support' *Psychological Reports*, **73** (4), 1312–4.

Tulgan, B. (1996) *Managing Generation X*, Capstone Publishing, Oxford.

Weber, M. (1976) *The Protestant Ethic and the Spirit of Capitalism*, 2nd edn, Allen and Unwin, London.

CHAPTER 23 The new manager

Introduction

Organizations are changing and the attitudes of individuals towards work are changing. Therefore, it should be no surprise that managers themselves will have to adapt as well. The population of managers is changing all the time. The tendency of organizations to promote internal candidates to middle and senior management positions is decreasing. The educational level and aspirations of managers are continually increasing. The demographics of managers are changing: managers are getting more responsibility at earlier stages of their career and an increasing number of managers are female.

Charles Handy recounted a meeting he had with a senior manager in a German organization: 'In Germany, our organizations are largely run by engineers. Such people think of the organization as a machine, something that can be designed, measured, and controlled—managed, in other words. It worked well for us in the past, when our organizations typically produced efficient machines of one sort or another. In the future, however, we can see that organizations will be very different, much more like networks than machines. Our brains tell us this, but our hearts are still with machines. Unless we can change the way we think and talk about organizations, we will stumble and fall' (Handy, 1997).

According to Drucker (1988) current managerial activities will be entirely inappropriate for the future. He argues that currently, managers:

● Do not like to create a climate which encourages change.
● Spend too much time protecting their own little territory.
● Are good at complaining, but poor at making good proposals.
● Rarely question the services they provide.
● Spend too much time organizing their activities, without checking whether or not they are doing the right thing.

Since organizations are changing rapidly toward decentralized, information-based, task-force dominated institutions (see Chapter 24), the new manager will need to possess a significantly different repertoire of skills and abilities. Certainly, he or she cannot operate as above. Attention will be centred upon flexibility, the possession of a general/corporate vision rather than a functional specialism, an ability to work easily in teams coupled with highly developed communication skills.

To cover all the potential changes for the managers of future organizations would be an impossible task in the short space allotted. Therefore, we will examine some of the areas and offer some perspectives on what managers might be doing, saying or thinking in the future.

Will we still require managers?

The urge is to say 'yes' and move on to the next topic! Yet, there has been a body of research and opinion which indicates that managers, top executives at least, have only a limited impact on the success of the organization (Lieberson and O'Connor, 1972). Theoretically, the population ecologists have argued that the latitude of managers has been limited to largely speeding up and slowing down organizational momentum along a particular direction. (Hannan and Freeman, 1977). Another body of researchers point out that managers often feel compelled to adopt a conservative course of action, which in most cases is to imitate what has gone on in the past. (Spender, 1989). Yet another reason why managers tend to have relatively little impact on organizational performance is that managers as a group have been homogeneous (March and March, 1977).

As one should expect by now, there is a body of opinion which indicates that managers do matter and can significantly affect organizational performance. (Tichy and Sherman, 1993, Virany and Tushman, 1986). Perhaps it is reasonable to say that the role of the manager is an important one and, depending upon the context, can be influential or not. The question then arises regarding whether the future will require a traditional managerial role or not.

Managers as change agents

For many large organizations, the term 'change agent' is reserved for external and sometimes internal individuals who are given the task of implementing some internal change project (see Chapter 14 for description of this role). By and large, this has suited managers since it has allowed them to stay focused on achieving their task-oriented objectives. From the organizational perspective, this has also meant that the managers were resistant to the change as it diverted their resources and attention to outcomes which were not directly and immediately related to what they were being measured upon.

In the future, managers are likely to be called upon to undertake the change agent role themselves. On one hand, this makes a great deal of sense in that the manager will know better than anyone the pressures driving and inhibiting change. On the other hand, the danger is that these change agent/managers may not wish to create the hassle for themselves or their teams by seeking out radical change solutions. Therefore, the role demands managers with a new perspective on their task and contribution (Schein, 1996). Schein identifies two key criteria for this new managerial role: a) the emotional strength to deal with the conflicting pressures in their role; and b) to have a profound understanding of organizational issues and the management of change, such managers are leaders of change. Schein goes on to highlight the characteristics required by these effective leaders in the future:

- exceptional levels of perception about the external environment and their own motivations and beliefs.
- high level of self-motivation to see them through periods of change.
- emotional strength and caring to coach themselves and others through constant change.
- skilled in analysing cultures and developing processes to overcome such change blockages.
- the confidence to share power and control with others and to develop this skill in colleagues.

Fishman (1997) offers a set of 10 guidelines for potential change agent managers:

1   *Change begins and ends with the business—not with change*   One of the reasons why change programmes often fail is that they are not clearly and succinctly linked with what really matters in the organization. To succeed, change agents must constantly highlight the link between the change and what is important to the organization. This is one of the reasons why external change agents—who may not fully understand the business—often fail.

2   *Change is about people. People will surprise you*   The standard approach to change programmes is to establish the vision, design the programme, and implement it. The reality is often somewhat different. Senior management might change, key political supporters might move on, and political allies might lose interest. Therefore, it is vital that the outcome of the change programme is also somewhat ill-defined to cope with such predictable shifts in organizational life.

3   *There is information in opposition*   Although as the change agent/manager you may believe that you are right and those who resist you are wrong, it is not always true. There may be a body of data and knowledge which might indicate another solution entirely. The correct response is to listen very carefully to the information in opposition and use that information to develop new outcomes which better fit all of the available knowledge.

4   *The informal network is as powerful as the formal chain of command—and you get to design your informal network*   The building and cultivation of internal and external support networks is vital to achieving change. As organizations become flatter, power and authority will lie with those individuals who can access the greatest range of information sources and mobilise the knowledge when and where necessary.

5   *You can't draft people into change—they have to enrol*   A common failing of change agents is that they *inflict* change upon people rather than *lead* it. The result is often a cynical one where people superficially go along with the change agent's demands, but don't perform or enact the required behaviour changes. The solution is to convince the individuals who will be affected of what is 'best practice'. If it is truly better—and they are convinced, they will subscribe.

6   *It's not a calling, it's a job*   One of the more depressing events in organizational change is to see a change agent adopt a messianic approach to their role and push fanatically for their preferred outcome. The result is often that these change agents lose their objectivity: those that agree are disciples to be rewarded, those that disagree are defined as heretics.

7   *Forget balance, create tension*   The traditional managerial role has been one of using personal knowledge or experience to inform others. The change agent role differs in that no one knows what the final outcome will be. This ambiguity creates a tension within the organization. Successful change agents seek to identify these tensions and use them to develop new solutions.

8   *No change agent ever succeeded by dying for their organization*   As the famous World War Two US general George S. Patton said: 'No bastard ever won a war by dying for his country'. The same principle applies to change agents. Although there sometimes is a tendency to see a change initiative as a noble calling, the effective change manager also knows when to call a tactical retreat to re-group and reformulate a new strategy.

9 *You can't change the organization without changing yourself* For any change initiative to proceed, the first change has to be to the change agent. As the leader of any change effort, the manager will be seen as the role model for behaviour and belief. In this way, the change agent must think carefully about their 'public' persona.

10 *Even if the company doesn't change, you will* The experience of most change agents shows that change programmes often do not achieve their intended outcomes. By the very nature of the task, change agents/managers feel more organizational pressure than their run-of-the-mill counterparts. In some sense, change agents need to self-select themselves for the role. As organizations enter a more turbulent period, they will require significantly greater numbers of change agents/managers than ever before. As a consequence, the desire to be engaged in change (even if they don't always succeed) is often sufficient to ensure that the change agent is recognized and attains a higher organizational profile than would otherwise be the case.

Managers of conflict

One aspect of management which is often seen as undesirable is the need to sub-optimize due to conflicts they are asked to resolve. One major aspect of the management function of the future will be the need to use conflict to generate discussion and consensus as to the overall direction of the organization or team (see Chapter 9). There are a variety of different forms of structural conflicts which managers must handle:

- *Workload–budget conflict* This is the pressure placed on managers to meet targets in terms of output and budgeted costs. As is often the case, the external variables influence both workload and budget considerably.
- *Profit–capacity conflict* This tension is caused by the desire to show profits to your shareholders while at the same time investing sufficiently in operating capacity to meet future demands.
- *Long-term growth–short-term profit conflict* The pressures to deliver a sufficient return on investment to shareholders will sometimes lead to a desire to cut costs (and headcount). This can often conflict with the long-term viability of the business.
- *Decentralization–centralization conflict* The conflicting demands of organizational integration and managerial empowerment and autonomy can create a cynical and confused workforce. As decisions are the means by which power is exercised in organizations, it is often a difficult change to get individuals and groups to accept a power diminution.
- *Growth–stability conflict* Given the other conflicts and pressures inherent in organization, it is not surprising that organizations are often reluctant to seek out new external challenges and continually 'reinvent' themselves. Therefore, there is often an in-built resistance to further growth opportunities—largely due to lack of excess energy than to desire.

As organizations become flatter and managers are asked to assume broader areas of responsibility, the importance of managing conflict and competing interests will increase.

Knowledge managers

As will be discussed in more detail in Chapter 24, organizations will increasingly derive their value out of the knowledge that they create and retain. Therefore, managers can be seen, to some extent, as curators of knowledge within their organization. The study of the creation of knowledge is known as epistemology. It contains some useful perspectives which help understand the role of knowledge managers in the future.

Self-referencing criteria   All individuals have their own unique frame of reference. We use these to make sense of our surroundings. However, it also is the source of significant difficulty when managing others since the 'frames' you have will almost certainly be different from the 'frames' of others. When you are managing others who have significant knowledge (which you might not be aware of), it is likely that their frame of reference will draw upon a different set of experiences than yours. To overcome this problem, a significant amount of time must be set aside for exploring each other's views, opinions and interpretations of events. It is only by sharing everyone's frames of reference (to the extent we are willing or able) that we can overcome the predisposition to view everything from our own, local, perspective.

Use of language   Many professions have developed their own unique set of jargon and interpretations of words as a short cut to discussing some complex issues. (You will no doubt have discovered a great many such jargon terms in this textbook). To communicate effectively with experts requires some linguistic ability on both sides. As a manager, it is largely your responsibility to establish the *lingua franca* and seek not to stray too far from it. Our experience has shown that even words such as 'profit' can mean a number of different things to different people. For example, accountants might view profit in terms of the final tally on a profit & loss statement. Department managers might view profit as meeting some form of cost/volume target. Strategic planners might view profit as a longer-term measure of organizational success. Therefore, care must be taken to ensure that the correct interpretations have been made.

Pattern seeking   In Chapter 17 we introduced the concept of chaos theory as a perspective for management. It fits in with the need for knowledge managers to seek to determine patterns of similar behaviours. Therefore knowledge management requires the constant search for patterns or processes reoccurring within a system. Called fractal analysis, this is often undertaken by sophisticated software analysis of large stores of data (data warehouses) to seek out common features. Without the aid of complex computer systems, knowledge managers must use their own pattern-seeking skills to link together existing knowledge in new ways for the organization (and themselves) to benefit.

Educating managers

The educating and training of managers has always received a great deal of lip-service. In quite a few organizations, the reality is that development is seen as an 'on-the-job' activity. Time off for attending courses is hard to negotiate, particularly in an organization trying to control its costs.

An important distinction which is not always made clear is the difference between 'business education' and 'management development'. In an attempt to define the two terms, Handy *et al.*, (1988) allocate business education to the responsibility of each individual. Generally, business education is provided through some sort of course presented by an educational institution, though it could also include reading and updating of knowledge by individuals. Management development is seen as much more the responsibility of the organization which employs the individual. The assumption is that the benefits which are derived from management development accrue both to the individual as well as the organization. Among the activities which can be considered as management development there are: experience through job rotation, on-the-job training, as well as bespoke courses to upgrade particular skills or knowledge areas.

One reason why management development has, until recently, been overlooked is the long timescale involved. It takes time for a manager to gain experience and it is often necessary to look at events over a five to ten-year period in order to put his or her development into proper perspective

In the UK, the drive to upgrade the education and training of managers has over the last decade been undertaken by what has become known as the 'Management Charter Initiative'. The idea is to provide a recognized professional qualification to managers in much the same way as there are professional accountancy or other qualifications. Behind this undertaking lies the Council for Management Education and Development. They have called upon large and small organizations in the private and public sector to subscribe to a code of practice on management development. The code calls on companies to:

1 improve leadership and management skills throughout the organization;
2 to provide managers with support and time off to enable them to pursue learning opportunities;
3 to review progress annually;
4 to set new targets for the organization and the individual manager;
5 to publicize both the review and the targets.

Though not part of the code itself, there is also a desire to raise the profile of management development so that it becomes a board level responsibility. In terms of the amount of time which organizations should grant managers to undertake development activities, one suggestion is that ten days per year should be seen as the average. This contrasts sharply with the fact that in 1987 British managers received, on average, only one day's formal training, and that the majority received no training at all (Keep, 1989).

The ability to reward employees with promotion and responsibility (rather than provide management education) may decline in the future. Byrne and Konrad, (1983) noted that many organizations that had established a management 'fast-track' when business was expanding have begun to slow the process as business stabilizes. Instead, these organizations are emphasizing higher-quality management development in job assignments for young managers with potential rather than highly visible and rapid advancement up the hierarchy. So advancement up the hierarchy is likely to become less common. The new manager is mobile, trained and self-developed and is likely to seek rewards by moving from organization to organization as a promotional route (Drucker, 1988).

Management techniques—a help for the future?

Mangers have always sought new techniques in an attempt to better both themselves and their organizations. Today, however, the number of available techniques is unsurpassed. Some are more fashionable than others, but in less than 50 years we have seen:

● *Henri Fayol and Weberian bureaucracy (1930s)* offered a militaristic design to decrease organizational ambiguity while allowing organizations to grow and increase their economies of scale.

- *Management by objectives*   (attributed to Peter Drucker in 1950s). Providing clarity of purpose and consistency to organizational relationships.
- *Programme evaluation and review techniques (PERT) (1950s)*   by studying how a company brings a new idea to market or project to fruition, one can emphasize those components that contribute to this process while eliminating or cutting back those that don't.
- *Management and leadership styles*   (especially Theory X and Y from Douglas McGregor and the Managerial Grid from Blake and Mouton) in the 1960s.
- *Zero-based budgeting (1970s)*   to regularly re-assess costs to avoid unnecessary duplication.
- *Portfolio management theory*   relating to market share and growth (1970s) (Buzzell and Gale, 1987).
- *Team building, quality circles*   (making decisions in small groups through consensus and co-operation) (1970s–80s)
- *Theory Z*   (Ouchi, 1981) to import Japanese people management practices into Western organizations by establishing overall goals that become more specific as they are implemented down through the organization allowing greater employee independence while still keeping the company oriented toward its long-term targets.
- *The 'one-minute manager'*   (Blanchard and Johnson, 1982) which advocates making decisions alone but quickly.
- *Searching for excellence*   the 'excellent' market-led, close-to-the-customer organizations of Peters and Waterman (1982) and many others.

Other techniques include:

- *Decentralization*   Making corporate groups and divisions more independent, complete with their own infrastructures, makes them more adaptive and competitive. (1970s onwards).
- *Total quality management*   An attempt to improve the quality of organizational operations toward a goal of perfection to improve competitiveness and customer satisfaction and loyalty. (1970s and 1980s).
- *CAD/CAM*   (Computer-aided design and manufacturing). By installing a combination of computer databases, process control systems, and robotics so that the organization can reduce operating costs, improve quality, and make possible high-margin mass customization, (1980s).
- *The learning organization*   In the rapidly changing modern world, successful companies will be those that can adapt quickly because they are built on continuously upgraded employee skills and knowledge, (1990s).
- *Business process reengineering*   The new competitive environment not only demands that companies revize their products and services but that they also re-think their organization in light of advances in information-technology telecommunications, (1990s) (Hammer and Champy, 1993).
- *Virtualization*   New technologies make possible companies 'without walls' that have a new, more integrated relationship with suppliers, distributors, retailers, customers, and even competitors. (See reading 16 by Chris Barnatt), (2000s?).
- *Flat organizations*   New information processing technology eliminates the need for the middle layers of corporate hierarchy that used to act as information filters and now enhances the ability of senior managers to handle a larger span of control, (1990s).
- *Chaos theory*   With the rapid shifts currently taking place in commerce and society, the best company organization is one that is essentially

chaotic within a well-defined structure designed to use that energy. Hence: 'chaos' and 'order,' (1990s).

- *Alliances, networks and co-operation* The emerging global economy will require a new type of business strategy, one that de-emphasizes winner-takes-all competition for new co-operative ventures that reward everyone concerned, (Brandenburger, 1998).

There are countless more, but we're sure you get the idea! None of those listed above are wrong, misguided or flawed. All have their place as tools which a manager can call upon to help in any particular situation. In this way, managers are similar to a craftsperson who needs to know the purpose and use of a wide variety of tools in their job. They may not use all of the tools all of the time—indeed some tools they may never use or take out of their toolbox. Nevertheless, the expertise of the craftsperson, like that of the new manager depends on their ability of knowing what techniques or resources they can call upon in any given situation.

A management style for the 21st century: is it identifiable?

Drucker (1988), Peters and Waterman (1982) and Kanter (1982) are among those authors who believe management thought has currently reached a state where particular management styles will be appropriate for the future. Their arguments are:

- Organizations of the future will be staffed predominantly by professionals, (knowledge workers), (Drucker).
- Organizations of the future will have to be more responsive to the needs of clients and customers (Peters and Waterman, Kanter).

Managing knowledge workers

A growing problem for many organizations is the need for specialists in a wide variety of disciplines. As the role of the generalist wanes (at least until senior management levels), the need to attract and retain the very best skills and knowledge has risen. At the same time, more and more people are working for 'professional' organizations such as accountancy firms, consultancies and high technology companies. In organizations where high levels of expertise are the firm's most valued asset, great care must be taken regarding how knowledge workers are managed.

The conventional approach is to take the best individual and appoint him or her the manager. The problem with such an approach is that the organization may lose their professional contributions as well as risk making them dissatisfied over time. Many professionals have spent years studying to achieve a professionally recognized status. For such individuals, their own identities are derived from their work. They choose their careers because they found the work exciting and challenging—not because they wanted to be managers. In many cases, the nature of managerial work conflicts with the very things which makes professional work exciting. According to Lorsch and Mathias (1987), some of the characteristics of the professional employee are:

1 Professionals enjoy their work since it provides rapid and measurable results. As a group, professionals tend to have a greater need for quick feedback from their action. Examples include: a consultant working on a project for a client and getting immediate feedback from the client, or a merchant banker working on a merger deal for a client. Managers, on the other hand, usually achieve results gradually and even then there may be

no concrete outcome. A good example is the need to develop new people in the organization.

2   Professionals enjoy the content of their work. Usually, they have chosen their profession because of its intellectual challenge and stimulation. Being a manager normally involves the control of small details which may lack the glamour of their profession. While managerial issues can be as complex as any professional task, they don't necessarily have to interest the specialist.

3   Professionals often prefer working alone or in small teams of colleagues. People who focus all of their energies on project assignments value the freedom that such work entails. Given their objective, individuals or small project teams of specialists can do whatever they can to accomplish their task. Managers rarely find life so simple. They are forced to deal with the complex set of relationships with superiors, peers and subordinates which all require some of their attention.

The dilemma for organizations which employ many specialists is clear. Do you leave your top specialists in the job which they are best at and choose the less able professionals to be managers? If so, the organization runs the risk of confirming the traditional specialists' complaint about management: that they are second-rate. An alternative which some organizations are trying is to bring in managers from outside. The difficulty with this approach is that the new managers may lack the necessary expertise to fully understand the tasks they are asked to oversee.

Management of innovation

If we can accept that the speed of response and intensity of competition in our markets is increasing, it will become necessary for organizations to be much better at innovation as a means of survival. Managers will therefore have a role in encouraging and nurturing the innovation process within their organization. In 'traditional' bureaucratic organizations, creativity and innovation was reserved for the research & development department which was filled with specialist engineers and scientists. The tendency in such departments was to undertake incremental innovations to existing products. (Schwartz, 1992) However, the view now is that innovation can emerge from a variety of different sources and that managers must be encouraged to develop these creative actions. (Drucker, 1992; Rosenfeld and Servo, 1992)

These sources are detailed in Table 23.1.

Table 23.1
Sources of innovation

Within the organization's operating environment	Outside the organization's normal environment
Unexpected occurrences/product launch failures	Demographic changes
Competitive market changes/new competition	Public perceptions
Process/manufacturing improvements	New knowledge

Source: adapted from Drucker (1992)

By studying patterns of innovation in the past, we can identify where innovations emerged and how they were put into practice (Utterback, 1994). However, just as important is the need to develop managerial processes designed to translate new ideas into valued products and services (Kao, 1997). As a guide to managers to encourage the creativity process, Kao highlights seven key skills:

1 Allow ideas to develop by keeping all options open. Avoid closure on ideas—however good or dumb they might be. It might spin off to something even better.

2 Do not shut down communication by being critical or judgemental. Consider the use of some creativity techniques such as 'six thinking hats'—see Table 23.2 (De Bono, 1986).

3 Avoid negative feedback, try to find the positive. Ideas must be heard and honoured before you go on to something else.

4 Need to harmonize timetables and perceptions of degrees of lateness or delay. Exceptional people sometimes need exceptional boundaries.

5 To define some clear boundaries to clarify resource availability, time pressures, competitive requirements, etc.

6 To create an open forum for dialogue: use 'open' questions (ones which cannot be answered just with a 'yes' or 'no'), ask 'why' frequently.

7 Deal with each individual as uniquely as possible. Seek to determine what each individual wants/expects from a manager.

Management styles for flexible, responsive firms

Beyond the challenge of managing professionals lie the questions of appropriate management styles for the 21st century. Linked into the market-led, customer-driven culture (see Chapter 13), are some fairly evangelical statements about the qualities of the future manager. Table 23.3 summarizes some of these key qualities.

Evidence for whether these styles work is mixed. Certainly, some of Peters and Waterman's companies turned in rather less than excellent performance in the late 1980s (although others such as 3M and Disney managed to sustain their success). Companies in Britain such as Eagle Star and Barclays Bank, which have emphasized quality and customer service are currently successful. Yet others manage well without total quality programmes and the like. Fads and corporate cure-alls are not new of course and it is likely that the future manager could add 'healthy scepticism' to his or her list of necessary knowledge for the future, at the same time acknowledging that these techniques do work for some organizations some of the time.

A management style for the 21st century: fads will not help

Two authors who argue that the above management styles are founded on little other than fads and fashion and therefore will be of little use for the future are McGill (1988) and Gunz (1989). McGill (1988) argues that every style and approach has worked for some organizations in the past and the tendency is to view these organizations as role models for the rest. He declares that the marketing of management style packages for the future has become itself big business with acronyms (such as LEAD—Leader Effectiveness and Adaptability Description) abounding, and often taking precedence over rigorous, academic content.

Gunz (1989) disagrees with the notion of an appropriate management style based upon a mixture of individual knowledge, skills and traits. Based upon empirical evidence from executives in the British operations of four large manufacturing organizations, he argues that successful management for the future seems to depend largely upon the organization rather than the individual. Specifically, organizations create the conditions in which particular management styles will flourish. The conditions are called 'command-centred', 'evolutionary', 'constructional' and 'turnaround'.

The command centred organization consists of managers who have

Table 23.2
De Bono's six
thinking hats

Explanation: One of the reasons why we find creativity difficult is our Western tradition of argument in which we tend to take a position and argue. For example, if X has one opinion and Y disagrees. De Bono found that this approach allowed those involved to get locked into their position and therefore increasingly interested in winning their argument rather than exploring the subject. The six hats method was to generate more productive discussions.

Each colour hat symbolizes a particular approach all participants should adopt. For example, if X and Y were to 'wear' the black hat at the same time, they could explore some of the dangers. If X and Y wear yellow hats, they must explore the benefits, etc. The approach reduces the tendency for adversarial thinking and encourages co-operative exploration.

Hat colour	Purpose	Typical questions
White hat	• Put aside the argument and focus solely on the information • To collect data and information	• What information do we have? • What information is missing? • What information would we like to have? • How might we get the information?
Red hat	• To provide your feelings and emotions about the topic • Allow expressions of 'gut instinct' • It can be right or wrong	• Putting on my red hat, this is what I feel about the project . . . • My gut instinct about this idea is that it will not work because . . . • I am not comfortable with the way this is being done because it makes me feel . . . • My intuition tells me that the demand for this product will fall off quickly because . . .
Black hat	• The 'caution' hat • For critical judgement • Why something cannot be done • Identify all the weak points in the argument • No defending allowed at this stage	• The industry regulator would not allow us to do that • We do not have the manufacturing capability to fulfil that request • The last time we tried that, this is what happened . . . • He does not have the necessary competencies to do the job
Yellow hat	• For optimism and the logical positive view of things • Looks for feasibility and how something can be done • Looks for benefits—but they must be logically based • Usually difficult due to a natural desire to avoid errors	• This might work if we moved the production plant nearer to the customers • The sales reps would benefit because it would save them time by . . . • Product quality would be enhanced because . . . • The high cost of energy would make everyone more energy efficient
Green hat	• For creative thinking and generating new ideas • Highlight additional alternatives and new hypotheses	• We need some new ideas here! • Are there any additional alternatives? • Could we do this in a different way? • Could there be another explanation?
Blue hat	• Meeting management • To redress balance of 'hats' used • Setting the agenda • Suggesting the next step in the thinking • Used for summaries and decisions	• Could we have a summary of your views? • I think we should take a look at the priorities • Can we try some green hat thinking to get some new ideas?

Source: adapted from De Bono, (1986)

Table 23.3
Management styles
for the future

Traditional management based upon role culture and bureaucratic structures	Future management based upon task cultures and flexible decentralized structures
Police officer	Guide
Disciplinarian	Cheerleader/coach
Paper shuffler	Enthusiast
Office bound	Walking around/verbal communicator
Allocates jobs	Delegates tasks
Focus on control	Focus on quality
Focus on markets	Focus on customers
Maintains bureaucracy	Sheds bureaucracy, creates and lives the vision

advanced through commanding a succession of bigger and bigger business units, but where the actual management process remains substantially the same. Retail banks are examples. Management style is inflexible (they are good at a narrow range of skills) and resistant to change. The evolutionary organization is one where management style is predominantly achieved through expanding a particular part of the business (their own) and growing with it. The problem here is often that efficiency of existing operations suffers in the quest for diversification.

The constructional organization is one which appoints managers deemed to have the 'right' qualities to run very different sections of the business at short notice. Such styles develop political and procedural skills above all else, but detailed understanding of either the business or its customers is lacking. The turn-around organization favours management styles which favours fast-track, well-reputed managers who grasp the nettle and effect change quickly and sometimes brutally. The problem is that management skills here often become focused on manipulating the grapevine, so that reputations are made (often without any supporting evidence).

Gunz (1989) argues that specific styles are appropriate for each of the four organizational contexts. It is a case of horses for courses. Change the organizational context and most managers will not be able to adapt. It seems that management styles are not easily transferable.

Summary

So, the question of whether we can identify a specific set of factors for an appropriate future management style remains not only unanswered, but the subject of polarized debate. As a student of organizational behaviour, you would have been suspicious of any other finding! We can, however, say some relatively concrete things about the future.

While it is difficult to say whether the environment facing managers will be any more or less challenging in the future, there is no doubt that it will be different. Managers will not only have to respond to the pressures of change, but also be the agents of change themselves.

As more organizations realize the value of an educated workforce, the gap between management development and business education may narrow. Forecasts for the future growth of organizations indicate an extended period of stabilization. This implies that fewer promotions will be able to be offered as rewards for top performers. In its place, increased learning opportunities may be offered to retain key staff.

As the service economy grows and organizations become more specialized, the assumptions of a flexible workforce must be reconsidered. The complexity of many tasks—computers, law, accounting, etc., mean that organizations will have to value the amount of expertise which an individual brings to the organization. To attract and retain such people, the organization will have to construct a work environment which allows the individual to maximize his or her utility, while at the same time, permitting the organization to monitor and direct the energy of its human resources. We approach the question of the organization in the future in Chapter 24.

References

Blanchard, K. and S. Johnson (1982) *The One-Minute Manager*, Prentice-Hall, Englewood Cliffs, New Jersey.

Brandenburger, A. M. (1998) *Co-opetition*, Doubleday, New York.

Buzzell, R. D. and B. T. Gale (1987) *The PIMS Principles: Linking Strategy to Performance*, Free Press, New York.

Byrne, J. A. and W. Konrad (1983) 'The fast track slows down', *Forbes*, 18 July, 77–8.

De Bono, E. (1986) *Six Thinking Hats*, Little Brown & Co., Boston, Mass.

Drucker, P. (1988) 'The coming of the new organization', *Harvard Business Review*, Jan–Feb., 21–7.

Drucker, P. (1992) 'The discipline of innovation', in J. Henry and D. Walker (eds.), *Managing Innovation*, Sage Publications, London.

Fishman, C. (1997) 'Change: The 10 laws of change that never change', *Fast Company*, **8**, April–May, 64–75.

Gunz, H. (1989) *Careers and Corporate Cultures*, Blackwell, Oxford.

Hammer, M. and J. Champy (1993) *Re-engineering the corporation: A Manifesto for Business Revolution*, Harper Business, New York.

Handy, C. (1997) 'The new language of organizing and its implications for leaders', in F. Hesselbein, M. Goldsmith and R. Beckhard (eds.), *The Leader of the Future*, Jossey-Bass, San Francisco.

Handy, C., C. Gordon, I. Gow and C. Randlesom (1988) *Making Managers*, Pitman, London.

Hannan, M. and J. Freeman, (1977) 'The population ecology of organizations' *American Journal of Sociology*, **82**, 929–1064.

Hendy (1996)

Kanter, R. M. (1982) *The Change Masters: Corporate Entrepreneurs at Work*, Allen & Unwin, London.

Kao, J. (1997) *Jamming: The Art & Discipline of Business Creativity*, Harper Collins Business, London.

Keep, E. (1989) 'A Training Scandal?', in K. Sisson (ed.), *Personnel Management in Britain*, Blackwell, Oxford.

Lieberson, S. and J. F. O'Connor (1972) 'Leadership and organizational performance: A study of large corporations', *American Sociological Review*, **3** (7), 117–30.

Lorsch, J. W. and P. E. Mathias (1987) 'When professionals have to manage', *Harvard Business Review*, July–Aug., 78–83.

March, J. C. and J. G. March (1977) 'Almost random careers-the Wisconsin school superintendency, 1940–1972', *Administrative Science Quarterly*, **22** (3), 377–409.

McGill M. E. (1988) *American Business and the Quick Fix*, Henry Holt & Co., New York.

Ouchi, W. (1981) *Theory Z: How American Business Can Meet the Japanese Challenge*, Addison-Wesley, Reading, Mass.

Peters, T. and R. Waterman Jr. (1982) *In Search of Excellence: Lessons from America's Best Run Companies*, Harper & Row, New York.

Rosenfeld, R. and J. C. Servo (1992) 'Facilitating innovation in large organizations', in J. Henry and D. Walker (eds.), *Managing Innovation*, Sage Publications, London.

Schein, E. (1996) 'Leadership and organizational culture' in F. Hesselbein, M. Goldsmith and R. Beckhard (eds.), *The Leader of the Future*, Jossey-Bass, San Francisco.

Schwartz, W. K. (1992) 'From idea to implementation: Pitfalls along the stony road between idea creation and the marketplace'. in J. Henry and D. Walker (eds.), *Managing Innovation*, Sage Publications, London.

Spender, J. C. (1989) *Industry recipes: The Nature and Sources of Managerial Judgement*, Blackwell, Oxford.

Tichy, N. and S. Sherman (1993) *Control your destiny or someone else will*, Currency Doubleday, New York.

Utterback, J. M. (1994) Mastering the Dynamics of Innovation, *Harvard Business School Press*, Boston, Mass.

Virany, B. and M. Tushman, (1986) 'Top management teams and corporate success in an emerging industry', *Journal of Business Venturing*, **1**, 261–74.

CHAPTER 24 The new organization

Introduction

The nature of organizations is changing all the time. Living in and observing them in the present, it is difficult enough to pick out trends in the ways in which organizations currently function. If one tries to look out for discontinuities in the future, it becomes even more impossible. Unlike businesses in the past, which were characterized by manufacturing oriented towards the domestic economy, organizations in the future are likely to be information-based, operating globally. As we observed in the previous two chapters, the people who inhabit these organizations will also have changing expectations about their role, their employment relationship and about the broader role of the firm in society.

To provide a final perspective on the attributes which organizations may have in the future, five areas are explored. These have been identified by recent organization theorists:

1 The learning organization
2 Intellectual capital
3 Intrapreneurialism
4 The growth of the small business sector
5 Globalization of business
6 The increasing importance of business ethics

As you might expect, the list is useful, but incomplete. The role of organizations in our society is as complex as the people which populate them. The study of organizational behaviour in the future will have to cope with an even greater diversity of views and objectives. The challenge will be, as always, to try and seek coherence out of such diversity.

The learning organization

One of the current topics in organizational behaviour is the 'learning organization'. It is obvious to anyone who has ever worked in an organization for a prolonged period that they continually make mistakes over and over again. The reasons for this are diverse, but generally, it is a reluctance by the individuals populating the organization to think that there might be lessons that can be learned from others in the business. The solution to this organizational forgetfulness (Rosenfeld, 1985) is to develop processes which capture lessons learned and disseminate them internally as and when required (Garvin, 1993).

One of the leaders in the field of the learning organization is Senge (1990). His book, *The Fifth Discipline* puts forward a view that the old methods and procedures of quality improvement, learning from mistakes, etc., are insufficient to enable organizations to survive in the future. Senge puts forward five 'component technologies' as prerequisites if an organization wishes to become learning focused:

- *Systems thinking* Managers need to be aware of the open linkages between their own actions and the actions of those around them, within and outside the organization. Senge's view is that managers do not fully grasp a systems perspective because they only perceive and act upon one aspect of a problem rather than understand the broader prespective.

- *Personal mastery* Organizations need to encourage their employees to continually learn and improve their own skills and abilities. Traditionally, organizations have sought to train and develop a select few ('the fast trackers') with the rest placed on a career 'scenic route'. Senge argues that organizations have wasted a valuable resource by not encouraging all individuals to become constant learning organisms.

- *Mental models* Mental models are deeply embedded assumptions and generalizations we all carry regarding how the world works and our own actions. It is often subconscious, yet can influence our behaviour in organizations substantially. Senge's view is that these mental models can serve as powerful constraints on an organization's ability to gain new insights and innovations. Arie De Geus (1997) confirmed the prevalence of this approach when he pointed out that managers only see what is relevant to their future.

- *Building shared vision* Senge has observed that, throughout history, a shared vision has been a critical component to organizational success. There is an important difference between a vision built around a charismatic leader—which is often transitory and that built around shared goals. For the development of a learning organization, the building and maintenance of a shared vision offers individuals the support to excel and learn. To develop a shared vision involves communicating descriptions of what the future might hold rather than seeking compliance to a prescribed view.

- *Team learning* In Chapter 8, we examined some of the characteristics of operating in teams. Working and sharing information among team members is a vital element of the learning organization. Senge recognizes that many teams exhibit signs of negative synergy or 'groupthink' (Janis, 1972). Senge stresses the need to overcome such difficulties by encouraging meaningful dialogue. This is accomplished by seeking to suspend assumptions and judgement and to engage in 'free-thinking' with other group members.

Other management thinkers have contributed to the growing literature on developing the learning organization (Pedler *et al.*, 1994; Garratt, 1987). All of these works work towards the same overriding message. Organizations that continue along their present trends will find themselves increasingly misaligned with their marketplace. Business history is littered with examples of companies which were unable to learn from their customers, their environment and their employees. As organizational life-spans are being reduced (De Geus, 1997), it will become increasingly vital that those which wish to live longer need to evolve more quickly than other members of their species.

Knowledge organizations and intellectual capital

Many organizations now recognize that their value (to their customers, to their shareholders, to their suppliers and to their employees) does not derive solely from the value of the capital invested in the fixed and working capital assets of the business. As organizations become more dependent upon the knowledge embedded in its employees they have tried to organize and codify that knowledge; they write handbooks, maintain files, provide training, and collect data. But knowledge management has mostly been historic and difficult to communicate.

The world of business is changing. Modern financial engineering has meant that the entrepreneur does not need to purchase vast amounts of fixed assets upfront—they can be leased, rented, etc. Instead, the critical input for the entrepreneur's business is his or her own ideas (innovation) and the dedication of the employees to fulfill that initial vision and to build on it. What is needed in these organizations is the knowledge and creativity of the individuals within it. Any future success of the business depends on the continued presence and contribution of those within it. This is where the concept of intellectual capital began (Peters, 1992).

Intellectual capitalism is different. In knowledge-intensive companies, it's not clear who owns the company, its tools, or its products. Whereas in the traditional organization, the entrepreneur/shareholders bought and owned the assets of the company, it is unclear who makes the investments on which intellectual capitalism depends—the people. The manager may have paid his or her own way through business school. At the same time, the employees may be taking evening or part-time courses, though the organization might reimburse them for a proportion of the cost when it is completed.

Many jobs still and always will require big, expensive machines bought by someone else. But in the age of intellectual capital, the most valuable parts of those jobs are the human tasks: sensing, judging, creating, building relationships. Far from being alienated from the tools of his trade and the fruit of his labour, knowledge workers carry them between their ears.

This change upsets the nature and governance of corporations. For example, in December 1994 institutional investors, unhappy with the senior management of Saatchi & Saatchi (the large UK-based advertising agency) forced the board of directors to dismiss the chief executive, Maurice Saatchi. In the aftermath, several other executives left as well, taking with them some of their clients (notably, Mars and British Airways). As far as the company's balance sheet was concerned, Saatchi's dismissal was a non-event. Nevertheless the stock, which had been trading on the New York Stock Exchange around $8.00, immediately fell to $4.00. The lesson learnt was that even though the investors thought they owned the assets of Saatchi & Saatchi, in fact they owned only half of it (judging from the drop in market capitalization). The remainder of the value of the company (which had disappeared with the departing executives and their clients) was intellectual capital. For a management consulting company, the assets of the business are largely intellectual, with only a very limited amount of fixed assets (offices, computers, desks, etc.)

Although there is plenty of evidence of the value of intellectual capital, organizations tend to manage these assets badly, (Edvinsson and Malone, 1997). One reason is that they have a hard time distinguishing between the cost of paying people and the value of investing in them (Jackson, 1997). One implication of this trend towards valuing the intellectual capital of an organization is that those employees who will not and can not contribute to the intellectual asset base are most at risk of losing their jobs.

Routine, low-skill work, even if it's done manually, does not generate or employ much intellectual capital for the organization. Often the work involved in such jobs can be automated, which is why these are the jobs most at risk. This should not be taken to imply that these employees lack skill or talent—only that it is not being fully utilized by the employer.

Therefore, the issue of intellectual capital is one of growing concern to the organization rather than to the individual. The question for companies is how to acquire as much human capital as they can use profitably. Intellectual capital grows in two ways: when the organization uses more of what people know and when more people know more about what is useful to the organization.

To maximize the return on intellectual capital already in the organization will require minimizing mindless tasks, meaningless paperwork, and unproductive infighting. The Taylorized workplace squandered human assets in such activities. Many organizations can recount stories of employees who spent their work time undertaking some mindless task, and then going home to spend their evenings and weekends rebuilding entire cars from scratch or running volunteer organizations. Clearly, the organizations were getting the work from the individual but no intellectual capital investment. To get more people to know more relevant information, organizations need to focus and amass talent where it is needed. The link to strategy is essential.

For most organizations, the challenge is to find and enhance talents that truly are assets for the future rather than information collected about the past (for not all skills are created equal) and turn them to advantage by making them, in some sense, organizational property.

Some knowledge can be owned and protected by intellectual-property laws while others can be codified in processes, procedures, manuals, databases, files, knowledge-management systems, etc., that the company owns. But the individual employees themselves can be rented, but not owned. Ceding 'ownership' of human capital to a corporation has to be voluntary. The most obvious way of achieving this is to develop a sense of cross-ownership between employee and company (Handy, 1995). However, a fundamental paradox is that at the same time that employers have weakened the ties of job security and loyalty, they more than ever depend on human capital. For their part, knowledge workers, because they bring to their work not only their bodies but their minds—even their souls—are far more loyal to their work (though not to their employer). Compounding the problem is the fact that the most valuable knowledge workers are also best able to leave their employers, taking their talent and their work with them.

To create human capital, a company needs to foster teamwork, communities of practice, and other social forms of learning, (Edvinsson and Malone, 1997). Individual talent is great, but it walks out of the door. Interdisciplinary teams capture, formalize, and capitalize talent; it becomes less dependent on any individual. A vibrant learning community gives the company an ownership stake.

The knowledge worker is as much an investor as the shareholder (Stewart, 1997). Share option schemes and other processes designed to encourage employees to have an equity stake in the business is an example of how the information age has changed the nature of the corporation.

Intra-preneurialism

The traditional dichotomy between being an employee of an organization and an entrepreneur (who founds his or her own organization) is crumbling. The first signs of this lay in the introduction of individual profit centres within large organizations. By allocating financial and product/market decisions to distinctive groups, the intent was to create a sense of ownership and responsibility among the profit centre managers. They could be their own entrepreneurs under the larger corporate banner.

In an attempt to achieve both innovation and a sense of ownership in large organizations, many firms have adopted policies of 'corporate venturing' or intrapreneurialism to remain competitive. Corporate venturing is a practice by which 'venture capital' is provided by the company to a set of its employees for them to set up a business on their own. As an alternative to seeking venture capital funding from outside the organization, corporate venturing offers budding entrepreneurs a staged withdrawal from the firm. In many cases, the start-up company is provided with cheap accommodation and access to many of the company's resources. In return, the company would own a percentage of the share capital of the new company. The argument is that if the firm were not willing to accept this proportion of control, then the potential for the innovation succeeding would be lost forever.

Most people are familiar with the term 'entrepreneur'. It generally refers to the founder(s) of a start-up company who have risked their financial livelihood on their confidence that their business idea can succeed. The term 'intrapreneur' was created in the US by Gifford Pinchot III, a management consultant. Pinchot argued that organizations can retain creativity and innovation within by creating an infrastructure which rewards entrepreneurial behaviour and yet, protects such people from the financial ruin which a failure can bring.

To encourage the potential of creating an organization of intrapreneurs requires the entire organization to reconsider its culture and processes of assessing performance. The rewards and punishments for success or failure have to be reconsidered. Many intrapreneurial projects are likely to fail and potential innovators must see that such set-backs will not unduly harm their careers. Similarly, the organization will also have to be more flexible in determining the appropriate rewards for successful innovation. One approach could be to create separate subsidiaries for successful innovations and to allow the intrapreneurs an equity share of the business as well as the opportunity to run the new operation. Atterhed (1985) illustrates the required change in attitudes between the traditional cultures of large firms and an intrapreneurial culture (see Table 24.1).

One of the key aspects of the intrapreneurial culture will be that of 'adding value' to the existing organization. This can occur on a number of levels, from adding value by creating new profitable firms in which the mother firm has a stake, to adding value in specific product lines and

Table 24.1
The corporation and intrapreneurial cultures

Big corporation corporate values	Intrapreneurial culture values
Control	Trust
Meddling	Protection
Boss	Mentor
Instructions	Visions
Planning	Flexibility
Orders	Viewpoints
Alienation	Participation
Fragmentation	Wholeness
Rules	Customers

Source: Atterhed (1985: 81).

services. Either way, the future organization is likely to face some or all of the following 're-thinking' if added value is to take place:

- assess strengths and weaknesses;
- transform from bureaucracy into leadership and
- flexibility;
- achieve effectiveness rather than efficiency;
- always ask 'why are we doing this?'

The growth of the small business sector

A significant part of the success of Germany's economy has been put down to the *Mittelstand*, small and medium-sized companies, often family-owned and frequently operating in the manufacturing sector. Many other European countries are now seeking to emulate Germany's success. However, cracks in the German economic model have started to emerge. In 1997, German unemployment was at its highest since 1933, and some German companies are moving overseas because of high domestic costs.

In the UK, the development of the Unlisted Securities Market (USM) and its successor, the Alternative Investment Market (AIM) has created a new source of capital for smaller, fast-growing companies. On the supply side, the growth of venture capital funds that began in the 1980s has a greater number of investors with an appetite for young stocks. Tax and labour market reforms have also made the UK a much better place in which to run a small business than it was in the darker days of the 1970s.

In the UK, the government has consistently encouraged the small business sector through a variety of means. Though the government would undoubtedly accept some (if not all) of the credit for the resurgence of small businesses, there are also a variety of social and economic pressures which have helped to nurture the entrepreneur.

One social factor which seems to be encouraging the small business is the increasing recognition in the workforce that the job security offered by the larger organizations can be matched by many smaller firms. Profit-sharing schemes, share options and company pension plans can be offered just as easily by most small businesses. Similarly, the recognition which one can receive in a small business for work well-done can be more immediate than in many large, impersonal organizations.

Economic factors are also providing opportunities for the small business. The continual demands of investors in large organizations for adequate returns means that they must pay closer attention to short-term profit targets. Small businesses are generally privately held and can, subject to the agreement of the directors, forego short-term profits to create a market presence. The expense and risk involved with starting up a new business has also been reduced. The government, through a variety of local and national programmes offer grants and loan guarantees to help the entrepreneur find the financial backing required. The increasing popularity of franchising is another route to creating new businesses. By agreeing to pay a royalty on future sales, a franchisee can take advantage of the larger companies brand image, marketing, production and management expertise.

Globalization of business: the optimistic scenario

A major advantage which Western societies have had since the 1900s has been a relatively affluent domestic market, characterized by ever-increasing levels of consumer demand. Industries in other countries have found it difficult to produce goods of equal quality or sophistication. The competitive advantage enjoyed by Western firms was largely based on the domestic market which they served.

The dominance of Western firms in serving their own domestic markets has been thrown into doubt by the spectacular rise of the Japanese since 1960. Though many Western firms have taken the lead in becoming multi-national, very rarely do these firms think in truly global terms.

The potential effect of the relaxation of trade and customs barriers within the European Union is frequently discussed, but rarely completely understood. Most countries have, over the years, erected substantial legal and procedural barriers to restrict foreign companies entering domestic markets. As discussed in Chapter 19, the process of dismantling national protectionist barriers is a long and arduous one.

The effect is likely to be profound, though not immediately apparent. Pan-European mergers and acquisitions are likely as firms try to gain market share. Previously heavily controlled sectors such as financial services will be opened up to allow for new competitors. The possibility of a Continental financial services firm purchasing one of the major UK clearing banks is conceivable.

One likely effect of the EU will be the increasing competitive pressure for companies to operate in as many of the EC countries as possible. Mitchell (1989) identified some of the characteristics of organizations which would be likely to have greater success in the wider EU marketplace. The 'Euro network' organization predicted by Mitchell will contain the following attributes:

1 Dividing the company up into identifiable business units with clear business objectives.
2 Implementing an organizational control system which minimizes the need for referral across the structure or above.
3 A recognition that duplication of support services is preferred over the greater complexity of centralization.
4 Management must adopt the vision of a single European market before it is a reality.
5 Increasing the span of control at all levels of the organization to allow for fewer organizational levels and for greater delegation.
6 A central services function which exists to serve the various operating units rather than supply the centre with resources.

In terms of human resource concerns, the increasingly global outlook of organizations may mean that managerial careers will be more likely to require some time spent abroad. Managers will have to exhibit cross-cultural qualities. For firms which operate globally, its managerial resource base will also have to be assessed in terms of its ability to function globally. One potential effect of this shift will be to increase the numbers of managers who speak more than their native language. Many academic institutions such as business schools have recognized this need and encourage students to improve their understanding of at least one non-native European language.

One of the effects of the globalization of business may be the creation of a truly international labour market. Organizations will have to offer compensation and working conditions which will meet or better the inducements of work elsewhere. Perhaps the most important result of the EU will be the changes it brings to the human resource management practices of European companies.

One of the most well-respected economic 'futurists' is John Naisbitt. He has published a number of books (*Megatrends, Reinventing the Corporation, Megatrends 2000, Megatrends for Women, Japan's Identity Crisis*) examining the trends which he perceives in our society. His book, *Global Paradox* (1995) looks at some of the social and economic trends at work in today's international community. Naisbitt's major theme is that the development of telecommunications is a driving force creating a giant global economy. At the same time, he feels that the concept of nation-state is becoming obsolete. The paradox, however, is that small organizational units are gaining greater power as national boundaries are rendered permeable by communication and information technology. Both countries and companies are deconstructing into smaller and smaller entities with greater economic power. As a consequence, Naisbitt concludes that economic power will shifting from the vertically integrated (large) firm to the horizontal (networked) organization.

Naisbitt suggests that in a globalized economy the market niche becomes smaller and smaller, and this favours the flexible, specialty company. Naisbitt contends that big companies will have to break up and become 'confederations of small, entrepreneurial companies in order to survive' and that 'webs' of strategic alliances will enable small and middle-size companies to produce products anywhere to the specific quality and market requirements found everywhere.

The Globalization of business: the pessimistic scenario

Just as Chapter 22 detailed some of the changes in working patterns as deleterious to individuals and as helping to create a divided society, then global scenarios of business also suffer from the same dual perspectives. Of course, globalization is good for those countries which benefit economically from the process. For those which do not, the process is rather like being a country which is long-term unemployed. There are going to be many winners and losers in the global economy.

We can begin to see some of these fissures in the strata of globalization. For example, it is only a few years ago that Asian firms thought they would benefit from continuous growth by globalization. They were wrong. As this book is written, many of Asia's top firms are struggling to survive. With the Indonesian rupiah at 10 000 to the dollar, it is a small fraction of its value even a few months ago and overall reductions in the value of the currency are predicted to be around 80%. Indonesia's economy and the companies in it are entering the twilight zone of global business. Even the biggest and most international Indonesian firms (such as Bakrie & Brothers—a conglomerate mainly of telecommunications, construction and agricultural businesses) have declared a moratorium on corporate debt and virtually all companies are technically bankrupt.

For many students, the purchase of this book may have been impossible. Only two years ago, a Malaysian student, for example, would have thought this book affordable and an integral part of their business studies degree. Today, with the Malaysian currency at a third of its value against sterling, the same student maybe cannot afford the book and would perhaps have to borrow a copy. He or she is also likely to have trouble paying university fees unless savings or family wealth can come to the rescue. The reduction in income for European universities which have substantial numbers of Asian and Indonesian students is likely to be significant.

The Asian economic meltdown also includes Japan, once heralded as the country to emulate for management, production and economic success. The

slowing down and reversal of the Japanese economy has prompted many
Western asset management firms to cut their weightings in Japanese and
other Asian equities by over 50%. Pulling out like this is likely to increase the
countries' economic problems even further. Neither are China and Russia
immune. China, often heralded as the great marketplace of the future for
Western businesses, is facing economic and social unrest as vast numbers of
former workers in old-fashioned manufacturing enterprises become
unemployed as the factories close down. The factories which still operate do
so at catastrophic losses. Neither can such factories be easily sold to Western
organizations. Not profitably, at least. There are rumours of whole Chinese
factories being valued and sold to Western buyers for less than one pound
sterling! The Russian financial markets have continued to drop significantly,
with the Russian stockmarket down by 35% between January and February
1998. There are continued fears that the rouble will collapse as foreign
investors who are some of the biggest sellers in both debt and equity markets
were pulling out of dealing in roubles. Only time will tell the true outcome.
But social unrest on an unprecedented scale would seem likely in both
China and Russia.

What is clear is that globalization will see rich winners and very
poverty-stricken losers. Countries in which investment remains high and
which can provide and sustain the educational base for the knowledge
workers of the future will prosper. Those which cannot will wither. The social
and political unrest which such inequality will produce globally can only be
guessed at. One could speculate, for example, that the historic pattern of
superpower confrontation will fade away completely to be replaced by
international military intervention in regional struggles (which are not
officially classed as 'war'). The most recent example of this at the time of
writing is the stand-off between Iraq and the United Nations. A total clash was
avoided and military intervention was not needed. Many thought that the
conflict was over. But a different 'war' has started in Iraq. Saddam Hussein is
turning Iraq to Islam. A huge mosque is to be built on the site of al-Muthana
airport (bombed and abandoned in the Gulf War). Even the national flag
now has Allahu Akbar (God is great) in its centre (and the mosque is to be
called the Saddam mosque!). The rise of Islamic fundamentalism can also be
seen as one reaction toward Western-style globalization. The ripples of this
backlash have only just begun, but they are evident in the West as, for
example, demonstrations, demands for separate schooling, attacks against
Mecca bingo halls in the UK and the killing of Western tourists in Egypt.

Within Western capitalism, such changes and conflicts may only be felt
incrementally and somewhat remotely. Nevertheless, even between countries
which are the 'haves' in the economic equation, global businesses will have
to adapt to the local conditions in which business takes place and they will
have to place a greater emphasis on ethical behaviour. We summarize the
ethical debates in the following section.

Business ethics

Increasing social and some governmental pressure is being placed upon
organizations to consider their contribution to wider social objectives. It is
likely that the future will bring even stronger expectations that businesses
must consider social issues alongside the pursuit of profit. Shareholders of
the future are likely to have to become used to a lower return on their
investment as firms attend to being corporately socially responsible (see
Chapter 16).

Business are being held increasingly accountable for improving the quality of the environment, making safe products, providing for worker health and safety and seeking to advance broad social objectives such as equal opportunity programmes. Many of the larger organizations have begun to recognize this trend and have initiated public relations campaigns which highlight their public-spiritedness. Others, such as the British motor car industry, are more tardy, particularly in their lack of response to cutting down the levels of exhaust pollution from cars. In this case, it seems that pressure from the British and European governments will have to be exerted on car manufacturers, rather than it be a voluntary decision.

One reaction many large firms have taken to this growing pressure to have a social conscience has been to issue 'corporate codes of conduct' (Chatov, 1980). These codes represent an effort to specify behaviour that the company does or does not sanction. The behaviours which are most commonly frowned upon include:

1 Extortion, gifts and kickbacks
2 Conflicts of interest
3 Illegal political payments
4 Violation of laws in general
5 Use of insider information
6 Bribery

Though these may not sound particularly innovative, for many firms, particularly those operating in many different national contexts, they represent a major challenge. The difficulties emerge where the local views on what is appropriate business behaviour differs from that proposed by the codes. Nevertheless, the movement towards an ethical approach to doing business is gaining momentum and it deserves to succeed.

Despite the increasing expectations about the role of organizations in fulfilling social objectives, Naisbitt (1982) argues that general confidence in large organizations is decreasing. The ability and desire of the government to satisfy the basic needs of citizens and provide for their welfare seems to be declining. Decentralization and greater emphasis on the role of the individual is the replacement.

Business leaders have done little in the past to modify the misconceptions and prejudices held by the general public regarding their activities. Too often managers have been overly defensive or have placed excessive attention on how good everything is. Because businesses have been reluctant to talk about their problems openly, the public can frequently feel that there is something to hide.

Managers must become more adept at convincing a sceptical public that the organization and its members maintain high ethical standards. To achieve this recognition, business leaders must establish long-term commitments to social action. In many cases, the programmes adopted in a blaze of publicity have been ill-conceived, hastily adopted and lack the long-term commitment of all parties.

Some observers of the past records of businesses in ethical behaviour remain sceptical. Many people argue that the only effective way to get businesses to pay attention to social issues is to continually mount aggressive attacks on companies. To convince the public otherwise, organizations will have to display sincere concern for the well-being of society. Most definitely, it is a long-term objective.

Summary   The kind of organization which will be operating successfully in the future seems to be one which incorporates either the small business orientations, or the global conglomerate approach, or is the bustling, innovative organization crammed full of intrapreneurs. How realistic is this picture? Of course, it is impossible to be sure. We speak from our own perspective of today. The way we currently view organizations effectively places parameters on the way we think about them in the future.

It is unlikely, however, that none of the foregoing characteristics will be present. Summarizing the arguments so far, we can construct some predictions for the future characteristics and values of organizations, even if we cannot accurately predict their size or structure (see Table 24.2).

Table 24.2
Characteristics of the future organization

In the short term ...	In the long term ...
An emphasis on quality	Establishing a 'vision' for the future (Imagineering)
High degree of customer orientation and a concern for the client	Developing the notion of integrating informally with suppliers and customers to provide seamless transition of value to all partners in the chain
Organizing around existing markets and/ products	Creating and developing new competencies and knowledge which will lead to evolving new markets and products
HR strategies based on coaching, counselling, progress reviews, and personal goal setting	HR strategies oriented towards enhancing the intellectual capital that the organization can call on when required. Realigning individual knowledge workers' goals and those of the organization
Flexibility and an ability to respond to change	An appetite for change driven by the need to enhance creativity and innovation in products, markets and internal processes

Perhaps the issue of greatest long-term importance will prove to be the social conscience of organizations. As concern over protecting our environment grows, the call for organizations to regulate their own actions has grown. The frequently conflicting pressures between maximizing shareholder returns and preserving the greater good of society will have to be addressed, confronted and resolved. The role of organizations as fellow citizens of our global society will have to be resolved very quickly, otherwise organizations may still be profitable, but to what end? Globalization may also produce very quickly a sharply divided world between exploiters and exploited; between nations which 'have' and those which are 'have-nots'. Political and social unrest which occurs as a result could eventually undermine the processes of business globalization as we envisage them from today.

As keen observers of organizations and the people which populate them, we are very aware of the social, political and economic pressures for change. During the course of writing this book, we have re-emphasized to ourselves the fundamental changes which societies are experiencing. The impact of technology on organizational design and behaviours is only now coming into focus. Our experience indicates that the research and results of the many thousands of researchers in organizational behaviour may need to be re-assessed in terms of their applicability to the new contexts and challenges now emerging. It all makes for a very exciting 21st century.

References

Atterhed, S. G. (1985) 'Intrapreneurship: The way forward', in D. Clutterbuck, *New Patterns of Work*, Gower, Aldershot.

Chatov, R. (1980) 'What corporate ethics statements say', *California Management Review*, **22** (4), 22.

De Geus, A. (1997) *The Living Company*, Harvard Business School Press, Boston, Mass.

Edvinsson, L. and M. S. Malone (1997) *Intellectual Capital: Realizing your Company's True Value by Finding its Hidden Roots*, Harper Business, New York.

Garratt, B. (1987) *The Learning Organization: And the Need for Directors Who Think*, Gower, London.

Garvin, D. A. (1993) 'Building a learning organization', *Harvard Business Review*, Jan.,

Handy, C. H. (1995) *The Age of Paradox*, McGraw-Hill, New York.

Jackson, T. (1997) 'Brains before dividends' *Financial Times*, 15 Mar., I

Janis, I. L. (1972) *Victims of Groupthink: A Psychological Study of Foreign Policy Decisions and Fiascos*, Houghton-Mifflin, Boston, Mass.

Mitchell, D. (1989) '1992: The Implications for Management', *Long Range Planning*, **22** (1), 32–40.

Naisbitt, J. (1984) *Megatrends: Ten New Directions Transforming Our Lives*, Warner Books, New York.

Naisbitt, J. (1995) *Global Paradox*, Nicholas Brearley Publishing, London.

Pedler, M., J. Burgoyne, and T. Boydell (1994) *The Learning Company: A Strategy for Sustainable Development*, McGraw-Hill, London.

Peters, T. (1992) *Liberation Management: Necessary Disorganization for the Nanosecond Nineties*, Fawcett Books, New York.

Rosenfeld, R. H. (1985) 'Understanding organizational precedents', *Proceedings of the 1985 Business Archives Council Annual Conference*, London.

Senge, P. (1990) *The Fifth Discipline: The Art and The Practice of the Learning Organization*, Random House, New York.

Stewart, T. (1997) *Intellectual Capital: The New Wealth of Organizations*, Doubleday, New York.

Embracing the virtual organization

Christopher Barnatt

Organizations, their employees, and their customers, are increasingly connecting together electronically across computer networks. As just one example, electronic data interchange (EDI) links are commonly employed to permit companies to operate automatic ordering and stock replenishment systems. Indeed, large retail chains such as Tesco in the UK, and WalMart in the US, now place the vast majority of their orders electronically without laborious human intervention. By using EDI systems, organizations not only improve their efficiency and reduce the likelihood of stockouts, but additionally strengthen customer–supplier relationships as the costs of switching to an alternative supplier almost inevitably increase (McFarlan, 1984: 99).

Within many businesses today, computer systems of all sizes are now being utilized for communications purposes as well as for information storage, processing and retrieval. From electronic mail (email) to PC video-conferencing, the development of computer-mediated communications (CMC) is providing a rapidly advancing armoury of new business tools. As a result, there is a need to appraise investments in new computing systems not just in terms of the internal processing benefits that they may bring to their parent organization. Additionally, investments in CMC systems now also need to be appreciated as providing organizations with an increased stake within the global system of computer networks across which an increasing proportion of business is being conducted.

No company would appraise the benefit of a new telephone exchange purely in terms of its novel *internal* communications and call-routing facilities. It is therefore surprising that some firms still see CMC systems as capable of delivering only internal business benefits (Barnatt, 1995b: 11–12). Indeed, it is almost alarming how many companies are using email as an effective internal communications tool, while not employing this low-cost, high-speed medium for external correspondence. In 1993, the average company spent 15% or less of its information technology (IT) budget on setting up external connections to its customers or suppliers. Reliable estimates predict that by the year 2000 this figure will have to rise to around 60% (Bird, 1995: 79).

The sprawling synthesis of computer networks that comprise the Internet—the *international network*—is continuing to grow at an almost exponential pace. At the time of writing, there were approaching 50 million people using the Internet to communicate, to publish, and to trade electronically around the globe. Like it or not, 'cyberspace'—the electronic world of information existing within computers and across computer networks—is *the* new business frontier that no manager dares ignore.

This reading examines how the increasing business adoption of the technologies of cyberspace will enable the creation of new 'virtual' organizational forms. Over the past few years, the phrase 'virtual organization' has entered the popular managerial lexicon, with reports, papers and books detailing 'virtual companies', 'virtual factories', 'virtual offices' and 'virtual corporations' appearing with increasing regularity (Barnatt, 1995a). However, just what is meant by the term 'virtual organization' is still far from clear. By examining recent developments in organizational structures and CMC-empowered new working practices, this reading offers its own interpretation of the virtual organization phenomena. In doing so, it also addresses some of the varied managerial challenges that may lie ahead.

Definitions and developments

A 'virtual organization' may be defined as any productive system enabling individuals separated by distance and/or time to work together towards a common goal. Almost inevitably, virtual organizations rely upon computer-mediated communications technologies to bridge the previously insurmountable barriers between their members. Virtual organizations are engineered around work processes, rather than being based upon the physical bureaucracies and infrastructures that have traditionally governed organizational formation. As Charles Handy explains, we are now seeing signs of:

> . . . organizations which do not need to have all the people, or sometimes any of the people, in one place in order to deliver their service. The organization exists but you can't see it. It is a network not an office. As technology continues to turn the unlikely into the familiar, it becomes cheaper and quicker to communicate with people electronically and telephonically rather than face-to-face in a room. (Handy, 1995: 212).

In May 1994, the Department of Trade and Industry (DTI) launched a three-year initiative to increase awareness of the possibilities for computer-supported co-operative work (CSCW) in the UK. The launch event carried the title *The Virtual Corporation*, and set forth to explore how to reengineer 'Tomorrow's Organization' with new information technologies. Across the world there are a whole host of similar governmental and industrial CSCW initiatives, such as the ESPRIT COMIC project across the European Community. A recent EC Commission report stated that, by the turn of the century, 60% of employment across the Community would be dependent in some form upon the 'information superhighway'. Just as staggeringly, the Japanese Government has predicted that, by 2020, 30% of Japan's gross domestic product will be generated across broad-band network links (Sherman and Judkins, 1993: 86). Whether or not you happen to like the abstraction of business processes away from the warm, tactile domain of the flesh, the virtual organization phenomena seems certain to play an increasingly prominent role across advanced economies in the years ahead.

The evolution of organizational forms

In order to appreciate how virtual organization developments fit within a wider ontology, it is useful to briefly step back and consider the broader evolution of organizational forms. Up until the early 1980s, the reasoning behind Henry Ford's declaration that his 'Model T' 'would come in any colour so long as it was black' was still identifiable as driving the bureaucratic, mass-production philosophy of 'Big is best' Western industrial organization. Larger and larger firms strove to streamline their product ranges so that they could be mass-produced by semi-skilled labour along standardized production lines. Rigid hierarchies dependent upon rules and strict job demarcations governed organizational construction in the name of unquestioning efficiency. Production plant was also dedicated to a single task. Change the business process, and you had to restructure, retrain and retool the organization.

Following the oil crisis of the 1970s, and with innovations in programmable computer-controlled machinery and the 'new competition' from strengthening Far Eastern economies, rigid hierarchical, mass-production structures have increasingly begun to flounder. The Japanese in particular led the way in customizing their outputs with programmable plant, and in reading their markets to produce the products that consumers most wanted. As Piore and Sabel (1986) contend, the 1980s marked the beginning of the end of the mass-production paradigm. From this time onwards, firms started to cross the 'second industrial divide' in order to embrace the fresh organizational paradigm of 'flexible specialization'.

Flexible specialization involves the flexible coupling of specialist resources into production *networks* only as and when required. In order to reduce costs and to concentrate upon their key business competencies, many organizations are choosing to work flexibly by outsourcing non-core activities to specialists within the marketplace. The resulting organization bears little resemblance to a rigid hierarchy, with networks instead being dynamic with no clearly defined boundaries. Operating within what Miles and Snow (1986) have termed a 'subcontracting mode', organic or dynamic network organizational structures consist of loosely-coupled webs of production agents co-ordinated by a central core or 'broker'. As Morgan explains, network organizations 'operationalize ideas' that the core wishes to develop:

> For example, the organization may be in the fashion industry. It has created a name and image—'its label'—but contracts out market surveys, product design, production, distribution and so on. In the public eye, the firm has a clear identity. But in reality, it is a network of firms held together by the product of the day. (Morgan, 1989: 67).

The concept of the 'virtual organization' simply extends the notion of dynamically-networked organizational forms one stage further. By using new working practices empowered via new CMC technologies (or 'cybertechnologies'), the core of the organization may be increasingly downsized. At the same time, a wider and wider range of agents may be drawn into the production web electronically. No longer do physical distances have to constrain who can and cannot work for a company. No longer does time have to be a boundary. With new software applications known as *groupware*, knowledge employees may work together where and when they choose. Contracts and deals may also in future be constituted and monitored electronically, removing even legal and administrative complexities from organizational formation and adaptation. Indeed, one key development likely to drive the construction of virtual organizations concerns the creation of 'intelligent' *software agents*.

Electronic servants

Software agents are electronic slaves, crafted in computer code, that will in the not-too-distant future roam cyberspace in order to undertake productive work for their human masters. Already General Magic, a spin-off company from Apple Computer, has created a control language—*Telescript*—which will allow software agents to communicate as they travel the myriad of computer networks that span the business world. As more and more business is conducted across computer network links, software agents will protect human beings from the repetitive drudgery and complexity of the on-line electronic marketplace. As Gelernter contends, in future agents will 'make everything happen'—reacting to information and synthesizing it, displaying it, studying it, investigating it, double-checking and analysing it (1992: 185). Want to book a holiday, conduct a data search or buy some shares? In future, software agents will be able to undertake all such tasks and many, many more. As virtual employees, software agents will undoubtably work at the very heart of many of tomorrow's virtual organizations.

Virtual working practices

While software agent virtual employees are still very much in development, other CMC developments are already leading to a plethora of new 'virtual working practices'. Although few companies today would describe themselves as virtual organizations, many openly employ advanced CSCW systems to empower so-called 'virtual offices' and/or 'virtual teams'. The adoption of teleworking—of employees working from home from where they connect into corporate computing facilities—is becoming increasingly widespread. According to the Institute of Management, there are now at least 400 000 people in the UK who can be classed as teleworkers. In the US, there are at least 6 million people registered as teleworkers. The EC has a target for 10 million teleworkers by the year 2000 (Pancucci, 1995: 78).

By working from home, employees are freed from the time and expense involved in travelling to work. They may also arrange their working day to more readily accommodate family and leisure commitments. Organizations also greatly benefit when their employees can be persuaded to take the 'teleworking option', with employment overheads plummeting even after sometimes hefty IT investments have been taken into account. American Express have reported savings per employee of $30 000 per year due to teleworking. In the UK, firms such as Burger King and British Telecom have also reaped major cost benefits (Pancucci, 1995: 79–80). In spite of the potential social problems of employee isolation, teleworking seems here to stay.

While teleworking provides the most obvious means of using CMC media to allow physically dispersed employees to work together, various 'half-way houses' for reducing corporate expenditures on office space are also becoming more popular. 'Hot-desking' is one such development, whereby office space no longer comes to be 'owned' by any specific employee. Rather, all office space is communal to be used as desired and required when workers need to be within the building. With white collar workers in many organizations frequently out on the road or visiting clients, companies that have introduced hot-desk systems have been able to drastically reduce the number of desks, computers, telephones and other office accoutrements that they have needed to supply. As Digital noted when it set up its 'office of the future', a permanent desk for an individual within a traditional office may cost around £6000 a year to maintain. By providing communal desks and computers in an airy, open-plan, hot-desk environment, Digital managed to reduce office space requirements by 50%, desktop equipment costs by 60%, and lighting bills by 70% (Digital Equipment Corporation, 1993).

At US advertising agency Chiat-Day, a similar 'come and go as you please so long as the job gets done' hot-desk working arrangement is in operation. Employees are allocated a locker in which personal possessions may be kept. Aside from this locker they own no personal space within the office. At Digital, at Chiat-Day, and within many other modern hot-desk environments, personal cyberspaces within the organization have become more important than personal physical spaces. No longer will an employee always be greeted by Jane on one side, Harry on the other, and the same stained coffee cup, fluffy toy and family photograph on their desk when they arrive at work each morning. Instead, around them co-workers will come and go and use different computers to get their work done as business processes demand. And with personal space and physical human contact at work diminished, for many the 'telecommuting' option will become more and more attractive.

Towards virtu-commuting

With corporate interest in reducing expenditure on office space and employee travelling costs increasing, CMC developments with far more radical implications than telecommuting or hot-desking will soon also become a reality. One such future form of computer-based communications is entitled 'virtucommuting'. As the name implies, virtucommuting means telecommuting in virtual reality (VR). Hence, rather than sitting in front of a keyboard and possibly a video link, people will don a virtual reality headset, dataglove, and perhaps other VR clothing, in order to be transported into a computer-generated working domain. In the UK, a project entitled *Virtuosi* has already crafted an office in virtual reality within which participants may share desks and chairs, whiteboards, documents, and even virtual TV monitors. Another *Virtuosi* development is the 'virtual catwalk', which will soon allow designers to create clothes on computers which will be 'worn' by computer-generated mannequins within a virtual reality fashion show.

Developments in distributed virtual reality (that is, virtual reality systems allowing multiple participants to join together in VR from different physical locations) indicate that some organizations may one day be crafted solely in the virtual medium of cyberspace. A fantasy? Far from it. As Pruitt and Barrett note, strategic advantage now lies in the acquisition and control of information within 'bewilderingly diverse and geographically far-flung' organizations (1993: 383). The ability to bring together human beings across cyberspace as seamlessly as possible will inevitably lead to future business success. So termed 'corporate virtual workspaces' (CVWs) in virtual reality are a logical means towards such ends. What's more, everybody will be able to have access to largest office in the (virtual) building, and will even be able to make their door invisible to unwanted visitors!

The management challenge

Telecommuting, hot-desk environments, virtucommuting, and other CMC developments, will clearly present future managers with fresh new dilemmas in the area of human resource management. Perhaps the most common question to be raised is 'How can you motivate *and control* workers who you cannot see?' As Handy argues, trust becomes a critical resource within virtual organizations, meaning that thorough recruitment methods will become more and more important (1995: 213).

While many companies seem to fear that teleworkers may prove unproductive and difficult to manage when out of sight, evidence to date suggests quite the contrary. In his book *The Telecommuters* (1987), Kinsman reported that teleworking makes employees more productive as they experience fewer interruptions and hence may concentrate more clearly throughout the working day. Kinsman also found that skilled people employed as teleworkers were easier to retain (although in gaining remote working skills they clearly become potentially far more occupationally mobile). Teleworkers are also reported to work hard to ensure that their contributions to the organization do not go unnoticed. Indeed, one common fear among those working from home is that they will be overlooked when promotions are being considered.

This last point leads us to consider the challenge for management of treating teleworkers with equity in comparison to more traditional, office-bound staff. When there are redundancies, let alone promotions, to be made, will teleworkers be treated the same as those 'real, live, flesh-empowered people' that managers regularly meet within the office? (Barnatt, 1995b: 203). The answer is almost certainly not, with it being far easier to sack a teleworker (an 'entity down a wire') rather than a 'real' person who may have become much more of a friend, lunch companion, tennis partner or whatever in addition to a productive organizational component. Leaning how to trust, to manage, and to integrate, networks comprising both 'real' *and* 'virtual' workers will undoubtedly provide one of the greatest managerial challenges in the years ahead.

Summary and conclusions

It is still hard to define exactly what is meant by the term 'virtual organization'. For some, a virtual organization may 'simply' involve the use of groupware and video-conferencing links to integrate telecommuters and virtual teams into more traditional organizational forms. For others, developments in virtual organizations will depend upon the creation of virtual offices and virtual factories into which human beings may virtucommute in a computer-generated virtual reality. What we may reasonably conclude, however, is that virtual organizations will exhibit the following three key characteristics:

- A reliance for their functioning and survival upon the medium of cyberspace.
- No readily identifiable physical form.
- Boundaries defined and limited solely by the available information technology. (Barnatt, 1995b: 82–83).

What we may also conclude is that there is no possibility of all—or even the majority—of organizations becoming 'virtual'. Any virtual organization can only exist across the physical hardware of a computer network infrastructure. In other words, virtual organizations, however flexible, will be *dependent* upon more traditional organizational forms to provide their infrastructural habitat. Virtual organizations represent new patterns of doing business within the new business medium of cyberspace. Virtual organizations will oil the wheels of the traditional economy by supplying information services and linking employees together in different ways. Yet virtual organizations will never *replace* their real counterparts so long as flesh-and-blood human beings continue to demand solid, physical products and services within the tangible 'real' world.

References

Barnatt, C. (1995a) 'Office Space, Cyberspace and Virtual Organization', *Journal of General Management*, **20** (4), 78–91.

Barnatt, C. (1995b) *Cyber Business: Mindsets for a Wired Age*, Wiley, Chichester.

Bird, J. (1995) 'Connect it up', *Management Today*, June, 78–80.

Digital Equipment Corporation (1993) 'A More Natural Way of Working', *Business Update*, **7**, 6–7.

Gelernter, D. (1992) *Mirror Worlds: The Day Software puts the Universe in a Shoebox; How it will Happen and What it will Mean*, Oxford University Press, New York.

Handy, C. (1995) *Beyond Certainty: The Changing Worlds of Organizations*, Hutchinson, London.

Kinsman, F. (1987) *The Telecommuters*, Wiley, Chichester.

McFarlan, W. (1984) 'Information Technology Changes the Way You Compete', *Harvard Business Review*, May–June, 98–103.

Miles, R. E. and C. C. Snow (1986) 'Organizations: New Concepts for New Forms', *California Management Review*, **XXVIII** (3), 62–73.

Morgan. G. (1989) *Creative Organizational Theory: A Resource book*, Sage Publications, Newbury Park, CA.

Pancucci, D. (1995) 'Remote Control', *Management Today*, April, 78–80.

Piore. M. J. and F. S. Sabel (1984) *The Second Industrial Divide: Prospects for Prosperity*, Basic Books, New York.

Pruitt, S. and T. Barrett (1993) 'Corporate Virtual Workspace' in M. Benedikt, (ed.), *Cyberspace: First Steps*, MIT Press, Cambridge, MA.

Sherman, B. and P. Judkins (1993) *Glimpses of Heaven, Visions of Hell: Virtual Reality and its Implications*, Hodder & Stoughton, London.

The factory of the future

J. Martin Corbett

Popular wisdom within the production engineering and computer science fraternity has it that 'peopleless' production will have become a reality by 2010 (Wright and Bourne, 1988). Governments and large corporations are investing large sums in the factory of the future. Since 1982, the Commission of European Communities has invested £600 million of public money developing ideas for the factory of the future. In America, private industry spent nearly $50 billion on automated production systems between 1981 and 1986. By the mid-1980s, Japanese manufacturers were using more robots than American and European manufacturers put together.

The aim of this reading is to outline the social dynamics behind the well-publicized drive towards full automation. An alternative vision is then outlined. The reading ends with a brief discussion of the job-design implications of these two opposing visions, or scenarios, of the future. The reader is encouraged to consider the implications and ramifications of the information contained in the reading for, and within, the wider sphere of organizational behaviour and theory.

In order to examine the social dynamics of technological development, Kurt Lewin's (1952) 'fields of force' model of change will be employed. This model views the change process in terms of a dynamic equilibrium between 'driving' and 'restraining' forces. In any situation there are forces which push for change (driving forces) as well as forces that hinder change (restraining forces). Change occurs when one of these forces is stronger than the other.

Scenario 1: the fully automated factory

Figure R17.1 illustrates a number of driving and restraining forces which currently effect the drive towards the 'peopleless factory' of the future. These are discussed in more detail below.

Driving forces

Management desire for control

Writers have argued that the design of production jobs is heavily influenced by the desire of higher management and top organizational decision-makers to achieve greater control over the production process (Braverman, 1974; Noble, 1984). Tighter managerial control can be achieved by adopting higher levels of automation and centralized production control technology. This managerial strategy is an important driving force towards the 'peopleless factory'. Braverman and others argue that shop-floor and line-management tasks have become increasingly fragmented and simplified, which leaves their jobs ripe for automation at each successive step of an organization's technological development.

In a recent survey of UK manufacturing, 20% of organizations cited the desire to increase management control as the main objective of their automation investment plan (Industrial Computing, 1987). Many suppliers of advanced manufacturing technology have used the predictability of

Figure R17.1
Force field analysis
1—full automation as
desired state

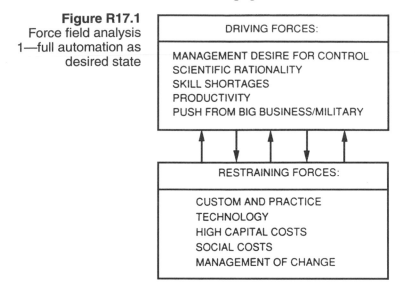

machines as powerful marketing images to bolster this managerial perspective (e.g. 'Robots don't strike').

Scientific rationality   Since the turn of the century, science and technology have been ideologically linked with the idea of economic progress (Rose, 1979). It is indisputable that they have contributed to the economic prosperity of the industrialized world. Cottrell (1986) argues that the competitive nature of scientific and technological development is such that an advance in one country raises fears in other countries that they may be missing some great opportunity for the future unless they add it to their own national list of scientific and technological activities. Hence, 'We have, in effect, a scientific and technological "Olympic Games" in which every technically advanced country can hardly resist the temptation to enter a candidate for every event' (Cottrell, 1986:113). Within manufacturing, the pervasiveness of an 'automate or liquidate' philosophy adds poignancy to this process.

Skill shortages   In recent years, one of the most cited reasons for the need to automate has been based on the perception that traditional metal working and craft skills are in short supply. Given the cost of training employees to demanding standards, many companies have looked to technology to enable them to employ less skilled (lower cost) operators. It was common for the vendors of the early numerically controlled (NC) machine tools to boast that 'even an idiot can operate them' (Noble, 1984).

With the advent of the 'information technology revolution' (Forester, 1982), it not only became possible to embody craft skills into software and hardware, but also to integrate previously discrete stages of the production process—propagating the belief that automation can replace entire groups of skilled labour.

Productivity   The economic benefits of automation most frequently cited by manufacturers are: reduced throughput times; reduced inventory and work-in-progress; reduced labour costs; increased flexibility; increased quality; increased managerial control of the production process; and increased overall productivity.

These are impressive claims which are substantiated by the publicized experiences of large corporations. General Electric's factory of the future in Louisville, Kentucky has raised productivity levels of dishwasher manufacturing by nearly a third, cut warranty calls by a half and boosted the company's market share from 31% to 43%. Similarly at IBM's highly automated typewriter factory in Lexington, Kentucky, 2000 employees can now turn out 1.4 million units per year, where 6000 used to produce 0.7 million units. Not only that, the new typewriters cost $1000 less than the models they replace.

Push from 'big business' and the military

Both large corporations and the military have invested huge sums in the drive towards the fully automated factory. Noble (1984) shows how the development of NC—the basic building block of automated production systems—was driven by huge investments by the US Air Force to fulfil a technical need (machining helicopter rotor blades) and a political need (to place control of production in the hands of management). Other designs, equally viable in economic terms, found it impossible to compete with the NC design, primarily due to lack of comparable capital resources.

The role of large, often multi-national corporations in the development of full automation is considerable. Many of these companies (e.g. General Electric, General Motors, Yamasaki and Boeing) design, manufacture and service innovative technological products which are the basis for production process innovations for their customers (Roy and Wield, 1986). For example, General Motors in Detroit invested $40bn between 1979 and 1987 on automation. They are currently imposing their own 'manufacturing automation protocol' (MAP) on the rest of the industry. MAP is a significant development towards full automation as it consists of a set of rules which govern how different machines should communicate with each other to enable full integration of design, manufacture and sales.

Restraining forces

Custom and practice

Organizations—particularly long-established organizations—are not renowned for their ability to respond rapidly to change. Simply because certain avenues are open to organizational decision-makers does not guarantee that they will take them. Established patterns of behaviour can prove highly resistant to change (Mirvis and Berg, 1977).

There are cases of trade unions and management groups successfully redirecting executive implementation strategies when the process was seen to lead to labour displacement or loss of power or status (Clegg *et al.*, 1984; Wilkinson, 1984; Burnes, 1988). Hence, even if full automation *can* be achieved, there is no guarantee that it *will* be achieved.

Technology

The present levels of safety, integrity and reliability of advanced manufacturing and information technology are such that a number of commentators seriously question whether the fully automated factory of the future is a realizable goal (e.g. Brodner, 1986).

Documented cases of robotic homicide (e.g Nagamachi, 1988), major software modelling errors (Wray, 1988), and computer-aided malpractice and misjudgement (Cooley, 1987) support this view. Proponents of full automation argue that the development of artificial intelligence (AI) and expert systems will enable 'intelligent' manufacturing systems to take contingent, as opposed to pre-programmed, actions to deal with unforeseen and unexpected occurrences reducing error and failure. Whether or not this argument is based on misplaced optimism is a matter for debate, although

AI system designers openly profess serious difficulty encapsulating human intelligence in a machine-readable form (Wright and Bourne, 1988).

High capital costs

Full automation is capital-intensive and only the wealthiest of companies seem prepared to enter the arena. With the number of small-to-medium-sized companies increasing steadily (Brodner, 1987); full automation may be restricted to large multi-national corporations, while the smaller, less wealthy companies stand aside evaluating the appropriateness of technological developments for their particular needs.

Social costs

There has been much debate on the social effects of automation, particularly with regard to labour displacement and job design. The literature offers a cloudy picture of the social impact of automation, ranging from optimistic (Forester, 1982) to pessimistic (Noble, 1984). As the drive towards the peopleless factory continues, shopfloor jobs will start to disappear. If the displayed employees fail to find alternative employment, the financial and social costs to society will inevitably increase.

In a US case study of three shop-floor employees displaced by one robot, Mital and Genaidy (1988) calculated that the loss of revenue to society (through loss of income tax, the payment of unemployment benefits, etc.) outweighed gains (increased tax levied on company profits and sales owing to productivity gains, etc.) by a factor of two over a three-year period.

The dynamic productivity model proposed by Rosenbrock (1981) and developed by Seliger (1984) demonstrates that such short-term productivity benefits occasioned by labour displacing automation can lead to unfavourable economic and social consequences in the long term. This analysis questions the economic viability of full automation.

Management of change

The productivity increases which support the drive towards full automation appear to be more a reflection of executive and managerial aspirations than of the current reality in manufacturing organizations. Majchrzak (1988) argues that American manufacturers are experiencing an estimated 50 to 75% failure rate when implementing advanced automated technology.

It is difficult to assess failure rates in organizations because companies are reticent to publicize negative experiences. From what is known about the management of technological change, researchers agree that successful implementation of automation crucially depends on the development of human resource and management practices which support, rather than undermine, factory automation (e.g. Buchanan and Boddy, 1983; Wall, Clegg and Kemp, 1987; Majchrzak, 1988). The economic success of Japanese manufacturing companies is often attributed to developments in organizational and managerial techniques as opposed to any inherent properties of automation *per se* (Schonberger, 1982).

Scenario 2: Hybrid factory automation

Hybrid factory automation refers to production systems which are designed to facilitate shared, concurrent control between skilled human operators and machines. The goal of hybrid automation is the design of systems which encourage a synergy between the creativity, flexibility and skills of users on the one hand, and the accuracy, data storage capacity and speed of new technology on the other. Figure R17.2 illustrates driving and restraining forces which currently influence developments towards the hybrid factory of the future.

Figure R17.2
Force field analysis
2—hybrid
automation as
desired state

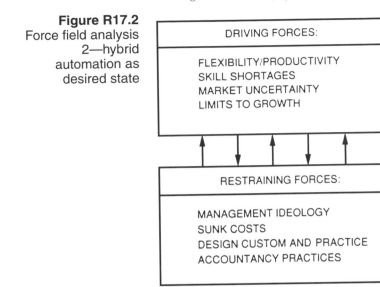

DRIVING FORCES:

FLEXIBILITY/PRODUCTIVITY
SKILL SHORTAGES
MARKET UNCERTAINTY
LIMITS TO GROWTH

RESTRAINING FORCES:

MANAGEMENT IDEOLOGY
SUNK COSTS
DESIGN CUSTOM AND PRACTICE
ACCOUNTANCY PRACTICES

Driving forces

Flexibility and productivity

This driving force towards hybrid automation has two components. First, the experience of many companies suggests that high levels of automation can reduce (or at best emulate) rather than increase productivity and flexibility levels and associated with lower levels of automation. Hence a number of companies are now looking towards alternative hybrid automated systems.

At General Motors, their $500m Hamtramck facility in Detroit contains 310 robots in a 'factory for the day-after-tomorrow'. Yet, the factory can only boast similar product quality and productivity as the ageing (less capital-intensive) General Motors factory in Fremont, California. Similarly, the $400m Buick City fully automated factory in Michigan can only achieve half the production throughput rate of the factory it superseded.

The second component of the driving force towards hybrid automation is the success of companies attempting to achieve human—technology synergy. Toyota's success in flexible manufacturing is based more on organizational practices and hybrid automation than on full automation. The company's famous 'Kanban' production technique—a key to the company's control of work-in-progress and inventory levels—is based on the very low technology of cards or chits which travel with containers of parts through the factory. The aim is to reduce the number of cards in circulation through removing bottlenecks in order to achieve just-in-time manufacturing. No cumbersome computer scheduling programs are involved—Toyota have concentrated their efforts on reducing waste and production bottlenecks and not on implementing increasingly sophisticated levels of automation. Toyota's success has driven many companies to re-assess their automation strategies.

Skill shortages

One of the key stumbling blocks to full automation is the inherent difficulty transferring production and craft knowledge from humans to machines. This is crucial as advanced manufacturing systems rely on skilled intervention for their operational performance. This human intervention is problematic in the monitoring and diagnosis of system error because machine 'minders' cannot develop the requisite skills simply from observing automated machinery in action (Bainbridge, 1983).

Hence, there is a two-fold skill shortage which hinders the development of full automation and promotes the embracement of hybrid systems. On the one hand, there is a growing shortage of shop-floor operators with the skills to manually control or override malfunctioning highly automated systems. On the other hand, there is a shortage of computer and social scientists with the skills to extract and codify the important craft knowledge of skilled operators. A number of commentators argue that such skill, by its very nature, cannot be codified into machine-readable form (e.g. Cooley, 1987).

Market uncertainty

The key word in the manufacturing world of the 1980s and 1990s is 'flexibility'. Companies no longer think in terms of mass production, but market niches, small batches and customized one-offs (Brodner, 1987). Manufacturers of advanced automation technology claim flexibility to be a key attribute of their products. Others argue (Brodner, 1986) that companies following strategies of full automation suffer from relative inflexibility with regard to batch changes and process innovation. Every change of a customer order or a piece of production equipment first needs to be modelled in a computer system. 'In the long run, the firm might even lose its innovation capability, since production knowledge and creativity on the human side would have been wasted away over time. All this is in contrast with market requirements' (Brodner, 1986: 147).

Limits to growth

The social costs outlined in the previous scenario are one example of the possible limits to the growth of full automation. Other limiting factors include ecological considerations such as energy resources and pollution.

Despite fierce controversy over the methods used to predict the likely effects of pollution and resource shortage in the future, it is becoming increasingly clear that there are real finite limits to material consumption. Dickson (1975) argues that 'It is physically impossible for the world to continue tracing out current patterns of industrial and technological growth without taking into account the physical limits imposed by the finite nature of the earth and its resources' (p. 21). An economy based on rapid growth demands a particular type of technology which is capable of producing the maximum innovation of new products with little consideration of real social need.

Restraining forces

Management ideology

A major obstacle to the development and diffusion of hybrid automation is management ideology—particularly management's desire for control of the production process. Managers often resist changes (whether technological or organizational) which result in a reduction in this control even when such a change brings undisputed gains in performance.

Emery and Thorsrud (1976) report the instance of a Norwegian electrical company who experimented with semi-autonomous work groups. Within the first year of the experiment, productivity rose by 20%, in the next year by a further 10%. Yet management refused to extend these new methods of working to the main plant.

> The management argument was that the workers were not really interested and that the old system gave better management control. Individual piece rates were assumed to be necessary to keep up productivity. In retrospect one can easily see that what was really at stake was management's basic idea of work organization (Emery and Thorsrud, 1976: 97).

Sunk costs

Investment in full automation is costly. For a large company to shift their emphasis to hybrid automation would involve writing off considerable investment.

It is also likely that large corporations which have invested heavily in the drive towards the 'peopleless factory' will attempt to regain control over the market if a shift towards hybridization became evident. Recent history shows that companies may attempt to manage their environments by suppressing the development and diffusion of competing technologies through patents and information manipulation (Dunford, 1987) or through influencing or 'tying in' customers to continue their present purchasing strategy (DeLamarter, 1988). This 'tying in' effectively excludes other competitors from supplying alternative manufacturing technology.

Design custom and practice

The design of hybrid automation which seeks to retain and develop the skills and knowledge of users is not unproblematic. Designers and production engineers (even when committed to developing hybrid automation technology) have great difficulty incorporating unpredictable human components into their design practice (Corbett, 1987a; 1990). Until new techniques and design methods are developed, this problem will restrain the development of exemplary hybrid systems. However, there are encouraging signs that the new methods which are now emerging can help overcome these problems (Clegg and Corbett, 1987; Corbett *et al.*, 1989).

Accountancy practices

In many companies there is a tendency to justify investments in automation by forecasting substantial savings in direct labour cost. This practice is biased against investment in hybrid automation which does not explicitly aim to displace labour.

Management accountants generally experience great difficulty in quantifying the inherent flexibility of hybrid systems in monetary terms (Primrose and Leonard, 1984). Others argue that the unsophisticated nature of manufacturing accounting is directly connected with a falling off in relative competitive performance, particularly against Japan (Kaplan, 1983). Until accountants develop methods to appraise investments in advanced manufacturing technology in broader terms, strategic investment in hybrid automation will remain 'unjustifiable'.

Job design and the factory of the future

Research into the impact of automation on job design is dominated by case-study analyses from which generalizations are difficult to articulate. Recent research (Corbett, 1987b; Zuboff, 1988; Corbett *et al.*, 1989) suggests that the centralized, highly integrated production systems (the precursors of full automation) are associated with stress and low motivation among operating personnel. The degradation of tacit craft skills may lead to a loss of innovative potential and an over-reliance on theoretical knowledge and systems analysis divorced from the production process itself. These findings are of crucial importance because an organization's technology choice today will carry over into the future.

Job designs associated with hybrid automation are less problematic since they are linked into the technical design process itself. The participation of company personnel in the design process enables job specific knowledge to be included into the system specification and thus allow a company to retain and develop its innovative capabilities.

Drucker (1988) argues that organizations of the future will be 'knowledge-based', with the knowledge resting in the minds and actions of employees at the lower levels of the organization hierarchy. Drucker forecasts that 'knowledge workers' will resist the command-and-control model that business took from the military a hundred years ago.

Full automation is incompatible with this new form of organization. It remains to be seen if organizations will develop a sufficiently broad vision of the future (encompassing technology and job design in its broadest context) into their strategic planning. This reading has briefly sketched out the fields of force which impinge on this vision of the factory of the future. It is for the new generation of management to convert such information into action.

References

Bainbridge, L. (1983) 'Ironies of automation', *Automatica*, **19**, 775–9.

Braverman, H. (1974) *Labor and Monopoly Capital*, Monthly Review Press, New York.

Brodner, P. (1986) 'Skill based manufacturing versus "unmanned factor"—which is superior?', *International Journal of Industrial Ergonomics*, **1**, 145–53.

Brodner, P. (ed.), (1987) *Strategic Options for New Production Systems*, CEC-FAST Publications, Brussels.

Buchanan, D. A. and D. Boddy (1983) *Organizations in the Computer Age*, Gower, Aldershot.

Burnes, B. (1988) 'New technology and job design: the case of CNC', *New Technology Work and Employment*, **3**, 100–11.

Clegg, C. W. and J. M. Corbett (1987) 'Research and development in "humanizing" advanced manufacturing technology', in T. D. Wall, C. W. Clegg and N. J. Kemp (eds.), *The Human Side of Advanced Manufacturing Technology*, Wiley, Chichester.

Clegg, C. W., N. J. Kemp and T. D. Wall (1984) 'New technology: choice, control and skills', in G. C. Van de Veer, M. J. Tauber, T. Green and P. Gorny (eds.), *Readings on Cognitive Ergonomics: Mind and Computers*, Springer-Verlag, Berlin.

Cooley, M. J. E. (1987) *Architect or Bee?: The Human Price of Technology*, Hogarth Press, London.

Corbett, J. M. (1987a) 'Human work design criteria and the design process: the devil in the detail', in P. Brodner (ed.), *Skill Based Automated Manufacturing*, Pergamon Press, Oxford.

Corbett, J. M. (1987b) 'A psychological study of advanced manufacturing technology: the concept of coupling', *Behaviour and Information Technology*, **6**, 441–53.

Corbett, J. M. (1990) 'Human centred advanced manufacturing systems: from rhetoric to reality', *International Journal of Industrial Ergonomics*, **5**, 83–90.

Corbett, J. M., R. Martin, T. D. Wall and C. W. Clegg (1989) 'Technological coupling as a predictor of intrinsic job satisfaction: a replication study', *Journal of Organizational Behaviour*, **10**, 91–5.

Cottrell, A. H. (1986) 'Technological thresholds', in R. Roy and D. Wield (eds.), *Product Design and Technological Innovation*, Open University Press, Milton Keynes.

DeLarmarter, R. T. (1988) *Big Blue: IBMs Use and Abuse of Power*, Pan Books, London.

Dickson, D. (1975) *Alternative Technology and The Politics of Technical Change*, Fontana/Collins, Glasgow.

Drucker, P. (1988) 'The coming of the new organization', *Harvard Business Review*, **66**, 15–21.

Dunford, R. (1987) 'The suppression of technology as a strategy for controlling resource dependence', *Administrative Science Quarterly*, **32**, 512–25.

Emery, F. E. and E. Thorsrud (1976) *Democracy at Work*, Martinus Nijhoff, Lieden.

Forester, T. (1982) (ed.), *The Information Technology Revolution*, Blackwell, Oxford.

Industrial Computing (1987) 'Survey supplement', October, EMAP Publications, London.

Kaplan, R. S. (1983) 'Measuring manufacturing performance: a new challenge for management accounting research', *The Accounting Review*, October, 23–4.

Lewin, K. (1952) 'Group decision and social change', in G. E. Swanson, T. M. Newcomb, and E. L. Hartley (eds.), *Readings in Social Psychology* (rev. edn), Holt, New York.

Majchrzak, A. (1988) *The Human Side of Factory Automation*, Jossey Bass, San Francisco.

Mirvis, P. H. and D. N. Berg (eds.), (1977) *Failures in Organizational Development and Change*, Wiley, Chichester.

Mital, A. and A. M. Genaidy (1988) 'Automation, robotisation in particular, is always economically desirable. Fact or fiction?' in W. Karwowski, H. R. Parsaei and M. R. Wilhelm (eds.), *Ergonomics of Hybrid Automated Systems, I*, Elsevier, Amsterdam.

Nagamachi, M. (1988) 'Ten fatal accidents due to robots in Japan', in W. Karwowski, H. R. Parsaei and M. R. Wilhelm (eds.), *Ergonomics of Hybrid Automated Systems I*, Elsevier, Amsterdam.

Noble, D. (1984) *Forces of Production*, Knopf, New York.

Primrose, P. L. and R. Leonard (1984) 'Optimizing the financial advantages of using CNC machine tools by use of an integrated suite of programs', *Proceedings of the Institute of Mechanical Engineers*, **198**, 147–51.

Rose, M. (1979) *Industrial Behaviour*, Penguin, Harmondsworth.

Rosenbrock, H. H. (1981) 'Human resources and technology', *Proceedings of the Sixth World Congress of the International Economic Association of Human Resources, Employment and Development*.

Roy, R. and Wield, D. (1986) (eds.), *Product Design and Technological Innovation*, Open University Press, Milton Keynes.

Schonberger, R. J. (1982) 'The transfer of Japanese manufacturing management approaches to US industry', *Academy of Management Review*, **7**, 479–87.

Seliger, G. (1984) *Wirtschaftliche Planung automatisierter Fertigungssysteme*, Sringer-Verlag, Berlin.

Wall, T. D., C. W. Clegg and N. J. Kemp (eds.), (1987) *The Human Side of Advanced Manufacturing Technology*, Wiley, Chichester.

Wilkinson, B. (1984) *The Shopfloor Politics of New Technology*, Heinemann, London.

Wray, T. (1988) 'The everyday risks of playing safe', *New Scientist*, 8 September 1988, No. 1628, 61–5.

Wright, P. K. and D. A. Bourne (1988) *Manufacturing Intelligence*, Addison-Wesley, Reading, Mass.

Zuboff, S. (1988) *In the Age of the Smart Machine*, Heinemann Professional Publishing, Oxford.

Oticon Holding A/S

Robert H. Rosenfeld

To compete in today's global information-based and customer-driven economy, organizations have to be efficient, innovative and competitive. This means being able to respond just-in-time, focus on quality, and implement 'mass-customization' (Pine, 1995). To achieve this, organizations will have to leverage the information and communication technologies to fit better in their environment, establish more co-operative relationships internally and with other organizations and compete on the international markets (Bobin, 1995). In order to monitor the changes in their environment and to gain the advantages of both an innovation and an efficiency strategy, organizations must also take into account the restraining force which exists within their own structure and culture and managerial processes (Martin, 1996). This case study illustrates the changes a medium-sized Danish company is undertaking to fulfil the dual need for innovation and efficiency.

Oticon Holding A/S is a Danish designer and manufacturer of hearing aids. Founded in 1904, Oticon is the oldest hearing instrument manufacturer in the world. Oticon is owned by William Demant Holding, which is owned by a charitable trust (William Demant og Hustru Ida Emilie's Foundation) who control 65.5% of the share capital, as well as by its' employees (approximately 20%) and other shareholders. As one of the world's largest manufacturers of hearing instruments, Oticon is also a major supplier to government hearing programmes in many countries. The Group employs 1443 staff, of which 676 are based in Denmark. Their head office employs 150 people and is located in an elegantly converted Tuborg soft drink factory.

They are one of the four largest hearing aid manufacturers (the others are Sony, Siemens, and Philips). Oticon have a large subsidiary in the US as well as smaller operations around the world. Although the £750 million market for hearing aids has been static in terms of sales growth for the past five years, Oticon has managed to grow quickly, with sales doubling from approximately £60 million to £120 million between 1990 and 1995. Profits rose even faster: in 1995, profits were £15 million compared to £1.5 million in 1990.

Today Oticon is seen as an innovator in the hearing instrument industry. Oticon's impressive growth figures were due in large part to their ability to launch a series of innovative products into the stagnant hearing aid market. From 1992 to 1997, the company has introduced 10 major new products. Its' most important innovation has been the world's first entirely digital technology hearing aid, launched in 1995. Called DigiFocus, it has subsequently been continuously improved. The latest version weighs only 4 grams. Technically, it has miniaturized the power of a desktop computer into a 'ear-level' hearing instrument. For the hard of hearing, the impact of this is analogous to the transition from a old-fashioned radio with only bass and treble controls to a fully digitized recording studio.

The President of Oticon is Lars Kolind. Kolind joined the firm in 1988 with a brief to turnaround the company's fortune. Kolind holds a MSc degree in mathematics and statistics and a B.Com in Organization Behaviour. Throughout the 1980s, Oticon's profits had steadily declined due to high costs, low productivity and increasing competition from large international companies such as Sony, Philips and Siemens. Out of necessity, Kolind took drastic action to stabilize the business by cutting costs and increasing productivity. However, it gradually became clear to him that the firm would find it difficult to compete in its chosen market by emulating its competitors' strategies and structures. Kolind was determined to compete in the market on the basis of innovation and rapid product development. To make up ground on its much larger competitors would require an organizational revolution.

In response to this concern, Kolind introduced a new and very flexible organizational structure in 1991. In an introduction to his organizational vision, Kolind distributed a document to everyone in Oticon outlining his views. 'Oticon needs breakthroughs,' Kolind wrote, 'and breakthroughs require the combination of technology with audiology, psychology, and imagination. The ability to "think the unthinkable" and make it happen. In organizations of the future,' he continued, 'staff would be liberated to grow, personally and professionally, and to become more creative, action-oriented, and efficient.'

Kolind's (1994) view was that one of the key restraining factors was the formal organizational structure. So Kolind radically reengineered the organization, developing something which he called the 'spaghetti organization'. Job titles were abolished. Projects, not functions or departments, became the defining unit of work. Project management is led by project leaders. Anyone can become a project leader. Essentially, they are individuals who come up with an idea that the project owners (members of Oticon's 10-member top management team) sponsor and support. At Oticon, teams form, work together, disband, and form again as the work requires. Similar in some sense to an internal 'free market', project leaders compete to attract the resources and people to deliver results. Project owners provide advice and support, but make few actual decisions. The company has about 100 projects at any one time, and most people work on several projects at once. Kolind's wish is to encourage the project teams to behave entrepreneurially. As Kolind says, 'We allow a lot of freedom. We don't worry if we use more resources than planned. Deadlines are what really matter,' (Labarre, 1996). And it has worked, according to Kolind, Oticon is developing products twice as fast as anyone else.

The company's head office reflects Kolind's desire for rapidity and flexibility. All three floors of Oticon's head office have large open-plan areas. All vestiges of hierarchy have disappeared. There are no physical offices, employees are issued with a 'caddie', which are metal desks mounted on large wheels. Each caddie provides a workspace with room for about 30 hanging folders and some binders and a state-of-the-art networked computer. Employees are constantly on the move internally, relocating their caddie/office wherever they choose—which can be for a couple of days to a few months. The office technology was expressly designed to support face-to-face interaction. According to Torben Petersen, designer of Oticon's

IT systems, 'If you can't talk to someone because they're sitting behind a secretary and a potted plant, they won't know what you know. People need to move around'.

When they were designing the technology to support Kolind's philosophy, the design team identified a number of 'constraining technologies'. One of these was paper documents. They found that one reason why individuals want their own office or workstation was the need to store paper documents. The hassle of moving paper was seen as a key constraint on mobility. Now, every morning, employees visit the second floor 'paper room' to deal with their incoming post. With the exception of very few documents, all material is put through electronic scanners and the original paper is put into a shredder—which empties down a large glass tube strategically placed in the middle of the first floor employee cafeteria. Oticon estimates that the paperless system and new workflow methods allowed them to bring products to market in half the time (relative to their experiences during the previous two and a half years). Paper storage was decreased by 70% and Oticon easily reached their goal of 30% productivity improvement. To eliminate the umbilical cord of telephones, the company has switched almost entirely to mobile telephones. Company-issued mobile phones are small and an almost surgical attachment to every employee's waist. Employees walk and talk constantly.

Conference and meeting rooms are available as well. Each room incorporates the very latest groupware systems to encourage electronic brainstorming techniques. This includes video conferencing facilities, whiteboards linked to computers. According to Kolind, 'These technologically supported creativity tools speed up the creative process by a factor of five. We can do in one day what we used to do in one week. We use them whenever we come to a critical decision-making point. We also use groupware for collective writing of technical manuals. It is fascinating to watch 10 people simultaneously working on one document,' (Labarre, 1996).

Despite the success of Oticon over the past few years, Kolind continues to surprise. After the launch of DigiFocus, their most recent product innovation, Kolind perceived that the organization was too focused on the continuing success of that one product. He began to feel that the longer-standing project teams were ossifying into something similar to departments. As a consequence, Kolind intervened to re-structure the physical space of the business so that project teams focusing on short-term topics (sales, marketing, customer service) relocated to the top floor. Medium-term projects (current product improvements) and long-term research located on the second floor, with technology, infrastructure and support moving to the first floor. As Kolind describes it, 'It was total chaos. Within three hours, over a hundred people had moved. To keep a company alive, one of the jobs of top management is to keep it disorganized', (Labarre, 1996).

Note   1   The information presented in this case study is partly derived from Labarre (1996).

References   Bobin, S. (1995) 'European CEOs Should Prepare Now for the Information
Superhighway', *Gartner Group*, **XI**, (6), Feb., 5.

Kolind, Lars. (1994) 'Thinking the Unthinkable: The Oticon Revolution', *Focus on Change
Management*, April.

Labarre, P. (1996) 'This organization is dis-organization'. *Fast Company*, **3**, 33–9.

Martin, J. (1996) '*The Great Transition—Using the Seven Disciplines of Enterprise Engineering to
Align People, Technology, and Strategy*', American Management Association, New York.

Pine, J., D. Peppers and M. Rogers (1995) 'Do you want to keep your customers forever?'
Harvard Business Review, **73**, 2, Mar., 103–14.

Questions   1   If you were in charge of employee recruitment for Oticon, what personal
characteristics and competencies might you look for in potential recruits?

2   In more traditional organizations, individuals often form social
relationships with their immediate work colleagues. At Oticon, would the
requirement for mobility reduce the social closeness among work
colleagues?

3   A lean, flexible organization such as Oticon requires employees who have
a broad understanding of the business. How would this requirement fit
with individuals who see themselves as 'professionals' in their area of
chosen expertise?

4   Are there likely to be limits to Oticon's organizational strategy? Can it be
sustained as the company grows? What might be some of the factors
which could cause it to breakdown?

Author Index

Subject Index